D1148035

POWER ACROSS THE PACIFIC

Power across the Pacific

A Diplomatic History of American Relations with Japan

WILLIAM R. NESTER

Associate Professor
Department of Government
St John's University, New York

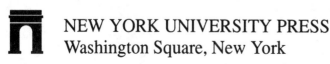

NEW YORK UNIVERSITY PRESS
Washington Square, New York

First published in the U.S.A. in 1996 by
NEW YORK UNIVERSITY PRESS
Washington Square
New York, N.Y. 10003

Library of Congress Cataloging-in-Publication Data
Nester, William R. , 1956–
Power across the Pacific : a diplomatic history of American
relations with Japan / William R. Nester.
p.   cm.
Includes bibliographical references and index.
ISBN 0–8147–5788–X
1. United States—Foreign relations—Japan.   2. Japan—Foreign
relations—United States.   3. United States—Foreign relations—1865–
4. Japan—Foreign relations—1868–   I. Title.
E183.8.J3N366   1996
327.73052—dc20   95–51997
                                                      CIP

Printed in Great Britain

Contents

v

To Andrea
with deepest love

May we always be . . .
neck and neck!

Introduction: Power, Perceptions, and Policy

CYCLES OF HISTORY

America's relationship with Japan recently passed its 140th-year anniversary. Over those years, hundreds of books and thousands of articles have explored different issues or periods of the relationship. Yet within that vast library no book has analyzed the entire relationship from beginning to present.

The void can perhaps be explained by the relationship's complexity and changes over time. Two great cycles of initial partnership and eventual rivalry have shaped American–Japanese relations, one geopolitical (1853–1945) and the other geoeconomic (1945 to the present).

In 1853–4, American gunboats forced open an isolationist Japan to bilateral trade and diplomatic relations. Then, for the rest of the nineteenth century, the United States served as Japan's patron in its drive to modernize its society and expand within the global political economy. But from the twentieth century's dawn, as both the United States and Japan seized colonies in the Far East, their national power and interests diverged and increasingly clashed. American perceptions of Japan as protégé correspondingly withered and that of Japan as geopolitical rival swelled. Where once the White House had encouraged Japanese expansion, it now tried to contain it. Then, from 1931 to 1941, America's latent fears of Japan were realized as Tokyo embarked on its brutal conquest of first China and then the entire Far East and western Pacific. Pearl Harbor brought the United States and Japan into a "war without mercy" which ended with Hiroshima and Nagasaki three and a half years later.

A geoeconomic version of this cycle has characterized the relationship since 1945. During the American Occupation (1945–52), the United States instituted revolutionary economic, political, and social changes that laid the foundations for Japan's subsequent rise into a political economic superpower. Cold War realities rather than altruism shaped these policies – the success of America's Far East containment policy depended on building Japan into the region's "workshop" and "aircraft carrier." In September 1951, Washington and Tokyo signed security and peace treaties which implicitly contained a grand bargain – in return for American bases in Japan and a bilateral alliance, the United States would tolerate Japan's industrial, trade, and technology policies that, among other elements, included closed home markets and economic expansion overseas, while America's vast market would be kept open to Japanese exports and investments. It also meant integrating Japan into global markets. During the 1950s and 1960s, Washington sponsored Tokyo's membership into the GATT and OECD, often in the face of harsh objections of other members who feared Japan's export machine.

But as Japan's geoeconomic power grew, once complementary national interests clashed ever more bitterly. As Japan has enjoyed increasingly larger trade and investment surpluses from the mid 1960s through today, a broader range of American businessmen have screamed for relief from Japanese dumping and closed markets. They have been joined by an ever-more vociferous body of American political and intellectual leaders who have criticized the grand bargain of bases for markets as obsolete and detrimental to American power and interests. Japan was no longer a weak, struggling economy that needed coddling, they argued, but had become an economic superpower with which the United States should insist on reciprocal economic and military relations. This perspective, however, remains subordinate to that of other influential Americans that the alliance must still take precedence, the bilateral deficits do not matter, and, finally, liberalism rather than neomercantilism shapes Japan's policies. Although the old relationship of America as patron and Japan as protégé continues, it is becoming increasingly fragile as the underlying geoeconomic power balance shifts in Tokyo's favor.

Up to now, Washington and Tokyo have been able to manage a growing number of trade, investment, and technology conflicts. Both sides have become adept at playing a game of economic brinkmanship while avoiding a full-scale economic war. As in the Cold War, the potentially disastrous results of going over the brink tempers the actions of both sides. With the two countries' combined economies accounting for over 40 per cent of global GNP, a trade war between Washington and Tokyo might well scuttle the world economy. Most analysts argue that the possibility of a bilateral trade collapse is unlikely, and a global economic meltdown remoter still. Yet, the possibility still haunts the governments and citizens of both nations.

THE MAKING OF POLICY

While the relationship's broad patterns are easily defined, what shapes the handling of specific issues? The making and implementation of American policy toward Japan differs little from that towards any other country.

In America's diplomatic history, the startling foreign policy initiatives of a Wilson or Truman are the exception. Continuity rather than change characterizes both domestic and foreign policy. Presidents and congresses largely carry on the work of their predecessors. Revisions of existing policies are rare; complete shifts in policy rarer still. Change, when it occurs, is mostly incremental.

Foreign policy making is a complex process that varies from one issue and time to the next, and can be shaped by key political and administrative leaders, bureaucratic politics, public opinion, and the impact of international events. Sometimes the bargaining over an issue is sharper within rather than between governments; the time, effort, and differences to be overcome among government institutions over policy may be greater than asserting that policy with another government. Much policy comes from the complex bureaucratic procedures and adjustment of conflicting interests over years rather than specific, decisive decisions. Policy becomes the sum of countless and often conflicting minor decisions or non-decisions throughout interested bureaucracies. The policy process is "decentralized and policy outcomes are subjective and often unstructured. No one is really in control . . . the bureaucracy [is] . . . a kind of automatic pilot [which manages routine issues] while the president . . . takes the control at critical junctures."[1]

The responsibilities and powers for foreign policy have shifted over time. Before World War II, foreign policy was made largely by the White House and State Department, with inputs from other affected bureaucracies, congressional committees, and interest groups. But throughout the postwar era, as the range of international issues proliferated, foreign policy making powers diffused among other ever more numerous and powerful players; the ability of relatively obscure bureaucrats, congressmen, and interest groups to impede or promote policy has accelerated.

Given these constraints, policy debates between presidential candidates have been largely over means rather than ends. Even presidents who come to power with the promise of abandoning existing policies and embarking on new ones usually end up tinkering with a few specifics. Political realities at home and abroad reined in Carter's human rights concerns and Reagan's military build-up, for example.

To further complicate matters, as with any other country, America's policy toward Japan is thoroughly entangled in the processes and decisions of Japan's policy toward the United States. In Japan too, policymaking is a multi-stranded tug of war among ever more diverse interests, many of which hold veto power. As power diffuses within Japan, gridlock is increasingly prevalent. Within broad policy guidelines there is enormous debate. Neomercantilism is to Japan's postwar foreign policy what containment was to

America's. However, within that broad orientation toward the world, there are bitter and endless battles among Japan's bureaucrats and politicians over how to implement it in specific economic sectors and overseas markets, and how much to adjust those policies if challenged by foreigners. Thus, what often appears as deliberate Tokyo stonewalling is actually the inability of Japan's leaders to form a policy consensus. Consensus building takes a long time in Japan, and often is still being forged even after negotiations begin. This both reflects and contributes to Tokyo's tendency to cope with or adapt to challenges rather than initiate change.

POLICIES, PERCEPTIONS, AND POWER

Ultimately, both nations' foreign policies are deeply rooted in their respective cultures and histories. American and Japanese foreign policies reflect the completely different economic orientations of liberalism and neomercantilism. As Gilpin notes, "whereas Western economies are based on the belief in the superior efficiency of the free market and individualism, the market and the individual in Japan are not relatively autonomous but are deeply embedded in a powerful nonliberal culture and social system."[2]

American policymakers and policies are often prisoners of the "city on the hill" syndrome in which the United States is the economic, political, and social model for all humanity. The American creed of free markets and decentralized politics prevents the government and public alike from conceiving of Japan, or any other country, outperforming the United States by carefully managing its economy through such means as government–business cooperation, widespread business cartels, five-year indicative plans, import barriers, and dumping. Japan's "managed market" system produced four times more wealth than America's "free market" system between 1950 and 1973, and twice as much since. Yet, because Americans are so thoroughly socialized into their nation's values and beliefs, most simply cannot comprehend that reality.

The American belief that the United States is a morally, politically, and economically superior country and model to all others has guided relations with Japan from the relationship's beginning. A 1852 editorial in the *Democratic Review* asserted idealistically that the Japanese, "naturally a trading nation, are debarred from external trade; an inquiring nation, they are denied the means of research; an ingenious nation, they are deprived of the benefits of ingenuity; an ambitious nation, they are reduced to arbitrary distinctions which paralyze all individual enterprise."[3] If only the Japanese had the opportunity, the reasoning went then and now, they would become "more like us."[4]

That conversion is unlikely to happen. Like every other country's foreign policy, Japan's is as much embedded in its culture as geography. In Japan, groups rather than individuals compose society's foundation. The individual is compared to an unturned nail that must be hammered down (deru kugi wa utareru). An individual's identity, purpose, and esteem comes from his or her group. There is no conception of equality in Japan. Everyone is either above or below everyone else. Before the Meiji revolution (1868), one's place in society was fixed; Japanese society held four broad classes – samurai, peasant, artisan, and merchant. There was little mobility within a class and virtually none between them. But as Japan began to modernize during the mid nineteenth century, opportunities arose for individuals to rise and fall in socioeconomic status and wealth. Yet, mobility is always in the context of a group to which the individual devotes himself and derives his or her basic identity.

Hierarchy and groupism shape the Japanese conception of international relations in which countries are either relatively superior or inferior to each other. Nineteenth-century Social Darwinism reinforced these traditional Japanese values. International relations is a perennial struggle in which the strong naturally and rightfully subdue and exploit the weak. Before 1945, Japanese tended to rank countries by their military prowess; since then by their economic prowess.

The Japanese sense of groupism does not include other humans (gaijin). Instead, Japanese groupism tempers its foreign relations with a fierce nationalism. Japanese are socialized to put the interests of their ultimate group – Japan – before all others. During World War II, Japanese soldiers and civilians tossed their lives away in suicidal charges or just suicide rather than surrender. While their sacrifice to the nation since 1945 has not been grisly, it is still fervent. For the last half century, Japanese have devoted themselves to their work groups as part of a greater obligation to make Japan an economic superpower.

Along with Japan's cycles of foreign relations were swings in Japanese perceptions of themselves and foreigners. While Japanese are in the "tutor stage" of their foreign patronship, they feel inferior to their benefactor. But after they have absorbed as much as possible of foreign practices and ideas into their own culture, and benefit materially, a sense of inferiority turns to superiority and an increasingly haughty nationalism.

Despite 140 years of association, Japan remains inscrutable for most Americans. In 1854, Perry wrote that "Japanese diplomats are certainly very pertinacious in holding out. They fall back from their advanced positions step by step, preserving their equanimity, nor do they take offense at any hasty expression of their opponents. . . . A Japanese never takes offense at being charged with disingenuousness or even with duplicity. One would suppose that they consider it a compliment to be thought tricky and deceitful."[5] A century later, Henry Kissinger offered a more sophisticated but similar view:

> [the Japanese] avoid commitment in the early stages of the process, to enable a serious deliberation to go forward in which participants have the option of changing their minds and the need for decision is avoided until genuine agreement exists. Thus, even if outsiders could obtain correct information about the internal state of play – no easy matter – it would do them little good because the early stages of the process are amorphous and its subsequent evolution depends on group psychology. Japan thereby acquires an enormous advantage. There is literally no one capable of making a decision by himself. Only amateurs would seek to pressure an individual Japanese minister; even when he yields out of politeness, he cannot carry out his promise. But when the consensus is formed, for whatever reason, it is implemented with speed, determination, and breadth unmatched by any Western country. . . . What could be more effective than a society voracious in its collection of information, impervious to pressure, and implacable in execution.[6]

More often than not, these profound cultural differences cause Americans and Japanese to talk past each other. International conflicts can then become crises because of "muddled perceptions, stifled communications, disappointed expectations, and paranoid reactions. In turn, each 'friend' misreads the other, each is reticent with the other, each is surprised by the other, each replies in kind."[7] Misperceptions abound in this atmosphere. Often there is a tendency to see one's own side as hopelessly divided, bumbling, and weak and the other side as invincibly united in purpose and method. A different but no less debilitating perception is to assume that the other side's politics and perspectives mirror one's own, that they are, or at least should be, "just like us."

Perceptions rule our actions. Power is as much psychological as material; like beauty, it may well lie in the beholder's eye, causing him to act accordingly. Many forces shape a nation's perception of its interests and the power it needs to protect or enhance those interests. As much as anything, perceptions and culture shape policy. In democratizing societies, the rise of a mass media and mass opinion increasingly channel the parameters within which leaders lead. The mass media both shapes and is shaped by mass opinion. Once an image becomes cemented in the minds of most, the public and the media it serves will rarely tolerate alternative views.

Perhaps no country's image has varied as widely in the American imagination as Japan's. Americans once scoffed at the label "Made in Japan;" more recently they view it with mingled awe, gratitude, and fear. Perceived Japanese perfidy and honesty are like opposite sides of a revolving door in America's consciousness. Within a generation spanning the mid twentieth century, America's image of Japanese shifted from armies of dutiful factory and office workers toiling at their assembly lines and desks, to masses of brutal, mindless soldiers tossing babies atop bayonets, and then after the surrender, back again. More recently, the serene image of monks raking a zen sand garden gives way to the hectic clamor of crowds charging through Tokyo streets and subway stations. American actions toward Japan have varied just as widely, from the loftiest altruism to the harshest retaliation.

The kaleidoscope of images shifts with the headlines. Yet despite a bitter war and more recent economic battles, most Americans admire and like Japan and the Japanese. In between newspaper, television, and congressional revelations of the latest Japanese dumping attack, buyout of a Silicon Valley firm, or discrimination against competitive American products, the public's image of Japan is decidedly positive. Surveys consistently indicate that three-quarters of Americans have positive feelings toward Japanese; only two-thirds of Japanese feel the same about Americans.

One more complicating factor in policymaking is the complexity of today's issues compared to those of the past. Before 1945, diplomats addressed a few large geopolitical issues with Japan like the power balance, naval size, immigration, and, ultimately, war. Since then, the issues have mushroomed from a few to hundreds, most of which are geoeconomic. It was much easier for American policymakers and diplomats to deal with those few relatively straightforward pre-1945 issues of war and peace than the contemporary complexities and paradoxes of simultaneously finessing an economic challenge and nurturing a military alliance.

Policies are promulgated and justified as a means of securing national interests. The calculation of national interests is rarely simple. Interests – and the power to defend or enhance those interests – may well vary considerably over time. A nation's military, economic, and cultural power relative to its rivals both shapes its interests and means to realize those interests. And sometimes a nation's interests may seem to conflict with one another. Washington's uncertainty about how to respond to Japan's rising geoeconomic power may lie in its ambivalent and insidious nature. As Akira Iriye reminds us, "not all expansion is imperialistic. . . . Ideas can expand, as can goods and capital."[8] The reverse side of Japan's trade and investment surplus – in the short run at least – is the American consumer's enjoyment of access to inexpensive Japanese goods and capital.

Although the relative, constantly shifting power among states has always been more difficult to calculate than national interests, it becomes more so as countries become ever more politically, economically, and culturally interdependent. Traditionally, a state's geopolitical and geoeconomic power were autonomous and interwoven. A state could not be a military and imperial power unless it was an economic power, and vice versa.

That is no longer true. Territorial expansion for the great and superpowers is now an anachronism. As the world becomes more interdependent, military power has increasingly retarded rather than enhanced national interests. The most successful states have become powerful by minimizing geopolitical entanglements and focusing on geoeconomic expansion. The accumulation and assertion of power and wealth now largely depend on denying rivals one's home market while capturing foreign markets. In an increasingly interdependent global economy, multinational corporations play the role that marines and gunboats once did in the perennial struggle to assert national interests.

Despite these changes, at least one facet of international relations endures. In the geoeconomic great power game, as in geopolitical struggles, some governments are more adept at fostering expansion at home and abroad than others. No country has been more successful at this strategy than Japan. Tokyo's interrelated industrial, technology, and trade policies resulted in annual average 10 per cent economic growth rates between 1950 and 1973, and 4 per cent increases since – four and two times, respectively, those of the United States during the same periods. During the 1980s, Japan surpassed the United States by most financial, technological, manufacturing, and trade indicators.

Once again, American and Japanese interests and power are grinding against each other, not just across the Pacific but around the world. But the United States seems just as bewildered today about Japan's challenge as it was in the 1930s. Despite the Cold War's end, the peace dividend has proven to be rather skimpy as the United States continues playing the old great power game. Even with the Soviet empire and communism dead, the White House has found new geopolitical bullies to confront. In so doing, it continues to avoid systematically addressing problems of immense trade and budget deficits, declining productivity and real income, crumbling cities, infrastructure, health care, families, education, bloody streets, and polluted landscapes.

EXPLORATION OF RELATED THEMES

This is an analytical history of American policy toward Japan; it does not simply chronical events, it tries systematically to make sense of them. All along this study will attempt to untangle the interrelated perceptions, convergent and divergent national interests, and shifting power relations which have shaped American policies toward Japan. More specifically, it will highlight the personalities, national moods, domestic issues and political alignments, and other pressing international concerns within which Washington has attempted to define and assert its interests toward Japan. America's two great cycles of relations with Japan will be analyzed in three parts, with the first cycle analyzed in Part I and the second cycle in Parts II and III.

Part I
From Geopolitical Protégé to Rival

1 Pacific Patron, 1853–94

During his presidential farewell address in 1796, George Washington articulated the guidelines for American foreign policy that had been followed since the United States achieved independence and would guide policymakers for another century: "The great rule of conduct for us in regard to foreign nations is, in extending our commercial relations to have with them as little political connection as possible. . . . Europe has a set of primary interests which to us have none or a very remote relation. Hence . . . it is our true policy to steer clear of permanent alliances with any portion of the foreign world."[1] To the admonition "Trade with All, Ally with None," President Monroe added the warning in 1823 against any Great Power encroachment in the Western Hemisphere.

American isolationism thus was never economic or even political. America's commercial interests were global; political interests were hemispheric and occasionally extended further. The perennial wars rearranging the frontiers of Europe and European imperialism in Africa and Asia were of concern to the United States only so far as they impeded American trade. And the United States would not hesitate to use force to preserve its trade interests. In the 1790s, American and French warships fought on the high seas. Between 1801 and 1807, President Jefferson dispatched America's small fleet to battle the Barbary states of North Africa for free trade in the Mediterranean.

American isolationism was essentially moral; Americans believed their political, economic, and social system superior to the corrupt, vicious practices of European and other despotic regimes around the world. Americans universalized their national ideals and interests, assuming that America's institutions, values, and behaviors were natural to all humankind, but elsewhere stunted by evil governments. This moral self-righteousness shaped the justification if not conduct of American foreign policy, as leaders and the public evaluated all international conflicts in terms of right and wrong, with the United States personifying the former and foreign countries the latter.

For much of its history, the United States got away with this policy. Geography and British naval power, however, rather than American diplomatic efforts, were primarily responsible. With the Atlantic and Pacific oceans serving as vast moats east and west, and with weak neighbors north and south, the United States could remain aloof as a "shining city on a hill," unsullied by foreign cultures and power struggles. The Monroe Doctrine asserting an American sphere of influence over the entire hemisphere was protected by the vast British rather than the tiny American navy. London was no more eager than Washington to see continental powers reestablish empires in Latin America.

America's policymakers heeded Washington's advice to avoid Europe's great power entanglements. When the United States did identify and act to protect a "sphere of influence" outside the western hemisphere, it occurred first in Asia rather than Europe.

AMERICAN EXPANSIONISM AND THE FAR EAST

If imperialism is the conquest of one nation by another, then the United States has been imperialist from its historical origins. Following independence, the United States simply followed an expansionist policy already 150 years old. From the arrival of the first English colonists on the east coast in the early 1600s until the U.S. Census Bureau announced the disappearance of the "frontier" in 1890, America's government and people worked to take and subdue from European powers and native peoples large chunks of land from the Atlantic to the Pacific. Although Washington's farewell address warned his countrymen against "entangling alliances," the United States has been anything but isolationist. The national consensus to heed Washington's warning resulted in neutrality not isolation. Merchants and diplomats took advantage of any opportunities for commercial and territorial expansion.

Thus, the national debate was not over expansion *per se*, but on its pace, means, and, most importantly, whether the new territories should be "free" or "slave." Several congressional compromises – 1820, 1850, 1854 – ensured a political power balance until the Civil War ended that "peculiar institution" of slavery. Whether it preceded or followed the Civil War, America's expansion was justified by such idealist visions as "Manifest Destiny" and the spreading of democracy, and such realist arguments as the international military and commercial power balance and Social Darwinism. Idealist and realist expansionist arguments complemented each other – they all promoted national interests.

America's expansion to and across the Pacific proceeded in an untidy series of acquisitions and settlements. The United States acquired large expanses of the continent from foreign sovereign countries – Britain, Spain, and Mexico – and then within the new territory subdued the Indian tribes or "domestic dependent nations" as the Supreme Court labeled them. Before the end of the nineteenth century, America's only successful war for territory was with Mexico (1846–8); the 1812 War with Britain was a draw. All other acquisitions were achieved through diplomacy – Mississippi River navigation (1795), Louisiana Purchase (1803), Canadian boundary (1815, 1818), West Florida and Spanish empire boundary (1819), northern Maine and Minnesota boundary (1842), Texas (1845), Oregon territory from Britain (1846), Gadsden Purchase from Mexico (1854), and Alaska from Russia (1867).

Even when the United States was still relatively weak, its leaders identified national security as dependent on a much broader international region. In 1823, President Monroe issued a warning that the United States would not tolerate any European attempts to crush the independence struggles by Latin Americans against Spanish rule. The Monroe Doctrine's importance was largely symbolic. Britain shared America's interest in seeing Spain's empire crumble and small, weak states emerge from the ruin. It was Britain's navy which provided the real deterrent to the ambitions of other European powers. The Monroe Doctrine, however, asserted an American security and commercial interest across the entire western hemisphere – a remarkable claim for a young and militarily weak republic.

As if the entire western hemisphere were not enough, almost from American independence, national security and interests became increasingly entangled with the Far East. American expansion did not end on the shores of California and the Oregon territory. Boston merchant ships traded for hides, tallow, and sea otter pelts off the Pacific coasts of North and South America even before the American revolution. Within a decade after achieving independence, the United States began developing interests across the Pacific basin. In 1784, the "Empress of China" became the first American merchant ship to arrive in Canton. In 1788, Captain Robert Gray discovered the mouth of the Columbia river and claimed the watershed for the United States. Gray then sailed to China via Hawaii. In 1796, the American merchant ship "Astrea" sailed into Manila Bay to begin trade with the Philippines. And in 1791, Captain John Kendrick, commanding the American ships "Columbia" and "Lady Washington" broke Japanese law when he anchored briefly in an isolated cove on the Kii peninsula. The scores of American merchant and whaling ships criss-crossing the Pacific by the late eighteenth century rose to hundreds by the mid nineteenth century.

America's growing ties with the exotic lands, peoples, products, and customs of the Far East soon seized the popular imagination as a natural extension of America's "Manifest Destiny." Secretary of State William Seward captured the mingling of idealism and materialism behind that vision when he asked fellow Americans to "consider what a magnificent destiny you have before you, to lay your hand on the Atlantic coast, and to extend your power to the Pacific Ocean and grasp the great commerce of the East, you will fully appreciate the responsibility."[2]

THE WESTERN POWERS AND CHINA

The United States was not the only country with expanding interests in the Far East. In the early nineteenth century, Spain and the Netherlands were the two leading imperial powers in the western Pacific with colonies in the Philippines and Dutch East Indies, respectively. The Portuguese had the tiny colony of Macao on the southern Chinese coast. But China allowed only a limited trade through Canton, and Japan and Korea were tightly shut to most outsiders.

Dreams of access to China's potentially vast markets dominated western aspirations in Asia. Foreign merchants and missionaries eyed China's 400 million population as a vast potential market in which they could either enrich themselves or save souls. These dreams remained largely unrealized; tapping China's vast potential market remained limited. Throughout the late eighteenth and early nineteenth centuries, Britain, the United States, and other western powers suffered trade deficits with China as their demand for tea, rhubarb, and porcelain far outweighed the Chinese desire for sandalwood, furs, hides, cotton, and ginseng. Chinese Confucianism and bureaucracy were as important as mass poverty in limiting the demand for western products. Tribute rather than free trade ruled the Chinese conception of foreign economic relations. China was the self-sufficient, culturally superior "Middle Kingdom." All other surrounding or distant realms were peopled by barbarians. China's foreign economic relations were to be harmonious, limited, and unequal. The barbarians would periodically journey to China to prostrate themselves (kowtow) before officials and offer tribute. The Chinese in turn would reward the supplicants with riches of perceived equal or even greater value. The foreign trade through Canton was channeled through a guild (Co-hong) of a dozen merchant firms. Foreign firms established "factories" or warehouses and residences in a section of Canton from which to conduct trade with the Co-hong.

The British solution to their limited and unequal trade with China was opium. In the late eighteenth century, the East India Company, which had a monopoly over Britain's trade with China until 1834, began illegally smuggling opium into China. American and other foreign merchants soon joined the opium trade which was channeled into the pipes of increasing thousands of Chinese addicts. Every American firm except Oliphant and Company participated in opium smuggling, and America's share of the market may have been as high as one-third.[3]

As a result, China suffered increasingly sharp trade deficits. Alarmed at the ever-larger outflow of silver, China's imperial government at Beijing periodically ordered crackdowns on the opium trade. But the foreign merchants simply bought off the Canton bureaucrats and Co-hong merchants charged with stamping it out.

Then, in 1839, Beijing dispatched incorruptable and steadfast imperial commissioner Lin Tse-hsu to Canton. Lin confiscated and burned tons of opium in the foreign settlement there. Rather than yield to China's sovereign right to enforce its own laws, Britain declared war. Throughout the Opium War (1839–42), Britain's modern navy and army repeatedly routed China's massed feudal levies and flotillas of war junks. Under the Treaty of Nanking (1842), China's Ching dynasty agreed to open five ports to British trade and residence, permanently cede Hong Kong island, abolish the Co-hong monopoly, limit Chinese tariffs on imports, and pay a 21 million Mexican dollar indemnity. In a supplementary treaty (1843) China also agreed to grant Britain "most favored nation" status in which Britain would automatically receive any trade concession China made to other countries.

Throughout the 1840s and 1850s, other western powers, including the United States, demanded and received similar concessions. On July 3, 1843, American and Chinese diplomats signed the Treaty of Wang-hsia in which China granted the United States the same privileges that Britain enjoyed, plus allowed for extraterritoriality or the right for Americans accused of committing crimes in China to be tried in an American court. During the 1850s, the United States followed up this success by negotiating and signing a series of agreements with China which opened an additional eleven ports, maintained tariffs at 5 per cent, allowed missionaries to travel anywhere in China, legalized the opium trade, and permitted an embassy in Beijing. American gunboats patrolled China's coasts and rivers to protect American merchants or missionaries.

China's sovereignty eroded with each "unequal" treaty. The Imperial Maritime Custom Service was run by the British and other foreign representatives. More than eighty ports and cities were eventually opened to foreign diplomats, merchants, and missionaries. By the late nineteenth century, Britain, France, and Germany had staked out entire regions along China's coast in which they claimed exclusive privileges.

Having opened China, the western imperial powers increasingly eyed an even more remote and potentially rich source of trade – Japan.

CYCLES OF JAPANESE HISTORY AND CULTURE

Japan's recorded history stretches back over 1,500 years, during which time its foreign relations were largely peaceful. Foreigners tried to conquer Japan only twice – the Mongolian attacks of 1271 and 1281. And Japan only once attempted to overrun another country – between 1592 and 1598 Japanese armies invaded Korea and then withdrew. Japan's foreign relations consisted largely of periods of intensive cultural borrowing and trade, followed by isolation.

Throughout its history, Japanese political struggles and foreign relations have been closely linked. Challengers to a regime frequently tried to bolster their legitimacy and power by using foreign technology, institutions, weapons, and ideas. Once enthroned, the new regime would then expand the importation of foreign products and incorporation of foreign ideas into Japanese culture. At some point, Japan's elite would satiate their capacity and interest in assimilating foreign ideas and practices. A reaction would then occur in which trade was restricted and "traditional" culture asserted.

Before the mid nineteenth century, Japan had passed through four of these cycles. During the sixth and into the seventh centuries, the Yamato clan unified and ruled most of Japan through a skilful mixture of diplomacy, alliances, and conquest, and legitimized their rule by integrating within traditional Japanese culture aspects of Buddhism, Confucianism, China's imperial system, and Chinese and Korean fine arts. By the eighth century, the Japanese desire for foreign institutions, ideas, and arts became satiated and the inevitable reaction occurred. The imperial court stopped sending ambassadors to China; foreign trade withered. Many of the political institutions and practices borrowed from the continent were abandoned or allowed to atrophy. The once powerful emperor became a figurehead and power in the capital of Kyoto passed into the hands of the aristocratic Fujiwara clan. New power centers outside Kyoto arose and opponents to the regime proliferated among the Buddhist sects and armed landowners. Ambitious feudal lords periodically rebelled and Kyoto found it increasingly difficult to crush them.

By the twelfth century, the wheel had turned again. Japan dissolved into civil war between the Kyoto-based Taira and rural-based Morimoto clans. The rebel Moritomo crushed the government's Taira forces and, after receiving the imperial title of shogun, or military commander, moved the administrative capital to Kamakura, leaving the impotent imperial line in Kyoto. Embassies to China were renewed and trade with East Asia increased. The shogunate integrated Chinese Zen Buddhist concepts into their "way of the warrior" (bushido) and instituted Zen Buddhism throughout Japan to help assert and legitimize Kamakura's power. With Zen from China came new forms of fine arts and crafts. The renewed cultural, economic, and diplomatic ties with the mainland, however, were relatively short-lived. It was during the Kamakura era (1185–1333) that Japan faced its only foreign invasion of the premodern era. Japan's samurai armies defeated massive Mongol attacks in 1274 and 1281.

Although the Kamakura regime decisively destroyed the foreign threat, it failed to crush the steady rise in power of the rival Ashikaga clan. The Ashikaga (1338–1573) attempted to legitimize their revolt by championing a claimant to the imperial throne. Eventually they defeated the Kamakura regime and relocated the administrative capital to Kyoto. Like previous new regimes, the Ashikaga renewed ties with the continent and immersed themselves in Chinese styles, arts, ideas, and institutions. Embassies and regular trade missions were exchanged. In 1401, the Ming Emperor formally acknowledged the shogun as the "king of Japan." Zen monasteries and temples experienced a renaissance as art and philosophy centers. Peace and foreign trade stimulated rapid economic growth and new centers and classes of wealth. Japanese merchants, pirates, and mercenaries spread throughout East and Southeast Asia.

Once again, a Japanese regime's power began to slowly crumble after periods of ascendancy and consolidation. A dispute within the Ashikaga clan led to a decade of civil war (1467–77) which gutted Kyoto and severed the regime's control over feudal lords across Japan. For the next century while the Ashikaga clung to Kyoto, Japan experienced incessant warfare as hundreds of ambitious warlords (daimyo) sallied forth from their castles to battle others in constantly shifting alliances and fortunes. As in Europe, Japan's decentralized feudalism was ended by cannon which battered down thin castle walls and muskets which destroyed the centrality of mounted warriors in warfare. That military technology came from overseas – this time not from China but from Europe.

In 1542, Portuguese priests were the first westerners to reach Japan. The first Portuguese merchant ship arrived in 1545, and Spanish, Dutch, and English merchants soon followed. By the late 1550s, some daimyo were manufacturing their own muskets and cannon. By the 1570s, most daimyo fielded musket corps alongside their archers and pikemen. In addition to European armaments, the Japanese quickly adopted tobacco, clocks, velvet, wool, and glassware. Although probably no more than 2 per cent of Japan's population ever converted to Christianity, many daimyo used the exotic faith to bolster their strength much as previous clans had used various Buddhist sects.

Throughout the late 1500s, a succession of three great military leaders

– Oda Nobunaga, Toyotomi Hideyoshi, and Tokugawa Ieyasu – unified Japan. Each leader in turn destroyed rival power holders: daimyo were defeated or coopted; armed monasteries burned and the monks slain; peasants disarmed; rich merchants looted or made financiers. Hideyoshi was the most ambitious of the three. He launched two invasions of Korea (1592– 6, 1597–8) with the hope of eventually conquering China. But the Japanese armies suffered unexpected defeats and were recalled after Hideyoshi's death in 1598. In 1,600, Tokugawa Ieyasu defeated his opponents at the battle of Sekigahara, and eliminated the remnants of resistance by destroying Osaka castle in 1614.

The Tokugawa clan then instituted one of the most authoritarian states in history and ruled Japan for another 250 years. They forced all remaining daimyo to raze all castles but one in their respective realms (han). The capital was moved to Edo (modern Tokyo). Land was redistributed among victors and vanquished alike in measures of grain called "koku" (5.2 bushels). There were four classes of daimyo – the immediate shogun's family (tenryo) whose lands were located mostly in and around Edo, the twenty-three related han (shimpan) whose lands were largely just beyond the tenryo's, the allied daimyo (fudai) beyond the shimpan's, and the former enemies (tozama) which were assigned lands on the far reaches of Japan. In return for these lands each daimyo swore an oath of allegiance to the Tokugawa regime or bakufu. The Tokugawa decreed a series of laws which strictly designated the duties and rights of the daimyo and emperor. Every daimyo was forced to spend either half of every year or one of every two years in Edo, and when he returned to his own realm he was forced to leave his family as hostage (sankin kotai). Although the daimyo were not directly taxed, the Tokugawa periodically undermined their accumulation of wealth by assessing contributions for expansive public works projects including temples, shrines, roads, pilgrimages, and the shogun's castle and palace. Tokugawa agents infiltrated all the han and reported all activities back to Edo. Meanwhile the emperor remained in Kyoto and had legitimized Tokugawa rule by formally designating them as the new shogunate. Four official classes – samurai, peasant, artisan, and merchant – were designated with no mobility between classes allowed. However, there were two other significant classes – the priests and the "untouchables" (hinin or eta). Each official and unofficial class was strictly regulated by law. Tokugawa ideology blended traditional Japanese values with neo-Confucianism which extolled the state, class divisions, and the promotion of social harmony.

Having used European ideas, technology, weapons, and even advisors to unify Japan, the new Tokugawa regime steadily reduced the influence of foreigners in the country to prevent any upstart clan from challenging their rule. By 1641, a series of decrees implemented an isolationist policy (sakoku) in which virtually no foreigners would be allowed to enter Japan, no Japanese could travel abroad, or Japanese currently overseas allowed to return. Any violators would be executed. Only the Chinese and Dutch could trade with Japan and then only from the tiny island of Deshima in Nagasaki harbor. Christianity was banned and any adherents who did not convert to Buddhism were executed. For over two centuries, except for the trickle of foreign goods and ideas through Nagasaki, Japan remained isolated from the rest of humanity.

The long peace of the next two and a half centuries transformed the samurai from fierce warriors into bureaucrats. Internal trade boomed, cities grew and proliferated, and the merchant class became increasingly rich and diverse. A cash economy arose alongside the barter system based on koku of rice. Inflation steadily undermined the samurai's fixed incomes from their rice crop. A symbiotic relationship developed between the samurai and merchants: the samurai protected the merchants in return for finance. By the mid nineteenth century, Japan's population leveled off at around 30 million, while Edo had expanded into a sprawling city of over 1 million people and Osaka half a million. As much as 40 per cent of males and 15 per cent of females had achieved literacy by attending the Buddhist temple schools and over 1,400 private schools.[4]

Despite Japan's isolation, the Tokugawa remained remarkably well-informed about the world. The "Dutch school" (rangaku) of scholars were allowed to study the latest western books and news from the Dutch trading post at Deshima island off Nagasaki. In 1811, the Bakufu established the "Institute for the Investigation of Barbarian Books" to explore systematically the wisdom, institutions, history, and customs of the west. By the time Japan was forced to open up to the west, many leading scholars and government leaders were familiar with western politics, history, science, medicine, mathematics, and inventions. The importance of these studies was reinforced by the periodic intrusions of foreign ships into Japan's waters. Japanese officials rejected visits by Russian, British, and American ships requesting trade relations. During this time the Russians were the most aggressive. Russian traders and colonists advanced into the Kurile islands, Sakhalin, and Hokkaido, precipitating clashes with Japanese settlers. After news of China's defeat reached Japan, debate intensified over just how to repeal western imperialism.

By the mid nineteenth century, the Tokugawa regime faced increasingly severe political and economic challenges at home. Natural disasters and subsequent famines sparked periodic peasant revolts. Most people became poorer from inflation as the government debased the currency nineteen times

in the early nineteenth century. The daimyo increasingly resented their diminishing incomes, growing debt to the merchants, and continuing repres-
sion by Edo.

Despite Edo's elaborate system of controls, several of the tozama han
became ever more economically and militarily powerful. Satsuma in southern Kyushu and Choshu at Honshu's western tip both benefited from financial (tempo) reforms which decreased debt and stimulated economic
growth, diversified crops and light industries, vigorous military training,
shipping, banking, and, in Satsuma's case, trade through the Ryukyu islands
and a near monopoly on sugar cane. By 1850, Satsuma and Choshu would
be ranked second and nineth in income among the 273 han. Unlike most
han, they were free of debts to Edo. Their animosity toward the Tokugawa
continued to burn even after 250 years. They would become the leading
opponents to Tokugawa rule.

By 1853, the Tokugawa faced severe internal and foreign challenges.

PERRY, HARRIS, AND JAPAN'S OPENING

Early Visits

Where was Japan's place in America's commercial expansion across the
Pacific?

Throughout the first seventy years of American trade with the Far East
Japan remained a distant, mysterious land. Yet it was not inaccessible; Commodore Perry and his sailors were not the first Americans to visit Japan. As
early as May 1791, Captain John Kendrick of Massachusetts briefly defied
Japan's nearly two centuries of seclusion when he anchored his ships, the
"Columbia" and the "Lady Washington", at Kashinora on the Kii Peninsula.
Unable to sell his sea otter pelts to the locals, he "made but a short tarry"
then sailed away. He left behind a note explaining "the stress of wind and
wave" forced him ashore and he would set sail as soon as the weather
cleared.[5]

Sporadically over the next half century, a score or more intrepid, none-
too-scrupulous American sea captains would enter Japan's waters from
necessity or design while plying the triangular trans-Pacific trade routes
among Canton, Hawaii, and America's northwest coast. Like Kendrick,
those who came to trade would find their ambitions frustrated by the stern
refusal of Japanese officials and the populace to buy foreign goods. Between 1797 and 1807, eight American ships flying the Dutch flag sailed

into Nagasaki. With its country at war with France and later England, the Dutch East India Company had employed the Americans to avoid the loss of their own ships.

Aware that the penalty for violating Japan's exclusion order was death, the American captains and their crews anchored in Nagasaki bay with considerable trepidation. To their relief, the Japanese turned a blind eye to the subterfuge. Merchant William Cleveland wrote that although "we were taught to look upon the Japanese as a cruel people before coming in, many stories we now think exaggerated and some entirely unfounded." Like so many other visitors who have since followed, Cleveland remarked on the people's courtesy, kindness, cleanliness, and obedience to authority, but complained of the long and tedious chore it took to sell "this little invoice, which would not have been an hour's work in Salem."[6]

One American visitor to Nagasaki during this period audaciously sailed under his own colors in 1803. Along with the usual trade goods, Captain William Stewart carried with him a camel, donkey, and water buffalo as presents and claimed to carry a letter from President Jefferson authorizing him to open trade with Japan. Japanese guard boats surrounded his ship, christened the "Nagasaki Maru", and officials took Stewart into custody. The Japanese accepted the menagerie but ordered Stewart to leave forthwith.

In 1807, Captain Joseph O'Cain at the helm of the American ship "Eclipse" flying Russian colors tried to succeed where Stewart failed. O'Cain fared no better. His request for trade was dismissed with the timeless Japanese response that "they had plenty of everything we had to offer."[7] Before sending her away, the Japanese officials supplied the "Eclipse" with vegetables, water, fish, and four hogs.

For the next quarter of a century, no more Americans ships are known to have sailed into Japanese waters. The reasons why are lost. Perhaps American merchants had given up on Japan's closed markets or had heard that the government had adopted a much more severe policy toward foreign intrusions. After a brawl between English sailors and Japanese villagers, in 1825 Edo issued its "no second thought" (ninen nahu) edict in which Japanese troops should immediately fire on foreign ships and kill any crew who came ashore. But in 1842, after learning of China's fate in the Opium War, the Bakufu chose to soften its "no second thought" policy. Now local officials could provision foreign ships and should only open fire if they refused to leave.

Captain Stewart had falsely claimed to represent President Jefferson. Although Jefferson was clearly interested in expanding America's commercial ties to the world's far corners, there is no record that he authorized

Stewart or anyone else to attempt Japan's opening. The first official suggestion that the United States pursue diplomatic and trade relations with Japan was an October 31, 1815 letter to President James Madison by US navy Captain David Porter. Madison pondered then rejected the idea.

Within a generation, the attentions of a succession of American presidents would be briefly diverted from pressing domestic problems to the need to establish diplomatic and trade relations with Japan. In 1832, President Andrew Jackson dispatched the diplomat Edmund Roberts with a small squadron to make treaties protecting American trade rights with various kingdoms and principalities bordering the Indian and western Pacific Oceans. Unfortunately, after securing treaties with Siam and Muscat, Roberts died in 1836 in Macao en route to Japan. Jackson did not appoint a successor.

Shortly thereafter, several American merchants tried to enter Japan. Charles King sailed on the "Morrison" to Japan in 1837 with seven castaway Japanese fishermen. Saving Japanese souls was as important in motivating King's expedition as garnering profits. He hoped his kind treatment and return of the Japanese would be the key to opening Japan to his ambitions. But when the "Morrison" anchored off Uraga at the mouth of Edo bay, Japanese shore batteries opened fire. Discouraged, King sailed off to Kagoshima. Initially he was treated well by Japanese officials who sent fresh water to his ship. But word arrived from Edo and the day after his arrival Kagoshima's batteries opened fire. The "Morrison" fled to Canton and King abandoned his dream of opening Japan.

In 1845, the "Manhattan" commanded by Captain Mercator Cooper anchored off Uraga after previously sending ashore some Japanese castaways. The Japanese did not fire upon the "Manhattan" but surrounded it with a thousand armed boats in three concentric circles. Among the Japanese officials who boarded the "Manhattan" was Moriyama Einosuke who spoke some English and would act as an interpreter at nearly every official meeting between the two countries for the next two decades. Cooper and the officials exchanged gifts and courtesies. The Japanese thanked Cooper for returning the castaways but pointedly told him to deposit any future derelicts at a Dutch port.

Commodore James Biddle sailed with two ships, the "Columbus" and "Vincennes" to Uraga in 1846. He anchored off Uraga on July 20 and was immediately surrounded by a flotilla of armed boats. Although officials refused to negotiate with Biddle, they offered him fresh supplies. The Americans were not allowed to go ashore. Japanese officials and commoners alike swarmed over the boats examining everything. At one point when Biddle attempted to board a Japanese boat, a sailor pushed him back into his own boat. When Biddle complained, the officials promised to severely punish the seaman. A week after Biddle's arrival, the officials handed him an unsigned and undated Bakufu document to "explain the reasons why we refuse to trade with foreigners. . . . This is the habit of our nation from time immemorial . . . the emperor positively refuses the permission you desire: He earnestly advises you to depart immediately, and to consult your own safety by not appearing again upon our coast."[8] Biddle reluctantly complied.

Unbeknownst to Biddle while he was anchored off Uraga, the Japanese were holding prisoner seven survivors of the shipwrecked crew of the American whaler "Lawrence". For nearly half a year, the Japanese confined the Americans in a dank cell, frequently struck them and forced them to tread on an image of the cross or Virgin and Child. They were shipped in chains to Nagasaki for repatriation and finally sailed for the Dutch East Indies in November 1846. Newspaper accounts of this ill-treatment of the castaways' bodies and souls and the incarceration of fifteen other Americans in Nagasaki incensed public opinion.

An incident like this was almost inevitable. In the early 1820s, whalers discovered the rich hunting grounds east and north of Japan's archipelago, and their numbers steadily increased over the next decades. In 1841 alone, Japanese officials counted nearly ninety whalers sailing through the straits separating Hokkaido and Honshu. The pounding of wave and wind inevitably disabled some ships and drove them onto Japanese shores.

The United States, however, did nothing about the reports of imprisoned Americans until 1849 when Commander James Glynn was ordered to sail his sloop of war the "Preble" to Nagasaki to investigate. After entering Nagasaki bay on April 17, Glynn immediately demanded the release of the American seamen. After five nerve-wracking days surrounded by war junks and batteries on the hills, Glynn finally received the seamen. The "castaways" were actually deserters from an American whaler, something Glynn clearly addressed in his official report. The press, however, treated those rescued as heroes who had endured months of ill-treatment.

The Perry Mission

By the mid nineteenth century, the United States had become a continental power with a 25 million population and global commercial interests. Although its industrial takeoff would not come until the Civil War and its military remained miniscule, American commercial power had grown steadily. As early as 1851, America's merchant fleet surpassed Britain's in tonnage.[9]

The Far East was an essential part of America's global trade and, increasingly, religious ties. While thousands of American merchants raked the lands of the Pacific basin for profits, they were followed by scores of American missionaries searching for converts. Japan's isolation, ill-treatment of ship-wrecked sailors, and potential riches were common knowledge. A growing chorus of prominent Americans called for opening Japan to trade and lib-erating it from feudalism and isolationism as an integral part of their nation's manifest destiny.

In 1852, Secretary of State Daniel Webster and Secretary of the Navy William Graham decided to revive the Japan mission, and quickly received President Millard Fillmore's approval. The Fillmore administration sought three major goals with Japan. First, it wanted an agreement that shipwrecked sailors would be treated humanely and property protected. It also wanted coaling stations established in Japan so that American steamships could resupply in their long arc from China to California across the northern Pacific. And finally, they desired an open port in which Americans could trade and supply their vessels. Ideally, the Americans could also negotiate advantages similar to what they had wrung from China, including diplomatic relations, fixed tariffs, extraterritoriality, residence, and freedom for mis-sionaries to proselytize. The White House chose Matthew Calbraith Perry to command the expedition. On March 24, 1852, Perry received orders to prepare his ship to join the small American East India Squadron, and then lead it to Japan.

Who was this man who would forever be associated with gunboats and America's forced opening of Japan? Matthew Calbraith Perry was born into a seafaring family of valour and distinction. His father fought at sea during the American Revolution, three of his brothers were naval officers, and two of his three sisters married naval officers. Most famous was his brother, Oliver Hazard Perry, nine years senior who commanded the Amer-ican fleet on Lake Erie which destroyed the larger British fleet at the Battle of Put-in Bay.

During his long career, Perry served with distinction, bravery, and initi-ative in the Atlantic, Caribbean and Mediterranean. One of the first advoc-ates of a steam powered navy, Perry commanded America's first steam warship, the "Fulton II" from 1837 to 1842. Based on his experience with the "Fulton II", Perry supervised the construction of the sea-going "steam-frigate" the "Mississippi" which served as his flagship during both the Mex-ican War and his expedition to Japan. Fearless, hard-driving, decisive, and popular with his men, he continually exposed himself to enemy fire during his amphibious raids along the Mexican coast during the Mexican War. At the battle of Tabasco, Perry charged ashore at the head of 1,000 men.

A fellow commander, Franklin Buchanan described Perry as "an aston-ishing man, the most industrious, hard working, energetic, zealous, perse-vering, enterprising officer of his rank in our navy."[10] He looked like an old hound dog, with his thick black hair, sad brown eyes framed by heavy eyebrows and bags, drooping jowls, downturned mouth and thick lips, double-chin, and ample belly. His natural sternness was occasionally softened by grog. Although ruled by Perry's strict discipline, his men admired him by the example of bravery and rectitude he set and justness with which he commanded. An amateur scientist, he read widely and had special interests in botany and conchology. He also had an eye for the ladies and commented in his journal on the varying female beauties and dispositions among the nationalities he encountered in his voyage.

Perry described his mission as the "great object of my life," one he hoped would be as renowned scientifically as diplomatically. Using the large contingent of scientists that accompanied Napoleon to Egypt as a model, Perry tried to interest the president in mounting a similar expedition. But the White House regarded the expedition as primarily diplomatic and dismissed asking the penny-pinching Congress for funding. He did hire on several artists and scientists at a master's mate pay of $25 a month.

He prepared for his mission by first obtaining all available information about Japan. He had agents scour the bookstores and libraries of New York, Philadelphia, and elsewhere for every book on Japan. He interviewed Commander Glynn and Charles King, and even traveled to New Bedford to interrogate whaling captains about the currents and winds off the Japanese coast. He collected a range of technological marvels to awe the Japanese including clocks, a daguerreotype camera, colt pistols and rifles, a telegraph system, and even a quarter size steam train and 350 feet of track. Before leaving he sent word to the shogunate of his mission via the American minister to the Netherlands who passed on word to the Dutch government which in turn sent the message through their trade post at Deshima.

To fulfill his mission, Perry was assigned one-quarter of the American navy – two steam frigates, his flagship the "Mississippi" and the "Susquehanna", four sloops of war, and three supply ships. Although presumably Perry could have achieved his objective with only one ship, the squadron would be assembled to impress the Japanese with American might and determination. While his primary mission was diplomatic, Perry was authorized to defend himself if attacked. But Japan's opening would be established through diplomacy not force. In November 1852, Fillmore made Perry an envoy extraordinaire and minister plenipotentiary.

Perry set sail aboard the "Mississippi" from Norfolk on November 24, 1852 to join the Far East squadron. In China he engaged two interpreters – at Macao S. Wells Williams, a Sinologist and missionary, and at Shanghai the Dutchman Anton Portman. His squadron dropped anchor off Naha in the Ryukyu Islands on May 26, 1853, and for a week negotiated with the government for supplies and diplomatic relations. As he would later in Japan, he used constant diplomatic pressure, lavish presents, and periodic saber-rattling to gain his objectives. Letters were delivered refuting every government excuse for not permitting an audience with the court; two marine companies were paraded on the beach, bands played, cannon fired salutes. The Ryukyu government finally allowed an audience and supplied Perry's warships. However they refused "to open their markets to us."[11] Foreign diplomats and businessmen have been echoing the same complaint about the Japanese ever since. Perry rewarded the Ryukyu diplomats with presents and had them send mirrors and perfume on to the reigning queen. In the Ryukyu Islands and later Japan, Perry insisted on paying for any supplies to his fleet to avoid being entangled by obligations.

Perry's four ships steamed from Naha on July 2. He had two steam-powered gunboats, the "Susquehanna" (which he now made his flagship) and the "Mississippi", and two sloops of war, the "Saratoga" and "Plymouth". Perry realized that his mission's success was not preordained. He arrived on the shores of Japan believing that the Japanese were unsurpassed "in chicanery and diplomatic treachery," and everything he experienced during his negotiations reinforced that image. Throughout his journal, Perry complains of Japanese "lying and deceitful cunning." He admitted that, given their power, the Japanese "may for a long time succeed in maintaining their system of exclusiveness. But the time will come when they will be obliged to give way to the march of civilization and human rights, and it may be hoped that the Americans will have the honor of opening the first avenues to a prosperous and happy intercourse with them."

On July 8, 1853, Perry's small fleet arrived at the small port of Uraga at the mouth of Edo Bay. A flotilla of Japanese guard boats immediately surrounded Perry's ships. Perry issued strict orders that no Japanese would be allowed on board any ships but the "Susquehanna", and only then Japanese officials. He wanted to avoid the carnival atmosphere that accompanied Bibble who allowed Japanese of all classes to swarm over his two ships and thus violate the most basic rules of dignity and security.

A low ranking official, Nakajima Saburosuke, who claimed and was at first believed to be the vice-governor, appeared with a note in French warning Perry to sail away or remain at his peril. Perry refused to see the official and sent word through Lieutenant John Contree that he brought a letter from the president to the emperor and would not leave until he had met with someone of corresponding rank to whom he could present the letter. Nakajima replied that any business could only be conducted through Nagasaki and demanded that the Americans set sail at once. Perry sent word that he would remain until he accomplished his mission and further insisted that the guard boats be withdrawn, and if not, "I would disperse them by force." Nakajima hastily complied. Perry noted that in his long battle of wits with the Japanese, "here was the first important point gained."

The Japanese had never seen steamboats before and were awed by the appearance and power of these "black ships." Japanese troops in scarlet uniforms massed the hills and headland and manned the batteries around Uraga. In Edo the Bakufu boiled with debate over how to respond to the invasion. Edo's populace panicked: "The whole city was in an uproar. In all directions were seen mothers flying with their children in their arms, and men with mothers on their backs. . . . The tramp of war-horses, the clatter of armed warriors, the noise of carts, the parade of firemen, the incessant tolling of bells, the shrieks of women, the cries of children, dinning all the streets of a city of more than a million souls, made confusion worse confounded."[12] Shinto priests at Japan's sacred shrine at Ise prayed for divine intervention to sweep the barbarians away.

The next day, a higher ranking official, Kayama Eizaemon, who claimed to be Uraga's governor, appeared and repeated the demands that the Americans depart immediately. Perry sent word through Commander Franklin Buchanan and Captain Henry Adams that "if the Japanese government did not appoint a suitable person to receive the documents addressed to the emperor, I would go on shore with a sufficient force and deliver them, whatever the consequences might be." The document's elaborate box was shown to Kayama who nodded and offered water and food supplies. Buchanan replied that the Americans wanted nothing but an audience with the government.

Meanwhile, Perry had a longboat dispatched to survey the surrounding waters. Kayama demanded that the surveying be stopped immediately since it violated Japanese law. Perry sent word that the surveys would continue since they were required by American law. Once again Perry completely disregarded Japanese sovereignty. Buchanan handed Kayama a letter from Perry to the Japanese government explaining his mission and requesting an interview. Kayama then departed promising to bring a reply in several days from Edo. The surveys continued over the next few days. Several tense hours passed on July 11 when around forty guard boats approached the surveying party but then dispersed when the "Mississippi" sailed towards them.

Kayama returned on July 13 with word that a high government official had arrived at Uraga with a document empowering him to accept the letter. He would meet with Perry the following day. Perry sent word accepting the offer.

On July 14, Perry's two steamboats lined up stern to bow with their port guns covering the beach at which the meeting would be held. Adverse winds prevented the two sloops from moving to the anchorage. Along the shore for "more than a mile was crowded with Japanese troops, from five to seven thousand drawn up under arms . . . composed of cavalry, artillery, infantry, and archers; some of the infantry with flint muskets, others with matchlocks." Around four hundred American marines, sailors, and band members clambered into a score of longboats and were rowed ashore. After they had lined up in review in two long lines leading to the audience hall, Perry and his officers embarked and were rowed to the beach. Ashore, the officers were preceded by two huge negroes carrying the American flag and "Powhatan's pennant"; they turned just aside outside the conference hall. Following Perry and his officers were "two of the best looking boys in the squadron" carrying the "rosewood boxes, about twelve inches long, with locks, hinges, and other mountings, all in solid gold" containing the letters "bound in blue silk velvet, with the seal of the United States attached to each by cords made of gold and silken thread, at the end of which were large gold tassels. The seals themselves were encased in circular boxes, made of pure gold." Two powerful, heavily armed negroes marched along with each boy. They strode between the ranks of marines and sailors presenting arms with fixed bayonets while three bands played the Star Spangled Banner.

Toda Izu no Kami and Ido Iwami no Kami, Uraga's two governors, stood waiting stoically in the audience hall. Inside the hall, the American and Japanese delegations bowed solemnly to each other. The boys delivered the rosewood boxes. President Fillmore's letter, dated November 30, 1852, called for "friendship, commerce, a supply of coal, and provisions and protection for our shipwrecked people," and pointed out that if the government would "allow a free trade between the two countries, it would be extremely beneficial to both." American diplomats have been making the same point ever since, despite the solid evidence that Japan's carefully managed rather than free markets are actually a superior means of achieving economic development and wealth. Commodore Perry's accompanying letter was much longer and stressed such things as American power, justness, friendliness, and determination to create relations with Japan based on equality and international law. The Japanese then handed the Americans a document acknowledging the letter's receipt and maintained that "we cannot now bring about any alterations in the ancient laws." The letter did hold out the possibility of a future softening of the isolationist policy but in the meantime ordered the Americans to leave. Perry replied that he would return for a definitive answer within a year. The delegations exchanged no presents or refreshments.

Rather than immediately leave as he was commanded, Perry boarded the "Mississippi" and ordered it to survey its way up the bay, eventually within six miles of Edo. Perry's intention was to "work up the fears of the emperor" and "might have gone still higher but was apprehensive of causing too much alarm." Perry's impetuosity was successful, "the nearer we approached the imperial city the more polite and friendly they became." While he was gone, Kayama appeared at the "Susquehanna", expressed his regret that the "Mississippi" had sailed up the bay, and offered presents to the officers. The American officers refused the presents but plied Kayama and his underlings with food and whiskey.

Perry returned three days later on July 17 whereupon the squadron steamed away. He claimed five achievements for his diplomacy, including the dispersal of the guard boats, extensive surveys, conferring with someone of equal rank, the receipt of the president's letter on the basis of diplomatic equality rather than tribute, and impressing the Japanese that the United States "is superior in power and influence to Japan."

During the winter, Perry's ships dispersed on various missions throughout the Far East. Perry must have had a restless winter, worrying over what decision the Japanese government would deliver the following spring and whether meanwhile another great power – Russia, France, or Britain – might be the first to force a treaty from the Japanese. At Macao, Perry encountered a French frigate which soon departed with a French minister under sealed orders; at Shanghai, three Russian ships had just returned from Nagasaki and rumour had it they would soon return. The European powers had known of Perry's mission and were soon to mount their own expeditions. Perry wrote of the Russian admiral that he suspected "his design of returning again to Japan, and apprehensive that he might ultimately go to Edo, and there interfere very seriously with my operations, and believing also with many others that the French commodore had been ordered by his government in the same direction, I became anxious . . . [to prevent] either the French or Russian to gain an advantage over me." Perry was determined that the United States would be the first nation to open Japan, and he would be the agent of that historic mission.

Meanwhile, the Bakufu was bitterly divided over the best response to Perry. Although the first Tokugawa shoguns had been powerful leaders, as the long peace proceeded, in typically Japanese fashion, shoguns became figureheads; real power centered in the shogun's closest advisors. At the time of Perry's visit, Abe Masahiro, the head of the shogun's Senior Council (Roju), had duties and powers similar to that of a prime minister. Abe had been in power since 1845 and was widely respected.

Abe and the other Roju members faced the dilemma of losing face whether they acceded to Perry's requests or fought and lost. The Roju chose to share the dilemma by "consulting" the other daimyo, an unprecedented action and signal to all that the Tokugawa regime was even weaker than most supposed. Of the roughly fifty recorded replies, most advocated resistance: thirty-four called for outright rejection of Perry's request and fourteen for further negotiations while Japan strengthened itself so that it could eventually expel the barbarians, and eight advocated an attack on Perry. Only two called for Japan's opening.[13]

Abe had achieved his consensus at the price of power-sharing. From now on, outspoken and ambitious daimyo freely voiced their perspectives whether they were solicited or not.

By January 24, 1854, Perry's reinforced squadron had reassembled at Hong Kong and set off that day to the Ryukyu Islands. His squadron included three steamships, the "Susquehanna", "Mississippi", and "Powhatan", the sloops of war "Vandalia", "Macedonia", "Plymouth", and "Saratoga", and the supply ships "Lexington", "Supply", and "Southhampton". On his departure's eve, Perry's race to open Japan was complicated when he received orders from Navy Secretary J. C. Dobbin to dispatch a steamship to meet America's new minister to China, R. M. McLane, and then patrol China's troubled waters. Exasperated, Perry wrote a reply complaining how the order disrupted his mission; he promised to dispatch a steamship only after he had achieved his prime objective. Nonetheless, his nine ships only briefly sailed together as Perry dispatched several to accomplish missions related to opening Japan. Throughout the expedition, Perry was in the thick of the action, transferring his flag among the three steamships as each was best able to accomplish his immediate objectives.

For two weeks, Perry tarried in the Ryukyus refitting his ships, negotiating with the government for a fair currency exchange rate, and visiting the palace. While he was pleased to see the populace friendly and eager to trade, he blasted the government for its perpetual "crooked policy of deceit."

The squadron arrived off Uraga on February 13, 1854 and anchored around twelve miles north of the town. This time the guard boats kept their distance while a boat containing a local delegation approached Perry's flagship, the "Powhatan". Captain Henry Adams greeted them. Conflict immediately arose. The officials said the Bakufu would be happy to meet the Americans, but only at Kamakura which was twenty miles south of Uraga and outside Edo Bay. Perry insisted that they meet somewhere between their present anchorage and Edo, and he himself be received at Edo before the court. The negotiations were deadlocked for ten days. Then the Japanese dropped Kamakura and maintained that they could only meet at Uraga. Perry steadfastly adhered to somewhere nearer Edo, arguing that Uraga's anchorage was poor and the proposed meeting hall situated in a deep gorge; he left unsaid his fear the gorge would be a death trap should the Japanese prove treacherous. All along, the four Bakufu ministers designated for the actual treaty negotiations waited in Uraga. Despite the impasse, the Americans and Japanese liberally exchanged courtesies, refreshments, and small gifts, quite a contrast from the tension and cool correctness of the previous July's meetings.

Frustrated with the deadlock, Perry determined that "it was better to have no treaty than one that would in the least compromise the dignity of the American character; and to agree to any arrangement that would recognize in the remotest degree the restrictions submitted to by the Dutch, could not for a moment be thought of." He severed the Gordian knot by sailing his squadron eight miles further up Edo Bay and dispatching survey boats in all directions.

The Japanese finally accepted Perry's proposal. Perry noted that it "is probable that arrogance may be charged against me for persisting as I did; and against, the judgement of all about me, in changing the place of conference, and thus compelling four princes of the empire to follow the squadron, and subjecting the government to the trouble and expense of erecting another building, but I was simply adhering to a course of policy determined on after mature reflection, and which had hitherto worked so well."

On March 8, 1854 Perry began negotiations with the Japanese at Kanagawa, a Yokohama suburb. He was determined "to distinguish the occasion of our second landing in Japan by all necessary parade, knowing as I well did the importance and moral influence of such show." His escort,

consisting of about 500 officers, seamen, and Marines fully armed – embarked in twenty-seven barges in command of Commander Buchanan, and forming a line abreast, pulled in good order toward the shore. The escort having landed and drawn up, I followed in my barge under an appropriate salute. Upon landing I was received by the escort and a party of Japanese officials and conducted to the hall prepared for the conference, where I found in waiting the five commissioners, and was invited to be seated opposite the chief personage. At this moment salutes were fired from the howitzers mounted in the launches, of twenty guns in honor of the emperor, and seventeen for the Japanese commissioners.

Perry was accompanied by Captain Adams, his secretary and son Oliver Hazard Perry II, and the two interpreters S. Wells Williams and Anton Portman. The Japanese delegation included Hayashi Daigaku no Kami, who was well-formed, grave, and reserved, about 55; Ido prince of Tsushima, "aged about 50, tall and rather corpulent, with a pleasant expression, resembling somewhat Mr. Buchanan [the future 15th president] our present minister to London"; Izawa, prince of Mimasaka, aged 41,

> the best looking of the number, he was quite gay, fond of fun and frolic, and had the reputation of being a Lothario . . . he entertained more liberal views with respect to foreign intercourse than either of his coadjutors, and seemed to be a favorite with the Japanese and he certainly was with us. He manifested a great fondness for music, and could not keep his hands and feet quiet when the bands were playing enlivening airs; Udono Nagatoshi, of the Revenue Board, was about 55, tall and had prominent features; and Matsuzaki Michitaro about 60 tall and lank, very near-sighted, outwardly grave and unsociable but rather fond of the gaudy things of the world.

Moriyama Einosuke was the chief interpreter. Perry would speak in English to Portman who would be interpreted by Moriyama to the Japanese, and then back again.

The Japanese presented Perry with a letter from the shogun who "prepared to concede much more than was anticipated by many, but, entertaining the opinion that something still more advantageous might be gained, I thought it good policy to hold out for a specific treaty." For the next three weeks, Perry countered the shogun's seven points with his own, including five open ports in addition to Nagasaki, fixed exchange rates, coaling stations, a consulate, and humane treatment for shipwrecked sailors all of which would be codified by treaty. He also raised and reached agreement on several side issues, including burial places for Americans who died in Japan, free movement up to twelve miles from a treaty port, the American customs of foregoing business on Sundays and breaking bread after negotiation rounds.

Perry's demands strained his counterparts and, within the Bakufu, the fragile consensus on negotiation rather than war. The Japanese recognized that "resistance would be useless, and very wisely determined to adopt peaceful measures and the exercise of a system of diplomacy peculiarly Japanese to evade by every possible means of falsehood and deceit the reasonable concessions demanded by my government." Of course, to the Japanese, it was the Americans who were being unreasonable. At one point Moriyama pleaded that Perry "give us more time. It is all very plain to you, but we are people coming out of a dark room into the glare of sunshine, and we do not yet see the bearing of things clearly."[14]

Throughout the negotiations, Perry tried to bolster his hand with the full range of diplomatic strategies. He flexed American power with cannon salutes and parades of his five hundred marines on the Yokohama beach. He presented his hosts with his fantastic machines and delighted the topknotted and robed Japanese samurai officials with rides on the small train and track and messages on the telegraph. He amused and undoubtedly puzzled them with a minstrel show and concert by the "Ethiopian" band of white men in blackface.

He softened his counterparts by plying them with large quantities of champagne, whiskey, and Madeira, and elaborate banquets which were enjoyed by all with "much hilarity and good feeling. . . . The party on deck was very uproarious, the Japanese taking the lead in proposing toasts and cheering 'à la Anglaise' at the top of their lungs whilst two bands stationed nearby added to the din." At the ranking officer table below, although Hayashi drank and ate sparingly, Matsuzaki got "gloriously drunk and the other three quite mellow." During one drunken party, Matsuzaki threw his arms around Perry, crushing his new epaulettes, and gaily repeated, "Nippon and America, all the same Heart!" When later asked whether he was offended by the man's affection, Perry replied that "if he will only sign the treaty, he may kiss me."[15]

Japan's display of might and pomp was even more colorful. Batteries and forts and phalanxes of archers, spearmen, and musketeers lined the hills. The Japanese entertained the Americans with sumo wrestling, and presented Perry and his officers with beautiful porcelain, lacquerware, silks, and paintings, and the fleet with two hundred bales of rice.

Although the Japanese negotiated with the massed guns of Perry's squadron pointed at them, the commodore determined to exercise his military power with discretion, "the rather to convince these misgoverned people of the leniency and humanity of our laws, than of the means by which a compulsion may be enforced." His official account, however, downplays his saber-rattling to intimidate the Japanese into agreement. Hayashi reported Perry's warning that if his proposals were not accepted he "was prepared to make war at once . . . [and] if he sent word he could summon a command of one hundred warships within twenty days."[16] S. Wells Williams confirms Hayashi's account, noting that Perry "threatens them in no obscure terms with a 'larger force and more stringent terms and instruction.' "[17] Although Williams lauded Perry's skilful diplomacy, he regretted the commodore's threats.

Perry's feelings about Japan and the Japanese were mixed. Throughout his journal he continually denounced Japanese deceits and chicanery, yet grew fond of his Japanese counterparts. The Japanese sense of decorum impressed him: "No person in the world exceeded the Japanese in politeness and courtesy as well as to strangers as to each other, and they are systematic in that as in all other matters, suiting the forms of their salutations to the rank and position of the person saluted." He contrasted Japan "where I have never seen a city or town exhibiting a greater degree of cleanliness . . . from the filthiness of all Chinese cities." Cleanliness, order and safety had a price, Japan's feudal system and the mass poverty offended Perry. Never in his travels except perhaps in Mexico had he seen "such an amount of apparent wretchedness as these squalid slaves would seem to suffer." He abhorred the "army of spies and policemen who throng the highways, and whose eyes are constantly upon everybody and everything going on, whether by night or day." He longed to "relieve these oppressed people of the burdens which are now grinding them to dust." When he and his men gave small presents to the peasants they would, "like hungry hounds, whilst snatching a morsel from a strange hand, tremble in fear of being seen by their master." As for sensual stimulation, he preferred Okinawan over both Japanese and Chinese cuisine, and observed that if they did not blacken their teeth Japanese women "would be tolerably good looking. . . . The young girls are well formed and rather pretty;" he then patriotically added that in regards to "beauty, the women of the United States undoubtedly deserve the palm."

Both sides were eager to learn all they could about the other. The American scientist Dr James Morrow wrote a report on the minerals, birds, fish, plants, climate, and topography. He collected several plants including soybean, yew, dwarf cypress, juniper, lily, and clover which within several years became well established in parts of the United States. The artist Peter Heine produced numerous sketches and watercolors of the pageants, people, and wildlife. Those Japanese officials invited on board the ships asked incessant questions as they poked and examined everything. Japanese townspeople and peasants thronged around the sailors and marines who strolled and cavorted ashore freely. Perry remarked that the "Japanese are remarkable for their inordinate curiosity and, in the display of so many of the inventions of our ingenious countrymen, they had ample means of gratifying this propensity."

After three weeks of tough negotiations, Perry and his Japanese counterparts signed the Treaty of Kanagawa on March 31, 1854. The Japanese agreed to most of Perry's requests, including safe treatment for shipwrecked sailors, two ports at which American ships could resupply, a consulate and most-favored-nation status. In return, Perry promised America's good offices should Japan become embroiled in a dispute with other western powers. There was a catch, however. The two ports were the tiny towns of Shimoda on the tip of the rugged Izu peninsula down the coast from Edo Bay and Hakodate on the southern end of Hokkaido. And although the Japanese agreed to most-favored-nation status, they had not formally agreed to trade with the United States.

The Japanese had conceded much but they rejected Perry's demand for an audience with the shogun. Perry did not press the point, fearing that to do so "would endanger the very friendly disposition which we have already held with these people" and not wanting to see his fellow negotiators commit seppuku (ritual suicide).

With the treaty signed, Perry dispatched his ships on various missions. He steamed first to Hakodate and then back to Shimoda to inspect them as treaty ports, pronounced them satisfactory, and then proceeded to the Ryukyu Islands where on July 11 he concluded a treaty with that kingdom similar to the Treaty of Kanagawa. Finally on July 17, he steamed away for the United States aboard the "Mississippi" and arrived in New York on January 12, 1855, after an absence of two years and two months. The Senate approved the Kanagawa Treaty on July 15, 1854; President Fillmore signed it into law on August 7; ratifications were exchanged at Shimoda on February 21, 1855.

After hearing of the American success, the other western powers quickly negotiated their own deals with Edo. The Japanese signed similar treaties with Britain on October 14, 1854, and Russia on February 7, 1855. The Russian treaty included extraterritoriality and the opening of Nagasaki.

The Realities and Illusions of American Power

Perry's expedition was extraordinarily successful. How did a few American gunboats manage to humble a nation of 30 million people governed by a fiercely nationalistic military clique? First, the Japanese understood that the mighty Chinese empire had bowed to western military superiority only a decade earlier. And the Tokugawa regime was much more vulnerable than the Ching dynasty. At least Beijing was inland; Edo was within range of the American cannon. Coastal shipping supplied most of the food and fuel for Edo's million people. A prolonged American blockade could have starved the city into submission. Although Japanese cannon guarded the approach to Edo and may have had a slightly longer range than the American smooth-bore guns, an intensive night bombardment of the city's wooden structures with red-hot shot could have fired a conflagration that would have reduced much of Edo to ashes. According to Perry, "Edo can be destroyed by a few steamers of very light draft, and carrying guns of the heaviest caliber."

Yet another reason was the power balance. The Tokugawa regime understood that Britain was the greatest sea and industrial power. Although Britain was preoccupied with China, it would only be a matter of years before it attempted to open Japan. Russia was a more immediate threat. In the over two centuries since Russian explorers first reached the Sea of Okhotsk in 1637, they had established a chain of forts and trading posts across Siberia and Manchuria, imposed unequal treaties on China, took over Alaska and claimed northern California, and maintained a northern Pacific fleet. The Japanese reasoned that they were better off striking an immediate deal with the relatively weak United States than resisting and eventually confronting a United States allied with the other western powers.

The appearance of the American gunboats in Edo Bay came as no surprise to the Bakufu. Two years earlier, the Dutch had forewarned the Bakufu of the expedition. And not only did the Bakufu have two years to prepare psychologically for the visit but, to the surprise of the Perry expedition, the Japanese already knew a great deal about the United States. Just before Perry's visit, the Bakufu published the "New Account of America" (*Meriken Shinshi*) which sympathetically and somewhat accurately portrayed American history and culture. They had gained the information from translations of western books and interviews with visiting Americans. The Bakufu's most remarkable informant was a Japanese castaway named Nakahama Manjiro (John Mung) who had actually lived in the United States for several years and served aboard American whalers until he made it back to Japan. Most of the American officers and merchants who had appeared in Japan over the previous half century had been gentlemen. Thus the Bakufu's image of the United States was positive.

The opening of Japan was one of many important stages in the fulfillment of America's "Manifest Destiny." Perry himself clearly recognized this. Five years after he returned to the United States, Perry reflected on the significance of his successful mission as one decisive step in American expansion: "'Westward' will 'the course of empire take its way.' But the last act of the drama is yet to be unfolded; . . . to me it seems that the people of America will, in some form or another, extend their dominion and their power, until they have brought within their mighty embrace the Islands of the great Pacific, and placed the Saxon race upon the eastern shores of Asia."[18]

While a fervent believer in America's "Manifest Destiny," President Franklin Pierce wisely rejected Perry's call for colonizing the Ryukyu Islands, arguing that "if, in the future, resistance should be offered and threatened, it would also be rather mortifying to surrender the island, if once seized, and rather inconvenient and expensive to maintain a force there to retain it."[19] Forty-five years later, President Mckinley would make a very different decision when Admiral Dewey presented him with the Philippines.

Edo Politics

The Tokugawa regime lasted another fourteen years (a period known as the bakumatsu or "end of the shogunate") following its decision to open Japan. During that time, opponents rallied against Edo with the battle cry "Revere the Emperor! Expel the barbarian! (Sonno joi!)." As in previous power struggles, the emperor became a political football in which possession meant legitimacy. And while the opposition reviled the "southern barbarians" (nanbanjin), it soon sought out western supplies of arms and money.

Abe's dilemmas continued. Edo had signed the treaties because they were too weak to resist the western powers' gunboat diplomacy. Abe had justified the agreements to the daimyo by promising that Japan would reverse the unequal treaties once it was strong enough to defeat the foreign barbarians. But to strengthen Japan, Abe had to strengthen the daimyo. He agreed to lift the limits on each han's military forces and allow the construction of ocean-going ships. In 1855, he founded a naval school at Nagasaki and an army training school at Edo with Dutch and French advisors, respectively. Severely criticized by the Tokugawa for giving so much away and by the dissident daimyo for not giving enough away, Abe resigned in 1855 and was replaced by Hotta Masayoshi.

The Harris Mission

It was amidst a Japan slowly convulsing from dynastic decay, intrigue, xenophobia, and violence, that Townsend Harris (1804–78) arrived at Shimoda on August 21, 1856 to serve as America's first consul-general to Japan. Harris would spend the next five years in Shimoda and Edo during which time he negotiated two treaties that codified commercial and residential opportunities for Americans in Japan.

Harris's tenure in Japan was the pinnacle of a remarkable career in business, education, and diplomacy. He served as president of the New York Board of Education and founded the Free Academy of New York which was later renamed City College. Restless to see the world and exploit its business opportunities, he journeyed to the Far East aboard his own merchant ship in 1849. He spent the next six years crisscrossing much of the South Pacific, India, Australia, and the Far East pursuing various enterprises and adventures. He was at Shanghai in May 1853 when the Perry expedition briefly dropped anchor before steaming away to Japan. Harris tried to join the expedition but was rejected. Instead, he applied for a diplomatic post at either Hong Kong or Canton and was appointed consul at Ninpo. He never served at the post and instead returned to New York, arriving on July 27, 1855.

The position of consul at Shimoda was open. Harris and his influential New York friends and Democrats wrote President Pierce nominating him for the position. Harris journeyed to Washington to meet with Pierce at the White House. On August 4, Harris received his treasured appointment for Japan, en route to which he was to conclude a commercial treaty with Siam.

On October 17, 1855, accompanied by his secretary Henry Heusken, he embarked by steamer for the Far East via Liverpool, Paris, Marseilles, Suez, Columbo, Penang, and Singapore, finally arriving at Menam, Bangkok's port, on April 13, 1856. There he waited until April 21 before receiving permission to proceed to Bangkok and officially begin his mission. Although Siam was already open to foreign trade and Britain had earlier concluded a commercial treaty with the kingdom, Harris faced a bewildering array of court factions arrayed around two kings with opposing views on the wisdom of restricted or free trade and residence. For the next few weeks, Harris made the diplomatic rounds of key court officials and the kings and finally concluded and signed a treaty on May 29. He steamed away on the U.S.S. "San Jacinto" on June 1 for Japan with stops at Hong Kong and then Macao where he hired several Chinese servants.

He approached Japan's coast in mid-August with mixed emotions of excitement and anticipated loneliness and frustration. He was well aware of his mission's importance: "I shall be the first recognized agent from a civilized power to reside in Japan. This forms an epoch in my life and may be the beginning of a new order of things in Japan. I hope I may so conduct myself that I may have honorable mention in the histories which will be written on Japan and its future destiny."[20] He also wondered whether his efforts were "for the real good of Japan?" Harris was prescient on nearly all counts.

Harris was 51 when he arrived at Shimoda. Of average height and somewhat portly, he had graying hair swept back from a wide forehead, slightly arched eyebrows, was double-chinned and fleshy-faced, and had thick lips framed by a walrus mustache and porkchop sideburns. His Dutch assistant, Henry Heusken, was only 24 and had only arrived in America in 1853.

Harris's initial reception on August 21 was disappointing. Claiming illness the governor refused to meet with Harris for several days, and only then if he were accompanied by the "San Jacinto's" commodore, James

Armstrong, who actually was bedridden with sickness. On August 25, Harris finally met alone with the governor and vice-governor, who made it clear that they had not expected a consul and urged him to leave. Several days later, when Armstrong accompanied Harris to a meeting with the officials, the governor bluntly asked the commodore "if he had no power to take me away." To worsen matters, Shimoda had been nearly destroyed by an earthquake nineteen months earlier and the Japanese insisted that the only accommodation available was in a small temple called Gyokusen-ji in the nearby village of Kakizaki.

Thus began for Harris over two long, lonely, frustrating years of nearly constant negotiations in which he broke through a seemingly endless series of both vital and trivial walls obstructing his mission. Isolated and unable to back his demands with military power, Harris attempted to win over the Japanese with a dogged, rational persistance in advancing his diplomatic objectives, softened by "such friendly intercourse as I may have to establish a kindly feeling toward me." He constantly warned the Japanese that they were better off striking a deal with the peaceful United States now than knuckling under to much harsher terms by one of the imperial European powers later. However, on several occasions he threatened that the United States would use force to win its demands if negotiations floundered.

Like Perry and most diplomats and businessmen since, Harris complained of Japanese "deceit, falsehood, flattery, and politeness" and "reasoning in a circle and trying to gain their point by simple pertinancy." Harris dealt with the perfidity by bluntly warning them that "I knew they lied; that if they wished me to have any confidence in them, they must always speak the truth. . . . I am determined to take firm ground with the Japanese. I will cordially meet any real offers of amity, but words will not do. They are the greatest liars on earth." He dealt with these difficulties by reminding himself that the Japanese "were like children; therefore I must have patience with them." Ninety years later, MacArthur would compare the Japanese to twelve-year-olds. Harris did appreciate that "the Japanese took a great while to consider every question; in this respect they differed from the Americans who decided promptly on all questions." He soon established good personal relations – the agreements took considerably longer – noting that the "Japanese officials are daily becoming more and more friendly and more open in their communications with me."

Harris suffered from his own government's neglect. He complained that:

I am nine days distant from Hongkong, yet I am more isolated than any American official in any part of the world. I have important intelligence to send to my Government – intelligence that will give an immediate spur to our trade with Japan; yet here it remains, month after month, without my being able to communicate it to my Government, or enabling my countrymen to benefit by it. The absence of a man-of-war also tends to weaken my influence with the Japanese. They have yielded nothing except from fear, and any future ameliorations of our intercourse will only take place after a demonstration of force on our part.

Few foreign ships took advantage of Shimoda's open port. Harris's isolation was broken briefly by the visit of the Russian corvette "Olivuzza" in November 1856 which allowed him several weeks of socializing with her worldly officers. The first American warship, the U.S.S. "Portsmouth", arrived on September 8, 1857 for several days of provisioning but brought no letter. When he finally did receive twenty-eight letters on October 20, they were all from friends; none arrived from the State Department. The least they could do, Harris complained, was acknowledge his treaty with Siam.

Although frequently exasperated by Japanese stonewalling and deceit, he genuinely liked them and their country. Harris found the Japanese "superior to any east of the Cape of Good Hope . . . clean in person and civil in manner. You see none of the squalor which usually attends poverty in all parts of the world. . . . The people are of a genial disposition and are evidently inclined toward intercourse with foreigners; but the despotic rule of the country, and the terror they have of their so-called inflexible laws, forbids them to express their wishes." The terror may be gone today but the government is just as skilled in restricting the Japanese people's opportunities to buy foreign goods. Harris admitted sometimes doubting whether "the opening of Japan to foreign influences will promote the general happiness of this people. It is more like the golden age of simplicity and honesty than I have ever seen in any other country."

He loved Japanese cuisine, and worked off his banquets with gardening and long walks and horserides in the countryside. He revelled in Japan's beauty, changing seasons, and mild climate. Some Japanese customs like mixed bathing embarrassed Harris' prudish sense of propriety. The entreaties of the officials to supply Harris with any woman he fancied likewise discomforted him. Heusken was less inhibited on both counts. A teetotaler, Harris abstained from the boisterous drinking bouts with his Japanese counterparts. And as a devout Christian, Harris insisted that he would neither conduct business nor receive visitors on Sunday. Given Harris's puritanical character and disinterest in women – he was a lifelong bachelor – his celebrated affair with the "geisha" Okichi-san was undoubtedly a myth. Although Okichi-san existed, she was no geisha but merely a "washerwoman and prostitute." Overall, Harris was a good sport, shrugging off plagues of mosquitos, rats, bats, and cockroaches. He weathered serious illnesses and bouts of homesickness, and the occasional earthquake and typhoon. Although he welcomed his Dutch companion, Harris complained that "Mr. Heusken only remembers when to eat, drink, and sleep – any other affairs rest very lightly on his memory."

After ten months of negotiations, Harris's first major success occurred on June 17, 1857 when he and Japanese officials signed the Treaty of Shimoda which allowed: (1) the opening of Nagasaki to American merchant ships; (2) the right of permanent residence for Americans at Shimoda and Hakodate and the right to appoint a vice-consul at the latter; (3) a fixed exchange rate in which the Japanese received no more than 6 per cent commission on equal weights of gold and silver – they had held out on 25 per cent; (4) the trial of Americans accused of crimes by the American consulate under American law; (5) the ability of American merchants to barter rather than pay currency for supplies; and (6) the right of the consul to travel anywhere in Japan.

During the first year, Harris also resolved several personal issues. Henceforth, he was allowed to mingle with the Japanese people, dismiss the guards around his residence and spies which trailed him everywhere, hire Japanese servants, visit the homes of officials and townspeople, buy anything in the Japanese shops at the same rates charged the locals, and receive a Japanese twenty-one gun salute on Washington's birthday. But despite these successes, three goals still eluded him – an audience with the shogun, a commercial treaty, and residence in Edo.

It was not until September 22, 1857, that Harris received permission to journey to Edo for an audience with the shogun. It took two months to prepare for the mission. On November 23, 1857, Harris set out along the Tokaido to Edo with all a daimyo procession's pomp and power. He was preceded by:

a military officer with a rank corresponding to captain. He had his horse and norimon and usual bearers and attendants, but before him went three lads each bearing a wand of bamboo with strips of paper attached to the top; they cried out, alternately . . . "Sit down". . . . They kept some four hundred yards in advance and their cry sounded quite musical. Next . . . came the American flag guarded by two of my guards. Then I came on horseback with six guards, next my norimon with its twelve bearers and their headman; bearers. . . . Then Heusken on horseback with two guards, then his norimon, bearers. Next followed a long retinue bearing packages containing my bedding, chairs, food, trunks, and packages containing presents; my cook, and his following. The Vice-governor of

Shimoda followed by his train, then the Mayor of Kakizaki, and last the private secretary of the Governor of Shimoda. A Dutch intepreter was carried in a cango in Mr. Heusken's rear. The whole train numbered some three hundred and fifty persons. . . . The people [along the route] were perfectly well behaved, no crowding on me, no shouting or noise of any kind. As I passed, all knelt and cast their eyes down (as though they were not worthy even to look at me). Only those of a certain rank were allowed to salute me, which was done by "knocking head" or bringing the forehead actually to the ground.

On November 30, Harris finally entered Edo, recognizing fully the historic significance of his act. Lying prostrate and silent, the people massed along the road from Shinagawa to Nihonbashi. He rested a week in his lodging awaiting final preparations and receiving high ranking Bakufu officials including the Tairo Hotta Masayoshi. To nearly the last moment before his audience, Harris had to settle diplomatic subtleties in which he succeeded in making his visit a diplomatic act rather than the receipt of a favor granted by a benevolent shogun.

Ironically, the day of his audience was December 7, 1857, eighty-four years before Japan's attack on Pearl Harbor. Harris and Heusken were brought by norimon from their lodgings through the streets of Edo into the shogun's palace. There they proceeded through corridors and a great hall in which nearly four hundred daimyo and nobility sat on the floor in exact rows until they finally entered the audience hall. The shogun was seated before them while the five members of the Great Council of State and the shogun's three brothers lay prostrate. Upon entering, Harris bowed toward the shogun, advanced to the room's middle and bowed again. He offered greetings from the president and the desire for enduring friendship, ending his short speech with another bow. The shogun replied briefly that he was pleased with the president's message and the ambassador's discourse, and stated the "intercourse shall be continued forever." Heusken then advanced into the room bearing the president's letter and solemnly handed it to Hotta. The shogun bowed slightly, indicating the audience had ended. Harris and Heusken then left the room, bowing three more times en route. Shortly after being ushered to the vestibule, Harris and Heusken returned to the daimyo's vacated chamber to meet with the Council of State where more courtesies and presents were exchanged.

Negotiations over a commercial treaty formally began on December 12 and continued for several months. A preliminary agreement opening up additional ports, allowing free trade, foreign residence, and equal currency exchange was agreed to by mid-February. But when the Council presented it to the Daimyo on that February 17 "instantly the whole castle was in an uproar. Some of the most violent declared that they would sacrifice their lives before they would permit such great changes. . . . Of the 18 Great Daimyo, 4 were in favor and 14 opposed . . . of the 300 Daimyo . . . 30 of every 100 were in favor." The Council and Daimyo then agreed to submit the treaty for the emperor's approval, whereupon the Daimyo would withdraw their opposition.

Harris and Hotta signed the Treaty of Amity and Commerce between the United States and Japan on July 29, 1858. The Treaty's most important tenets included: (1) a minister at Edo and consuls at any treaty port, all of which have the right to travel freely through Japan; (2) if requested, the President can choose to mediate disputes between Japan and third countries; (3) in addition to Shimoda and Hakodate, Kanagawa and Nagasaki would by opened by July 4, 1859, Niigata by January 1, 1860, Edo by January 1, 1862, and Osaka and Hyogo by January 1, 1863; (4) Americans can reside, lease ground, and purchase buildings, hire labor, and buy and sell any product except opium in any treaty port; (5) duties shall be fixed and determined by an import's value; (6) foreign and Japanese currencies can be freely exchanged according to their metals' weighted value; (7) extraterritoriality for American citizens; and (8) free exercise of religion. Within weeks the British, French, Dutch, and Russians signed similar treaties with the Japanese.

The Treaty of Shimoda was ratified by the Senate on June 15, 1858 and signed by President Buchanan on June 30. The American legation opened in Edo on July 7, 1859. Pleased with the treaty, President Buchanan appointed Harris the American minister in Edo. Harris tendered his resignation upon learning of Lincoln's election. He remained in Japan another year before being finally relieved in October 1862.

Although exaggerated, British consul Joseph Longford's tribute to Harris's accomplishments echoed other contemporary perspectives. "The story of how, unbacked by any display of force under his country's flag, he succeeded by his own personal efforts in overcoming the traditional hatred of centuries to even the smallest association with foreigners, is one of marvelous tact and patience, of steady determination and courage, of straightforward uprightness in every respect that is not exceeded by any in the entire history of the international relations of the world."[21]

AMERICA AND THE END OF THE SHOGUNATE (BAKUMATSU)

In 1860, Edo sent a delegation of seventy-seven officials to the United States to exchange treaty ratifications. Among them was Fukuzawa Yukichi who later became Japan's leading advocate of westernization. The delegation's leaders were Shimmi Buzen no Kami, Muragaki Awaji no Kami, and Oguri Bungo no Kami.

They crossed the Pacific on the three-hundred ton warship, the "Kanrin Maru", which Japan had bought from Holland. After a two months voyage, the delegation arrived in San Francisco on March 17, 1860. The delegation then journeyed to Washington via Panama, arriving in the capital on July 20.

Congress had appropriated $50,000 for the Japanese delegation's entertainment, and lavishly feted them during their several days sojourn in Washington. The Japanese met similar boisterous receptions during their journey to Baltimore, Philadelphia, and New York. Finally, the delegation left New York on July 29 aboard the U.S.S. "Niagara" for Japan via Cape Horn.

Like most of the delegation, Muragaki was appalled by American brashness, ill-manners, food, familiarity between the sexes, and haughtiness, and bored by the endless rounds of dinners, toasts, and balls. He wrote in his diary: "these foreigners did not earn their name of barbarian for nothing." Fukuzawa saw things slightly differently: "Almost all of us, seventy-seven members of the mission, have in the past hated Westerners. But now that we have come to understand their attitudes, we have changed our mind. To despise foreigners at all times as if they were dogs and horses, would be discourteous and a great mistake."[22] The Japanese did benefit from visits to the Patent Office, National Observatory, Naval Yard, and Smithsonian Institution in Washington, and the Philadelphia mint.

In contrast to the barely concealed contempt which the Japanese felt for the Americans, the Americans were enthralled by the Japanese delegation. Like many observers of Japanese, Frank Leslie's *Illustrated Newspaper* remarked that the Japanese clearly had "a higher degree of culture and organization than prevails in any other of the Asiatic races." *Harpers Weekly* noted presciently that "civilized as we boast of being, we can learn much from the Japanese."[23]

The elation greeting the Japanese was short-lived – America would soon tear itself apart in four years of civil war. Japan would not send another delegation to the United States for another twelve years. The delegation had accomplished its simple mission of exchanging ratification papers and boosting Japan's image.

After leading the western parade into Japan during the 1850s, the United States then largely followed the lead of others. Throughout the early 1860s, American efforts in Japan were eclipsed by the other powers as the United States was torn apart by civil war. Secretary of State William Seward ordered his ministers in Japan and around the world to cooperate with the British and French whenever possible to help forestall their possible recognition of the Confederate States of America.

Japan, too, was increasingly torn by violence among rival samurai factions. While the Harris treaty sparked great enthusiasm and a quick ratification in the United States, it split Japan apart. Hotta's belief that most daimyo supported him was shattered after the treaty's provisions were publicly announced and most daimyo erupted in a chorus of denunciations. Hotta journeyed to Kyoto to plea for the emperor's approval of the treaty. The emperor refused. Hotta returned to Edo to urge the Bakufu to sign the treaty even without imperial approval. The Bakufu hesitated.

To make matters worse, Shogun Iseda soon died heirless. The Tokugawa, daimyo, and even the court split bitterly over two claimants to the shogunate's throne – Tokugawa Yoshitomi and Hitotsubashi Yoshinobu. To help resolve the impasse, a consensus agreed that Hotta should be eclipsed by Ii Naosuke who was named Great Councilor (Tairo), a position only filled in times of crisis. It seemed like an auspicious choice for Japan's foreign if not domestic problems. He had been one of the two daimyo to unequivocably agree to opening Japan in 1853. Displaying a decisiveness not displayed by Edo in living memory, Ii signed the treaty. The emperor, however, still refused to ratify it. He then threw his weight behind the shogun candidate Tokugawa Yoshitomi and consolidated his position by house arresting or executing all those who had supported the Hitotsubashi.

However, hopes that the Tokugawa regime had revived were dashed in 1860 when Ii was assassinated. Two years later in 1862 the Bakufu bowed to daimyo pressure to appoint Hitotsubashi regent to the shogun. That same year, the emperor asked Satsuma rather than Edo to supply troops to maintain order in Kyoto. Later, fearing that Satsuma's influence would grow too popular and attracted by the more fervent support of Choshu and Tosa for the emperor, the court asked those two han also to supply troops for Kyoto. The power balance was steadily shifting away from Edo and toward Kyoto and the dissident han.

The foreign presence in Japan offended not just ultranationalist pride. Free trade disrupted Japan's economy. The influx of currency and demand for Japanese silk and tea severely inflated prices, while cheap western goods such as cotton textiles damaged their rival Japanese industries. The foreigners resisted any attempts by the shogunate to stem the influx of foreign money and goods.

Violence was not confined to participants in Japanese politics. Under the banner of "Revere the Emperor! Expel the barbarians (Sonno joi)", disgruntled samurai – most of whom came from Satsuma and Choshu – known as "shishi" (men of determination) launched their first attacks on foreigners in 1859. For the shishi, hating and murdering foreigners "became for them an act at once of utility, loyalty, and piety."[24]

Although the Bakufu surrounded the foreign delegations with guards (betto), the shishi succeeded in cutting down several foreigners. On January 15, 1861, shishi murdered Harris's secretary Henry Heusken. Harris requested Edo to arrest the murderers and pay Heusken's widowed mother $10,000. Amidst this settlement, shishi unsuccessfully attacked the British embassy in Edo. Although the other ministers temporarily fled Edo, Harris remained until he was replaced by Robert H. Pruyn in October 1861.

The most consequential attack occurred in September 1862. A party of four English were riding down the Tokaido road when they encountered the Satsuma daimyo's delegation. Rather than politely stand aside while the procession passed, the English arrogantly tried to ride through it. Outraged at the insult to their lord, the samurai attacked the English and killed one of them, an English visitor at the consulate named C. L. Richardson. The others fled to the Edo consulate where the English minister, Sir Rutherford Alcock, promised redress.

Alcock demanded huge indemnities from both the Bakufu and Satsuma. The Bakufu knuckled under and paid Britain 100,000 pounds. Satsuma refused. A British squadron appeared in Kagoshima Bay in August 1863 and issued an ultimatum. On August 15, after Satsuma forts fired on the foreign fleet, the British responded with a bombardment that destroyed much of the city. The British warships then sailed away. Four months later, Satsuma handed over 25,000 pounds to British diplomats.

That same year, Choshu also attempted a direct challenge to the western powers and was similarly humbled. Choshu had convinced the shogun to come to Kyoto for important talks in the spring, and then forced him to agree to expel the barbarians by June 25, 1863. Although the shogun did nothing on that day, Choshu batteries fired on foreign ships sailing through the Shiminoseki straits while Choshu shishi burned the British embassy in Edo. Among those foreign ships shelled was the American steamer "Pembroke".

The United States was the first foreign power to retaliate. On July 16, the U.S.S. "Wyoming" steamed into the Shiminoseki straits, bombarded the Choshu batteries, and sank two Choshu gunboats. Then four days later, French warships landed troops which destroyed the Choshu forts and spiked their guns. Choshu's fortunes sank lower when Satsuma and Hizen forces forced their troops out of Kyoto.

Choshu, however, remained defiant. The forts were rebuilt and continued to fire on foreign ships throughout 1864. In August, Satsuma and Hizen samurai defeated a Choshu attempt to capture Kyoto. Then in September, a combined fleet of seventeen British, French, American (only the "Wyoming" participated), and Dutch ships attacked and destroyed Choshu's batteries. The allies then forced Choshu's daimyo to promise not to rebuild the batteries and demanded a $3 million indemnity from the shogun. The indemnity was eventually paid. Twenty years later, the United States strengthened its prestige in Japan by returning its share of the indemnity.

Faced with this latest crisis, the shogun, emperor, and most daimyo formally agreed to a power-sharing arrangement known as the "court–daimyo coalition" (kobu-gattai) in which the shogun became in effect the emperor's prime minister in a cabinet of daimyo representatives. A Tokugawa-led expedition of 15,000 men marched on Choshu to punish it in retaliation for the rebel han's earlier attack on Kyoto. On January 24, 1865, Choshu's leaders agreed to the government's terms. The coalition army then marched away and dispersed.

The peace and unity, however, was short-lived. Differences within the coalition caused its dissolution. Civil war within Choshu followed. The radicals took power on March and immediately demanded the shogunate's resignation. Meanwhile, an allied fleet, to which the Americans contributed the "Wyoming", anchored off Kobe and demanded that the emperor ratify the various treaties signed by Edo including those containing a 5 per cent ceiling on tariffs. The emperor complied. The result for the shogunate was a further loss of power. Now all major decisions made in Edo had to be carried to Kyoto for approval.

After their attacks on the foreigners were met with humiliating defeats, Satsuma and Choshu chose to work with rather than against the western powers for the time being. Both resumed buying foreign arms and even accepted British military advisors. Satsuma concentrated its efforts on acquiring foreign naval ships and training which later became the basis of the Japanese navy. Two of Choshu's most prominent shishi, Inoue Kaoru and Ito Hirobumi, who had participated in attacks on foreigners in Yokohama, sailed to Britain for study and later became leaders in the Meiji government. British military aid proved decisive in allowing Choshu to defeat a second Tokugawa expedition in August 1866. The shogunate's prestige plummeted. One han had not only defied but actually defeated Edo. Despite the fierce rivalry between the two han, Satsuma had refused to support the expedition against Choshu. Following the Tokugawa defeat, Choshu and Satsuma formed a secret alliance.

Japan's political crisis worsened in 1867. Emperor Komei died and his 14-year-old son, Mutsuhito or Meiji as he was officially renamed, ascended the throne. Hitotsubashi reluctantly became shogun, and was renamed

Tokugawa Yoshinobu. Yoshinobu tried but failed to forge another emperor–shogun–daimyo coalition. Meanwhile, the British and French became more deeply involved than ever in Japanese politics, with the former supporting the rebels and latter the government. Fearing civil war and the growing power of Choshu and Satsuma, Tosa's daimyo proposed that the shogun resign and a council of daimyo and the emperor take power. On November 8, 1867, Yoshinobu agreed to the "Tosa Memorial" and resigned.

Fearing their power would be limited in the new government, the Satsuma and Choshu leaders and their allies from other han conspired to seize power. On January 3, 1868, their army captured the imperial palace in Kyoto and declared the emperor's restoration to power (which theoretically had already occurred when the shogun resigned), and the abolition of the shogunate and confiscation of its lands.

The fighting which followed was short-lived. On January 27, the "imperial army" routed a Tokugawan army marching on Kyoto at Toba-Fushimi. The imperial troops marched on and, after a short fight on July 4, seized Edo where upon Yoshinobu peacefully surrendered. Sporadic fighting in northern Honshu continued until November when the remaining Tokugawa land forces gave up. The Tokugawa navy finally surrendered in Hokkaido in May 1869.

Throughout this decade, the United States continued to support the shogunate, even after the other western powers tilted toward the revolutionaries. The American minister R. B. Van later wrote that he "used every means at his disposal to prevent the revolution in Japan because he thought it was a retrograde movement. . . . I little dreamed that the restored Mikaido would excel the dethroned Tycoon in emulating western civilization."[25] Fortunately, the revolutionary leaders did not begrudge the United States for its former support of the Bakufu.

THE MEIJI REVOLUTION

The new Meiji regime (named after Emperor Meiji) quickly consolidated power. In April 1868, the government issued its Charter Oath or five promises to the Japanese people: (1) policy would be based on wide consultation through deliberative assemblies; (2) individuals would be allowed to pursue their own interests; (3) national interests would transcend all others; (4) outdated customs would be abolished; and (5) knowledge shall be sought throughout the world to strengthen the foundations of imperial rule. The government also promised to adopt a constitution. In 1868, the government moved from Kyoto to Edo which it renamed Tokyo, and in early 1869 brought the emperor to the new capital.

The coalition of rebel leaders was dominated by Choshu and Satsuma men, with several prominant samurai from Tosa and Hizen. On March 5, 1869, the daimyo from these four han agreed to return their domain's titles to the emperor and convinced most other daimyo to follow suit; in July, they ordered the other daimyo to do so. The emperor then appointed the former daimyo governors, thus establishing the emperor's power. On August 29, 1871, the "governors" were called before the emperor who announced their retirement and their han's dissolution and conversion into seventy-two prefectures (reduced to forty-five in 1889) and three municipalities headed by governors appointed by Tokyo. The central government pensioned off the daimyo and samurai and assumed their debts.

The Meiji government abolished all han troops and confiscated han castles. In their place an "imperial army" was formed with largely Satsuma, Choshu, and Tosa troops, and the following year created a national navy with Satsuma forces as its core. In 1873, the government inaugurated a national draft with all men liable and abolished the difference between samurai and commoners.

The government reorganized itself into a Grand Council of State (Daijokan) of seven departments, including a Legislative Department of an upper council and lower assembly of han representatives, Executive, Shinto, Finance, War, Foreign Affairs, and Civil Affairs. A Department of Justice was established outside the Council structure to provide some measure of judicial independence.

The Meiji government split in 1873 in debate over whether or not to war immediately against Korea and conquer it. Those who favored postponement won out and the disgruntled losers resigned from the government, including their outspoken leader, Saigo Takamori. Throughout the early and mid 1870s, several revolts flared in the provinces by samurai and other malcontents, all of which were soon crushed by government forces. The most serious occurred in 1877 when Saigo gathered 40,000 ex-samurai in Kyushu and rebelled against the government. After six months of fierce fighting, the government conscript army succeeded in destroying the samurai rebels and killing Saigo. The result was not only the last serious challenge to Meiji rule, but the defeat of the samurai forces by a national conscript army which represented the victory of modernity over feudalism.

These revolts and the peaceful "popular rights movement" (minken shido) of opponents to the Meiji government pressured Tokyo to create the "representative assemblies" it had promised in its Charter Oath. Tokyo gradually created new institutions which encompassed the representatives of larger numbers of the public. It established a Senate (Genroin) in 1875 of appointed officials which were charged with drafting a constitution. But the government rejected each of the four drafts submitted for being too liberal. In 1884, the government created an aristocracy of five classes and converted the Legislative Department into a House of Peers from which they could advise the government. The following year, the remaining departments of the Council of State were transformed into a western style cabinet whose ministers served at the emperor's discretion. In 1888, a Privy Council of appointees was created to advise the emperor, approve the constitution, and approve and guide Cabinet policies.

The 1889 Constitution elaborated the structure, duties, and power of these institutions and joined a newly created House of Representatives with the House of Peers to make a Diet or parliament. The lower house was largely a debating society whose only power was to withhold a vote on the national budget – in which case the previous year's budget would take effect. According to the Constitution, sovereignty lay not in the people, but in the "divine" emperor who personified Japan's "national essence" (Kokutai). The Constitution was ambiguous concerning the emperor's powers, with some tenets making him beholden to the law and others allowing him to supercede it. Another problem, which would not become evident until later, was the army and navy ministers' legal and moral duty to the emperor, the Commander-in-Chief, rather than the cabinet.

In typically Japanese fashion, real power resided in none of these new institutions. Nowhere mentioned in the constitution was the Genro, a small group of Satsuma and Choshu leaders which had led the Meiji Restoration and now "advised" all other branches of government – including the emperor. The Genro ruled Japan throughout the nineteenth and into the early twentieth century until most of its members died off or retired. The Cabinet then filled some of the power vacuum led by the tough, wise Genro leaders. But in the 1930s the military increasingly pushed aside the civilian leadership in important policies.

Having eliminated or neutralized any possible contenders for power, the Meiji government embarked on a massive, systematic modernization program, to rally elite and popular support under the new slogan "rich country, strong military" (fukoku kyohei). Unlike so many other developing countries, Japan did not accumulate large foreign debts. Tokyo floated loans in London in 1869 to help finance railroad construction and again in 1872 to help pay for the dismantlement of the han. But nearly all of Japan's modernization was financed from within. A national tax system was created with payments based on the individual rather than village and paid to the central rather than local government. Throughout the 1870s, Tokyo invested in modern industries and then sold them off to private investors during the

1880s. In 1881, the Finance Minister, Matsukata Masayoshi, implemented sweeping financial reforms that included the creation of the Bank of Japan and the deflationary policy of cutting back on government spending and the money supply. Despite a rapid industrialization, Japan's exports during the late nineteenth century were mostly silk and tea, followed increasingly by textiles. By 1905, however, manufactured exports comprised half of Japanese exports.

Japan's modernization was boosted by the dispatch of researchers and students overseas, particularly to the United States. The Meiji government was determined to modernize Japan and reverse the unequal treaties. In November 1871, the Iwakura mission left Japan for an extended diplomatic visit through the United States and Europe. In addition to its leader Iwakura Tomomori, the delegation included such illustrious Meiji leaders as Okubo Toshimichi, Kido Koin, and Ito Hirobumi. The Japanese were open about their mission's objectives. At a banquet in Sacramento, Ito declared that: "We come to study your strength so that, by adopting wisely your better ways, we may hereafter be stronger ourselves."

The Iwakura mission failed to convince the western powers to equalize relations. Nonetheless, the Japanese did return home in September 1873 with countless ideas for Japan's modernization. Although the mission's report noted Japan's backwardness, it pointed out that the western powers had only recently industrialized themselves and advocated a range of policies to speed Japan's development. However, not all of those who departed with the Iwakura mission returned. Fifty-four young Japanese students were placed in various American schools. These first students were followed, between 1865 and 1885, by an additional three hundred Japanese young people, including several girls, who were dispatched by the Meiji government to America to enroll in its universities and learn its ways.

Meanwhile, strenuous efforts were being made in Japan to modernize its education system. Education Minister Mori Arinori and Keio University founder Fukuzawa Yukichi were the leading advocates of westernization, and particularly cited the United States as a model for Japan's development. They, along with several other leading Meiji figures, founded the Meirokusha in 1873 as a forum for discussing and studying the west. Among its members were Kato Hiroyuki, later president of Tokyo University, Nishmura Shigeki, the emperor's tutor, Nishi Amane, later principal of Tokyo Normal College, and Nakamura Masanao, founder of Tokyo Women's Normal School. Dozens of other clubs formed across Japan to debate and adapt to modernization.

The new slogan for modernization became "Civilization and Enlightenment" (bummei-kaika). Fukuzawa published a number of books advocating specific modernization measures which drew on his own western experiences. In such books as "Conditions in the Western World" (*Seiyo jijo*, 1866), "Encouragement of Learning" (*Gakumon no susume*, 1872), and "Outline of Civilization" (*Bunmeiron no gairyaku*) he advocated mass education, social equality, and women's rights, and attacked feudalism and Confucianism.

The craze for all things western lasted decades. Japanese men adopted western suits, hats, and umbrellas; former samurai grew out their hair and curbed their swagger; meat-eating became increasingly popular in the Buddhist nation; some of the wealthy built frame houses with high-pitched roofs; mixed nude public bathing was banned. Mori went so far as to advocate intermarriage between Japanese and westerners to strengthen the former.

Japan's tradition of assimilating foreign ideas, technologies, and institutions was a major reason for its successful modernization. When its traditional model, China, was humbled by the west, the Japanese quickly accepted the western powers as their new patrons. The nationalism of Japan's elite quickly spread to the mass populace as news of the foreign threat spread across the land. The entire nation rallied around the idea that Japan had to modernize as quickly as possible in order to throw off the unequal treaties and achieve equality with, or even superiority over, the west. Japan's samurai tradition gave it the discipline and fervor with which to transform a feudal realm into a modern and eventually imperial nation. Even before Perry's visit, Japan enjoyed a significant degree of economic development. Japan's transportation and communications system was intricate. Japan's widespread, wealthy, and powerful merchant class and its symbiotic relationship with the samurai bureaucrats provided the capital and entrepreneurship to create modern industries. By the century's turn, Japan was one of the world's industrial and commercial great powers.

AMERICA'S ROLE IN JAPAN'S MODERNIZATION

What was America's part in Japan's modernization throughout the late nineteenth century? One observer extolled America's role in the revolutionary changes which took place in Japan following Perry's visit which "unmoored Japan from the coast of Asia, and towed it across the Pacific, to place it alongside the New World, to have the same course of life and progress."[26] In fact, although America's mission to "awaken" Japan continued throughout the late nineteenth century, the United States played a relatively minor role in Japan's prewar modernization.

Advisors

Tokyo eventually brought about 3,000 foreign advisors to Japan to help plan and implement all aspects of Japan's modernization. Many stayed for years until their expertise was mastered and they were sent home. Americans, of course, supplied only part of the foreign advisors. The French and British also contributed hundreds of advisors. Britons continued to advise Japan's fleet and French the army. German legal experts helped Japanese draft their first constitution while professors structured Japanese universities along German lines.

Americans were particularly prominent in foreign affairs, finance, education, and agriculture. Henry Willard Denison assisted the Foreign Ministry between 1880 and 1914. Former banker and customs commissioner George Williams was hired to help write up Japanese banking laws, coinage systems, and patent office procedures. Matthew Scott and Hillard Miller assisted the Foreign Ministry in organizing the custom service. David Murray of Rutgers University advised the Education Ministry for five years starting in 1873, and most notably helped set up a national elementary school system and curriculum. For four years, Horace Capron helped Japanese develop their frontier, Hokkaido, along American farm lines including big red barns. Samuel Bryan developed Japan's postal system, negotiated several postal treaties, and served as Superintendant of Foreign Mails for four years. John Berry promoted prison reform. Erastus Smith advised the Foreign Ministry on power politics and expansion. William Clark, president of what is now the University of Massachusetts, helped found in 1875 what is now Hokkaido University, and was famous for saying to his Japanese students: "Boys! Be ambitious!"

One of the most remarkable of these American advisors was General Charles LeGrande who resigned an American consulship in China to join Japan's Foreign Ministry. During the 1870s, LeGrande was involved in plotting most of Japan's foreign policies, including its punitive 1874 expedition against Taiwan aborigines who had previously attacked Japanese fishermen and 1876 gunboat diplomacy forcing Korea to open. Emperor Meiji rewarded LeGrande with the Order of the Rising Sun in 1875.

Some of the advisors wrote books and articles which helped Americans understand Japan better. William Griffis returned from Japan to write the largely sympathetic *Mikado's Empire*, which was "perhaps the most widely read American book on Japan for a quarter of a century or more."[27]

Far more important to Japan's development were those Americans who helped Japanese understand themselves by preserving and analyzing traditional arts, temples, shrines, religion, myths, fables, music, and history.

Edward Morse discovered the shell mounds at Omori, contributed several works to the fields of archeology, zoology, architecture, biology, and anthropology in Japan, and founded several marine biology laboratories. William Sturgis Bigelow wrote books on Japanese Buddhism. Between his arrival in Japan in 1878 and his death in 1904, Lafcadio Hearn collected and popularized Japanese fables. Ernest Fenollosa studied and taught in Japan for fifteen years and became the western world's leading expert on Japanese art.

Trade

Meanwhile, then as now, American businessmen struggled to squeeze through doors theoretically opened by international treaties. The first attempt after the Treaty of Kanagawa by an American entrepreneur to sell in Japan occurred in June 1854 when the clipper "Lady Pierce" and its owner Silas Burrows arrived at Shimoda. Perry's treaty, of course, contained no commercial clauses, a point which the Shimoda authorities sternly made to Burrows. He sailed away without selling any of his own goods or purchasing Japanese products. The following year two other merchants, W. C. Reed and T. T. Dougherty, arrived aboard the "Caroline E. Foote" with their families and goods in Hakodate. There they planned to open a store in Hakodate to cater to foreign whalers. Although the Hakodate officials refused to let them set up shop, they did allow them to buy local products. Reed and Dougherty returned to San Francisco where they made a small fortune disposing of their cargo of Japanese goods, the first officially imported into the United States.

Although no one understood it at the time, the transaction was richly symbolic. Despite the strenuous efforts to open Japan by Perry with his gunboats and the first pioneer American businessmen with their heavily laden cargo ships, Japanese exports to the United States preceded American goods into Japan. Ever since then, American businessmen have found it far easier to buy from than sell to the Japanese, even if they did enjoy a trade surplus for the first half century.

It was not until after Harris signed his commerce treaty with Edo, that Japan's officials grudgingly allowed American and other foreign merchants to begin selling in Japan. Within weeks of the opening of the American consulate in July 1859, the first American merchant house, Walsh, Hall and Company, set up shop in Yokohama. Others followed and bilateral trade rose steadily, with anywhere from twenty to forty American ships anchoring in Yokohama annually.

Civil war, however, restrained America's trade potential with Japan. In 1864–5, American merchants accounted for only $690,000 of the

$6.2 million worth of goods imported from Japan, and exported only $1.328 million of the $13 million in goods which flowed into Japan. By 1900, America's $16 million of exports to Japan were double its $8.7 million of imports. American clocks, watches, petroleum, tobacco, leatherware, and shoes were exchanged for Japanese silks, fans, porcelain, lacquerware, sulphur, camphor, and tea.[28]

Americans took a leading role in the international settlements in Yokohama and Japan's other open cities. Sixty of the 250 foreign merchants residing in Yokohama in 1865 were American, as were five of the twenty-six members of the municipal council. Although the council had eleven British members, its first president was the American Ralph Shoyer, who also started Japan's first English-language newspaper, the *Japan Express*. The foreign settlement burgeoned in merchants, their families, sailors, and warehouses, and also such amenities as churches, theaters, clubs, hotels, billiard halls, bars, bowling alleys, boat regattas, shooting matches, and brothels.

The Americans had an impact on Japan that transcended their relatively small numbers or trade figures. Among the American cultural exports to Japan were baseball, circuses, sewing machines, ice cream and milk, oil lamps, photography studios, stagecoaches, buttons, and jinrikishas or pedal cabs. One of the first ships in Japan's navy was the American made "Fujiyama".

Americans composed most of the Christian evangelists in Japan. Although Tokyo would not issue a toleration edict until 1873, the first six American missionaries arrived in 1859. Two of these first missionaries were more successful in enhancing Japanese education than "saving" Japanese souls. James Hepburn standardized the romanization of Japanese while Guido Verbeck started an interpreters school in Nagasaki and later helped start Tokyo University and served in the education ministry.

The trickle of missionaries entering Japan became a flood after 1873 when the government lifted the ban on Christianity. But these missionaries had little better luck than their predecessors three centuries earlier. By 1900, the number of American missionaries had grown to nearly 500, and they had founded over 250 churches. Yet, the converts of American and other foreign missionaries reached little more than 100,000.[29]

CONCLUSION

In the summer of 1879, former General of the Army and President, Ulysses S. Grant, traveled for six weeks in Japan as part of a round the world trip. In a talk with Emperor Meiji and the government, Grant gave the Japanese government very candid advice on dealing with modernization and international relations. He warned them against foreign debts, pointing out that "some nations are very desirous to loan money to weaker nations whereby they might establish and exercise an undue influence over them. They lend money to establish political power." He went on to advise that "on all matters at issue, do not invite or permit so far as you can avoid it, the intervention of a foreign power. European powers have no interest in Asia, so far as I can judge from their diplomacy, that does not involve the humiliation and subjugation of the Asiatic people."[30] Grant's sympathy for the Japanese exemplified the first decades of American–Japanese relations.

And most Japanese appreciated America's patronage. As Fukuzawa Yukichi put it in an 1886 editorial in his *Jiji Shimpo*: "When we remember that it is to the United States of America that we owe our success and our advancement to our present proud position, we cannot help entertaining for them sentiments of peculiarly deep respect and esteem."[31]

These sentiments on both sides of the Pacific would gradually but steadily change over the next half century.

2 Pacific Rival, 1894–1930

At the century's turn, America's relationship with Japan shifted from patronage to rivalry.[1] Until this time, although increasing numbers of American businessmen haggled in the world's bazaars, and American gunboat diplomacy had forced Japan's opening, the United States was not yet a full-fledged imperial power. An American overseas empire emerged from its successful war with Spain in 1898, just as three years earlier Japan had carved out its own empire after victory over China.

Imperialism was not preordained for either country; a diverse vocal spectrum of interests in each advocated everything from peaceful to military expansion. For both countries territorial expansion occurred from opportunity rather than design. There were parallels between Japanese and American imperialism during this era, including on the eve of the Sino-Japanese and Spanish–American wars, the respective "concern with the need to extend national interests commercially and peacefully, . . . awareness of racial and cultural diversity."[2] During international crises, the military expansionists won out and tipped the political balance toward imperialism.

Successful wars and imperial acquisitions dramatically changed the relationship between the United States and Japan. During the three subsequent decades, the United States and Japan rose from secondary to great powers; as they did so their perceived national interests increasingly clashed. America's Far East policy during this era was largely shaped by fear of Japanese imperialism and desire to maintain open trade doors in China and elsewhere. Meanwhile, Japan's actions in Northeast Asia were largely attempts to revise the power balance in its favor, along with the need for commercial expansion and emigration. As Akira Iriye put it, after 1900, "hitherto almost exclusively concerned with such matters as tariff revision and extraterritoriality, Japanese–American relations would now be those between rival empires."[3]

Throughout the era, American policy for dealing with Japanese ambitions changed markedly. President Roosevelt actually encouraged Japan's leaders to expand into Manchuria to divert their attention from American interests in China proper and the western Pacific, while he sent the US fleet on a worldwide cruise largely to impress Japan's leaders with American resolve and power. President Taft's "dollar diplomacy" emphasized business expansion rather than saber rattling to reinforce American interests in the region. Although President Wilson strongly protested Japan's "21 demands" on China, he was more conciliatory toward Japan's ambitions at the Versailles peace conference, inaugurating a decade-long détente in US–Japan relations. The détente ended in 1931 when the White House perceived Japan's conquest of Manchuria as a threat to the security of all America's Far East interests. Secretary of State Henry Stimson's "non-recognition" policy toward Japan's actions in Manchuria signaled the end of the mostly friendly rivalry between the two countries and beginning of a Cold War that ended with Pearl Harbor a decade later.

THE PRESSURES FOR AMERICAN IMPERIALISM

America's acquisition of an overseas empire at the century's turn happened largely by chance. Outright imperialists were a vocal minority among the elite and public alike. Until 1899, presidential vetos or congresses torpedoed opportunities to acquire Santo Domingo, Cuba, Haiti, and Hawaii.

With or without colonies, the United States was a rising global power. America's industrialization had begun in the early nineteenth century but did not take off until the almost insatiable demand for steel, armaments, railways, coal, textiles, iron-ore, ships, and medicine brought by Civil War. By the late nineteenth century, the United States had become the world's largest and most populated industrial power, with industrial production almost as great as that of Britain, Germany, and France combined, and was second only to Britain in exports. Most American exports went to Europe or Canada and only slivers to Latin America, Asia, and Africa. Asia's importance to America's economy was insignificant. But with a population of 63 million in 1890, most American manufacturers could safely reap profits at home rather than in risky foreign markets.

However, there were risks in this "fortress America" business strategy. The severe depressions of 1873, 1885–6, and 1893–7 were blamed on a glut of capital and products which the American public could not consume. The solution to this problem, increasingly prominent voices argued, was to seize colonies which could absorb excess finance and products, and the sooner the better. Many argued that if the United States did not jump into the imperial race its access to foreign markets would be severed. Others countered that what the United States needed was not colonies, but better wages, an expanding middle class, the breakup of monopolies and price-fixing, and more competition. Then as now, three-quarters of American trade and investments were with other industrial countries. But those businesses which traded and invested in Asia, Africa, and Latin America often had powerful friends in Congress and even the White House to aid their expansion.

Economic interests in expansion were joined by intellectual arguments. In 1890, the Census Bureau announced that the frontier was officially closed. In 1893, Frederick Jackson Turner expounded the thesis that America's culture, history, wealth, and vitality depended on frontiers to conquer. With the frontier's demise, he feared that America would wither. Others picked up this theme. In his *Influence of Seapower Upon History* (1890), Alfred Thayer Mahan argued that national power depended upon naval and trade power. Thus the United States had to expand its fleet to control the world's trade routes, and had to support the fleet with a global system of fortified supply bases.

Some advocated American imperialism simply because it could be done. Advances in transportation and communication such as steamships, railroads, and telegraphs, military technologies such as rapid firing rifles and artillery, and medicine to combat tropical diseases enabled the United States and other ambitious powers to penetrate, conquer, and administer formerly inaccessible regions around the world.

In the United States and other great powers, expansionist ideologies such as free trade, Social Darwinism, and Orientalism reinforced these economic and strategic rationales for overseas empires. "Free trade" was imperialism's most important tool. When they did not outright conquer a country, the great powers used the free trade doctrine to justify their imposition of unequal treaties on weaker nations in Asia, Africa, and Latin America in which native craft industries were soon bankrupted by the free inflow of mass manufactured goods. Contrary to the theory's grandiose claims, free trade further impoverished rather than uplifted most of the countries upon which it was imposed. "Social Darwinism" applied notions of the survival of the fittest to international relations. Civilizations, like species, evolved through a constant struggle for power in which the strong vanquished the weak. Not only was imperialism "natural," it was "just" as civilization's benefits spread to the world's "lesser breeds." "Orientalism," the study of cultures from the Mediterranean to the Pacific, reinforced imperialism and Social Darwinism by developing the image of exotic but corrupt, unjust, and often cruel "other" cultures. Established by western scholars, Orientalism was popularized by journalists and, inevitably, politicians and the public. Kipling's line personified this perception of the "other:" "East is east and west is west and never the twane shall meet." Irrationally, the presence of the "other" threatened many westerners. Some argued that western civilization must either expand over or succumb to Asia's "yellow hordes." No one publicly pointed out that there was no threat from the east, and had not been since the Turks besieged Vienna in 1683. The yellow horde myth was too valuable for justifying western imperialism.

Perhaps the most articulate American advocate for imperialism was Josiah Strong, a Congregationalist minister, who wrote several popular books advocating American imperialism which included "white-man's burden" and "Social Darwinian" arguments: "The world will enter upon a new stage of its history – the final competition of races, for which the Anglo-Saxon is being schooled."[4] Roosevelt was one of many prominent voices which equated imperialism with the spread of civilization, and maintained that the civilized nations had a moral responsibility to civilize the world's darker races.

By the century's turn, powerful pressures had arisen in the United States for overseas imperialism. Yet another reason to expand overseas was the rise of Japanese imperialism.

THE RISE OF JAPANESE IMPERIALISM

Japan got the jump on the United States in seizing an overseas empire. As early as 1861, Choshu had asked the emperor to urge the shogun to adopt a policy of foreign expansion. While such a policy was hardly a realistic option for the beleaguered Bakufu, it remained a popular dream for some time. Although the leaders behind the Meiji coup and subsequent revolution had struggled for years to expel the barbarians, by the time they took power they had accepted the reality that it might be decades before Japan could directly challenge the west.

Yet, within years of the Meiji coup, Japan was expanding her territory and trade overseas. Japan's first significant foreign policy success was to secure a trade treaty with China in 1871. In 1872, Tokyo asserted control over the Ryukyu Island kingdom which had paid tribute since 1609 to both China and Satsuma, and the following year over the Bonin Islands. In 1874, to help legitimize its conquest, Tokyo ordered a punitive expedition sent to Taiwan to avenge the deaths of fifty-four Ryukyuans who had been shipwrecked in Taiwan in 1871. China could do nothing more than protest the expedition. In 1875, using the same gunboat diplomacy as the western powers, Tokyo dispatched a fleet to Pusan, Korea to force that country's opening to trade. The Koreans eventually signed the Treaty of Kanghwa on February 27, 1876. Japan gained two open ports in addition to Pusan and, perhaps more importantly, received the right to maintain a powerful legation guard at its embassy in Seoul. In 1879, Tokyo converted the Ryukyus into a prefecture called Okinawa after its largest island.

Then, for two decades after this initial burst of imperialism, Japan concentrated on modernization at home rather than overseas expansion. Yet, the dream of conquest never died among Japan's elite or mass public. In 1882, Fukuzawa Yukichi, Japan's leading liberal of the Meiji era, clearly expressed the Japanese desire for expansion: "We shall someday raise the national power of Japan so that not only shall we control the natives of China and India as the English do today, but we shall also possess in our hands the power to rebuke the English and to rule Asia ourselves."[5] Sixty years later, the Japanese almost succeeded in achieving this dream.

Eventually, as in the United States, political, economic, and intellectual pressures steadily built for another expansion round. By the 1890s, Japan's absorption of western ideas, technologies, and practices had reached the psychological saturation point, and the inevitable reaction set in. The imperial court helped lead the rejection of many superficial western customs and the readoption of traditional Japanese values. The Imperial Rescript on Education of 1890 meshed aspects of Shintoism, Confucianism, and statism in which students would dedicate themselves to the emperor and Japan.

Japan's growing industrial and military power allowed Tokyo to extract a series of treaties with the western powers reversing the unequal treaties. The first of these occurred in 1894 when Britain agreed to eliminate extraterritoriality by 1899. Tokyo soon forged similar agreements with the other western powers.

Japan's imperialism at the turn of the century was primarily defensive – "less an appetite for territory than a desire for recognition and security."[6] For Japanese, it was clear that a modern country was an imperial country and the western powers only respected strength. Western concepts of "Social Darwinism" mirrored Japan's own views of an international hierarchy of superior and inferior races, constant struggle among them, and the right of the strong to conquer and exploit the weak. As in the United States, imperial sentiments had built up in Japan, which only needed an excuse to exercise them.

War between Japan and China in 1894 arose over their struggle to dominate Korea. China had been Korea's suzerain power for thousands of years. With the 1876 Treaty of Kanghwa, Japan had extracted the right to station troops in Korea. In April 1885, Japan and China attempted to reduce growing tensions by agreeing to withdraw their respective troops from Korea. Meanwhile, Japanese diplomats and agents continued their machinations to weaken China's influence over Korea and strengthen the pro-Japanese court faction, while Japanese businessmen captured one market after another.

In early 1894, Tokyo decided it was strong enough to risk war to dominate Korea. It presented a financial, administrative, and economic reform plan for Korea that it knew the Chinese would reject since it resembled those the western powers had tried to impose on Peking. Shortly after Peking rejected the plan, Tokyo declared war on August 1, 1894. Within weeks, Japanese troops overran most of Korea, the navy had destroyed China's fleet, and the embassy forced Korea's government to agree to a protectorate. In late October Japanese armies advanced into Manchuria and the Liaotung (Kwantung) peninsula. In March 1895, Tokyo forced Seoul to sign a loan agreement for 3 million yen in which Japanese advisors would be allowed to administer Korea's three southern provinces until it was repaid. With its armies routed and Korea's takeover a fait accompli, China sued for peace.

The Treaty of Shimonoseki, signed on April 17, 1895, gave Japan Taiwan, the Pescadore Islands, the Liaotung peninsula with its naval base and fortress at Port Arthur, an indemnity of 360 million yen, the opening of additional Chinese ports to Japan, the occupation of Weihaiwei until the indemnity had been paid, and recognition of Korean independence. Suddenly Japan was one of the great powers with the same rights in China and a small overseas empire.

The victory elation soon turned to mass bitterness. On April 23, 1895, Russia, Germany, and France threatened Japan with war if it did not renounce its acquisition of the Liaotung peninsula. Tokyo had no choice but to comply. The "Triple Intervention" outraged the Japanese, and that resentment deepened over the next few years as the three powers and Britain widened their spheres of influence over China. In 1897 Germany acquired the right to develop Kiaochow as a naval base and expand its economic influence over Shantung province. Russia acquired a similar lease over Port Arthur in 1896 and the following year the right to construct a railroad across Manchuria to Port Arthur. In 1898, France acquired a naval base at Kwangchowwan and Britain a sphere of influence over the Yangtze valley and port rights at Weihaiwei.

Despite the Triple Intervention setback, victory over China was a turning point in Japan's history and the regional power balance. In defeating China, Japan joined the ranks of great powers. Japanese imperialism literally payed for itself as Tokyo imposed and received a huge indemnity from China, which financed further ambitions. Increasing numbers of Japanese saw their central foreign policy mission as liberating "Asia for the Asians."

THE FIRST IMMIGRATION CRISIS

American actions temporarily diverted Japanese attentions from the great power struggle for spheres of influence in China and Manchuria. Throughout the late 1890s and periodically into the twentieth century, tensions erupted between Washington and Tokyo over Japanese immigration into Hawaii and California.

Throughout the nineteenth century, American merchants had slowly taken over Hawaii's ports and sugar plantations. Washington increasingly saw Hawaii's value as strategic as well as commercial. No foreign power could attack America's west coast without a coal supply in the islands, while possession of Hawaii gave the United States a huge stepping stone toward the western Pacific.

As early as 1842, Washington announced that it would not take over Hawaii nor tolerate its conquest by any other nation, renewed the pledge in 1851, and in 1854 cast aside its promise and tried to outright buy Hawaii. The deal fell through when the Hawaiian monarch died and his successor repudiated the treaty. Hawaii became a de facto American colony as businessmen acquired huge sugar plantations. Yet Americans were divided over whether to annex Hawaii. Domestic sugar producers protested the access of Hawaiian sugar to the American market.

King Kalakaua toured the United States in 1875 to promote a treaty in which the United States would acquire Pearl Harbor in return for free access for Hawaiian sugar to the United States. Unrest in Hawaii forced Kalakaua to revise his proposal so that he would not cede Pearl Harbor to any other power other than the United States. Congress passed the revised treaty and then in a 1884 treaty received the sole right to use Pearl Harbor. In 1881, Secretary of State James Blaine maintained that "the United States regards the Hawaiian group as essentially part of the American system of states . . . [and] could not regard the intrusion of any non-American interest in Hawaii as consistent with our relations thereto."[7]

Not all Americans appreciated Hawaii's strategic and commercial importance. In 1890, domestic sugar producers pressured Congress into increasing tariffs on Hawaiian sugar. To make matters worse for America's sugar planters in Hawaii, the compliant King Kalakaua was succeeded by his sister, Queen Lilioukalani who promoted a new constitution that would revoke the American participation in Hawaii's government.

In 1893, the planters organized a coup that overthrew the queen and asked for annexation by the United States. President Benjamin Harrison negotiated an annexation treaty with the new government, but his successor, Grover Cleveland, withdrew the treaty from the Senate because he feared the Hawaiian regime was a puppet of the American planters and did not represent the views of most native Hawaiians.

America's growing influence over Hawaii, and growing commercial and naval power across the Pacific, was accompanied by increasingly racist attitudes toward Asians in general, and Japanese in particular. Like other westerners, most Americans accepted a Social Darwinian view of international relations as a continual struggle in which the strong invariably and "naturally" conquered and exploited the weak. Americans were also affected by the "yellow peril" hysteria popular around the turn of the century. The Hearst newspaper chain was particularly vociferous in stirring yellow peril fears and pushing the government to keep the Asians at bay.

Fear of "yellow hordes" of immigrant invaders increasingly influenced American policy toward the Pacific throughout the late nineteenth and into the early twentieth centuries. Chinese began immigrating to the United States as early as 1848 to work the mines, railroads, and farms. Chinese immigrants suffered severe discrimination and were frequently the victims of violence, theft, and even lynchings. Anti-Chinese riots in Los Angeles in 1871 left eighteen Chinese dead and in Rock Springs, Wyoming, in 1885 twenty-eight murdered.

Congressional acts of 1882, 1888, and 1892 forbade further Chinese immigration, the reentry of Chinese who had previously resided in the United States, and required Chinese to register with the police and carry identification papers. In 1871, the United States Supreme Court upheld a California state law forbidding Chinese from becoming American citizens. In 1893, the Supreme Court ruled that the government could deport Chinese aliens without trial or even by demonstrating just cause. Ironically, this discrimination occurred while the United States insisted on the rights of Americans to travel freely, do business, evangelize, and even reside in China.

After the Chinese Exclusion Act of 1882, Japanese became the largest group of immigrants to Hawaii and from there to the United States. By the late 1890s, there were already 26,000 Japanese in Hawaii, more than one-quarter of the population. The Americans feared that any more immigrants would take over the islands. Rumours maintained that many "laborers" were actually disguised soldiers who were sent by Tokyo to lead a rebellion.

The first crisis over Japanese immigration occurred in 1897 when three Japanese ships carrying Japanese immigrants docked at Pearl Harbor. American officials forced nearly two-thirds of those hopeful immigrants to return to Japan. Tokyo protested and sent a warship with a foreign ministry official aboard to Hawaii to "observe relations." Rather than intimidate the Americans into allowing free immigration, Japan's gunboat diplomacy actually spurred them to complete their takeover of Hawaii. Secretary of the Navy John Long ordered American warships in Hawaii to assert a protectorate over the islands if the Japanese made any aggressive moves. Citing the Japanese threat, President William McKinley had a treaty of Hawaiian annexation signed and ratified in 1898.

Tokyo could do nothing more than protest America's annexation. Although many newspapers, politicians, and even Japan's minister to the United States, Hoshi Toru, advocated war, Foreign Minister Okuma Shigenobu pressured the cabinet to accept the annexation as a fait accompli. Okuma cabled Hoshi that: "Continuation without interruption or disturbance of our intercourse with the United States is of vastly more importance to Japan than interests that will be menaced by annexation. Consequently good policy dictates that our opposition to annexation must be within the limits of diplomacy."[8]

Okuma's patience paid off. Hawaii eventually paid a $75,000 indemnity to compensate those passengers returned to Japan. Immigration continued with Japan's population in Hawaii reaching 61,000 in 1900, double that of a mere four years earlier. The United States, however, rejected a Japanese request to codify rights for its immigrants in the United States. And in early 1900, it tightened its immigration controls to forbid contract labor. Japanese immigrants to Hawaii plummeted to 4,760 from 27,155 the previous year.

The Senate Foreign Relations Committee saw Japan's threat as apocalyptic. Its report concluded that "the present Hawaiian–Japanese controversy is the preliminary skirmish in the great coming struggle between the civilization and the awakening forces of the East and civilization of the West. The issue is whether, in that inevitable struggle, Asia or America shall have the vantage ground of the control of the naval 'Key of the Pacific,' the commercial 'Crossroads of the Pacific.'"[9] With these and other fears, America went to war with Spain.

THE SPANISH–AMERICAN WAR AND ITS AFTERMATH

Throughout the nineteenth century, certain American businessmen and politicians had coveted Cuba. Before the Civil War, southerners saw Cuba as a potential rich slave state to balance politically and economically the newly taken nonslave western territories. After 1865, those interested in Cuba mostly eyed its agricultural potential. But Washington had passed on numerous opportunities to expand its influence in Cuba. From Cuba's first aborted revolution in 1823 up through the Spanish–American War, there were nine failed attempts by revolutionaries to achieve independence. Presidents and most in Congress had repeatedly disdained involving the United States in a liberation struggle which would mean war with Spain and the possible acquisition of an alien culture and bitter people. Those who favored intervention remained a minority.

In 1895, however, for both self-serving and idealistic reasons, those advocating Cuba's liberation had grown more numerous, vocal, and powerful. Locked in a nation-wide business war, the Hearst and Pulitzer newspaper chains seized on the Cuban civil war as a hot news item. Each newspaper tried to outdo the other in depicting Spanish atrocities and the valour of Cuban nationalists, often printing verbatim the revolutionaries' propopanda handouts. This "yellow journalism" (so called because of the cheap yellow paper used) fired widespread public sentiments for intervention. Congress passed a resolution urging the Cleveland administration's recognition of the Cuban revolutionaries. Citing American neutrality laws, Cleveland rejected any American involvement and simply called on Spain to grant Cuba greater autonomy.

As if Spain were not challenged enough by the Cuban revolution, in 1896 a middle-class Filipino revolt broke out for reform rather than outright independence. Fortunately for the Spanish, the Filipino revolt was easily put down. After leading Filipino forces in several minor victories against the Spanish, Emilio Aquinaldo became the rebel leader. In 1897, Aquinaldo agreed to retire to Hong Kong in return for a Spanish payment of $800,000. In addition, Spain promised to reduce the Catholic Church's power and allow for more foreign trade. The revolt collapsed. But Madrid never did fulfill its promises to the rebels. Aquinaldo only received half the money he was promised, and used much of it to supply arms and training to rebels in the Philippines.

In the 1896 election, William McKinley won the presidency. Sympathizing openly with the rebels, McKinley informed Spain that the United States expected a just peace in Cuba by November 1, 1897 and asked Congress for $50,000 in relief to Cuban refugees. By early 1898, the crisis appeared to ease. A liberal government came to power in Spain and recalled General Weyler, who the American newspapers had depicted as a mass butcher, released Cubans swept up into concentration camps and Americans interned for pro-Cuban actions, and, most importantly, offered autonomy for Cuba.

Unfortunately, circumstances defeated these initiatives. Spanish loyalists rioted when they learned of Weyler's recall and the proposal for Cuban autonomy. Opposition in Spain surged against the liberal government. A letter intercepted from the Spanish ambassador to the United States, Enrique Dupuy de Lome, revealed his contempt for McKinley and advised negotiating with the United States only to play for time. Then, on February 24, 1898, the U.S.S. "Maine" exploded mysteriously in Havana harbor, killing 266 of the 350 crew. A naval board investigation concluded that an external rather than internal explosion had sunk the "Maine", leading to a frenzy of charges of Spanish sabotage. Spain denied any complicity.

McKinley resisted the increasing pressure for war. On March 26, he telegrammed his minister in Madrid to demand three things: the release of all Cubans, armistice, and independence by October 1, after which the United States would intervene. Spain agreed to the first two demands, but denied that it had done so because of American pressure. McKinley sent a message to Congress explaining the negotiation results and requesting the authority to use military force if necessary to resolve the conflict. On April 20, after considerable haggling among congressional factions, McKinley signed a resolution which authorized him to use force to achieve an independent Cuba. Spain then broke diplomatic relations with the United States. When McKinley ordered a naval blockade of Cuba two days later, Spain declared war.

Within six months, American forces defeated Spanish troops in both Cuba and the Philippines. During the war, McKinley ordered Hawaii's annexation, and the seizure of Guam and uninhabited Wake Island as stepping stones to the Philippines. America's "splendid little war," as Secretary of State John Hay called it, was achieved with relatively few losses – combat killed 379 Americans and yellow fever and malaria another 5,000. The enthusiasm of Hay and many other Americans aside, the war was and remains controversial, with many arguing that it should never have occurred let alone resulted in an overseas empire.[10]

On May 1, 1898, Commodore George Dewey sailed into Manila Bay with his fleet and defeated the Spanish fleet. Since there had been no plan to occupy the Philippines, there were no American troops aboard Dewey's ships. Dewey had transported Aquinaldo and his followers from Hong Kong to the Philippines, but later denied Aquinaldo's claim that he had promised the Philippines independence.

Having defeated Spain, the McKinley administration now had to decide what to do with the Spanish empire. The Tucker amendment to the declaration of war renounced any intention of colonizing Cuba, but it said nothing about the Philippines. Most prominent Americans like Grover Cleveland, Andrew Carnegie, Mark Twain, and William Jenning Bryan vociferously opposed seizing anything in the Philippines. A few like Mahan advocated taking Manila Bay and Luzon. Henry Cabot Lodge called for taking the entire archipelago and then trading all of it except Manila and Luzon to Britain for British islands in the Caribbean. After Dewey's easy victory, McKinley decided to keep Manila Bay as a springboard to the Asian mainland.

The successful Philippine revolution meant that Spain could no longer hold the islands and a weak Aquinaldo government would be prey to other foreign powers. Just four years earlier, Japan had conquered the nearby island of Taiwan and many feared that Tokyo would be the most likely country to move into a Philippine political vacuum if the United States did not stay. Reasoning that American possession of the Philippines would be the lesser evil, London urged Washington to take it over.

The McKinley adminstration shifted to the view that the United States had no choice but to take over the Philippines. Aquinaldo was considered too weak to rule a faction-ridden Filipino independence movement. Anarchy might well invite the Philippines' conquest by another imperial power. Public opinion surged in support of taking over the entire archipelago.

After being offered $20 million for the Philippines, Spain agreed to relinquish it and a peace treaty was signed. Under the peace treaty, the United States outright colonized the Philippines, Puerto Rico, and Guam, and asserted a protectorate over Cuba. It was largely a Japanese threat in the Pacific that stimulated America's takeover of the Philippines and Guam. The United States imposed severe trade and immigration restrictions on the Philippines, thus frustrating those Japanese who hoped America's takeover from Spain would allow new opportunities for Japanese capital and emigrants. As in Hawaii, Tokyo acquiesced in America's takeover of the Philippines.

Congress remained bitterly divided over the Philippines' acquisition. The treaty's ratification passed the Senate by only two votes on February 2, 1899. Two weeks later on February 14, the vice-president broke a Senate tie and voted against the Bacon amendment which would have promised the Philippines independence as soon as they established a stable government.

Shortly after American troops arrived in the Philippines, conflict arose between them and Filipino forces. The American commander, General Elwell Otis, refused to allow Filipino troops to join the liberation of Manila from Spanish rule and, in fact, actually arranged a mock battle with the Spanish to "preserve their honor." Although the Americans controlled Manila, the rebels occupied the countryside and established a government at Malolos. Even before a peace treaty was signed, McKinley ordered American military rule over the entire Philippines.

On February 4, 1899, two days after the peace treaty was signed granting the Philippines to the United States, fighting broke out between American and Filipino troops. The subsequent guerrilla war – called an insurrection by the Americans – lasted three years and resulted in the deaths of at least 20,000 insurgents in combat and perhaps as many as 140,000 Filipinos from disease and hunger, along with 5,000 Americans. It eventually took 70,000 men, or two-thirds of the American army, to crush the Filipino revolt. After Aquinaldo was captured in 1902, the movement crumbled.

After spilling considerable American blood and treasury to seize the Philippines, the United States soon committed itself to nurturing the country into independence. In 1907, Congress passed the Jones Act which allowed home-rule and promised eventual independence for the Philippines. In 1935, the Tydings–McDuffy Act promised independence within a decade. Japan's conquest of the Philippines in 1942 delayed independence until 1946.

THE OPEN DOOR NOTES AND THE BOXER REBELLION

American interests in China during the 1890s were paltry. China accounted for little more than 1 per cent of American exports. Although sales to China did increase steadily throughout the decade, they accompanied a general rise in American exports around the world. American investments in China were minimal. There were only about a thousand protestant American missionaries and their families scattered across China. America's treaty with China, like those of the other powers, guaranteed most-favored-nation status for the United States, thus preventing Beijing from economic discrimination.

Why then did the United States issue its Open Door notes in 1898 and 1900, warning the other foreign powers to maintain China's territorial integrity and open markets?

A scramble among the four great powers – Britain, France, Germany, and Russia – to carve out exclusive economic zones from China began with Germany's seizure of the port of Kiaochow in Shantung Province in November 1897. Within a couple of years, the French had taken over several southern provinces, the British parts of the Yangtze valley, the Germans the entire Shantung peninsula, and the Russians Manchuria. It was feared that the Europeans might eventually divide all of China among them as they had earlier chopped up Africa. If China's government dissolved, America's treaty rights would disappear with it.

In 1898, President McKinley rejected a British offer to issue a joint declaration in support of China's territorial integrity and equal access. Pressure was growing on the administration to join the imperial race in China. In 1899, the U.S. minister to China, Edwin Conger, advocated an American takeover of Chili province and Tientsin which guarded the approach to Beijing. McKinley rejected the idea. With its minuscule army and navy already tied up in the Philippines and Caribbean, the United States could not possibly stand up to a challenge by one or more of the other western powers. Public opinion in the United States, however, took up the demand that the United States take its own sphere in China.

The State Department China expert, William Rockhill, advised McKinley to do just the opposite. Fearing a scramble to break up China would not only squeeze out the Americans but lead to a world war, Rockhill drafted a message calling for China's territorial integrity and treaty rights. Hoping to undercut domestic criticism, President McKinley authorized Secretary of State John Hay to send it. On September 6, 1899 an identical letter was dispatched to each of the other great powers asking that they continue to allow Americans to trade freely in their respective spheres, honor existing treaty rights, and let the Imperial Maritime Customs Service gather revenue for China. The United States issued the statement alone since the British, after originally proposing the Open Door policy, now rejected it. The Open Door notes contained no threats and, given America's weak and vulnerable position, could have been easily discarded. Instead, each great power assented to America's request with reservations. The power balance was so fragile that each European power feared alienating and driving the United States into alliance with its rivals. Ignoring the reservations, Hay then announced that the Open Door policy was universally accepted, making it even more difficult for any great power to openly reject it.

In 1900, the Society of Righteous and Harmonious Fists (which became known by westerners as the Boxers because they practiced kung fu) carried out a systematic attack on foreign merchants and missionaries in northern China. Although the Boxers were as anti-Ch'ing dynasty as anti-western, in June 1900, the Ch'ing government secretly began arming the rebels and allowed them to take over Beijing and besiege the foreign legations.

McKinley responded by dispatching 2,500 troops from the Philippines to join a 14,000-strong international force massing in Tientsin. As the allied forces marched on Beijing, McKinley and Hay feared that the other powers would use this as an excuse to topple the Ch'ing dynasty and carve up China. They issued another series of notes stating the reasons for America's intervention which included the need to restore order, maintain the Open Door principles, and preserve China as a territorial and administrative entity. The notes did not threaten or even call on the other powers to reciprocate. And the message was certainly not new – Americans had been advocating an Open Door toward China and elsewhere throughout the nineteenth century. Hay simply codified a long-standing American policy.

Only Britain acknowledged receipt of the note, and the Open Door declaration probably had no practical impact on the western powers' policies toward China. There was little possibility of the European powers trying to take over all of China. Simply crushing the Boxer Rebellion had strained western military and logistical capabilities. China's conquest was out of the question. And ironically, shortly after issuing the notes, Hay asked China about acquiring a coaling station at Samsah Bay in Fukien Province, then withdrew the request after the Japanese got wind of it and pointed out to Hay that it violated his own principle.

Over time, however, the second Open Door note acquired a meaning far beyond its original intention and impact. Americans increasingly believed the Open Door notes saved China from dismemberment, and saw themselves as the champion of an underdog China bullied by the greedy great powers and, after 1931, by Japanese imperialism. In the popular imagination, the Open Door stood beside the Monroe Doctrine as a pillar of American purpose in the world. This image then became a reality for succeeding administrations as they felt compelled to follow its principles.[11]

THEODORE R. ROOSEVELT AND THE AMERICAN EMPIRE

McKinley may have won an empire for the United States, but Roosevelt gave it purpose, character, and spirit. As the prolific writer of thirty-six books and over 15,000 letters, rancher, gunfighter, cavalry commander, Spanish–American war hero, Nobel prize winner, doting father, big-game hunter in North America and Africa, Roosevelt personified an age of Horatio Alger's "rags to riches," the cult of the hero and "strenuous life," Social Darwinism, gunboat diplomacy, and Manifest Destiny. His boisterous energy and cheer carried his life. Roosevelt's sheer will freed him from a weak, asthmatic childhood and propelled him into being an accomplished boxer, horseman, rower, and weight-lifter. Cabinet meetings were filled with anecdotes and witticisms and free-ranging debate. To cajole his wife into excepting his planned African safari, he argued, "It'll be my last chance to be a boy!" Asked to comment on his seven years as president, Roosevelt replied, "I enjoyed myself immensely!" Of all the countless anecdotes of life, perhaps none personify his manifold nature more than the image of Roosevelt calmly reading *Anna Karenina* as he and two cowboys rowed down the ice-clogged Little Missouri River in pursuit of rustlers.

Roosevelt soared politically through such posts as New York City police commissioner, governor, navy secretary, vice-president, and finally the presidency. All along, deep-rooted morality and idealism fired his public "square deal" crusades against corruption, nepotism, machine politics, and monopoly-capitalism. Roosevelt captured his mixture of hard realism and lofty idealism with the maxim "Keep your eyes on the stars and feet on the ground."

As president, Roosevelt closely meshed the exercise of American power with the pursuit of American interests. "Speak softly but carry a big stick" was more than a political slogan for him, it was his foreign policy's essence. Few presidents have wielded power overseas as deftly or successfully as Roosevelt whose foreign policy revolved around manipulating the global and regional power balances in America's favor. Although he proudly built America's navy into a first rate power, he was no warmonger or insatiable imperialist. While Roosevelt dispatched American ships and marines to show the flag at a score of far-flung exotic ports, seas, and frontiers around the world, the country remained at peace. Roosevelt resisted pressure to annex Cuba and the Dominican Republic, and avoided intervention in other imperial powers' spheres of influence such as Japan's in Korea and Manchuria. He stepped back from the Open Door policy to avoid entanglements in a military quagmire on the Asian mainland. He recognized that the Philippines were a net drain on American wealth and power, a potential Achilles' heel that should be eventually released honorably and securely. He took the Panama Canal Zone only after ensuring that his actions were rooted in international law and exhausting all other means of settling the dispute.

Roosevelt's foreign policy was grounded in the noblesse oblige idea that the greater a nation's power, the more responsibly it should be wielded, and that "a nation is bound by the same moral code as the individual."[12] He preached right and wrong throughout his public speeches and policy debates, maintaining that whenever possible the golden rule should guide a nation's foreign policy and promises made should be firmly kept. Yet, despite his irrepressible non-stop talk, he was discreetly tightlipped with secrets. Roosevelt preferred and mastered secret diplomacy, both to allow others a face-saving way to compromise and to avoid exciting popular passions that would carry away policy. All along, Roosevelt's two secretaries of state, John Hay and Elihu Root, complemented and refined his strategic vision and solutions to complex international conflicts.

POPULAR PERCEPTIONS OF JAPAN

As the twentieth century began, Germany rather than Japan loomed as America's most potential enemy. The appearance of a German fleet in Manila Bay shortly after America's invasion helped convince McKinley that he should seize the Philippines for the United States. Germany's island colonies in the South Pacific and permanent naval squadron in the Caribbean seemed to directly threaten American interests. Berlin supplied arms and money to sympathetic political forces in Mexico, Venezuela, and Colombia, and frustrated early American attempts to secure a Panama Canal agreement with Bogota.

Japan, in contrast, had a largely popular image for the first few years of the new century. Tokyo had supported the United States in both the Open Door notes and Boxer Rebellion. Japan's contingent of 8,000 men was nearly half the total allied force of 17,000, and Japanese troops were admired for their discipline and professionalism. Perhaps no prominent American was a greater admirer of the Japanese than Theodore Roosevelt who continually lauded their discipline, industriousness, and fighting abilities.

But America's largely positive image of Japan steadily shifted throughout Roosevelt's administration and beyond as people increasingly saw the Japanese as rapacious bullies and the Chinese as virtuous underdogs. The Open Door policy had stimulated an already nascent view in the American imagination that the United States was China's patron, and as such had to protect and promote that benighted land much as it had for Japan a half century earlier. This image was shaped by several forces. Japan's military and economic power and ambitions contrasted with China's impotence, backwardness, chaos, and exploitation. While most would grudgingly concede Japan's military prowess, in comparing the respective attributes of Chinese and Japanese they would agree that "morally, and especially in truthfulness and in commercial integrity, the Japanese are greatly the inferior."[13]

Through books, articles, and speeches, some protestant missionaries were the most active in popularizing China's image as a downtrodden country that needed help. In 1905 3,107 of the 3,776 American protestant missionaries overseas were in China.[14] An example of these sentiments occurred in 1905 when the government and public responded with sympathy rather than resentment to a Chinese boycott of American goods because of immigration restrictions. While reluctantly admitting that the restrictions must continue, the Roosevelt administration promised to treat Chinese merchants, students, and travelers fairly; China's boycott was rescinded. While visiting Shanghai in 1907, Secretary of War Taft wrote Roosevelt that the Chinese "turn to us as the only country that is really unselfish in the matter of obtaining territory and monopolies, and I think it worthwhile to cultivate them."[15]

A minority of influential voices remained skeptical of America's tilt toward China. The American ambassador to Japan, Thomas O'Brian complained to Philander Knox in 1910 that China is unable "to meet her simplest obligations. She cannot or will not observe the terms of her solemn treaties, and the Government seems impotent to enforce its will even in her own provinces;" he concluded that it made no sense to alienate Japan in fruitlessly aiding China. The diplomat George Kennan observed that those "who expect in China the rapid national transformation that took place in Japan will certainly be disappointed."[16]

THE RUSSO-JAPANESE WAR AND ITS AFTERMATH

In the half dozen years following the Spanish–American War, while American perceptions of a Japanese threat gradually rose, Japan's perceptions of an American threat diminished and that of a Russian threat grew steadily until it dominated Japanese foreign policy efforts. Russia's construction of the South Manchuria railway linking the trans-Siberia railway with Port Arthur threatened Japanese interests in Korea and stifled them in Manchuria. During the Boxer uprising, Russia had poured 50,000 troops into Manchuria and refused to withdraw them.

In 1901, Tokyo actually approached Washington for an alliance against Russia. Secretary Hay replied that the United States was not "prepared to attempt singly, or in connection with other Powers, to enforce [the Open Door in China] . . . by any demonstration which could present a character of hostility to any other power."[17] Despite its nascent empire, militarily the United States was still a second-rate power. Of the seven great powers in 1902, America's battleship tonnage of 119,120 ranked sixth, after Britain's 561,900, France's 246,096, Russia's 193,311, Japan's 129,715, and Italy's 124,153, but ahead of Germany's 115,968.[18] In 1903, the Navy Department organized a permanent Pacific fleet comprising one-third of total American naval strength. The Navy Department also began constructing a chain of naval bases across the Pacific including Panama, Pearl Harbor, Wake, Guam, and Manila. But despite these measures, the United States remained unprepared for an alliance that could lead to war.

Tokyo then turned to London with which it shared a common threat of Russia whose empire's rapid expansion throughout the nineteenth century brought it grinding against Britain's domains in southern Asia and Japan's interests in northeast Asia. On January 30, 1902, Britain and Japan signed a security treaty in which each recognized the other's special interests in China and Korea, and right to defend those interests from internal or foreign enemies. Each agreed to come to the other's aid if it found itself at war with two or more other powers, but not if it were only fighting one enemy. Under a secret agreement both would maintain naval forces in the Pacific larger than any other naval power.

Understandably, Washington suspiciously eyed the Anglo-Japanese alliance as an affront to the Open Door policy and possible threat to the United States. Neither Britain nor Japan wanted to alienate the United States and attempted to reassure Washington that the treaty's purpose was largely to contain Russia. In 1911, the revised treaty stated that the alliance would not be evoked against any country with whom either Britain or Japan signed an arbitration agreement. That same year, Washington hastily negotiated and signed an arbitration treaty with Britain, although the Senate never ratified it.

Russia signed an agreement with China in April 1902 in which it agreed to withdraw its troops from Manchuria in three stages. After completing the first stage by April 1903, Russia refused to begin its promised next two stages. Instead, St Petersburg demanded that China employ only Russian advisors and refuse to open any more cities in Manchuria. China delayed while asking the United States for help. Washington responded by repeating its Open Door principles and asserting that Russia did have an "exceptional" interest in Manchuria. St Petersburg denied that it opposed any more open cities in the region, meanwhile threatening China with war if it did not sign the agreement.

Tokyo viewed Russia's imperialism in Manchuria with increased alarm. Washington's refusal to back its Open Door principles with force, at least in regards to Russia, disappointed the Japanese. In August 1903, Tokyo sent St Petersburg a draft agreement in which each would respect the others sphere of influence in Korea and Manchuria, respectively, but the latter would remain less restricted to Japanese trade and investments. Russia finally replied in October, rejecting most of Japan's demands and asserting rights in both Manchuria and Korea. Negotiations over the next several months failed to narrow the wide gap between the two sides.

Frustrated with Russia's refusal to concede, Japan's cabinet, the Genro, and Emperor Meiji met on February 3, 1904 and agreed to go to war to break the impasse. Tokyo hoped that war would eliminate Russia's presence in Korea and Manchuria, and allow complete Japanese control over the former and indirect control over the latter. On February 8, in a sneak attack Japan's fleet destroyed the Russian fleet at Port Arthur; two days later, Japan formally declared war on Russia. Japanese armies quickly drove Russian troops out of Korea and then advanced into Manchuria, besieging Port Arthur and battling toward Mukden. Despite these successes, Japan's war effort was becoming increasingly expensive, forcing Tokyo to raise money in international financial markets. Half of the initial funds came from American investors, and that support enabled Japan to garner loans in London.

From the war's beginning, other powers encouraged the United States to use its influence to contain and finally end the fighting. In February 1904 and January 1905, Hay sent identical notes to all signatories of the Boxer Protocal urging them to help maintain the Open Door and China's integrity. The White House also pressurized Germany to not enter the war on Russia's side. In December 1904, China implored the White House to mediate the war.

From the war's outbreak, Roosevelt hoped to mediate its end but waited to offer America's good offices until the time was right. Officially the United States attempted to maintain a strict neutrality. Ideally, the war would result in the two powers weakened but still threatening each other in northeast Asia, thus continuing to divert their attentions and energies from expansion elsewhere. In a March 1904 letter, Roosevelt clearly articulated his hope that "the two powers will fight until both are fairly well exhausted, and that then peace will come on terms which will not mean the creation of either a yellow peril or a Slav peril."[19] Roosevelt saw Russia as a greater threat than Japan, later writing his son that "I was thoroughly well pleased with the Japanese victory, for Japan is playing our game."[20]

Throughout the war, a series of relatively minor issues arose in which Roosevelt warned the Japanese to first stop abusing foreign correspondents in the war zone, and then return a Russian warship it had seized in Cheefoo, thus violating China's neutrality and international law. Tokyo refused to comply with Roosevelt's suggestions on either issue, thus dulling his enthusiasm for the Japanese.

Meanwhile, Japan's victories continued to mount. On January 2, 1905, Russian forces in Port Arthur surrendered. Japanese troops continued to battle their way north, taking Mukden in March. Yet these victories were enormously costly in blood and treasury, and Japan's government hoped for a negotiated end to the war.

During January 1905 in several meetings with Japan's ambassador to the United States, Takahira Kogoro, Roosevelt elaborated his views of a just peace which included a Japanese protectorate over Korea, the return of Manchuria to China, and no indemnity. Takahira cabled Roosevelt's views to Tokyo. On March 8, War Minister Terauchi informed Ambassador Griscom of Japan's desire to end the war, but only if it got Korea, Sakhalin, a huge indemnity, and Russian withdrawal from Manchuria. Griscom in turn cabled the White House that Japan would like the United States to help mediate the war's end, but only when it judged the time was right. Not wanting to appear too eager, Roosevelt cabled Griscom that he would only mediate if Tokyo could not find a more suitable go-between. After Mukden's surrender, Roosevelt offered his good offices to both Tokyo and

St Petersburg. Hoping to score yet more victories, Tokyo refused. Aware of Tokyo's humiliating peace terms, Russia also rejected Roosevelt's offer.

Russia's last hope was a decisive victory by its Baltic fleet which was steaming toward Korea. On May 28, 1905, the Japanese fleet met and destroyed the Russian fleet. Three days later, Foreign Minister Komura informed Roosevelt through Takahira that Japan's government desired the president simultaneously to offer mediation to both belligerents. Roosevelt agreed. On June 12, Russia reluctantly agreed.

Roosevelt first suggesting meeting at the Hague, but the Japanese refused to go to Europe. He then offered Washington, D.C., but the summer weather was so sweltering that the participants finally agreed to meet at Portsmouth, New Hampshire. In July, while the delegations were journeying to the United States, Japan invaded and overran Sakhalin.

The conference opened on August 9, 1905 and continued until September 5 when a treaty was signed. Japan's government charged its delegation, headed by Foreign Minister Komura, with three essential goals: (1) domination of Korea; (2) Russia's complete withdrawal from Manchuria; and (3) transfer of Russia's lease over Liaotung and the railroad from Harbin to Port Arthur, to Japan. Secondary goals included Sakhalin, an indemnity, surrender of Russian warships in neutral ports, limitations on the Russian navy in the Far East, and fishing rights off Russia's maritime provinces. St Petersburg allowed the Russian delegation, led by former Finance Minister Sergius Witte, to concede to any Japanese demands as long as they did not involve Russia ceding land or money. The negotiations stalled over Sakhalin, the indemnity, and the fate of Russia's warships.

Although Roosevelt stayed at his home at Oyster Bay, Long Island during the negotiations, through cables to Portsmouth and meetings with diplomats he pressed for a peace that would preserve the power balance. On August 18, Roosevelt proposed to the Japanese that if they relinquished their demands on Russia's navy and agreed to the nonbinding arbitration of an indemnity, they could take Sakhalin. Komura agreed and made the proposal to Witte who would only cede half of Sakhalin. Komura then said Japan would return the northern half of Sakhalin for a payment of 1.2 billion yen or about $600 million. Witte cabled St Petersburg for instructions. On August 23, the Czar sent word to Roosevelt that he would concede southern Sakhalin but no indemnity. Roosevelt pressed the Japanese to accept the offer. On August 28, the cabinet and Genro met before Emperor Meiji and unanimously agreed to accept Russian's concessions. The Treaty of Portsmouth was signed on September 5, 1905.

The long-term effects of the Russo-Japanese War were far more disruptive to the regional and global power balance than those of the Sino-Japanese

War. The war financially drained both Russia and Japan. Over the long-term, however, Japan not only recovered but expanded its industrial power; Russia did not. The defeat and wartime massacre of protesters before the Winter Palace discredited and weakened the Czarist regime; World War I would then destroy it. In November 1917, the communists overthrew the Russian government and established a revolutionary, totalitarian state.

Although Roosevelt later received a Nobel prize for his efforts, the Japanese public focused its wrath on him for pressuring Tokyo to forego an indemnity. When the Portsmouth Treaty's text was published, anti-American riots broke out in Hibiya Park in downtown Tokyo and continued for four days until the government declared martial law. The swell of anti-American feelings were ironic considering that without American loans Japan's victory would not have been possible.

In contrast, Roosevelt applauded Japan's victory and was delighted in Japan's growing interests on the mainland since it diverted Tokyo's attentions and energies from the Pacific. Roosevelt encouraged Japan's control over Korea, "just like we have with Cuba." Bowing to geopolitical realities, he admitted that the United States "cannot possibly interfere for the Koreans against Japan. They couldn't possibly strike one blow in their own defense."[21] In March 1904, Ambassador Allen refused to grant the Korean king asylum in America's embassy in Seoul. This policy was enshrined on July 27, 1905 when Roosevelt's special envoy to Tokyo, William Howard Taft, signed with Foreign Minister Katsura Taro what became known as the Taft–Katsura Memorandum in which Japan promised to recognize America's predominance in the Philippines and the United States Japan's in Korea.

The Portsmouth Treaty recognized Japan's paramount political, military, and economic interests in Korea. Tokyo quickly took full advantage of these terms, imposing a treaty on Korea's king in November 1905 in which Japan would assume complete control over all foreign affairs, defense, communications, and trade, appoint a Resident General and advisors in all ministries to "assist" Korea's government, and disband the Korean army and station Japanese troops throughout the country. Five years later, on August 22, 1910, Japan forced the Koreans to sign a treaty of annexation in which the king was deposed and Japan's emperor became the new ruler.

Under the Portsmouth Treaty, Russia transferred the rights to its South Manchurian railway to Japan, a transaction that had to be confirmed by China. Shortly after receiving this right, Japan almost sold part of it to the American multi-millionaire E. H. Harriman who aspired to create a global railroad and shipping system. On October 12, 1905, Harriman and Foreign

Minister Katsura signed a preliminary agreement to create a Japanese–American syndicate to develop the South Manchurian railway. Although desparately short of the capital which Harriman offered, Japan's cabinet vetoed the deal.

Japan's policymakers became increasingly locked into the logic of empire in which each successful conquest must be protected by further expansion. Having taken over Korea, it now became imperative to establish control over neighboring Manchuria and eventually China. As Iriye points out, from 1904 on "Japanese expansion would be as much continental as maritime, carried out by military as well as economic means."[22]

Although the Portsmouth Treaty called for Manchuria's restoration to China, over the next three decades, Japanese influence in the region steadily strengthened. Japanese troops had occupied southern Manchuria during the war with Russia. In return for a reduction in Japan's troop level in Manchuria, China signed the Treaty of Peking with Japan on December 22, 1905 in which it agreed to transfer the Russian lease of the South Manchurian railway to Japan along with complete civil and military control. China also promised not to build any parallel lines. Japanese corporations and settlers poured into Manchuria, establishing businesses and homes. Japanese officials used money and threats to manipulate Manchurian politics in Japan's favor and squeeze out other foreign businessmen.

American business interests were the most severely hurt of those foreigners with trade and investments in Manchuria. In 1905, American exports into Manchuria's open port of Newchwang were greater than those of all other foreign nations combined, but quickly dwindled as the Japanese asserted control.[23] In March 1906, the United States and Britain urged Tokyo to open the trade door in Manchuria. Tokyo promised an Open Door by June 1, but after that date continued to impede foreign business.

Willard Straight, the U.S. consul at Mukden, tried strenuously and ultimately fruitlessly to promote American commerce, strengthen Chinese influence, and stem Japan's domination of Manchuria. Straight's scheme to use the Boxer indemnity to finance an American–Chinese railway line parallel to Japan's was undercut when China admitted that it had promised not to construct such a railroad in the Peking Treaty.

Successful wars with China and particularly Russia had boosted Japan's self-image as a "superior" country. Japanese justified their growing regional hegemony with the concept of "Asia for the Asians" in which it was Japan's destiny to liberate the Far East from western imperialism and lead it into an age of prosperity and enlightenment. Foreign Minister Okuma captured these sentiments: "The War, the Japanese feel, proves there is nothing that Westerners cannot do that Asians cannot do."[24]

THE SECOND IMMIGRATION CRISIS

Tokyo continued to promote Japanese immigration as a means of alleviating crowding at home and expanding economic and political influence abroad. While Japan's imperial ambitions focused on continental expansion, its emigrants headed east across the Pacific. After 1900, Japanese immigrants sidestepped Hawaii's tightened immigration controls by sailing straight to the United States, particularly California. By 1905, there were 65,000 Japanese in Hawaii and 40,000 on the west coast, while only 5,215 lived in all of Manchuria, 50,000 in Taiwan, and 40,000 in Korea. Then a xenophobic backlash in California diverted Japanese immigrants toward Hawaii; in 1906, 30,393 immigrants arrived at Pearl Harbor, and from there on to the Pacific coast.[25]

Japan's horde of immigrants exacerbated "yellow-peril" fears, with some seeing disguised spies and soldiers wherever Japanese settled and even collusion with blacks to undermine American society.[26] In spring 1905, the California legislature and San Francisco government passed resolutions calling for restrictions on Japanese immigration, and San Franciscan toughs attacked Japanese and mobbed shops in Japan Town. The U.S. Congress debated but did not vote on amending the 1904 law prohibiting Chinese immigration to include Japanese. Although the xenophobia abated for a while, on October 11, 1906, San Francisco passed a resolution segregating Asian from white school children. Boycott and outright attacks against Japanese businesses followed.

Although there were only ninety-nine Japanese school children in San Francisco, the official discrimination and unofficial violence against Japanese led to a crisis in American–Japanese relations. Japan's ambassador Aoki Siuzo issued a strong protest. Japan's press fiercely denounced San Francisco's actions. Some prominent Japanese and newspapers called for war.

Roosevelt was appalled by Californian discrimination against the Japanese whom he greatly admired. Yet he favored immigration restrictions, "not because they were racially inferior, but because they were racially different."[27] Like many others, he also feared a Japanese backlash that could damage American trade with the Far East and perhaps even lead to war. While secretly preparing the fleet for action, Roosevelt tried to negotiate a compromise with both California and Tokyo. Thus Roosevelt once again exercised his "speak softly but carry a big stick" policy, which toward Japan he described as "behaving with absolute good faith, courtesy, and justice to her on the one hand, and on the other, of keeping our navy in such shape as to make it a risky thing for Japan to go to war with us."[28]

On December 4, 1906, the president appeared before Congress, strongly denounced San Francisco's discrimination and recommended that a law be passed allowing the naturalization of Japanese immigrants. He promised to use all legal means to protect the Japanese. Roosevelt then embarked on separate negotiations with Japan and California that lasted until February 1907. An impasse arose when the school board would not retreat unless Tokyo agreed to limit immigration. Tokyo refused to budge unless San Francisco stopped its discrimination. Roosevelt invited California's entire congressional delegation to the White House in January, and in February San Francisco's school board and mayor. He spoke openly of war with Japan, both to wring concessions from the Californians and larger naval appropriations from Congress. Meanwhile, Foreign Minister Elihu Root strongly refuted Tokyo's contention that the school discrimination violated the 1894 Friendship and Trade Treaty between the two countries.

The result was a "Gentlemen's Agreement" on February 24, 1907 in which, in return for Tokyo's promise to limit immigration to the United States, Roosevelt got Congress and San Francisco to drop their discrimination against Japanese. Over the next few months while Roosevelt and, after considerable arm-twisting, California upheld their end of the deal, Tokyo did not. Japanese immigrants continued to pour into Hawaii and the west coast, albeit at slightly reduced rates. An anti-Japanese riot in San Francisco in May caused a frenzied backlash among Japan's press and populace which included war cries.

On July 4, 1907, the White House announced that the fleet was sailing to the Pacific. Roosevelt hoped to accomplish several goals by dispatching the fleet: intimidating Japan's extremists, training the navy for action, and creating popular support for more battleships. The most important objective, of course, was deterring war. He wrote later that "I found the Japanese war party firmly believed that they could beat us . . . it was time for a show down."[29] From the beginning Roosevelt intended the fleet to sail around the globe, but did not announce the plan until February 1908.

Roosevelt's fleet action worked. In 1908, Washington and Tokyo strengthened their relationship by signing arbitration and trademark treaties. That same year, more Japanese left the United States than entered. The war talk subsided the closer the fleet steamed toward Japan. When the "Great White Fleet" dropped anchor in Tokyo Bay on October 18, it was greeted with thousands of Japanese school children singing American national songs, a thousand college students acting as volunteer guides, and a week of huge banquets for the officers and sailors alike. When it departed on October 25, the war scare had ended.

What had been at stake in the relationship was not war but good will. Given Japan's economic problems, the White House considered war unlikely. As in its war with Russia, Tokyo would have had to borrow extensively from international bankers to finance any struggle with the United States, and would not have been able to count on American financiers this time.

Roosevelt's policy toward Japan culminated on November 30, 1908 when Secretary of State Elihu Root and Foreign Minister Kogoro Takahira exchanged notes reaffirming their respective spheres of influence, the Open Door, China's territorial integrity, and peaceful resolution of conflicts. For eight years, Roosevelt had promoted American interests in the Far East through skilful manipulation of the regional power balance, deft diplomacy, and appropriate displays of the "big stick." Roosevelt's efforts had reinforced Tokyo's decision to concentrate on expanding on the Asia mainland rather than south and east across the Pacific.

Despite the resolution of these conflicts, Japan and the United States now viewed each other as their chief threat and potential enemy. In 1907 both sides secretly drew up war plans against each other.

America's Plan Orange was one of several contingency war plans devised by the Joint Army and Navy Board between 1903 and 1907 with each potential enemy given a color code (Japan was orange, Germany black, Mexico green, and Britain red). Plan Orange was nearly the mirror image of its Japanese counterpart. The plan involved holding out in the Philippines and Guam against Japanese attacks until the U.S. fleet could sail to the rescue. Japan's acquisition of the Marianas, Carolines, and Marshalls during World War I, which lay astride the American rescue route to the Philippines, enormously complicated Plan Orange.

The Joint Board recognized that the Philippines would undoubtedly fall to Japanese forces, but did not admit that probability in the revised Plan Orange of 1924. Instead, American forces in the Philippines would retreat to Manila Bay and hold out until the fleet arrived. In 1935, Plan Orange was expanded to include the capture of key islands in the Carolines and Marshalls to use as bases. A 1936 revision called for American forces to simply defend Manila Bay's entrance rather than the entire bay. In 1938, the operations in the Carolines and Marshalls were elaborated. In 1939, Plan Orange was incorporated into five new war plans, code-named Rainbow, which accounted for different scenarios of enemies and allies in the Pacific and Atlantic.

Japan's 1907 contingency plan for war with the United States was largely devised by the Navy Ministry. Japan's battle plan involved quickly overrunning the Philippines and Guam, then concentrating its naval forces while the American fleet steamed into the western Pacific. The Japanese fleet would then destroy the American fleet in a decisive battle. In 1928, the war plan was modified to account for Japan's takeover of the German islands during World War I and the Washington Treaty. Screens of Japanese submarines would lie waiting across the American fleet's path across the Pacific and pick off ships as they slowly advanced west. By the time the two fleets closed, the American fleet's advantage in numbers would be largely rusting on the ocean bottom. Japanese planes launched from carriers and bases in the islands would then attack the American fleet, sinking as many ships as possible. The Japanese fleet would then sail in to administer the coup de grace.[30]

DOLLAR DIPLOMACY

The Taft administration shifted American policy toward Japan. While American containment of Japanese ambitions in the Far East continued, the means changed. The Taft emphasis on loans and trade rather than guns to promote American interests became known as "dollar diplomacy."

This policy was promoted after the creation of a Far Eastern Bureau in the State Department in March 1908 at the end of Roosevelt's term. Pro-Japanese William Rockhill was replaced with other experienced diplomats like Willard Straight, William Phillips, and Huntington Wilson who had all served in Asia and feared Japanese expansion. They, along with a group of American businessmen interested in trading and investing in Manchuria, advocated an Open Door policy toward northeast Asia.

After taking office in 1909, President Taft and Secretary of State Philander Knox supported the efforts of E. H. Harriman to build the Chinchow–Aigun railroad in Manchuria which would compete directly with Japan's South Manchurian railroad. Although China's government initially supported the American project, it backed down after Japan protested, reasoning that the United States would not be willing to go to war over the railroad or to support China's sovereignty over Manchuria. Knox then proposed that all railroads in Manchuria be bought out by China, which would receive the money to do so with a loan from the great powers. The other powers rejected Knox's proposal. The Taft administration did succeed in getting American bankers to join a consortium of British, French, and German financiers which would loan China money with which to strengthen inself against Japan. Tokyo pressured the financiers to include Japan and Russia in the loan. Then, in 1912, revolutionaries overthrew the Ch'ing dynasty. Taft went along with the consortium's decision to delay recognizing the new government led by Sun Yat-sen and Yuan Shikai.

Fear of Japanese imperialism continued, enflamed in 1909 by the publication of two popular books, respectively addressing Japanese military and economic threats. Homer Lea's *The Valour of Ignorance* warned of a Japanese plan to surprise attack Hawaii and the west coast, and argued that the United States had to prepare for this threat.[31] Thomas Millard's *America and the Far Eastern Question*, popularized the views of those who advocated a tough stand against "Japan's goal [of] . . . commercial supremacy in the whole East."[32] Millard cites a litany of means by which the Japanese were asserting hegemony in the region including government–business collusion, corruption of local officials, export and investment subsidies for Japanese business, import barriers against foreign goods and investments in Japan and its empire, the copying of foreign technology, designs, and products, and so on, all of which are virtually identical to accusations about Japan since 1945.[33]

The Taft administration was more successful in its attempts to cooperate with rather than confront Japanese ambitions. In 1911, Washington and Tokyo signed a commercial treaty in which the United States abandoned its right to control Japan's tariffs on American goods and renewed the Gentlemen's Agreement.

WORLD WAR I AND THE VERSAILLES TREATY

American–Japanese relations experienced a new round of tensions and conflict during the Wilson administration over World War I and the Versailles Treaty. As with his predecessors, President Wilson was eventually able to overcome these problems, thus maintaining cooperative relations between the two countries.

Born deep in Virginia, Woodrow Wilson was the son of a sternly self-righteous Presbyterian minister. Like father, like son in disposition if not career, Wilson was the only American president to earn a doctorate, wrote a brilliant book on Congress, and served as a professor and then president of Princeton before plunging directly into politics to become New Jersey's governor. He was a classic liberal, promoting with almost religious fervor his faith in markets and individuals freed from government's heavy hand. Although unyielding in defending his beliefs, his thinking did evolve from fervent support for States' rights to an equally impassioned promotion for the New Freedom and New Nationalism for all America. America was for Wilson the "city on a hill," an oasis of liberty and civility and model for a corrupt, violent world.

Whether he admitted or even realized it or not, like other idealists, Wilson's beliefs and policies often rudely clashed.[34] There were distinct limits to Wilson's liberalism which allowed for discrimination against blacks and other "lesser breeds" while his internationalism was flavored with notions of the "White Man's burden." According to Wilson, East Europe's nationalities deserved self-determination; those of Africa and southern Asia did not. He sent the army into Mexico in 1915 as much to protect American oil interests as restore an aborted democratic revolution; then abruptly withdrew the troops as the United States edged closer to joining the war in Europe. He was reelected in 1916 partly on his promise to keep America out of the war, then shortly thereafter asked Congress for a war declaration.

Early on Wilson became embroiled in Far East politics. One of Wilson's first acts as president was to withdraw government support for American bankers involved in the six-nation consortium financing railroad construction in China. Upholding the Open Door policy, he denounced the consortium and other foreign machinations which bit deeply into China's sovereignty. Wilson then recognized China's new government, sparking the first clash with Japan. Tokyo protested Wilson's recognition by arguing that warlords were breaking up the country and the new regime controlled only its capital and a few provinces. Tokyo was right. President Sun stepped aside in 1913 and Yuan took power. Yuan negotiated a loan from the consortium and when he used the money to build up his private army rather than China, Sun's organization, the Nationalist Party (Koumintang, KMT) tried to overthrow him and the country dissolved into civil war.[35]

When World War I broke out, Japan used the excuse of its alliance with Britain to join the Allies and take over the German possessions in Shantung and the Pacific islands north of the equator while Australia and New Zealand took those south of the equator. In 1915, Tokyo sent China its infamous "21 Demands" which included: China's acceptance of Japan's control over Shantung; the extension of Japan's concessions in Manchuria; China's agreement not to grant any more harbors to other foreign powers; half of all China's arms had to be purchased from Japan; Japanese advisors would guide all Chinese political, military, and economic ministries; Japanese police to administer important points throughout China.

Although Tokyo warned China to keep the 21 Demands secret, the Chinese government leaked it to Washington and requested American help in maintaining the Open Door. Concerned with the war raging in Europe, Secretary of State William Jennings Bryan instead issued a statement recognizing Japan's new possessions in Shantung and Manchuria. Wilson reversed Bryan's policy after listening to a powerful plea from China expert and American minister to Beijing, Paul Renisch. Wilson wrote notes to Japan and China warning that the United States would not recognize any agreement that jeopardized American rights, China's territorial integrity, or the Open Door. Britain joined the United States in protesting Japan's 21 Demands.[36]

Tokyo responded by withdrawing its demands that China accept a Japanese shadow government but forced Beijing to accept the rest. Wilson then agreed to American support for a new consortium which would raise a loan for China. In 1917, the diplomats Robert Lansing and Ishii Kikujiro exchanged notes in which the United States would respect Japan's special interests in China in return for Japan's support of the Open Door, while a secret protocol required both sides to respect China's status quo throughout the war. American and Japanese interests in China obviously contradicted each other, something the Lansing–Ishii Agreement simply papered over.

When World War I had broken out in 1914, Wilson pledged America's strict neutrality. Two years later he was reelected with the slogan, "He Kept Us Out of the War." Wilson's instincts, American business, and German aggression pushed the United States ever closer to Britain and France. Between 1914 and 1916, American trade with Britain and France rose from $824 million to $3.2 billion, while its outstanding loans to those countries by 1917 had risen to $2 billion.[37]

It was German atrocities rather than Wilson's sentiments or business profits that brought the United States into the war. Starting in 1915, Germany followed a policy of unrestricted submarine warfare which resulted in the sinking of allied passenger ships with Americans on board. The German government disregarded protest letters from Wilson which followed each sinking. Finally in 1916, Wilson sent Berlin an ultimatum that any more sinkings would be considered a casus belli. The sinkings stopped.

Wilson's other endeavors were less successful. He repeatedly extended his "good offices" to mediate the war's end, but was just as often rejected. On January 21, 1917, Wilson denounced before Congress the "Old World" international relations shaped by the power balance and secret treaties, and called for collective security, self-determination, equality among nations, limited armaments, freedom of the seas, and a peace without annexation or indemnities, long-standing American principles which he ascribed to "the silent mass of mankind everywhere."

Germany resumed its submarine offensive in February 1917, gambling that with a hundred submarines it could blockade and starve Britain into submission before the United States could gather a large enough army to make a difference on the western front. After Berlin announced its new policy on February 1, the Wilson administration severed diplomatic relations. In late February, London passed to Washington a telegram from German Foreign Minister Arthur Zimmerman to the Mexican government in which he called for an alliance between Germany, Japan, and Mexico, and would return territory to Mexico taken by the United States in the mid nineteenth century. On February 26, Wilson responded to the Zimmerman telegram by asking Congress for permission to arm merchant ships, but a filibuster killed the proposal. On March 3, Wilson side-stepped congressional isolationists by arming merchant ships through an executive order.

Then in March, German submarines sank three U.S. merchant ships. On April 2, Wilson asked Congress for a Declaration of War to "Make the world safe for democracy." Congress declared war on April 6.[38] The United States joined France, Britain, Italy, and Russia on the Supreme War Council which coordinated their war effort as an "associate" rather than "allied" power, symbolizing Wilson's insistence on preserving America's freedom of action and ideals in its new relationship.

On January 8, 1918, President Wilson issued the fourteen points for which the United States was fighting, which included open covenants openly arrived at; freedom of the seas; free and reciprocal trade; arms reduction to minimum safety levels; and an impartial adjustment of territorial claims. Wilson's fourteenth point was a "general association of nations" which would resolve international conflicts through negotiation and compromise rather than war. He followed up this postwar vision with a speech on February 9 calling for lenient peace terms for Germany without indemnities or annexations. Wilson's presciption for the world's ills was harshly criticized across the political spectrum, with Roosevelt and Lodge the most vociferous opponents of the "sellout of American interests and ideals."

The first of what would become two million American troops began arriving in France in summer 1917. The doughboys stabilized a front threatened by the transfer of nearly a million German troops from the eastern front following Russia's withdrawal from the war with the Brest-Litovsk Treaty of March 3, 1918, and helped blunt vast German offensives between March and July.

Meanwhile, between November 1917 and June 1918, Wilson rejected British and French pressure to join their intervention in Russia's civil war on the side of the anti-Bolshevik forces, ostensibly to keep huge stores of war materials they had previously sent there from being transferred to the Germans. In February 1918, Tokyo dispatched the first troops of what became an army of 100,000 men into Siberia, Manchuria, and Sakhalin "to restore order" but actually to establish a Japanese regional sphere of influence.

On July 6, 1918, Wilson sent 7,000 American troops to Vladivostok, ostensibly to protect the huge store of American armaments and support the "Czech Legion" which had liberated that city from the Bolsheviks; it was actually to deter the Japanese from making "demands" on the Russians similar to their 1915 "21 demands" on China. Outwardly U.S. forces co-operated with the Japanese. Within months the American "watchdog" was dwarfed by Japan's huge army. Although the armistice removed the excuse for intervention, Wilson kept American forces in Siberia for another eighteen months and also in Murmansk where they joined French and British forces defending a huge storehouse of war materials. American support for the intervention withered. Two resolutions in the Senate demanding American withdrawal died by five votes on February 7, 1919 and a vice-presidential tie breaker on February 14, 1919. Wilson began withdrawing troops from Russia in June 1919, partly to garner Senate support for the Versailles Treaty. With America's inability to prevent the White Army's collapse in 1920 or Japan's plundering of the region, Wilson withdrew the last American troops by April 1, 1920. Always a bitter anti-communist, Wilson announced on August 20, 1920 that the United States would refuse to recognize the Soviet government.

Despite the withdrawal of Russia from the war, the weight of America's army on the western front had helped the allied forces break through and rout the German army in August and September; the Germans withdrew to their Siegfried Line on their border. On October 4, 1918, the German chancellor, Prince Max of Baden, appealed to Wilson for a peace based on his fourteen points. Wilson agreed, touching off a bitter squabble with the French and British. French premier Georges Clemenceau's remarks typified the European skepticism about Wilson's ideals: "God gave us the ten commandments and we broke them. Wilson gave use the fourteen points. We shall see."

After agreeing to Allied reservations concerning freedom of the seas and compensation for war damages, Wilson told the chancellor he would accept an armistice if the Germans adopted a cease-fire. The Germans agreed to do so a week later and Wilson submitted the correspondence to Paris and London for approval. Meanwhile, Germany's government collapsed; Kaiser Wilhelm abdicated on November 9 and fled to exile in Holland. The new government proclaimed a republic and quickly agreed to surrender. The armistice was signed on November 11, 1918. The Allies agreed to open a peace conference in January 1919.

In December, Wilson and his delegation – Secretary of State Lansing, close advisor Edward House, American representative on the Supreme War Council General Tasker Bliss, and career diplomat and Republican Henry

White – arrived in Paris amidst mass cheering and adoring crowds. The adulation would not last.

The Paris peace conference convened on January 18, 1919 and was attended by twenty-seven national delegations which in turn were organized into over fifty commissions which held over 2,000 meetings. Germany and Russia were not present. Wilson pushed the conference to put his proposed League of Nations first on the agenda, and got himself appointed to chair the commission to draw up the Covenant. After ten days of constant work, the commission presented their blue-print. The League of Nations would have an assembly in which all members would have one vote, and a Council, which would include the Big Five allied powers – Britain, France, the United States, Italy, and Japan – as permanent members and five other countries whose membership would rotate.

Having achieved agreement for his cherished League, Wilson then left on February 24, 1919 for a three-week sojourn in the United States to sign bills and nurture the public's acceptance of the League of Nations and Versailles Treaty. Wilson left his closest friend and advisor, Colonel Edward House, in charge of negotations. House and Secretary of State Lansing differed strongly with Wilson on what the United States should achieve at Versailles, with the two advisors pushing balance of power and economic interests over self-determination and the League.

When Wilson returned to Paris in March he learned to his horror that House had negotiated away many of his "fourteen points," the worst being his agreement not to include the League of Nations in the treaty. Sick and assailed by American and European critics, Wilson ended up conceding many of his goals and other important American interests in order to retain support for his League and insistence that the Allies pay back their $10 billion war debt to the United States.

Wilson had opposed a harsh peace for Germany which would alienate the German people and sow the seeds of future conflicts. The British and particularly the French demanded and got a peace in which a huge indemnity and a strict limit of only 100,000 troops was imposed on Germany. President Clemenceau and Prime Minister Lloyd George pressured Wilson to agree to turn over the reparations question to a special commission and leave the total sum open. Finally Wilson accepted the "war guilt clause" which pointed the finger solely at Germany. Wilson even gave in to some limitations on American power. For example, Prime Minister Lloyd George got Wilson to agree not to build up America's fleet to rival Britain's.

Politically and geographically, the postwar world would differ vastly from what preceded it. France not only received the return of Alsace-Lorraine taken in the Franco-Prussian War of 1870, but also the Rhineland industries and Saarland's coal mines for fifteen years after which the region's fate would be settled by plebiscite. Wilson acquiesced as the victorious allies carved up Germany's colonies among themselves. Britain received Tanzania and the Cameroons, South Africa, a mandate over Southwest Africa, and Japan a mandate over Germany's Pacific islands. In addition to the transfer of German colonies to other flags, the new states of Poland, Czechoslovakia, Hungary, Yugoslavia, Rumania, Latvia, Lithuania, and Estonia emerged from the ruins of the European empires. The Ottoman empire in the Middle East was carved into "mandates" for Britain and France.

From a strategic perspective, Wilson's most damaging give-away was Japanese control over the Caroline, Mariana, and Marshall islands. Japan's naval power now engulfed the western and central Pacific, threatening America's life-line to the Philippines and trade with China. The Japanese skilfully extracted other concessions from Wilson, pressuring him to set aside the Open Door policy and agree to a partial Japanese withdrawal from Shantung after an unspecified period which would allow Tokyo to maintain control over the province's railroads, industries, and infrastructure. Only after receiving Wilson's concession on the Pacific islands and Shantung did Tokyo agree to sign the Versailles Treaty. In return, Tokyo withdrew its demand that the treaty include a "racial equality" clause, a morally pyrrhic "victory" for the western allies.[39]

China never agreed to Japan's gains and later refused to sign the treaty. Announcement of the Versailles Treaty's terms prompted "the May Fourth movement" of Chinese mass protests and boycotts of Japanese goods. Senator Lodge denounced Wilson's sellout of China and castigated Japan as "the Prussia of the east" and harbinger of the "yellow peril."

On June 16, the Allies presented the Versailles Treaty to the German government as an ultimatum; war would result if it were not signed. After fruitless protests, Berlin finally signed the treaty on June 28, 1919. The Allies then negotiated and signed similar treaties with the other belligerents: Austria (September 10, 1919), Bulgaria (November 27, 1919), Hungary (June 4, 1919), and Turkey (August 10, 1920).

What little Wilson had gained for the United States in Paris he lost in Washington. There were Republican majorities of two in the Senate and forty-five in the House. Wilson's political and philosophical nemesis, Henry Cabot Lodge, chaired the Senate Foreign Relations Committee. Lodge stacked the Committee with Republicans who opposed the treaty. Public opinion favored a quick return to political isolation and rejected Wilson's proposed tax increases to pay for war and peace alike. The odds of passing the treaty would have been remote for a Democratic president in the teeth of a Republican Congress and hostile public opinion, even if he were genial and willing to compromise on minor points. For someone of Wilson's battered health and unyielding moralistic disposition, it would have been well-nigh impossible.[40]

During the Senate Foreign Relations Committee hearings, Lodge and others added fourteen reservations, the most important of which required congressional approval before the United States would aid victims of aggression. Wilson refused to compromise with Lodge over the reservations. On September 3, 1919, Wilson began a cross-country campaign to promote public support for the treaty during which he made thirty-two major and eight minor speeches and traveled 8,000 miles. Twenty days into his trip he suffered a massive stroke which incapacitated him for the next six months.

The Senate voted on three versions of the Versailles Treaty. On November 19, 1919, the treaty with Lodge's reservations was defeated 55–39, and the original treaty failed 53–38. The final vote on the treaty with Lodge's reservation occurred on March 19, 1920, with the 49–35 simple majority well below the two-thirds vote needed for ratification.[41] Most Democrats voted against the treaty with the reservations and Republicans against the original treaty. But some Democrats and Republicans opposed both treaties. Liberals objected that both treaties excluded many of Wilson's fourteen points and imposed a harsh peace on Germany. Conservatives deplored the League Covenant's failure to recognize the Monroe Doctrine, its power to negotiate issues like tariffs and immigration, and the general restrictions on American foreign policy. Wilson's intervention in Russia and refusal to recognize the Soviet Union had cost the support of several senators from across the political spectrum, regardless of how they viewed either treaty's merits.

THE REPUBLICAN ERA, 1920–32

For the twelve years following the Versailles Treaty, American diplomacy was guided by three Republican presidents – Warren Harding, Calvin Coolidge, and Herbert Hoover.[42] During this time, American foreign policy seemed schizophrenic as it seesawed between two extremes. On one hand, Washington pursued isolationist and protectionist policies that worsened the global economy and regional tensions. But among these actions Washington initiated several significant bilateral and multilateral negotiations which promoted disarmament and peace, and fulfilled America's duty as the banker for an increasingly troubled global economy.

Throughout this era, each White House steadfastly refused to attend conferences related to the League of Nations or the Versaille Treaty. The Harding administration even refused to open mail addressed from the League! In 1924, Washington rejected an invitation to a Geneva conference in which participants agreed to combine against any country that refused to submit a conflict to arbitration. Referring to the Monroe Doctrine, Secretary of State Hughes went so far as to threaten war with the League of Nations should it attempt to intervene in a conflict in the western hemisphere. And the United States clung to its traditional position that as a neutral country it had the right to trade or not trade with anyone.

These policies were wholly at odds with the dramatically new European, Asian, and global power balances spawned from World War I and the Versailles Treaty. The war materially and psychologically devastated the world's European victors – Britain, France, and Italy. Four empires – the German, Austro-Hungarian, Russian, and Ottoman – were destroyed. In stark contrast, the United States emerged into the 1920s more powerful than ever. In 1914, the United States was a debtor nation owing $3.7 billion to international bankers. Five years later in 1919, the United States was the world's creditor with $12.5 billion in outstanding foreign loans, including $10.3 billion in war loans. America's geoeconomic power grew steadily throughout the 1920s. By 1930, the United States had outstanding loans of $21 billion, produced nearly half of the world's manufactured goods, accounted for one-sixth of global trade, and enjoyed a GNP larger than the combined economies of Britain, France, Germany, Canada, Japan, and the next eighteen richest countries.[43] Understanding the drain defense spending inflicts on a nation's economic vitality, Washington refused to convert more than a fraction of America's vast wealth into military power. Although America's fleet remained second only to Britain's in tonnage, the army was mostly demobilized. By 1934, the American army ranked seventeenth in the world in its number of soldiers.

Other than the United States, only Japan's power was dramatically enhanced by joining the winning side in World War I. Unlike the United States, Tokyo did not hesitate to wield its growing power to expand its empire. Revelation of Japan's 21 Demands on China had frightened most Americans. Then, at the Versailles peace conference, Tokyo's success in winning Shantung province and a mandate over the three Pacific island chains, the Marianas, Carolines, and Marshalls, had tipped the region's power balance. A year after American troops left Siberia, an army of Japanese soldiers and administrators remained to plunder the region's resources and wealth. Meanwhile, Tokyo embarked on a massive program in which it would add sixteen new battleships to its fleet by the mid-1920s. With a powerful modern fleet and the Pacific islands, Japan threatened America's trade ties with China, the Philippines, and even Hawaii and the west coast. Although the League mandate insisted the islands could not be fortified, many feared that Japan was doing just that. When Japan refused to allow the United States to build a cable station on Yap Island, the Harding administration sought the elimination of Japan's mandate over the islands. But the League continued it.

In rejecting the Versailles Treaty, the United States freed itself from the provision restricting its fleet. In 1918, the United States had sixteen battleships compared to Britain's thirty-three. But that year Congress approved a Navy Department plan to make America's "navy second to none" by expanding its battleships to thirty-nine by 1925 and thus surpass Britain's fleet. The Harding administration then deployed fourteen of its newest battleships to Pearl Harbor and asked Congress to appropriate money to fortify America's Pacific islands to offset Japan's territorial and commercial expansion in East Asia and the Pacific.

Hoping to clip this budding naval arms race and growing tensions in the Pacific, Senator Borah introduced resolutions in December 1920 and April 1921 calling on the great powers to meet and negotiate an arms limitation treaty. While the Harding administration rejected the first resolution, it could not ignore the second which passed the Senate 74–0 and the House 332–4. Reasoning that through hard bargaining it could achieve parity without an expensive build-up, the Harding administration agreed not only to attend but also host the conference. Secretary of State Charles Evans Hughes invited all the world's naval powers to Washington. Hughes convinced Tokyo to attend by promising that the United States would maintain a strict impartiality in relations between Japan and China.

The Washington Conference began on November 12, 1921 and ended on February 23, 1922. America's primary objective at the Washington Conference was to contain Japan's rising power in the western Pacific. Weeks of tough bargaining resulted in three agreements which seemed to realize this goal. The Five Power Pact froze for a decade the number of capital ships like battleships and cruisers at a ratio of 5.25 or 525,000 tons each (with a maximum battleship size of 35,000 tons and 16 inch guns) for Britain and the United States, 3.15 or 315,000 tons for Japan, and 1.75 or 175,000 tons for France and Italy. Washington succeeded in pressuring Japan to accept this ratio instead of the 10:10:7 ratio that it initially demanded. In return for Japan renewing its pledge not to fortify its Pacific mandates, the United States agreed not to strengthen its defenses in the Philippines and Guam;

Hawaii and British Singapore, however, were exempted. America's agreement not to fortify its islands was hardly a concession – neither the White House nor Congress wanted to appropriate the funds.

Washington also succeeded in forging two other treaties. It convinced Britain and Japan to dissolve their alliance and join a Four Power Treaty with the United States and France in which each would consult the others should they be threatened. As a side-agreement, Japan allowed the United States to build a relay station on Yap Island for a trans-Pacific cable. Finally, Japan joined the United States, Britain, China, France, Holland, Portugal, Belgium, and Italy in signing a Nine Power Treaty which guaranteed China's territorial integrity and the Open Door.[44] In addition, Japan agreed to withdraw its troops from Siberia and return Shantung to China. This agreement, however, did not restore China's sovereignty – the unequal treaties allowing extraterritoriality, foreign control over tariffs, and leases on ports cities, railroads, and, other economic assets continued.

The Washington Conference and its treaties advanced American military and economic interests. Naval parity was achieved without an expensive build-up. The Japanese not only agreed not to fortify their islands or carve out any more exclusive economic zones in China, but also promised to retreat from Siberia and Shantung. In presenting his treaties to the Senate, Harding explained that the Nine Power Pact superceded the 1917 Lansing–Ishii agreement which had recognized Japan's special interest in China.

Tokyo reacted angrily to Harding's disavowment of the Lansing–Ishii agreement and maintained that it still held. There followed a series of notes throughout 1922 in which each side defended its position and demanded that the other accept it. Exasperated with the exchange, Washington finally played a trump card – it threatened to publish Lansing–Ishii's secret protocol that pledged both countries not to seek privileges in China which violated the rights of other nations. Tokyo pleaded with Washington not to do so, fearing that its revelation would enflame Japanese militarists committed to expansion. When the Harding administration persisted in its threat, Tokyo agreed in December to renounce Lansing–Ishii while continuing to maintain that it had special rights in China, and to deny that the Nine Power Pact applied at all to Manchuria and Inner Mongolia.

Japan's navy bureaucracy split over the Five Power Pact. Japan's Naval Ministry, with duties for the budget, ship construction, and dealing with the cabinet and Diet, and Naval General Staff which planned and implemented operations, were entirely separate institutions which battled continuously over policy. The Navy Ministry supported both the Washington and later London naval limitation treaties; the Naval General Staff were adamantly opposed to both treaties.

Despite these differences both within Japan and between Japan and the United States, the Washington Conference treaties "marked the end, at least in outward form, of the old era of imperial alliances and policies in Far Eastern international relations and inaugurated a new and relatively stable era of multinational agreements and peaceful coexistance among the Great Powers . . . [the Nine Power Treaty] contained at least one fatal flaw . . . it did not provide enforcement or coercive machinery that could be used in the event any power violated China's sovereignty or territory. The Nine Power Treaty rested on good faith rather than good works."[45]

The Washington Treaty system promised a new era of cooperation in the Far East. Instead, relations between the United States and Japan plummeted when Congress passed the Immigration Act of 1924 which established quotas for foreign nationalities in which only 2 per cent of the number already in the United States could immigrate in any year. The act also embraced any previous laws forbidding particular nationalities from entering the United States. Two years earlier, in 1922, the Supreme Court had upheld the series of laws between 1882 and 1913 that forbade any Asians the right to immigrate and become citizens.

As if America's immigration policies were not humiliating enough, Japanese increasingly objected to their trade relationship with the United States. During the 1920s, America's trade relationship with Japan was nearly the reverse of what it is today. The United States enjoyed a slight surplus and exchanged mostly manufactured goods for Japanese raw materials and semi-finished goods. Japan was by far the more dependent partner. The United States shipped Japan 75 per cent of its automobiles, lumber, and building materials, supplied 40 per cent of foreign investments in Japan, and purchased 90 per cent of Japan's raw silk, and 40 per cent of its total exports.[46]

REPARATIONS AND WAR DEBTS

On November 11, 1921, the United States and Germany exchanged ratifications of a bilateral peace treaty. This separate peace and America's refusal to work with various Versailles Treaty commissions eventually boomeranged against the United States. Without the moderating hand of the United States, the Reparations Commission charged Germany $33 billion, to be paid with annual installments of $375 million between 1921 and 1925, and $900 million thereafter.

Throughout the early 1920s, these payments deepened Germany's economic crisis with hyper-inflation and high unemployment. On January 10,

1923, French and Belgian troops occupied the Ruhr after Germany failed to deliver its scheduled reparations. To alleviate the crisis, the White House encouraged American bankers to loan the money to Germany which in turn paid off that year's reparations. The foreign troops were withdrawn. Then, in 1924, Germany once again defaulted. French troops once more marched into the Ruhr to enforce payments. This time the White House sent two American businessmen, Charles Dawes and Owen Young, to the Reparations Commission to help alleviate the crisis. In what became known as the Dawes Plan, Germany's reparations payments were temporarily reduced and French troops withdrawn from the Ruhr. Based on its capacity to pay, German reparations would henceforth annually range from $250 million to $625 million. But to pay this, Germany had to mortgage railroads and industries and accept a $200 million loan, half of which came from the United States. The plan worked for five years until 1929 when Germany's reparations were further reduced by the Young Plan in which $8 billion would be repaid over 58.5 years at 5.5 per cent interest, a payment which amounted to $153 million annually.

Washington backed the Dawes and Young plans by encouraging American industry to invest in Germany and the other major European countries to help promote economic growth. Germany's economy expanded steadily and by 1928 was 50 per cent larger than in 1913 while per capita income had risen from $178 to $279 million. As long as the United States remained Europe's banker, the system would flourish.

While they propped up Germany's economy, every president from Wilson to Roosevelt insisted that the allies repay their debts. In February 1922, the Harding administration established the War Debt Funding Commission which insisted that all war debts be repaid within twenty-five years at 4.25 per cent interest. The debtors offered counter-proposals and eventually the Commission struck agreements with thirteen countries. Yet, to Washington's dismay, the war debt and reparations issues became entwined. Throughout the late 1920s, London and Paris stated several times their willingness to cancel 90 per cent of Germany's war reparations if Washington would allow a similar reduction in British and French war debts to the United States. Washington refused and the impasse on both issues continued.

As if the threats to the world's financial system were not serious enough, the security arrangements of the Versailles Treaty itself appeared uncertain. In April 1922, the world's two pariahs, Germany and the Soviet Union, signed the Treaty of Rapallo in which they publicly reestablished diplomatic relations and renounced any outstanding claims against each other, and secretly allowed military and economic collaboration. Then, in December 1925, European security seemed to strengthen with the signing of several treaties in Locarno among Britain, France, Italy, and Germany, in which France's rights to Alsace-Lorraine were assured, the Ruhr was permanently demilitarized, Britain and Italy agreed to guarantee the new border and diplomatic arrangements, France's security treaties with Poland and Czechoslovakia were recognized, and Germany was accepted into the League of Nations. Impressive as these agreements seemed, the Locarno treaties failed to settle Germany's eastern borders.

JAPAN'S POLITICAL AND ECONOMIC CRISES

Throughout the 1890s and up through the 1920s, Japan's political system remained highly authoritarian. At first, tax qualifications confined the electorate to about 450,000 or 1 per cent of the population. Although the opposition parties controlled the Lower House, they had no power. The Genro selected the prime minister, a post which rotated among the Satsuma and Choshu Genro representatives. But one by one the Meiji revolutionaries died off, with Yamagata Aritomo succumbing in 1922. The leadership vacuum worsened when Emperor Meiji died in 1912, and the new emperor, Taisho (1912–26), proved mentally unbalanced. From 1923, Taisho's son Hirohito served as regent.

Japan, however, weathered the loss of its Meiji leaders with increased democratization. The two main political parties, the Seiyukai (successor to the Jiyukai) and Minseito (called the Kenseikai before 1927), played an increasingly important role in Japanese politics. In 1918, the Genro allowed Hara Kei, the Seiyukai head, to become prime minister – the first time someone from outside of the oligarchy was allowed to do so. "Party governments" ruled Japan from 1918 through 1932. In May 1925, a bill passed by the Diet allowing the enfranchisement of all Japanese males aged 25 or older, thus increasing the electorate to 14 million. That same month the government reduced the Japanese army from twenty-one to seventeen divisions. Professor Minobe Tatsukichi of Tokyo University expounded his "organ theory of the state" in which the emperor was a constitutional monarch beholden to rather than above the law. Japan had become a highly urbanized, literate, industrialized nation with a relatively high standard of living. An array of political parties, interest groups, and mass publications often shrilly expounded a spectrum of views from extreme right to left.

Despite these advances, Japan's political system had deep flaws which eventually resulted in the abandonment of democratization and imposition of a totalitarian political and authoritarian economic system. Although there was a mass male franchise, the two largest political parties – the Seiyukai and Minseito – were not mass political organizations. Instead they largely represented the interests of the Mitsui and Mitsubishi zaibatsu, respectively, which spent enormous sums buying the voting blocs necessary to get their candidates into office. Although the 1918–32 period is described as one of party government, only six of the eleven prime ministers during that time were party men, five were bureaucrats or soldiers. Of the six party men, three were assassinated.[47] A "Peace Preservation Bill" was enacted in 1925 which widened police powers to arrest people for "dangerous thoughts" and further restricted the ability of citizens to speak or assemble freely. The communist and various socialist parties were outlawed and their members arrested or driven underground.

To worsen matters, Japan suffered an array of economic problems, including a vast and growing gap between rich and poor. Half of all peasants farmed someone else's land and paid the owners as much as half of the crop for the privilege. Most factory hands were overworked and underpaid in often miserable conditions and had no job security. Vast family-owned industrial groups (zaibatsu) dominated the economy.

The military would eventually fill the huge power vacuum that had opened with the deaths and retirements of the old Meiji era oligarchs. The tradition that the army and navy ministers had to come from senior active duty leaders gave them a veto power over cabinet decisions and composition. If either or both branches refused to submit a candidate for a new cabinet a government could not form; if they withdrew their minister the cabinet would fall. According to the 1889 constitution, the emperor, not the cabinet, had ultimate authority over the military. But with a weak emperor, the army and navy had few constraints.

While the military's highest officers largely came from old samurai families and were graduates of the exclusive Army War College, most of the lower- and middle-ranking officers had humble rural roots. They were appalled by the corrupt politicians, bureaucrats, and businessmen who ruled Japan, and resented their superior officers who seemed to collaborate with the ruling elite. Many joined the dozens of ultra-nationalistic groups which brazenly called for overthrowing the government and expanding Japan's empire. These young officers increasingly resorted to the tradition of "loyal insubordination" (gekokujo) in which junior officers could act decisively in political deadlocks or crises for the greater good of Japan and the military. As in other Japanese institutions, the military was riddled with fiercely competing factions, each of which conspired constantly for power and tried to outshout the others in ultranationalist sentiments and actions.

THE CRISIS IN CHINA

The Nine Power Pact did not inhibit Japanese expansion in China which increasingly became dependent economically and politically on Tokyo. Between 1921 and 1931, one-quarter of Japan's exports went to China and nine-tenths or $1 billion of its foreign investments. America's stake in China was much less, only 3 per cent of its total exports and $120 million in direct investments.[48] As Tokyo expanded its influence throughout China, conflict between the United States and Japan worsened accordingly.

Japan's deepening machinations in China were stimulated in part by fear that the country might be unified by one of those Chinese factions vying for power. Among the dozens of warlords which dreamt of occupying Beijing and ruling China were only two serious contenders. Chang Tso-lin controlled Manchuria and in September 1924 aided a coup d'état in China's capital, Beijing, which brought his ally Tuan Ch'i-jui and the Anfu Party to power. Meanwhile, Sun Yat-sen and his National Party (Koumintang, KMT) held a power-base around Canton. When Sun Yat-sen died in 1925, his military commander, Chiang Kai-shek assumed KMT leadership. Chiang had trained in Moscow for nearly two years; upon his return he reorganized the KMT on the Soviet communist party model. Soviet advisors helped found the KMT Whampoa military academy and were attached to every Chinese army division. The head Soviet advisor, Mikhail Borodin, helped Chiang's coup and consolidation of power over the KMT following Sun's death. Moscow's influence in the KMT increased even more in 1924 when it renounced Soviet extraterritorial rights in China and the Boxer indemnity. The KMT and Chinese Communist Party (CCP), which had been founded in 1922, formed an uneasy alliance dedicated to China's reunification and an end to the unequal treaties. In July 1925, the KMT declared itself China's legitimate government.

Recognizing the KMT's growing power and anxious to curtail growing Soviet and Japanese influence in China, Washington tried to support Chiang. Secretary of State Frank Kellogg convoked the Special Tariff Conference (October 1925–April 1926) in which he hoped to allow an increase in China's tariff rates and an end to extraterritoriality. The Japanese protested both these proposals, and the conference broke up without significant agreement on either issue. Despite this failure, Washington promised the KMT that it would continue to work to reverse the unequal treaties.

In July 1926, Chiang sent his armies north to defeat or coopt one warlord after another. Washington increasingly saw in Chiang China's savior. Not only did Chiang seem single-minded and powerful enough to unify China, he also seemed to personify important western values. In 1927, he married Soong Mei-ling, a Wellesley College graduate, Christian, and member of the rich and powerful Soong family. Chiang soon converted to Christianity.

This image was sullied on March 24, 1927 when some KMT soldiers rampaged through Nanjing and killed a half dozen foreigners. In response to foreign protests, Chiang promised an indemnity but disclaimed responsibility. Then a month later on April 12–13, Chiang redeemed the KMT in foreign eyes when he launched a surprise attack against his CCP allies, destroyed their strongholds in the eastern cities, and drove the remnants into Jiangxi province. Chiang's army occupied Beijing on July 3, 1928. The United States recognized Chiang's government on July 25, 1928 and, in return for most-favored-nation status, granted China tariff autonomy. The United States then urged the other foreign powers to cut similar deals with Beijing.

The KMT's growing power in China undermined Japan's position. Tokyo wanted a weak disunited China in which Japanese businessmen and officials could play off one corrupt warlord against the others to enhance Japan's economic and military power. Tokyo responded to Chiang's offensive by trying to get the Manchurian warlord, Chang Tso-lin, to accept a Japanese protectorate. Chang refused to cooperate. Chinese and Japanese troops skirmished. Former General Tanaka Giichi became prime minister in 1928 and allowed Japanese officers in Manchuria to issue an ultimatum to Chang for concessions. When Chang rejected the demands, Japanese officers assassinated him and expanded their military control over Manchuria.

Japan's brazen aggression encouraged Chiang and Chang Tso-lin's son, Hsueh-liang, to unite in outraged protest and Tanaka's government publicly diluted its demands while privately continuing to press Chang for a protectorate. Chang, however, was just as fiercely committed as his father to maintaining Manchuria's autonomy. Chiang and Chang negotiated Manchuria's formal reunification with China in December 1928. Rebuffed and embarrassed by the publicity of Japan's machinations in Manchuria and elsewhere, Tanaka then recognized Chiang's KMT as China's rightful government and accepted Manchuria as a integral part of China. Tanaka then resigned when the Japanese army refused to court-martial Chang's assassins. The new government tried to discourage further Japanese plots in Manchuria and China. Although one of the 21 Demands China had been forced to agree to in 1915 was to allow Japanese to lease or buy land in Manchuria, Chang Hsueh-liang issued a law in 1929 forbidding the practice.

FROM INTERNATIONALISM TO ULTRANATIONALISM

Amidst Japan's machinations in China, the Kellogg–Briand pact outlawing war was negotiated and signed. Ironically, the pact began as an attempt by the Coolidge administration to sidestep what it thought was a French attempt to entangle the United States in an unwanted alliance. On April 6, 1927, the tenth anniversary of America's entry into World War I, French Foreign Minister Aristide Briand proposed to the United States that they sign a bilateral nonaggression pact. Secretary of State Frank Kellogg agreed to informal talks on June 11, but ten days later Briand produced a treaty. Kellogg then delayed negotiations until December when the White House concluded that promoting a multilateral instead of bilateral nonaggression pact would at once earn the United States laurels as a promoter of peace and dilute any obligations to France. Over the next half year, Kellogg rounded up other participants. On August 27, 1928, representatives of fifteen countries, including Japan, signed the Pact of Paris which required them to renounce war as a national policy and resolve all disputes by pacific means. Most participants signed side agreements in which they retained the right of self-defense. By 1929, fifty-four countries were signatories.

While the Washington Conference had successfully capped the capital ship race, the 1922 Five Power Agreement had not included auxiliary ships like submarines, destroyers, and cruisers under 10,000 tons with 8-inch guns or less, and an arms race in these ships soon embroiled the three great naval powers. In 1927, Britain and the United States attempted to organize a naval treaty at Geneva. France and Italy, however, boycotted the negotiations because the conference did not include restrictions on land forces. Japan attended and demanded that its ratio be raised to compensate for its inferiority in capital ships. The United States and Britain refused Japan's demand. The conference ended with no agreement.

The powers took up these and other questions again at the London Conference that met between January and April 1930. The United States and Britain soon agreed to limits of 327,000 tons for cruisers, 150,000 tons for destroyers, and 53,000 tons for submarines. Then followed two months of hard bargaining between the Americans and Japanese in which Washington insisted on a 6:10 ratio for cruisers and Tokyo demanded it be nothing less than 7:10. The two chief negotiators, Senator David Reed and Ambassador Matsudaira Tsuneo compromised at 66 per cent for Japan's heavy cruisers, 70 per cent on light cruisers and destroyers, and parity for submarines – a 10:10:6.975 which was only a fraction from Japan's original demand. To gain this tiny symbolic reduction, Washington agreed that the United States would delay the contruction of its heavy cruisers until after 1936, and build eighteen rather than twenty-one cruisers with 8 inch guns.

The minuscule 0.25 difference between what Japan's negotiators promised they would achieve and what they actually got caused an uproar in Japanese politics. When the treaty's terms were announced, Japan's "fleet faction" rabidly denounced it and the "treaty faction" which had agreed to it. Prime Minister Hamaguchi Osachi promised higher naval appropriations, retired those naval officers who supported the treaty, and appointed outspoken imperialist Prince Fushimi Hiroyasu chief of the Naval General Staff. These compromises did not satisfy everyone. In November 1930, an ultranationalist murdered Hamaguchi.

Despite having taken the initiative on several arms limitation conferences and defusing the reparations crisis, the United States increasingly turned economically inward throughout the decade. The 1922 Fordney–McCumber Tariff slowed what might have been a rapid growth in global trade. Congress then followed up that tariff by raising it thirty-two times during the 1920s on products from countries which discriminated against American goods. The October 1929 New York stock market crash plunged the United States into depression. In a misguided attempt to save American jobs, Washington then enacted the 1930 Smoot–Hawley Tariff which raised tariffs 50 per cent. Thirty-one countries retaliated by raising their own tariff walls. Governments engaged in competitive currency devaluations in a desparate attempt to push exports and keep imports at bay. International bankers recalled their loans, exacerbating the trade and economic collapse. Denied sales for its products in America, those countries which owed the United States money had even less with which to service their debts. The result was the collapse of the global economy and trade, and subsequent rise during the 1930s of imperialistic dictatorships in Japan and Germany. Ironically, it was American policies which were primarily responsible for helping create the adverse economic conditions in which those fascist regimes came to power and which the United States would eventually have to destroy.

3 The Road to War, 1931–41

The United States and Japan pursued contradictory goals in the Far East during the 1930s. The Americans wanted naval superiority with Japan and the Open Door with an independent China. The Japanese wanted Washington to accept naval parity and Japanese hegemony over China. These conflicting goals eventually resulted in war.

American policy toward Japan between 1931 and 1941 was largely characterized by indecision and often outright appeasement of Japanese aggression, punctuated with periodic moral condemnations.[1] Simultaneously plagued by an intractable depression that had halved America's economic output and left one of four workers jobless, and Japanese, Italian, and German aggression, the Hoover and Roosevelt adminstrations seemed impotent to deal with either. Rather than resist a deepening national isolationism, both administrations' words and deeds seemed to encourage it.

Yet what else could the Hoover and Roosevelt administrations have done? Was war between the United States and Japan inevitable? Could the White House have pursued any policies that satisfied American interests without leading to war with Japan? And when the Japanese attacked Pearl Harbor, was it simply another stage in their ambition of carving out an empire from the central Pacific to the Himalayas, or did Roosevelt unwittingly force Tokyo into an war that neither country wanted?

THE MANCHURIA CRISIS, 1931–3

Manchuria's strategic importance to Japan increased steadily throughout the 1920s. Japan relied on Manchuria for nearly half of its food and pig iron, and one-third of its coal. Over 80 per cent of Japanese foreign investments beyond its colonies were in Manchuria and China. Manchuria increasingly became an outlet for Japan's surplus population. By 1930, 750,000 Japanese had settled in Manchuria; half of Dairen's population was Japanese.

Japanese perceived their national interests in Manchuria threatened by Chiang Kai-shek's growing power, the possible reunification of China and Manchuria, demands for the end of the unequal treaties, Chinese boycotts of Japanese goods, and attempts to build a railroad line in Manchuria to compete with the South Manchurian railroad. Tokyo claimed that, between 1928 and 1931, there were 120 cases of Chinese infringements of Japanese rights in Manchuria, ranging from unlawful detention to excessive taxation and confiscation of property. Manchuria's warlord, Chang Hsueh-liang, was fiercely anti-Japanese – understandably so, considering that Japanese agents had murdered his father – and moved steadily closer to Chiang Kai-shek and the KMT (Koumintang).

Echoing the conspirators (shishi) of the 1860s who demanded that Japan "revere the emperor, expel the barbarian (sonno joi)," those of the 1920s and 1930s rallied under the Imperial Way Faction (kodo-ha) that vowed to sweep away the corrupt government in Tokyo, allow the emperor to rule directly, and expand Japan's empire across Asia. The officer corps of the Kwantung Army, which was deployed along the South Manchurian railway, was permeated with ultranationalist groups and conspirators.

In 1930, the War Ministry and Kwantung Army agreed that Japan should take over Manchuria by one of three means: by agreement with Chang, overthrowing Chang and imposing a pro-Japanese regime, or outright conquering the province. When the attempt to browbeat Chang into compliance failed, the War Ministry and Kwantung Army agreed to pursue the other two means. They differed over the timing: the War Ministry favored waiting until spring 1931; the Kwantung Army preferred September 1931. Some of the more radical elements wanted to couple Manchuria's takeover with a coup d'état in Tokyo which would overthrow the corrupt regime and impose an imperial government.

On September 18, 1931, Japanese agents exploded a bomb on a stretch of track on the South Manchurian railroad outside Mukden. Claiming a Chinese attack, the Kwantung Army occupied Mukden and other Manchurian cities. On September 21, China appealed to the League of Nations for help, and the League promptly responded by requesting that both sides stop fighting. China also asked the United States to pressure Japan, but Secretary of State Stimson declared America's strict neutrality in the conflict. On October 17, the League invoked the Kellogg–Briand Pact and ordered Japan to withdraw its forces by November 16. On October 24, Stimson endorsed the League decision, but did not communicate America's position to Tokyo for another week and even then did not include the November 16 deadline.

The deadline passed with Japanese forces continuing their advance across Manchuria. Chang and the remnants of his troops retreated to Chinchow just north of the Great Wall. Tokyo halted its troops outside Chinchow and told the League it would only withdraw its forces if China agreed to grant concessions to Japan. On December 10, the League formed and dispatched an investigory commission led by Lord Lytton and including British, French, American, and Italian representatives. Japan's cabinet resigned. Although the new prime minister, Inukai Tsuyoshi, sympathized more openly with the military, he opposed any expansion into China. Nonetheless, Japanese troops attacked and occupied Chinchow on January 2, 1932. Chang's army collapsed and he fled to Beijing.

Although shortly after Japan's aggression broke out, the president and secretary of state agreed that America should make no more than moral protests, Stimson gradually changed his views as Japan's armies rampaged across Manchuria. After Chinchow fell, Stimson resolved not to accept any change in Manchuria's status. On January 7, 1932, Stimson sent notes to Japan and China asserting that the United States would not recognize any subsequent treaty or agreement which inhibited the "treaty rights of the United States or its citizens in China, including those which relate to the sovereignty, the independence, or the territorial and administrative integrity of the Republic of China, commonly known as the Open Door policy."[2] After echoing League pronouncements for several months, the United States had now taken the lead in confronting Japan's aggression in Manchuria. Stimson hoped that Britain and the League would soon respond with similar statements of nonrecognition. Although London did declare its support for the Open Door principle, nothing stronger followed.

On January 28, 1932, the Japanese responded to a continued Chinese boycott by bombarding the Chapei district of Shanghai. Although the United States and Britain reinforced their military units in and around Shanghai, Hoover completely ruled out economic or military sanctions, insisting that war with Japan was folly. Fearing the possibility of war over Shanghai, Tokyo on February 1, 1932 asked for America's "good offices." Stimson replied with a five-point plan which called for a cease-fire and simultaneous settlement of the Manchurian and Shanghai conflicts. Tokyo rejected the plan because it linked Shanghai and Manchuria. Then on March 10, 1932, Tokyo installed Pu Yi, China's last emperor, as Manchuria's new leader. Assassins gunned down Inukai on May 15, 1932.

Throughout these dramatic events, the United States and the League simply looked on. Finally, in October 1932, the Lytton Commission reported that Japan had not acted in self-defense in Manchuria, and recommended that Manchuria be restored to Chinese rule while safeguarding Japanese interests in the region. Yet it was not until January 1933 that the League formally adopted the Lytton report. Tokyo responded furiously to the League's decision. On March 27, 1933, Tokyo formally withdrew from the League of Nations. Japanese troops then overran Jehol and Hopei provinces, cutting off communications between Beijing and its port Tientsin. On May 31, 1933, China and Japan signed the Tangku Truce which allowed Japanese troops to operate freely north of the Great Wall. Chiang then turned his army's back on the Japanese and sent a quarter million troops against communist guerrillas in southern China. The course of world history might have been dramatically different if Chiang had instead launched an attack on Japan's outnumbered troops in Manchuria.

When Japan brutally conquered Manchuria, it clearly violated international law, including the Pact of Paris outlawing aggressive war which it signed only three years earlier. Yet it was not exactly clear who did have the right to rule the region. Despite Chiang's successful offensives against the warlords and communists between 1927 and 1931, he still only controlled eight of twenty-four Chinese provinces; Manchuria remained autonomous. When Tokyo signed the 1922 Nine Power Pact guaranteeing China's territorial integrity and the Open Door, it reserved the right to treat Manchuria separately from China.[3]

There were arguments to support Tokyo's position. Traditionally, Manchuria was not considered an integral part of China. After conquering China in 1644, the Manchus refused to allow Chinese immigration to Manchuria and the realm always remained a semiautonomous part of the Chinese empire. Manchuria's warlords flew their five barred flag rather than the Chinese white star flag and paid no revenue to China. When John Hay issued his Open Door notes, he acknowledged Manchurian autonomy. Teddy Roosevelt encouraged Japanese expansion into Manchuria to divert their attention from the Pacific. Although in 1928, Chiang and Chang agreed to integrate Manchuria with China, the agreement was never implemented.

Still Japan had no legal claim to Manchuria. The region's fate was for Chang and Chiang to decide. Nonetheless Manchurians soon adjusted to Japanese rule. Japan's soldiers provided order and its bureaucrats efficient administration. The economy grew steadily. Ambassador Grew reported in 1934 that most Manchurians enjoyed "a considerable degree of contentment" and warned that China's northern provinces might join Manchukuo "without force of arms."[4]

Stimson's nonrecognition policy after January differed little in principle and none in practice from his previous appeasement policy. But there was little else the United States could have done. A dilemma bedeviled American policymakers between 1931 and 1941. As a signatory to the Pact of Paris, the United States was committed to denouncing, though not necessarily acting against, aggression. Legality aside, appeasement might either divert war with an aggressor, or it might make it inevitable. Yet America's deep depression and isolationism inhibited the White House from even issuing moral statements.

A major inhibition on American diplomacy was the lack of American credibility on international issues. Not only had the United States rejected membership in the League of Nations, it had infected the world with its depression through its Smoot–Hawley tariff hikes that helped collapse world trade. It is hardly surprising that when Stimson announced his nonrecognition policy, his hopes that it would rally Britain and the League into a tougher stance proved illusury.

If the Europeans scoffed at the unreliable Americans, the Japanese were openly contemptuous. Typical was the attitude of then Colonel Ishiwara Kanji who was a key conspirator in Chang Tso-lin's murder but later opposed Japan's military expansion into Manchuria and China. When an American officer suggested that Ishiwara visit the United States after two years in Germany studying its military system, he replied: "The only occasion for which I plan to visit the United States is when I arrive there as chief of the Japanese forces of occupation."[5]

EYE OF THE HURRICANE, 1933–7

Franklin Delano Roosevelt had two powerful role-models for his presidency – one was Teddy Roosevelt, his fifth cousin. Yet FDR lacked his cousin's decisiveness, knowledge of international relations, appreciation for the world's ambiguities and complexities, and skill in manipulating the power balance to safeguard American interests. Instead, Roosevelt conducted his foreign policy with the same genial first-name banter over cocktails style that he did with domestic politics – with predictable results. Some maintain that Roosevelt lacked any coherent foreign policy strategy, with George Kennan, for example, dismissing his diplomatic style as "basically histrionic."[6] The world's Stalins and Churchills respect toughness and reliability, not charm. Roosevelt also deeply admired Woodrow Wilson under whom he had served as Assistant Secretary of the Navy. Although Wilson's democratic ideals and efforts deeply inspired Roosevelt, he lacked his predecessor's single-minded drive in achieving them: "Like Wilson, FDR asserted the universal validity of the democratic ideal, but unlike him possessed neither the mind of a philosopher nor the soul of a prophet."[7]

Roosevelt had a deep need to be loved by others. Hence, he went out of his way to avoid revealing or making decisions that might offend others, particularly the mass public. Unfortunately, this caused "a dichotomy between personal feeling and public statement, between what he said to public envoys privately and what he told his countrymen."[8] He frequently promised different people and groups different things, only to reverse himself later. Roosevelt has been described as a "chameleon" whose positions shifted with the audience and public opinion: "One theme which spans a full range of events from 1933 to 1941 is that of diplomatic dualism, the discrepancy between what Roosevelt said and what he thought, between what he promised to do and what he in fact did. It was not unusual for him to pursue contrary lines of policy simultaneously and to alternate between several lines of strategy."[9]

Another problem was that Roosevelt's White House lacked a clear organizing principal. Roosevelt would play off different advisors to prevent any one from gaining too much power. Without clear policy divisions, turf battles among the advisors were incessant. Roosevelt himself would send up a succession of foreign policy trial balloons and then back away from any proposals that were shot at. Abhorring direct conflict, Roosevelt had underlings submit controversial or tough decisions, a practice described as "leading with someone else's chin."[10]

Roosevelt's instinctive caution in foreign affairs was reinforced by the consistent advice by Secretary of State Hull, Assistant and later Undersecretary of State Sumner Welles, and Ambassador Joseph Grew that the United States appease Japanese, Italian, and German agression, and support the neutrality laws that prevented the president from distinguishing between aggressors and victims. Arrayed against these appeasers were several important administrators who consistently favored tough measures against foreign aggression, including Treasury Secretary Henry Morgenthau, Interior Secretary Harold Ickes, and chief of the State Department's Far Eastern Division Stanley Hornbeck. But the containers would not supercede the appeasers until the year before Pearl Harbor.[11]

A vital aspect of leadership involves shaping rather than following public opinion. Roosevelt once remarked wistfully that "it's a terrible thing to look over your shoulder when you are trying to lead – and to find no one there."[12] Yet, Roosevelt himself may have contributed to America's growing isolationist sentiments, to which he frequently catered and in so doing may have deepened them. He opposed American membership in the Legue of Nations in two books published shortly after he took office.[13] He repeatedly spoke out against American involvement in Europe's worsening diplomatic problems throughout the 1930s. His statement before a San Diego audience on October 2, 1935 was repeated throughout his first decade in office: "The United States of America shall and must remain . . . unentangled and free."[14]

Shortly after entering the White House, Roosevelt briefly enjoyed an opportunity for taking a tougher stand against Japanese aggression. Most Americans favored increased defense spending and 90 per cent wanted a larger air force. But Roosevelt failed to mold and lead this sentiment into a decisive stand against further Japanese aggression. By the mid-1930s, as the Manchurian crisis receded in public consciousness, a majority of Americans favored disengagement from world affairs.[15]

Roosevelt badly bungled the neutrality legislation. Although he privately favored a neutrality law that distinguished between victims and aggressors, he publicly see-sawed over whether or not he really supported such a law under debate in Congress in spring 1933. He refused to fight a rider removing the president's power to designate an aggressor. The bill was eventually tabled. Two years later, he still refused to fight publicly for his private sentiments, refusing to veto an August 1935 neutrality law which did not distinguish between aggressors and victims. Requiring him to prohibit the sale or shipment of arms, munitions, and other war goods to all sides of a conflict, the law subsequently straitjacketed his ability to respond to Japanese aggression in Asia and German aggression in Europe. In fact, by forbidding the president to discriminate in favor of the victims, the law actually favored the better armed aggressors. Roosevelt did nothing to prevent Congress from strengthening the law in February 1936 and add a January 1937 amendment specifically forbidding any American involvement in the Spanish Civil War. In May 1937, Roosevelt signed a neutrality bill empowering the president to boycott all goods to those involved in war. The bill did have a loophole – in the name of national security the president could order all trade on a "cash and carry" basis. But it would not be until November 1939 that Roosevelt succeeded in getting Congress to renounce the neutrality laws.

Roosevelt's timidity on foreign affairs was somewhat understandable given the economic crisis he faced at home. When he took office, fifteen million Americans were unemployed; 5,000 banks and their $9 billion in assets had disappeared; steel mills ran at 12 per cent of capacity; 100,000 Americans applied for jobs in the Soviet Union.[16] There is little evidence that he had a clear idea of how to confront the depression until after he settled into the Oval Office. Ironically, Roosevelt had assailed Hoover during the presidential campaign, not for doing nothing, but for his "radical" social measures and wasteful spending. During the presidential campaign, Roosevelt promised to cut government spending and balance the budget. Yet during his first three months in office, Roosevelt pushed through Congress fifteen bills which attempted to stimulate the economy with increased federal government spending and programs.

In contrast to the barrage of ambitious and largely successful domestic programs launched in his first one hundred days, Roosevelt's foreign policy initiatives stumbled badly; subsequent policies continued to backfire over the next half decade.[17] Like his predecessor, Roosevelt took office as a fervent nationalist on international economic issues. On April 20, 1933, he took the United States off the gold standard and thus devalued the dollar. In so doing, he was reacting against Britain which had abandoned the gold standard eighteen months earlier in September 1931.

As if to make amends shortly afterwards, Roosevelt invited eleven heads of state and forty-two foreign missions to the White House to discuss outstanding issues. Hitler refused his invitation. He dispatched an envoy to Geneva to observe the League Advisory Committee. And then on May 16, 1933, Roosevelt issued a statement addressing the heads of all fifty-four sovereign governments, including those represented at the London and Geneva conferences, and all of the world's peoples in which he called for international currency stabilization, free trade, the elimination of offensive weapons, and a nonaggressive pact to deter aggression.

Roosevelt choose not to attend the London Economic Conference devoted to freer trade and financial stability. Without firm presidential guidelines, the American delegation to the London Conference feuded incessantly over policy. Then on July 3, after Hull had managed to negotiate some preliminary free trade agreements, Roosevelt announced his rejection of any return to the gold standard, and admonished the Europeans to balance their budgets and pay their debts to the United States. By breaking up with no agreement, the London Conference strengthened rather than defused worsening economic nationalism.

Like his predecessors, Roosevelt continued to squabble with Britain and France over the war debt issue. In December 1932, France had defaulted on its payments to the United States. Congress responded by refusing to allow any reduction in the French and British debt. Publicly, Roosevelt denounced debt cancellation because a majority in Congress were opposed to it and he feared doing anything that might jeopardize his domestic policies. In 1934, he even helped draft the Johnson Debt Default Act which barred extending loans to deadbeat countries. Yet privately he favored debt cancellation and even encouraged Britain, France, and Germany to default to force the issue.

Italy invaded Ethiopia on October 3, 1935. Two days later, Roosevelt responded by invoking the neutrality act, thus severing trade with both countries. This action mostly hurt American exporters. Nearly six weeks later, on November 18, 1935, the League of Nations Council voted to embargo most trade with Italy. Fearing a tougher stand might push Mussolini into Hitler's arms, Britain refused to cut off oil, scrap iron, steel, or copper shipments to Italy, close the Suez Canal to Italian ships bound for Ethiopia, or blockade Italian ports. Any or all of these actions would have aborted Italy's takeover of Ethiopia.

Of the twin threats looming across the Atlantic and Pacific throughout the 1930s, the Roosevelt White House viewed Germany's as the more dangerous. The White House did find some ways to circumvent the neutrality laws. While it little more than protested Japanese imperialism in Northeast Asia, when German troops marched into the Rhineland on March 7, 1936, the White House withdrew most-favored-nation status and levied countervailing duties, which were then increased to 25 per cent after *Kristalnacht*.

POLICY TOWARD JAPAN AND THE FAR EAST, 1933–7

For nearly a half century, America's main goals in the Far East were as clear as they were potentially contradictory – peace with Japan and the maintenance of Chinese sovereignty and the Open Door. Following Japan's invasion of Manchuria in September 1931, the United States had to choose between its two goals.

Most Americans understood the nature of Japan's threat. In 1934, Nathaniel Peffer captured an increasingly widespread American image of Japan:

> That the country is completely under the rule of the military caste is self-evident, and that the people would follow the army into any adventure, however fantastic, is also clear. It is the combination of national centralization with feudal loyalty, of mysticism with technical efficiency, of medievalism with tanks and airplanes, that make the Japanese incalcuable by twentieth century criteria and beyond understanding by the modern mind, as well as peculiarly dangerous in a world at least somewhat rationalist. They dwell in a non-man's zone of time: their springs of action in the Middle Ages, their instruments of action out of the twentieth century.[18]

Despite this popular image of Japanese militarism, Americans were divided over how best to deter it. Like the Hoover administration, Roosevelt's policy toward Japan's widening aggression was substantially one of appeasement flavored with occasional dollops of criticism. For much of the decade, the most influential voice shaping America's Far East policy was that of Ambassador Grew, an old Yale University chum of Roosevelt's who spent ten years in Japan (1931–41). In 1933, he described the Japanese to Hull as "war-loving," "aggressive," "unscrupulous," and "menacing," and the following year reported to Hornbeck that the Japanese hoped to conquer the world.[19] Yet despite these views, Grew not only advocated appeasing Japanese aggression in China, but even opposed any concrete aid to Britain. He hoped that American appeasement would not discredit and alienate the political "liberals" who were momentarily eclipsed by the militarists. As will be seen, Grew completely misunderstood Japanese politics. There were no "liberals" in Japan's government at any time. All agreed on Japanese expansion; they differed only on the means and timetable.

Although there were two schools of thought on Far Eastern policy, both within the State Department and within his immediate circle:

> FDR's personal leaning was toward China, and this served to nullify any positive move made by American officials in the direction of Japan. At the same time, . . . when pressure from Europe mounted for concerted action against Tokyo, he refused to go beyond rhetoric, and his harsh-sounding words meant little when accompanied by subtle, behind-the-scenes gestures of friendship. Beyond this, there was the public image he chose to cultivate, which, by contrast with his equivocal diplomatic posture, never varied. To the people at home, he was always an uncompromising foe of autocracy and aggression.[20]

He just did little more than rhetorically confront these foes.

Relations with Japan quickly became an important part of Roosevelt's crowded foreign policy agenda. In January 1933, before taking office, Roosevelt conferred with Stimson and then announced at a press conference that his administration would continue the nonrecognition policy. However, Roosevelt said nothing when the League of Nations formally adopted the Lytton Commission report on February 24, 1933 or when Tokyo announced its withdrawal from the League of Nations on March 27, 1933.

Between 1933 and 1934, Tokyo dispatched nine high-ranking envoys to Washington to negotiate outstanding issues. In just the three months after he took office, Roosevelt met with Japanese envoy Viscount Ishiii Kikujiro four times, and at other times with other ranking diplomats Matsuoka Yosuke, Admiral Nagano Osani, Komatsu Takashi, and Nomura Nichisaburo. All of these talks were inconclusive. Roosevelt proposed a nonaggression pact with Japan but later backed off when the Japanese finally agreed. Roosevelt also rejected an Italian initiative for him to mediate a Far East settlement.

In December 1934, Roosevelt sent special envoy William Bullitt to Tokyo but the mission also failed to reach any understanding.

These negotiations failed because the respective positions were unbridgeable. The United States asked Japan to withdraw from Manchuria but refused to back its request with the threat of force. Japan asked the United States to recognize not only the state of Manchukuo, as it had renamed Manchuria, but also Japan's increased control over northern China.

Japan's civilian and military leaders were split over how far to challenge the west.[21] "Radicals" and "moderates" differed only over the timetable and means of imperialism. Radicals agreed that Japan's empire should expand across Asia and the Pacific even if it meant war with the west. Moderates feared that the radicals would plunge Japan into war with the United States and Britain before its navy and army were strong enough to prevail. Noting how powerful Japan's military power had become over the past fifteen years, the moderate Admiral Yamamoto Isoroku, who later planned the Pearl Harbor attack, wrote in 1934 that: "the time has come for this mighty empire rising in the east to devote itself, with all due circumspection, to advancing its own fortunes."[22] In other words, expand cautiously while continuing to build up Japanese forces for the decisive future battle with the United States.

On April 17, 1934, Japanese Foreign Ministry spokesman, Amau Eliji, issued what became known as the Amau Doctrine which declared China a special interest of Japan's and ordered China not "to avail herself of the influence of any other country in order to resist Japan" and warned against "any joint operations undertaken by foreign powers even in the name of technical or financial assistance." The 1934 Amau Doctrine was Japan's most important statement about its goals in China since its 1915 "21 Demands." Essentially, Tokyo renounced the 1922 Nine Power Pact guaranteeing China's sovereignty and the Open Door.

The Roosevelt administration's actions in response to Tokyo's demands for hegemony over China were contradictory and undoubtedly confusing to Japan. The White House remained silent when Tokyo issued its 1934 Amau Doctrine asserting an exclusive sphere of influence over China. Yet when Hull met with Ambassador Saito shortly thereafter he not only rejected a Japanese proposal that the United States withdraw from the western Pacific in return for continued trade rights with China, but warned that American bombers could devastate Japan in the event of war. Despite this stand, several months later Congress passed and Roosevelt signed the Tydings–McDuffie Act in which the United States would grant the Philippines its independence in 1945 after a decade of home rule. Shortly thereafter the White House refused a Japanese offer of a bilateral nonaggression pact, yet withdrew much of the Pacific fleet to the Atlantic. While Roosevelt was in Honolulu to negotiate with Japanese envoys, he spoke of American air bases in the Aleutian islands and support for China's air force. But Roosevelt refused to push for a naval buildup to the limits allowed by the London Treaty.

The 1930 London Treaty had continued a naval building holiday until 1936. On December 28, 1934, Japan denounced the 1922 and 1930 naval limitation treaties, and gave its two year notice of withdrawing from those treaties. Between December 1935 and March 1936, representatives of the United States, Britain, and Japan met in Europe to resolve their differences. The Japanese angrily stormed out after the Americans and British refused to accept parity among the three powers.

Japan continued to expand its control over China's northern provinces. Between 1933 and 1937, claiming that Koumintang forces had violated the 1933 Tangku truce, Japan forced the provincial warlords of Hopei, Chahar, Suiyuan, Shaxi, and Shantung to kick out the Nationalist troops and accept Japanese troops and advisors. In October 1935, Foreign Minister Hirota announced Japan's "Three Principles" for relations with China: (1) an alliance to destroy communism in China (which would allow Japanese troops to be stationed throughout China); (2) abandonment of China's policy of playing off one foreigner against the others (in other words, China had to abandon its desperate appeals to the west for help from Japanese aggression); and (3) recognition of Japan's takeover of Manchuria and complete "cooperation" (in effect, Japanese control) over China's development.

Meanwhile, between the 1933 Tangku truce and December 1936, Chiang Kai-shek concentrated on crushing the CCP. He almost succeeded. Chiang's armies drove the communists on an 8,000 mile "long march" which took them out of eastern and central China and into a last stand in Yenan near Mongolia. In December 1936, Chiang and, Chang Hsueh-liang, and other leading Chinese generals were in Xian planning the sixth campaign. Chang and the others "kidnapped" Chiang and forced him to agree to call off the campaign against the communists in northwest China and instead concentrate China's forces in the northeast to confront Japan's looming threat. Once Chiang had agreed, Chang surrendered to him and returned to Nanjing as his prisoner. Chiang reluctantly called off the sixth campaign and redeployed some Chinese units in northeast China.

Japan's expansion abroad was paralleled by increased authoritarianism at home. On February 26, 1936, officers of the 1st Division in Tokyo staged a coup against the government by occupying the ministries and attempting to assassinate key leaders – all in Emperor Hirohito's honor. Prime Minister Okada Keisuke narrowly escaped death, but the Finance Minister,

Lord Keeper of the Privy Seal, and Inspector General of Military Education were all murdered. Emperor Hirohito responded decisively to the crisis, ordering the rebels to lay down their arms and surrender. Within three days, loyalist troops had crushed the coup.

This aborted coup was the watershed in Japan's growing authoritarianism, shifting it decisively, in Maruyama's words, from "fascism from below" to "fascism from above."[23] The "control faction" which favored the creation of a totalitarian state and aggression abroad displaced the "Imperial Way faction" which actually supported less controls at home and negotiated advances abroad. Following the coup, the government retired rebel officers from the military in Japan and Manchuria.

While united on creating an "Asia for Asians," the army and navy differed where and when to attack first. The army favored expansion into China and Mongolia, the "strike north" strategy. The navy insisted on a "strike south" strategy to take over the resource-rich British, Dutch, and French empires in Southeast Asia. Both strategies were based on creating and seizing opportunities rather than adhering to strict timetables. In August 1936, the Cabinet adopted the "Fundamental Principles of National Policy" which embraced both strategies while insisting that the southern advance would best be achieved "gradually and by peaceful means" and the northern strategy only "by extreme caution . . . to avoid causing trouble with the Soviet Union."[24] Then in November 1936, Japan and Germany signed the Anti-Comintern Pact, in which they committed themselves to coordinating efforts to squash communism at home and helping the Soviet Union if it attacked either country.

In order to bring greater coherence to its strategic planning and implementation, the government created the Imperial General Headquarters in 1937 which included the ministers of war and navy, and the chiefs of their respective general staffs. An Imperial Liaison Conference was then created between the Headquarters and the Cabinet to coordinate overall strategy and diplomacy. The Liaison Conference was the most important decision-making body throughout the war years. It met twice weekly and was presided over by the emperor when particularly important questions were debated.

THE "CHINA INCIDENT" CRISIS, 1937–40

With both Japanese and Chinese forces massing in the region surrounding Beijing, a shooting incident was bound to happen eventually. On July 7,

1937, Japanese and Chinese troops clashed at the Marco Polo Bridge just southwest of Beijing. Although Tokyo wanted to limit the fighting, on July 11 it mobilized four additional divisions for the front, and demanded an apology and the withdrawal of Chinese forces. Chiang responded by sending four Chinese divisions into disputed northern provinces and on July 17 vowed that China would surrender no more territory to Japan. Japanese troops began a concerted offensive on July 27 which brought control over much of the area between Beijing and Tientsin. On August 14, Chinese troops attacked Japan's naval installations in Shanghai. Japan dispatched reinforcements to defend its Shanghai settlement and installations.

Japan's invasion of China triggered America's neutrality laws. The White House cancelled the planned shipment of nineteen bombers to China, forbade any American ships from carrying war goods to either country, refused to augment American gunboats in China to protect American lives, and warned that any Americans remaining in the war zone did so at their own risk. Hoping to revive the role Teddy Roosevelt played in the Russo-Japanese War, Roosevelt offered his good offices three times to help negotiate a peace treaty between China and Japan. Tokyo refused.

Throughout July, August, and September the British and French repeatedly urged Roosevelt to join them in such actions as offering good offices, calling a conference of the nine powers, organizing a joint fleet for a naval demonstration off China's coast, or even blockading Japan. The British alone appealed ten times during the rest of 1937 for a tough American response to Japan's aggression. Roosevelt sympathized but explained the neutrality acts tied his hands and that he had to act alone or not at all.

Initial American outrage at the invasion was soon muted by Chinese actions. In August Chinese troops had attacked the International Settlement in Shanghai and pilots had struck the U.S.S. "Augusta". However, for several reasons most Americans eventually condemned Japanese aggression and rallied around China. Most people saw a weak, struggling underdog China victimized by a ruthless, unprovoked aggression by the Japanese bully. Japan was the first nation to launch mass air attacks against crowded cities. Although the world would later become inured to the strategy, Americans and many other people around the world were appalled by these "crimes against humanity." Spector asserts that "American opposition to the Japanese conquest of China rested largely on revulsion against the Japanese use of air power on civilian targets."[25] Newsreels and photo magazines blared horrible Japanese atrocities – heaps of unarmed Chinese dead, bayoneted babies, raped women, burned out and looted cities – and thus imbedded deep into America's consciousness the image of barbarian, uncontrollable, and merciless Japanese hordes.[26]

But the White House remained extremely cautious in responding to Japanese aggression. In a speech at Chicago on October 5, 1937, Roosevelt declared that the "epidemic of world lawlessness is spreading . . . and when an epidemic of physical disease starts to spread, the community approves and joins in a quarantine of the patients in order to protect the health of the community against the spread of the disease."[27] Roosevelt called on the League of Nations to end the war. But Roosevelt had no specific plan and the following day when reporters pressed him on just what he had in mind he denied that the word "quarantine" implied coercion.

The speech did stiffen the League's backbone if not Roosevelt's. The day following the speech on October 6, the League Council called on the Nine Power Treaty signatories to convene in Brussels. Japan refused to join the conference; its interests were represented by Italy. At the Brussels Conference between November 3 and 24, 1937, Roosevelt's chief envoy, Norman Davis, attempted to enlist British envoy Anthony Eden and French envoy Yvon Delbos in proposing a settlement that Japan would likely reject, and then using that as an excuse to impose sanctions. He hinted that the president would ask Congress to revise the neutrality acts. Davis proposed such actions as banning loans to Japan, boycotting Japanese exports, nonrecognition, arms to China, and joint fleet action in the Pacific. But when the British and French asked for an American guarantee that it would be willing to use force if necessary in enforcing a peace in China, Davis demurred, claiming it was impossible to make such a commitment in a democratic country. When the press got word of Davis's proposals, Hull and Welles disavowed them and claimed he exceeded his instructions. The conference broke up without agreement.

By failing to act against Japanese aggression, the Brussels Conference encouraged it. Washington's indecisiveness caused the French to bow to a Japanese demand that they cut off any supplies to Chiang's regime funneled through Indochina. The Portuguese did the same in Macao. Italy joined Germany and Japan in the Anti-Comintern Pact. With its most recent "cry of wolf" revealed as meaningless, the United States was more discredited than ever.

French Prime Minister Camille Chautemps spoke for many at the conference when he angrily declared that:

> you Americans from time to time talk as if you really intend to act in the international sphere when you have no intention of acting in any way that can be effective. . . . I should infinitely rather have him [FDR] say nothing than make speeches, like his speech in Chicago, which aroused immediate hopes when there is no possibility that in the state

of American opinion and the state of mind of the Senate he can follow up such speeches with action. Such a policy on the part of the United States merely leads the dictatorships to believe that the democracies are full of words but are unwilling to back their words by force, and force is the only thing which counts in the world today.[28]

The crisis soon worsened. Japanese troops captured Nanjing in December and began a systematic month-long slaughter of its inhabitants in which at least 250,000 and perhaps as many as 350,000–400,000 Chinese were butchered. Amidst Japanese genocide in Nanjing and elsewhere, on December 12, 1937, Japanese bombers attacked American and British gunboats in Shanghai harbor which were taking on western refugees, and sank the U.S.S. "Panay". There was no doubt that the Japanese attack was deliberate. Japanese officers had inspected the "Panay" the previous day, the crew had draped huge American flags across the decks, and the weather was fine.

Roosevelt toyed with proposals for a joint Anglo-American naval demonstration, imposing economic sanctions, seizing Japanese financial assets, and outright blockading Japan. In the end Roosevelt did nothing; American isolationism prevailed. While Morgenthau advocated war, six other key Roosevelt advisors favored appeasement – William Bullitt, Hugh Wilson, Colonel Edward House, Joseph Grew, Francis Sayre, and J. Pierrepont Moffatt. Although sympathetic to the Chinese people, public opinion continued to run seven to three any against action other than withdrawing all their fellow citizens from China; few wanted revenge. Most newspapers, labor organizations, and churches supported the call for quarantine; the *Wall Street Journal*, *Chicago Tribune*, and Hearst newspaper chains along with most of the more prominent voices in the Senate were opposed.[29] Roosevelt merely reflected public opinion, and in so doing, of course, reinforced it.

On December 24, Tokyo apologized profusely for its attack on the "Panay" and offered to pay an indemnity. The White House accepted and the crisis died. The Roosevelt administration continued to turn a blind eye to Japan's rape of China and violation of the Nine Power Pact and other international agreements. In January 1938, it rejected a Chinese plea for a half billion dollar loan and war supplies. Subsequent British attempts in January and March 1938 to elicit an American commitment on applying firm economic or possibly military pressure against Japan were similarly rejected. On some issues, Roosevelt dithered. First he proposed and then disavowed a league of armed neutral states and international embargo against Japanese goods.

American isolationism had become deeply rooted. In January 1938, Roosevelt forced a vote on preventing the discharge from committee on the so-called Ludlow constitutional amendment which would require a national referendum on any war declarations. The House vote to bottle up the bill in committee was a slender 209–188 in favor. The Ludlow vote came a month after the Japanese sank the U.S.S. "Panay".

Although the public supported Roosevelt's appeasement policy, it was and remains controversial. Some have argued that it was correct; economics rather than concern for the victims of aggression should have guided America's policy toward Asia.[30] After all, 48 per cent of American exports and 21 per cent of imports with Asia were with Japan, and Americans had more than three times more trade and investments with Japan than China, along with a trade surplus.[31] In other words, if the policy was flawed, it was because it did not appease Japan enough. Marks, for example, faults the Roosevelt administration with failing to appreciate Japanese interests in China. While characterizing Secretary of State Hull's influence on Roosevelt's Asian policies as "secondary, if not tertiary," Marks maintains that "he never showed the slightest sign of understanding, or even of wanting to understand Japan's dilemma." Marks describes Treasury Secretary Morgenthau as "closest to the president" and dismissive of "Japan's grievances out of hand and vouched for the efficacy of economic sanctions down to the eve of Pearl Harbor."[32]

German aggression in Europe soon overshadowed Japan's in China. Between February and March 1938, Hitler engineered Austria's requests first for German troops to restore order and later unification of the two countries. Then in April, Hitler demanded that Czechoslovakia's Sudetenland with its 3 million Germans be joined to Germany. Threats and negotiations continued for the next half year until British Prime Minister Neville Chamberlain flew to Munich for a conference with Hitler on September 29–30 and agreed that disputed parts of Czechoslovakia be distributed among Germany, Hungary, and Poland.

Viewing Germany as the greater threat, Roosevelt was much tougher against Hitler's aggression. The White House cut off all helium exports to Germany after its takeover of Austria in 1938. Countervailing duties soared after Germany completed its conquest of Czechoslovakia. Roosevelt's most ambitious proposal was the 1938 Welles Plan, named after its architect and White House aide, Summer Welles, under which a conference of states at Washington D.C. would draft new principles of international law, including peaceful ways to revise treaties, guaranteed access to raw materials for all nations, arms reduction, and the revision of Versailles Treaty inequities. Fearing both domestic and foreign opposition, Roosevelt postponed presenting this ambitious agenda five times. And then he undercut these symbolic actions with periodic calls for hemispheric Monroe Doctrines. All along, Roosevelt refused to present a united front with Britain and France.

With the Sudetenland crisis "settled," international attention soon swung back to the Far East. Japan's armies continued to devastate and conquer more Chinese cities and provinces. On November 3, 1938, Prime Minister Konoye proclaimed a "Greater East Asian Co-prosperity Sphere" in which Tokyo would expel the western imperialists and create an "Asia for Asians" led by Japan. He urged China to accept a peace in which it recognized Manchukuo, allowed Japanese troops and advisors access to all China, Japanese "guidance" over China's economic development, and ejection of other foreign powers. On November 19, 1938, Foreign Minister Arita Hachiro bluntly told American diplomat Eugene Doorman that the Open Door no longer existed.

The White House was divided over how to respond to Konoye's statement. Morgenthau and Hornbeck pushed for a loan to China as the first step in reversing the neutrality laws and imposing sanctions against Japan. Hull and Grew favored doing nothing. Roosevelt finally agreed that the United States had to do something to show its displeasure at Konoye's blunt assertion of Japanese imperialist goals. On December 13, Roosevelt approved a $25 million Export–Import loan to China to finance the purchase of tung-oil. But the money would be a drop in the bucket of China's financial needs for fighting the Japanese.

While Roosevelt dithered, the American public increasingly supported tougher measures, with 75 per cent agreeing with an arms embargo and 66 per cent a boycott on Japanese imports. By 1940, 80 per cent would favor a boycott.[33] A majority on the Senate Foreign Relations Committee called on Roosevelt to revoke the commercial treaty with Japan and cut off all trade. Despite this political and public support, Roosevelt refused to follow, let alone lead, calls for tough measures; his embargo would be purely voluntary.

Japanese troops occupied Hainan in February 1939. Amidst these growing tensions, Saito Yoshie, Japan's ambassador to the United States, died in Washington. Saito had served as ambassador for five years and lived in the United States for twenty-eight years altogether. As a good-will gesture, Roosevelt on March 1 ordered Saito's ashes conveyed to Japan in a large funeral urn atop the American cruiser, "Astoria".

Roosevelt's decision was controversial. Roosevelt not only refused to protest Japan's takeover of Hainan, but continued with the Saito plan after the Japanese announced on March 31 their intention to take the French-claimed Spratley islands in the South China Sea. Japan's takeover tipped the region's military power balance. The Spratley's were in range of the Philippines, Vietnam, Singapore, and Borneo. Finally, two days before Saito's ashes were to arrive in Tokyo, Roosevelt gave in to French and British pressure, protested the Spratley takeover and ordered the American fleet to sail from the Atlantic to Hawaii. Undeterred, the Japanese took over the Spratleys.

In July 1939, Ambassador Grew returned to Washington to champion appeasement with Japan based on analyses by two State Department experts, Whitney Griswold's "Far Eastern Policy" and Robert MacMurray's hundred page memorandum. In both meetings with Grew, Roosevelt rejected his position and spoke not only of a possible future embargo but sending more naval forces to the Pacific. Yet he refused to act publicly until a majority on the Senate Foreign Relations Committee voted in favor of economic sanctions. On July 26, 1939, while Grew was still in Washington, Roosevelt gave the six months withdrawal notice from the bilateral 1911 Treaty of Commerce and Navigation. Grew returned to Japan and continued to warn the White House that economic sanctions would only lead to war.

Meanwhile, the German threat loomed ever greater across the Atlantic. In February 1939, Roosevelt had stated that America's frontier rested on the Rhine. This statement did nothing to deter the ambitions of Hitler and Mussolini. On May 21, 1939, Germany and Italy signed their "Pact of Steel" alliance, thus upsetting years of western appeasement of Italian aggression to inhibit Mussolini from joining Hitler. Italy stepped up its takeover of Albania which it had begun on April 7. Hitler made a series of demands on Poland for territorial and political concessions. On August 23, 1939, Germany and the Soviet Union signed a ten-year non-aggression pact; an accompaning secret treaty split up Poland between them. On September 1, German and Soviet troops invaded Poland. Britain and France reacted by declaring war on Germany.

Although Roosevelt initially reaffirmed American neutrality, on September 6, he began a secret correspondance with Churchill that evolved into a de facto alliance by Pearl Harbor's eve. Early on, Roosevelt and Churchill agreed to a "Europe-first" strategy in which their war effort would concentrate on defeating the more immediate threat of Germany, followed by Japan, even if war first broke out in the Far East.

The neutrality laws continued to tie Roosevelt's hands. His campaign to reverse them began in September and met severe resistance from isolationist congressmen. On October 27, 1939 the Senate and House revoked the neutrality laws and replaced them with a "cash and carry law" by votes of

63–30 and 243–172, respectively. Roosevelt signed the law on November 4. From then until Pearl Harbor two years later, Roosevelt could wage war although he could not declare it. Secretary of War Henry Stimson compared Roosevelt's strategy during this time to Lincoln's before the firing on Fort Sumter: "The vacillations of pulling back and forth, trying to make the Confederates fire the first shot. Well that is apparently what the President is trying to do here."[34]

Meanwhile, Japan intensified its effort to conquer China. Foreign Minister Arita Hachiro announced on February 29, 1940 that Japan was engaged in a holy war to defeat China and on March 30 that it had established Wang Ching-wei as president of a new Chinese government in Nanjing. The United States responded by denouncing Wang, reiterating support for Chiang Kai-shek's government in Chungking, and extending a $20 million export–import bank loan to China for tin. In April Roosevelt dispatched the fleet from the Atlantic to Pearl Harbor even though there were better training and supply facilities at San Diego. In early May 1940, special envoy Francis B. Sayre met repeatedly with Foreign Minister Arita and once with the emperor. The talks went nowhere. Sayre offered a Pacific nonaggression pact and extended America's good offices for a settlement. When pressed, Sayre admitted that a Pacific nonaggression pact would require a Japanese withdrawal from China. Tokyo rejected Sayre's proposal.

European events created opportunities for Japan. In May and June, 1940, German armies swept across the Benelux countries and destroyed France's armies; Berlin imposed puppet governments on its newest conquests. To Japan's militarists, the huge power vacuum opening in Southeast Asia made French and Dutch colonies ripe for the plucking. Tokyo forced France's Vichy government to cut off all trade with China and began pressuring it for Japanese base rights in northern Indochina. It also demanded that Britain sever its Burma Road supply line to southern China. The French and British reluctantly complied.

With France and Britain appeasing the Japanese, the White House felt it would be folly to do otherwise. In July 1940, Grew launched another series of talks with Arita over a possible Pacific nonaggression pact and war settlement. Grew's efforts seemed to be strengthened by Roosevelt on July 6 when he announced his support for three Monroe Doctrines, an American for the western hemisphere, while states in Europe and Asia settled their own problems.

The liberal press and China lobby severely criticized Roosevelt for this explicitly isolationist statement. Morgenthau, Stimson, Ickes, and Hornbeck instead called for an embargo against Japan under the July 2, 1940 National Defense Act which authorized the president to restrict exports necessary for national security. Roosevelt then about-faced, ordered Grew to suspend his talks with Arita and debated the pros and cons of an embargo for the next two weeks. On July 24, he learned that the Japanese were trying to corner the market on strategic goods by buying up all they could with long-term agreements. The following day, Roosevelt imposed a limited embargo on the export of aviation fuel, lubricants, and high grade scrap steel and iron to Japan – the first genuine American embargo of Japan.

Despite Roosevelt's worry about the upcoming presidential election, American policy shifted dramatically from appeasement toward confrontation from the embargo of July 25, 1940 through the fall. But Roosevelt's actions were limited by America's weak military and continued congressional and public isolationist sentiments. During this time Roosevelt pressed Churchill to reopen the Burma road which not only supplied Chiang's regime but conveyed Chinese tungsten on to American factories. But Roosevelt was not willing to back Churchill with anything more than private words. Twice Churchill asked for a firm American military commitment if Britain were attacked and was twice refused. Roosevelt also rejected Churchill's call for an American squadron and fleet in Singapore, and firm warning to Japan that any attempt to change the Pacific power balance would not be tolerated. Without American support and with his back against the wall in Europe, Churchill could not provoke a war with Japan; he kept the Burma road closed.

Congress continued to complicate Roosevelt's foreign policies. It had amended the naval appropriations bill on June 28, 1940 so that military equipment could not be exported unless it was deemed essential for national defense. This complicated Roosevelt's intention of swapping fifty aged destroyers to Britain in turn for base leases in British colonies in the Caribbean and Atlantic. After considerable negotiations between the United States and Britain, they signed the base-for-destroyer swap on September 2, 1940. Roosevelt justified it as an executive agreement which fell outside the appropriations bill and compared it to Jefferson's 1803 purchase of Louisiana from Napoleon. To his surprise, the storm of congressional and public opposition did not materialize. On September 13, by one vote, Congress passed a law authorizing a military draft.

By September 22, 1940, Japan had armtwisted from Vichy the right to station troops in northern Indochina for operations against the Chinese army. Goaded by the hardliners, Roosevelt agreed on September 26 to extend the embargo to all grades of scrap iron and steel, and promised yet another $25 million loan to China.

Throughout the late 1930s, the Japanese army had advocated an alliance with Germany and Italy, hoping that it would pressure the United States to abandon its support of China. The Japanese navy had opposed an alliance fearing it would inevitably lead to war with Britain and the United States. But by September 1940, changes in key leaders in the Navy Ministry and Naval General Staff had resulted in their reluctant approval. On September 27, 1940, the world's fascist powers forged a formal alliance by signing the Tripartite Pact pledging each to join in war if any member was "attacked by a power at present not involved in the European War." The Soviet Union was excluded from this tenet; while the United States was not mentioned, it was clearly the country the signatories had in mind. Among other things, the signatories recognized "the leadership of Germany and Italy in the establishment of a new order in Europe" and "Japan's new order in greater East Asia."[35]

This in turn provoked tougher White House measures. In October's first week, Roosevelt promised to double the amount of America's loan to China, ordered up the entire naval reserve, reinforced the Philippines, and ordered all Americans out of the Far East. Churchill responded by agreeing to reopen the Burma Road, and publicly announced on October 8 his intention to do so on October 17.

Even Grew began to awaken to the Japanese threat. On September 12 he cabled his "green light" message to the State Department, advocating war if the Japanese attacked any British possessions in the Far East. In December 1940, he wrote Roosevelt that "Japan has become openly and unashamedly one of the predatory nations . . . which wrecks about everything that the United States stands for. . . . We are bound to have a showdown some day."[36] One cannot help but wonder where Grew's mind had been for the previous nine years.

THE ARSENAL OF DEMOCRACY

On December 29, Roosevelt delivered his tough "Arsenal of Democracy" speech in which he clearly identified Japan among those threatening the United States. Yet, America's military itself was woefully unprepared for war. Despite the growing international tension throughout the 1930s, Roosevelt did not begin to build up America's military forces until 1940. In 1939, the American army ranked nineteenth in personnel in the world! As a percentage of the total population under arms it was forty-fifth. The military was less than 70 per cent of the peacetime strength of the 280,000 army and 180,000 navy authorized by Congress. Only one-quarter of all men under arms were considered combat ready. In 1940, the air force had only fifty-three modern bombers and 187 fighter planes.[37]

Roosevelt was largely to blame for America's military weakness. Throughout the 1930s he continually slashed congressional attempts to increase defense spending. In 1938, it was Congress rather than the president which initiated a $326 million program to strengthen twenty-five U.S. bases in the Pacific. Roosevelt then cut the figure to $65 million. That same year he chopped congressional proposals to increase the navy by 9,900 men to only 4,000 and the marines by 4,000 to 3,000. In 1940, he denounced the two-ocean navy and requested only $1 billion for the entire defense budget. In an emergency session, Congress finally approved a $5 billion defense budget which included a two-ocean navy. Roosevelt reluctantly signed the bill. Roosevelt's support for the draft was also belated. American support for the draft rose steadily in 1940, with 59 per cent in favor in June and 69 per cent in July. Yet it was not until August 2 that Roosevelt announced his support for a bipartisan congressional bill authorizing the draft. Congress approved a one-year military draft. By late 1940, Washington had agreed on a $10.5 billion defense budget, two-ocean fleet, the first peacetime draft in American history, and national guard mobilization. In December 1940, Congress approved a $100 million loan to China to help stabilize its currency.[38]

Roosevelt was more decisive in appointing able leaders. In November 1939, he selected General George Marshall for Army Chief of Staff and Admiral Harold Stark as Chief of Naval Operations. In June 1940, Frank Knox and Henry Stimson were appointed the secretaries of the Navy and War Departments, respectively. These men would lead America to victory in World War II.

That war seemed ever more likely. Throughout 1941's first few months, Japan's leaders increasingly saw war with the west as their best option. German Foreign Minister Joachim von Ribbentrop repeatedly urged the Japanese to attack British forces in Singapore and Malaya, and promised that Germany would immediately declare war on the United States if it entered the fight. German armies had swept over the Balkans and across North Africa, its air force reducing Britain's cities to rubble, and its submarine fleet sending an average of 115,000 tons of British shipping to the murky ocean bottom every month. Britain's demise seemed only a matter of time, and with it all of colonial southeast Asia except the Philippines would be ruled by defeated regimes that could be easily swept away by Japanese armies. Japan's ambitions were inhibited only by possible war with the United States. But given America's isolationist and effete society, war increasingly seemed a risk worth taking. The odds were that Washington would simply bow to the reality of a Japanese empire in the Far East. Facing victorious enemies across both the Atlantic and Pacific, what else could it do?

Meanwhile, the Roosevelt administration was preparing for that very possibility. In January 1941, the White House drafted and submitted to Congress the Lend-Lease Bill which authorized the president to have manufactured and "sell, transfer title to, exchange, lease, or lend" to any government any goods deemed vital for America's security. The Lend-Lease Bill passed the House on February 8 by a vote of 260–165. An amended bill passed the Senate on March 8 by 60–31 which would allow Congress to block the president. The House approved the amended bill on March 11 and Roosevelt immediately signed it. The next day Congress approved $7 billion of what would eventually become $50 billion in lend-lease commitments. The White House used lend-lease to force Britain to curtail its imperial preference trade discrimination.

Although the 1939 neutrality reform and 1941 lend-lease bills had strengthened his ability to aid China, Britain, and other besieged countries, Roosevelt was still constrained by the constitution which allows only Congress to declare war. Roosevelt continually rejected British pleas for a secret alliance. While a secret prior alliance commitment would be constitutional, there was no guarantee that Congress would honor it with a war declaration. Roosevelt did allow high ranking American and British officers to meet in Washington between January 29 and March 27, 1941 to discuss possible contingencies and joint actions. Yet, Roosevelt refused to approve the final report because it smacked too much of a formal alliance. Later the White House even repudiated a secret American, British, and Dutch naval conference which drew up an operational plan called PLENAPS if Japan attacked.

In April, Roosevelt approved a flurry of measures designed to help America's de facto allies and prepare the United States for war. On April 2, the United States seized thirty German and Italian ships interned in American ports and used them to supply Britain. On April 10, American forces negotiated with Denmark the right to base troops in Greenland. On April 15, Roosevelt ordered the navy to convoy merchant ships to the mid-Atlantic from where they would be escorted by the British navy. On April 18, he approved the lend-lease sale of 100 P-40 fighter planes to China, upped a promised loan to Chungking to $100 million, and allowed American pilots to fly as mercenaries for China's air force. On May 6, China became eligible for lend-lease aid. All that remained was for American forces to directly join the fighting.

NEGOTIATIONS TO DIVERT WAR, 1941

The 1941 negotiations between the United States and Japan were initiated by two diplomatic novices who were known within the State Department as the "John Doe" associates. In the fall of 1940, two American priests, Bishop James E. Walsh, the superior general of Maryknoll, the Catholic Missionary Society of America, and James M. Drought, the vicar general and treasurer, made the rounds of Japan's government to plea for better relations between the United States and Japan. Tokyo decided to enlist them as diplomatic go-betweens. In December 1940, the government instructed Walsh and Drought on Japan's position, and in January dispatched them to Washington to meet with Roosevelt and Hull. Among Japan's proposals was a summit between Roosevelt and Konoye in Tokyo or Honolulu.

In early February 1941, Roosevelt responded to the John Doe associates' message by returning Eugene Doorman, second to Grew at the Tokyo embassy, to strongly convey to Japan's leaders American determination to uphold the Open Door and power balance in the Far East. Doorman met with Japanese Vice Minister for Foreign Affairs Ohashi Chuichi on February 14. After listening to Doorman, Ohashi bluntly asked him: "Do you mean to say that if Japan were to attack Singapore there would be war with the United States?" Doorman diplomatically replied:

> It would be absurd to suppose that the American people, while pouring munitions into Britain, would look with complacency upon the cutting of communications between Britain and British dominions and colonies overseas. If, therefore, Japan or any other nation were to prejudice the safety of those communications, either by direct action or by placing herself in a position to menace those communications, she would have to expect to come into conflict with the United States.[39]

On February 26, with Foreign Minister Arita, Grew reiterated Doorman's remarks.

The same day that Doorman met with Ohashi, ambassador Admiral Nomura Kichisaburo and special envoy from the War Ministry Iwakuro Hideo met with Roosevelt at the White House. Roosevelt agreed that direct negotiations could be useful. It was not until March 8 that Hull and Nomura met for what would be the first of nearly fifty negotiation rounds between them. The first meeting was not unlike most of the others. Both men stated principles and proposals that would ultimately be unbridgeable.

To help bring coherence to Japan's position, Iwakuro and Drought wrote

the "Preliminary Draft of an 'Agreement of Principle'" and submitted it to
Hull on March 17. The Draft included a withdrawal of all Japanese troops,
Chinese independence, the severance of Japanese trade ties with Germany,
and trade embargo on countries supplying Germany. Hull was pleased with
the draft and agreed it could be a basis for negotiations. Iwakuro dispatched
the draft to Tokyo which was appalled by the concessions.

After conferring with Tokyo, Iwakuro and Drought wrote up and submitted on April 9 a final "Draft Understanding" in which none of the first
draft's clauses were included. Instead, the United States would recognize
Manchukuo, allow greater Japanese immigration, and support Japanese
demands for a British withdrawal from Hong Kong and Singapore. In
return, Japan would withdraw from China and recognize its sovereignty
and territorial integrity, refrain from any indemnity, and endorse the Open
Door. Chiang Kai-shek and the Japanese puppet Wang Ch'ing-wei would
form a coalition government. Tokyo and Washington would oppose any
transfer of territory in the Far East.

The preliminary draft certainly had attracted Roosevelt's attention but
the "final Draft Understanding" submitted in April disappointed him. Yet
he choose to enter negotiations with the hope that he might secure an agreement based on the preliminary draft. Regardless, he "wished to remain
noncommital while giving the impression of interest. Hull was advised to
state that if Tokyo approved the Draft, he would study it 'sympathetically'
and 'feel optimistic that on the basis of mutual good will our differences
can be adjusted.'"[40]

Unfortunately, Hull exceeded his instructions. On April 14, he called
the Draft a "basis" rather than "starting point" "of negotiations," implying
that the United States was committed to some version of the points that
were not outright rejected. Hull did discard the Draft's clauses on Britain's
surrender of Hong Kong and Singapore, and immigration. Then two days
later on April 16, Hull called on Japan to accept four guiding principles
for negotiations: the territorial integrity and sovereignty of all nations; non-
interference in the domestic affairs of others, free trade, and the noninter-
ference of the Pacific status quo except by negotiation. Only if Tokyo
accepted these principles and "abandoned its present doctrine of military
conquest" would the United States discuss the Draft Understanding.

Although Nomura agreed to these principles, he failed to inform Tokyo
of them for nearly a month and then gave the impression he had discarded
them. The result was that for five months each side talked past the other.
It was not until September that Tokyo actually understood how important
the principles were to Hull.

Foreign Minister Matsuoka Yosuke then rewrote the Draft and included demands that the United States immediately resume trade with Japan, pressure Chiang to accept Tokyo's conditions for a settlement, and acknowledge the New Order in Asia. In addition, while maintaining that Japan would adhere to the Tripartite Pact, Matsuoka deleted a pledge that Japan would use only peaceful means in the southwest Pacific and attend a future summit. Nomura submitted the revised draft to Hull on May 12. Hull was aghast at the new demand. Each of the two subsequent drafts was far harsher than the preliminary draft.

The negotiations soon swirled around four key issues: Japanese troops remaining in China to combat communists and defend Manchukuo, American commercial opportunities in China and Manchukuo, American recognition of Manchukuo, and Japan's neutrality in case the United States went to war in Europe. Hull eventually agreed that American recognition of Manchukuo would be part of a general peace treaty. Nomura promised that Americans would be free to trade and invest in China and Manchukuo. Although the Tripartite Pact bound its members to ally against any foes, Nomura pledged that Tokyo would loosely interpret the vaguely written document, but only in return for American toleration of Japanese troops in China.

In late May, Nomura agreed to withdraw 90 per cent of Japanese troops from China within two years and restrict the remainder to zones in northern China. Hull countered by demanding the withdrawal of all Japanese troops from China within one year; communist inroads could be limited by building up Chiang. Nomura rejected the proposal. While Hull and Nomura negotiated these and other points, Drought and Walsh continued to serve as intermediaries between Tokyo and Washington. Drought alone made seventeen trips. Despite all of this diplomatic activity, there was no significant narrowing of the two sides' positions over the next five weeks.

Foreign Minister Matsuoka blustered to Grew on May 14 and 19 that if the United States and Germany went to war, Japan would join its ally. Despite Matsuoka's threats, Grew continued to cable Washington that most Japanese leaders wanted peace, thus reversing his "green light" warning about the inevitability of war he had made the previous fall. Amidst these negotiations, Roosevelt ordered 40 per cent of the Pacific fleet to sail to the Atlantic.

On May 17, Morgenthau bluntly told Roosevelt it was time to enter the war. Roosevelt replied, "I am waiting to be pushed into this situation."[41] Yet just five days later when a German submarine sank the American freighter "Robin Moor", Roosevelt and Hull resisted the entire cabinet's pressure that the time had come to ask Congress for a war declaration. Roosevelt did declare an "unlimited national emergency" but refused to take the next logical step.

With the crisis deepening with the British and Americans over southeast Asia, Tokyo was anxious to settle affairs with the Soviet Union. Foreign Minister Matsuoka flew to Moscow and on April 13 signed a nonaggression pact with the Soviets. Despite the treaty, Tokyo was still nervous about Soviet power in northeast Asia. At a Liason Conference on April 16, the government decided to advance southward only through economic and diplomatic means. Tokyo drastically began to rethink its diplomatic strategy after June 22 when Germany attacked the Soviet Union and its armies quickly overran vast areas, capturing or killing hundreds of thousands of Soviet troops. By attacking the Soviet Union, Hitler at once relieved pressure on Britain in Europe and increased it in the Far East. With the Soviet Union likely to collapse within months, Japanese war planners could now concentrate on the "strike south" strategy without constantly looking over their shoulder toward Siberia.

On July 2, 1941, an Imperial Conference decided on three important policies: (1) establish the Greater East Asia Co-prosperity Sphere regardless of the international situation; (2) decisively settle the China "incident" by advancing south while securing relations with the Soviet Union; and (3) achieve these goals "no matter what obstacles may be encountered."[42] On July 12, Tokyo issued an ultimatum that Vichy allow Japan to take over southern Indochina. Faced with war, Vichy complied. On July 24, Japan disembarked over 50,000 soldiers into southern Indochina. With a naval base at Cam Ran Bay and nearby airfields, Japanese forces were within easy striking distance of most of southeast Asia including Singapore.

On July 26, Roosevelt responded by freezing Japanese financial assets in the United States and embargoing high octane fuel. Henceforth, Japan would have to apply for an export license before it could buy any American goods. Roosevelt thought his freeze on Japanese assets was a compromise between hardliners like Treasury Secretary Morgenthau and Assistant Secretary of State Acheson who favored an all-out embargo and softliners like the Navy Secretary who argued that the United States should not do anything provocative that could lead to a war for which the United States was unprepared.[43]

Instead, it advanced rather than deterred Tokyo's ultimate decision for war. Roosevelt did not intend to cut off all trade with Japan, but that occurred anyway. While Roosevelt had flown off for a secret meeting with Churchill, bureaucrats charged with enforcing the freeze rejected Japanese requests to license shipments of oil and gas to Japan. When Roosevelt found out about the policy, he decided not to reverse it for fear that he would appear weak in Tokyo's eyes. Britain and Holland also froze Japan's assets and cut off trade. While his cabinet fully supported the tougher steps, Roosevelt's embargo was not popular with everyone – at the time, only 19 per cent of American businessmen favored any economic sanctions against Japan.[44]

When Washington cut off oil and gas exports to Japan in July 1941, Tokyo had only an eighteen month fuel supply, and two years stockpile of other strategic minerals. Although many in Washington may have believed that an oil embargo would force Japan to accede to American demands to withdraw from its recent conquests, Tokyo saw only one choice. Military and civilian leaders alike agreed that by declaring economic war the United States had declared total war. With Japan's resource stockpiles steadily diminishing, it was imperative to attempt to cripple America's Pacific fleet and seize natural resource-rich southeast Asia as soon as possible. The seasons also influenced Japan's attack timetable. Any attack in southeast Asia after mid-December could be disrupted by bad weather and tides.

However, Tokyo still preferred to resolve the crisis peacefully, but the negotiations remained deadlocked as Nomura continued to demand more. On July 7, Hull had asked that Japan renounce the Axis pact. Nomura refused. Then on August 6, Nomura proposed that Japan would put no more troops into southern Indochina and withdraw those already there after a peace settlement according to Japan's terms was imposed on China. Meanwhile, the United States would resume trade, recognize Japan's special status in Indochina, and force Chiang to agree to Tokyo's demands. Hull rejected Nomura's proposal.

Roosevelt met Churchill in Newfoundland between August 9 and 12 to coordinate plans in the likely event that the United States entered the war. He resisted the prime minister's call for a highly publicized summit and instead shrouded their meeting in secrecy. Roosevelt pressed Churchill not to consider Japan's occupation of Thailand a cause for war, and resisted the prime minister's plea that they issue parallel warnings that further Japanese aggression in the southwest Pacific would invite retaliation. Roosevelt's primary goal for the summit was to propound a set of ideals for which the two countries stood. Issued on August 14, the Atlantic Charter contained four principles or freedoms to which the two countries were committed: (1) no territorial aggrandizement, territorial changes only with the agreement of those involved, and restoration of self-government to those countries which had been conquered; (2) freedom from fear and want; (3) freedom of the seas; and (4) denunciation of the use of force to resolve conflicts. Amidst this summit, on August 7 the Senate approved the military draft's extension by one year. On August 12, the House passed the bill by only one vote (203: 202).

True to the Atlantic Charter ideals, the president still hoped to resolve conflict with Japan through negotiation rather than force. On August 8 and 17, Nomura requested a summit. Preoccupied with the Newfoundland summit with Churchill, Roosevelt did not agree to a summit until August 28 when he proposed meeting Prime Minister Konoye in Juneau. Tokyo replied that Washington should tie down a specific summit date by September 20. Roosevelt then vacillated, fearing he would be accused of agreeing to a Munich-like appeasement of Japanese aggression. On September 3, he said he would not consider a summit until both sides agreed to Hull's principles. The next day, he announced that Japanese shipping could not use the Panama Canal.

On September 3, the Liaison Conference tentatively agreed to go to war unless by early October the United States resumed oil shipments and acceded to Japan's other demands. This policy was ratified by the Cabinet the next day and by an Imperial Conference three days later on September 6. Deciding to attack was easier than where to attack. Four options were considered: (1) taking the Dutch East Indies first, then the Philippines and Malaysia; (2) seizing the Philippines first then the rest of southeast Asia; (3) taking Malaysia first followed by the Dutch East Indies and finally the Philippines; (4) conquering them all simultanously. Although the most difficult of the four, the government decided on the last option as a compromise between conflicting army and navy plans.

Admiral Yamamoto Isoroku then argued that Japan abandon its 1907 plan to wait in the western Pacific and ambush the American fleet as it steamed to the rescue. He argued instead that if Japanese forces destroyed the fleet at Pearl Harbor with a surprise attack by carrier-launched planes then Japan could concentrate on conquering southeast Asia and beyond without continually looking east over its shoulder. A decisive blow could force the United States to sue for peace and accept Japan's empire. But even if the United States did decide on war it would be years before it could build another fleet and send it to the western Pacific. By then, Japan would have built an impregnable complex of island defenses and an invincible fleet to destroy anything the Americans could muster. After weeks of discussion, Yamamoto first won over the navy and then the government to his bold plan.

Over the next two months, Tokyo made several limited concessions. On September 6, Konoye assured Grew that Hull's principles were a fine basis for reviving the bilateral relationship. On September 13, Nomura agreed to eventually withdraw almost all Japanese troops from China following a peace settlement. Hull continued to insist on a one-year deadline. On September 25, Tokyo countered by proposing that Japanese officers command Chinese troops in northern China and said it might agree to a specific time-table for the withdrawal of regular Japanese troops if Roosevelt would agree to a summit with Prime Minister Konoye. Hull countered on October 2 by maintaining that a summit was only possible if the Japanese rejected the Tripartite Pact and withdrew some troops from China and Indochina. On October 8, Tokyo indicated a willingness to negotiate the presence of Jap-anese troops in northern China. Hull countered by insisting that the United States would not sign any treaty unless Japan showed its good faith by with-drawing some troops. Konoye resigned on October 15, and both sides gave up the idea of a summit.

In October and November Roosevelt once again passed up two opportun-ities to ask Congress for a war declaration. German submarines sank five American merchant ships early that month and on October 16 the U.S.S. "Kearney", a destroyer. Following the German sinking of the destroyer "Reuben James" on October 31, Roosevelt asked Congress to repeal the ban on arming merchant ships. By November 17, the ban was lifted. Yet Roosevelt's caution was justified – the same House that renewed the draft for a year by only one vote and lifted the ban on arming merchant ships by a simple majority would have been unlikely to declare war.

Prime Minister Tojo Hideki led a series of Liaison Conferences between October 23 and November 2 designed to create a consensus over Japan's last negotiating positions with the Americans and what to do if they were rejected. On November 5, an Imperial Conference ratified Japan's last nego-tiating position. If Washington rejected the proposal, an Imperial Con-ference would be held on November 25 to decide on war. The deadline was later moved to November 29. Meanwhile, Chief of Naval Operations Nagano Osami accepted Yamamoto's plan and ordered those units desig-nated for the attack to begin training for an attack on December 8 (Decem-ber 7 in Hawaii).

On November 8, Nomura presented Plan "A" to Hull, and two days later to the president himself. The plan included Japan's standard demand that if the United States immediately resumed trade and forced Chiang to accept Tokyo's peace terms, Japan would begin withdrawing troops from Indochina and China. Japanese troops in North China, Inner Mongolia, and Hainan Island would stay for twenty-five years. Tokyo would loosely interpret the Tripartite Pact if the United States did get involved in the European war. Finally, foreign countries would be allowed to resume trade in China if the Open Door principles became the basis of global trade.

Roosevelt replied that before he could consider the proposals, Japan had to show good faith by withdrawing some troops from China and Indochina.

Over the next two weeks, Hull insisted that Tokyo abandon the Tripartite Pact and argued that the United States could not agree to global free trade since it involved the sovereign rights of other countries. Amidst these negotiations, former ambassador to Germany Kurusu Saburo arrived in Washington to assist Nomura and together they met the president on November 17 to plea that he accept their terms.

The president proposed a six month agreement in which the United States would provide "good offices" between China and Japan and allow limited exports of oil and other goods if Japan halted any reinforcements to China or Indochina, and did not invoke the Tripartite Pact even if the United States went to war in Europe. Roosevelt hoped that a limited agreement could buy time for the United States to prepare for war and deal with the European situation.

Encouraged by the possibility of averting war, Nomura presented an agreement the following day on restoring the situation to before July when Japan took over southern Indochina and the United States froze Japan's assets. Hull agreed and Nomura cabled Tokyo for approval of the potentially war-averting proposal. But Tokyo rejected the agreement and ordered Nomura to submit the second plan.

On November 20, Nomura and Kurusu submitted Plan "B" in which Japan would halt its expansion in southeast Asia and immediately evacuate southern Indochina in return for the immediate resumption of American and Dutch trade, the fulfillment of Japan's oil needs (4 million tons a year from the United States and 1 million tons from the East Indies), the cutoff of American aid to China, and acceptance by Chungking of Tokyo's peace terms.[45]

Hull rejected these demands, later writing that they meant "condonement by the United States of Japan's past aggressions, assent to future courses of conquest by Japan, abandonment of the most essential principles of our foreign policy, betrayal of China and Russia, and acceptance of the role of silent partner aiding and abetting Japan in her efforts to create a Japanese hegemony over the western Pacific and eastern Asia."[46] He replied that the United States would continue to aid Chiang until Japanese troops were withdrawn from all of China. He demanded an immediate Japanese withdrawal from all of Indochina and the Tripartite Pact. He did agree to resume oil shipments to Japan, but only enough to satisfy civilian needs.

Early in 1941, the United States had broken Japan's secret diplomatic code, an operation code-named MAGIC. On November 22, the White House received a MAGIC intercept that revealed the negotiation deadline had been moved to November 29 "after which things are automatically going to happen." Unbeknownst to Washington, a Japanese task force of six aircraft carriers left its base in the Kurile islands on November 25 and sailed in strict radio silence toward Hawaii. Before his War Council on November 25, Roosevelt commented that he expected a Japanese attack as early as December 1. The War Council agreed to warn Tokyo that an attack on British positions in the Far East would be considered an attack on the United States.

Roosevelt still believed he could avert war. As late as November 26, he sought compromises with Japan that he hoped could delay or prevent war. On that day he drafted proposals for resolving the crisis that were similar to Tokyo's. But then Secretary of War Stimson called and informed the president of an intelligence report that Japanese troop transports were heading south from Formosa. Roosevelt tore up his conciliatory proposals and had Hull draw up a ten-point list of demands that would require Japan to withdraw from all of its conquests since 1931.[47]

On November 26, Hull presented to Nomura his Ten Point Note in which he offered trade resumption, unfrozen assets, and a fixed yen–dollar exchange rate if the Japanese withdrew all forces from Indochina and all of China including Manchuria, recognize only Chiang's government, sign a multilateral nonaggression pact covering the Far East and Pacific, and renounce the Tripartite Pact. In other words, Japan had to return to the pre-1931 status quo.

Although Nomura and Kurusu did not take Hull's Ten Points as an ultimatum, Tokyo thought it was as good as a war declaration. On November 29, the Cabinet voted in favor of war. A Liason Conference ratified the decision the following day. Finally on December 1, an Imperial Conference gave final approval. Emperor Hirohito insisted that a formal break in relations and negotiations be made before hostilities began. The next day, the War Ministry radioed the message "Climb Mt. Niitake" which gave Japan's fleet the go-ahead to attack Pearl Harbor.

After resisting Churchill's requests for years, Roosevelt finally pledged on December 3 to ask Congress for a war declaration not only if the Japanese attacked Britain's possessions but also the Dutch East Indies and Thailand. MAGIC intercepts on December 4–5 revealed Tokyo's order to its embassy to destroy all codes and prepare to leave the United States. War was clearly imminent.

Roosevelt decided on a last-minute appeal to Hirohito on December 5 in which he proposed a ninety-day truce and Sino-Japanese talks in return for a Japanese withdrawal from Indochina. Hoping to reach as wide an audience as possible, Roosevelt sent the message to Grew in a code he knew was broken and informed the press of the action but not the contents of his message.

Thirty minutes after Roosevelt's appeal to the emperor was dispatched, MAGIC decoded the first thirteen parts of a fourteen part message from Tokyo to the embassy. Most of it was a refutation of Hull's Ten Points, and ordered Nomura to deliver it at 1.00 p.m. on December 7. It was not until 10.00 on December 7 that the fourteenth part was received which ordered diplomatic relations to be broken. Nomura and Kurusu appeared before Hull at 2.15, nearly two hours after the attack on Pearl Harbor began.

At 7.53 a.m. on December 7, 1941, 181 dive and torpedo bombers and their fighter escorts flew in precision waves over Hawaii's air and naval bases. Japanese planes sank six battleships, and damaged two other battleships, three cruisers, and three destroyers, destroyed 180 planes and damaged 128 others, and killed or wounded 3,600 Americans.

On December 8 before a joint session of Congress, President Roosevelt declared December 7 a "day that would live in infamy" for Japan's "unprovoked and dastardly attack;" he then asked Congress for a war declaration. The Senate voted unanimously and the House 388–1 for war.

CONCLUSION

Was war between the United States and Japan inevitable? Until shooting actually starts, war is never inevitable. The seeds of potential future wars are sown in previous conflicts. Over time, the spectrum of options available to decision makers on either side may narrow considerably before one or both participants in a conflict choose war as the best option to serve national interests.

During this decade, Japan's leaders were united on a policy of a greater Japanese empire, if divided over the timetable and means.[48] There was no grand plan for Japanese imperialism during the 1930s and early 1940s. Tokyo simply took advantage of opportunities that arose to enhance Japan's national interests as they were then understood. Each opportunity presented choices to Japan's leaders. They were responsible for each escalation of the Far East war, whether they initiated it themselves or, as in 1931, when it was forced upon them by renegade officers in Manchuria. As Japan's armies bogged down in the China quagmire, Tokyo choose to widen the war rather than negotiate a settlement. Likewise, Tokyo decided to take advantage of the power vacuum in southeast Asia created by Hitler's victories in Europe, even though it made war with the United States more likely. Ultimately, Japan's leaders chose to attack Pearl Harbor, along with the Philippines, Malaysia, Singapore, and the Dutch East Indies, thereby going to war against the United States, the British empire, and Holland.

Just as Tokyo's policies were shaped by domestic politics and foreign threats and opportunities, so too were Washington's. American diplomacy between 1931 and 1941 was inhibited and distorted by many internal constraints, including powerful isolationist sentiments, a devastating depression, neutrality laws, misperceptions about Japanese politics and ambitions, a weak military, a vulnerable Far East colony, an unshakeable commitment to Open Door principles, and weaknesses of Roosevelt's policy making, political skills, and long-term goals and strategy to fulfill them. All along, the United States faced not only a direct threat from the Pacific but also an indirect and perhaps even more dangerous threat from across the Atlantic. Thus, the United States was necessarily on the defensive; American policy toward Japan, such as it was, simply reacted to Tokyo's initiatives.

Before 1940, the United States largely appeased Japanese aggression, thus encouraging it and making an ultimate confrontation more likely. By mid 1940, appeasement policies were thoroughly discredited in both Europe and the Pacific. The Roosevelt administration was able to push through Congress revisions of the neutrality laws that strengthened its diplomatic hand and thus allowed a more confrontational policy toward Japanese imperialism. Roosevelt, however, chose not to begin direct negotiations with Tokyo for a sweeping settlement of outstanding conflicts until February 1941, and even then largely because of a Japanese diplomatic initiative through the Maryknoll priests. Ironically, by this time, Roosevelt had decided that war was inevitable and sought to delay it as long as possible.

War between the United States and Japan would never have occurred had it not been preceded by a decade of brutal Japanese imperialism and genocide in Asia. Tokyo was responsible for each aggressive act including its direct attack on the United States. But American policymakers, too, must bear some responsibility. The Hoover and Roosevelt administrations mishandled both domestic and foreign policy, thus weakening the United States as it faced a worsening Japanese threat.

Both Hoover and Roosevelt had two clear choices in dealing with Japanese imperialism. They could have accommodated it and negotiated a new Far East power balance which curtailed American geopolitical and geoeconomic interests in the region. Or they could have boldly issued Japan an ultimatum that it accept the pre-1931 power balance, which would have resulted either in a Japanese retreat or war. They did neither and instead straddled these options. Writing of Roosevelt's diplomacy, Marks points out that he adopted Stimson's moral imperative but until the very end delayed the economic sanctions and military build-up necessary to back it up "despite clear indications of congressional support and the insistent prodding of his advisors . . . Roosevelt tended to substitute words for action, condemnation for policy."[49] Both administrations followed "firm but conciliatory" policies in which Washington protested and refused to accept each stage of Japanese aggression, but carefully avoided any actions that might provoke Japan to war.

In contrast to those who criticize Roosevelt as a diplomatic bumbler are those who claim that he deliberately exposed the fleet at Pearl Harbor to bring America into the war.[50] Conspiracy theories can make good novels and films but rarely good history. All the evidence points to Roosevelt doing all he could to avoid rather than accelerate America's entry into the war. For nearly a decade, Roosevelt appeased Japanese aggression. While the neutrality laws clearly hindered Roosevelt's ability to act, he had been instrumental in their becoming law. Likewise Roosevelt reinforced rather than resisted public isolationism. Roosevelt had no grand strategy for dealing with Japanese, German, and Italian aggression. White House actions were simply *ad hoc* reactions to momentary crises, and then were largely shaped by indecision and caution. While incensed at Japanese imperialism and genocide, Roosevelt repeatedly ducked any opportunities to rally the nation around containing Tokyo's expansion, even as late as November 1941 when all of his cabinet except Hull and Marshall urged him to go to war.

Roosevelt's tendency to appease rather than confront foreign aggression sprang partly from his belief that the Japanese, German, and Soviet dictatorships were unpopular and moderates waited in the wings. Thus it was reasoned that a harsh stand against Japanese or German and later Soviet expansion would strengthen the militarists while acquiescence would encourage the moderates. For a decade, Ambassador Grew reinforced this view with a stream of reports advising appeasement. Marks points out that "down to the bombing of Pearl Harbor, Tokyo council-chambers were thought to be dominated by a small military clique."[51]

This perception was mere wishful thinking, as the Japan expert, Sir George Sansom pointed out in an April 1941 article in *Foreign Affairs*: "We are inclined to postulate the existence of a numerous class of 'liberals' and we are misled . . . into supposing that there is in Japan a school of political thought which approves of democratic institutions. A further assumption, no less unjustified, allows us to picture this liberal element in Japanese life as a force hostile to what is called the 'liberal party'. . . . It is a mistake to suppose that there is a split between the military and civilian opinion in Japan. . . . Totalitarian . . . thinking has for years past been gaining strength . . ."[52] Japan's civilian leaders themselves promoted this view to foreign diplomats both before and after the war, in part to scapegoat the military leaders for policies that at the time the entire leadership thoroughly supported.

Misperceptions about the nature of Japan's political system and ambitions were not the only forces which warped American policy. Roosevelt was as much a prisoner of traditional American diplomacy as anything else. The United States continued to uphold principles of the Open Door and territorial status quo that it had articulated nearly a half century earlier. Any departure from this position would have required "not only a diplomatic–military reassessment but a sharp psychological break with traditions and modes of thinking past and present – perhaps even a reevalution of America's needs and responsibilities in Asia."[53]

But this moralizing over the Open Door, without the threat of economic or military sanction, proved useless at best and may have strengthened foreign aggression. As Marks put it, "Roosevelt's reliance upon words had little impact other than to embolden his enemies and demoralize many of America's friends."[54] By 1940, the momentum of Japan's conquests had grown too great to allow for serious negotiations.[55] Even if Roosevelt had caved in to Tokyo's demands, war between the United States and Japan would have most likely merely been postponed. Appeasement would not have worked any better in the Pacific than it had in Europe. When Roosevelt finally imposed economic sanctions against Japan in the fall of 1940, the effect was to encourage rather than inhibit Japanese imperialism. Morgenthau later admitted that the use of economic sanctions against Germany and Japan proved nothing more than "yapping at the heels of a world striding inexorably towards war."[56]

All along, most policymakers on either side wanted peace, but only on their own terms which meant the other side had to retreat either partially or fully from its declared position. This gap proved impossible to bridge. Allison and Halperin explored this dynamic:

> In the months leading up to Pearl Harbor, competing groups in Japan and the United States needed different actions from each other's government. . . . In Tokyo, those who opposed war with the United States needed to be able to show that the United States would not interfere with Japanese expansion by cutting off sources of scrap iron, oil, and other materials. They also needed the United States to avoid actions which would have enabled their opponents to argue that war with the United States was inevitable. . . . Roosevelt, who sought to avoid a Pacific war . . . had to resist pressures within the government from those who wanted to go to war with Japan. At the same time he did not want to so demoralize them that they would resign or reduce their efforts to

prepare for the war with Germany which he believed was necessary. Thus Roosevelt's purposes required that Japan avoid: (1) flagrant violations of international law, (2) linking up with Germany in ways that made it impossible to resist arguments that war with Japan was a part of the war against the Fascist alliance, and (3) threats to the British or Dutch colonies which could be seen as a threat to the Allies in Europe.[57]

Tokyo, of course, violated each of America's national security interests in the Far East. Roosevelt in turn responded by embargoing war materials to Japan and freezing Japanese assets in the United States.

Roosevelt's diplomatic style inhibited any decisive measures that might have forced an issue with Japan years earlier:

Whenever he moved against tolerable opposition, he did so by degrees. In 1933, for instance, he requested discretionary power to impose trade sanctions, but when faced with vociferous dissent from a handful of senators, he canceled the drive only to resume it at a later date. The same holds true for his campaign to persuade the Military Affairs Committee that America's frontier was on the Rhine. One is also reminded of his "unlimited national emergency" speech of 27 May 1941, which he took back at a press conference the next day despite telegrams running 95 per cent in its favor. Implying the need for convoys, he insisted that American supplies must reach Britain: "It can be done; it must be done; it will be done." Nonetheless, within hours, under heated interrogation, he announced that there would be no convoying and no request for revision of the neutrality law after all.[58]

Marks concludes that Roosevelt's foreign policies were an abject failure that made war inevitable: "no other American admininstration before 1933 had as many opportunities . . . to avert the coming of war, to settle wars in progress, or to shape the future of peace. . . . Not one of FDR's offers of mediation ever succeeded, and most were flatly rejected. He made at least thirty unsuccessful protests and appeals. . . . Out of dozens of prewar diplomatic initiatives and schemes emanating from the White House, all but a handful proved fruitless."[59] It is hard to argue with his tough judgement.

4 The Road to Peace, 1942–5

America's entry into and ending of the Pacific War have become clouded by controversy. Did Roosevelt cynically lure the Japanese fleet into attacking Pearl Harbor to bring America into the war? Did Truman just as cynically order the nuclear attacks on Hiroshima and Nagasaki to contain the Soviet Union in the Far East and elsewhere even though Japan's surrender may have been imminent? These questions form the bookends of American policy toward Japan during World War II.

From 1931 to 1945, Americans collectively viewed the Japanese as utterly ruthless, barbaric hordes determined to conquer Asia and die en masse for the emperor. This image was shaped by Japan's own official doctrines of race, genocidal policies, and battlefield fanaticism, filtered to the American public by skilled government propaganda writers and filmmakers. Some argue that this image led to an American "war without mercy" toward Japan. Is this true?

Although bilateral relations were severed throughout the war, American diplomacy with its allies during the wartime conferences largely determined Japan's fate in the postwar era.

PEARL HARBOR: WHO WAS RESPONSIBLE?

Some accuse Roosevelt of setting up the Pearl Harbor attack in order to bring America into the war, and claim that he deliberately exposed the fleet at Pearl Harbor, committed other aggressive acts, and delayed warnings to his commanders. John Toland, for example, argues that as early as December 4, Roosevelt, Marshall, and Knox may have known about the Japanese carrier task force sailing toward Hawaii. They welcomed the attack, assuming it would result in a Japanese defeat and a congressional war declaration.[1]

In fact, there is no hard and little circumstantial evidence for any White House knowledge that Japan's fleet had put to sea, let alone that it was headed toward Pearl Harbor. In his definitive analysis, Gordon Prange explodes all of the conspiracy theories and demonstrates convincingly that for many reasons no one in the American government suspected Pearl Harbor would be attacked, let alone wanted such an attack to occur.[2]

Roosevelt not only did not know of a Pearl Harbor attack but actually believed that he could prevent war by a last minute appeal to the emperor on December 5. The previous day Roosevelt shared this hope with British ambassador Lord Halifax, and two days later, turned down an Australian request that he sternly warn Japan not to attack because he wanted to first see how the emperor responded. And even if these were just smoke-screens and he really wanted the Pearl Harbor attack to occur, why did he not issue a specific warning to his Hawaiian commanders to ambush the Japanese and score a major victory? After all, whether it succeeded or failed, a Japanese attack would have elicited a congressional war declaration.

So then who was responsible for the Pearl Harbor disaster? A special commission of inquiry in January 1942 found Hawaii's two commanders, Admiral Husband E. Kimmel and Lieutenant-General Walter C. Short, guilty of dereliction of duty for failing "to take appropriate measure of defense required by the imminence of hostilities," a finding that was subsequently supported by six administrative investigations and a congressional investigation which produced thirty-nine volumes of documents and findings.[3]

The War Department was faulted for failing to explain to Short that he should prepare for an enemy attack as well as sabotage. The Hawaiian commanders' real fear was that Japanese-Americans would slip into the harbor and airfields and plant bombs among the ships and planes. Hence, the air fleet was parked wing-tip to wing-tip at the air bases and the fleet, including every American battleship in the Pacific, crowded into Pearl Harbor's narrow anchorage. Fortuitously, the American carriers, the "Lexington" and "Enterprise" and their cruiser, destroyer, and supply ship escorts, were far north of Hawaii delivering aircraft to Midway and Wake islands when the attack occurred.

Ironically, the Pacific fleet was stationed at Pearl Harbor entirely for show. Exposure to an unexpected attack was not the only weakness in keeping the fleet in Hawaii: the "logistical, repair, and training facilities at Pearl Harbor were inferior to those on the West Coast, and prolonged absence from their families in the western states had affected the morale of the men adversely."[4] If war broke out the fleet would have had to retire to the west coast for an extensive overhaul before it was ready for battle. Political rather than military strategy prevailed. When Pearl Harbor's previous commander, James Richardson, protested the fleet's unreadiness he was relieved of command.

Although the White House rather than Short or Kimmel was certainly responsible for sending the fleet to Hawaii, the commanders did have the freedom and responsibility for taking security measures to protect their forces. Between June 1940 and the attack, there were three major alerts and many drills. Military reports in 1936 and 1940 had warned of the possibility of a surprise attack. Despite clear warnings from the War Department in late November that war was imminent and all commanders should ready their forces, Short and Kimmel took no special measures. Scouting planes were sent aloft sporadically. Few patrol boats or destroyers were dispatched to sea for picket duty. Radar operated only part-time – between 4.00 and 7.00 a.m.

Short and Kimmel are not entirely to blame for the fiasco. Clearly, as Roberta Wohlstetter argues, there was a breakdown in intelligence collection and analysis at virtually all levels, and not just in Hawaii.[5] Just what did American intelligence know and when did it know it? As early as November 1940 American cryptologists cracked Japan's diplomatic code, a coup they labeled "MAGIC." In the week preceding the attack, MAGIC diplomatic and other intercepts which indicated possible attacks on a variety of targets including Pearl Harbor had piled up on various desks without being properly analyzed and forwarded to top decision makers. Wohlstetter points out that the Pearl Harbor attack was unexpected "not for want of the relevent information but because of a plethora of irrelevent ones. . . . There is a difference between having a signal available somewhere in the heap of irrelevancies and perceiving it as a warning, and there is also a difference between perceiving it as a warning and acting on it."[6]

While the possibility for a Japanese attack on Pearl Harbor was buried in piles of intercepts, Washington did act on its awareness that war was imminent. One diplomatic message said that "things were automatically going to happen" if there was no agreement by November 25, although Tokyo would continue negotiating until November 29. On November 30, a MAGIC intercept from Tokyo to its Berlin embassy warned that war might be imminent. At the time, five Japanese divisions on troopships were steaming south of Taiwan, their destination unknown. American intelligence, however, assumed that Japan's carrier fleet remained at Kure since they had not picked up any radio intercepts. The reason, of course, was that the fleet maintained strict radio silence as it steamed toward Pearl Harbor. On November 24, the chief of naval operations cabled the Pacific commanders that "a surprise aggressive movement [by Japan] in any direction . . . is a possibility." He followed this message up on November 27 by issuing a "war warning. Negotiations with Japan . . . have ceased and an aggressive move by Japan is expected within the next few days."[7] On November 28, the army commanders received a similar message.

On the early morning of December 7, Naval Intelligence intercepted and decoded a fourteen-part message to Ambassador Nomura who was ordered to immediately destroy his code machine and announce to Secretary of State Hull at 1.00 p.m. the next day that Tokyo was breaking off all negotiations. The analyst, Colonel Barton, reasoned that since the message mentioned a specific delivery time it might coincide with an attack somewhere in the Pacific. Barton awoke Marshall with the news, and he in turn consulted Navy Secretary Stark. Together they agreed to warn the Pacific commanders. Unknown to them, however, a temporary glitch in the communications system prevented the warning from arriving at Honolulu until shortly after the attack began.

Shortly before it switched down on December 7, one outlying radar station picked up the incoming Japanese bogey and promptly reported it to the Army Aircraft Service Information Center on Oahu. "Don't worry about it," the radar station was told, it was a scheduled flight of B-17's en route from the west coast.

Prange argues that a psychological rather than intelligence failure was the core reason for America's tragic defeats.[8] Call it hubris or cognitive dissonance, despite warnings to prepare for just such a possibility, neither the Hawaiian nor Philippine commanders thought that the Japanese were materially or psychologically strong enough to attack their respective realms. Although all of the commanders knew that war was imminent, they did have some good technical reasons to believe that attacks on their bases were improbable at best. Stark and Kimmel assumed that the Japanese would not target Pearl Harbor because it was too far from their homeland and, even if they launched a carrier-based attack, Pearl Harbor was too shallow for torpedo bombs. Both commanders believed that sabotage was the real threat so they acted accordingly by squeezing their ships and planes closer together. General Douglas MacArthur, commander of military forces in the Philippines, likewise believed that the colony was invulnerable because Japanese bombers based on Taiwan could not hold enough fuel to bomb and return. The Japanese overcame these technical problems, improving both their torpedoes so that they could run in shallow water and bombers so that they could fly further.

WINNING THE WAR

Preparations for War

Between 1922 and 1935, the U.S. army's strength averaged around 135,000 men, with a peak of 141,000 men in 1924. Then between 1936 and 1940, the army slowly increased from 135,000 to 268,000. In the year before Pearl Harbor, alarmed by Japanese and German aggression, Congress authorized the army's increase to 1.5 million. But these troops were poorly equipped and trained; most divisions remained undermanned and far from combat ready. The four top army field commanders in 1941 were Spanish–American War veterans, and their strategic outlook largely reflected the war era in which they had first experienced combat. Naval officers were just as ill-prepared for World War II as their army rivals. They graduated from an academy that was "parochial, spartan, intellectually sterile, and pedagogically backward."[9] Pooh-poohing the idea that aircraft carriers would render obsolete the traditional role of battleships, naval commanders continued to dream of refighting Trafalgar. America's officer culture and promotion system "was a sort of gentlemen's club" which "bred mental stagnation, reverence for routine, parochialism – and indifference."[10] Athletic rivalries rather than preparation for future wars was the major focus of officer's lives and promotion basis.

Neither the army nor the navy had yet adapted to Brigadier-General Billy Mitchell's 1919 prediction that "aerial warfare now ranked with naval and ground warfare in importance."[11] The military establishment rejected Mitchell's concepts of massed air attacks against the enemy's industrial centers and cities to cripple its warmaking capacity and the need for aircraft carriers to establish sea and air superiority. As it turned out, air power would be decisive in the Pacific War.

Despite clinging to a battleship strategy, the U.S. fleet was not completely unprepared for carrier warfare. Two of the battle cruisers which had to be scrapped under the 1930 London Naval Treaty were converted into America's first giant aircraft carriers, the "Lexington" and "Saratoga". The lessons learned from the operations of these carriers were built into the first American carrier built from scratch, the "Ranger", and improvments continually made with each additional carrier in the class, such as the "Yorktown" and "Enterprise".

But other parts of the U.S. fleet were deficient. While America's submarines were superior to Japan's, their torpedoes were nearly worthless. The torpedoes either plowed far beneath the targeted ship or failed to detonate when it did strike steel. It took two years before Washington replaced its defective torpedoes with effective ones.

Combat readiness aside, the revised versions of the original Plan Orange did prove to be an important preparation for the Pacific War. As early as 1921, Marine Corps Major Earl Ellis, who served in the Naval War College, devised a strategy for amphibious warfare against the Japanese in the Pacific. Adopted by Marine Corps commander, General John Lejeune, the plan was woven into Orange and became the basis for the strategy and tactics later used during the Pacific War. In 1937, talks were begun between the American and British navies over what to do in the event of war with Japan, and further adjustments in Plan Orange were made. Altogether American naval officers refought Plan Orange 127 times on board games at the Naval War College after 1907. Admiral Nimitz later declared that the "courses were so thorough that nothing that happened in the Pacific War was strange or unexpected."[12]

Plan Orange, however, did not include a scenario for simultaneously fighting a war in Europe, and had to be adjusted accordingly. In November 1940, Admiral Stark submitted four options to the president: (a) hemispheric defense; (b) attack in the Pacific, defend in the Atlantic; (c) attack in the Pacific and Atlantic; (d) defend in the Pacific, attack in the Atlantic. Stark and most other ranking commanders favored the "d" option or "Plan Dog" as it came to be called. Roosevelt approved it and the Joint Board eventually expanded it and incorporated Plan Orange within it as the basis for fighting Japan after Germany's defeat.

Success and Failures of Japan's 1941–2 Offensive

Japan's attacks across the Pacific and Southeast Asia in December 1941 through spring 1942 were brilliant except in one respect. Tokyo gambled that a decisive blow against the U.S. fleet at Pearl Harbor and rapid conquest of the Philippines would shrivel America's will to fight. But just the opposite happened. Japan's "sneak attack" galvanized Americans into an outpouring of fervent patriotism and mobilization for total global war.

Japan's attack on Hawaii was successful but not decisive. The sunken ships and destroyed planes were largely obsolete and their loss may not have set back America's war effort at all. The Japanese failed to destroy the carriers or, even more importantly, the oil storage tanks which held enough fuel for the fleet to operate for nearly two years. Even more crippling would have been a successful Japanese invasion of Hawaii which would have forced America's defenses back to the west coast!

In one important way, the Japanese did the Americans an enormous service by sending its battleships to rust on Pearl Harbor's sandy bottom. The brilliant success of Japan's carrier-launched attack and loss of America's obsolete fleet allowed for a quick shift from a battleship to carrier task force-centered naval strategy. The carrier advocates had previously been a minority voice within the tradition-bound American navy. After Pearl Harbor, they dominated.

Should Japan have attacked the United States in the first place? Some argue that the surprise attack on Pearl Harbor and the Philippines could not have given Roosevelt a better excuse for war. If Japan had by-passed American possessions and concentrated its attacks on the British and Dutch colonies in southeast Asia, Roosevelt "would have found it awkward trying to win support for a war in defense of distant European colonies in Asia, rather than leading a righteous crusade to avenge Pearl Harbor."[13]

But Tokyo's odds of winning the gamble that America would remain neutral despite a Japanese conquest of southeast Asia were far greater than the historic attack. If Congress did pass a war declaration then America's battleship fleet would be intact and, more importantly, its army and air force in the Philippines would lie directly astride Japan's supply lines to its Southeast Asian empire. Japanese forces would have had eventually to invade the Philippines anyway. The longer they put off such an invasion, the more time they would give MacArthur to bolster its defenses. Of course even then, there was no guarantee that MacArthur's defense of the Philippines would have been any less inept than what actually occurred. Nonetheless, Japan's strategic position would have been far more vulnerable and challenging than it was historically.

Japan's best option would have been to concentrate first on seizing Hawaii along with the Philippines, Malaya, and Singapore, after which the rest of Southeast Asia would have fallen easily. With America's defense thrown back to the west coast, Japan could have enjoyed a year or so breathing space within which to successfully conquer India and Australia. And afterwards, who knows, perhaps Japanese troops could have even linked up with German forces in the Middle East. World War II could have ended with a quite different set of victors.

How the War Was Won

Although they were brilliantly conceived and executed, Japan's offensives through the Pacific and southeast Asia which began in December 1941 eventually literally ran out of gas. Japan had depended on the United States for 80 per cent of its oil needs. Although Japan's onslaught quickly overran oil-rich Malaya and the Dutch East Indies, those energy sources never made up for Japan's loss of American oil. By April 1942, Japan's empire had reached its limits in the Pacific. American naval victories at the battles of the Coral Sea in May and Midway in June proved to be the Pacific War's turning points. For the next three and a half years, except for relatively limited offensives in Burma and China, Japan would simply defend and attempt to consolidate the newest additions to its empire.

America's strategy was controversial. Bowing to the fierce army–navy rivalry, Roosevelt agreed to divide the Pacific between a largely army operation in the southwest Pacific under MacArthur and a largely navy–marine operation in the central Pacific under Admiral Chester W. Nimitz. In subjecting sound strategy to politics, the two-pronged advance proved to be a vast waste of countless resources, lives, and time, and exposed both prongs to separate defeat. The war might have ended sooner if America's limited material and human resources had been concentrated on the navy-led thrust across the central Pacific toward Japan.

In July 1944, Roosevelt met with Nimitz and MacArthur at Honolulu to plot grand strategy. Roosevelt and Nimitz originally sought the strategy of bypassing the Philippines and invading Taiwan while the major strike took place straight across the central Pacific toward Japan. MacArthur made a typically eloquent and long-winded three-hour plea for the Philippines' liberation, arguing that American honor was at stake. Roosevelt eventually caved in to MacArthur's demands, perhaps not so much on their flimsy strategic rationale but possibly from a promise that MacArthur might endorse Roosevelt in the 1944 presidential election campaign.

Despite the flawed grand strategy, many factors contributed to the virtually unbroken series of American victories from the Battle of the Coral Sea onward – superior strategy, training, equipment, intelligence, and luck. A vital ingredient of victory was the ability to monitor radio traffic and crack Japanese codes. By March 1942, cryptoanalysts had unraveled parts of the new Japanese naval code, enabling them to learn much of Japan's Midway campaign strategy. Ronald Spector puts the codebreaking in perspective, arguing that it "did not assure the American victory at Midway but made it possible. Midway was the greatest single success produced by intelligence in the war with Japan."[14] Throughout the war, the Americans kept up with frequent Japanese code changes. But the decisive factors in the war were the quality of America's fighting men, weapons, and supplies, and the strategic and tactical skill with which they were employed against the enemy.

"WAR WITHOUT MERCY"

Race War?

Was the war between the United States and Japan simply over clashing geopolitical interests between two great powers, or was racism its basis?

John Dower argues that race was as important as geopolitics in determining why and how the war was fought: "stereotyped and often blatantly racist thinking contributed to poor military intelligence and planning, atrocious behavior, and the adoption of exterminationist policies."[15] Is Dower right?

For at least some of the participants, World War II clearly was as much a war over race as it was for territory, military supremacy, *lebensraum*, raw materials, oil, or markets. Both the Japanese and Germans fought and committed mass atrocities under banners of racial purity and supremacy. Dower admits that "Japanese behavior betrayed a racial supremacism as virulent in its own way as the master-race theories of the Nazis. . . . Pan-Asianism was thus a hydra-headed ideology involving not merely a frontal attack on the Western colonial powers and their values but also discrimination vis-à-vis the other races, nationalities, and cultures of Asia."[16] All of the combined Nazi racist literature and theories never equaled the massive Japanese government study completed between 1942 and 1943 entitled "Global Policy with the Yamato Race as Nucleus." However, unlike the Germans, the Japanese did not attempt to realize their racist ideology with a "final solution."

During the war, the initial enthusiasm with which many Asian nationalists greeted Japan's "liberation" of their homelands soon turned to a bitter disillusionment and often outright armed resistance. Although many newly "liberated" Asians rallied around Japan's slogans of "Asia for the Asians" and the "Greater East Asian Co-prosperity Sphere," they soon awoke to the reality that the Japanese were even more racist, exploitive and brutal than the western powers they had replaced. After first embracing the Japanese, Burmese independence leader Ba Maw eventually decried their "brutality, arrogance, and racial pretensions."[17]

Japanese racism was self-defeating – it turned potential allies into bitter enemies. In the Philippines, for example, over 200,000 people actively resisted Japanese rule. While the Filipino resistance never threatened to defeat the Japanese, it did divert thousands of troops from fighting the Americans. Similar guerrilla movements arose against the Japanese in each occupied region. Throughout the war, the American Office of Strategic Services (OSS) parachuted men and equipment to many of these guerrilla forces.

While preaching racial solidarity, Japanese practiced racial genocide. The exact atrocity figure of Japanese imperialism between 1931 and 1945 will never be known. Certainly millions of Asians died directly from Japanese bayonets and bombs, and millions of others indirectly from labor camps, starvation, and disease. Conservative estimates are that at least 20 million Asians died during World War II; some argue the number of dead may have been twice that.

Despite native resistance to the Japanese, the western colonial powers genuinely feared Japan's slogan to liberate an "Asia for the Asians" and attempt to create a "Greater East Asian Co-prosperity Sphere." While no significant pan-Asian armies arose during the war, the western colonial powers assumed that they would have trouble reasserting control over their colonies after the war. That fear was realized.

While Germany and Japan were the most outrageous proponents of racism and mass murder, no participant in World War II completely escaped such charges. After all, racism was an integral and explicit force shaping international relations. The second great wave of western imperialism that extended from the mid nineteenth through mid twentieth centuries was justified by notions of Social Darwinism and the "white man's burden." During the Versailles Conference in 1919, the western allies rejected Japan's plea for a racial equality clause. Britain, France, and the Soviet Union commanded vast empires of many nationalities and races.

Certainly no country was more hypocritical than the United States in the discrepancy between the ideals for which it fought and its actual policies. While the Roosevelt administration proclaimed the ideals of the Atlantic Charter and democracy, racial discrimination permeated American culture, politics, and economy. White and black Americans served in separate and unequal units. During World War II, the White House ordered the arrest and imprisonment without trial of 110,000 Japanese residents of the United States, most of whom were American citizens.

Yet, while racism was clearly important in shaping World War II, it was a secondary factor in determining the actions of all participants except the Germans and perhaps the Japanese. Although Dower's book is well researched and written, he grossly exaggerates the impact of racism on the conduct of bilateral diplomacy or warfare.

Japanese Views of Themselves and the World

Ironically, although Dower criticizes Americans for their racist views of Japan during the war, most of these stereotyped images came from the Japanese themselves. The government's publication in 1937 of the "Cardinal Principles of the National Polity" (*Kokutai no Hongi*) elaborated the Japanese conception of themselves and their place in the world. The *Kokutai no Hongi* was required reading in all of the schools and its essence propagated through the mass media. It called upon all Japanese to purge themselves of all western influences, live austerely, and devote their lives to fighting and, if need be, dying for the emperor and Japan. In August 1941, the Ministry of Education issued the "Way of the Subject" (*Shinmin no*

Michi) which caricatured Japanese and westerners alike and commanded Japanese to continue to think, act, and look the same. No one could deviate from devoting themselves to such values as loyalty, hierarchy, collectivism, filial piety, and emperor worship, all for the glory of imperial Japan. These views were elaborated in the 1942 "Way of the Family" (*Ie no Michi*). The government issued each soldier a copy of its Field Service Code (Senjinkun) which also subscribed uniform attitudes, perceptions, and behavior. If Japanese saw themselves as "100 million hearts beating as one," why should foreigners have seen the Japanese any differently?

What was the purpose of this collective thinking and acting? In December 1942 and July 1943, the Ministry of Health and Welfare finished, respectively, "The Influence of War upon Population" and "An Investigation of Global Policy with the Yamato Race as Nucleus." These reports were the blueprints and justifications for Japan's exploitation of its conquests. The Greater East Asian Co-prosperity Sphere would "simultaneously provide a secure defense zone, a self-sufficient economic bloc, and a new living space."[18] Tokyo would be the headquarters of a vast, integrated autarchic political economic system. In this realm, Japanese and foreign nations would be one happy family under the emperor in which relations would be like "parent and child, elder and younger brother," and Japanese and foreign subjects alike would be treated with a "combination of benevolence and stern justice" (oni heiyo). Japanese would become the empire's common language and all of its subjects would bow toward and worship the emperor in Tokyo.

Japanese justified this ambition by bestowing upon themselves the title of "master race" (shido minzoku) or "divine country governed by an emperor who is a deity incarnate."[19] The "pure, unique" "Yamato race" (Yamato minzoku) was destined to rule not only over the "Greater East Asian Co-prosperity Sphere" (Daitoa Kyoeiken) but the "eight corners of the world" (hakko ichiu). Japan's "Greater East Asian Co-prosperity Sphere" allowed each race its "proper place" and "suitable work." Japan was fighting a holy war for the liberation of "Asia for Asians" from the western imperialists, particularly the "devilish Americans and English" (Kichiku Bei-Ei). Eventually Japan hoped to unite all the nations and races of the world under its leadership. All obstacles to these goals would be overcome by an outpouring of "Japanese spirit" (Yamato damashii).

Obviously it takes more than fighting spirit to win a war. The Japanese victimized themselves by their belief in their racial invincibility. Carried away by a frenzy of assumed moral and spiritual superiority, Japan failed to weigh carefully such realities as America's production which was ten times larger than Japan's, its seemingly inexhaustible riches of natural resources, its vast expanse of continental-wide territory that would be virtually impossible for foreign armies to invade let alone conquer, its population half again larger than Japan's, and America's own fighting spirit.

In the first half year after Pearl Harbor, Japan's military spirit and audacity did seem to carry all before it. But after the Battle of the Coral Sea, the Japanese military was forced onto the strategic defensive and suffered a continual chain of devastating defeats that left its once invincible fleet rusting at the bottom of the Pacific Ocean, the bodies of millions of soldiers rotting across jungle and coral islands across Asia and the Pacific, and its cities burned to the ground. Human wave "Banzai" attacks infused with Yamato damashii only made Japan's defeat easier.

Japanese imperialism, racism, and atrocities were stimulated both by traditional Japanese cultural values and victimization by western imperialism. Hierarchy, groupism, and conformity rather than equality, individualism, and liberty were the foundation of Japanese culture. Before the 1868 Meiji revolution, the social class hierarchy was fixed; afterwards individuals and groups were allowed to rise or fall in society by their own relative strengths and efforts. Japanese likewise saw international relations as the same struggle in which the strong subjected and ruled over the weak. Japan's unabashedly Social Darwinian view of international relations contrasted with the hypocritical western view which embraced at once the justness of imperialism and the theoretical concept that sovereign states enjoyed equal rights and duties.

Having been forced into the modern world at gunpoint, Japanese before 1945 can be forgiven for assuming that modernization and imperialism went hand-in-hand. Japan's successful imperialism and modernization was rewarded with the dismantlement of the unequal treaty system in the early twentieth century and designation as one of the "Big Five" nations at the Versailles peace conference in 1919. Yet genuine equality remained elusive. The western powers rejected Japan's proposal for a racial equality clause in the Versailles Treaty and the United States deepened Japan's humiliation by passing the 1924 Immigration Act which upheld previous laws preventing Asian immigration and citizenship.

American Views of Japan and Japanese Actions

Not long after Pearl Harbor, in order to understand who they were fighting and the best way of defeating that enemy, the White House began tapping into the knowledge of scholars, diplomats, and businessmen who had studied Japan.

Perhaps no American was as knowledgeable about contemporary Japan as Joseph Grew who served in Tokyo for ten years before being repatriated after the Pearl Harbor attack. As ambassador, Grew had almost continuously called for appeasing Japanese agression for fear of undermining Japan's "moderates" against the "militarists." Stateside, however, Grew described the Japanese as a "closely disciplined and conformist people – a veritable human bee-hive or ant-hill" and culturally "totalitarian." He argued that "the Japanese will not crack. Only by utter physical destruction or utter exhaustion can they be defeated."[20] Grew's prediction proved correct.

The government asked numerous scholars to analyze Japanese national character and use that understanding to undermine Japan's war efforts. These "national-character" studies attempted to identify the central values, social institutions, and behavior patterns of Japanese culture. They tried to explain such phenomena as how the Japanese could be so polite in one instant and so brutal the next, why Japanese fought so fanatically without seeming care for their own survival, and then, among those few who were captured, why four of five would betray their country by supplying their captors with information about Japanese troop deployments, supplies, and plans.

Some studies were more helpful and sophisticated than others. The crude Freudian explanations of toilet training, castration fears, Oedipal complexes, anal stage arrested development, and penis envy as the sources of Japanese aggression were not only shallow but not based on empirical evidence.[21] Much more sophisticated were studies by Margaret Mead, Clyde Kluckhorn, and Ruth Benedict.[22] Of all the wartime cultural studies, Benedict's *Chrysanthemum and the Sword* was the most influential, best written, and profound of the lot.[23]

How influential were these national-character studies on the war effort? After reviewing the literature, Dower concludes that before "Japan's surrender . . . it is difficult to point to a single area where the wartime studies brought about a major change in public opinion or government policy."[24] Readers of these studies were largely confined to the tight academic circles which produced them.

More practical if not influential were the studies of the Foreign Morale Analysis Division of the Office of War Information (OWI). Several studies concluded in late 1944 that both frontline and home-front Japanese morale was crumbling and a concerted propaganda campaign that emphasized the retention of the imperial system and punishment only for the war leaders might provoke its collapse. But no one higher up took the studies seriously let alone acted upon them. As OWI chief for Japanese studies, Alexander Leighton, later put it: "the administrator uses social science the way a drunk uses a lamppost, for support rather than illumination."[25]

Superficial as most of these studies were, they were more sophisticated than the popular American and allied view of Japanese as "ungodly, sub-human, beastly, sneaky, and treacherous."[26] Burned permanently in the minds of Americans and other foreigners were images of Japanese soldiers tossing babies into the air and impaling them on their bayonets, beheading and machine-gunning POWs, and mass-raping girls.

The feeling that Japanese were somehow inhuman was borne out in a psychological survey of American soldiers: only 5–9 per cent of those polled said they "would really like to kill a German soldier" while 38–48 per cent expressed the desire to kill Japanese soldiers.[27] In Europe, 54 per cent of combat soldiers said that seeing German POWs made them feel that "they are men like us; it's too bad we have to be fighting them," while only 18 per cent felt like killing the German POWs. Among Americans fighting the Japanese, only 20 per cent felt the Japanese were just like us while 42 per cent wanted to kill them. Despite these attitudes, the survey concluded that in fact "the men fighting the Japanese were less vindictive toward the Japanese than were either soldiers in training in the United States or soldiers fighting the Germans in Europe."[28]

Many Americans favored a Carthaginian peace for Japan and Germany alike. A December 1944 poll revealed that 13 per cent of Americans supported exterminating the Japanese as a nation, while 33 per cent favored destroying their political independence. The same poll did not ask whether Americans favored exterminating the German people, but did find that 34 per cent wanted to destroy Germany's sovereignty.[29]

American propaganda films directed by such masters as Frank Capra and Joris Ivens carefully distinguished between the evil Axis governments and their misled and captive peoples. Viewers witnessed the evil of Japanese, German, and Italian fascism through newsreels of their leaders' speeches. In their films, Capra and Ivens simply spliced together the most explicit examples of Japanese atrocities and totalitarianism.

Throughout the war, the most effective source of anti-Japanese propaganda was the Japanese themselves whose behavior continually reinforced western images. Japanese "leaders and ideologues constantly affirmed their unique 'purity' as a race and culture, and turned the war itself – and eventually mass death – into an act of individual and collective purification."[30] Confronted with a merciless enemy who fought to the death with massed Banzai and kamikaze attacks, murdered, raped, and pillaged civilians, and beheaded or worked to death POWs, western images of the Japanese as somehow subhuman were understandable.

Until the war's end, there was never a battle in which more than 5 per cent of Japanese forces surrendered; the usual figure was closer to 1 per cent.[31] Japanese resistance seemed to rage all the fiercer with each coral atoll and jungle island the Americans invaded closer to Japan. The image of Japanese fanaticism was reinforced by the waves of kamikaze pilots which began crashing into the decks of American ships during the Philippines campaign in October 1944. In the fighting for Iwo Jima in February 1945, the marines lost 6,821 men dead and 20,000 wounded; all but several hundred of the 21,000 Japanese defenders died by fighting or suicide. For the first time, the Japanese had inflicted more casualities on the Americans than they had suffered. It took nearly four months of an incessant bloodbath from April 1, 1945 until June 21 for the Americans to secure Okinawa. Over 12,000 Americans died and as many were wounded, a casualty rate of 35 per cent! Over 70,000 Japanese soldiers and 80,000 civilians died from fighting, suicide, or murdering each other in the emperor's name.

The Japanese violated virtually every international law of war. They would booby trap their own wounded and fake surrenders to lure the Americans into the open. The Japanese were far more brutal than the Germans toward POWs. Twenty-seven per cent of Anglo-American POWs died (35,756 of 132,134) in Japanese camps compared to only 4 per cent (9,348 of 235,473) in German camps.[32] While some died from disease, many others died from being overworked, bayoneted, or beheaded by their Japanese captors.

What could the Americans do in the face of such ruthless fanaticism in which the Japanese seemed to value no human life at all, including their own? Not surprisingly, faced with such fanatical and merciless foes, many American GIs eventually fought just as brutally. One correspondent who witnessed fighting in Europe and the Pacific admitted that on both fronts some Americans: "shot prisoners in cold blood, wiped out hospitals, strafed lifeboats, killed or mistreated enemy civilians, finished off the enemy wounded, tossed the dying into a hole with the dead, and in the Pacific boiled the flesh off enemy skulls to make table ornaments for sweethearts, or carved their bones into letter openers."[33]

America's commanders encouraged this behavior. Drill instructors half-humorously admonished their marine recruits that: "Every Japanese has been told it is his duty to die for the emperor. It is your duty to see that he does so." A May 1943 conference of high-level American naval commanders concluded: "All agree that the only way to beat the Japs is to kill them all. They will not surrender and our troops are taking no chances and are killing them anyway."[34]

If anything, the fighting in a future invasion of Japan would be even bloodier than previous campaigns, and planners and soldiers alike dreaded the thought of such a campaign. The invasion of Kyushu Island in Japan was scheduled for November 1945, and an attack on the main island of Honshu for March 1946. In Kyushu alone, the Japanese had concentrated fourteen Japanese divisions and five independent brigades, numbering nearly as many troops as the American invasion force. For the Kyushu campaign, 767,000 American soldiers were earmarked, of which it was estimated at least one-third or 268,000 would be either killed or maimed.[35]

Japan's vast army would be supplemented by the entire civilian population. A Japanese government order maintained that "all able-bodied Japanese, regardless of sex, should be called upon to sacrifice their lives in suicide attacks."[36] Armed with bamboo spears and swords, Japanese old men and women would rush American soldiers in mass banzai attacks or, wired with explosives, throw themselves under the treads of American tanks. Meanwhile, Japan's remaining planes were filled with bombs for waves of kamikaze attacks against the American fleet. With its forested, rugged mountainous terrain, Japan was perfect for guerrilla warfare. Even after Japan's main armies were wiped out to the last man, armed resistance could continue for years or even decades. There was no distinction between Japanese civilians and soldiers. All were willing to die for the emperor even when there was no military rationale for their sacrifice.

An invasion was essential for defeating Japan; bombing alone would not do the job. After all, Germany's cities had been systematically destroyed and yet the government had surrendered only after the allies had completely destroyed all German armies and occupied the entire country. And this was from a foe whose soldiers did surrender when there was no chance of success and whose civilians were not combatants.

Perceptions and Policy

What were the effects of these attitudes on policy?

Such stereotypes alleging Japanese near-sightedness and thus inability to fly well, and dearth of fighting, production, and innovation skills, and mental and physical weaknesses caught the Americans and British flat-footed when the war broke out. Perhaps more than any other factor, the surprise Pearl Harbor and Philippine attacks resulted from the American inability to imagine that the Japanese could plan and pull off such an audacious and brilliant attack.

After suffering a string of disastrous defeats, Americans abandoned the stereotype of the Japanese subhuman for the Japanese superhuman who could fight indefinitely and to the death on handfuls of rice and bullets in the worst jungle or desert island conditions. Despite a nearly unbroken series of American battlefield victories, this image of the Japanese as utterly ruthless and immune to emotions and physical limits persisted to the war's end. As Roosevelt recognized, the result of building up Japanese soldiers as "a sort of superman–superdevil, in ability, ferocity, and training" meant that American soldiers went "into battle with an inferiority complex."[37]

Within hours of the war declaration against Japan, the White House ordered unrestricted submarine warfare against Japanese shipping, thereby violating international law and a long-standing American policy which had led the United States into World War I. The White House justified its policy by arguing that the Germans and Japanese already conducted unrestricted submarine warfare. Unrestricted warfare was soon expanded to include air attacks. Any merchant ships at sea would be sunk by air or submarine attack at once without warning.

Although American submarines managed to sink 725,000 tons of Japanese shipping in 1942, the Japanese were able to replace it and supply lines to southeast Asia remained unimpeded. But the deployment of improved torpedos in the fall of 1942, code-breaking, and "wolf pack" tactics enabled American submarines to eventually sink about half of Japan's merchant fleet and two-thirds of its tanker fleet by 1944. Oil imports from the East Indies fell to a trickle and total imports dropped to 40 per cent. Although accounting for no more than 2 per cent of navy personnel, America's submarines accounted for 55 per cent of Japan's total shipping losses, including a battleship, eight aircraft carriers, and eleven cruisers.[38] Meanwhile, Japanese submarines were diverted from sinking allied shipping to supplying Japan's isolated island garrisons throughout the Pacific.

America's policy of unrestricted air warfare against Germany and Japan remains highly contentious. As with unrestricted submarine warfare, the White House claimed it was literally fighting fire with fire by launching massive attacks on German and Japanese cities. After all, as early as 1937 in China, Japanese had inaugurated mass air warfare against civilians.

The first detailed plan, code-named Matterhorn, to bomb Japanese cities did not appear until April 1944. Matterhorn involved mass attacks of long-range B-29 bombers from Chinese bases. The first bombing raid against Japan from Chinese bases occurred on June 14, 1944, and other raids against targets in Japan and Manchuria followed. But the scarcity of fuel in China and Japanese offensives which overran some of the bases limited the effectiveness of these raids. After seizing the Marianas, the Americans quickly built large air bases on those islands and began launching increased attacks on Japanese industrial centers. These raids were also ineffective because the bombs were dropped from 30,000 feet and were high explosive rather than incendiary.

In January 1945, General Curtis LeMay took over America's bombing campaign and switched the strategy from "precision" bombing of industrial targets to the incendiary bombing of Japanese cities. The first incendiary attack occurred against Kobe on February 4, 1945 and proved effective in reducing Japan's industrial production. The bombing assessment reported that the B-29s damaged five of the twelve targeted factories and reduced shipbuilding at the two shipyards by half.

Soon LeMay was systematically reducing Japan's cities to ashes with mass B-29 attacks. The March 8, 1945 attack on Tokyo was second only to the Dresden bombing in destructiveness and exceeded the destructiveness of either atomic bombing. Sixteen square miles of Tokyo were completely destroyed, 83,000 people killed, and one million left homeless. By the war's end, sixty-six Japanese cities suffered conventional air raids and almost 400,000 died. Firebombs composed 98,000 tons of the 153,000 total tons of bombs dropped on Japan.[39] The 393,367 Japanese who died from the bombing included 97,031 in Tokyo and 86,336 in sixty-three other Japanese cities.[40]

Perhaps the only impact of the wartime studies on policy were their virtually unanimous conclusion that any direct attack on the emperor would simply harden the Japanese will to fight to the death. Paradoxically, retaining the imperial institution would hasten rather than impede the postwar transition to democracy. But while the War Department refrained from bombing the imperial palace or ancient capital of Kyoto, the unconditional surrender policy in which Japanese would not know the emperor's fate until after they gave up made them all the more unwilling to do so.

The most egregious policy shaped by American racism was inflicted, not on the Japanese, but on American residents and citizens of Japanese ancestry. On February 19, 1942, in what was arguably the grossest miscarriage of justice in American history, the president signed Executive Order 9,066 in which 110,000 Japanese-Americans were rounded up and interned in ten camps for the war's duration. This massive civil rights violation occurred amidst the national hysteria following the attack on Pearl Harbor which many feared was the prelude to a Japanese invasion of the west coast. Racism, not reason, fueled this policy. There was no evidence of an organized sabotage campaign within the Japanese-American community. Italian- and German-American groups, including the Bund which openly supported Hitler, remained free.

Did the United States fight a "war without mercy" against Japan? No more so than it did against Germany. Americans certainly perceived the Japanese as more fanatical than the Germans. But Japanese wartime behavior was responsible for this attitude. After all, German soldiers, let alone civilians, did not fight to the death nor pilots divebomb their planes into allied ships. Only after the allies liberated the concentration camps at the war's end did they realize that Germany's government, if not population, was even more systematically genocidal than Japan's.

If America's racial animosities were as deeply ingrained as Dower maintains, then how could a war without mercy against Japan so quickly become an occupation of mercy and reform? Unfavourable American images of the Japanese, like those of the Germans, dissipated quickly after the war, raising the question of how deep-rooted they were during the fighting.

WAR DIPLOMACY

Japan's postwar fate was decided in a series of wartime conferences among the allied leaders.[41] American policy toward Japan was shaped primarily by the goal of defeating the Axis powers as quickly as possible, and secondarily by Roosevelt's vision for the postwar world. By the war's last year, conflicts with the Soviet Union stimulated a reappraisal of the future of Japan and Germany that would not be complete until Washington's containment policy emerged several years later.

Arcadia, Casablanca and Quebec

The first wartime summit between Roosevelt and Churchill occurred only a few weeks after Pearl Harbor. In late December, they met in Washington to reaffirm the previously agreed upon strategy of defeating first Germany and then Japan, and establish a Combined Chiefs of Staff of American and British officers to coordinate grand strategy. Following this "Arcadia" conference, the Americans adopted Britain's Joint Chief of Staff system. Despite the "Germany-first" strategy, Roosevelt, Churchill and their joint command continually approved American offensives in the Pacific.

A year later, Roosevelt and Churchill met at Casablanca in January 1943 to celebrate recent victories in North Africa and across the Pacific, and plot their next moves. Under pressure from Roosevelt, Churchill agreed to curtail his "soft-underbelly" of Europe strategy through the Mediterranean and accepted an Allied landing in northern France by mid-1944. He also approved planned offensives in the central and southwest Pacific. Then Roosevelt, with Churchill beside him, announced at a press conference the Allied resolve to accept nothing less than Axis forces' "unconditional surrender".

The Joint Chiefs of Staff incorporated the Pacific and Asian strategy into its "Strategic Plan for the Defeat of Japan" which was completed by spring 1943. The plan focused on liberating south China, Luzon, and Formosa and using them as springboards for the bombing, blockade, and eventual invasion of Japan.

At a meeting at Quebec in August 1943, Roosevelt and Churchill approved detailed plans for the invasion of France in 1944 and Germany's defeat in 1945. The war leaders grimly resigned themselves to a timetable in Asia and the Pacific that would take five long bloodsoaked years to vanquish Japan. In 1944, the British would battle their way through southeast Asia while the Americans continued their two-pronged offensives in the Pacific with the ultimate goal of liberating the Chinese coast from which Japan's bombing and blockade would begin. Throughout 1945 and 1946, allied forces would invade and conquer the Philippines, Taiwan, and finally the Ryukyus. Japan itself would not be invaded until 1947 with its defeat completed sometime late in 1948.

Chungking

In January 1942, the White House selected General Joseph Stillwell as the American liason general with President Chiang Kai-shek's headquarters. Stillwell would have two other duties – commander of all American forces in southeast Asia, India, and China, and administrator of lend-lease to China. Stillwell was an excellent choice. In addition to being a brilliant, tough officer, he had spent nearly a decade in China and spoke fluent Chinese.

Like most strategists, Stillwell initially believed that China, with its virtually limitless manpower and ports and airfields would be the ideal springboard for the future invasion of Japan. Conditions in China quickly disabused Stillwell of this notion shortly after he settled at Chiang's capital of Chungking. Although Chiang designated Stillwell commander of Chinese forces in Burma, he limited the American's forces and operations. Stillwell's first offensive in Burma failed and his subsequent operations scored limited successes. Stillwell's worst defeats involved his continual attempts to pressure Chiang to curb his corruption and send his armies against the Japanese: "Chiang had not the slightest intention of allowing Stillwell or any other foreigner to command his troops, upset the delicate balance of forces between the generalissimo and the war-lord generals, unleash the communists in the north, or cause him to lose face before his own people."[42]

Stillwell was not the only American commander in China. General Claire Chennault had first gone to China in 1940 to command the "Flying Tigers," the American volunteer pilots fighting the Japanese. In 1942, Chennault pushed a plan that he claimed would defeat the Japanese if he only had enough air power. Both Chiang and Roosevelt supported the plan, the former because he could keep his armies safe from combat and the latter because it was less costly than supplying Chiang's armies. Stillwell rejected Chennault's plan as naive and vainglorious, arguing that the Japanese would simply attack west and seize Chennault's airfields. Chennault received his requested bombers and fighters, and in 1943 began his offensive. As Stillwell predicted, Japanese armies soon surged westward and overran Chennault's airfields.

Cairo and Tehran

Roosevelt and Churchill met with Chiang at Cairo from November 6 to 22, 1943. Roosevelt included China among the world's "four policemen" and promised Chiang that China would recover all of Outer Mongolia and Manchuria, including Port Arthur, Dairen, and the railroad system. In addition, Roosevelt pledged to renounce extraterritoriality and repeal the Chinese Exclusion Act, which Congress did later that year.

But Roosevelt failed to fulfill one important promise to Chiang. Only 10 per cent of the aid pledged was actually shipped (only 0.5 per cent of all lend-lease aid) and a $1 billion loan was never delivered. There were good reasons not to support China. Chiang's regime was hopelessly corrupt and inefficient, squandered most of the aid it did receive, and refused to fight the Japanese, preferring to hoard its strength for the inevitable postwar battle against the communists. Half a million of Chiang's troops were deployed against communist forces in northern China rather than against the Japanese.

At Cairo, Roosevelt and Churchill also approved revised Combined Chief of Staff strategies against Germany and Japan. Ironically, while designating Chiang one of the four policemen, Roosevelt and Churchill abandoned the dream that China would get off the bench and into the field with its vast armies. Henceforth, the major allied effort would be in the Pacific. Even the British offensive in Southeast Asia was reduced to liberating Burma. Recent victories over Japanese forces allowed the planners to shorten the timetable by a year.

From Cairo, Roosevelt and Churchill flew on to Tehran to meet with Stalin from November 28 to December 1. It was at Tehran that Stalin promised to join the war against Japan after Germany's defeat, but in so doing he extracted a high price from Roosevelt. Not only did Roosevelt agree to Stalin's demand that the Americans and British open a second front in France as soon as possible, but also allowed Stalin a free hand in Poland

and the Baltic states, the shift of Poland's eastern and western borders west, a postwar Soviet "protectorate" over Mongolia, the transfer to the Soviet Union of Japan's southern half of Sakhalin and the Kurile Islands, Dairen's internationalization, Port Arthur's ninety-nine year lease to the Soviet Union, and allied and enemy war and merchant ships. And, of course, the Soviets would only attack Japan after Germany's defeat.

Roosevelt essentially acquiesced to Soviet hegemony in northeast Asia. In so doing, he violated an understanding with Chiang Kai-shek over the postwar Asian power balance. If China was to be one of the four world policemen, Stalin would be the police superintendent in northeast Asia. The president failed to understand that it was in Soviet interests to enter the war against Japan. Stalin did not demand Dairen, the Kuriles, or ships – Roosevelt volunteered them. He admitted to Stalin that his concern for Poland and the Baltic states was solely shaped by the possible effect of Polish- and Baltic-American voters in the 1944 election. Roosevelt agreed to move Poland's eastern and western borders west and allow Moscow to incorporate the three Baltic states – Estonia, Latvia, and Lithuania – into the Soviet Union. And in return for all of this, Roosevelt asked for nothing else but Stalin's promise to attack Japan. As part of his "charm" offensive to extract the "concession," Roosevelt tried calling Stalin "Uncle Joe." Stalin was not amused let alone charmed by the nickname.

Chungking and Yenan

While the White House by 1943 had accepted the unlikelihood that Chiang would ever mount a vigorous and sustained campaign against the Japanese, China was still considered essential to the war effort. Not only did China absorb over 2 million Japanese soldiers and the supplies to sustain them, it, along with India, served as symbols of a pro-western Asia. Roosevelt faced two problems with his Chinese ally – relations between Stillwell and Chiang, and between the KMT and CCP. Neither was successfully resolved.

In early 1944, Roosevelt dispatched Major-General Patrick Hurley to China to help adjust relations between Chiang and Stillwell. Hurley assured Roosevelt that the problem's essence was personality. In October 1944, Roosevelt recalled Stillwell and replaced him with Major-General Albert C. Wedemeyer. Stillwell was recalled just when his two year's efforts in Burma began to pay off. Throughout 1942, a scant 3,700 tons of supplies reached China; when he left 30,000 tons of supplies poured into Chungking each month.[43] Wedemeyer built upon Stillwell's successes and encountered the same frustrations.

The KMT and CCP had not cooperated since Chiang's army attacked and defeated the communist New Fourth Army in 1941. Fighting had sporadically continued between them ever since. But while the battle-lines stagnated between the rival Chinese armies, the CCP steadily infiltrated and captured large areas of Japanese territory. By late 1944, the CCP controlled most of four northern provinces.

In April 1944, Vice-President Henry Wallace traveled to Chungking to urge Chiang to forge an alliance with the CCP against the Japanese and allow the United States to send a military mission to Yenan. Chiang grudgingly agreed. In July 1944, Colonel David Barrett led the "Dixie mission" (so-called because it went to the other side of a civil war) of military and foreign service officers to Yenan. The Americans and communists hit it off, with the former impressed by the latter's efficiency, austerity, friendliness, and, most importantly, willingness and ability to fight. The Americans filtered limited supplies to the communists. But these budding ties were clipped when anticommunist Hurley replaced Clarence Gauss as ambassador to Chiang, and he helped squash America's growing ties with the CCP.

The brief flowering of US–CCP relations raises a set of intriguing and unanswerable questions. How different would history have been if the Americans had expanded rather than severed their ties with the Red Chinese? The friendship opportunity with Mao was similar to that with Ho Chi Minh in Vietnam. Could a concerted effort to forge relations with either have made them the Titos of Asia? Would then the tragedies of the Korean and Vietnam wars have been averted?[44]

Yalta

The Yalta summit of Roosevelt, Churchill, and Stalin lasted from February 4 to 11, 1945. Some historians have harshly criticized Roosevelt's diplomacy at this conference. In return for Stalin's agreement to support the United Nations and enter the war against Japan within three months of Germany's defeat, Roosevelt accepted the communist dominated Lublin government of Poland, and promised Stalin the Soviet–Chinese management of the Manchurian railroad system and other special rights, and, from Japan, southern Sakhalin and the Kurile Islands. Critics accuse Roosevelt of giving away eastern Europe and inviting Soviet hegemony in northeast Asia in return for simply nailing down a firm commitment to attack Japan within three months of Germany's surrender, something Stalin would have done anyway to enlarge the Soviet empire in the Far East.

Other historians are more charitable to Roosevelt. After all, a 3-million strong Soviet Red Army had conquered almost all east Europe and now sat in central Germany. The Soviet Union's 290 divisions dwarfed the ninety of the United States and Britain. What else could Roosevelt have done? Communists would have taken over Poland just as they eventually did every east European country even if Stalin had agreed to include in the Lublin government more Polish exiles. Roosevelt, like Churchill, was simply accepting the brutal realities of the postwar power balance.

The United Nations, not Poland, was Roosevelt's obsession. Roosevelt assumed he got a good deal when he received Stalin's nod for the American Dumbarton Oaks plan and headquarters in New York. In addition, Washington solidly believed that a Soviet promise to attack Japan within three months of Germany's defeat was essential to the war effort. A Soviet attack would tie down millions of troops that might be diverted for Japan's defense.

The Atomic Bomb

By the Yalta conference, the United States had committed three years, billions of dollars, and hundreds of thousands of skilled personnel to building an atomic bomb. Yet no one knew whether an atomic bomb would work, let alone how effective it would be. Hence Roosevelt's war diplomacy and strategy had to be planned and conducted as if the atomic project did not exist.

The American idea of creating an atomic bomb dates back to October 1939 when two physicists and Hungarian refugees, Leo Szilard and Otto Hahn, convinced Albert Einstein to sign a joint letter to President Roosevelt warning of a possible German attempt to devise such a bomb. Roosevelt responded by creating the Uranium Committee to study the feasibility of such a project. In July 1941, the committee warned that the Germans had a two year head start on atomic research. Roosevelt supported a greater American effort. On October 9, 1941, Roosevelt, Stimson, and other advisors first met to organize the atomic bomb project.

It was not until August 1942, however, that the War Department actually began work on the bomb. Directed by General Leslie Groves and codenamed the Manhattan Project, America's atomic effort cost $2 billion and employed 150,000 people at plants and laboratories at Hanford, Washington, the University of Chicago, Oak Ridge, Tennessee, and Los Alamos in New Mexico. War Secretary Stimson helped shape all of the Manhattan Project's major decisions and from May 1, 1943 directly advised the president on atomic policy.

President Roosevelt died on April 12, 1945. Harry Truman was quickly sworn in as president. On April 25, Stimson and Groves met with Truman and extensively briefed him on the bomb project, including not just its ability to end the war with Japan but the probability that other nations would eventually master the technology. Astonished at the project's scale and potential, Truman enthusiastically supported it.

Around the same time as Truman's endorsement, some scientists began reconsidering whether the bomb should be used at all. Ironically, Szilard, the man most responsible for the Manhattan Project's origins, now led the opposition to the bomb's use. In April 1945, Szilard sent Roosevelt a memorandum that argued the bomb's explosion could provoke an arms race with the Soviet Union and war that could destroy civilization. But Roosevelt died before the memorandum reached him. Szilard then tried to contact Truman but was referred to Secretary of State designate James Byrnes. Byrnes rejected Szilard's arguments, asserting that the bomb was vital to forcing Japan's surrender and forestalling Soviet expansion in the Far East. Szilard continued his efforts of pressuring those involved in the decision to give a full warning and demonstration to Japan before dropping the bomb. Other scientists also expressed their misgivings. In April 1945, James Franck and Arthur Compton presented a memorandum to Commerce Secretary Henry Wallace which outlined the atomic bomb's dangers to civilization and advocated strict controls on its use.

Meanwhile, acting on Stimson's advise, Truman appointed a civilian advisory group called the Interim Committee, composed of Stimson, Secretary of State Byrnes, Under Secretary of the Navy Ralph Bard, Assistant Secretary of State William Clayton, MIT President and Chief of the government Office of Science Research and Technology Dr Karl Compton, Chairman of the National Defense Research Committee and Harvard President James Conant. Between May 9 and May 31, the Interim Committee conducted wide-ranging discussions on the bomb's political, military, and scientific ramifications, including possible postwar domestic and international controls. Most of the debate centered on the bomb's wartime use, and soon swirled around two questions: (1) where should the bomb be dropped, and (2) should there be prior warning? The Committee did not address the question of whether the bomb should be exploded.

On June 1, the Interim Committee submitted its unanimous conclusion that the bomb should be dropped on a "dual target" – a military base or industrial complex near a civilian population – as soon as possible without prior warning. Bard later dissociated himself from the report and urged a prior warning. In reaching these conclusions, the Committee discussed and discarded the idea of demonstrating the bomb in an uninhabited area as impractical at best, and a potential disaster if the bomb proved to be a dud.

And with just two operational bombs, neither could be squandered on a demonstration that the Japanese might disregard.

Although the June 1 Interim Commission decision became the policy for the bomb's use, the controversy in scientific circles continued. In April, a group of University of Chicago scientists had formed the Committee on the Social and Political Implications of Atomic Energy with James Franck as chairman. On June 12, the committee submitted its Franck Report to Stimson, who then forwarded it to the Interim Committee's Scientific Advisory Panel. The report called for demonstrating the bomb on an uninhabited island before international observers. If Tokyo still refused to surrender, only then should the bomb be dropped on Japan. It also warned of an arms race with the Soviets and called for strict controls on its possession and use.

Four days later, the Scientific Advisory Panel concluded that, after reviewing diverse suggestions for the bomb, "we can propose no technical demonstration likely to bring an end to the war; we see no acceptable alternative to direct military use."[45] Stimson summed up the government's perspective: "to extract a genuine surrender from the Emperor and his military advisors, they must be administered a tremendous shock which would carry convincing proof of our power to destroy the Empire. Such an effective shock would save many times the number of lives, both American and Japanese, that it would cost."[46]

Meanwhile, concerned with the increasingly vocal opposition to the existing policy, Groves conducted a poll of all top scientists at Chicago and Los Alamos. Only 15 per cent wanted the bomb used "in the manner that is from the military point of view most effective in bringing about prompt Japanese surrender"; 46 per cent favored "a military demonstration in Japan to be followed by a renewed opportunity for surrender before full use of the weapon;" 26 per cent called for an experimental demonstration preceding military use; and 13 per cent rejected any military use.[47] Groves interpreted these results as support for the bomb's prompt use.

These last-minute second thoughts challenged long-standing conclusions. As early as April 1944, a committee of air force officers and scientists explored ways in which the bomb could be used. In June 1944 they concluded that there was "no technical demonstration of the bomb likely to bring an end to the war . . . no acceptable alternative to direct military use."[48] Planning for possible bomb targets did not begin until spring 1945 when American B-29s had already devastated over sixty Japanese cities. The only prominent city yet untouched was Kyoto, spared because of its cultural importance and lack of military targets. The air force advocated dropping the first atomic bomb on the old imperial capital. Stimson protested, arguing that destroying Japan's holy city might stiffen rather than collapse the enemy's will to fight to the last. Tokyo was scratched because of the need to retain a government that could surrender. Truman wrote in his diary that "even if the Japs are savages, ruthless, merciless and fanatic, we as the leaders of the world for the common welfare cannot drop this terrible bomb on the old and new capitals."[49]

By mid-summer 1945, America's atomic bomb policy was determined. All that remained was the successful testing of an atomic bomb.

Japan's Peace Efforts

Some Japanese civilian leaders had recognized as early as the summer of 1944 that a Japanese victory was impossible and it might be better to negotiate the best deal possible with the Allies. Such ranking officials as former foreign minister Togo Shigenori, diplomat Yoshida Shigeru, and imperial advisors Konoye Fumimaro, Okada Kasuke, and Kido Koichi realized that the longer a surrender was delayed, the harsher the peace would be. By early 1945, Emperor Hirohito began conferring with these "jushin" or very important subjects in his Privy Council.[50]

But this "peace faction" had no power in Japan in a political system which was perhaps only exceeded by the Soviet Union in its totalitarianism. Whatever sentiments might be whispered among trusted allies behind closed doors, the government allowed no public dissent or even doubts from the official dogma that Japan would soon win an overwhelming victory against the western barbarians. Anyone who said otherwise would be quickly executed.

Following the American victory in the Marianas Islands in July 1944, Tojo resigned and was replaced as prime minister by General Koiso Kuniaki. While Koiso had misgivings about the war, he carried it on. Koiso agreed to put out peace feelers through Japanese embassies in Moscow and Stockholm, and the Russian embassy in Tokyo. Unfortunately, the Soviets snubbed the Japanese request.

Despite these reverses, the Japanese faith in somehow achieving Soviet mediation continued. Logically, this faith should have been destroyed in early April when Moscow informed Tokyo that it was withdrawing from the bilateral non-aggression pact. Although Koiso resigned on April 5, 1945 after Moscow's announcement and the American invasion of Okinawa, inexplicably Tokyo still clung to a Soviet mediated peace.

Koiso's successor, Admiral Suzuki Kantaro, who took office on April 7, also had mixed feelings about Japan's prospects, as did his foreign minister Togo Shigenori. But the military chiefs only accepted Suzuki and

Togo's appointment if they promised to fight to the death. Suzuki and Togo complied, issuing public statements as warlike as those of any Japanese leader. Germany's surrender on May 7 only quickened the urgency among the peace faction to end the war, yet they remained impotent. Instead, on June 8, the Supreme Council resolved to "prosecute the war to the bitter end."[51] Suzuki responded to Okinawa's fall with a public broadcast describing the event as "an improvement in Japan's strategic position" and a "spiritual blow to America;" he ended by fiercely denouncing "peace agitators."

Marquis Kido convinced Emperor Hirohito to intervene. On June 22, for the first time during the war, the emperor called for an Imperial Conference. During the meeting, Hirohito asked the Supreme Council to negotiate the war's end, stating that "it was necessary to have a plan to close the war at once as well as a plan to defend the home islands." This was the first explicit imperial statement in favor of a negotiated peace. The conference agreed and efforts were resumed to induce the Soviets to act as mediators. However, it was not until July 12, nearly three weeks later, that Foreign Minister Togo actually instructed Ambassador Sato in Moscow to approach the Soviets about mediation. Stalin rejected the proposal.

The Fate of the Emperor and Japan

The same sensitivity over sparing Japan's ancient capital of Kyoto from destruction eventually also saved Emperor Hirohito. As early as autumn 1943, the State Department had recommended retaining the emperor as a constitutional monarch presiding over a postwar democratic Japan. Subsequent committees agreed that the emperor should be preserved to aid the transition to democracy. Historically, the emperor had always been a political football in Japan's periodic power struggles. The emperor was the ultimate source of political legitimacy and the Americans wanted his blessing for the postwar occupation and reforms. Throughout the war, American propaganda avoided criticizing the emperor and concentrated on denouncing the war clique within Japan's government. B-29s avoided bombing the imperial palace in Tokyo or the ancient capital of Kyoto.

The White House policy of preserving the emperor ran counter to sentiments of America's public and allies. A June 1945 Gallup poll revealed that 33 per cent of Americans wanted Japan's emperor executed as a war criminal, 11 per cent wanted him imprisoned, 9 per cent wanted him exiled, and only 7 per cent wanted him to retain his throne.[52] America's allies, too, favored executing Hirohito. Fearing to offend its allies and the American public, both the Roosevelt and Truman administrations kept secret their decision to retain the emperor.

On May 26, 1945, former ambassador Grew called on Truman to beg him to announce publicly that Hirohito could retain his throne after Japan's surrender. Truman deferred a decision until after Grew had spoken with his key advisors. Grew then spoke with Marshall, Stimson, and Forrestal. Although they were all sympathetic, they feared that Tokyo would interpret a public announcement as a sign of weakness while the United States was bogged down in the bloody Okinawan campaign. On June 18, after the Okinawan campaign had been won, Grew once again implored the president to issue a public statement concerning the emperor. Truman replied that it was inappropriate for him unilaterally to make such a momentous decision, and he would settle the matter with the other Allied leaders at the Potsdam conference a month later.

By reading the MAGIC intercepts, the White House knew of Japan's peace efforts in Moscow. The details of these meetings were revealed when Harry Hopkins met with Stalin on May 27. Hopkins cabled Truman that some Japanese leaders knew their cause was doomed and thus were putting out peace probes. However, weighing the peace feelers against the stream of Japanese government invectives about fighting to the end, the White House chose the latter as more representative of Tokyo's position. The administration feared that any American peace proposals would only encourage the Japanese to fight harder.

Meanwhile, Truman established a committee composed of War Secretary Stimson, Navy Secretary James Forrestal, and Under-secretary of State Joseph Grew, to study ways to induce Japan's surrender. The committee concluded on June 29 that it signal to Tokyo that in return for the complete surrender of Japanese forces and an allied occupation, a reformed Japan "may include a constitutional monarchy under the present dynasty if it be shown to complete satisfaction of the world that such a government shall never again aspire to aggression."[53] This policy led to the Potsdam Declaration.

On July 2, 1945, Stimson presented Truman with a memorandum reviewing the enormous cost in lives and capital that Japan's invasion would cause. He then argued that "Japan is susceptible to reason . . . [and] is not composed wholly of mad fanatics. . . . I think the Japanese nation has the mental intelligence and versatile capacity in such a crisis to recognize the folly of a fight to the finish and to accept the proffer of what will amount to an unconditional surrender."[54] He concluded with a detailed list of terms for what became the Potsdam Declaration for Japan's surrender. Nowhere in the memorandum does Stimson refer to the atomic bomb or Soviet expansion in Northeast Asia. He focuses his arguments on the possibility of averting a costly invasion with a carefully worded call for Japan's surrender, and

Japan's eventual "reconstruction as a responsible member of the family of nations."

Potsdam

The United States and some Japanese leaders wanted a peace without any more fighting. Both hesitated to explicitly state their desire for fear of sounding weak. Yet, even when the United States, Britain, and China issued the Potsdam Declaration calling for Japan's surrender, Tokyo chose to reject publicly the message and vowed to fight to the end.

The Potsdam summit of Truman, Churchill (who was replaced by the new prime minister Clement Attlee), Stalin, and Chiang met between July 17 and August 2 to discuss the war against Japan and the postwar world. The previous day on July 16, 1945, the world's first atomic device was successfully detonated at Alamogordo, New Mexico. Receiving the news of the successful test at Potsdam, Truman was jubilant. As Byrnes noted, "the bomb had met our highest hopes and . . . the shock of its use would very likely knock our already wavering enemy out of the war."[55] With the atomic bomb, the Americans no longer needed Soviet help in the war against Japan.

Shortly after Truman received the atomic bomb news, Stalin informed him that Soviet forces would attack the Japanese army in northeast Asia around the middle of August. The only obstacle to Soviet intervention was the negotiation of a treaty with China which incorporated the promises Roosevelt made at Yalta for Soviet acquisition of Chinese concessions in Manchuria, Mongolia and elsewhere. China's foreign minister, T. Y. Soong had arrived in Moscow on June 30 and negotiations were continuing. Stalin also presented Truman with the latest Japanese requests for mediation, but added that "it might be desirable to lull the Japanese to sleep . . . with an unspecific answer."[56] Truman concurred. After all, he and the other Allied leaders would soon issue the Potsdam Declaration.

If Truman really wanted to use the bomb to limit Soviet advances in northeast Asia, this would have been time to tell Stalin that with the atomic bomb Soviet forces were no longer needed to induce Japan's surrender. Yet Truman would not inform Stalin of the atomic bomb for another eight days until after the operational bombs were ready for use. And even then he did not discourage Stalin's commitment to enter the war. The reason, of course, was that the bombs might not work technically or politically and the Soviet entrance into the war would still be necessary.

On July 22, Truman received word that operational atomic bombs were ready to be sent to the Pacific theater. Two days later, on July 24, Truman signed a directive ordering the atomic bombs to be used against Japan. The following day General Carl Spaatz, Commanding General of the U.S.

Strategic Air Force, ordered the 509th Composite Group to "deliver its special bomb as soon as weather will permit visual bombing after 3 August, 1945," and other bombs dropped as soon as they were ready.

The same day that Truman ordered the bombs to be used, he casually informed Stalin that the United States had developed "a new weapon of unusual destructive force." Stalin nodded; his spies had already told him of American progress on the bomb and Truman's annoucement was no surprise.

On July 26, Truman, Attlee, and Chiang issued the Potsdam Declaration, which included the following: (1) Japanese militarism would be "eliminated for all time;" (2) "a new order of peace, security, and justice" would be established during an Allied occupation; (3) the Cairo Declaration would be enforced which stated that Japan would be stripped of all its conquests since Commodore Perry opened Japan in 1853; (4) Japan's military would be dissolved and its soldiers sent home; (5) freedom of speech, religion, thought, and other fundamental rights would be ensured for the Japanese people, but war criminals would be prosecuted; (6) war industries would be dismantled but Japan would be allowed to retain other industries and participate in international trade; (7) occupation forces would be withdrawn when Japan established a responsible and peaceful government; (8) the Japanese government should proclaim the unconditional surrender of all Japanese armed forces.

The Declaration's final wording was a compromise between the committee draft and public and allied opinion. It followed the committee draft in most respects but changed the explicit promise of a constitutional monachy if the Japanese sincerely renounced aggression for the vaguer promise that the allies would help establish "in accordance with the freely expressed will of the Japanese people, of a peacefully inclined and responsible government."[57] The Truman administration hoped that the Japanese government would read between the lines and realize that acceptance of the "freely expressed will of the Japanese people" committed the victors to allowing the emperor's retention if the people wanted it. Although the atomic bomb was not mentioned, the Allies clearly stated that "the full application of our military power, backed by our resolve, will mean the inevitable and complete destruction of the Japanese armed forces and just as inevitably the utter devastation of the Japanese homeland."

Mokusatsu

Against both Germany and Japan, the Allied policy of accepting nothing less than their enemy's unconditional surrender complicated their ability to negotiate the war's end. Every Allied war conference from the war's beginning concluded that Japanese and German imperialism must be crushed for all time. The assumption was that any peace agreement which allowed the Nazi or Japanese totalitarian governments to remain in power would not have lasted. The Allied conversion of both Japanese and German total-itarianism into liberal democracy is perhaps the best justification for the un-conditional surrender decree. The trouble with this policy was that German and Japanese leaders, facing the probability of being executed, resolved to fight to the death rather than surrender to a noose.

Despite the official unconditional surrender policy, the Potsdam Declara-tion itself was quite conditional. The Allies promised the Japanese demo-cracy, industry, demilitarization, and peace. Some terms, however, were ambivalent. Both human rights and democracy were promised. What if the Japanese people chose a dictatorship again? While war criminals would be prosecuted, the Japanese could choose their own government. What if Hirohito were placed on trial and the Japanese people wanted to retain him as emperor?

Japan's government was understandably confused about these ambiguit-ies and interpreted them in the worst way. When asked at a press confer-ence on July 28, Suzuki publicly declared that he would treat the Potsdam Declaration with "silent contempt" (mokusatsu).

The Atomic Bombings and Surrender

Understandably, the allies intepreted Suzuki's remarks as a rejection of negotiations and his intention to fight the war to the end. With Tokyo's rejection of the Potsdam call for surrender, the White House gave the green light to the atomic bombing of Japan. Stimson had narrowed the list of cities to four, including Hiroshima and Nagasaki. General LeMay then chose to have the bombs dropped on Hiroshima and Nagasaki. In addition to heavy industries and military bases, Hiroshima was the army headquarters for forces defending southern Japan; Nagasaki was a major seaport and indus-trial city.

On August 6, 1945, the "Enola Gay" and two escort B-29s packed with scientific equipment of the 509th Composite Group flew over Hiroshima. At 9.15 a.m. at an altitude of 31,600 feet, Colonel Paul Tibbets ordered the Enola Gay's bomb bay opened and "Little Boy" released. Forty-two seconds later most of Hiroshima disappeared in a titanic whirlwind of blast, heat, and radiation. The initial Japanese casualty count was 71,379 dead, 19,691 wounded, and 171,000 homeless. The government published a revised account on July 31, 1959 which stated that 60,175 people were killed.[58]

Receiving word of the successful blast, Truman remarked: "This is the greatest thing in history." The White House announced Hiroshima's destruction several hours later and warned that unless the Japanese surrendered they "may expect a rain of ruin from the air, the like of which has never been seen on this earth."[59]

Two days later on August 8, the Soviets declared war on Japan and shortly thereafter launched a massive offensive in Manchuria and Mongolia that quickly broke through and routed Japanese forces. On August 9 at 11.01, the atomic bomb ("Fat Man") was dropped on Nagasaki, killing instantly nearly 40,000 people.

Despite these three devastating blows to their empire, Tokyo gave no sign of surrender. Initial reports of the Hiroshima blast downplayed its destruction and experts even claimed to have recovered a bomb fragment that proved the bomb was made in Germany. Indeed, the Supreme Council did not meet until three days after Hiroshima's destruction. Togo urged that Japan accept the Potsdam Declaration. War Minister Anami, Army Chief of Staff Umezu, and Navy Chief of Staff Toyoda agreed to surrender only under three conditions: (1) Japan would disarm its own troops; (2) war criminals would be tried in Japanese courts; (3) Japan's foreign military occupation would be limited. Togo warned that the Allies would reject these conditions and urged the militarists to accept the Potsdam Declaration. Amidst this debate news arrived of Nagasaki's destruction. Yet the deadlock continued until the meeting broke up at 2.30 a.m.

Suzuki and Togo then went before the emperor and requested that he convene an Imperial Conference. That night Hirohito appeared before them to listen to their debate. The peace and war factions repeated their positions. Suzuki then made the unprecedented request that the emperor resolve their deadlock. The emperor rose and declared the need to end the fighting if the imperial institution could be preserved. He then left the room. Suzuki then stated that "His emperor's decision should be made the decision of this conference as well." It was 2.30 in the morning of August 10. A cabinet meeting was convened a half hour later to unanimously accept the decision.

At 7.00 a.m. on August 10, Tokyo sent a message to the United States, Britain, China, and the Soviet Union announcing that it would accept the Potsdam Declaration as long as "it does not compromise any demand which prejudices the prerogatives of His Majesty as a Sovereign Ruler."[60] Later that morning the cabinet debated whether or not to tell the Japanese people. Fearing a military coup, they decided not to issue a public statement until after an imperial rescript had been declared. General Anami gathered all officers in Tokyo of lieutenant colonel rank and above to explain the decision and appeal for acceptance. Admiral Yonai issued the same explanation to navy officers of the same rank.

Truman gathered Stimson, Byrnes, Forrestal, Leahy, and other top advisors at the White House to debate America's response to Japan's offer to surrender if the emperor were retained. Public opinion favored the harshest terms for the Japanese and even the emperor's execution as a war criminal. There were fears that agreeing to the emperor's retention might actually encourage the Japanese to continue fighting. Ever the pragmatist, Stimson argued that only the emperor had the authority to ensure Japan's surrender, retaining him "would save us a score of bloody Iwo Jimas and Okinawas."[61] Stimson then added that the longer a surrender was delayed the greater the Soviet influence in postwar Asia.

Truman agreed and asked Byrnes to draft a compromise message including the following: (1) from the moment of surrender the emperor and government would be subject to a Supreme Commander for the Allied Powers who will institute the surrender terms; (2) the emperor will order his government and military to sign the surrender and all troops to lay down their arms; (3) upon surrender Japan's government will transport all POWs and civilian internees to safety where they can be repatriated; (4) Japan's ultimate government will be decided by Japan's people; (5) occupation forces will remain in Japan until the surrender's terms are achieved. Byrnes did so and, after receiving British, Chinese, and Soviet approval of the note, dispatched it to Japan's Swiss embassy. Meanwhile, Truman ordered the conventional bombing of Japan's cities and industrial areas resumed.

After receiving the American offer, Japan's leaders debated it for the next three days, with the military determined to reject Washington's terms and the civilians resigned to accept it. Suzuki morosely sat on the fence. On August 13, Japan's Swiss embassy passed on word from the White House that it had resisted pressure from China and the Soviet Union to remove the emperor. Although the message should have cleared up the ambivalance concerning the emperor's fate, the deadlock continued. That night seven B-29s dropped the most explosive payload ever on Tokyo – five million leaflets with the text of Japan's surrender proposal and America's reply. Then the next day on August 14, 828 B-29s and 186 fighters pounded Tokyo with thousands of tons of explosives and incendiaries.

Inured to months of bombing, it was the leaflets that moved Marquis Kido to action. Terrified that news of the negotiation could spark a military coup, Kido met with Hirohito at 8.30 that morning and urged him to convene an Imperial Conference to resolve the impasse. Suzuki then joined them and echoed Kido's plea.

The Imperial Conference began at 11.00 that morning. The factions repeated their arguments. After hearing them out, Hirohito requested that they "bow to my wishes and accept the Allied reply forthwith. In order that the people may know of my decision, I request you to prepare at once an imperial rescript that I may broadcast to the nation."[62] Only the emperor's direct decision could relieve his military commanders of much of the surrender's shame and humiliation.

By appealing directly to his subjects, the emperor and his advisors hoped to forestall a military coup. At 2.49 that afternoon, Tokyo broadcast its acceptance of the Potsdam Declaration to the Allied capitals. The emperor signed an imperial rescript at 10.50 that night. Ten minutes later the official decision was communicated to the Allies. The emperor then issued two imperial rescripts to the military ordering them to ground arms. Finally he recorded an announcement of Japan's surrender that would be broadcast to the nation the next morning.

As expected, some military leaders continued to resist surrender. That night of August 14, army officers appeared before Lieutenant-General Mori Takeshi, commander of the Imperial Guards Division in Tokyo, and ordered him to disobey the surrender order. When he refused they murdered him and then used his seal to stamp orders to confiscate the recording of Hirohito's surrender. After hearing of Mori's murder and the attempted coup, General Tanaka of the Eastern District Area Army assumed command of the Imperial Guards and used them to round up the coup leaders. By 8.00 in the morning of August 15 the coup had been squashed. Yet some resistance continued. During the day unsuccessful attempts were made to assassinate Suzuki, Kido, and Hiranama. Although he took no part in the coup, War Minister Anami committed suicide to avoid hearing the emperor's surrender. The four coup leaders also killed themselves, followed by General Tanaka, who had aborted the coup. Dozens of other officers also killed themselves with revolvers or swords.

Throughout the morning of August 15, the radio had announced that an important broadcast would be made at noon. Promptly at noon, Emperor Hirohito's reedy voice appeared and in courtly Japanese announced, in one of the great understatements of history, that "the war had not gone exactly according to our wishes." He never mentioned the word surrender.

Truman received word of Japan's surrender at 3.50 in the afternoon of August 14 and announced a two-day celebration. Byrnes meanwhile cabled back to the Japanese an order for them to immediately lay down their arms, which was received in Tokyo at 4.00 on August 16. The White House ordered all American forces to ground arms. On September 2, 1945, Japanese and American representatives signed a surrender document aboard the U.S.S. "Missouri" anchored in Tokyo Bay. It was only then that Emperor Hirohito formally announced Japan's surrender to the nation.

THE BOMB CONTROVERSY

The controversy over the bomb's use revolves around whether Japan would have soon surrendered anyway, and thus whether the second or even the first bomb was necessary. Some argue that negotiations rather than atomic bombs could have ended the war. Baldwin states that "it is quite possible that the atomic bombs shortened the war by a day, a week, or a month or two – not more. . . . By using the bomb we have become identified . . . as inheritors of the mantle of Genghis Khan and all those of past history who have justified the use of utter ruthlessness in war. . . . Its use may have hastened victory . . . but cost us in peace the preeminent moral position we once occupied."[63] Most historians, however, argue that without the atomic bombings, the Japanese would have surrendered only after a massive invasion in which hundreds of thousands of Americans and millions of Japanese would have died. Whose interpretation is correct?

Surrender Politics?

Discussions about the politics behind Japan's surrender usually explicitly or implicitly blame the United States for not trying harder before incinerating Hiroshima and Nagasaki. Revisionists argue that Japan's surrender was imminent and could have been induced without atomic bombs. By early August Japan was already defeated and its surrender was a matter of time, if only the Americans had stated that the emperor would be retained.[64]

Most of the revisionist arguments are heavy in polemic and weak in fact and logic. Their assertions fail to understand the dynamics of Japan's government. When asked by MacArthur why he did not end the war earlier, Hirohito pretended to cut his throat. Leaders like Konoye, Suzuki, and Togo favored a negotiated peace. But these desires, like the emperor's, had to remain buried behind frenzied cries that victory was just around the corner.

Peace negotiations did not seriously begin until after the atomic bombs were dropped because there was no previous opportunity to do so. The White House did not ignore the succession of Japanese peace feelers to the Soviets between February and July 1945; the Potsdam Declaration was a direct answer to them. True, the Potsdam Declaration was ambiguous over the emperor's fate. But Japan's government remained split even after the White House clarified that the emperor would be retained. Japan's military leaders continued to reject the Potsdam Declaration and instead maintained that Japanese forces would disarm themselves, Japanese courts would prosecute war criminals, and a foreign occupation would be limited.

As both Germany and Japan demonstrated, there can be a huge difference between being defeated and admitting defeat. The German government fought on for several days even after Hitler committed suicide in his bunker and Allied troops had overrun nearly the entire country. There was no reason to believe that Japan would not fulfill its pledge to fight to the last devoted subject.

Although they favored the war's end, the emperor and civilian leaders had been unable even to discuss surrender openly. The atomic bombs made Japan's surrender possible, giving those who wanted to give up the excuse to do so. Still, it took eight days of constant and acrimonious debate before the emperor finally forced the government to accept surrender. Without the shock of the bombs, Japan's peace faction could never have gotten the emperor to break the impasse with the military.

Even then, Japan's surrender was not certain. As Morrison reminds us, "even after two atomic bombs had been dropped, the Potsdam Declaration clarified, the guards' insurrection defeated, and the Emperor's will made known, it was still touch and go whether the Japanese actually would surrender."[65] A military coup could have deposed the civilian leaders and forced the emperor to lead Japan to total destruction. Japan's kamikaze pilots at Atsugi air base boasted of crashing into the U.S.S. "Missouri" when it sailed into Tokyo Bay. It took the appearance of Hirohito's younger brother, Prince Takamatsu, to restrain them.

Conventional Bombs Alone?

The seemingly strongest revisionist arguments come from some American commanders, including Secretary of the Navy Forrestal, Undersecretary of the Navy Bard, Admiral Leahy, Admiral King, who maintained that Japan could have been defeated without an invasion through a tightened blockade and B-29s. After the war, the Strategic Bombing Survey declared that "interrogation of the highest Japanese officials . . . indicated that Japan would have surrendered . . . even . . . if the atomic bombs had not been dropped. . . . [C]ertainly prior to 31 December 1945, and in all probability prior to 1 November 1945, Japan would have surrendered even if the atomic bombs had not been dropped, even if Russia had not entered the war, and even if no invasion had been planned or contemplated."[66] In a talk before the National Geographic Society on January 25, 1946, Admiral Nimitz also argued that Japan could have been defeated by conventional means alone, concluding that the "atomic bomb merely hastened a process already reaching an inevitable conclusion."[67] Eisenhower later wrote that he informed Stimson at Potsdam of his belief that "Japan was already defeated and dropping the bomb was completely unecessary. . . . I thought our country should avoid shocking world opinion by the use of a weapon that was no longer mandatory as a measure to save American lives. . . . Japan was . . . seeking some way to surrender with a minimum loss of face."[68] Alfred McCormack, Director of Military Intelligence for the Pacific Theater of War, argued that even conventional bombing was unnecessary in August 1945; the continued naval blockade would have brought Japan to its knees through starvation.[69]

There is no evidence that Japan could have been starved and bombed into submission. If Hiroshima and Nagasaki had been reduced to ashes by "conventional" incendiary bombs like sixty-three other Japanese cities, would Japan's government have been any more willing to wave the white flag? Once again, Japan's peace faction needed a shock to allow them to bring the emperor before the Supreme Council and break the deadlock. And even in the unlikely event that Japan would have given up from conventional bombing alone, many times more Japanese would have died before they did so.

Saving Lives?

The atomic bombs were dropped to spare hundreds of thousands of Allied and millions of Japanese lives. In his June 19 diary entry, Stimson wrote that the "last chance warning . . . must be given before an actual landing of the ground forces in Japan and fortunately the plans provide for enough time to bring in the sanctions to our warning in the shape of ordinary bombing attack and S-1 (the atomic bomb)."[70] Stimson did not expect that the Potsdam warning of complete destruction alone would bring Japan's surrender. Conventional and atomic bombing might bring Japan's government to the peace table if they were convinced that the United States could simply destroy Japan without an invasion. Like everyone else in the project, Stimson could have had no idea until the atomic bomb's successful test whether it would even work, let alone its ability to win the war. He is still equating the atomic bomb with lots of conventional bombs and assumes that without a pointed surrender demand an invasion will still be necessary.

An invasion would be a bloodbath for the Americans and Japanese alike. Army intelligence estimated that a massive invasion of the Japanese islands would not have forced a surrender before late 1946 at the earliest, and even then would have cost an additional one million American casualties.[71] Japan's military and people were committed to fighting to the last. Unlike the German army whose troops would give up when they were clearly defeated, millions of Japanese soldiers had already died in distant jungles and coral islands rather than surrender, throwing their lives away in mass banzai charges or with gun barrels in their mouths. The Japanese army remained a formidable fighting force; it fielded over 5 million troops, including over 2 million in the home islands, 2 million in northeast Asia and China, 200,000 in southeast Asia, 500,000 in the East Indies and Philippines, and 100,000 in other Pacific islands. Japanese civilians were just as committed as the soldiers to dying for their emperor-god. Thousands of Japanese civilians had already committed suicide on Saipan, Okinawa, and elsewhere rather than face the shame of surrender: schoolgirls held grenades to their breasts and pulled the pins; mothers tightly held their children's hands and plummeted from cliffs to blood-soaked rocks below. American B-29s had been systematically pounding Japan's cities and industrial complexes for over a half year before the surrender, killing over 400,000 Japanese. The two atomic bombs killed another 100,000 Japanese. Nonetheless, the government was training its entire adult population to charge the American invaders with bamboo spears and grenades.

Japan's military leaders compared the 1945 situation with the year 1281 when the Mongols invaded Japan and were fortuitously destroyed by a "divine wind" or typhoon. However, now the Japanese people would be the kamikaze which would save the empire. Although 2,550 kamikaze pilots had already died trying to fly their planes into enemy ships and positions, 5,350 planes remained and were being packed with explosives; 7,000 additional planes were in repair or storage. There were more than enough kamikaze volunteers to fly that vast air force against the invaders.[72] Before the war's end, Japanese kamikazes "had sunk 34 American ships, including 3 aircraft carriers, and damaged 285 (including 36 aircraft carriers . . . 15 battleships, 15 cruisers, and 87 destroyers). During the Okinawan campaign alone, 16 of our ships had been sunk and 185 damaged (including 7 carriers, 10 battleships, and 5 cruisers)."[73]

Atomic Diplomacy?

Another revisionist argument is that whether or not Japan would have surrendered without the atomic bombing, Hiroshima and Nagasaki were as much directed against Moscow as Tokyo.[74] There is no empirical evidence to support this claim.[75] If the administration viewed "atomic diplomacy" as a means to deter the Soviets as a top priority, why then was Roosevelt's major goal and triumph at Yalta to secure Stalin's agreement to enter the war against Japan? Roosevelt was not concerned about a Soviet threat. He still believed that the Soviets would be a constructive member of the postwar collective security system and worked hard to gain the Kremlin's trust and cooperation.

Although Truman was more suspicious of Soviet ambitions, he too hoped for the best. Once the bomb was successfully tested, Truman could have bluntly told Stalin that the Soviet attack against Japan was no longer necessary, thus limiting Soviet advances in northeast Asia. Instead Truman enthusiastically greeted Stalin's announcement of Soviet intervention. As Feis argues, while "knowledge of the successful test may have stiffened Truman's resistance to some of the furthest reaching Soviet wishes, it did not cause him to alter American aims or terms as previously defined. . . . Even as the American government proceeded to use the bomb against Japan, it was brewing proposals for controlling its production and banning its use, except possibly as an international measure to enforce peace."[76] Truman's assertion of American interests and denunciations of Soviet aggression did not begin after he got word of the successful atomic test. Eleven days after taking office, Truman tore into visiting Soviet Foreign Minister Molotov for Soviet machinations. Molotov later angrily complained: "No one ever talked like that to me before!"

Certainly, the White House never considered "surprising" the Soviets with the bomb because as early as 1943 they knew that the Soviets knew about the Manhattan Project. Stimson convinced Roosevelt it was better not to inform Moscow of the Manhattan Project so they did not have to turn down a possible Soviet request to share the technology.[77] But the White House was just as leery of sharing atomic secrets with the British. By December 1942, the White House had decided to end British participation in the project. At the Quebec Conference in August 1943, Roosevelt agreed to once again enlist British help in the project, but this time as junior partners. Roosevelt and Churchill began discussing the role of atomic energy in the postwar international order they were building.

Undoubtedly, both Roosevelt and Truman appreciated the bomb's potential for deterring possible Soviet aggression after the war. As early as December 1944, Roosevelt and Stimson agreed that the bomb might help deter Soviet infringement on American interests in the postwar world. But the Soviets had largely cooperated throughout the world. Interests clashed in some areas but the relationship remained sound. In 1945, Truman did discuss with Stimson and Byrnes the possibility of trading access to atomic bomb technology for the resolution of outstanding international problems. He thus saw the bomb as a big bargaining chip, not a means of browbeating the Soviets into unilateral concessions. It was not until 1947 that the accumulation of grievances against Soviet machinations in east Europe and elsewhere prompted Truman to declare Cold War. However, never then nor since has the United States devised an effective means of achieving American interests through atomic diplomacy.[78] Atomic diplomacy worked only against Japan.

Atomic diplomacy was solely directed against Japan, not against the

Soviet Union. Possession of the atomic bomb did not change American policy toward the Soviet Union. In his July 2 memorandum, Stimson nowhere mentions any Soviet threat to northeast Asia. As he later maintained, "the principal political, social, and military objective of the United States in the summer of 1945 was the prompt and complete surrender of Japan. Only the complete destruction of her military power could open the way to lasting peace."[79] For both the Roosevelt and Truman administrations the bomb was the means to avoid an invasion of Japan which would result in at least a half million American and untold millions of Japanese casualties.

Bureaucratic and Political Imperatives?

Some argue that bureaucratic and political pressures were the most important forces behind the decision to drop the bomb, that the decision to do so was as much decided for as decided by Roosevelt and Truman.[80] Once the assumption that the bomb would be used was established in the minds of all involved, the only question was when and where. After Roosevelt approved the project, it acquired a bureaucratic life of its own. The ethical and strategic justification for the bomb's use was never seriously questioned thereafter. Truman did not even know about the project until after he became president; he simply signed off on a decision that had been made nearly four years before. Accompanying these bureaucratic pressures was the political fear of a severe congressional reaction if it discovered that $2 billion had been secretly spent on an atomic dud. And having successfully tested a bomb, the Truman administration had to use it to justify its cost. While the bureaucratic pressures clearly were there, they were of secondary importance. There is no evidence the bombs were dropped to justify their expense.

Demonstration Effect?

Revisionists criticize the White House for not demonstrating the bomb before dropping it on a Japanese city. But that option had been carefully debated and rejected. Until the bomb was successfully tested the biggest fear was that it would be a dud. The strongest argument against inviting Japanese and international observers to the Los Alamos test was that its failure would only stiffen the Japanese will to fight to the death. And even the successful Los Alamos test under ideal conditions did not guarantee the bomb would explode if dropped from an airplane. These fears may well have been exaggerated. The Japanese would have fought just as hard whether they knew of the failed bomb test or not. But in the psychology of the time, such fears seemed rational and they shaped policy.

Moral Dilemmas?

No human activity is more filled with moral dilemmas than war. All the world's major faiths and philosophies condemn murder – except in extra-ordinary circumstances. Self-defense is an exception; one can kill to avoid being killed. But "just war" doctrines insist that the killing must be kept to a minimum.

Ethical debate about the atomic bombing of Hiroshima and Nagasaki boils down to one question – did it save or waste lives? Three and a half years of death and destruction had inured all the participants to war's horrors. Japan's government had mobilized nearly its entire population for the war, thus erasing the distinction between soldiers and civilians. Thus, carpet bombing Japanese cities with incendiaries was seen as morally justifiable. To the White House, the difference between destroying a city with one bomb rather than thousands was one of efficiency rather than ethics. As Stimson put it, the bomb "was considered to be a new and tremendously powerful explosive, as legitimate as any other of the deadly explosive weapons of modern war . . . at no time, from 1941 to 1945, did I ever hear it suggested by the President or any other responsible member of government that atomic energy should not be used in the war. All of us understood the tremendous responsibility. . . . [Yet] the exact circumstances in which that weapon might be used were unknown to any of us until the middle of 1945."[81]

The moral and strategic assumption since the project's inception was that the bomb would end the war early and save lives. If this assumption was correct, it would thus be immoral not to use the bomb. Daily bombardment by B-29s would have killed dozens of times more Japanese in the months leading up to the November invasion. Millions more Japanese would have died after the invasion began.

If the Truman administration can be faulted, it is for waiting ten days between the bomb's successful test on July 16 and the Potsdam Declaration of July 26. The White House could also have accompanied the Potsdam Declaration with the scientific proof of the bomb's successful explosion.

However, these two actions would most likely not have broken Japan's government deadlock. The militarists would have dismissed any photographs and eyewitness testaments as faked. Ultimately, Hiroshima and Nagasaki would still have been incinerated. But a clearer warning would have made the ethics of Truman's decision as sound as its strategic rationale.

A Second Bomb?

If the Hiroshima bomb was justifiable, what about the Nagasaki bomb? The second bomb was dropped shortly after the first to give the impression the Americans had a huge stockpile with which to systematically reduce Japan's cities to radioactive rubble. This strategy worked. After analyzing records of the Japanese government meetings, Feis argues that one bomb was not enough – both were needed to shock the government into surrender: "if the second bomb had not been dropped, the Japanese rulers would have delayed, perhaps for weeks, the response which was preliminary for capitulation. The military heads would have been so firm in opposition that the emperor would probably have waited until the situation became more hopeless before overruling them."[82] Meanwhile, tens and perhaps hundreds of thousands of Japanese would have died from continued conventional bombings, while thousands and perhaps tens of thousands of more Americans would have died from kamikaze attacks.

The Tokyo Wall?

Finally, if the atomic bombs had never been dropped and the war ground on for another year or so with millions more lives lost, maimed, and shattered, what would Japan's fate be today? An American invasion in southern Japan would have eventually been joined by a Soviet invasion of northern Japan. Like Germany, Japan would have suffered a postwar division between Soviet and American spheres. Under these conditions, Japan's economic and constitutional development would have differed greatly. There would have been no Article 9 "peace" clause forbidding Japanese rearmament. Instead vast sums of money would have been diverted to maintaining an army, navy, and air force to deter Soviet forces defending a communist north Japan. Reunification would probably not have occurred any sooner than that of Germany. Investing more money in the military–industrial sector means less would have been spent in far more productive civilian industries and enterprises. Japan would not be as economically rich or dynamic as it is today, though how much less is impossible to determine.

Atomic Purification?

Finally, Japan would have been denied the atomic bombings' psychological as well as material benefits. Hiroshima and Nagasaki did not just save perhaps millions of Japanese lives and Japan's postwar division by ending the war before an invasion was necessary. Perhaps more importantly, the atomic blasts purified the Japanese of any deep guilt or responsibility for the atrocities they committed between 1931 and 1945. For most Japanese, psychologically if not intellectually, World War II began with Hiroshima and ended with Nagasaki, three days later. The atomic bombings overshadow all other steadily fading images the Japanese hold of World War II.[83]

This may be salve for the Japanese psyche but complicates Japan's relations with other East Asian states where memories of Japanese genocide, destruction, and exploitation are kept vivid. Japan's aggression between 1931 and 1945 cost the lives of perhaps 39 million Asians! Of these dead, about 2.5 million were Japanese – 2.1 million soldiers and 500,000 civilians. Japanese do not remember all of the atomic bomb victims. At least 10,000 of those who died at Hiroshima and Nagasaki were Korean and Chinese slave laborers.[84]

Evaluation

The atomic bomb decision was made with the highest strategic and ethical considerations. The White House was not omniscient; they could not read the minds of Japan's war leaders. The policies of the Roosevelt and Truman administrations were shaped by a Japanese aggression so seemingly fanatical that the government was mobilizing the entire adult population to fight to the death. The Roosevelt and Truman administrations believed that the bombs would save lives and shorten the war. As a means to this end, Truman claimed he never lost a night's sleep over the decision: "When you deal with a beast you have to treat him as a beast."[85] Spector writes that the "fanaticism and contempt for life conveyed by kamikaze tactics may have contributed to American willingness to employ the atomic bomb as an alternative to confronting an entire nation of kamikazes in an invasion of Japan itself."[86] Stimson is convinced that "the controlling factor in the final Japanese decision to . . . surrender was the atomic bomb."[87]

The atomic bomb's psychological impact was even more important than its destruction. More humans were incinerated in Tokyo than Hiroshima or Nagasaki. Yet, as Compton points out, "it was not one atomic bomb or two which brought surrender; it was the experience of what an atomic bomb will actually do to a community, plus the dread of many more, that was effective."[88]

CONCLUSION

On March 17, 1854, Commodore Perry signed with Bakufu officials the Treaty of Kanagawa which began a seventy year revolution that would transform Japan into an industrial, quasidemocratic, and imperial great power. But between 1931 and 1945, Japanese modernization self-destructed into fascism and imperialism. The United States was chiefly responsible for initiating and then eventually ending Japan's first modernization era.

On September 2, 1945, ninety-one years after Perry's squadron anchored in Tokyo Bay, Japan was opened once again when its government formally signed the surrender documents aboard the battleship USS "Missouri." Among the Allied leaders present was General Douglas MacArthur who would command the allied occupation of Japan and help implement a political, economic, and social revolution that has endured and deepened where the first modernization revolution failed.

Part II
The American Revolution of Japan

5 Demilitarization and Democratization, 1945–7

If a revolution is a complex of sweeping, systematic political, economic, and social changes, then the policies implemented during America's seven year Occupation of Japan (1945–52) were profoundly revolutionary. American policies transformed Japan politically from fascism into liberal democracy, and laid the foundation for Japan's eventual development from a poverty-stricken industrially backward country into an economic superpower and middle class society.

General Douglas MacArthur headed the Supreme Command for Allied Powers (SCAP), the Occupation's headquarters. SCAP, in turn, was ostensibly controlled by the Far East Commission (FEC), which included representatives of eleven allied nations. FEC's powers, however, were largely symbolic. Americans composed virtually all of the Occupation's administration and most of the military forces. SCAP policy originated in Washington and served American interests. Despite his megalomania, MacArthur was largely faithful to most of Washington's directives.

The American Occupation had two phases, each with its own ends and means. MacArthur's initial orders were to destroy Japan's military institutions and psychology, and democratize the country. The demilitarization and democratization phase lasted from September 1945 through 1947 and included the imposition of a democratic constitution, land, labor, and industrial reforms, demobilization of Japan's military, purge of many leading militarists, and war crimes trials.

During this first phase, growing animosities with the Soviet Union little affected SCAP's democratization and demilitarization policy – although both Truman's White House and MacArthur's SCAP feared and attempted to check Soviet ambitions in postwar Asia. Washington was prepared for these challenges. Intelligence estimates during World War II had foreseen "an Asia wracked by nationalist rebellions and susceptible to Soviet influence."[1] After the war, as one after another Far East country disintegrated into chaos and rebellion, Japan became an oasis of stability and growing prosperity. Despite this, few American officials could have envisioned Japan's subsequent rise from ruins to riches. Many feared that Japan would be an American ward indefinitely; others that Tokyo would quickly dump the American-imposed constitution and other political, economic, and social reforms as soon as the Occupation ended, and resort to authoritarianism and perhaps even membership in the Soviet bloc.

Although the White House had encouraged Soviet advances in northeast Asia as the price for joining the war against Japan, it tried to limit those advances once the guns fell silent. Truman and MacArthur bluntly rejected Stalin's attempts to gain an occupation zone and greater voice in administering Japan. On August 16, 1945, Stalin asked Truman to allow Soviet troops to accept the surrender of Japanese forces in the Kurile Islands and northern Hokkaido. Truman replied that Soviet troops could only occupy the Kuriles which had been previously promised to Moscow. Throughout the Occupation, MacArthur ignored attempts by the Soviet representative in Tokyo, General Kuzma Derevyanko, to influence policy.

By 1947, America's wartime alliance with the Soviet Union had broken down into bitter confrontation on a range of geopolitical and geoeconomic issues. The Cold War and fears that Japan might be a perpetual financial burden on the United States prompted Washington to shift its policy from demilitarization and democratization to economic revival. Having defanged Japan, Washington now saw it as the potential keystone of a future Far East trade system whose prosperity might keep communism at bay. SCAP now encouraged Japan's government to adopt policies of fiscal conservatism, an undervalued currency, high savings and investment rates, industrial targeting, foreign investment barriers, capital controls, technology acquisition, import barriers, and export drives. In other words, after forcing Japan to accept political liberalism, Washington then reinforced its traditional neomercantilism. The United States also began encouraging Japan's trade ties with southeast Asia, or in Kennan's words, "getting Japan back into the old co-prosperity sphere." This "reverse course" became complete after the Korean War broke out in June 1950 when Washington pressured Tokyo into rearmament. On September 8, 1951, Tokyo signed both a peace treaty with forty-nine other countries and a security treaty with the United States. The Occupation ended six months later.

WARTIME PLANNING

The American Occupation has been described as "perhaps the single most exhaustively planned operation of massive and externally directed change in world history."[2] Even before the attack on Pearl Harbor, the State Department had convened a "special research division" of area specialists like Robert Fearey, Hugh Borton, and George Blakesee to discuss a possible postwar settlement. After the war began, this planning was expanded under the State Department's Postwar Programs Committee (PWC) and the army's Civil Affairs Division (CAD).

PWC's policy proposals shifted with its leadership and its rivalry with other planning agencies. At first PWC, like CAD, pushed for demilitarization and democratization reforms that would root out Japanese militarism. In March 1944, PWC submitted a plan for a postwar Japan in which there would be no zonal divisions and a predominantly American occupation which would use Japan's government and the emperor to demilitarize and democratize the country. But shortly thereafter, former ambassador to Japan Joseph Grew replaced "China hand" Stanley Hornbeck as head of the Office of Far Eastern Affairs. Grew had pushed for the appeasement of Japanese aggression during the 1930s and now attempted to appease Japan's defeated power elite. Stacking the staff deck with "Japan hands," Grew advocated a limited Occupation that would disarm Japan but leave its authoritarian government and society intact. Grew's former secretary in Japan, Robert Feary, submitted a State Department policy paper in November 1944 which stated that "Occupation authorities should not attempt long-range reforms or reorganization of the internal economy."[3] As late as May 1945, Grew tried to convince President Truman that "the best we can hope for is a constitutional monarchy, experience having shown that democracy in Japan would never work."[4]

But while Grew and Feary were advocating "softline" policies, the original planning group within the State Department continued to push for reform policies. Despite "Japan hand" opposition, these reformers reemerged because most Foreign Service Officers (FSOs) were largely conservative generalists who knew nothing about civil administration or the intricacies of economic and social policy. To supply the policy details, the State Department created the Special Research Division in 1944 and later renamed it the Territorial Studies (TS) office. New Dealers George Blakesee and Hugh Borton headed the TS and pressed to shift State Department policy from tolerating Japanese authoritarianism to replacing it with liberal democracy. Grew's influence on Japan policy declined after he was promoted to Under Secretary of State in December 1944. Then in March 1945, former Office of Strategic Services (OSS) Japan expert Edwin Martin was named head of PWC's economic section and proved "to be the key figure in transforming State Department policy into one of radical economic reform for Japan."[5] Martin authored the economic reform section of SWNCC 150/4.

External forces were as important as internal ones in shifting the State Department's orientation. Cohen writes that over time "those involved in Japan's occupation planning grew from a handful to a hundred, and from one obvious office to more than a dozen in five departments (State, War, Navy, Agriculture, Treasury) plus two independent agencies (the Office of Strategic Services and the Foreign Economic Administration."[6] This expansion of policymaking institutions and perspectives steadily diluted the State Department's power over policy.

Among these institutions, CADD head John Hilldring proved the most powerful figure shaping U.S. policy toward Japan. Hilldring flatly rejected Grew's belief that Japan's system was sacred and neither could nor should be tampered with. He staffed CAD with experts on Japan, law, civil administration, and economics, and encouraged them to devise specific reform policies. Realizing that the State Department and CAD were devising widely diverging policy tracks, Hilldring pressed the White House for some coordinating agency.

The White House responded in December 1944 by organizing the State–War–Navy Coordinating Committee (SWNCC) composed of assistant secretaries to coordinate planning for a postwar settlement and occupation.[7] SWNCC set up the Subcommittee on the Far East (SWNCCFE) which met fifty-one times during 1945 and had the final word on plans for Japan's occupation. Meanwhile, the Joint Chiefs of Staff (JCS) worked with CAD to supplement SWNCC's efforts.

Although SWNCC brought a badly needed coherence to the policy process, the White House largely ignored its efforts. For example, Roosevelt did not even inform SWNCC after he secured Stalin's agreement at Yalta to enter the war against Japan in return for privileges in Manchuria and the return of Sakhalin and the Kurile Islands. SWNCC also competed with other planning committees, particularly Treasury Secretary Henry Morgenthau's Informal Policy Committee on Germany (IPCOG) which advocated the elimination of Germany's government and heavy industry, and the country's division into occupation zones. When rumours swept SWNCC in April 1945 that the same measures would be applied to Japan, the committee rushed to finish its "U.S. Initial Post-Surrender Policy," which essentially elaborated PWC's earlier proposal. SWNCC strongly opposed the complete dismantlement of Japanese industry.

After Truman took office in April 1945, he dismantled Morgenthau's group and allowed SWNCC to determine American postwar policy toward the Axis powers. He also purged the "Japan hands" from State Department positions and filled them with "China hands." John Carter Vincent replaced both Eugene Doorman as SWNCCFE head and Joseph Ballatine as Office of Far Eastern Affairs head. Hugh Borton took Earle Dickover's job as Japan Division chief. George Atcheson rather than Doorman was named SCAP's State Department liaison.

Truman then reinforced the planning process by bringing in advisors like War Secretary Henry Stimson, Navy Secretary James Forrestal, diplomats Joseph Grew and W. Averell Harriman, and former president Herbert Hoover. Grew and Hoover, not surprisingly, broke sharply with existing policy. Both urged that the United States should induce Japan's surrender before the Soviets intervened and thus prevent Moscow from expanding its empire in northeast Asia. Grew called again for a soft peace which left in place Emperor Hirohito and Japan's political and economic system. Hoover went further, arguing that Japan be allowed to retain its Taiwan and Korean colonies. Truman's other advisors blasted these radical proposals. Most White House war leaders still saw Japan as the primary enemy and the Soviet Union as a difficult but vital ally. With the atomic bomb still untested, Soviet intervention was seen as essential in defeating Japan. Like Germany, Japan would be thoroughly demilitarized, democratized, and stripped of its empire.

Even if the White House had accepted the intellectual arguments for a soft peace toward Japan, they would not have been able to sell it politically. Popular wartime sentiments favored the harshest peace for Japan; two-thirds of Americans, along with all of its allies, favored Emperor Hirohito's execution as a war criminal. Thus the July 26 Potsdam Declaration could only hint at Hirohito's survival subject to the "freely expressed will of the Japanese people." Any explicit guarantee would have caused an uproar among the American people and allies.

The submission of SWNCC 150/4/A in late August 1945 represented the height of the committee's policy influence. These views were elaborated in JCS 1380/15 whose first version was complete by September 1, 1945. These reports presented a revolutionary program of demilitarization and political and economic reforms. Afterward SWNCC and JSC would quickly fade in importance. For the next six years Japan's fate would largely rest in the hands of one man, General Douglas MacArthur.

MacARTHUR

On August 15, 1945, General Douglas MacArthur received orders from Washington to prepare for commanding the allied occupation of Japan. Who was this man who would lead Japan's transformation from fascist totalitarianism into liberal democracy and create the foundation for its future rise into an economic superpower?

If MacArthur had not gone into the army he might well have become a preacher. MacArthur loved pontificating, sometimes for hours, on strategy, history, the "Asian mind," and virtually any other subject. Those Japanese subject to these sessions called them "sermons" (sekkyo). Among his most fervent beliefs was that Christianity would eventually sweep over Asia and form the spiritual basis for an alliance between East and West which could resist communism. He noted excitedly in 1946 that Japanese prime minister Katayama, Philippine president Roxas, and China's KMT president Chiang were all Christians.

Although he was a hero to millions of Americans, allies, and eventually even Japanese, those who have critically analyzed his character and military record find it wanting in many areas. Schaller describes MacArthur as a man of "little intellectual depth. An exceptionally good memory, a repertoire of quotes and anecdotes, a love of convoluted or even archaic language and a wealth of historical trivia formed the core of the general's wisdom. The geopolitical sweep and absolute certainty of his assertions left audiences gasping. Even if he said little original or profound, the vivid style, cadence, and metaphor convinced many they had heard an oracle."[8] Not everyone was swept away by MacArthur's charisma. The British liason to MacArthur's World War II headquarters, Lieutenant-Colonel Gerald Wilkinson, characterized him as "shrewd, selfish, proud, remote, highly strung and vastly vain. He has imagination, self-confidence, physical courage and charm, but no humor about himself, no regard for the truth, and is unaware of those defects. He mistakes his emotions and ambitions for principles."[9] Yoshida had kinder words for MacArthur, ascribing to him "innate friendliness" and "a genuine understanding of the country and its people. . . . It was fortunate for Japan that the Occupation was guided by a person of General MacArthur's calibre and conviction."[10] Yoshida's kind remarks about MacArthur are understandable given the prime minister's ability to bend the general on so many SCAP policies.

The primary source of MacArthur's ambition was his parents. His remote Civil War hero father and domineering stage mother controlled him long after they departed; he strove constantly to live up to their lofty expectations.[11] He seemed to have always been trying to overcompensate for deep insecurities and failings. For example, his first wife divorced him because "he's a buck private in the boudoir."[12]

MacArthur was America's first and most enduring World War II hero, adored by millions. Yet his career would have been exceptional even if it had ended before Pearl Harbor. No cadet has ever surpassed his West Point grades. During World War I he earned thirteen combat metals and seven citations for exceptional valor, was injured twice and gassed once. At age 50 he became the army's youngest chief of staff. He retired in 1937 and journeyed to Manila to serve as the Philippine's military advisor. Six months before Pearl Harbor, he accepted the White House offer to command U.S. forces in the Philippines. His pre-World War II career, however, was not flawless. Many criticize him as the commander of the troops which in 1932 brutally dispersed the "bonus marcher" World War I veterans encamped in Washington D.C., and in 1942 for pocketing $500,000 in Philippine funds from President Manuel Quezon for his services as "special advisor."

While his personal valor was unquestioned, MacArthur's "military genius" was produced not so much on the battlefield as by his own public relations machine and the American public's need for a hero to worship. Spector states bluntly that MacArthur "was unsuited by temperament, character, and judgement" for high command and reveals his numerous "errors of judgement and . . . refusal to face reality."[13]

Yet MacArthur flourished despite these flaws. The Pearl Harbor commanders, Kimmel and Short, were cashiered for failing to prepare for a possible attack. MacArthur's defense preparations for the Philippines were as inept as those of his colleagues. He received a message that Pearl Harbor had been attacked ten hours before Japanese bombers appeared over the Philippines. Parked wing to wing, his air force was destroyed on the ground. The Japanese invasion later in December quickly overran most of Luzon and bottled up MacArthur's troops in the Bataan Peninsula. After the Japanese invasion, he holed up on Corregidor Island in Manila Bay and refused to visit the front. His troops contemptuously called him "Dugout Doug."

There was no investigation despite MacArthur's devastating defeat. In desparate need of heroes, Americans elevated MacArthur into the pantheon of national demi-gods. Always sensitive to public opinion, Roosevelt ordered "the hero" to abandon Corregidor for the safety of Australia. Roosevelt then awarded MacArthur the Medal of Honor and named him commander of American forces in the southwest Pacific. As Eisenhower put it: "The public has built itself a hero out of its own imagination" and called MacArthur's Medal of Honor and high command a reaction "to public opinion rather than military logic."[14]

Historians are generally critical of both America's grand strategy in the Pacific and MacArthur's subsequent World War II campaigns. Many argue that the White House's compromise to the navy and army allowing a two-pronged attack by Admiral Nimitz's forces across the central Pacific and MacArthur's across the southwest Pacific was a risky, wasteful strategy. Ideally, Washington would have allocated enough troops to MacArthur to hold the line in the southwest while Nimitz received most troops, ships, and supplies to strike more quickly and overwhelmingly toward Japan's heart.

Having received equal billing in the Pacific War, MacArthur pushed across Papua-New Guinea and then the Philippines in a series of rapid leaps broken by long pauses. While his casualty rates were among the highest in the Pacific, he grossly exaggerated the enemy losses. MacArthur could have neutralized the Philippines through bombardment and blockade then bypassed it for the strategically superior Taiwan. But he swept sound strategy aside to fulfill his promise to return. Roosevelt eventually agreed to his strategy. MacArthur later claimed Roosevelt did so to pay off the general for a determined 1944 presidential push. Schaller notes that "removing the general from Corregidor, giving him a theater, and approving the return to the Philippines were all examples of how politics had triumphed over sound strategy."[15] During the Korean War, he suffered yet another humiliating defeat. After his brilliant, risky landing behind the enemy lines at Inchon in September, he pushed his army far into North Korea and was routed by Chinese armies in November 1950.

MacArthur's ambitions were not confined to war and occupation. He believed that the White House was the logical destination of the five star general who had helped defeat, occupy, and reform Japan. In the 1944 and 1948 elections, he encouraged his stateside backers to promote his name in Republican Party primaries; he suffered humiliating defeats both times.

So why did Truman choose this controversial and politically ambitious general to be SCAP commander? Schaller argues that the White House had no choice; "having built the SWPA commander up to nearly mythic proportions, they would be hard pressed to justify passing him over." Apparently Truman originally intended to nominate Nimitz for SCAP but changed his mind after someone warned him that slighting MacArthur would cost him five million votes in 1948. Interior Secretary Harold Ickes admitted that denying MacArthur the post would only make "a martyr out of him and a candidate for president."[16]

INITIAL OCCUPATION

After the emperor's historic broadcast on August 15 in which he admitted the war had not exactly gone in Japan's favor, Japan's government attempted to restrain maverick army officers who remained determined to die fanatically to the last Japanese, and to prepare for a foreign occupation. Prime

Minister Suzuki resigned and was replaced by Prince Higashikuni Naruhiko, the emperor's uncle-in-law. On August 19 and 20, a sixteen-member Japanese delegation met with MacArthur in Manila, received the surrender documents, and worked out the ceremony details. On August 28, a unit of 146 engineering and communications troops became the first Americans to land in Japan. Two days later, 4,200 American troops flew into Atsugi air base outside of Tokyo and Yokosuka naval base in Tokyo Bay. MacArthur accompanied these troops.

On September 2, 1945, the official surrender took place aboard the U.S.S. "Missouri", which was the centerpiece of a vast armada of 260 American ships which had anchored in Tokyo Bay. Two huge American flags towered above the Japanese delegation, one flown by Commodore Perry when he steamed into Tokyo Bay in 1853, and the other which flew over the U.S. Capitol on December 7, 1941. With stoic bitterness the Japanese signed the surrender document which declared that: "We hereby proclaim the unconditional surrender to the Allied Powers. . . . The Authority of the Japanese emperor and the Japanese government to rule shall be subject to the Supreme Commander." That same day, the emperor issued a rescript ordering his troops and people to lay down their arms and obey the Occupation forces.

The surrender became symbolically complete on September 27 when Emperor Hirohito traveled from his palace to nervously meet MacArthur at SCAP Headquarters. Two days later, the newspapers published photos of the diminutive emperor wearing a black suit and tie standing rigidly beside tall, lanky, casually attired MacArthur. The photos caused a sensation as they helped further demystify the emperor and symbolize the totality of Japan's defeat.

After preparing to charge the American invaders with bamboo spears and grenades, why did the Japanese so meekly lay down their arms and comply with the Occupation? The emperor's direct order that they do so was certainly vital. Without it violent resistance might well have lasted for years in Japan and among Japanese troops overseas. Japanese Social Darwinism also helps explain the peaceful transition. Japan's philosophy of "proper place," argues Dower, "facilitated the superficially drastic transition from leading race to defeated power. It had been foolhardy for the Japanese to step out of line and challenge the older and more powerful imperialist powers, the postwar line of reasoning went. Now, confronted with a ruined landscape and undeniable defeat, Japan had no choice but to redefine its proper place."[17] Dower also points to the divided nature of the "visiting gods" (marebito) in Japanese folklore, which can either ravish or enrich its unwilling hosts. The Americans were seen as benevolent gods whose gifts should be eagerly accepted and their presence tolerated in hope they would eventually go away.

And why was the Occupation so constructive and peaceful? Although 100,997 Americans died and 291,543 were wounded fighting the Japanese, and the war began with an attack on Hawaii, the United States escaped direct destruction and its economy boomed during the war years.[18] While even today, many Pacific War veterans still hate and mistrust the Japanese, soon after the fighting ended most Americans supported a policy of reconstruction rather than revenge for Japan. Unlike Japanese culture which tends to bow to the strong and exploit and denigrate the weak, Americans tend to sympathize with underdogs.

Yoshida tells a story that captures the Occupation's psychological dynamics and American character. He was driving to Tokyo when

> two American GIs suddenly appeared and signaled my driver to halt. I imagined them to be on some kind of marauding expedition, but they turned out to be soldiers returning to Tokyo who had lost their way, and they politely requested a lift. . . . Relieved that their intentions were strictly honorable and benevolent, I invited them into the car and we had not proceeded far before they were pressing chocolates, then chewing gum, and finally cigarettes upon me. The incident surprised and pleased me; feelings which were probably shared by the majority of the Japanese people in their initial contacts with the men of the Occupation forces. I recall thinking at the time that it was this natural way of acting on their part, and the inherent good nature of the average American, which enabled the Occupation of Japan to be completed without a shot being fired.[19]

OCCUPATION POLITICS AND POLICYMAKING

SCAP

While flying toward Tokyo Bay on August 30, MacArthur summarized the "initial policy" to his staff, which he described in his *Reminiscences* as: "First, destroy the military power. Punish war criminals. Build the structure of representative government. Modernize the constitution. Hold free elections. Enfranchise the women. Release the political prisoners. Liberate the farmers. Establish a free labor movement. Encourage a free economy. Abolish police oppression. Develop a free and responsible press. Liberalize education. Decentralize political power. Separate the church from state."[20] Although he conveyed the impression to his awed staff that the vision he presented was his own, he had actually summarized SWNCC 150/4/A which he had received a few hours earlier, along with the even more comprehensive policy blueprint JSC 1380/15 whose early versions he had seen several weeks earlier.

MacArthur wore two hats and theoretically served two masters. As the American commander of U.S. Far East Command (GHQ FEC), MacArthur was subject to the Joint Chiefs of Staff and ultimately the president as commander in chief. As SCAP commander he was obedient to the eleven-nation Far Eastern Commission (FEC) which was formed in 1946 with the power to make Occupation policy, and had to listen to the advice of the Tokyo-based Allied Council for Japan (ACJ). Of the 111 directives MacArthur received while SCAP, fifty-one were from Washington and sixty from the FEC. The most important directives were the Potsdam Declaration, which provided the fundamental statement of Occupation goals and principles, and were in turn elaborated in the SWNCC 150/4/A "Initial United States Post-Surrender Policy", and the even more detailed JSC 1380/15 "Basic Directive for Post-Surrender Military Government in Japan Proper" whose final version MacArthur received on November 3, 1945. While SWNCC 150/4 was largely a statement of Occupation principles, JSC 1380/15 was a twenty-five page blueprint for Occupation policies. MacArthur divvied up JCS 1380/15's 179 paragraphs and 7,500 words for implementation among the appropriate staff sections.

On MacArthur's SCAP office wall was a framed quote from Livy citing a speech by Roman general Lucius Aemilius Paulus: "Rest assured that we shall pay no attention to any councils but such as shall be framed within our own camp." Beneath the quote was written "Amen. Douglas MacArthur."[21] MacArthur did all he could to live up to that motto. In a nation whose people pride themselves on being "rugged individuals," few American generals have consistently disregarded orders more than MacArthur. At times that "independence of command" edged over into outright insubordination. In fall 1945, for example, MacArthur rejected two Truman requests that he return to the United States for consultations. He declined, claiming his duties in Asia were too urgent.

In practice, MacArthur acted autonomously within Washington's general directives while largely disregarding FEC instructions. MacArthur only met once with the ACJ – its first session in April 1946. He later wrote that the FEC and ACJ issued "not one constructive idea to help with the reorientation or reconstruction of Japan."[22] Yet, he did not hesitate to use FEC to stave off unwanted Washington orders. When pressed, MacArthur claimed that as SCAP he represented the FEC rather than his commander-in-chief, an ironic claim considering his open contempt for the former along with his barely concealed dismissal of the latter. Washington tried to end this argument by sending MacArthur orders under his title as "Commander in Chief in the Far East" (CINCFE). Yet MacArthur still resisted with legalistic arguments. For example, he declared that the shift from democratization to economic revival embodied in "NSC 13/2 has not been conveyed as an order to SCAP by appropriate directive as prescribed by international agreement and therefore SCAP is not responsible in any way for its implementation."[23] Meanwhile he issued appropriate orders for the implementation of much of 13/2 without mentioning it by name, thus taking credit for the new policy.

Until the Cold War, the Truman White House largely let MacArthur rule Japan and implement broad policy guidelines as the general wished. Even then until MacArthur's dismissal in April 1951, the White House continued to treat his insubordination with kid gloves. Orders were watered down into memos of suggestions and requests. Truman put up with MacArthur's repeated snubs and even his aborted run for the presidency in 1948.

Throughout Japan's Occupation, despite his extravagant verbiage and rakish dress, MacArthur followed an austere, almost monkish lifestyle. He rarely strayed from his daily routine of driving the mile from his home to SCAP headquarters in the Dai Ichi Insurance building in downtown Tokyo just across the moat from the emperor's palace. He did not travel around Japan or even Tokyo. He met with few Japanese, and those mostly government officials. He did meet in his office with Prime Minister Yoshida Shigeru seventy-five times, and Emperor Hirohito eleven times (once every six months), and several times each with the other Occupation prime ministers, Higashikuni Naruhiko, Shidehara Kijiro, Katayama Tetsu, and Ashida Hitoshi. During his six years in Japan, he left only twice for quick visits to Manila and Seoul to attend their respective national independence ceremonies. And once for an infamous meeting with Truman on Wake Island.

MacArthur surrounded himself with a loyal and fawning staff of mixed administrative abilities. At its height, SCAP had thirteen staff sections and 3,600 personnel. The staff was divided between army officers whose chief pursuit was to maintain order and New Deal-oriented civilians who hoped to revolutionize Japan. The three most important offices were the Government Section (GS) headed by General Courtney Whitney, intelligence (G-2) by General Charles Willoughby, and the Economic and Scientific Section (ESS) by William Marquat. SCAP Civil Affairs teams of roughly fifty personnel each were assigned to fifty-three places around Japan to monitor conditions and compliance with policy. These teams assisted rather than controlled the local governments.

SCAP's powers were sweeping. What freedom SCAP gave to the Japanese with one hand, it sometimes took away with the other. Although it pushed for constitutional provisions guaranteeing freedom of the press, SCAP heavily censored Japan's mass media throughout the Occupation. And it is often forgotten that SCAP also commanded a huge occupying army – 600,000 initially which were reduced to 250,000 by December 1945 and then gradually diminished to 100,000 in 1952. Virtually all of these troops were either American or British Commonwealth forces. SCAP's only nonmilitary office was the Office of the Political Advisor filled with a State Department official, George Atcheson. MacArthur ignored this position.

Allied Powers

Although the Allies accepted a predominantly American role in Japan's occupation, the British and Soviets pressed for some policy and administrative responsibilities. On August 21, 1945, the White House proposed setting up the Far Eastern Advisory Commission (FEAC) in Washington to advise Occupation policies. The FEAC's first of ten meetings took place on October 30 and each generally rubberstamped decisions already made by Washington.

While both London and Moscow demanded a more authoritative Occupation role for themselves, the Soviets outright boycotted the proceedings. Averill Harriman, ambassador to Moscow, also urged a less assertive American policy toward Japan and the Far East. He argued that Moscow sought "nominal parity rather than real influence in Japan," and overall desired more "a relationship of equality with the United States than with expansionist plans."[24] By offering the Soviets a token role in Japan, Washington and Moscow could better deal with other Asian and global issues.

On December 26, 1945, at the Big Three Foreign Ministers meeting in Moscow, Secretary of State Byrnes agreed to create two new institutions, a Far Eastern Commission (FEC) in Washington and an Allied Council for Japan (ACJ) in Tokyo. FEC would include representatives of eleven (later thirteen) nations – United States, Britain, Soviet Union, China, France, Netherlands, Australia, New Zealand, Canada, the Philippines, and India. Its role would be to debate and formulate policies for SCAP to implement. Each of the Big Four would wield veto power. ACJ would be a four-member – United States, Britain, Soviet Union, and China – advisory body attached to SCAP. In return for the nominal role in Japan that Byrnes offered Stalin, he demanded and received an equally nominal role in administering the Balkan countries.

These institutions helped SCAP in two ways. In rubberstamping SCAP policies, FEC gave them an international legitimacy. And when FEC or

AJC debated harsher policies for Japan, MacArthur could always pressure Tokyo to accept his own milder policies or suffer the consequences. Thus MacArthur played "good cop" to the FEC and ACJ "bad cops."

Japan's Government

SCAP issued "instructions" (SCAPINs) to Japan's government which in turn passed them on to the appropriate ministry or agency for implementation. During the Occupation, Japan's government issued 293 imperial ordinances (known as cabinet ordinances after the constitution took effect) to implement SCAPINs.

Theoretically, SCAPINs were orders that had to be obeyed. Japan's officials, however, greeted SCAP policies with anything but docile acceptance. As SCAP's directives were filtered through Japan's bureaucracy, they were often stubbornly resisted and sometimes altered or even derailed, a strategy known as "following orders to a superior's face, and reversing them behind his back" (menju fukuashi). The Japanese government and bureaucracy continually blocked or watered down policies and tested the Occupation's will. Without strict American supervision, the Japanese were able to "ignore or defy many unpleasant demands or, more important, to distort the information on which SCAP relied."[25] Yoshida admitted that "we Japanese . . . never lost an opportunity to demand the revision and readjustment of those Occupation policies which we judged to be impractical and not suited to the actual conditions existing in Japan."[26] During the Occupation's first phase, these "unsuitable" policies tended to be nearly every democratic and economic reform on SCAP's agenda.

Japanese officials soon became adept at distinguishing between hard- and soft-line SCAP sections and personnel and playing them off against each other. The Japanese found MacArthur an easy mark despite his aloof and stern demeanor. GS head Courtney Whitney warned MacArthur in a November 8, 1946 memo that Japan's "government manifests a continuing tendency to negotiate with you . . . rather than to proceed to implementation within the letter and spirit of your policy and decisions already determined and communicated to it."[27]

When outright delay and arguments did not work, Japan's leaders tried using scare tactics to impede SCAP policies. Every prime minister and many ministers echoed Prince Konoe's dire warning that "if you wipe out in one blow the established feudal forces and the zaibatsu as well, Japan will immediately go communist."[28]

At times, the Japanese were able to assert their positions without a struggle. For example, SCAP originally intended to replace army script for

Japanese yen as the nation's currency and its own military courts for Japanese courts. The Higashikuni government's protests caused SCAP to abandon these proposals even before the September 2, 1945 surrender ceremony. After a brief talk Yoshida got MacArthur to table indefinitely plans to force the zaibatsu to adopt new names.

Yoshida Shigeru was prime minister for five of the Occupation's six and a half years. He had had an illustrious diplomatic career. Upon graduating from Tokyo Imperial University, Yoshida joined the foreign ministry and worked his way steadily up through the ranks until he served as ambassador in Rome and London. As one of the peace advocates during the war's last year, he was briefly imprisoned by the Kempeitai for his actions. Rotund, cherubic, barely five feet tall, Yoshida could be witty and caustic, eloquent and obtuse. MacArthur berated Yoshida as "monumentally lazy" and "inept," and condemned him for derailing many SCAP reforms.

SCAP had to exert continual tough pressure to get the Japanese to sincerely implement its policies. That SCAP was ultimately successful is attributable to its patience and perseverance.

DEMILITARIZATION

Emperor

Democratization could not be accomplished unless Japan was completely demilitarized. Shortly after the Occupation began, SCAP began overseeing the demobilization of Japan's military forces and destruction of its equipment. Yet, the emperor, who many believed was the most responsible for Japanese imperialism, remained enthroned.

During the autumn of 1945, the Allies debated the emperor's fate as they drew up lists of suspected war criminals. Australia and New Zealand argued that the emperor should be persecuted. Britain and the Soviet Union were mildly opposed to putting him on trial. The State, War, and Navy departments agreed that the emperor should not be immune from trial, but a decision should await the evidence currently being collected in Tokyo.

The issue came to a head on January 21, 1946 when Australia's representative to the United Nations War Crimes Commission in London demanded that the emperor be charged with war crimes. When MacArthur received word of the possibility that the emperor would be charged, he drafted and fired off to Washington a cable in which he argued that the emperor was Japan's symbol of historical and cultural unity and his trial could spark a "vendetta for revenge . . . whose cycle may well not be complete for centuries, if ever. It is quite possible that a million troops would be required, which would have to be maintained for an indefinite number of years. In addition, a complete civil service might have to be recruited and imported, possibly running into a size of several hundred thousand."[29]

MacArthur's powerful appeal for removing the emperor from charges convinced the White House. On January 30, the State Department intervened in London and succeeded in tabling the Australian and New Zealand proposal. Over the next two months, Washington forged a reluctant consensus among the Allies for the emperor's immunity. The FEC approved the policy on April 3.

War Crimes Trials

The United Nations War Crimes Commission was created in October 1943 and immediately began collecting evidence against Germany and Japan. The Allies, however, were divided over whether or not accused criminals should be tried. Churchill favored summarily executing those accused as they were apprehended. The Americans and, surprisingly, the Soviets favored due legal process. Churchill finally agreed.

The Potsdam Declaration clearly called for war crimes trials. On October 3, 1945, Washington defined three war criminal categories. Class A criminals were those who committed crimes against peace by planning or waging an aggressive war, and would be tried jointly by the eleven major allies. Class B criminals were those who violated war's laws and customs, and would be tried by those countries against whom or in which the crimes occurred. Class C criminals were those who committed inhumane acts against civilians such as enslavement or murder, and would also be tried separately by each power.

SCAP's investigation of war crimes was complicated by Tokyo's August 16, 1945 order to all military units to destroy all military documents. The Army and Navy ministries and Imperial Staff Headquarters, which had escaped the bombing, were burned down to destroy the evidence. Tokyo's action violated the unconditional surrender agreement it had accepted on August 14 in which all government documents, as well as forces, supplies, and equipment, would be given up. In contrast, Germany's archives were largely captured intact.

Despite these constraints, by January 1946, SCAP had arrested 103 suspects. On January 19, 1946, MacArthur convened the International Military Tribunal for the Far East's (IMTFE) charter which empowered it to investigate the era from 1928 to 1945 and prosecute any suspected war criminals.

Three months later, on April 29, IMTFE issued indictments against twenty-eight Class A suspects on fifty-five counts, of which thirty-six were for crimes against peace, sixteen for murder of prisoners of war and civilians, and three for conventional war crimes and crimes against humanity. Among those indicted were fifteen high ranking army officers, three admirals, five senior government officials or advisors, and five diplomats. An additional thirty-one suspects were held in custody without indictment and would not be released until the trial ended in 1948. The remainder of those 103 suspects were set free.

The IMTFE opened on June 3, 1946 and concluded on November 12, 1948. It held 818 sessions, listened to 419 witnesses, received written evidence from 779 additional witnesses, admitted 4,336 evidence exhibits, and produced 48,412 pages of transcripts. The final judgement was 1,218 pages. Of the eleven judges, three dissented. Of the twenty-five defendants, seven were sentenced to death, sixteen to life imprisonment, one received twenty years, and the last two years. None were acquitted. The seven were executed at Sugamo prison on December 23. Thirty years later, in 1978, Japan's government officially enshrined fourteen of the twenty-five convicted Class A war criminals at Yasukuni Jinja, Japan's national shrine to its war dead.

Of the Class B and Class C war crimes held elsewhere in the Far East, the Soviet Union and People's Republic of China have not completely released their war crime trial statistics. Elsewhere in the Far East, of more than 5,500 Japanese tried, 920 were executed, 475 received life sentences, 2,944 lesser prison terms, and 1,018 acquitted. The United States alone tried 1,344 of whom 140 were executed, 145 received life sentences, 877 lesser prison terms, and 182 acquitted.[30]

Were these trials and their decisions just? There is no question that Japan's government and commanders ordered wars of aggression and genocide. Japanese aggression murdered either directly or indirectly anywhere from 25 million to 44 million Chinese, and elsewhere in the Far East an additional 10 million to 20 million people.[31] The government indoctrinated all soldiers with the "three all policy" (sanko seisaku) – "Kill all! Burn All! Destroy all!" Yet, the responsibility for many Japanese atrocities "is destined to remain controversial – particularly if responsibility is understood to include not merely direct orders, but also socialization, indoctrination, and indifference."[32]

Was the United States also subject to war crimes trials for its carpet bombing of German and Japanese cities? After all, on September 28, 1937, the State Department denounced Japanese atrocities in China, declaring that "any general bombing of an extensive area wherein there resides a large population engaged in peaceful pursuits is unwarranted and contrary to the principles of law and of humanity." On June 3, 1938, the State Department proclaimed when "these hostilities take the form of ruthless bombing of unfortified localities with the resultant slaughter of civilian populations, and in particular of women and children, public opinion in the United States regards such methods as barbarous . . . [and] in violation of the most elementary principles of those standards of humane conduct which have been developed as an essential part of modern civilization."[33]

These American policy statements were in accord with international law which clearly distinguishes between combatants and noncombatants. But some belligerents in modern wars have blurred this distinction. In that sense, perhaps America's later carpet bombing of Japanese, if not German, cities was justified. After all, Japan's government had mobilized all of its subjects, armed them with bamboo spears and grenades, and ordered them to hurl themselves at the American invaders. Were not all Japan's subjects, by definition, potential combatants to be treated accordingly? A similar argument carries for production. Japan had mobilized virtually all of its economy for war. Was the factory or farm hand any less an effective soldier than those with rifles and tanks? And if the production army is as important as the fighting army in the war effort, should they both be considered legitimate targets?

Perhaps a better case for American hypocrisy on the war crimes trials can be made for its selection of whom would be prosecuted. Among those suspects which the United States chose to absolve were those in Unit 731 which was located in Harbin and conducted gruesome medical experiments on more than 3,000 allied POWs, including Americans. SCAP interrogated Unit 731's commander, Lieutenant-General Ishii Shiro, in spring 1946 but apparently granted him immunity in return for full information on Japan's biological warfare research and weapons.[34]

While the Class A Tokyo trial was being set up, the United States independently tried two suspected war criminals in late 1945, General Yamashita Tomoyuki and General Homma Masaharu who were, among other charges, respectively accused of perpetrating the 1945 Manila massacre and 1942 Bataan death march. The key charge was that they had ordered "the wholesale destruction of human lives, not alone on the field of battle . . . but in the homes, hospitals, and orphanages, in factories and fields; and the victims would be the young and old, the well and infirm – men, women, and children alike."[35] Both were found guilty and hanged. While no evidence was found that either general had directly ordered such atrocities, they were convicted for failing to prevent the crimes as they happened. The judgements have been heavily criticized as "victor's justice."[36]

Purges

SCAP purged those war leaders whom they could not directly try. On January 4, 1946, SCAP issued SCAPIN 550, the "Removal and Exclusion of Undesirable Personnel from Public Office." Yoshida protested MacArthur's purge order and pleaded with the general to himself take responsibility for implementing it. MacArthur refused, arguing that democratization would not be complete unless Japan purged itself. Japan's government, however, did not officially act until a year later on January 4, 1947 when it issued six imperial ordinances implementing SCAP's order. Meanwhile SCAP itself screened and purged officials.

The purges involved no legal proceedings, no arrest or imprisonment, and only limited appeals; those designated were simply removed from their careers. Of 2,308,863 people listed for investigation, over 200,000 Japanese from the military, government, zaibatsu, ultranationalist groups, and education were eventually purged. The exact figure of those purged will never be known because many designates quietly stayed in their positions. Along with Japan's entire military establishment and the Home Ministry, 80 per cent of the Diet members and 147 ultranationalist organizations were dissolved. Of the 3,384 people running in the April 1946 election, 252 were declared ineligible. Of national government officials, 1,809 were officially purged and thousands of others were pressured to resign. Around 4,800 officials, mostly policemen, were purged from the Home Ministry before it was officially abolished on December 31, 1947. Of hundreds of thousands of city and prefectural officials, 3,960 lost their jobs. After the military, the education system was the most heavily depleted with 5,211 directly purged and 115,778 forced to resign. Among the government and private mass media, 605 institutions were investigated and 1,066 of 1,328 people screened were purged.[37]

Yet, Japan's ministries were not purged across the board. Bureaucratic continuity rather than shakeups characterized most ministries, particularly the economic ones. For example, "only 42 higher officials (bureau chiefs and above) were purged from the Ministry of Commerce and Industry – the wartime Ministry of Munitions – and only nine from the Ministry of Finance."[38] SCAP viewed most bureaucrats as simple soldiers obeying orders from elsewhere, a nonpolitical body implementing rather than making policy. In this, of course, SCAP was profoundly wrong.

The purge of Japan's corporate elite did not begin until January 1947. MacArthur colorfully stated the logic behind SCAP's purge of Japan's corporate leaders: "It was these very persons, born and bred as feudalistic overlords, who held the lives and destiny of the majority of Japan's people in virtual slavery, and who, working in closest affiliation with its military, geared the country with both the tools and the will to wage aggressive war. . . . These are the persons who, under the purge, are to be removed from influencing the course of Japan's future economy."[39]

Japan's government found ways to mitigate SCAP's purge directive. For example, the order to purge "standing directors" was translated as targeting "managing directors" which was one step higher in Japan's corporate hierarchy, and thus reduced significantly the number who lost their jobs.[40] Of over 100,000 firms, only 154 were targeted out of which 8,309 ranking managers were screened and 914 were forced to resign.[41] Overall the Japanese got off much more lightly than the Germans who had a much higher percentage of their total population investigated and purged or even tried. Over 100,000 Germans were jailed and fined, and the property of a million more confiscated.[42]

The purges were an effective if blunt instrument for rooting out Japanese militarists and opening the way for a less authoritarian leadership. As Cohen points out, if the "purge brought little concrete benefit, failure to purge could have brought psychological disaster. Who among the Japanese people would have believed that Japan had really changed if the same old crowd was still running the country."[43] Even Yoshida grudgingly admitted that the purges were a "bloodless revolution" which exerted "a considerable influence in bringing about the democratization of all spheres of activity in Japan."[44]

DEMOCRATIZATION

Initial Reforms and Elections

On October 4, 1945, MacArthur issued a "bill of rights" which ordered the government to "remove all restrictions on political, civil, and religious liberties; free all political prisoners; abolish secret police organizations; permit unrestricted comment about the emperor and the government; and remove the minister of home affairs and all high police officials responsible for the enforcement of measures limiting freedom of thought, speech, religion, and assembly."[45] Rather than preside over these initial democratization steps, the Higashikuni cabinet resigned in protest. On October 9, a cabinet led by Shidehara Kijuro reluctantly took over.

The human and civil rights measure soon released 439 political prisoners, ended the surveillance of 2,026 others, and fired 4,800 thought police.[46] It also allowed the emergence of a spectrum of political parties from left to right which were soon competing fiercely for votes and finance.

The separation of church and state followed with a December 15 decree which cut off all state funding for Shinto and stated that all religions had equal rights. Emperor Hirohito reinforced these religious reforms on New Year's Day, 1946, when he issued a "declaration of humanity" (ningen sengen) and renounced his divinity. Afterward, Hirohito complied with MacArthur's request that he travel around the country and meet the people.

Japan's first postwar election on April 10, 1946 was a liberal democratic triumph. Over 3,000 candidates representing a score of political parties jostled for 466 House of Representative seats. The conservative Liberal and Progressive parties won 140 and 93 seats, respectively, giving them a comfortable majority. On the left, the Socialist Party garnered 92, the People's Cooperative Party 14, and the Communist Party 5. The remaining seats were divided among independents of widely varying perspectives and tiny parties that soon faded or were consolidated into the larger parties. Among those elected were 39 women, the largest number to reach the Diet to date.

At times SCAP's goals of demilitarization and democratization clashed, providing strangely mixed political lessons for the Japanese. Shortly after the election, SCAP purged Liberal Party leader Hatoyama Ichiro for his wartime sentiments. Hatoyama handed the party's reins over to Yoshida Shigeru who then became prime minister.

The April 1947 election was even more vast – 205,092 candidates competed for both the upper and lower Diet houses, prefectural, and local elections. With 143 seats the Socialists actually surpassed the Liberal and Democrat (formerly the Progressive) parties with 132 and 126, respectively, while the communists took 4 seats. Of the 466 house seats, 221 were new but only 15 were women. On May 24, Socialist Party head Katayama Tetsuo became Japan's first socialist prime minister. Following the revelation of a scandal, Katayama resigned in February 1948 and was replaced by Democrat Party leader Ashida Hitoshi.

The Constitution

In August 1945, although both Washington and SCAP expected constitutional revision to be democratization's central pillar, there was no blueprint for what Japan's new law of the land would include. Tokyo bowed to the need for "revision" yet had no intention of submitting a draft that differed significantly from the 1889 Constitution that made the emperor supreme. MacArthur first broached the constitutional reform issue to Prime Minister Shidehara on October 11, two days after he took office. Two days later Shidehara asked Matsumoto Joji to head a committee to study and suggest constitutional changes.

On January 11, 1946, Washington finally submitted to SCAP SWNCC 228 entitled "Reform of the Japanese Governmental System," which detailed the current constitution's defects and suggested specific changes. The report warned that "only as a last resort should the supreme commander order the government to effect the above-listed reforms, as the knowledge that they had been imposed by the allies would materially reduce their acceptance and support."[47]

The Matsumoto committee submitted its first draft on February 1. Upon examining it, GS head Courtney Whitney rejected it as still too authoritarian and demanded that the committee devise a genuinely liberal democratic constitution. Matsumoto returned on February 8 with another version that differed little from its successor.

Meanwhile on February 3, despairing that the Japanese could achieve that goal, MacArthur decided to draft a "model" constitution for Matsumoto's "guidance." MacArthur's instructions to twenty-seven GS members charged with the task included making the emperor the head of state, denouncing Japanese military forces, and abolishing the nobility. The GS committee was divided into seven subcommittees and took only seven days, from February 4 to February 10, 1946, to complete a revolutionary new constitution for Japan.

As MacArthur ordered, the emperor was made Japan's symbol while real sovereignty rested in the people. A dozen tenets guaranteed full human and civil rights for the Japanese. Representative democracy was enshrined in a unicameral parliamentary system from which the prime minister and his cabinet would be drawn. A separate supreme court was charged with judicial review. Constitutional amendments required a two-thirds Diet approval, followed by majority approval in a national referendum. The constitution's most controversial clause was Article 9 which explicitly stated that Japan would abandon the sovereign right of self-defense and military forces.

Whitney, his deputy, Charles Kades, and several other SCAP officials met with Matsumoto and other committee members on February 13. He started out by criticizing the second Matsumoto draft and then, to the shock of the Japanese, submitted the SCAP constitution. Whitney made it clear that while Matsumoto was not compelled to use the SCAP draft, it would be in Japan's interests to do so. Without a sincere Japanese commitment to liberal democracy, Whitney argued, MacArthur might be unable to keep the emperor from trial as a war criminal.

Despite Whitney's tough talk, Matsumoto resisted. On February 18 he submitted yet another version of Japan's authoritarian constitution. Whitney once again rejected it. The cabinet took up the SCAP draft the following day, and split over the emperor's powers and Article 9. Shidehara met with MacArthur on February 21 to plead for the Matsumoto version. MacArthur clearly stated that only the SCAP-drafted version was acceptable and warned Shidehara to take full credit for its inspiration, particularly Article 9 in which Japan renounced its participation in war and retention of military forces. And if Shidehara did not accept his "advice," MacArthur threatened to present the draft constitution to the Japanese people and let them decide. Shidehara and his cabinet had no choice, and the next day sought the emperor's approval. Hirohito fully accepted the SCAP constitution as the best possible deal for himself and Japan.

While the Americans were firm, Yoshida denies there was anything "coercive or overbearing in the attitude of the Occupation authorities towards us. They listened carefully to the Japanese experts and officials charged with the work, and in many cases accepted our proposals. When it happened that our discussions with them reached a deadlock, they would often adopt the attitude that we were perhaps too steeped in the ways of the old constitution to look at the problems in any other light; we might at least give their suggestions a trial and then, if they did not work, we could reconsider the whole question at the proper time and revise the necessary points. And they meant it."[48]

On March 4 and 5, the American and Japanese committees met to discuss the final draft. The only significant change the Japanese elicited from SCAP was a bicameral rather than unicameral legislature. Other than that there were minor changes in wording but not substance. All along, the constitutional drafts and negotiations were conducted in the strictest secrecy and the impression given that the final draft was solely the Matsumoto committee's creation. The more controversial the new constitution's tenet, the more vigorously SCAP claimed the Japanese were responsible. For example, although MacArthur and Shidehara later claimed that Article 9 was the latter's idea, all evidence points to the general as the author.

But before SCAP's draft became Japan's new constitution, it had to be approved by the existing political system. The new constitution was submitted as an amendment to the 1889 constitution, at once abolishing and replacing the older system. Under the 1889 constitution only the emperor could submit constitutional amendments. The emperor issued an imperial rescript approving the draft late on March 5. The text was publicly unveiled on April 17, 1946, and then debated in Diet committees, the Privy Council, the mass media, and political parties over the next six months. On October

7, the lower house approved the constitution 342–5, with only the communist members voting against it, while the upper house voted unanimously in favor. On October 29, the Privy Council approved the constitution. On November 3 the emperor signed the constitution. Six months later on May 3, 1947 it formally became law.

The Japanese made some thirty-one minor changes to the constitution. While the emperor's status and the peace clause were the most bitterly contested tenets of the proposed constitution, in the end they remained unaltered. The most controversial issue was the clause denying equal rights to non-Japanese residents, thus allowing the government and society to continue to discriminate against Korean, Chinese, and other foreign residents, many of whose ancestors were originally brought to Japan as slave labor. Japan's official and unofficial discrimination against other Asians has remained a bitter issue in its relations with those countries.

In the half year before the constitution became law, SCAP and the government wrote and the Diet passed eleven laws changing Japan's existing legal and judicial system to bring it into compliance with the new system. Within a year after the new constitution was enacted, an additional seventeen bills were passed which completed the revolutionary transformation of Japan's former authoritarian system into a liberal democratic system. The most important of these laws was the revised Civil Code which was passed on July 1, 1948.

Education

A central goal of Japan's school system was to indoctrinate children into an unquestioning obedience to authority and reverence for the emperor. Judging by the willingness of Japanese to die en masse during the war, the school system was extremely successful in achieving these goals. The school system was as unequal as it was authoritarian. School was mandatory and free only up to grade six, after which families had to pay. Only 1 per cent of elementary school graduates went on to college.

In December 1945, SCAP directed the Education Ministry to purge all ultranationalist teachers, books, teachings, and practices from Japanese schools, and completely revise the curriculum and textbooks to promote liberal democratic values. Eventually 115,778 teachers and administrators or 22 per cent of 700,000 resigned before the screenings and another 6,000 were later purged.[49] Textbooks were written by independent authors and published by private firms, and used with the Education Ministry's approval.

On March 31, 1946, an education mission led by George Stoddard, later president of the University of Illinois, arrived in Japan to supervise and advise the education reforms. Three weeks later, Stoddard issued a mission report in which he advocated compulsory, free, coeducational education which would include six years of primary, three of lower secondary, and three of upper secondary education; higher education as "an opportunity for the many, not a privilege for the few"; teaching based on class participation as well as lectures and textbooks; locally elected school boards and a reduction in the Education Ministry's powers to mostly supervisory; and some romanization of Japan's written language. SCAP overruled the government's attempts to delay implementation of the Stoddard program. In March 1947, the Diet finally passed the "Fundamental Law of Education" and the "School Education Law" which included all of the Stoddard recommendations.

The education reforms were largely a success. Today, about 95 per cent of Japanese children graduate from high school and of them 25 per cent go on to college. There were revolutionary gains in higher education. Between 1945 and 1952, the number of universities rose from twenty to 304, including 200 junior colleges. Japan Teacher's Union (Nikkyoso) soon became and remains a powerful force against any revival of nationalism and authoritarianism.

Yet, after the Occupation ended, Tokyo recentralized controls under the Education Ministry, made school boards appointed and advisory rather than elected and independent, and eliminated the internationalist perspectives in textbooks in favor of nationalist ones.

ECONOMIC RECONSTRUCTION

Humanitarian and Economic Development Aid

Although JSC 1380/15 had ordered MacArthur not to accept any responsibility for reviving Japan's economy, conditions soon forced him to do so. Japan was devastated by the bombing and blockade. The war destroyed one-quarter of Japan's economy, or $26 billion.[50] Industrial production in 1946 was only 30 per cent of what it had been a decade earlier. In 1947, Japan imported $526 million and exported a mere $174 million. Of Japan's 72 million people, over 2.1 million had died during the war, millions more were physically or emotionally scarred, and 7 million troops and civilians remained stranded overseas. Two million Korean and Chinese slave laborers awaited liberation in Japan. Around 13 million Japanese were unemployed.

These problems were exacerbated by the Japanese government. Between

August 14 and September 2, 1945, in direct violation of the surrender agreement, Tokyo dispersed an estimated 70 per cent of its vast supply stockpiles to Japan's business elite. Despite strenuous efforts, only about 30 per cent of those looted supplies were ever recovered; the rest ended up on the black market, thus simultaneously netting the sellers huge fortunes and bringing yet more hardship and despair to Japan's exploited masses. The value of these looted military stores may have "exceeded the total of all American aid ($2.2 billion) during the seven years of occupation."[51] And against SCAP orders, the government expanded the money supply twenty-six times between September 1945 and December 1946 alone. The result of these irresponsible policies designed to protect the business and political elites was hyperinflation and an ever wider gap between the rich few and mass of urban and rural poor. SCAP in turn had to request more money to address these Japanese government-created problems, thus increasing the burden for American taxpayers.

As if these problems were not enough, the 1945 crop was two-thirds its usual level; Japan faced mass starvation and disease. Tokyo residents received only 150 calories daily from Japanese sources, one-tenth of that necessary to survive and one-seventh the prewar level of 2,260 calories.[52] Yoshida admitted that the "food situation at that time was so serious that the Government was advised that ten million persons could be expected to die of starvation."[53]

SCAP instituted a massive food aid program which peaked during the summer of 1946 when a quarter of all Japanese food calories (two-thirds for Tokyo residents) came from American supplies. By reducing the Occupation forces from 600,000 to 200,000 in the fall of 1945, MacArthur was able to divert two-thirds of his army's allocated food supplies to the Japanese people. Altogether, the United States distributed 3.8 million tons of food worth $500 million and perhaps saved as many as 11 million Japanese lives.[54] SCAP also instituted a mass innoculation program against smallpox, cholera, typhoid, tuberculosis, and other infectious diseases, while the fields were sprayed with DDT to fight malaria. MacArthur estimated that these health measures saved an additional 2 million lives.[55] America's official humanitarian aid was largely administered under its Government Aid and Relief in Occupied Areas (GARIO) program. Altogether Washington sent to Japan over $1 billion in humanitarian aid between September 1945 and June 1948 alone. There was obviously a huge political as well as humanitarian payback in the GARIO program. As MacArthur admitted, "starvation . . . renders a people an easy prey to any ideology that brings with it life-sustaining food."[56]

America's Economic Recovery in Occupied Areas (EROA) program was

Japan's equivalent of the Marshall Plan or Economic Recovery Program (ERP) for Europe. Under this program, the United States gave Japan $1.8 billion in agricultural supplies alone, including fertilizer, machinery, fuel, seeds, and subsidies.[57] An additional billion dollars was pumped into the government to help overcome its balance of payments deficits.

SCAP authorized the creation of the Reconstruction Finance Bank (RFB) in 1946 to help finance development projects. The RFB immediately became a huge channel of public money to business leaders. On October 18, 1946, the Diet finally passed a law implementing an earlier SCAP directive that the government pursue deflationary policies which included ending postwar subsidies and imposing taxes on the vast wartime profits made by companies and businessmen. Yet, the government refused to implement this law, leading SCAP to fire Finance Minister Ishibashi Tanzan on May 16, 1947.

In addition to these measures, SCAP helped organize Japanese business into two powerful institutions, the Federation of Business Organizations (FEO, Keidanren) which helps propose and implement industrial policies, and the Japanese Management Association (JMA, Nikkeiren) which concentrates on labor policy.

Land Reform

After the constitution, SCAP's most revolutionary act was land reform. By 1945, peasants comprised 30 million people or 40 per cent of Japan's population, of which 65 per cent partially or wholly worked the fields and handed over at least half of the crop to the nearly one million absentee landlords. These tenant peasants paid additional costs for fertilizer, seed, animals, housing, and equipment. Most existed on a hand-to-mouth subsistence existence. Peasants often reluctantly sold their daughters into prostitution.[58]

SCAP pressured the government for sweeping land reform measures. The government replied with a December 6, 1945 law setting limits of 12.25 acres for absentee landlords. The law would have had little effect on farm tenancy. On December 9, SCAP ordered the law suspended and demanded a more comprehensive plan. Negotiations between SCAP and the government continued throughout the first half of 1946. A SCAP-approved bill passed the cabinet on July 26 but did not pass the Diet until October 11, 1946. When the government continued to drag its feet implementing the law, SCAP issued another directive in February 1948 ordering it to do so, and backed its order by arguing that if Tokyo refused to implement the existing reforms it might have to accept far harsher ACJ proposals which involved no compensation for landowners. The government finally complied.

Under the land reform bill, the government bought land from its owners with government ten-year bonds and resold it at cheap prices to the peasants who cultivated it. Low-interest loans were extended to the peasants. By 1949, Japan's tenant-farmers had been reduced from nearly 65 per cent to 10 per cent of all farmers, and 3 million had acquired ownership of 5.5 million acres. Farmers were organized into "agricultural cooperatives" (nokyo) through which the government extended subsidies, cheap credit, technology, equipment, fertilizer, seed, and markets.

Even the hyperinflation helped the peasants. Forced debts had stolen land from peasants during the previous century. The land reform and hyperinflation allowed the peasants to acquire land and pay off past debts at minimal costs. By 1948, the farm debt had fallen to 1 per cent in real terms of its 1934–6 level![59] That same hyperinflation allowed the government to buy out land from the landowners at minimal costs and simultaneously stripped the rich rural elite of much of their wealth.

No SCAP economic reform was more revolutionary than land reform. The reforms transformed millions of poverty-stricken peasants, for whom communist and socialist slogans had considerable appeal, into middle class conservative farmers who ever since have provided the backbone of Liberal-Democratic support and a vast affluent market for Japanese business.

Labor Reform

A labor movement had struggled in Japan since the early twentieth century. By the mid-1930s it embraced about 420,000 workers, only a fraction of Japan's total labor force. In 1940, the government banned all labor unions and organized the remnants into the Imperial Rule Assistance Association (IRAA).

From the Occupation's start, MacArthur pressured the government to enact labor reforms. The government reluctantly complied. On December 21, the Diet passed the Labor Union Law which was patterned after the 1935 Wagner Act which legalized labor unions, collective bargaining, and the right to strike. The result was a dramatic increase in union membership, from none to 5 million members and 17,266 unions by December 1946.[60] These unions were virtually all enterprise rather than trade unions, and were organized into several federations of which the most important were the moderately leftist Japan Federation of Labor (JFL, Nihon Rodo Kumiai Sodomei) with a million members and the radical Congress of Industrial Unions (CIU, Sanbetsu Kaigi) with 1.6 million members.

SCAP followed up this law with several other important labor reforms.

On September 28, 1946, the Diet passed the Labor Relations Adjustment Law which provided labor relations boards at the prefectural and national levels to mediate any disputes. On April 17, 1947, the Diet passed the Labor Standards Law which promoted an eight-hour day and forty-eight hour work week with 25 per cent overtime premiums, cash salaries, protection for women and child labor, and safety, sanitation, sick leave, accident compensation, and other workplace standards.

A mission led by Blaine Hoover arrived in Japan in late 1946 to investigate Japan's public workers and led to the third sweeping law. Of the then 2.5 million government employees, 1.5 million were civil servants in ministries and agencies and 1 million were in public enterprises like the railroads, communications, salt, and tobacco. The Hoover mission report on June 16, 1947 advised that civil servants be allowed to organize but not bargain collectively or strike while government enterprise workers be allowed to organize and bargain collectively but not strike. These proposals were embodied in the National Public Service Law passed by the Diet on October 21, 1947. The Katayama government created a Labor Ministry on September 1, 1947 to uphold these and other labor laws.

Zaibatsu Reform

The zaibatsu were huge family owned industrial conglomerates that controlled most of Japan's economy. The ten largest zaibatsu owned 53 per cent of Japan's financial and insurance business, 50 per cent of mining, 68 per cent of machinery and equipment production, and 38 per cent of chemical production.[61] The zaibatsu cooperated rather than competed with each other, divvied up markets "with other cartels, fixed prices, allocated materials, operated joint subsidiaries, and often enforced business agreements on nonparticipating companies. Through their banking outlets, they even controlled credit to small businesses."[62]

A number of prewar and wartime studies such as William Johnstone's *The Future of Asia*, Owen Lattimore's *Solution in Asia*, Andrew Roth's *Dilemma in Japan*, and Thomas Bisson's *Japan's War Economy* created the widespread belief in Washington that Japan's zaibatsu contributed to Japanese expansion by their demands for foreign markets and resources.[63] MacArthur agreed, stating that the zaibatsu's "record is thus one of economic oppression and exploitation at home, aggression and spoliation abroad."[64] Under these assumptions, a major source of Japanese imperialism would disappear if the zaibatsu were eliminated.

Aware that there were moves to eliminate the zaibatsu, in October 1945, Japan's Big Four zaibatsu (Sumitomo, Mitsui, Mitsubishi, and Yasuda) leaders met with SCAP and proposed that the family members sell off their shares. SCAP viewed this as a first step but warned that the reform had to be much more sweeping and include all of the zaibatsu. After persistent SCAP pressure, the government unveiled a plan on November 4, 1945 to transfer the stocks of the Big Four zaibatsu, which controlled one-third of the economy, into a newly created holding company liquidation commission (HCLC) which would in turn sell the stocks to private investors. The zaibatsu would be compensated with government bonds.

Meanwhile, the JSC "Basic Directive" which MacArthur received on November 3, 1945 called for the drastic restructuring of Japan's economy which involved the "reduction or dismantlement of certain branches of Japanese production" including steel, iron, chemicals, nonferrous metals, ships, aluminum, magnesium, synthetic rubber, machine tools, automotive vehicles, heavy machines, and so on, and also a wider "distribution of income and of ownership of the means of production and trade."[65] MacArthur acted on this policy on November 6, 1945 by issuing SCAPIN 244 which ordered the dissolution of all family-owned zaibatsu. On December 8, SCAP ordered the government to increase the number of those zaibatsu targeted to eighteen holding companies and 326 subsidiaries. Even tougher measures would follow.

A half year earlier, in April 1945, Truman had appointed Edwin Pauley the head of a special committee to propose industrial reforms in Japan and Germany. In November and December 1945, Edwin Pauley led a mission to Japan to study ways in which Japan's war industries could best be dismantled. On December 18 Pauley issued a report sharply critical of SCAP's antimonopoly program. Instead, he called for the sweeping dissolution of Japanese zaibatsu and corporations, including machine tools, ball bearings, and shipbuilding, the reduction of steel from 11 million to 2.5 million annual tons, and the elimination of the aircraft industry. Pauley concluded by arguing that Japan not be allowed an industrial base larger than its 1930–4 level. These targeted industries would be dismantled and sent abroad as reparations in an amount based on Japan's ability to pay rather than the war damage Japanese imperialism had caused.[66] Secretary of State Byrnes supported the plan; MacArthur strongly opposed it as too severe.

Then, from January to March 1946, a mission led by Corwin Edwards further investigated the zaibatsu. The Edwards Report also criticized SCAP's antimonopoly program. It defined "excessive business concentration" as that which "restricts competition or impairs the opportunity for others to engage in business independently, in any important segment of business."[67]

SWNCC passed on the report to the FEC which did not get around to approving it as FEC-230 until October 1947. By that time, the deconcentration policy was well underway.

MacArthur eventually complied with these policies. On August 13 and 14, 1946, SCAP issued eight directives designating 505 factories for reparations, and later upped the number to 700 in January 1947. Yet, SCAP actually dismantled and sent abroad only a handful of these factories. In January 1948, SCAP began to send overseas the first of 19,000 machine tools worth $20 million from seventeen army and navy arsenals and completed the program seven months later. China received half, the Philippines one-fifth, and the Dutch East Indies and British Commonwealth the rest. These shipments represented only 15 per cent of all Japan's machine tools.[68]

Meanwhile the Holding Company Liquidation Commission (HCLC) raised the total number of targeted corporate and individually owned holding companies to 83 and 56, respectively. The HCLC bought the stock with government ten-year bonds and then resold it to private investors. By late 1947, the HCLC had bought and sold $670 million of stock. But of those 83 holding companies targeted, only 16 were actually dissolved, 26 were dissolved and reorganized, 11 were reorganized, and the remaining 30 were untouched. Of the targeted subsidiaries, 250 were forced into independence.[69] SCAP did not target banks, which, along with insurance and trading firms, bought up most of the stocks and quickly replaced the holding companies as the industrial group's financial core. All along SCAP repeatedly urged the Japanese to pass and implement deconcentration legislation, but Tokyo continued dragging its feet. Finally, on March 12, 1947, the Diet passed the "Law for Prohibition of Private Monopoly and Methods of Preserving Fair Trade."

The deconcentration was shortlived. For example, when "SCAP broke up Mitsui and Mitsubishi trading companies [which together had accounted for 70 per cent of Japan's prewar trade] into hundreds of fragments – 213 successor companies in all. . . . Within five years, like droplets of mercury coalescing into ever bigger drops on contact with each other, both the Mitsubishi and the Mitsui trading companies were substantially reconstituted as before."[70] The zaibatsu reforms failed to prevent excessive corporate collusion and concentration; they simply made Japan's industrial groups more efficient, transforming them from "cordial" to "cutthroat" oligopolies and transferring ownership from feudal families to professional money-managers.[71] Japan's economy remains dominated by hundreds of industrial groups and cartels in which markets, products, contracts, and prices are carefully managed so that the insiders prosper at the expense of entrepreneuers and foreign firms.

CONCLUSION

Washington's policy toward Japan was shaped by the tugging and pushing of three positions scattered throughout the administration. The "Japan hands" advocated the soft-line policy of keeping Japan's political, social, and economic system intact while simply demobilizing its military. The moderate-line favored extensive political, economic, and social reforms designed to thoroughly demilitarize and democratize Japan. The hard-line pushed for a punitive peace that would destroy Japan's industry as well as military and ensure that the country would never again be more than a second-rate power in the world. The policy that emerged from this tug-of-war was largely a mix of the moderate- and hard-line positions during the first phase up through 1947, and soft-line thereafter.

During the Occupation's first two years, SCAP followed up Washington's orders by pushing through sweeping political and economic reforms that created the foundation for Japan's interrelated liberal democracy and prosperity. Impoverished, landless peasants were tranformed into middle class conservative farmers; unions and the number of affiliated workers rocketed, with five million members by December 1946. The constitution and new civil code transformed Japan from authoritarianism to a multiparty liberal democracy.

All along, Japan's government and interest groups resisted all of these essential reforms. If SCAP had given in to the Japanese resistance, the country would have remained authoritarian and underdeveloped in many ways. Rather than developing into the economic superpower of today, Japan's current socioeconomic level would fall somewhere behind the United States and West Europe and ahead of Mexico and Brazil.

At the time, however, many in the Japanese elite rejected the American reforms. Throughout his *Memoirs*, Yoshida particularly blasts the labor reforms as being "utilized by the destructive Left-wing elements in the country, enabling them to stage demonstrations and engage in labor disputes of a political character which intensified the general social unrest prevailing in Japan after the defeat."[72] As a conservative, Yoshida's views are unsurprising. He was socialized in a highly authoritarian environment in which government and business collaborated in exploiting labor.

Rather than criticize the reforms, Yoshida should have embraced them because they made his task of governing infinitely easier. Politically, SCAP's labor and land reforms gutted the political left's issue agenda, making possible solid conservative rule throughout the postwar era. The reforms converted impoverished masses of peasants and workers into middle class voters largely committed to the status quo. Japan's postwar labor and other protests occurred within newly created democratic institutions rather than against a repressive, exploitative system. The ten-year bonds which the government paid out to land and business owners were quickly eroded by inflation until they were nearly worthless, and thus helped narrow the formerly vast discrepancies between rich and poor.

MacArthur later claimed that the democratic constitution was "probably the single most important accomplishment of the occupation."[73] Without American pressure, the Japanese would have simply continued the prewar authoritarian system which was not terribly different from that of Mexico's current system.

While most laud the 1947 constitution's liberal principles, to MacArthur and Japanese officials, the constitution's most profound tenet rested in Article 9 which read: "Aspiring sincerely to an international peace based on justice and order, the Japanese people forever renounce war as a sovereign right of the nation and the threat or use of force as a means of settling disputes with other nations. For the above purpose, land, sea, and air forces, as well as other war potential, will never be maintained. The right of belligerency of the state will not be recognized."

Yoshida expressed the feelings of many Japanese and Americans alike when he said "we feel unbounded pride and responsibility in leading the world by our renunciation of war."[74] To Yoshida, Japan renounced even self-defense. In his arguments before the Diet for Article 9's acceptance, Yoshida maintained "since both the right of belligerency and the maintenance of all forms of war potential were renounced in Clause 9 of the new Constitution . . . , it followed that war as a means of self-defense was also denounced."[75]

The elation over the "peace clause" soon faded. While Washington had ordered Japan's military abolished during the Occupation, it had no intention of removing Japan's sovereign right of self-defense. Washington and most Japanese conservatives reject Yoshida's argument and have argued that Japan still retains the right of self-defense, and simply cannot use force overseas. Washington and Tokyo, however, have periodically debated the size and structure of Japan's military. Like Yoshida, Japan's leftist parties take Article 9 literally and argue that there should be no Japanese defense forces. A half century after the Occupation ended, that debate continues.

6 The Reverse Course, 1947–52

By 1947, American policy toward the Soviet Union had shifted from serving a World War II ally to fighting a Cold War enemy. Henceforth the United States would "contain" rather than accommodate Soviet ambitions. The founder of America's containment policy was George Kennan who "came as close to authoring the diplomatic doctrine of his era as any diplomat in our history."[1] Kennan, and to a lesser extent Defense Undersecretary William Draper, was also largely responsible for making Japan the subject of a "shift of occupation policies from democratization of a former enemy to reconstruction of a future cold-war ally."[2]

MacArthur at first resisted Washington's new policy. However, his humiliating loss in the 1948 presidential primaries and Republican convention where he received only eight votes, emboldened the White House: "the political verdict heralded the end of MacArthur's independence in Japan."[3] Now, the White House would push through its policies toward Japan whether MacArthur joined them or not. On December 10, 1948, Truman issued a nine-point economic revival directive to SCAP (Supreme Command for Allied Powers) and dispatched Chicago banker Joseph Dodge to implement it. Although MacArthur protested and tried to delay such intrusions, he ultimately conformed.

During the implementation of these new policies, SCAP personnel and direct supervision of many aspects of Japan were steadily reduced. Between 1947 and 1949, SCAP's number of American civilian employees at headquarters was cut from 3,660 to 1,950, its civil affairs teams which supervised the prefecture capitals from 2,758 to 326, and its troop level to 150,000.[4]

While united on transforming Japan into Asia's "workshop," the White House was split on when a peace treaty with Japan should be signed and what terms it should include. North Korea's attack on South Korea in June 1950 brought the Defense Department into ranks with the State Department on negotiating both defense and peace treaties with Japan that would cement that nation's ties with the United States. Henceforth, Japan would be America's central military as well as economic Far East ally.

THE INTERNATIONAL MATRIX: THE COLD WAR, CONTAINMENT, AND JAPAN

Who was responsible for the Cold War in which for nearly forty-five years the United States and Soviet Union sought to strengthen their influence and weaken the others around the world by every means short of all-out war? In the years following World War II both Moscow and Washington became ever more tightly locked into a mentality whereby they perceived the other's actions as expansionist and aggressive and their own actions as justified and defensive. For example, while Washington was demanding a role in the fate of the eastern European regimes that Stalin was rapidly subjecting, it was simultaneously asserting its domination over Japan's Occupation and pressuring the United Nations to grant the United States complete control over the western Pacific islands.

The White House would have probably eventually attempted to contain rather than outright war against the Soviet Union. It was George Kennan who initiated the containment policy and carefully formulated its conceptual framework and grand strategy. In doing so, Kennan gave President Truman a cohesive program to sell to an increasingly isolationist and financially stingy Congress and public.

Who was containment's author? Kennan was a Princeton graduate and foreign service officer with a distinguished series of postings in different Eastern European capitals and during 1933–4, 1935–7, and 1944–6 in Moscow. He returned to Washington in April 1946 to serve first as lecturer at the National War College and then from 1947 as director of the State Department's Policy Planning Staff (PPS). Quietly intense, highly intelligent, gentlemanly, dutiful, and self-effacing, Kennan personified the model diplomat and foreign policymaker.

Kennan's containment policy evolved through his "long telegraph" from Moscow to the State Department in August 1946, "Psychological Background of Soviet Foreign Policy" in January 1947 which was later published as the "Mr X" article in *Foreign Affairs* in July 1947, lectures at the National War College, and a series of PPS papers. In these works and others, Kennan rejected Roosevelt's universalist foreign policy for a focus on concrete American interests and the strategy to best secure those interests. Rather than through the United Nations as Roosevelt had hoped, American security would rest on the White House's skilful manipulation of the power balance and spheres of influence. As a conservative realist Kennan recognized "that all choice exists along a spectrum of evil; one must distinguish gradations and choose the least imperfect policy from various unhappy possibilities."[5]

American foreign policy would center on countering the Soviet Union which, in the postwar world, posed a threat to the west. But just what was that threat? According to Kennan, although it did involve the expansion of Soviet power, it was not one of outright military aggression like that the Allies just defeated. Moscow's foreign policy under the commissars differed little from that of the Czars. Centuries of foreign invasion had led Moscow to create a highly autocratic state, and ingrained in Russians a fierce xenophobia and obsession with secrecy. The Soviets, like their czarist predecessors, sought not to conquer the world but carve out buffer regions in eastern Europe, central Asia, and the Far East that would leave the vast empire relatively invulnerable to attack. There was no grand plan and timetable to Soviet foreign policy, only priorities. Opportunities for expanded influence in those priority regions and issues would be seized or, if need be, created. Soviet influence in West Europe and other regions would be achieved through communist subversion rather than invasion. However, Soviet, like Russian, foreign policy was flexible. Faced with firm opposition, Moscow would retreat temporarily and probe elsewhere for weaknesses and opportunities.

Kennan's strategies for thwarting Soviet ambitions were political and economic, not military. Communism breeds in economic chaos, stagnation, and inequality, and subsequent political instability. By creating or restoring a country's economic vitality and political moorings, the United States would wither the base of communism's appeal and thus blunt Soviet expansion. American policy would succeed not with bluster and saber-rattling but with a quiet, confident, tough diplomacy – "as long as we show that our purposes are decent and that we have the courage to follow them through, the Russians will never challenge us."[6]

American military security could rest on nuclear power and a small conventional army, navy, and air force. Having been devastated by Germany's invasion which cost at least 20 million Soviet lives, Moscow would avoid another war – one that it would likely lose – at all costs. Although the Soviets might occasionally test western resolve as in Berlin and later Cuba, Moscow would retreat if faced with unblinking American resolve. America's containment strategy would take decades to succeed. Eventually, however, contained within its vast polyglot empire, the Soviet threat would crumble because of communism's failures and the growth of nationalism.

Kennan's containment policy was highly "selective" compared to the "global" containment of American policy after 1950. He identified three centers of industrial and military power in the world besides the United States and Soviet Union – Britain, Germany and West Europe, and Japan. American security depended on keeping those three powers firmly allied to the

United States. If any of them should fall under Soviet domination, Moscow would have the potential industrial and military might to threaten directly an attack on the United States. While the Persian Gulf lacked military and industrial power, Kennan increasingly saw its vast oil reserves as an additional fulcrum of global power that had to be kept from Soviet control.[7]

Kennan wrote off eastern Europe and much of the Third World, including China, as insignificant in the geopolitical contest between Washington and Moscow. There was nothing the United States could or should do about the Soviet subjection of eastern Europe. The Soviet Red army occupation and imposition of communist governments was a reality that the United States had no interest in challenging. Kennan's containment policy was not anti-communist per se, but anti-Soviet. To Kennan, many liberation struggles in the Third World were nationalist first and communist second. Neighboring countries which became communist would be little better able to resolve their often ancient conflicts and unite against the west. And if a poor country or even region became communist, it would eventually have to accommodate itself to a global economy controlled by the western powers.

Kennan warned against confusing human rights concerns with concrete American strategic and economic interests; worries over the former would at best obscure and at worse undermine the latter: "We should stop putting ourselves in the position of being our brother's keeper and refrain from offering moral and ideological advice. We should cease to talk about vague and – for the Far East – unreal objectives such as human rights, the raising of living standards, and democratization. The day is not far off when we are going to have to deal in straight power concepts. The less we are then hampered by idealistic slogans the better."[8]

According to Kennan, American power was as limited as its interests; thus policymakers had to be extremely careful where and how it was wielded, for fear of squandering it in marginal issues and areas. For example, while acknowledging the political necessity to continue to provide some "minimum aid" for the KMT, Kennan urged Truman to "liquidate as rapidly as possible our unsound commitments in China."[9] A communist victory in China would not bolster Soviet power, and might undermine it as Moscow poured billions of dollars into the world's most populous poverty-stricken country to support the new regime.

Influenced by Kennan's perspectives, other agencies offered similar analyses. The March 1947 SWNCC 360 report offered a sweeping analysis of the threats facing American interests around the world. It identified West Europe and Japan as economically and politically vulnerable to Soviet influence, and advocated a $500 million American aid program to strengthen them. The report explored Japan's potential importance as the Far East's engine of growth.

The growing animosity between the United States and Soviet Union, along with Kennan's conception of that struggle and how best to wage it, coincided with a growing conservatism in American politics. In the November 1946 congressional elections, Republicans and Southern Democrats won out over New Deal liberals. Many of the conservatives were isolationist and virtually all favored tax and spending cuts, particularly for foreign aid. The Truman administration had increased difficulty getting a tight-fisted Congress to appropriate its spending requests; it could break the logjam only by rallying the people and politicians around some idealistic crusade.

Despite these compelling foreign and domestic reasons to accept Kennan's containment policy, the catalyst did not arrive for Truman until early 1947 when Britain announced that it could no longer afford to maintain the eastern Mediterranean's political stability, currently threatened by two crises, the civil war in Greece and Soviet pressure on Turkey to revise its eastern provinces. The White House feared that communist victories in Greece and Turkey would inspire similar efforts throughout the region. But before Truman could act, he had to receive congressional and public approval.

In 1947, America's containment policy was announced in two major addresses, that of President Truman on March 12 and Secretary of State George Marshall on June 5. Someone once said that you cannot rally the American people to a cause unless you scare the hell out of them with the consequences of their failure to act. Truman's speech attempted to do just that. To Kennan's alarm, Truman espoused a global rather than selective containment. While attempting to win support for massive American aid to Greece and Turkey, Truman maintained that every country and region was vulnerable to communism. Thus the United States would have to intervene – militarily if need be – anywhere communism threatened. Truman's apocalyptic vision, however, seemed to work; in May it wrung congressional appropriations for Greece and Turkey and prepared the way for Marshall's far more ambitious aid plan.

In contrast to the "Truman Doctrine," Marshall's plan captured Kennan's emphasis on using primarily economic means to revive the most essential regions and countries. Congress finally passed Marshall's European Recovery Program (ERP) in March 1948 under which the United States would extend massive aid to Europe only if those countries which desired it organized themselves to receive and disburse it in the most effective manner. This cooperation helped lay the foundation for the European Community. The American extension of $13.3 billion in aid to Europe and $2.2 billion to

Japan was decisive in reviving those countries and integrating them within an expanding global economy.

To wage Cold War, Truman also revamped the White House's personnel and institutions. Truman had replaced Byrnes with Marshall as Secretary of State in January 1947. Marshall then embarked on a complete reorganization of American foreign policies and policymaking institutions. In May, Marshall founded the Policy Planning Staff (PPS) within the State Department to act as a long-range planning center, and named Kennan as its first chief. In July 1947, Congress passed the National Security Act which created the Defense Department, Central Intelligence Agency (CIA), and National Security Council (NSC) which replaced SWNCC.

Where did the Far East fall into containment's ends and means? Immediately following World War II, the Americans and Soviets largely cooperated in Asia. In August 1945, China and the Soviet Union signed a treaty in which Moscow agreed to withdraw its forces from Manchuria within three months, promised to not interfere in China's internal politics, and granted support to Chiang's government. By early 1946, Moscow had recalled its troops from Manchuria while Washington withdrew its 50,000 from China. Stalin favored a negotiated end to China's civil war and applauded George Marshall's appointment as special envoy to the KMT (Koumintang) and CCP (Chinese Communist Party) in 1946. Moscow grudgingly went along with Washington's "strategic trusteeship" over the Pacific islands.

Another area of cooperation was Korea. The Truman administration's decision to occupy Korea was prompted by the Soviet entry into the war against Japan. On August 10, two days after the Soviets attacked Japanese forces in northeast Asia, Truman ordered American troops to land in Korea, and then told Stalin that they should divide Korea at the 38th parallel between a southern American zone and northern Soviet zone. Korea's capital, Seoul, would be in the American zone. To the administration's surprise, Stalin complied. He may have done so hoping that Japan would similarly be divided. Or he simply may not have cared about Korea's fate and was happy to receive an explicit half of it.

As in Germany, neither Washington nor Moscow anticipated Korea's permanent division. Yet both powers followed policies that reinforced the artificial division. Each power imposed its own dictator to govern its half. Washington brought in Rhee Syngman who had exiled himself in the United States during most of the Japanese occupation. Communist leader Kim Il Sung rode into the northern capital, Pyongyang, on a Soviet tank after having spent years fighting Japanese forces in Manchuria. Soviet and American forces occupied their respective sides of the 38th parallel in Korea until they both withdrew in 1948.

Meanwhile, in the years following Japan's defeat, Washington strove to build a defense in-depth across the Pacific. Washington pressured the United Nations in April 1947 to grant the United States a "strategic trusteeship" over the Marshall, Caroline, Marianas, and Marcus islands. One price Tokyo eventually would pay for a peace treaty was to relinquish indefinitely the Ryukyu islands to the United States. These island chains along with anchors in Japan and the Philippines and, after 1950, South Korea and Taiwan, formed a vast bulwark to defend against or assault any threat from mainland Asia. Washington further solidified this defense in 1952 with several security treaties. World War III scenarios envisioned U.S. planes carrying atomic bombs toward the Soviet Union from bases in Japan and the Ryukyus as well as West Europe and Turkey. The JSC described the rationale behind this strategy in March 1946: "the experience of the recent war demonstrated that the defense of a nation, if it is to be effective, must begin beyond its borders. The further away from our own vital areas we can hold the enemy, through the possession of advanced bases . . . the greater our chances of surviving successfully an attack with atomic weapons and of destroying the enemy which employs them against us."[10] However, until the Korean War, the Far East ranked third in strategic importance and war planning priority behind West Europe and the Middle East. A Soviet attack was deemed most likely in Europe, less so in the Persian Gulf, and least likely in Northeast Asia.

By early 1946, the White House began to write off Chiang's KMT and China's strategic importance. It had become apparent that China would remain so wracked by civil war, chaos, and poverty that it would probably never fulfill Roosevelt's vision of it as one of the "four world policemen." Virtually every American envoy dispatched to China reported back the KMT's corruption, inefficiency, poorly trained soldiers, unwillingness to fight aggressively, and lack of popular appeal. Chiang was seen as the leader of a "feudal-fascist" regime that could not possibly survive let alone win the civil war against the communists with their grass roots support and brillance at fighting a guerrilla war. Prolonged U.S. support for the KMT would only make relations more difficult with the ultimately victorious CCP.

Yet, despite this unofficial White House consensus, American support for Chiang continued. As the Cold War deepened, pressure from the powerful China lobby in Washington built on the White House to increase its support for Chiang's regime. In 1947, the Truman administration lifted its arms ban imposed the previous year. The following year, the White House asked Congress for an additional $400 million in economic aid and $125 million in military aid to the KMT. Congress complied with the China Aid Act of April 1948.

Meanwhile, the power balance in Europe and Asia seemed to tilt against the United States and its allies. Between July 1948 and April 1949, Stalin imposed a blockade on Berlin which the United States circumvented through a round-the-clock airlift to the beleaguered city. Then the Soviet Union exploded its own nuclear bomb in 1949, ending America's nuclear monopoly. In October 1949, Mao Zedong proclaimed the creation of the People's Republic of China. Kennan aside, most influential Americans saw China's "loss" as a disaster for American interests. The result, many feared, would be a domino effect of one Far East country after another experiencing revolution, including ultimately, Japan itself. In January 1950, the Chinese communists seized American consular property and briefly detained consul general Edward Clubb. Mao Zedong and Josef Stalin signed a thirty-year friendship treaty on February 14, 1950 which pledged Soviet aid and both countries to ally against "aggressive action on the part of Japan or any other state which should unite with Japan, directly or indirectly, in acts of aggression."[11]

On January 5, 1950, the Truman White House finally decided to cut its losses and run from China's civil war when it announced that it would end its aid and advice to the KMT holed up on Taiwan. The KMT could, however, still purchase arms and equipment with already appropriated money. On January 12 before the National Press Club, Acheson tried to put the administration's new policy toward the KMT in a larger context. He explained that the Soviet threat was primarily directed against West Europe and only indirectly connected with the political and economic chaos afflicting many countries and regions worldwide. Nationalism rather than communism was the primary cause of anti-colonial struggles and the assertiveness of newly independent states. China's civil war and the communist triumph followed from the breakdown of traditional Chinese society in the nineteenth century from imperialism and modernization. Given the power of Chinese nationalism, Acheson expected Beijing's new communist rulers to break eventually with Moscow despite their common ideology. American policy would attempt to widen differences both within and between communist states and ameliorate revolutionary conditions elsewhere through economic and military aid. American interests lay not on mainland Asia but along a "crescent or semi-circle which goes around . . . [it] with Japan at one end and India at the other." Acheson identified Japan as the key to this rim strategy, the workshop that could boost those countries' economic dynamism and political stability. But despite the Occupation reforms Japan's economy remained weak. The United States would have to continue aiding Japan and promoting its trade before the country could become Asia's engine of growth.

The image which captured American fears about communist expansion in Asia during this time was not dominos but bowling. In a highly influential March 1950 *Saturday Evening Post* article, Stewart Alsop wrote: "The head pin was China. It is down already. The two pins in the second row are Burma and Indo-China. If they go, the three pins in the third row, Siam, Malaya, and Indonesia, are pretty sure to topple in their turn. And if all the rest of Asia goes, the resulting psychological, political, and economic magnetism will almost certainly drag down the four pins of the fourth row, India, Pakistan, Japan, and the Philippines."[12]

In other words, as Indochina goes so goes Japan, along with the rest of Asia. Unless, of course, the United States entered the fray with the determination and skill to counter the communists with massive economic and military resources. The efforts of Alsop and other journalists prepared the public to accept a interventionist policy in the region which the White House was busily formulating. In March 1950, Truman got Congress to allocate the first direct aid – $15 million – to French forces fighting the communists in Indochina. A quarter century later, the United States would finally withdraw from Indochina after squandering 58,000 American lives and $200 billion.

The government and public were rapidly adopting a rigid, hardline anticommunist position which would eventually lock the United States into a role as the economic, military, and/or covert patron of noncommunist forces in virtually all the world's regions and countries. At the time, these policies seemed eminently reasonable to most Americans, given the Berlin crisis, Soviet explosion of a nuclear bomb, communist victory in China, and Beijing–Moscow alliance, along with the rise of anti-communist hysteria fired by Senator Joseph McCarthy, the Committee on Un-American Activities, and the damning accusation "Who lost China?"

This new hardline, military-oriented, global containment was conceptualized in NSC 68 which was issued in April 1950. Composed largely by new PPS head Paul Nitze, NSC 68 assumed that "in the context of the present polarization of power a defeat of free institutions anywhere is a defeat everywhere."[13] NSC 68 called for a massive American military build-up and U.S. military and economic aid to any country besieged by communist insurrection. The rationale was that every country was important to American security, since the loss of one country to communism anywhere would provide a base for the subversion of neighboring states. All American resources must be mobilized toward winning the Cold War, no matter what the economic or moral costs: "Considerations of priority and economy might be appropriate in normal times, but in the face of a threat such as that posed by the Soviet Union, preoccupations of this sort had to go by the board.

... The integrity of our system will not be jeopardized by any measures, covert or overt, violent or non-violent, which serve the purpose of frustrating the Kremlin design." The administration quickly adopted it as official policy.

Then, on June 25, 1950, North Korea invaded South Korea. The Truman administration quickly concluded that Moscow had encouraged North Korea's attack, hoping to test American resolve, intimidate Japan away from future peace and security treaties, and possibly bog down U.S. forces in Asia before another Soviet probe or even all-out attack in West Europe. JCS head Omar Bradley later admitted that "in those days we held the rather simplistic belief that all communist moves worldwide were dictated from Moscow and by Stalin personally."[14] Thus, an American defeat of North Korea would simultaneously thwart Soviet aims. Acting decisively and successfully would also regain the Democrats' prestige lost with China, and thus perhaps regain seats in upcoming congressional elections.

The Korean War marked a decisive shift in America's containment policy from Kennan's "selective" to Nitze's "global" strategy. Truman's immediate response was to send American troops to defend South Korea and the 7th U.S. fleet to protect Taiwan, dramatically increase American aid to anti-communist forces in Indochina, the Philippines, and elsewhere, and push through peace and security treaties with Japan. Washington attempted to knit the Far East together with several defense treaties, including ones with Australia and New Zealand (1952), South Korea (1953), Taiwan (1954), and the Southeast Asian Treaty Organization (1954). American military spending rose from $13 billion to $50 billion between 1950 and 1953 alone.

Why did the invasion occur? How much a series of American statements about an American offshore chain of allies stretching around Asia and seeming to exclude the Korean peninsula encouraged the attack will never be truly known, but were probably insignificant. In December 1949 and January 1950, high-ranking State and Defense Department officials including Dean Acheson, Louis Johnson, and Omar Bradley did speak of an American defense rim around Asia that seemed to leave out Korea and Taiwan. Yet in January Acheson lobbied Congress for aid to South Korea and Taiwan. Congress complied, granting additional aid to Korea and extending the China Aid Act six months. In March, Acheson once again pointedly included South Korea in America's defense perimeter. Special envoy John Foster Dulles visited South Korea in June shortly before the North's attack. Acheson bluntly warned Kim against an attack.

Assuming Pyongyang even paid attention to these mixed statements, it is unlikely that they provoked much more than confusion among North

Korea's leaders. For months before the invasion, Kim and Rhee had threatened to unify Korea by force; bloody skirmishes broke out along the border. America's last occupation troops had withdrawn in 1949; several hundred officers remained to advise South Korean forces. Kim gambled that a lightning attack would crush the Rhee regime and unify Korea before the Americans could intervene. While Stalin and Mao were aware that Kim contemplated an attack and gave him an uneasy blessing, they probably knew not the day or even month.[15]

Regardless, the North Korean attack on 25 June 1950 shifted American policy decisively from a "selective" to "global" containment, and brought Japan back into the world as an independent country and firm American ally.

ECONOMIC REVIVAL

While Washington recognized the Far East's strategic importance well before its economic value, it identified Japan's economic importance by 1947 but did not reach a consensus on Tokyo's military role until after the Korean War broke out in June 1950. As the Cold War in Asia heated up, Washington increasingly saw Japan as playing the regional role once envisioned for China. On May 8, 1947, Dean Acheson declared that both Japan and Germany should be transformed into the respective "workshops" of Asia and Europe.[16] In October 1947, SWNCC 384 called for an immediate shift in policy from democratic reform to economic revival. To achieve this end, Washington would allocate an additional $180 million to the $400 million in development aid already earmarked for Japan for April 1948 to April 1949. Army Secretary Kenneth Royall noted on January 6, 1948 that "there has arisen an inevitable conflict between the original concept of broad demilitarization and the new purpose of building a self-supporting nation."[17]

Despite this elite consensus, it was not until January 22, 1948 that the White House ordered MacArthur to implement SANACC (State–Army–Navy–Air Coordinating Committee) 384 which called for taking "all possible and necessary steps consistent with the basic policies of the occupation to bring about the early revival of the Japanese economy on a peaceful, self-sustaining basis."[18] Army Under-Secretary William Draper followed up this order by forwarding to MacArthur a plan called "Crank Up" which pressed for a self-supporting Japan by 1950. To this end, the United States pledged $1.2 billion in aid. Draper pressed MacArthur to eliminate or curtail reparations and deconcentration.[19]

Secretary of State Marshall named Kennan head of the State Department's new policyplanning staff in 1947. After submitting a study on European recovery that formed the basis of the Marshall plan, Kennan traveled to Japan in February 1948 where he completed a similar study. He was highly critical of SCAP officials and their "shrill cackling wives" who acted as though the war had been fought so that they could have "six Japanese butlers with the divisional insignia on their jackets." He admitted that while "many of the Japs deserve a worse fate than to have the tastes and habits of American suburbia imposed upon them," SCAP reforms were simply not "intelligible to most Japanese."[20]

Kennan's report identified Japan and the Philippines as the "cornerstones of a Pacific security system . . . which should deter any threat to our security from the East within our time."[21] He recommended Japan's economic revival, the end of the purges, reparations, and industrial deconcentration, and fundamental reforms in its economic institutions, policymaking process, and policies. He also requested that the State Department share the then exclusive U.S. military administration of Japan. Kennan eventually developed these ideas in his NSC 13/2 which shifted American policy toward Japan from economic punishment to promotion. Truman signed NSC 13/2 on October 9, 1948, and a more refined version called NSC 13/3 on May 6, 1949, which was forwarded to SCAP on May 12. Although the White House acted quickly on Kennan's economic recommendations, the Defense Department succeeded in blocking Kennan's proposal that the State Department establish an agency in Japan to take over all non-military American policies.

What was Kennan's impact on the reverse course policy? He later wrote that he had made "a major contribution to the change in occupation policy that was carried out in late 1948 and 1949; and I consider my part in bringing about this change to have been, after the Marshall Plan, the most significant constructive contribution I was ever able to make in government. On no other occasion, with that one exception, did I ever make recommendations of such scope and import; and on no other occasion did my recommendations meet with such wide, indeed almost complete acceptance."[22]

As if the increased pressure from Washington were not enough, MacArthur was increasingly criticized by influential Americans who felt the Occupation democratization and economic reforms had gone too far. James Kaufman, a prominent lawyer who briefly worked with the Occupation, Harry Kern, *Newsweek's* publisher, and Tokyo correspondent Compton Packenham formed the American Council on Japan (ACJ) to reverse the Occupation's reforms, particularly its anti-zaibatsu program. The ACJ soon included other powerful military, business, and diplomatic leaders who believed the United States should economically build up Japan to help contain the Soviet Union, and denounced SCAP's reforms as "socialistic."

Even without the Cold War, the White House would eventually have switched policy gears. Japanese reparations, food, fuel, reconstruction, imports, and production were all underwritten by American taxpayers who increasingly demanded that Washington grant them their promised peace dividend. The White House was also feeling the financial pinch. With only so many financial resources, the more aid Washington injected in Japan's economy, the less it had available for other needy strategic countries. Unless Japan's economy revived, the United States would have to support it indefinitely.

Deconcentration Policy

Army Under-Secretary William Draper visited Japan in September 1947 just when SCAP's anti-cartel policy was taking off. Alarmed, Draper returned to Washington determined to reverse American policy toward Japan from economic punishment to revival. Two 1947 missions led by Clifford Strike of Overseas Consultants, Inc. concluded that the list of firms targeted for dissolution by the Pauley mission should be drastically cut back. Defense Secretary Johnston increased the Strike mission's recommended 33 per cent cuts in the Pauley targets to 50 per cent, while cutting back reparations to only 25 per cent of the 1945 target.[23]

As MacArthur received an ever heavier barrage of reverse course orders from the Defense Department, he continued to follow those with which he agreed and table those with which he disagreed. In October 1947, Draper ordered MacArthur to hold up a deconcentration bill then awaiting a Diet vote. MacArthur refused, arguing that it was popular and was in Japan's best interests: "that system . . . has permitted the major part of the commerce and industry and natural resources of [Japan] to be owned and controlled by a minority of feudal families and exploited for their exclusive benefit. The world has probably never seen a counterpart to so abnormal an economic system. It permitted the exploitation of the many for the sole benefit of the few . . . and set the course which ultimately led to war and destruction."[24] When he wrote this, MacArthur may not have only had justness in mind; it was later revealed that MacArthur's adherence to deconcentration was motivated as much by his presidential ambitions as Japan's interests. He passed on word to Prime Minister Katayama to push the bill in order "not to embarrass the general who expected to be nominated for president." Katayama was even threatened that if the bill were not passed, SCAP "would not be so kind in the future."[25] The bill passed on December 8.

The State and Defense Departments were so "appalled by this action . . . [they] resolved to throttle MacArthur. From this point on, they viewed the Supreme Commander as the greatest single danger to Japan's security."[26] Fearing to attack MacArthur directly, Draper encouraged *Newsweek* to savage the "socialistic" deconcentration policy. Other newspapers including the *Chicago Tribune*, *San Francisco Chronicle*, and *Washington Times-Herald*, along with prominent senators like William Knowland (Republican, California), took up the outcry. MacArthur, however, continued to stand firm.

On March 11, 1948, a mission led by Ralph Young, a member of the Federal Reserve Board, arrived in Tokyo to investigate Japan's economic malaise and propose remedies. The Young mission recommended sweeping fiscal reforms including a balanced budget, higher taxes, credit controls, and undervalued yen. MacArthur bluntly rejected the Young report shortly after it was released, saying it would lead to economic depression and political chaos.

Exasperated, Draper announced on April 7, 1948 that Washington had abandoned FEC 230, then bypassed MacArthur by forming a Deconcentration Review Board and sending it to Japan in May 1948. The Board quickly removed 150 corporations from the 325 targeted for dissolution, and delayed decisions on the remainder. By the time the Board was disbanded on August 3, 1949, 297 firms were exempted from dissolution, seventeen were being dissolved, and eleven were ordered to dissolve. By the Occupation's end, only eighteen corporations were actually broken up and these all soon recombined. In June 1949, the 1947 anti-monopoly law was rewritten to allow cartels, mergers, and other anti-free trade practices, which Japanese businesses have enthusiastically and extensively enjoyed ever since, much to the dismay of foreign businesses and governments which are legally forbidden such advantages.

Reparations

Meanwhile, Washington ordered SCAP to discontinue Pauley's program of dismantling equipment and factories and exporting them to the Far East as reparations. Pauley had recommended sending overseas equipment valued in prewar yen of 990 million. But the program had harmed Japan and failed to help the region. Although little equipment was actually shipped overseas, Japan's industrialists refused to invest in capital equipment for fear it would be expatriated, thus holding back Japan's economic recovery. Meanwhile, the recipients lacked the markets, skills, and natural resources to run it profitably or the infrastructure to integrate the equipment.

Much of the equipment ended up rusting away in unused factories and warehouses.

MacArthur finally came on board the new policy. On March 21, 1948, he declared that "the decision should be made now to abandon entirely the thought of further reparations. . . . In war booty Japan has already paid over fifty billion dollars by virtue of her lost properties in Manchuria, Korea, North China and the outer islands. . . . Except for actual war facilities, there is a critical need in Japan for every tool, every factory, and practically every industrial installation which she now has."[27] He warned Washington on July 25, 1948 that the new policy required new expectations of Japan's industrial structure and power, with its future "export trade . . . will have a substantially different pattern than prewar. With the rapid expansion of the cotton textile industry in other countries in the Far East . . . it is indicated that future Japanese exports will consist much more of machinery, other capital goods and chemicals. . . . This will require a larger steel and machinery capacity to support export industries."[28] In May 1949, Washington announced that the reparations program had been successfully completed.

Not surprisingly, Far East and European countries bitterly protested the reverse course. Far East recipients of Japanese reparations like the Philippines, Taiwan, and Indonesia demanded their continuance. European powers feared Japan's industrial revival would compete head-to-head with their own industries. Washington ignored their pleas.

Macroeconomic and Industrial Policy

SCAP's democratic revolution did not spark an economic revival. Although American aid saved Japan from mass starvation and helped rebuild its shattered cities, the economy continued to be plagued with hyperinflation, hoarding, falling real wages, poor productivity, huge government deficits, corruption, and low growth. Inflation alone rose 20,000 per cent between 1945 and 1949, largely because the government printed vast amounts of paper money despite the economy's debility.

On December 8, 1948, Draper ordered MacArthur "to achieve fiscal, monetary, and price and wage stability in Japan as rapidly as possible, as well as to maximize production for export."[29] Draper's directive would be completed within three months and included nine points: (1) balanced budget; (2) stronger price controls; (3) better tax collection; (4) increased production; (5) more efficient food collection; (6) more foreign trade; (7) a single fixed currency value; (8) reduction in the money supply; (9) cuts in government spending.

MacArthur protested the directive, claiming that its sweeping economic controls would "require the reversal of existing trends toward free enterprise ... and negation of many of the fundamental rights and liberties heretofore extended to ... Japanese society." He concluded by stating that although "explosive consequences well may result ... I shall do my best."[30] When MacArthur forwarded the order to Yoshida on December 19, he acknowledged that it was a Washington directive rather than his own. The general wanted to deflect the subsequent blame for economic restructuring pain from himself to Washington. MacArthur was right about the directive's effects on curbing free enterprise and personal liberties – these remain limited in Japan. Yet the shift from a free-wheeling market to careful government managed economy was a decisive reason for Japan's subsequent rise into an economic superpower.

Well aware that MacArthur had received the directive under protest and having no idea whether or not he would even attempt to fulfill it, the White House dispatched Joseph Dodge with the rank of minister to oversee the policy's implementation. Dodge was a tough fiscally conservative Chicago banker who had previously served as advisor to General Lucius Clay, the American commander of occupied Germany. Dodge arrived on February 1, 1949 and over the next three months imposed macroeconomic policies that revamped Japan's economy and set the stage for the subsequent remarkable growth and development.

When Dodge arrived, Japan was still mired in economic stagnation. The worst problem was hyperinflation with wholesale prices 20,876 and retail prices 24,337 times higher than the 1934–36 level which had only risen from 100 to 350 and 308, respectively in 1945. Japan's trade deficit had risen from $352 million in 1947 to $426 million in 1948. Industrial production had risen and then stalled at 70 per cent of the 1934–36 level. The ministries and public companies were overstaffed by 20–40 per cent.[31]

Dodge carefully investigated Japan's economic problems and the reasons for them before meeting with Japanese officials on February 9. Negotiations between Dodge and the recalcitrant officials led by Finance Minister Ikeda Hayato lasted nearly two months. During that time, Dodge came to know "more about the details of each ministry's budget than the ministers and of every special account more than the specialists. More important he understood the impact of each entry on the economy."[32] He argued that Japan's economy was "walking on stilts" of American aid and massive subsidies funneled through the Reconstruction Finance Bank (RFB), and that these artificial legs would have to be removed before it could walk on its own two legs.

Finally, on March 20, they reached agreement on a budget for the next fiscal year that drastically cut spending and raised revenues so that there would actually be a surplus of $460 million, the first since 1931![33] Public employees were cut by 160,000. The RFB was abolished and replaced with a U.S. Aid Counterpart Fund that extended long-term loans to strategic industries. The Japanese strictly adhered to the "Dodge line" policy of balanced budgets until 1965 when it first used fiscal policies to stimulate the economy.

On April 23, the Japanese agreed to set the exchange rate at 360 yen for a dollar, a level undervalued enough to allow all of Japan's industries to export competitively. This rate would continue until December 1971 when it was revalued 10 per cent to 308 yen to a dollar. During the twenty-two years of this fixed exchange rate, Japan's economy would expand an average 10 per cent annually, four times America's growth rate, thus continually undervaluing the exchange rate, making Japan's products and economy all the more competitive, and the rate ever more undervalued. Even when the yen was revalued 10 per cent in 1971 it remained grossly undervalued.

In May 1949, Dodge's efforts were reinforced by a mission led by Carl Shoup of Columbia University. Shoup's recommendations for repealing the sales tax for basic commodities in favor of direct business and household taxation were implemented in 1950 and have remained the essence of tax policy ever since.

The "Dodge line" was essential for reforming Japanese macroeconomic policies whose irresponsibility had caused hyperinflation and stagnation. Japan's officials lacked the political will and incentives to enact these vital reforms on their own. Only severe and unrelenting external pressure could have shifted Japan's macroeconomic course. Yet without the Korean War stimulus the following year, Dodge's deflationary policies would have plunged Japan into a deep recession.

SCAP created new institutions and revamped old ones to guide Japan's economic development. In 1949, the Ministry of International Trade and Industry (MITI) was founded to command Japanese industrial, technological, and trade policies.[34] MITI's powers were and remain sweeping, and the ministry has continued to act as Japan's "economic general staff" or "defense department," targeting "strategic" industries and technologies for development while protecting inefficient but politically powerful other industries.

SCAP then enhanced MITI's power by pushing through additional powerful laws and institutions. The 1949 Foreign Exchange and Foreign Trade Control Law and 1950 Foreign Capital Law gave MITI sweeping powers to develop Japan's economy. SCAP used American financial aid to set up the Japan Export–Import Bank (Eximbank) in 1950 and Japan Development Bank (JDB) in 1951, and attached both to MITI. SCAP also got the Ministry of Finance (MOF) to combine all of its accounts into one huge Fiscal Investment and Loan Program (FILP) from which various ministries could lend money at low interest rates to their key industries.

Trade Policy

Japan's trade revival faced two huge obstacles – the loss of its most important markets and a dollar gap. Between 1943 and 1945, nearly all of Japan's overseas trade was with Manchuria, Korea, northern China, Taiwan, and Sakhalin. Now all of those territories were ruled by hostile regimes. Japan's trade with China alone had dropped from $600 million in the early 1940s to $7 million by 1948. Meanwhile, Japan suffered a severe dollar trade gap. While about 90 per cent of Japan's imports came from the United States, about 65 per cent of its exports went to Asia. Thus Japan needed hard currencies to pay for American imports, but received mostly soft nonconvertible currencies from its exports.

Kennan summed up these problems in an October 1947 report: "the loss of its markets and raw material resources in Soviet dominated portions of the mainland, with highly unstable conditions prevailing in China, in Indonesia, in Indochina, and in India, and with no certainty as to the resumption of certain traditional exports to the dollar area, Japan faces, even in the best of circumstances, an economic problem of extremely serious dimensions."[35] At several meetings, Kennan argued that Japan would not revive "unless they again reopen some sort of empire to the South. Clearly we have got . . . to achieve opening up of trade possibilities, commercial possibilities for Japan on a scale very far greater than anything Japan knew before."[36]

In a highly influential August 1949 *Washington Post* report, Stewart Alsop popularized Kennan's argument:

if Southeast Asia goes, Japan should not prove a difficult target, unless American troops are to hold Japan indefinitely by brute force. China and Southeast Asia comprise Japan's whole natural trading area, and economic pressure alone could be enough ultimately to bring Japan into the Soviet sphere. With Japan's industrial potential added to the great riches and huge population of Southeast Asia and China, and the whole area under Soviet control, a vast upset in the world power balance will have occurred. It is worth recalling that we fought a long, cruel war with Japan to prevent such an upset in the balance of power. It is also worth recalling that Japan was not a European power, and the Soviet Union is.[37]

With a communist victory in China imminent, Washington began considering alternatives to Japanese trade with the mainland. Japan State Department experts deemed southeast Asia the only viable alternative. In July 1947, MacArthur received SWNCC 381 which was based on a State Department study. The document called for an additional $400 million in development aid to Japan, the reduction of reparations, and encouragement of industrial expansion and trade. The most interesting proposal involved allowing Japan to repay its debts to the United States with soft currencies which Washington would in turn use to buy more southeast Asian natural resources for Japanese industries. This would evolve into a triangular trade spanning the Pacific basin composed of American high technology, capital goods, and finance, Japanese intermediate products, and Southeast Asian natural resources, to everyone's betterment.

Not to be outdone, in November 1948 SCAP's Economic–Scientific Section (ESS) issued its "Blue Book" report in which it advocated a $1.3 billion U.S. aid program over four years to help regional integration by using yen and dollars to underwrite Southeast Asian purchases of Japanese goods and services. Japan would be the supply source for Southeast Asia even if the prices were more expensive than equivilent American goods. Dodge later described this as a multiplier process whereby each American aid dollar "may be used several times over in the achievement . . . of recovery and reconstruction throughout the Far East."[38] Draper approved the report and urged the State Department to make it the basis of its Far East policy.

The proposal to economically marry Japan and Southeast Asia pitted the State Department's European and Japan specialists against each other. Japanese trade with Southeast Asia would compete directly with British, French, and Dutch trade with their own colonies – a relationship that was important for Europe's economic revival. Europe had annually exported nearly a billion dollars worth of goods and services to Southeast Asia before World War II. Britain, for example, used the dollar earnings from Malayan rubber and tin to bridge its own dollar gap with the United States. About 20 per cent of the Netherlands' economy was generated by trade with the Dutch East Indies. As for the Southeast Asians, most favored political independence but did not want to replace their economic dependence on Europe with a probably more exploitive relationship with Japan.

Washington was thus caught in a dilemma. If it succeeded in rebuilding Japan's co-prosperity sphere, Southeast Asians would be bitterly resentful and Europe would suffer, requiring the United States to prop it up with billions of dollars in more aid. But if Japan lacked markets, it too would remain an American ward. In March 1949, PPS 51 attempted to placate conflicting Japanese, European, and Southeast Asian interests, by calling for an American commitment to "vigorously develop the economic interdependence between Southeast Asia as a supplier of raw materials, and Japan, Western Europe and India, as due recognition, however, of the legitimate aspirations of Southeast Asian countries for some diversification of their economies."[39]

In practice, however, the United States favored Japan over Europe in the "strategic fulcrum" of Southeast Asia. Washington reasoned that Europe's economy and businessmen were more resilient and could find overseas markets relatively easily. Japan, in contrast, given its prewar reputation for predatory trade tactics and wartime savagery, remained an international pariah and desperately needed American patronage. While Europe appeared on the road to recovery, the Far East remained in political and economic flux. Japan could anchor the region with trade and help build a prosperous, integrated Far East political economy composed of all countries that "are potential sources of raw materials for Japan and potential markets for Japanese products." SWNCC 360 saw the failure to accomplish Japan's trade revival as apocalyptic not just for the Far East but the entire global economy, resulting "in a breakdown, gradual or precipitous, that would represent a complete loss in the American investment in a stable democratic, and peaceful Japan and would seriously jeopardize the U.S. program for world-wide economic recovery and political stabilization."[40]

Throughout 1949 and 1950, the United States dispatched a series of high-ranking missions to Japan and Southeast Asia to study and promote trade. The White House followed these missions up with a policy linking all American Mutual Defense Assistance Program (MDAP) aid to Southeast Asia to purchases of Japanese goods and services, regardless of cost. MDAP thus economically pumped up both Japan and Southeast Asia. Washington encouraged Japan to grant yen credits to regional customers and dispatch trade and technical missions to expand economic ties. Japanese would pay for their American imports with yen which Washington would then distribute to Southeast Asian countries which would in turn use them to purchase Japanese goods and services. SCAP helped Tokyo set up an Export Finance Corporation that loaned Japanese firms money to promote foreign trade. This package of "yen credits," "counterpart funds," and other American policies gave Japanese businessmen an enormous advantage over their European and American rivals, and was the essential reason behind Japan's eventual assertion of economic hegemony over the region.

By early 1949, it was clear that the communists would soon conquer China. This reality accelerated Washington's debate over Japan's future trading partners. The State Department hoped to wean China from potential Soviet control, and make Mao the "Tito of Asia." Thus it was open to continued Japanese trade with the mainland as one means to moderate the new regime and lessen its dependence on the Soviets. In contrast, the Defense Department saw a monolithic Soviet–Chinese bloc in northeast Asia that Japan must completely avoid; Moscow would use any tie to pull Japan into its bloc. The White House was just as split over American policy toward Taiwan. Should the United States, as the State Department argued, accept the inevitable communist conquest of Taiwan since to do otherwise would only further antagonize Mao and make a rapprochement more difficult? Or should the United States defend Taiwan as an essential link in America's offshore western Pacific defense chain as the Defense Department advocated, at the risk of permanently alienating communist China?

While he would not resolve the Taiwan question until the Korean War broke out, Truman did settle the Sino-Japanese trade question. On March 3, 1949, he passed on NSC 41 to MacArthur ordering him to "encourage trade with China on a quid-pro-quo basis but should avoid preponderant dependence on Chinese sources for Japan's critical food and raw material requirements. Every effort should be made to develop alternative resources on an economic basis, particularly in such areas as southern Asia where a need exists for Japanese exports."[41] The 1950 Chinese–Soviet treaty did not dampen State Department support for this policy. From then until Chinese forces intervened in the Korean War, Acheson believed that a break between the two communist giants was imminent given their age-old unresolved conflicting ambitions, xenophobia, and animosities over territory. The Defense Department remained skeptical.

Truman's decision relieved Tokyo which had favored a revival of trade with China. Prime Minister Yoshida declared in November 1948 that he viewed "without any anxiety the possibility of a total seizure of China by the communists. . . . I don't care whether China is red or green. China is a natural market, and it has become necessary for Japan to think about markets."[42]

CHECKS AND BALANCES TO DEMOCRATIZATION

MacArthur had actually begun to curb some civil liberties in Japan nearly a year before the White House consensus emerged on the reverse course. Symbolically, the reverse course began on January 31, 1947 when MacArthur issued a press statement ordering the labor unions to call off a general strike scheduled for the following day. MacArthur's statement read: "I have informed the labor leaders . . . that I will not permit the use of so deadly a social weapon in the present impoverished and emaciated condition of Japan, and have accordingly directed them to desist from . . . such action. . . . I have done so only to forestall the fatal impact upon an already gravely threatened public welfare. . . . I do not otherwise intend to restrict the freedom of action heretofore given labor in the achievement of legitimate objectives."[43]

The threat of a general strike had been preceded by months of dead-locked negotiations between government unions for greater wages, benefits, and job security, and government officials who were trying to hold down costs through salary ceilings and personnel cutbacks. The final monthly salary gap between the two sides was only 70 yen wide, or about one dollar. Radicals in the labor movement prevented negotiators from bridging that small gap and mobilized unions for the general strike. MacArthur's moratorium on the general strike discredited the radicals and allowed the government and moderate union leaders to cut a deal three weeks later in which the latter's proposed wage increase was accepted.

Yoshida painted the general strike threat in the worst terms: "Had the general strike materialized, a situation of indescribable confusion would have been created, and the stoppage of all transport, food, and fuel alone might well have driven the Japanese people, already suffering from acute shortages of the necessities of life, into a state bordering on desperation. Despite the specious reasons for the strike given by the leaders, it was clearly aimed at producing just such a condition of affairs in order to serve Communist ends."[44]

In February, MacArthur followed up his suppression of the planned general strike by approving Yoshida's proposal that large electoral districts be redrawn to the pre-1946 system of 117 districts in which each voter could vote for only one of three to five representatives. Yoshida had argued that the larger districts and multiple votes had given the advantage to leftist candidates.

Yet the new districts did not save Yoshida's Liberal Party which lost heavily in the April 1947 election and was replaced by a socialist-led coalition government. When scandals torpedoed first Katayama's socialist-led coalition in February and Ashida's democratic-led coalition in October 1948, the Liberal Party remained the only credible party. On October 14, 1948, the House of Representative elected Yoshida prime minister. At first Yoshida's power base was shaky and he ruled in coalition with the Democratic Party. Following the last election on April 25, 1947, the Liberals held only 153 seats compared with the democrats 90, the socialists 143, and the communists a mere 9.

But with the January 23, 1949 election, Yoshida's Liberal Party seats soared to 264 while the democrats were left with 68, the socialists 49, and the communists 35. This election was the turning point in Japan's postwar politics; the conservatives established an unshakeable power in the Diet which continued until the June 1993 election which brought a moderate coalition to power.

With its political power diminished, labor leaders sought other means of asserting influence. Although they did not dare to try another general strike, the more radical labor leaders instigated thousands of company and industry strikes. The communist party provoked many of these strikes. As irritating as these strikes may have been, the communist "threat" to Japan was grossly overstated. In 1948, among 80 million Japanese there were only an estimated 15,000 Communist Party members and about 70,000 close supporters.[45]

MacArthur, however, perceived a threat. He fired several shots across the Communist Party's bow in the year preceding his "red purge." In April 1949, SCAP got the government to pass the Organization Control Law which prohibited any extreme right-wing or left-wing groups which threatened to overthrow democracy, and required all political associations to register with the government and provide key information about membership, money, and activities. The Justice Ministry's Special Examining Bureau was authorized to uphold this law and actually dissolved several organizations including the League of Koreans and National Liaison Council of Labor Unions affiliated with the communist front World Federation of Labor Unions. The Diet, meanwhile, set up a committee on subversion similar to the U.S. committee on "un-American activities."

On July 4, 1949, MacArthur questioned "whether any organization that persistently and publicly advocated a program at variance with the aims of democracy and opposed established order should be permitted to function as a legal party." A year later on May 3, 1950, he declared that the Communist Party "has cast off the mantle of pretended legitimacy and assumed instead the role of an avowed satellite of an international predatory force and a Japanese pawn of an alien power policy, imperialistic purpose and subversive propaganda. That it has done so . . . raises doubt whether it should be regarded as a constitutionally recognized political movement."[46]

While Japan's Communist Party was anathema to SCAP and conservative Japanese, it apparently was too moderate by Moscow's standards. On January 6, Cominform, the Kremlin's official organization for coordinating the efforts of communist parties around the world, issued an editorial blasting Japanese Communist Party General Secretary Nozaka Sanzo and his "lovable communist party" policy as "anti-democratic, anti-socialist, anti-patriotic, and anti-Japanese."[47] Cominform urged Nosaka to abandon his accommodation policy with SCAP and become more militant. Nosaka apologized and promised to uphold Cominform's line.

While Nosaka's new policy increased tensions, the crisis did not occur until a May 30 demostration in which Japanese Communist Party toughs roughed up several American soldiers taking photos. SCAP responded on June 6 and 7 by ordering the government to arrest twenty-four members of the Communist Party's Central Committee, and on June 26 suspended publication of "Red Flag" (*Akahata*), the party newspaper. MacArthur justified the arrests in a June 6 public letter in which he asserted that "their coercive methods bear striking parallel to those by which the militarist leaders of the past deceived and misled the Japanese people, and their aims, if achieved, would surely lead Japan to an even worst disaster. To permit this incitation to lawlessness would risk ultimate suppression of Japan's democratic institutions in direct negation of her chance for political independence, and destruction of the Japanese race."[48]

The arrest of the Communist Party leaders was only the start of a "red purge" in which the government eventually dismissed 11,000 from its own ranks, including 2,591 from the railroads, 1,750 from the schools, and 2,741 from communications.[49] As in the earlier purge, those affected had no legal due process. However, despite his earlier warnings, MacArthur never outlawed the Communist Party. Only after the Occupation ended would those arrested be released and *Akahata* allowed to resume publication.

This "red purge" had a chilling effect on political demonstrations and labor strife. In the 1950 election, the Communist Party lost all of their Diet seats. A new, moderate labor federation called Sohyo formed on July 11, 1950 and soon commanded over half of all labor union membership.

Ironically, MacArthur had admitted a year earlier in March 1949 that "there was no evidence of any connection between the Japanese Communist Party and Moscow. For three years his G-2 had been looking for it and it had not been found yet. In his view, the Japanese were essentially conservative. . . . SCAP said that he was not worried by communism in Japan. There were more socialists than genuine communists in the JCP."[50]

PEACE AND SECURITY

The United States initially favored an early peace with Japan and Germany. In November 1945, Washington proposed to its Big Four allies that they negotiate treaties with their former enemies. Treaties were drafted but Moscow repudiated them before negotiations actually began. As the wartime alliance between the United States and Soviet Union crumbled into Cold War, Washington backed away from its quick peace policy. Washington's initial treaty drafts for Japan were harsh, calling for heavy reparations, complete demilitarization, and U.S. control over Okinawa, all of which would last for twenty-five years. These terms were no longer appropriate now that Tokyo was seen as a potential ally to be built up rather than an enemy to be repressed.

Then, in March 1947, two new peace treaty proposals emerged. After several months' work, a State Department committee led by Hugh Borton produced a draft surrender proposal that called for the Occupation's formal dismantlement followed by the FEC's close supervision of a neutral Japan for twenty-five years to ensure that it maintained its democratic reforms and limited its industrial and military power. At a news conference on March 19, 1947, shortly after learning the details of Borton's draft, MacArthur proposed concluding a peace treaty with Japan the following summer. His terms were lenient – no limits on Japan's sovereignty and a U.N. security guarantee to back its permanent neutrality. He opposed any American bases in Japan or defense treaty with Tokyo. He argued for the early peace because, in his words, "history points out the unmistakable lesson that military occupations serve their purpose at best for only a limited time, after which a deterioration rapidly sets in."[51]

The White House condemned both proposals. MacArthur's was viewed as particularly dangerous not just because it eliminated Japan as a potential American ally but an early peace would free the general for a 1948 presidential run. (MacArthur's name did appear in the Wisconsin primary the following year, but the general got a humiliatingly low number of votes and he later withdrew his name from other primaries.)

The peace proposals had broken the ice – Japanese officials increasingly pressed SCAP and other American officials for a peace treaty. Prime Minister Ashida submitted his own draft treaty the following month to SCAP and then to Washington. Although both SCAP and Washington rejected the "Ashida memorandum," the issue would not die.

Trying to regain the initiative, on July 11, 1947, the State Department proposed to FEC that they convene a peace conference in August. But Moscow, London, and Taipei blocked the American proposal, insisting that only the Big Four shape the peace. Britain, representing not only itself but the Commonwealth, feared that a sovereign Japan would rapidly expand economically into Southeast Asia. The Soviets and Chinese wanted to write the treaty in the Big Four Council of Foreign Ministers (CFM) where each country had a veto. Washington favored FEC because proposals would carry with a two-thirds vote, and it thought it could rally that number behind its proposals. The debate dragged on for months until the White House finally dropped the proposal.

The Truman administration had concluded that an independent Tokyo would be extremely vulnerable to Soviet subversion and communism given Japan's political and economic weaknesses. Any peace treaty had to be accompanied by a security treaty that tied Japan inexorably to the United States. A September 22, 1947 PPS meeting agreed that: "A major shift in U.S. policy toward Japan is being talked about under cover. Idea of eliminating Japan as a military power for all time is changing. Now, because of Russia's conduct, the tendency is to develop Hirohito's islands as a buffer state. The peace treaty now being drafted would have to allow for this changed attitude."[52]

After the three western allies negotiated a peace treaty with West Germany in 1948 that would take effect in 1949, Tokyo again pressed SCAP and Washington for a treaty. If Germany's sovereignty could be returned, Japanese asked pointedly, why not Japan's? Washington remained adamant, with the Defense Department particularly opposed to any peace treaty that could allow Japan to drift away from the United States toward the Soviet Union and China. Following his visit to Japan in February 1948, Kennan submitted a report that concluded that "in no respect was Japan at that time in a position to shoulder and to bear successfully the responsibilities of independence that could be expected to flow at once from a treaty of peace."[53] Japan's rockhard economic revival and political stability had to precede any peace treaty.

Some notable voices dissented from this distant peace policy. After becoming Secretary of State in 1949, Dean Acheson soon saw things differently: "To me, one conclusion seemed plain beyond doubt. Western Europe and the United States could not contain the Soviet Union and suppress Germany and Japan at the same time. Our best hope was to make these former enemies willing and strong supporters of a free-world structure."[54] Acheson's views were shared by Prime Minister Clement Attlee whose cabinet feared that the United States favored Japan with more aid than America's allies and was building up Japanese industries to the point where they could overwhelm Britain's. Foreign Minister Ernest Bevin visited Washington in 1949 to propose cutting Japan loose with a soft peace treaty without a security treaty or special economic benefits. The Truman White House rejected his proposal. Throughout these years, while various governments and officials debated the appropriate time for a peace treaty, the Japanese were kept in the dark over their country's fate.

NSC 13/2 had called for Japanese rearmament, something that none of America's allies or other Far East countries wanted. MacArthur, too, was firmly opposed. Having inspired Article 9 forbidding Japan any military forces or participation in war, the general was not about to reverse himself and accept Washington's new policy. Until the Korean War he resisted attempts by Washington for him to armtwist Tokyo into a limited rearmament. MacArthur argued that Article 9 was unalterable and even if it were, a rearmed Japan would alarm other Far East countries and provide a target and rationale for Soviet aggression. However, he did agree in September 1949 to maintain American forces in Japan for an indefinite period as part of any peace treaty.

While Washington wanted a security treaty rather than a peace treaty, Tokyo pressed for the opposite. Yoshida offered MacArthur the Ryukyu islands in return for an early peace treaty as long as Japan did not have to sign a security treaty. Not only would rearmament and American bases distort Japan's economic development, they would antagonize the Soviet Union and China. Trying to allay American fears that Japan would follow a peace treaty with neutrality or even membership in the Soviet bloc, Yoshida bluntly told a State Department official on April 7, 1950 that "Japan must rely on the United States for protection as it will process no armaments of its own."[55] Meanwhile he lobbied unceasingly for a peace treaty.

In May 1950, Yoshida bypassed MacArthur and dispatched Finance Minister Ikeda Hayato to Washington to plea for a peace treaty. The Ikeda mission was notable for two reasons. It was the first official diplomatic mission to the United States since Pearl Harbor. More importantly, the Japanese reluctantly agreed to allow American troops to remain based in Japan after a peace treaty. Despite this concession, the Pentagon remained firmly opposed to an early peace treaty.

Schaller nicely summarized the rationale and mindset behind the departmental differences:

> The Defense Department and the JSC retained a deep suspicion about Japanese loyalties and feared that Tokyo might take advantage of its sovereignty by becoming neutral or even reaching an accord with the Soviet bloc. Hence a treaty ought to be postponed as long as possible and must include ironclad provisions for keeping Japan in the Western camp. Acheson and his advisors shared some doubts about Tokyo's inclinations, but they argued that a prolonged Occupation would only undermine the still predominant pro-American, anti-Communist consensus. Thus a "reasonable" treaty providing for limited bases and a general commitment to limited rearmament represented the surest way to affirm Japanese–American ties.[56]

On May 18, 1950, Acheson succeeded in getting Truman to appoint John Foster Dulles in charge of future negotiations. Dulles had participated in the Versailles peace conference and subsequent international negotiations as both a diplomat and lawyer. As a Republican, he contributed to the bipartisan foreign policy Truman was trying to hold together. In June, Dulles traveled to Japan and South Korea to conduct preliminary talks with officials. MacArthur once again championed an early peace treaty, but also argued that the United States garrison not only Okinawa but also Chiang Kai-shek's Taiwan. To confuse matters further, Defense Secretary Louis Johnson and JSC chair Omar Bradley arrived in Tokyo to loudly voice their fears that Japan would not be a reliable future partner after independence and pressure MacArthur to abandon his support for a peace treaty. Hoping to maintain MacArthur's support and sway Johnson and Bradley, Dulles conveyed to them Acheson's new position that Taiwan be "neutralized" rather than abandoned to the communists. Dulles failed to get the Defense Department to accept an early peace treaty or Yoshida to agree to Japanese rearmament. He did, however, get MacArthur to accept American bases in Japan and Japanese rearmament.

On June 25, 1950, amidst Dulles's efforts, 90,000 North Korean troops invaded and overran much of South Korea. Truman's reaction was reasoned and decisive. On the day of the invasion, he succeeded in getting an United Nations Security Council resolution condemning the North Korean invasion. The Soviets were not present to veto the resolution since they were boycotting the United Nations because it refused to seat the communist Beijing government. Two days later, Truman ordered U.S. air and naval forces to assist the South Korean army; on June 30, he authorized MacArthur to use the four army divisions under his command to repel the North Korean invasion. On July 8, Truman complied with a Security Council resolution to name a commander for the United Nations forces that would liberate South Korea by tapping MacArthur.

This crisis broke the impasse on both the rearmament and peace treaty issues. On July 8, 1950, MacArthur ordered Yoshida to create a 75,000 strong "national police reserve" (NPR) and add 8,000 men to its existing 10,000 strong "maritime safety force." Yoshida reluctantly complied and the NPR was officially created on August 10, 1950. MacArthur equipped these forces with heavy weapons, uniforms, and ammunition. While Japan's NPR was never sent overseas, its minesweepers did help the allied navy in clearing sea-lanes around South Korea.

In a July 24 meeting, Acheson convinced Truman that an early peace treaty was in American interests. The Defense Department finally agreed with the stipulation that permanent American bases in Japan be part of any treaty. These concerns were included in NSC 60/1 which Truman signed on September 8, 1950. Acheson then gave Dulles the green light to build upon his preliminary negotiations. On September 14, Truman publicly announced the intention of negotiating a peace treaty with Japan and the FEC countries. The following day, Dulles publicly stated that the United States would not restrict Japanese rearmament. Negotiations among the FEC countries then began in New York while Dulles traveled to Japan to negotiate directly with Yoshida. In Tokyo the talks stalled over the questions of Japanese rearmament, a bilateral security treaty, and Okinawa's fate.

The Korean crisis also accelerated the reverse course's political and economic aspects. As part of the deal for the NPR, MacArthur agreed to allow amnesty for many of those previously purged. The amnesty board eventually recommended that 10,094 of 32,089 people examined be released.[57] In October 1950, SCAP approved all those recommended.

The Korean War jump-started Japan's economy. Japanese industries received $2.3 billion in direct procurement orders (Tokuju) during the war while Allied soldiers passing through Japan poured billions more dollars into the economy. By October 1950, industrial and mineral production finally exceeded the prewar level. Japanese firms cut increasing numbers of technology licensing deals with foreign and largely American firms – 27 in 1950, 101 in 1951, 133 in 1952.[58] The procurements allowed Japanese industries to achieve economies of scale production.

While American policy toward Japan was succeeding, it was bogging down in Korea. The triumph of MacArthur's bold September 15 landing behind the North Korean lines in Inchon, and subsequent rout of communist forces and drive deep into the north was followed in November by the humiliating rout of his forces by the Chinese army. By early 1951, MacArthur's forces had retreated to roughly the present border and for the next two years the U.N. and communist armies slugged at each other along that line. Truman fired MacArthur on April 11, 1951 for the general's repeated semi-public pleas for allying openly with Taiwan, bombing Manchuria, dropping atomic bombs on China, and, finally, his telegram to House Minority Leader Joseph Martin urging the unleashing of Chiang's KMT troops against the mainland.

About the time the war on the Korean peninsula reached a stalemate, the American–Japanese peace talks achieved a breakthrough. On February 1, 1951, Yoshida presented to Dulles a draft security treaty which included: (1) U.S. guarantees of Japan's security; (2) if the U.N. judged aggression had occurred against Japan, the U.S. would protect Japan; (3) U.S. forces could be stationed in Japan; (4) Tokyo and Washington would consult whenever either was threatened; (5) the agreement would last ten years.

Dulles agreed with these points but pressed Yoshida for details on Japanese rearmament. The following day, Yoshida presented the "Initial Steps for Rearmament Program" which included the creation of a 50,000 man land, air, and sea military forces separate from the NPR.

Dulles presented draft security and peace treaties on February 5. The security treaty included most of Yoshida's points. The peace treaty had no restrictions on Japan's economic or political activities, no reparations, allowed self-defense, kept the Ryukyu (Okinawa) and Bonin islands under U.S. control, and reduced Japan's territory to the four main islands. Yoshida agreed to these two treaties on February 6. Finally, on February 9, the two leaders initialed five documents, the peace treaty, collective self-defense treaty, agreement by Japan to supply bases and supplies to U.N. forces, status of U.S. forces in Japan agreement, and facilities and services Japan would provide to U.S. forces agreement. The two men postponed negotiations over fishing, dumping, and war damage claims.

There remained negotiations over the details of these agreements and FEC approval of the peace treaty. Dulles flew to Manila on February 11 and met a wall of protests from the Philippine government and population that reparations were not included in his draft treaty. Dulles continued on to Australia and New Zealand where he met their worries over Japanese rearmament by negotiating with them a multilateral defense alliance (ANZUS).

Upon arriving back in Washington, Dulles presented the draft peace treaty to the fourteen member FEC and South Korea. Nearly all the FEC members protested some or all aspects of the Dulles draft, particularly the lack of reparations and delimitation of Japanese territory. There was also controversy over whether the Taipei or Beijing government should be allowed to sign the peace treaty. Washington addressed some of these concerns in June by agreeing that neither Chinese government should sign the treaty, and forcing Japan to renounce sovereignty over Taiwan, southern Sakhalin, and the Kurile islands, to pay reparations, and to negotiate deals on shipbuilding and fishing.

In August, Tokyo finally agreed to pay reparations, but without an actual amount mentioned in the peace treaty. Instead, after signing the peace treaty Japan would negotiate with each country separately for the amount and payment schedule. Under this agreement, Japan could stonewall any reparations negotiations. In fact, the $1.15 billion in reparations Tokyo eventually paid out to ten Far East nations served largely as an export subsidy for Japanese firms and helped them reestablish economic footholds throughout the region.

Between September 4 and 8, 1951, the representatives of fifty-two nations met in San Francisco for the "Conference for the Conclusion and Signing of the Treaty of Peace with Japan." President Truman opened the conference with a televised nationwide speech, the first in American history, on September 4. As conference president, Acheson succeeded in controlling the proceedings. The peace treaty's draft was already written and the conference's purpose was simply to provide a forum for representatives to make lofty speeches and then vote for and sign it. Attempts by Soviet representative Andrei Gromyko to open up the treaty's terms to debate and alterations were voted down by 36 to 3 and 47 to 3.

On September 7, Prime Minister Yoshida gave his country's acceptance speech in which his attempts to reassure Japan's neighbors of his country's commitment to peace included an ambiguous statement over who the war's true victim really was: "My people have been among those who have suffered greatly from the destruction and devastation of the recent war. Purged by that suffering of all untoward ambition, of all desire for the path of military conquest, my people burn with a passionate desire to live at peace with their neighbors in the East and in the entire world."[59]

The following day on September 8, 1951, the representatives of forty-nine countries signed the peace treaty. The Soviet Union, Czechoslovakia, and Poland refused to sign. That same day, the United States and Japan signed the security treaty whereby Tokyo agreed not only to allow American bases in Japan from which American forces could freely operate throughout the region without permission, but renounced its right to make any military agreements with other countries and could ask for U.S. troops to put down "large-scale riots and disturbances in Japan, caused through instigation or intervention by an outside Power or Powers." In the previous days, the United States had signed security treaties with Australia and New Zealand, and the Philippines. These three treaties became the foundations for America's defense perimeter in the western Pacific. With these peace and security treaties, the United States had completed its transition from the "internationalism" of the "Yalta system" of Big Four consensus on global relations to the American "hegemony" of the "San Francisco system."[60]

DENOUEMENT

The adoration with which most Japanese viewed MacArthur as their "blue eyed shogun" faded quickly after his departure. Japan's press widely reported some unfortunate remarks MacArthur made in May 1951 before the Senate Foreign Relations Committee. Asked about democracy's chances of taking root in Germany and Japan, he replied: "If the Anglo-Saxon was, say, forty-five years of age in his development in the sciences, arts, divinity, culture, the Germans were quite as mature. The Japanese however, measured by the standards of modern civilization, would be like a boy of twelve as compared with our development of forty-five years."[61] The general meant that the Japanese understanding of democratic institutions and values was relatively underdeveloped compared to that of the west – an uncontroversial conclusion. Japanese interpreted his remarks as meaning he thought the Japanese were psychologically and culturally immature.

On April 14, 1951, General Matthew Ridgway replaced MacArthur as SCAP and Far East commander. Shortly after Ridgway took office, Yoshida pressed him to approve a list of conservative measures including the centralization of police and education, reduction of suspects' rights, the relaxation of anti-monopoly and labor rights laws, and the legal recognition of the household head as the center of family life. Ridgway had the new GS head, Frank Rizzo, reject the list. Yet on May 3, 1951, Ridgway authorized Yoshida to reexamine all laws passed under the Occupation. Yoshida created a committee for the review which eventually adopted many of the prime minister's original list of suggested changes. To Yoshida's disappointment, SCAP never approved the controversial list. While he succeeded in achieving most of his conservative agenda after the Occupation ended, Yoshida obviously would have preferred that SCAP bear the political heat.

Ridgway was largely a caretaker administrator for the next year until the Occupation ended. With the peace and security treaties negotiated, there were no new significant American interests to pursue. Initially, Ridgway concentrated on relaxing the purge. By the Occupation's end, he had authorized the release of over 200,000 purgees.[62] The Japanese largely welcomed the depurging of these men, although Yoshida and his followers resented the reappearance of former political foes.

NSC 125/2 was issued in January 1952 and, among other things, called for building up Japanese ground forces to 325,000 in ten divisions. After receiving the report, Dulles and SCAP began pressuring Yoshida to comply with the targets and join a multilateral defense alliance. Yoshida bluntly rejected Washington's troop numbers and instead proposed increasing Japan's military to 100,000 men. In 1952, Yoshida did agree to change the name of the National Police Reserve to the National Security Force, and raise its personnel from 75,000 to 110,000, a number far below Dulles's.

Yoshida skilfully resisted all of Dulles's pressures and enticements for Japan to join a Far East equivalent of NATO. In doing so, Yoshida recited the litany of Japanese economic and political problems, a strategy Nagai Yonosuke calls "blackmail by the weak."[63] He also frequently cited Asian suspicions of a revival of Japanese militarism and even went so far as to encourage leftist demonstrations during Dulles's visit to exaggerate the perception of Japanese weakness.[64] Although during the Korean War, Japanese mine sweepers operated off the peninsula, Yoshida minimized Japan's involvement to simply enjoying the billions of dollars in procurement windfalls that the Allies spent for supplies and R&R. Part of Yoshida's reluctance to contribute more was rooted in traditional Japanese isolationism and cultural supremacy: "Yoshida never desired the cultural or political integration of Japan with the West or with neighboring Asian nations. Although he was eager for international economic integration, he wished to maintain a distinctive cultural identity for the Japanese people."[65]

Despite China's intervention in the Korean War in November 1950, Acheson and Dulles remained split over the proper policy toward China. Acheson still hoped eventually to entice China away from the Soviet Union. Dulles assumed that they had already forged an unbreakable, monolithic communist front. Thus while Acheson sought to encourage Japanese trade with China, Dulles tried to sever and divert it to Southeast Asia.

Both Britain and Japan supported Acheson's position. London favored diplomatic and trade relations with the new communist government not just to divert Beijing from Moscow, but also to divert Japanese trade from Britain's southeast Asian colonies to China. Having already recognized the Beijing government, the British were opposed to anything but trade relations between Japan and Taiwan. London threatened to withhold allowing Japan to join GATT as an observer nation unless Washington allowed it to trade freely with China.

When they met during the September 1951 peace conference, Acheson gave Yoshida the green light for expanded trade with China. Dulles noted bitterly that "Acheson left the door open for Japan to recognize and make a treaty with Communist China and not nationalists."[66] Working with likeminded senators, Dulles managed over the next three months to undercut Acheson and force Tokyo to support Taiwan.[67] On September 12 fifty-six senators sent Truman a letter stating that they favored Japan recognizing Taipei as China's legitimate government, and implied they might not ratify the peace and security treaties unless Tokyo complied. At this point Acheson gave in, but asked Dulles to reconcile the British and Japanese.

On December 13, Dulles met separately in Tokyo with both Yoshida and British ambassador Esler Denig and presented his case for Japan's diplomatic relations with Taiwan rather than mainland China. Yoshida tentatively agreed if the British would go along; Denig was opposed. Dulles turned up the heat on Yoshida by ushering in visiting senators Alexander Smith and John Sparkman who clearly said ratification depended on Japan's support for Taiwan. On December 18, Dulles handed the prime minister a draft letter which Yoshida would sign, agreeing to open diplomatic relations with Taipei. Yoshida agreed, but said he had to first prepare public opinion. Dulles left on December 20 without an agreement. On January 7, 1952, Dulles received a letter from Yoshida dated December 24 which was nearly identical to his original draft. In the letter, Yoshida promised that Japan would normalize relations with Taiwan for all territories under its immediate control. But this agreement had a price. The prime minister stated that a sizeable American loan to Japan would help sway public opinion in favor of diplomatic ties with Taipei. The White House agreed to Yoshida's demand, and then released Yoshida's letter to the press.

Ratification passed relatively smoothly in both governments. On October 26, 1951, Japan's Diet ratified the peace treaty by 307 to 47 in the lower house and 174 to 15 in the upper house, and the security treaty by 284 to 71 in the lower house and 147 to 76 in the upper house. On January 19, 1952, the Senate passed the peace treaty by 66 to 10, and the security treaty by 58 to 9. Japan and Taiwan began negotiations on February 20 and eventually signed a peace treaty on April 28, 1952. The peace treaty became law and the Occupation officially ended on April 28, 1952. The war was finally over.

CONCLUSION

Virtually all scholars agree with Japanologist Herbert Passim that the U.S. Occupation of Japan "ranks as one of . . . the proudest achievements of post-war American foreign policy [and] central to the development of Japan's 'modern miracle.' "[68] SCAP official Theodore Cohen asserts that "nothing the United States had ever attempted in any other land, or even in its own, was as grand in conception."[69]

Throughout the Occupation, there was a creative and at times antagonistic dynamic between Washington and SCAP. Generally, Washington formulated policy; SCAP implemented it. But this process was often complicated and distorted by the "role of individual ideas, vested interests, ideologies, MacArthur's political ambitions, foreign policy concerns, personal relations, and conflicting interpretations in the end product."[70] In implementing the government's broad directives, SCAP often embarked on policies unexpected and sometimes unwanted by Washington such as the constitution's Article 9. These actions in turn prompted Washington to shift its own policies. With the reverse course, the White House attempted to implement those policies directly by dispatching a series of "missions" to Japan.

All along, MacArthur was the wild card of American Occupation policy. While Dean Acheson declared as early as September 1945 that MacArthur was "the instrument of policy, not its determinant," historians have concluded that the general "was allowed perhaps the greatest leeway ever accorded an American officer in peacetime."[71] Most observers concurred with Cohen who "was astonished at the degree to which the Occupation had become personalized. Every Occupation action, every policy, every decision was MacArthur's. His name appeared countless times in the newspapers, those of his immediate subordinates, themselves men of great power and influence, hardly ever. All the Washington policies, so diligently hammered out in 1944 and 1945, were ascribed to MacArthur . . . the General had, in effect, displaced the U.S. government as far as the Japanese people were concerned."[72]

Even without the Cold War, domestic political pressures would have stimulated the reverse course. Republicans demanded America's return to political isolation; taxpayers their promised "peace dividend." Yet, the Cold War and Kennan's containment policy made imperative Japan's conversion into Asia's workshop and America's ally. The Occupation was as successful in achieving its objectives in the second phase as it was in the first phase. Building on the democratization and demilitarization reforms, SCAP completely revamped Japan's public and private economic institutions and policies, and integrated the country into what has become a Pacific basin trade and investment system that has surpassed that of the Atlantic basin in volume. Japan would not be the economic superpower of today without all of America's Occupation policies – democratization, demilitarization, the reverse economic course, and the Korean War procurements.

Tokyo continued the reverse course after Japan's sovereignty was restored. The industrial groups (keiretsu) regrouped around banks rather than holding companies and remain as concentrated and domineering in Japan's economy as ever; police and education power were recentralized in Tokyo. Japan would be economically and socially weaker if Tokyo had not reversed the SCAP policies of industrial, police, and education decentralization. The keiretsu are Japan's economic workhorses and the global economy's Trojan Horses. No country does a better job of teaching its youth the basics of reading, writing, and arithmetic. Japan's cities are among the world's safest.

While the reverse course clearly benefited Japan, how well did it serve American interests?

What neither MacArthur nor other officials recognized at the time was that America's policy of upgrading Japan's industrial structure and exports would inevitably bring it into direct conflict with American industries, to the detriment of the latter and American economic growth and living standards. Yet, no one could have possibly foreseen how powerful Japanese industry and technology would eventually become. The priority of that time was to revive Japan's economy so that it could be the centerpiece of a prosperous Far East economy and bulwark against Soviet expansion.

Was America's policy correct? Although it made geoeconomic sense to those who conceived it, it may have replaced one extreme policy of industrially castrating Japan with another extreme policy of building Japan into an economic superpower that overcame its Far East neighbors and eventually the United States. Finn argues that "if the Allies had reached quick agreement on reparations and early deliveries had been carried out by Japanese technicians under Allied supervision, the program might have been beneficial to Asian nations. In fact . . . the Allies probably took too little from Japan after World War II."[73]

A well-conceived and implemented reparations program could have simultaneously accelerated the Far East's economic and industrial development while moderating Japan's, thus serving two American interests at costs far lower than the historical account. American industries would have prospered longer before they were undermined by foreign competition, the economy and living standards would have grown faster, and the aid burden to American taxpayers would have been much less. But, of course, these perspectives benefit from hindsight.

Washington had essentially represented and forced the acceptance of Japan's national interests, often before those of the other countries, including the United States. In his *Memoirs*, Yoshida calls on all Japanese to express gratitude to MacArthur "for his consistent advocacy of an early peace treaty" and Dulles "for making the terms of the treaty of such advantage for Japan."[74] Yoshida opposed rearmament but supported alliance with the United States: "Our national interests coincided with those of the United States . . . and I continue to believe that allying ourselves with the United States remains the best means of providing for the defense both of the United States and of ourselves."[75]

What then was the Occupation's legacy? Virtually all scholars would agree that for "Japan the Occupation was indispensable, for only a powerful force from outside could have broken the immensely tenacious traditional mold, and without breaking it Japan could not have made its postwar transformation."[76] Japan's political, economic, and social "miracles" would not have occurred without the American Occupation policies. And also remarkable was the transformation of bitter enemies into allies. As Yoshida put it, the "Americans came into our country as our enemies, but after an Occupation lasting little less than seven years, an understanding grew up between the two peoples which is remarkable in the history of the modern world."[77]

Part III
From Geoeconomic Protégé to Rival

7 America Triumphant: The Eisenhower, Kennedy, and Johnson Era, 1953–69

America's interrelated policies of rebuilding the global economy and containing the Soviet Union blossomed during this era. Geoeconomically, the European Community became ever more cohesive and prosperous and stimulated economic expansion throughout the rest of West Europe. Japan achieved average growth rates of 10 per cent annually and became the world's second largest capitalist economic power in 1968. The GATT increased its members and brought down formal trade barriers through a series of negotiation rounds. Geopolitically, with a stable power balance having emerged between West and East Europe, Washington and Moscow instead sublimated their conflict into battles for hearts and minds throughout the Third World. Stalin's death and the Korean ceasefire in 1953 briefly lowered the fears that one of these Cold War struggles would escalate into World War III. But these fears reemerged in 1958 with the second Berlin crisis and culminated with the November 1962 Cuban missile crisis. The nearness of nuclear war over Cuba sobered both Washington and Moscow. Although throughout the 1960s, the United States became increasingly bogged down in an unwinnable war in Indochina, Cold War temperatures dropped overall as Washington and Moscow cooperated on forging the 1963 Nuclear Test Ban Treaty and 1968 Non-proliferation Treaty, thus setting the stage for the détente era of 1969–79.

For all three presidents during this era, foreign policy and geopolitics were almost synonomous. There were few significant geoeconomic issues. Global trade and investments were expanding robustly. America's economic power remained dynamic and unchallenged. Ninety-six per cent of American wealth was generated within the United States, only 4 per cent from foreign trade and investments. The United States enjoyed continual though shrinking trade surpluses. Only the dollar "overhang" problem threatened the global economy. After 1960, foreign governments held more dollars than the United States had gold to redeem them. Although French President de Gaulle did demand gold for dollars, fortunately he sparked no international run on America's gold reserves and subsequent breakdown of the global fixed currency system. Serious as that threat was, it remained an abstraction to most American policymakers and the public. Presidents and their foreign policy staff concentrated on managing crises and wars.

Of all the images that shaped American foreign policy between the Korean War and the Nixon Doctrine, the "domino effect" was the most powerful. America's key domino in Asia was Japan whose importance was still seen as primarily geopolitical, and its loyalty, economic health, and political stability fragile. Throughout this period, Japan continued to serve as the keystone of America's Far East defense and economic system. With its huge population, advanced industrial base, conservative dominated democratic system, and position off northeast Asia, Japan was perhaps second only to West Germany as the most strategically valuable country in America's containment policy. American bases in Japan proved invaluable during the Korean War; Okinawan-based B-52's pounded Indochina from 1965 through 1972. And by taking advantage of the Occupation reforms and American efforts to integrate Japan into foreign markets, Tokyo was rapidly building Japan into the "workshop" of not only Asia but the world.

Under the domino logic, America became ever more deeply committed to South Vietnam to defend ultimately Japan. If Indochina was lost, so the logic went, so too would communism eventually overwhelm Japan and the rest of Asia. On January 23, 1953, newly appointed Secretary of State John Foster Dulles said on national radio that:

> The Soviet Russians are making a drive to get Japan, not only through what they are doing in the northern areas of the islands and in Korea but also through what they are doing in Indochina. If they could get this peninsula of Indochina, Siam, Burma, and Malaya, they would have what is called the rice bowl of Asia. That's the area from which the great peoples of Asia . . . such as Japan and India get a large measure of their food. And you can see that, if the Soviet Union had control of the rice bowl of Asia, that would be another weapon which would tend to expand their control into Japan and into India. That is a growing danger.[1]

During these years, Washington's geopolitical concerns with Japan and the region overshadowed bilateral geoeconomic conflicts. American economic policy toward Japan involved providing Japanese exporters access to American, Southeast Asian, and global markets, and tolerating Tokyo's web of import and investment barriers. By simultaneously enjoying protected home markets and access to foreign markets, Japanese reaped vast economies of scale in production, profits, and investments.

Japan's economic expansion during this era was boosted not only by American and other foreign consumer demand. American military procurements during the Korean War had jumpstarted Japan's stalled economy, launching it into average annual 10 per cent growth for the next quarter century. As Japan's economy expanded, American procurements played an important but diminishing role:

> Between 1945 and 1955, [Japan's] cumulative dollar gap totaled some $6.2 billion, balanced by $2 billion in economic aid and $4 billion in military expeditures. During the next decade, military procurements increased by about $3.2 billion. As American spending for the Vietnam War accelerated from 1965 to 1970, military orders placed in Japan rose by nearly another $3 billion. The total of about $10 billion worked out to an average annual American military subsidy for Japan of some $500 million per year over twenty years. These expenditures cemented the relationship between Japanese recovery and American security throughout Asia.[2]

Washington's encouragement of Japanese neomercantilism – government development of strategic industries, technologies, and firms through subsidies, cartels, export promotion, and import and investment barriers – inevitably provoked conflicts. Starting with the Japanese dumping of "dollar blouses" in the mid-1950s, each president worked with Tokyo against beleaguered American industries which vainly pleaded for protection. A diplomatic pattern emerged in which an American industry would pressure the White House for relief from Japanese dumping; the White House would then reluctantly raise the issue with Tokyo; after considerable stonewalling and denial that a problem even existed, Tokyo would offer a "voluntary" cutback in exports that alleviated but failed to halt the predatory attacks; the White House would then announce victory and refocus its full attention on the Cold War. Likewise, Washington ignored American firms trying to sell or invest with Japan's systematically protected markets. American policymakers acted consistently on the belief that beefing up Japan geoeconomically was vital to strengthening American geopolitical interests throughout the Far East. And they were largely right.

DWIGHT D. EISENHOWER, 1953–61

Policymaking and Implementation

Dwight D. Eisenhower became the Republican Party's presidential nominee largely because moderates wanted to head off the drive of right wing

Senator Robert Taft for the nomination. It was Taft's talk of reducing American support for NATO that pushed Eisenhower into the race. Eisenhower was a popular choice for the Republicans and nation. Although best known as the European commander for Allied forces during World War II, Eisenhower subsequently served as President of Columbia University and then NATO commander after the Korean War broke out. Eisenhower was admired for his diplomatic and management skills rather than his limited battlefield experience. He won a resounding victory over Democratic challenger Adlai Stevenson by a vote percentage of 55–45.

President Eisenhower and Secretary of State John Foster Dulles dominated the administration's foreign policy. After leaving office, Eisenhower exploded the popular image of his secretary of state controlling foreign policy by asserting that "I'm supposed to have left too much to Dulles. Well . . . he has never done a thing that I did not approve beforehand."[3] Technically Eisenhower was right, but his administration's policies were often shaped by elements of a hard right agenda with which he sometimes disagreed.

Eisenhower was a model of foreign policy supervision, decision, and delegation. He relied heavily on his NSC by constructing it as the clearing house for policy proposals drafted elsewhere in the executive bureaucracy. The NSC Planning Board reviewed each proposal and passed on appropriate ones to the president for approval. These policy steps were merged in those frequent times when Eisenhower participated actively in Planning Board meetings. The decision was then sent to the NSC Operations Coordinating Board for implementation. Planning and operations were thus distinct aspects of the policy process linked by the President's decisions.

Though not a politician, Eisenhower was politically astute. He preferred to manage things with a "hidden hand" and let subordinates take the credit or blame for the results. When confronted by journalists, he would intentionally dissemble with a rambling discourse that confused rather than enlightened. Yet, to the American public Eisenhower offered a vision of American resolution against communism and commitment to prosperity at home. To Eisenhower, leadership's essence involved finding "a way to bring men to a point where they will give to the long-term promise the same value that they give to immediate and individual gains."[4]

Policy Priorities

Eisenhower stepped into the White House as one Asian war was winding down, left the White House as another Asian war was gearing up, and in between fought the Cold War around the world. The White House's first task was to end the Korean War. As in previous wars, policymakers learned "lessons" from Korea that were supposed to guide their conduct of foreign policy. General Matthew Ridgway recounted the central lesson: "Before Korea, all our military planning envisioned a war that would involve the world, and in which the defense of a distant and indefensible peninsula would be folly. But Korea taught us that all warfare from this time forth must be limited. It could no longer be a question of whether to fight a limited war, but of how to avoid fighting any other kind."[5]

As one of many historians has pointed out, the Korean War

did for the Cold War what Pearl Harbor had done for World War II. It globalized the Cold War. Prior to Korea the only American political or military commitment outside the Western Hemisphere had been the North Atlantic Treaty, by 1955 the United States had about 450 bases in thirty-six countries and was linked by political and military pacts with some twenty countries outside Latin America. Also, the United States' foreign aid program, appropriately named the "mutual security program," no longer had as its purpose economic and social reconstruction but military support for recipient countries. Most important, the communist menace was now perceived in Washington in global terms rather than in terms of Europe alone, as had largely been the case prior to 1950.[6]

While the Korean War's "lesson" might have helped American policymakers avoid World War III, it led to American involvement in dozens of limited wars around the world, the most intensive of which was in Indochina.

Largely because of Japanese resistance, Washington choose not to unite the Far East into a regional alliance like NATO. Instead, Washington knit the Far East together by forging a series of bilateral and multilateral treaties throughout the region. In 1952, in addition to its security treaty with Japan, the United States signed a multilateral defense treaty with Australia and New Zealand (ANZUS), and bilateral treaty with the Philippines. In July 1953, the Eisenhower administration negotiated defense treaties with South Korea, and in December 1954 with Taiwan. The most symbolically important of all America's regional treaties was that creating the South East Asian Treaty Organization (SEATO) in September 1954, and signed by the United States, Britain, France, Thailand, Pakistan, the Philippines, Australia, and New Zealand. Japan, Burma, Indonesia, and India refused to join.

Eisenhower had a very sophisticated conception of national power as a mix of military, economic, political, and psychological factors levened by public opinion and morale. Emphasizing other components of American power, Eisenhower cut back defense appropriations to 70 per cent of the amount Congress wanted. Between fiscal 1954 and fiscal 1961, absolute spending rose only $800 million, from $46.6 billion to $47.4 billion while military spending fell as a percentage of the budget from 65.7 per cent to 48.5 per cent. He tried to avoid using military force at all costs, but when forced to act he used it overwhelmingly as when he sent the marines into Beirut in 1958.[7]

Throughout the 1950s, containing communism in Vietnam loomed more important on the White House's policy priority agenda. The Truman and Eisenhower administrations had given France $2.5 billion in military aid to underwrite its efforts to quell the communist insurgency in Vietnam. When France withdrew from Indochina in 1954, the United States stepped into the void. The Geneva Accords of May 1954 temporarily divided Vietnam between communist northern and noncommunist southern halves which would be reunited after a 1956 election determined the country's political fate. Estimating that North Vietnam's leader Ho Chi Minh would win as much as 80 per cent of the vote, the White House advised South Vietnam president Ngo Dihn Diem to call off elections and began massively supplying him with military weapons, equipment, and training that totaled $1 billion between 1955 and 1961; military aid accounted for 78 per cent of America's total aid to South Vietnam during that time. When Eisenhower left office, there were 1,500 American military advisors in South Vietnam.[8] Yet, the communists' strength continued to spread despite all the billions of dollars or thousands of personnel the United States poured into South Vietnam.

Ironically, while the Eisenhower administration was implementing its global containment policy, the Soviet Union was moderating its own interventionist policies. Stalin died in 1953, and for the next three years moderates ruled the Kremlin. Yet, the only significant cooperation between Washington and Moscow during this time was their 1955 agreement to withdraw from their respective halves of Austria and reunify it as a neutral country. By the late 1950s, the Cold War worsened again as Moscow, in 1957, launched the world's first satellite (sputnik) and intercontinental ballistic missile (ICBM) into space, and the following year prompted another Berlin Crisis. During the 1960 presidential campaign, Democratic challenger John F. Kennedy spoke of a "missile gap" in which the Soviets had surpassed the United States in nuclear power. The world seemed ever more mired in the Cold War, with apocalypse just over the horizon.

Eisenhower addressed these concerns in his presidential farewell speech, warning the American people that their democratic and economic future was threatened by the uncontrolled rise of a vast "military industrial complex." In waging the Cold War, Eisenhower feared the United States was becoming a "garrison state" which increasingly subjected civil liberties and economic development to feeding an ever more voracious obsession with communist threats at home and abroad. He called on Americans to remain ever vigilant against the more insidious dangers at home as well as more obvious foreign threats. Unfortunately, he was more effective in countering the latter than the former.

Policy Toward Japan: Geopolitical Issues

Unlike virtually all presidents, Eisenhower actually understood something about Asia. Eisenhower had served on MacArthur's staff in the Philippines for several years before World War II, although he was by no means an expert on the Far East, let alone Japan.

Throughout the Eisenhower years, Dulles continually pressed Tokyo for greater defense contributions but rarely got more than a fraction of what he asked, and often nothing at all. During the early 1950s, Dulles envisioned creating a Far East version of NATO. From 1952 through 1954, he negotiated the building blocks of a regional military alliance but Tokyo was largely responsible for preventing him from putting them together. Yoshida bluntly refused Dulles's repeated requests to join a collective Asian defense alliance, citing Article 9, Japan's need to focus on economic expansion, and the mistrust of Japan by other Asian countries.

Dulles had better luck getting Yoshida to expand Japan's military forces and equip it with the latest American weapons. Yoshida consistently opposed rearmament, but bowed to persistent American pressure in return for far more important economic advantages. The 75,000 man National Police Reserve (NPR) which MacArthur ordered Yoshida to create in July 1950 rose to 110,000 by the time the Occupation ended in April 1952. In August 1952, after considerable American pressure, Tokyo rechristened its nascent army and navy the National Security Force and Maritime Security Force, respectively, both managed by a Security Board attached to the prime minister's office. In November 1952, Washington and Tokyo signed an agreement whereby the United States would "lend" Japan eighteen frigates of 1,500 tons each and fifty landing craft of 25 tons each. Under a subsequent May 1954 agreement, Washington lent an additional two destroyers of 1,600 tons and two destroyers of 1,400 tons each. On July 1, 1954, the Diet passed the National Agency Establishment and Self-Defense Force laws which transformed the National Security Force into the Self-Defense Force (SDF) under the command of the National Defense Agency (Boeicho) attached to the prime minister's office. Troop strength was increased to 152,000 men.

With Japan's military industry dismantled, Tokyo had to look to Washington to supply the SDF. Washington was happy to oblige. In October

1951, Congress had passed the Mutual Security Assistance (MSA) Act which was supposed "to consolidate the American alliance system through the supply of weapons and equipment, participation of allied officers in training programs in the United States, and the overall coordination of military strategies."[9] In March 1954, Washington and Tokyo signed an MSA agreement whereby the United States would help equip Japan's military in return for which Japan "will increasingly assume responsibility for its own defense . . . [but] Overseas duty for Japan's internal security forces will not arise" and its contributions would be limited by economic and constitutional considerations.[10] Between 1954 and 1965, Washington gave $866 million in military aid to Japan, and $1.4 billion and $2.3 billion to the front-line states, Taiwan and South Korea, respectively.[11]

As Japan's military forces increased in number, American forces were correspondingly reduced. American troops in Japan dropped from 200,000 in 1954 to 90,000 by December 1956. Japanese troops began to take over from American units military bases in Hokkaido. As this transfer occurred, Moscow tested American resolve in Hokkaido by overflying it with MIG fighter-bombers. In January 1954, American fighters shot down a MIG. Henceforth Moscow cut back its violations of Japanese air space.

The United States also reduced some of its forces in the Ryukyu Islands which remained under military rule after Japan's sovereignty was returned. The U.S. military administration of the Ryukyus began with their subjection after fierce fighting in July 1945. Following reconstruction and the 1952 peace treaty, some Okinawan groups became increasingly vocal in demanding the Ryukyu Islands' reversion to Japan. In November 1953, Vice-President Nixon stopped in Naha, the Ryukyu capital, and declared that "the United States will control Okinawa as long as a Communist threat exists." The White House, however, was willing to return portions of the Ryukyus that had no strategic importance. On December 25, 1953, Dulles gave Yoshida a much desired Christmas present when he signed an agreement returning the northernmost of the islands, Amami Oshima with its population of 214,000, to Japan. The White House was relieved to be rid of Amami Oshima – the island had been convulsed by anti-American demonstrations and its military significance was slight. But to underscore American determination to hold on to the rest of the islands, Eisenhower declared two weeks later that: "We shall maintain indefinitely our bases in Okinawa. American freedom is threatened so long as the world Communist conspiracy exists in its present scope, power, and hostility."[12]

America's troop reductions in Japan were part of Eisenhower's "more bang for the buck" policy of cutting back American conventional forces and relying increasingly on the threat of massive nuclear retaliation to deter a potential Soviet attack. In 1955, the United States introduced into Japan its "Honest John" medium range ballistic missiles (MRBMs) which could hold nuclear warheads. When asked whether the Honest Johns actually were nuclear armed, American diplomatic and military spokesmen offered the standard "we can neither confirm nor deny" response. Japan's opposition parties and much of the mass media erupted in protests that called for the missiles' removal. The Hatoyama government asked Washington for an informal agreement that it would not bring in nuclear missiles unless Tokyo agreed. Washington complied. The issue subsided.

Yoshida was followed as prime minister by Hatoyama Ichiro in December 1954. Hatoyama was determined to distance Tokyo somewhat from Washington and pursue better relations with Moscow and Beijing, a strategy known as "multi-directional diplomacy" (zenhoi gaiko). While building on previous trade agreements with Beijing, Hatoyama broke new ground in relations with Moscow. The Soviet Union had refused to sign the 1951 peace treaty with Japan. Outstanding issues remained, including the fate of hundreds of thousands of Japanese soldiers still held as prisoners in Siberia and the ownership of what the Japanese called the "Northern Territories" or the four islands of Kunashiri, Etorofu, Habomai, and Shikotan north of Hokkaido.

Negotiations over these issues with Moscow began in June 1955 and were concluded in the days after Hatoyama arrived in Moscow on October 15, 1956. On October 19, 1956, Hatoyama and Khrushchev signed a Joint Declaration in which they agreed to reopen diplomatic relations and the restoration to Japan of Habomai and Shikotan upon the conclusion of a peace treaty. Both countries' parliaments ratified the agreement. In a side understanding, Moscow promised to withhold its veto on Japan's United Nations membership. Japan joined the United Nations in December 1956. In 1957, Tokyo signed a trade treaty with Moscow, granting the Soviet Union "most favored nation" status.

The Japanese and Soviets cut this deal in the face of American opposition. At first, believing the talks would stall, the White House assumed an "interested by-stander" stance. But as they progressed, Dulles became increasingly concerned, fearing they represented the first step of Japan's inevitable slide from the American into the Soviet orbit. On August 19, 1956, he warned that if Tokyo settled for only two of the four disputed islands and "gave better terms to Russia we could demand the same status by ourselves," thus implying the United States might annex part of Okinawa.[13] To no avail, Dulles protested Tokyo's granting of MFN to Moscow.

But in the end, it was not Washington but Moscow which scuttled the islands deal. A week after Tokyo and Washington signed the 1960 Mutual

Security Treaty, Moscow attached a condition (the Gromyko memorandum) to the 1956 treaty that said the islands would only be returned when all foreign troops were withdrawn from Japanese territory.

Eight years of Eisenhower policy toward Japan ended ignominiously in 1960 with a bitter conflict within Japan over the Mutual Security Treaty that replaced the controversial 1951 treaty. Even many Japanese who favored an alliance with the United States abhorred those clauses of the 1951 treaty in which the United States did not explicitly guarantee Japan's defense yet allowed American troops based in Japan to fight from the country against foreign enemies but also within it "at the express request of the Japanese government to put down large-scale internal riots and disturbances in Japan, caused through instigation or intervention by an outside Power or Powers."

Hatoyama took office determined to forge an equal relationship with the United States on the security treaty and other issues. In August 1955 he dispatched Foreign Minister Shigemitsu Mamoru to negotiate the security treaty's revision and reversion of the Ryukyu and Bonin islands. Dulles bluntly refused to consider these requests. Dismissing Shigemitsu's call for a clear defense guarantee, he cited the Vandenburg amendment to the security treaty which said the United States would only defend Japan within a multilateral defense community.

In his first press conference as prime minister in February 1957, Kishi Nobusuke asserted that "the Japanese people desire that the present security treaty and administrative agreement between Japan and the United States should be abolished."[14] Because Kishi was pro-American, the White House was more willing to negotiate. On a summit's eve, Dulles wrote Eisenhower that Kishi "has emphasized that he desires the establishment of a full partnership with the United States . . . on a basis of cooperation than on a basis of the exercise by the United States of unilateral rights. . . . I feel the time has come to take the initiative in proposing a readjustment of our relations with Japan and to suggest to Mr. Kishi that we work toward a mutual security arrangement which could . . . replace the present Security Treaty."[15]

During the June 25, 1957 summit, Eisenhower agreed to Kishi's requests for a new security relationship, and offered him three options: a base-lease agreement, amendment of the current treaty, or a new treaty. Although advised to amend the existing treaty to avoid a ratification debate, Kishi chose to negotiate an entirely new treaty, thus leaving behind the stigma of the 1951 treaty imposed upon Japan as a defeated country.[16] Their joint communiqué acknowledged that the 1951 security was transitional and also blasted the communist threat and need to stand united against it.

A joint committee was set up to analyze the issue, while parallel talks took place between Ambassador Douglas MacArthur II and Foreign Minister Fujiyama Aiichiro from September 1957 to September 1958, whereupon Fujiyama flew to Washington to deal directly with Dulles. Both men submitted draft agreements which found common ground in a mutual security treaty which would hold for a decade after which either side could terminate it after one year's notice. After that agreement, Dulles and his successor Christian Herter, who took office in April 1959, met periodically with Fujiyama to dicker over the proposed treaty's details.

The treaty was signed in the White House by Kishi and Herter on January 19, 1960. Under the treaty's provisions, the United States was pledged to aid Japan if it were attacked, and for Japan to aid American forces attacked in Japan. Tokyo pledged to build up its military to resist an attack, and Washington to consult Tokyo if its troops based in Japan would be used in combat elsewhere. The Prior Consultation Notes appended to the treaty required the United States to notify Japan of any restructuring of its personnel or weapons within Japan or against a target elsewhere.

The treaty's revision was supposed to inaugurate the relationship's evolution into a more equal partnership. Unfortunately, Kishi failed to forge a consensus within the Liberal Democratic Party (LDP) and with the opposition parties over the treaty. To undercut Kishi's power, opposition LDP factions criticized parts of the proposed treaty. Meanwhile, the opposition parties were already incensed by Kishi's submission of a police bill in December 1958 that would have drastically increased police powers. They mobilized against the bill by creating a National Congress which coordinated demonstrations, strikes, and teach-ins from political, union, and student organizations. When Kishi conceded on the police bill by withdrawing it from Diet consideration, the opposition shifted its focus to defeating the security treaty.

As a result of Kishi's blunders, the National Congress' efforts, and increased tensions following the shooting down of an American U-2 spy flight over the Soviet Union, public opinion shifted dramatically against the treaty. At the treaty's signing, Japanese public opinion was split with 29 per cent regarding it as "good" and 25 per cent as "bad." In March, the percentage of those who thought it was bad increased to 36 per cent while those who thought it good dropped to 21 per cent.[17]

The vote was scheduled for May 20. The opposition party members tried to block the lower house speaker in his office to prevent him from initiating a vote before the Diet session ended. Kishi responded by ordering 500 police to clear the Diet of all opposition members. The remaining LDP members then voted unanimously to ratify the treaty. Kishi had won his treaty's ratification, but his hardline tactics provoked criticism from across Japan's political spectrum. Kishi replied that he had to act as he did in order to ratify the treaty before President Eisenhower's scheduled visit on June 19. A treaty approved by the House is automatically ratified if the upper House of Councilors fails to vote within a month.

In pushing the treaty through the LDP and Diet, Kishi had violated basic Japanese norms of consensus in which all major participants, including opponents, should indicate their consent if not approval. In doing so, the "participant is indicating satisfaction that his point of view has been fairly heard, and while he may not wholly agree that the decision is the best one, he is willing to go along with, and, even more, support it."[18] Without this formal nod in his direction, the dissenter may actively resist the policy.

Concerned with the increasingly violent political disruptions in Japan, Eisenhower suggested delaying the visit for two months until passions died. Kishi urged him to stick to the original schedule. Eisenhower complied. On June 10, Eisenhower's press secretary James Hagerty was mobbed at Tokyo's Haneda airport when he arrived to prepare for the president's visit. The White House again requested a postponement. Kishi refused.

On June 12, Eisenhower left for a two-week journey through several Far East countries including the summit in Japan. On June 15, radical students invaded the Diet; a female college student was killed in the mêlée. The Kishi government agreed reluctantly that they could not guarantee the president's security and abruptly cancelled the summit. Eisenhower received word of Tokyo's cancellation on June 16 just after he arrived in the Philippines. The cancellation was particularly embarrassing since Premier Khrushchev had cancelled an earlier scheduled summit following the shooting down of the U-2 spyplane. Eisenhower's trip to the Far East was supposed to be an important part of a diplomatic effort to promote the western alliance's coherence and determination to contain the Soviet Union, of which shaking hands with Kishi in Tokyo over the Mutual Security Treaty was to have been the highlight. Eisenhower did fly to Okinawa where no serious disruptions occurred. Presumably he could have met Kishi outside of Tokyo or even, with heightened security, in the capital itself.

The dust over the treaty settled quickly despite all the controversy. Japan's ratification occurred automatically on June 20 when the upper house failed to vote. Although 6.25 million workers struck for a day in protest, there were no prolonged disruptions. When the United States Senate ratified the treaty two days later it immediately took effect. Kishi and his cabinet resigned on July 15, and three days later Ikeda Hayato was elected prime minister. In November, a general election strengthened the LDP domination of the Diet. By resigning, Kishi satisfied Japanese notions of justice allowing his successor Ikeda to win soundly in the fall election.

Although called a "mutual" security treaty, the relationship remained grossly imbalanced. While the United States was firmly committed to defending Japan if it were attacked, Tokyo was only required to aid the United States if American troops were attacked at their Japanese bases. Japan did not have any regional commitments. Yet, that was the best Washington could do given the political realities of Article 9 which literally interpreted forbids any Japanese military forces.

Policy Toward Japan: Geoeconomic Issues

The United States not only sheltered Japan under its conventional and nuclear arms umbrella, but exerted enormous efforts to build up Japan economically by allowing Japanese products nearly uninhibited access to America's vast market, and forcing Southeast Asia and GATT nations to follow suit.

The Eisenhower White House repeatedly called on American consumers and businesses to "buy Japanese." On September 15, 1953, the United States and Japan signed a commercial treaty in which Japan's manufactured goods were allowed free access to the United States while only farm products, technology, and raw materials were allowed into Japan, and only then if they did not compete with any Japanese products. Competitive American products or investments in Japan were highly restricted or outright barred.

This arrangement, of course, did not prevent American industries from complaining about Japanese dumping and other unfair trade practices. The first U.S.–Japanese trade dispute in the postwar era was over textiles. Massively restructured by American fiancial, technical, and managerial aid during the Occupation, Japan's textile industry expanded at fantastic rates throughout the 1950s. In 1955, over 4 million Japanese "dollar blouses" were sold in the United States, up from none as recently as 1952, and captured one-quarter of the market![19] This tidal wave of Japanese exports hit America's textile industry which had been contracting over the previous decade from 1.325 million workers in 1947 to less than one million in 1957. Not surprisingly, America's textile producers lobbied the White House and Congress for relief.

The White House opposed efforts in Congress to impose quotas on Japanese textiles and instead pressured Tokyo to "voluntarily" limit exports. Secretary of State Dulles argued that the alliance with Japan was too important for the United States to retaliate against Japan's predatory trade practices. Writing to Senator Margaret Chase Smith, Dulles maintained that setting "import quotas on Japanese textiles would be most unfortunate. . . . It would serve to restrict trade at a time when the free world must depend for so much of its strength on the expansion of trade and the economic viability of countries such as Japan."[20] Dulles foresaw disastrous results if Washington strongly resisted Japanese dumping: "the Japanese would almost assuredly have begun to develop closer relations with Communist China."[21]

The textile conflict was resolved in a diplomatic pattern that has been repeated hundreds of times since. The White House promised to relieve the beleaguered American industries; Tokyo dragged out the subsequent negotiations until the United States threatened sanctions, whereupon it offered "concessions." In December 1955, Tokyo agreed to restrict textile exports, and in January 1957 accepted a five year agreement with more comprehensive restrictions involving total exports and quotas in specific areas of cloth and clothing. The latter represented a Japanese concession since they wanted to be free to determine the mix of exports within broad limits so they could shift production to meet changing fashions and demands.

Meanwhile the White House continued to deepen Japan's trade ties with Southeast Asia. American embassies throughout the region continued to help Japanese exporters sell locally, often by tying American aid to purchases of Japanese goods and services. Not content with this assistance, Tokyo pressured Washington for ever more massive aid to the region to expand Japan's economic power at home and abroad. During his 1954 visit to Washington, Yoshida later recalled that he demanded that the:

> United States recognize Japan's status in Asia as an independent country, with the two nations co-operating on an equal footing for the maintenance and promotion of peace in Asia. Next, I desired to make it clear that Japan was ready to do all in her power to contribute to the economic development of the free countries in Asia and also our two Governments had reached an understanding to the effect that the economic welfare of Japan was a question of importance to the free world in general so that while the United States would be ready to consider any means for the improvement of the economic status of the Japanese people, Japan herself would do her best to promote overseas trade and strengthen her economic position in the world.[22]

In other words, Washington should give Japan equal status in promoting Asian peace and prosperity while massively boosting its aid program which already strengthened Japan's economy and overseas trade. One Japanese historian concludes that "the Japanese were interested in purely economic aspects of the U.S. security program and other related programs in Asia, giving only lip service to American beliefs about the military–strategic importance of these programs."[23] Eisenhower assured Yoshida that the United

States would continue to aid Japan's economic expansion throughout Southeast Asia and the world, but could not afford the vast Marshall Plan Tokyo envisioned.

Washington was also instrumental in forcing Japan's reintegration into the global economy against the resistance of other industrial countries. On May 29, 1952, Japan was admitted to the International Monetary Fund (IMF) and on August 12, 1955 into the General Agreement on Trade and Tariffs (GATT) which allowed it membership as a developing country.

Eisenhower even tolerated Japan's expanding trade with China. Washington had forced Japan to cutback its trade with China after Beijing intervened in the Korean War. Japan's trade with China was further restricted in July 1952 when Tokyo joined the Coordinating Committee for Exports to Communist Areas (COCOM), and its China Committee (CHINCOM). Tokyo had little choice in joining. Mutual Security Assistance (MSA) forbade American aid to any country which sold strategic goods to communist countries. Fearing that Tokyo could be sucked into the Chinese orbit, Washington restricted Japan's trade with China more tightly than it did Britain, France, and other European countries. While it tolerated limited trade between its allies and China, Washington continued to prevent any American trade with the mainland.

Tokyo's eagerness to trade with China was obvious. On July 27, 1953, the same day as the Korean ceasefire was signed, the Diet resolved that Japan promote trade with China. Yoshida pressed Eisenhower to grant permission. The White House was split over the issue; Eisenhower favored and Dulles opposed allowing Japan to expand its trade with the mainland. Echoing Kennan's arguments of the late 1940s, the president argued as early as 1953 that "there was no future for Japan unless access were provided for it to the markets and raw materials of Manchuria and North China," and Washington should not only "permit" but "encourage" that trade.[24] Dulles maintained the global containment idea that the United States faced a monolithic communist bloc – to allow Japan to trade with it would mean Japan's eventual loss to it.

In early October 1953, Walter Robertson, the Assistant Secretary of State for Far Eastern Affairs, and Finance Minister Ikeda Hayato began negotiations with Washington over expanding its China trade to the same products as the Europeans. Robertson demanded a quid pro quo. In return for allowing Japan an expanded trade with China, the United States asked that Tokyo beef up its military. He asked Tokyo to increase its ground troops to 350,000 men. Tokyo rejected the troop target. On October 21, Washington agreed to allow expanded trade in return for Tokyo's promise to increase its ground forces from 110,000 to 180,000 men within five years. Although Dulles had reluctantly gone along with that agreement, he fruitlessly opposed the agreement signed a week later between Tokyo and Beijing on October 29 to exchange trade representatives.

To Dulles's consternation, Sino-Japanese trade expanded rapidly from $35 million in 1953 to $150 million in 1956. However, relations between China and Japan deteriorated after Kishi Nobusuke became prime minister in February 1957. Mao plunged China into the disastrous "Great Leap Forward" of decentralized industrialization which resulted in the vast misallocation of material and human resources and starvation deaths for 20 million people. China's trade with Japan and other foreign countries contracted. Negotiations to revive it were marred by disputes over whether the Chinese flag should be flown over China's trade office in Tokyo and Kishi's visit to Taipei in 1958.

In the late 1950s, the Allies divided over COCOM's more restrictive list toward China, known as the "China differential." Britain and Japan led the charge against the China differential. Eisenhower also denounced not only the China differential but the entire restrictive trade policy toward communist countries. It was naive, he argued, to believe that cutting off trade would weaken the communist countries. Instead, the trade policy simply pushed the communist countries closer together and reinforced their governments' totalitarianism and imperial policies. Freer trade would not only spur western economic growth but open the communist countries to western economic and cultural influences, and thus gradually soften them. This would be the logic behind Nixon's détente policy a decade later. Despite this understanding, Eisenhower still yielded to Dulles and other hardliners on policy in the White House and Congress. The president admitted that "our trouble was that our domestic political situation compelled us to adopt rigid policy respecting trade with Communist China and the Soviet Union."[25]

Following a deadlocked COCOM meeting on the China differential in May 1957, Japan and the other allies simply denounced it and used an expanded list of trade goods. Increasing numbers of congressmen also agreed to eliminate the differential, hoping it might divert some Japanese textile exports from the United States to China. Ironically, since an executive order rather than law restricted American trade with China, the decision was up to the president rather than Congress. Yet while Eisenhower's "views were clear, publicly and privately stated . . . he was unwilling to use any more of his political capital to force a policy change on the rest of his administration."[26] Throughout the summer, the White House gradually forged a consensus that it made more sense to accept the reality that America's allies had abandoned the differential rather than resist it on principle or retaliate. On August 6, 1957, Washington accepted the differential's formal elimination.

A vital element of Japanese economic expansion involved the acquisition of foreign and particularly American technology. By the mid 1950s, Japan's Ministry of International Trade and Industry (MITI) had targeted a range of high technology industries for nurturing, including microelectronics, semiconductors, and computers. MITI had vast powers to develop Japan's economy, of which one of its most important was its ability to act as "gatekeeper." MITI was able to pressure competitive foreign firms to sell their technology to their Japanese rivals by preventing them from either trading or investing in Japan, and playing them off against each other.

IBM was the world leader in many of the technologies MITI had targeted for Japan's corporations. Chalmers Johnson vividly describes MITI head Sahashi Shigeru's attempts to shake down IBM's high technology secrets before it would be allowed a limited ability to trade or invest in Japan: "Sahashi wanted IBM's patents and made no bones about it. . . . 'We will take every measure possible to obstruct the success of your business unless you license IBM patents to Japanese firms and charge them no more than a 5 percent royalty.' In one of his negotiation sessions, Sahashi proudly recalls, he said that 'We do not have an inferiority complex toward you; we only need time and money to compete effectively.'"[27]

In 1960, MITI and IBM cut a deal whereby it was allowed to build and sell some of its products in Japan in return for licensing its basic technology to fifteen Japanese microelectronics firms. MITI's official management of IBM's market share and products continued until 1979; unofficially IBM's market and product shares remain limited even today by a range of Japanese restrictions.

The White House sat on the sidelines throughout MITI's successful attempts to shake down technology from IBM and scores of other leading American corporations. By refusing the requests of American firms to help them break through the walls protecting Japan's economy, it aided their Japanese rivals. The incessant and growing conflicts between Japan's corporate behemoths and America's battered firms throughout the 1980s and 1990s are rooted in White House decisions of the 1950s and 1960s.

JOHN F. KENNEDY, 1961–3

Policymaking and Implementation

When he took office, Kennedy faced formidable hinderances to effective policymaking. Having won by only 120,000 votes out of 69 million cast, he could hardly claim a popular mandate. Although there were large Democratic majorities in the Senate and House, several key committees were ruled by Republicans or conservative Democrats. Many in Congress and among the public were suspicious of a 43-year-old patrician and catholic whose father was the notorious Joe Kennedy. There was the danger that with Kennedy's lack of a clearly defined political philosophy or policy goals, his tenure might well be the triumph of style over substance.

Yet Kennedy carried into the Oval Office such vital strengths as high intelligence, self-confidence, and openmindedness. He gathered around himself a "brain trust" from among the nation's "best and brightest" policy experts and managers, including a dozen Rhodes scholars. Of the top 200 White House officials, 18 per cent were from universities or foundations and only 6 per cent were businessmen; in contrast, businessmen made up 42 per cent and scholars only 6 per cent of Eisenhower's White House.[28]

Kennedy essentially served as his own Secretary of State and created a small informal State Department among his staff. Among the formal foreign policymakers, Kennedy relied much more heavily on his gifted, imaginative, assertive NSC advisor McGeorge Bundy and Defense Secretary Robert McNamara than his intelligent but reticent and conservative Secretary of State Dean Rusk.

Kennedy's free-wheeling administrative style contrasted starkly with Eisenhower's bureaucratized approach. Kennedy abandoned Eisenhower's elaborate NSC bureaucracy and instead relied on "informal meetings and direct contacts – on a personal White House staff, the Budget Bureau and *ad hoc* task forces to probe and define issues for his decisions – on special Presidential emissaries and constant Presidential phone calls and memoranda – on placing Kennedy men in each strategic spot."[29]

The decisions for the Bay of Pigs invasion of April 1961 and Cuban Missile Crisis of October 1962 have become the respective models for how not and how to make decisions. Group-think, over-reliance on experts, and rashness characterized the first; prudent analysis of the problems and possible solutions, the second. Sorenson recalls the debates during the Cuban Missile Crisis, including "the sense of complete equality. Protocal mattered little in a crisis which had no precedent. Even rank mattered little when secrecy prevented staff support. We were fifteen individuals on our own, representing the President and not different departments."[30] The transition from one policymaking process to the next rested on Kennedy's flexibility and eagerness to learn.

Policy Priorities

Many who remember Kennedy for his wit and panache, forget that he was a hardnosed realist. During his State of the Union address in January 1961,

Kennedy admitted to the American public that: "Our problems are critical. The tide is unfavorable. The news will be worse before it is better."[31]

Kennedy was prescient. Like his predecessors, he soon became bogged down in a range of Cold War conflicts and issues around the world. In 1961, the Soviets built the Berlin Wall while the American-sponsored invasion of Cuba by a small anti-Castro exile army was destroyed at the Bay of Pigs. Communist insurgencies in the Congo, Laos, South Vietnam, and Cambodia gained in strength. Kennedy, like most Americans, feared that "the whole world . . . would inevitably begin to move toward the Communist bloc."[32]

Like other administrations, Kennedy's pursued a two-track international economic policy in which it retaliated against unfair foreign predatory trade and promoted freer multilateral trade. In May 1961, two months after taking office, the Kennedy White House submitted a seven-point plan to aid America's textile industry, which included international negotiations to regulate trade. Negotiations over the International Trade in Cotton Textiles (LTA) began two months later, were completed in February 1962, and took effect in October 1962. Under the LTA, any country could restrict imports if they were causing or threatening to cause damage to domestic industries. The importing country first had to attempt to negotiate with the exporting country, and could only act unilaterally if it failed to cut a deal within sixty days. Under the LTA, however, quotas on imports could expand by 5 per cent annually. While the LTA seemed restrictive, textile-exporting countries actually welcomed it because the quotas gave them footholds in restrictive markets in Europe and elsewhere.

The agreement emerged from a Kennedy campaign promise in 1960 to restrict growing textile imports which increasingly squeezed American producers. Although Japanese exports fell from $84.1 million to $74.1 million in the three years following the 1957 bilateral accord, textiles from other countries rose from $154.3 million to $248 million.[33] Kennedy's support in depressed textile states in the northeast and southeast may have won him a very close election.

The Trade Expansion Act of 1962 empowered the president to negotiate multilateral free trade agreements. The president launched what became known as GATT's Kennedy Round which, when it was completed in 1967, had succeeded in drastically lowering tariffs.

Throughout his administration, Kennedy struggled over what to do in Vietnam. He leaned toward the pervasive arguments that if America could save Vietnam, it would save the rest of Southeast Asia from communism. Between 1961 and 1963, he increased the number of American advisors from 1,500 to 16,000. Then, days before he flew to Dallas in November

1963, he signed an order withdrawing one thousand of those advisors and spoke of bringing them all back by 1965. Nonetheless, until the day he died, Kennedy was haunted by the dilemma over whether to re-escalate or withdraw America's military commitment to Saigon's dictatorship completely.

Policy Toward Japan: Geopolitical Issues

Like other presidents, Kennedy had trouble squeezing the resolution of American squabbles with Japan into his crowded policy agenda. One of the first bilateral issues arose over the Ryukyu islands which the army had administered for over fifteen years. In 1961, the State Department raised the issue of Okinawa's future with Kennedy. The president asked White House aide, Carl Kaysen, to prepare an analysis of Okinawa's importance to the United States and alternative policy proposals. The subsequent December 1961 Kaysen Report captured the dilemmas of American bases in the Ryukyu islands: "Okinawa is our most important base in the Western Pacific. Its value reflects not only the installation and facilities . . . but . . . our use of it is free from the restraints imposed by the existence of another political authority. Yet although we have exclusive administrative authority, our effective control is . . . conditioned by both the domestic situation in Okinawa and by the reflection of that situation in Japan."[34]

Acting on the report's recommendations, Kennedy ordered American civilian administrators to replace the military officials ruling the islands, expanded the Okinawan legislators' terms from two to three years and allowed them to nominate the chief executive with approval by the High Commissioner. The president also increased economic aid to the Ryukyus and asked Tokyo to encourage the expansion of business investments there. With Kennedy concerned by many geopolitical crises elsewhere, few issues flared between the United States and Japan during his brief tenure in the White House.

Policy Toward Japan: Geoeconomic Issues

Paradoxically, Japanese nationalism grew with its global economic power. The GATT and OECD pressure on Japan to dismantle its trade and investment barriers sparked a vehement reaction. Chalmers Johnson describes

the crisis atmosphere that existed in Japanese industrial circles during 1961. The press prattled on endlessly about the "second coming of the black ships," "the defenselessness of the Japanese islands in the face of attack from huge foreign capitalist powers," and "the readying of the Japanese economy for a bloodstained battle between national and foreign capital." [MITI chief] Sahashi himself invoked the name of the National General Mobilization Law of 1938 and said that Japan again required a "national general mobilization" in order to create an economic system that could withstand the rigors of international competition.[35]

In July 1963, Tokyo applied for membership with the Organization for Economic Cooperation and Development (OECD), and was finally admitted on April 29, 1964. As with GATT, Washington had sponsored Japan's membership in the OECD in the face of strong opposition. Tokyo joined only after insisting on more reservations to the OECD's capital liberalization code than any other members except Spain and Portugal.[36] In return, seventeen OECD countries agreed to accept Japan's membership only if they got temporary reservations from granting Tokyo full privileges. The result was another Japanese spasm of xenophobia.

Tokyo, of course, had no intention of complying with the GATT or OECD requirements. Japanese neomercantilism remained as vigorous and systematic as ever. For example, MITI continued to nurture Japan's microelectronics firms with a range of cartels, import barriers, joint technology development, subsidies, export promotion, "buy Japanese" practices, and foreign technology infusions.

During the Kennedy years, MITI succeeded in wringing from Texas Instruments (TI) a deal similar to that it negotiated with IBM during the Eisenhower years. It granted TI no more than a 10 per cent market share in exchange for TI's promise to license its technology to its Japanese rivals. The Kennedy White House, like Eisenhower's, refused to intervene on the side of a beleaguered American high technology champion. MITI outright excluded from Japanese markets other American high technology firms which lacked the power of IBM or TI.

Overall, the Kennedy White House was more concerned about Japan's trade with China than its trade with the United States. When Kennedy raised the issue during their June 1961 summit, Prime Minister Ikeda replied that "Japan historically and traditionally has had special relations with the Chinese continent. I think it would be reasonable for Japan to engage in at least as much trade as the Western European countries are currently doing."[37] Kennedy agreed to the seemingly sensible argument that Japan's trade with China should be on the same basis as Europe's.

In fact, Ikeda was distorting the facts. By 1960, Tokyo had become Beijing's leading trade partner with a volume exceeding that of the European countries' combined total. Ikeda's policy toward China was shaped by three elements: expanding trade, not recognizing Beijing before Washington did, and serving as diplomatic bridge between the United States and China. Tokyo forged agreements with Beijing in 1962 and 1964 which further expanded not only trade but Japanese investments and Export–Import Bank loans to facilitate those economic ties.

Washington became alarmed that Japan's economic ties were changing "from trade to aid." During a U.S.–Japan Joint Trade and Economic Committee meeting on December 3, 1962, Kennedy warned that "the major question facing us today is the growth of Communist forces in China, and how to contain Communist expansion in Asia. I hope [this committee] will consider what the United States and Japan as allies can do, and what roles they can play in order to prevent the Communist domination of Asia."[38] Tokyo ignored Kennedy's pleas and continued to expand its trade, investment, and financial ties with China.

LYNDON B. JOHNSON, 1963–9

Policymaking and Implemention

For his first eighteen months as president, Johnson largely used Kennedy's staff. However, he used it differently. Perhaps no administration has been more characterized by "group think" than Johnson's. While Kennedy stimulated open debate, Johnson demanded yes-men who would support and faithfully carry out his decisions. Not surprisingly, Johnson preferred the obsequious and loyal Secretary of State Dean Rusk to any of the other policy "whizkids." When McNamara began to express doubts about the Vietnam War, Johnson excluded him from his inner foreign policymaking circle, the "Tuesday lunch" group which also included Rusk, CIA Director Richard Helms, and National Security Advisor Walt Rostow.

Johnson appeared to organize his foreign policy system to reinforce the State Department. Policymaking was focused in the Senior Interdepartmental Group (SIG) which include the Defense Secretary, CIA Director, Joint Chief of Staff Chair, USIA Director, and NSC advisor, and presided over by the Assistant Secretary of State. SIG in turn was supported by a dozen Interdepartmental Regional Groups (IRG) which corresponded to the State Departments' regional bureaus. The Planning–Programming–Budgeting System (PPBS) further augmented the State Department's role by providing it with a budgetary overview of all departments and agencies involved in foreign policy.

Yet, Johnson bypassed this elaborate machinery by concentrating foreign policy decisions in his own hands. Intimidated by the "eastern establishment" intellectuals surrounding him, Johnson sought to rule by intimidating them. He forced through his wishes by sheer force of his personality and physical presence. And he demanded unquestioning loyalty. In addition to his character flaws, Johnson was profoundly ignorant and parochial about foreign affairs.

Johnson was a master of duplicity, egotism, and cynicism: "The reasons he will give for his actions will not be those he really believes because" he says what he thinks you want to hear. He "will not change course even when he knows he is wrong. The only advisors he will listen to are those who will tell him what he wants to hear, for he is not a man who tolerates listening to both sides of a problem. . . . Furthermore, since his entire training has been that of a politician trying to overpower other politicians, he will rely on personal diplomacy to buy off, threaten, and coerce other nations."[39]

Throughout his life, Lyndon Johnson had struggled to overcome deep feelings of inadequacy and insecurity. While highly intelligent, Johnson was no intellectual and boasted of having read no more than six books during his entire public life.[40] In each domestic or foreign conflict, Johnson saw himself as a valiant defender of American values and interests besieged in an Alamo-like trap by ruthless opponents. More than most presidents, Johnson personalized his conflicts, for example, seeing North Vietnamese attacks on American forces as direct attacks on himself.

Perhaps no president has taken his role as commander-in-chief more seriously; Johnson micromanaged the war to the point where he poured over maps to find bombing targets. Johnson did have considerable background in defense issues. Throughout his congressional career, he served on virtually every defense committee and subcommittee. While Johnson despised the Pentagon, he exalted America's military machine and sought constantly to aggrandize it.

While Johnson dismissed the idea of having a political philosophy, he did have a clear mind-set. Like many of his generation, "Johnson's ideas were set in thick concrete by World War II. Every big action he takes will be determined primarily on the basis of whether he thinks any other action will look like a Munich appeasement. . . . [He] sees the Cold War as permanent, the enemy unchangeable, and every anti-United States activity anywhere . . . as a deliberate act controlled by an international monolithic Communist network operating from the Kremlin."[41]

Policy Priorities

Throughout its five and a half years in office, the Johnson administration struggled to achieve two vastly ambitious and competing goals: building a "Great Society" in America and winning a war in Vietnam.

With Democratic majorities in both houses of Congress, Johnson's "Great Society" programs were relatively easy to enact. Within two years of taking office, Johnson had signed a score of laws creating housing, income, health, and welfare programs, and protecting civil rights. Ambitious as these programs were, they did not eliminate poverty but at their height merely helped reduce the number of Americans living in absolute poverty from 15 per cent to 11 per cent.

Like Kennedy, Johnson faced the question of what to do about America's commitment to South Vietnam. The choices were stark: withdraw America's 15,000 military advisors, maintain them, or escalate America's involvement from training South Vietnam's army to combatting the Viet Cong and North Vietnamese forces directly. Unlike Kennedy, Johnson did not brood Hamlet-like over the decision. At Kennedy's funeral, Johnson told U.S. Ambassador to South Vietnam, Henry Cabot Lodge, that "I am not going to lose Vietnam. I am not going to be the President who saw Southeast Asia go the way China went."[42]

Swearing he would not be the first president to lose a war, Johnson used the excuse of a reported attack (that may never have occurred) on August 1, 1964 by North Vietnamese gunboats on two U.S. destroyers to ask Congress essentially for a blank check to fight the war. Congress responded with the Tonkin Gulf Resolution authorizing the president "to take all necessary measures to repel any armed attacks against the forces of the United States and to prevent further aggression." The Senate voted 88–2 and House 317–55 in favor. Johnson's popularity rating soared from 42 to 73 per cent overnight.[43]

Policy Toward Japan: Geoeconomic Issues

Obsessed with simultaneously pushing through his "Great Society" welfare legislation and fighting the Vietnam War, Johnson had little time left to think about let alone act on outstanding issues with Japan. American policy toward Japan was thus shaped by bureaucratic politics rather than grand strategy. And the bureaucrats most concerned with Japan were the Defense and State Departments which continued the trade off of Tokyo's alliance with the United States and tolerance of American military bases in Japan for Washington's commitment toward maintaining unimpeded Japanese access to American markets and breaking down barriers to Japanese products around the world.

The Johnson administration viewed Japan's surging economic power without trepidation. In 1964, Ambassador Edwin Reischauer sent a report to the White House which argued that it continue to support Japan's geoeconomic expansion and display "firm Executive Branch resistance of American industry demands for curtailment of Japanese imports."[44] Johnson essentially followed this advice.

One of the clearest statements of Washington's policy of promoting Japan's economy, often to the detriment of America's, was contained in a 1964 U.S. State Department report which declared that "looking ahead over the next ten years, we can expect to find ourselves dealing with an increasingly strong, confident, and nationalistic Japan. . . . It's difficult to see how Japan's minimum economic goals can be attained unless Japan is afforded opportunity to expand its sales in the U.S. market at least in proportion with the growth of the U.S. GNP. . . . This will require firm Executive Branch resistance of American industry demands for curtailment of Japanese imports. . . . It is only less important that when the U.S. must act contrary to Japanese trading interests, time and effort be taken to put the best possible face on the action."[45]

This report was issued when Japan had enjoyed annual average growth rates of 10 per cent for the previous fourteen years, had become the world's second largest economy, and was about to enjoy its first trade surplus with the United States. Yet the image persisted of a frail, unstable, poor Japan that might well join the communist camp if the United States curbed its special treatment.

It was on President Johnson's watch in 1965 that Japan's persistent trade deficit with the United States was transformed into a trade surplus that has soared ever since. Johnson and Rusk became concerned not that Tokyo continued to maintain huge trade and investment barriers and dump its goods in the United States and elsewhere, but that Japanese firms were merely selling in Southeast Asia and not trying to develop the region. After all, "a fundamental reason for the original American involvement in Vietnam between 1949 and 1954 had been the assumption that Vietnam had to be held as part of a security package (including capitalist economic development) for the entire region – especially for Japan. Only by keeping Southeast Asian markets open could the United States prevent intolerable Japanese–Chinese relations."[46] Nonetheless, Washington continued to promote Japanese trade and investments throughout the region – at the expense of American firms. And Japan continued to enrich itself from billions of dollars in annual American military procurements, although they only financed about 7–8 per cent of Japan's exports compared to 63 per cent during the Korean War.[47]

Ironically, despite the logic of America's involvement in Vietnam, the Johnson White House abandoned attempts to restrict Japanese and other allied trade with China. In talks with LDP Secretary General Miki Takeo on January 13, 1965, Vice-President Hubert Humphrey essentially gave Japan the green light to increase its economic if not political relations with China, and even stated that by doing so "Japan could act to reduce some of the aggressive, militant spirit of Communist China."[48] A June 1966 CIA report entitled "Economic Benefits to Communist China of a Removal of U.S. Trade Controls" stated bluntly that they were minimal and actually hurt American industries because "the Chinese can usually satisfy their needs by buying in Western markets or Japan."[49] If Japan could reduce China's aggressiveness through trade, why could not the United States do the same, and in so doing boost its own economy? For domestic political reasons, American policymakers did not dare to follow the logic to its obvious conclusion.

During 1967, Prime Minister Sato toured several Asian countries to promote Japanese exports and investments. That was not the subject of his November speech before the National Press Club in Washington. There Sato announced that he had found "widespread support" for "free-world efforts to cope with Communist intervention." During their summit meeting shortly thereafter, Johnson told the prime minister that of the eighty-seven government leaders he had met over the previous year, "none had been more direct or helpful than Sato."[50]

Policy Toward Japan: Geopolitical Issues

Like other administrations, Johnson's sought but failed to achieve a larger Japanese defense role. After China exploded its first nuclear device in 1964, the Johnson administration actually discussed the possibility of encouraging Japan's acquisition of nuclear weapons to create a regional nuclear power balance. Dean Rusk reportedly argued: "Why shouldn't Japan have a nuclear weapon? Why shouldn't our friends have nuclear weapons now that our enemies have them?"[51] But the administration finally agreed that Japan's acquisition of nuclear weapons would exacerbate rather than ease regional tensions and the nuclear arms race. Nor did the Johnson White House strongly encourage Japan's conventional build up.

While over 300,000 men of America's ally South Korea fought in Vietnam (a force two-thirds larger than Japan's entire military), Tokyo actually decreased its defense role. In 1967, Prime Minister Sato issued the "three non-nuclear principles" whereby Japan would not produce, possess, or permit the introduction of nuclear weapons in its territory. Although Sato's policy was in response to China's nuclear build up, it complicated Japan's alliance with the United States. Later that year, Sato announced the "three principles of arms exports" under which Japan would not export to communist countries, countries embargoed by the United Nations, or countries likely to be or currently involved in war. Then, in a 1968 speech before the Diet, Sato stated that Japan's nuclear policy rested on the: (1) reliance on America's nuclear umbrella; (2) three nonnuclear principles; (3) promotion of worldwide disarmament; and (4) development of nuclear energy for peaceful purposes. Few questioned the irony or contradiction of claiming that Japan had a "nuclear allergy" yet relied on another nation's nuclear umbrella for defense and built up its own nuclear energy industry, nor did many point out that Tokyo has done nothing substantial to encourage nuclear disarmament. Yet, for his brief statement, Sato was awarded the Nobel Peace Prize.

The long-standing opposition of many Japanese and Okinawans to the U.S. bases in the Ryukyu Islands soared during the mid 1960s as knowledge leaked that they were being used for B-52 raids on Indochina, MACE missiles capable of being armed with nuclear weapons, and nuclear submarines.

In 1964, Sato Eisaku chose to demand the reversion of the Ryukyu and Bonin islands partly because of conviction but also to distinguish himself from his opponents running for LDP president. Ikeda won the presidency and thus prime ministership but had to resign four months later because of ill health. Sato renewed his pledge upon taking office and worked steadily toward that goal throughout his eight years in office.

At their first summit in 1965, Johnson disappointed Sato by dismissing his request with the argument that Okinawa was central to America's Pacific defense and war in Vietnam, and Tokyo had not given any good rationale for the Ryukyu's reversion to Japan. Sato and the Japanese public were disappointed with Johnson's position. Throughout the next few years, Japanese and Okinawan demonstrations against America's war in Vietnam and for Okinawa's reversion increased. American Ambassador Edwin Reischauer took up the Japanese side on Okinawa and continually pressured the White House to concede.

In 1966, in order to study and propose policies on the complex of issues and conflicts in that part of the world, the White House formed a Far East Interdepartmental Regional Group (IRG), and included a Ryukyus Working Group which included High Commissioner designate Lieutenant-General Ferdinand Unger and new ambassador to Japan U. Alexis Johnson. After assuming his post in late 1966, Unger publicly admitted the group's conclusions that preparations for Okinawa's reversion should begin.

America's failure to prevail in Vietnam undermined talks over Okinawa's return to Japan. By late 1967, Johnson had increased American troops in South Vietnam to 460,000 and ordered massive bombing across North and South Vietnam, and yet victory seemed unobtainable. In the months leading up to the November 1967 summit, the Ryukyus Working Group and Assistant Secretary of State for Far Eastern Affairs William Bundy agreed that the Ryukyus should be returned and pressured Johnson to accept that position. The Pentagon, however, remained opposed. On August 30, 1967, Defense Secretary McNamara urged the President to tell Foreign Minister Miki at a pending meeting that the Okinawan bases "are there at least as much for the protection of the Japanese as they are for the defense of the United States" and thus Japan should share "the very heavy political and economic costs of providing security to the area."[52] On the November summit's eve, Senate Armed Services Committee Chair Richard Russell strongly objected to the Ryukyu's reversion under conditions limiting American use of the bases. Russell was one of Johnson's most important allies on Capitol Hill for funding and supporting the Vietnam War.

Facing two different policy proposals, Johnson decided on a compromise. On November 16, 1967, President Johnson and Prime Minister Sato issued a joint communiqué that, among other things, announced that the Bonin (Ogasawara) islands would be returned to Japan the following year and the Ryukyu islands "within a few years." A controversy immediately arose over the communiqué's different wording in English and Japanese. The Japanese version converted within a few years to "two or three years" (ryosannen), thus adding a specific deadline that the Americans had been careful to avoid. The White House denied the Japanese version, causing relief at the Pentagon and disappointment in Tokyo and across Japan, particularly in the Ryukyus. Sato returned to criticism from across the political spectrum for his "sell out" to Washington.

Shortly after the summit, Sato announced his "blank sheet" policy whereby a decision over whether nuclear weapons could be installed in the Ryukyus would be decided after their reversion. Sato's position was hardly comforting to the Pentagon which feared that Tokyo would simply forbid a nuclear presence after it took over the islands. In 1968, Johnson returned the Bonin islands to Japan by executive agreement. The United States continued to maintain two bases there.

Despite these American concessions, Japanese pressure on the United States for a complete reversion increased. In February 1968, Okinawa's legislature resolved that B-52s based on the island should leave. In Japan's

Diet, the Japan Socialist Party (JSP) submitted a similar motion but it was voted down. In November 1968, a JSP candidate won Okinawa's governorship and immediately created a commission to study the closing of American airbases and the island's reversion to Japan.

The pressure was building on the Johnson administration over the Ryukyus. However, this issue was lost amidst a range of other crises that eventually caused Johnson to announce in 1968 that he would not seek re-election.

CONCLUSION

After nearly twenty years of largely positive feelings and shared interests between the two countries, tensions emerged in the mid 1960s over Japan's growing trade surplus and America's increasingly bloody intervention in Vietnam. Japanese psychology exacerbated these disagreements. Just as Japanese "amae" or the "indulged dependence" of the junior partner in return for loyalty had earlier reinforced American–Japanese relations, the Japanese tendency to "be meek toward the strong, and arrogant toward the weak" increasingly manifested itself as Japan's 10 per cent annual growth transformed the country into an economic superpower.

Throughout this era, increasing numbers of Americans saw Japan as an economic rival as much as a military ally. Not just Japan's trade surplus, but more importantly the composition of bilateral trade became major concerns in Washington. Japanese manufactured goods captured an increasing share of bilateral trade while American manufactured goods dwindled. Americans once noted that a product was "Made in Japan" with condescension and pity; increasingly and, for many, fearfully, they acknowledged the label symbolized high-quality.

Yet, none of the three administrations addressed these growing fears. Each administration promoted America's geopolitical alliance rather than addressed its growing geoeconomic rivalry with Japan.

8 America and Japan Neck and Neck: The Nixon, Ford, and Carter Era, 1969–81

By the late 1960s, the United States was groaning under the weight of geopolitical and geoeconomic commitments all around the world. Geopolitically, the United States had military alliances and assistance agreements with nearly fifty countries, had 560,000 troops fighting in Vietnam, was feverishly trying to stay ahead in the nuclear arms race with the Soviet Union, and watched impotently as France and China joined the nuclear club in the mid 1960s and acted increasingly independently of the two superpowers. Geoeconomically, Japan had become the world's second largest economy and from 1965 enjoyed continually larger trade surpluses with the United States, the European Community became more cohesive and prosperous, while the United States suffered low growth, higher inflation and unemployment, and a deteriorating trade balance.

Richard Nixon entered the White House in 1969 vowing to realign American commitments with its relatively declining military and economic power. At Guam in June 1969, the president announced the principles of what would become known as the "Nixon Doctrine." American policy henceforth would fight communist insurgencies indirectly by aiding governments determined to defeat them. During the decade from the 1969 Nixon Doctrine to the 1979 Soviet invasion of Afghanistan, the United States steadily reduced its military commitments to the Far East and elsewhere. Nixon's "Vietnamization" policy of turning over the fighting to the South Vietnamese while withdrawing American troops was an integral part of the new policy. He pursued détente with China and the Soviet Union, and signed a "peace with honor" with Vietnam.

On economic fronts, Nixon threw the White House's weight behind some American industries like textiles besieged by foreign dumping. On August 15, 1971, he announced his New Economic Policy which included the suspension of the dollar's convertibility into gold, a 10 per cent surcharge on import tariffs, and later the dollar's devaluation. The Ford and Carter administrations largely followed the broad outlines of Nixon's strategy.

Nixon's policies slowed rather than reversed America's declining power. In 1971, America suffered its first trade deficit since 1893. The White House could do nothing to prevent OPEC's quadrupling of oil prices in late 1973, nor its further doubling in 1979. In the mid 1970s, America's trade across the Pacific basin surpassed that with the Atlantic basin, while Japan's trade surplus with the United States soared. American prestige fell with Indochina to communism in 1975. Then in 1979, several geopolitical challenges ended a decade of détente and complicated those forces undermining America's geoeconomic power. Anti-American revolutions toppled friendly regimes in Iran and Nicaragua, and the Soviet army invaded Afghanistan. To top things off, Iran kidnapped fifty-two American diplomats and held them hostage for what would be 444 days. American power seemed impotent before all these challenges and affronts.

Throughout this decade, Washington and Tokyo squabbled ever more frequently over economic and military issues. As Japan's trade surplus with the United States, economic growth rate, and per capita income continued to soar while it continued to bask under America's nuclear and conventional umbrella and enjoy largely uninhibited access to American markets and technology, increasing numbers of prominent Americans began to accuse the Japanese of "free riding" and called for "get tough" policies to redress the imbalance. Although America's economic stakes were far more serious in the 1970s than before, the White House continued to dance to Japan's waltz of American accusation, Japanese denial, American threats, and Japanese promises. All the while Japan's trade surplus continued to rise.

Even the hitherto solid bilateral alliance showed some strains throughout the 1970s. Although the Japanese happily received Okinawa's return in 1972, they viewed most other American policies toward the Far East from 1969 through 1979 with a mixture of fear and resentment. The Nixon Doctrine, recognition of China, communist conquest of Indochina, and Carter announcement of troop withdrawals from South Korea all increased Japanese anxieties over the strength of America's commitment to Japan itself.

RICHARD M. NIXON, 1969–74

Policymaking and Implementation

President Nixon and National Security Council head Henry Kissinger have been perhaps the most dynamic foreign policy duo in American history. Kissinger served as the president's foreign policy gatekeeper by chairing the NSC or Senior Review Group which included the secretaries of State and Defense, Joint Chief of Staff Chair, CIA Director, and representatives from other departments and agencies depending on the issue. The Senior

Review Group was the hub of six Interdepartmental Groups which addressed specific issue areas and devised policy proposals. However, to tighten his foreign policy domination, Kissinger increasingly bypassed NSC and dealt directly with the Interdepartmental Groups. In 1969, NSC met thirty-seven times; in 1971, only ten times; in 1973 twice. In contrast, few secretaries of state have been weaker in influence or expertise than William Rogers. In 1972, Nixon replaced Rogers with Kissinger.

Superficially, Nixon and Kissinger were quite different. Nixon grew up in a Quaker family in southern California, served as a commissary officer in the Pacific during World War II, and after a brief law stint became a politician whose rollercoaster career was marked by controversy and as many defeats as victories. At twelve years old, Kissinger fled Germany with his Jewish family, served as an interpreter in Europe during World War II, and afterward developed a brilliant academic career at Harvard.

However, Nixon and Kissinger shared an understanding of global politics and a formula for securing American interests within rapidly shifting geopolitical and geoeconomic power relations. And while their backgrounds differed, they shared an obsession with power, security, anti-communism, and loyalty, and could be consumed with rage and ego. Few men got to know Nixon better than Kissinger who described him as composed

of several warring personalities struggling for preeminance. One was idealistic, thoughtful, generous; another was vindictive, petty, emotional. There was a reflective, philosophical, stoical Nixon; and there was an impetuous, impulsive, and erratic one. Sometimes one set of traits prevailed; sometimes another; occasionally they were in uneasy balance. One could never be certain which Nixon was dominant from meeting to meeting. . . . Strangely enough, the thoughtful analytical side of Nixon was most in evidence during crises, while periods of calm seemed to unleash the darker passions of his nature. . . . No modern President could have been less equipped by nature for political life. Painfully shy, Nixon dreaded meeting new people; only the anonymity of large, approving crowds could make him feel secure. Fearful of rejection, he constructed his relationships so that a rebuff, if it came, would seem to have originated with him. Fiercely proud, he could neither admit his emotional dependence on approbation nor transcend it. Deeply insecure, he first acted as if a cruel fate had singled him out for rejection and then he contrived to make sure that his premonition came to pass.[1]

As befitting a diplomat, Kissinger was more adept at human relations. Through a mixture of flattery and browbeating, he skilfully manipulated other administrators, the press, his public image, and ultimately Nixon. In a November 4, 1972 interview with journalist Oriana Fallaci, Kissinger admitted that he loved power and "when one wields power, and one has it for a long time, one ends up thinking one has a right to it." He also admitted that he "always acted alone. Americans admire that enormously . . . the cowboy."[2]

Neither Nixon nor Kissinger deeply admired Japan. Like most other prominent Americans, Nixon and Kissinger still believed that "real diplomacy" only addressed geopolitics, not geoeconomics, a prejudice that would be merely curious had it not so undermined American power and wealth over the decades. Both could denigrate the Japanese with racial slurs. Although Kissinger lauds the Japanese excessively in his memoirs, he was known privately to disparage them "as 'little Sony salesmen,' or 'small and petty book-keepers' who confused their trading ledgers with diplomatic documents."[3]

Policy Priorities

During the 1960s, global power became increasingly multipolar both geopolitically and geoeconomically. There was a stable nuclear and conventional power balance between the United States and Soviet Union, the Sino-Soviet break, the Chinese and French acquisition of nuclear weapons in 1964 and 1966, respectively, and France's break with NATO in 1966 created two new maverick, rising geopolitical powers. Geoeconomically, Japan's transformation into an economic superpower and the world's second largest economy and the European Community's growing prosperity and cohesion likewise marked the defusion of global power. The old colonial empires of Britain, France, and other great powers had largely broken up into scores of newly independent nation-states.

America's power crumbled economically and militarily relative to these new challenges. The biggest drain of American material and psychological power was its war in Indochina which became increasingly unpopular with the American public and allies. As the United States continued to bog down deeper in Vietnam, the risks for America and the world were vast. As Kissinger put it,

American self-doubt proved contagious; it is hard for foreign nations to have more faith in a country than it has in itself. . . . The agony of Vietnam threatened a new disillusionment with international affairs that could draw America inward to nurse its wounds and renounce its world leadership. This would be a profound tragedy, far more grievous than the tragedy of Vietnam itself. We would be back in our historical cycle of exuberant overextension and sulking isolationism. And this time we would be forsaking a world far more complex, more dangerous, more dependent on American leadership than the world of the 1930s.[4]

Nixon and Kissinger responded decisively to these great power shifts by pursuing policies which realigned America's commitments and goals with its power. The bottom line for protecting American interests amidst this array of geopolitical and geoeconomic challenges was the skilful manipulation of the power balance. Kissinger nicely summed up his foreign policy philosophy thus: "If history teaches anything it is that there can be no peace without equilibrium and no justice without restraint. But I believed equally that no nation could ever face or even define its choices without a moral compass that set a course through the ambiguities of reality and thus made sacrifices meaningful. . . . History knows no resting places and no plateaus. All societies of which history informs us went through periods of decline; most of them eventually collapsed."[5]

According to this view, Moscow and Beijing were motivated primarily by the concrete interests of nationalism rather than the ideological interests of communism. Nixon and Kissinger realized that they could diminish the power and moderate the policies of both the Soviet Union and China by playing them off against each other. Thus the White House simultaneously pursued détente with Beijing and Moscow, enhancing relations with each country by exploiting territorial, ideological, and cultural differences between them. Likewise it used its improved relations with China and the Soviet Union to pressure Hanoi for concessions in its continuing negotiations for a face-saving way of withdrawing from Vietnam.

The United States no longer had the wealth or will solely to uphold the global political economy and contain communism. Kissinger maintained that "it was in American national interest to encourage a sharing of responsibilities. If the United States insisted on being the trustee of all the non-Communist areas we would exhaust ourselves psychologically long before we did so physically. A world of more centers of decision . . . was fully compatible with our interests as well as our ideals."[6] Nixon's June 1969 speech at Guam was the first public articulation of a policy that made allied "burden sharing" a central foreign policy goal. From now on the United States would assist rather than underwrite its allies' defense needs.

Burden sharing also meant that Washington would no longer tolerate the lopsided relationship whereby its economic competitors enjoyed largely free access to America's vast market while they kept their own markets largely closed to competitive American products and investments. Nixon's point man in this policy was former Texas governor John Connally whom he appointed as Treasury Secretary in December 1970. Connally immediately pushed for tougher positions on trade, currency, and "burden-sharing" issues, and shoved aside those high-ranking officials who supported free trade ideals.

At Munich on May 28, 1971, Connally pointed out that the United States spends

> nearly 9 per cent of our Gross National Product on defense. . . . Financing a military shield is a part of the burden of leadership; the responsibilities cannot and should not be cast off. But 25 years after World War II, legitimate questions arise over how the cost of these responsibilities should be allocated among the free world allies who benefit from that shield. . . . No longer does the U.S. economy dominate the free world. No longer can considerations of friendship, or need, or capacity justify the United States carrying so heavy a share of the common burden.[7]

America's defense commitments had outstripped its ability to pay for them. This trapped the United States in a vicious cycle of economic decline in which the more resources diverted to defense meant less for consumer industries which in turn suffered from more competitive foreign rivals, which decreased national wealth, which made the defense burden greater, and so on. Connally eventually convinced Nixon that only a sweeping set of tough policies could reverse America's economic decline.

On August 15, 1971, Nixon announced before a nation-wide television audience his "New Economic Plan" which included investment credits, a $4.7 billion cut in government spending, a ninety-day freeze on wages and prices, the postponement of government pay increases, the repeal of the excise tax on automobiles, a 10 per cent cut in foreign aid, a 10 per cent surcharge on import tariffs, and the suspension of the dollar's convertibility into gold, with the latter the plan's most vital part. In doing so, Nixon not only attempted to reverse America's relative economic decline, but more importantly avert the danger of a run on gold as the amount of dollars piled up in overseas bank vaults reached ten times the existing U.S. gold supply. A month later, Nixon declared at a press conference that he would only lift the tariff surcharge if America's allies agreed to share more burdens in defense and reduce trade barriers and surpluses. The dollar was devalued in December 1971 and floated in February 1973. With these actions, Nixon destroyed the Bretton Woods fixed currency system in order to save the global political economy.

Asia played an essential role in Nixon's geopolitical and geoeconomic policies. In a 1967 *Foreign Affairs* article, Nixon had written: "The United States is a Pacific Power. Europe has been withdrawing the remnants of empire, but the United States, with its coast reaching in an arc from Mexico to the Bering Straits, is one anchor of a vast Pacific community. Both our interests and our ideals propel us westward, across the Pacific, not as conquerors but as partners." Yet America's Pacific power and interests also posed dangers: "During the final third of the twentieth century, Asia, not Europe or Latin America, will pose the greatest danger of confrontation which could escalate into World War III."[8] In the same article, Nixon spoke of the need to pull "China back into the world community" and for the United States and China to resolve their differences.

Although Japan remained the keystone of American military and economic security in the Far East, the White House continued to address bilateral conflicts piecemeal rather than as part of a broad strategy to secure American interests. American attempts to assert its interests vis-à-vis Japan were often pushed aside amidst the life and death issues negotiated with Hanoi and Beijing.

Despite Japan's growing power, it played a minimal role in the Nixon administration's calculus of global power and the strategy to achieve American interests. Kissinger admitted that upon taking office "there was no major country I understood less than Japan." That admission can certainly be echoed by virtually every government official, before, then, or since. In his memoirs, Kissinger realizes that as "I write these pages I find it astonishing that no record can be found of any effort to consult Japan in advance about its attitude, even though we planned to include it in our [1973 Year of Europe] initiative . . . the joke of naming an initiative including Japan in the 'Year of Europe' apparently struck no one. Japan was indeed part of the larger community of the industrialized democracies . . ."[9]

The day following Nixon's inauguration, Kissinger ordered an interagency review of American policy toward Japan. On April 30, 1969, the White House had formally agreed to continue to make Japan the cornerstone of American security in Asia and to encourage Tokyo to increase its own defense capabilities and foreign aid to the region. This paper was followed up in June 1969 when NSC staff member Fred Bergsten submitted an "options paper" which

> analyzed the four major problems in U.S.–Japan economic relations: the bilateral payments imbalance, Japan's import restrictions, Japan's investment restrictions, and textiles. The paper concluded that the United States would have to clarify its priorities among the four issues in order to make any progress at all and recommended the ordering just indicated. The

president was unwilling to set any priorities, however, the practical effect of which was to focus most of the U.S. effort on textiles.[10]

Unfortunately, despite these plans, Nixon failed to address systematically the bilateral problems. As in every administration before or since, instead of establishing priorities and single-mindedly achieving them, the Nixon White House's policies toward Japan were largely shaped by politics. Kissinger admits this fatal weakness in America's policy toward Japan: "Our economic agencies, each representing a different constituency, were bombarding the Japanese with a barrage of demands. . . . The plethora of proposals was actually self-defeating; the Japanese were choosing the least onerous ones. The Japanese had a coherent policy; we had only a set of separate demands."[11] Kissinger tried to forge a more coherent policy but failed to enlist Nixon's support.

Policymakers were divided over whether the United States should continue to extend special economic privileges to Japan as a vital ally, or embark on a two-track policy of maintaining the military alliance while demanding reciprocity from an increasingly fierce economic rival. Increasing numbers of prominent Americans criticized Tokyo for "free riding" on America's defense alliance and open markets while Japan's economy remained largely closed to competitive foreign imports or investments.

By 1971, America's worsening trade deficit with Japan and Tokyo's stonewalling on textile negotiations strengthened the hand of those who advocated a systematic, tough policy toward Japan that served America's geoeconomic as well as geopolitical interests. That year, Commerce Secretary Maurice Stans captured the growing fears of many Americans that "the Japanese are still fighting the war, only now instead of a shooting war it is an economic war. Their immediate intention is to try to dominate the Pacific and then perhaps the world."[12] Stans favored resisting rather than encouraging foreign neomercantilist practices that undermined America's economy and power. Japan's growing power and the increased inadequacy of America's laissez-faire policies to serve national interests were the central themes of the 1971 "Peterson Report," written by Assistant for International Economic Policy Peter Peterson.[13] The term "Japan, Inc." was coined to explain the tight government–business relationship that devised and implemented Japan's neomercantilist industrial, trade, investment, and technology policies.

A diminishing number of White House advisors sided with C. Fred Bergsten in supporting the old policy of special treatment for Japan. In 1972, Bergsten harshly condemned Nixon's détente with the communists and tough trade line with western allies: "the new economic approach, coupled with the coming presidential visits to Peking and Moscow, produced the most bizarre U.S. policy imaginable: war on our friends, concessions to our adversaries."[14]

In reality, if not rhetoric, the old policy of pampering Japan continued. Nixon's textile and dollar devaluation policies did no more than briefly check Japan's geoeconomic power, while his China and soybean shocks to Japan were solely psychological. Throughout the 1970s and beyond, Japan's trade and investment surplus continued to soar while America's relative economic power just as steadily diminished.

Policy Toward Japan: Geoeconomic Issues

Although there had been periodic bilateral trade conflicts before, nothing compared to the bitterness and tenacity with which Washington and Tokyo fought over Japan's textile exports during the Nixon administration's first term. Mirror image accusations of "arrogance," "intransigence," and "deceit" colored the conflict. President Nixon's rage at Prime Minister Sato's failure to fulfill a secret November 1969 promise to settle promptly the dispute may have motivated him to retaliate against Japan with three "shocks:" announcements in July 1971 that he would visit China the following year, in August 1971 of his New Economic Policy, and April 1973 the threat of a boycott of soybean exports. Altogether the textile conflict took three years and "two summit conferences, two cabinet-level ministerial conferences, and at least nine other major negotiations" to resolve.[15]

Washington and Tokyo had been managing textile conflicts for fifteen years before President Nixon took office. Japan's textile industry recovered quickly after World War II by combining advanced equipment and then cheap labor. The first battle took place in 1955 and was settled with a Japanese promise to restrain some textile exports. But America's textile industry received only short-term relief. Throughout the 1960s, textile imports from Japan and increasingly from Hong Kong, South Korea, and Taiwan captured an increasing share of America's textile market. In 1969, textile imports were 4.0 per cent of America's total production in value and 8.1 per cent in weight. While overall imports were still relatively modest they took larger shares of market niches. Man-made fiber imports took a 4.5 per cent share, cotton a 11.5 per cent share, and wool 21.6 per cent. Japanese products accounted for 28.7 per cent of all imports while the combined total of Hong Kong, Taiwan, and South Korea accounted for 31.6 per cent. Textile workers numbered 2.4 million in the United States and 1.8 million in Japan, with workers in the latter representing about twice the share of the total population.[16] The battle was increasingly over synthetic rather than natural fibers.

Although textile producers had been pressuring Congress and the White House for import relief for years, the issue did not become important until the 1968 presidential campaign. Nixon openly supported textile quotas, along with other southern causes, to secure both the Republican nomination and the presidency. In return, highly influential South Carolina Senator Strom Thurmond swung his regional support behind Nixon against first Republican challenger Ronald Reagan and later in the general election against Democratic nominee Hubert Humphrey and third party candidate George Wallace. Nixon first committed himself to quotas at a meeting with textile industry heads and Thurmond on June 1. Then, on August 21, 1968, Nixon reiterated to Thurmond his support for quotas in a telegram which was released to the press. He justified "voluntary" quotas by arguing that if they were not concluded Congress would enact even more restrictive measures. But Nixon also preferred voluntary quotas because he rather than Congress could take credit for them. Nixon's victory margin of 500,000 votes of 73 million cast in November 1968 was razor-thin; if he had not carried the two leading textile states, North and South Carolina, his electoral college vote would have been only 281 or eleven above the victory margin.[17]

In January 1969, the initial plan for implementing Nixon's campaign promise was posed by White House staff member Robert Ellsworth who advocated a low-key, behind-the-scenes strategy to cut a deal and save the face of Japan's elite. But Ellsworth soon left to become American ambassador to NATO. The void was quickly filled by outspoken Commerce Secretary Maurice Stans who pushed for a tough high-profile approach. Nixon agreed to Stans's strategy. At a February 6, 1969 press conference, the president asserted again his commitment to achieving Japan's voluntary textile export restraints.

Stans followed up Nixon's comments with a series of public announcements criticizing Japan's export floods and the harm to American textile producers. Then, on April 11, he led a fourteen-man delegation repesenting seven government agencies to Europe to garner support for a multilateral conference on textiles. The U.S. delegation visited six countries over two weeks; everywhere the American proposals were received unenthusiastically. Most European countries already severely restricted imports and the governments feared that any multilateral deal would force them to ease those restrictions, as they had in the Long-term Agreement (LTA).

Although puzzled by his failure to enlist European support against Japanese and other Asian textile exports, Stans proceeded on to Tokyo in May, followed by visits to South Korea, Taiwan, and Hong Kong. In Japan, Stans found all relevant bureaucratic, political, business, and media elites opposed to any export restrictions. The Japanese had been arguing all along that Japan's exports to the United States had been flat rather than increasing and, regardless, were not harming America's industry. Thus no quotas were necessary. This Japanese position hardened between Nixon's February 6 announcement and Stans's May 10 arrival. During his three days in Tokyo, Stans's call for export restraints met with repeated rejections by Japanese officials of any bilateral talks let alone quotas. Instead, the Japanese told Stans to take his case to GATT.

For the next two months, each side retreated into their respective positions. The Americans periodically pressed Tokyo to accede to their demands, which the Japanese simply rejected. To break the deadlock, Stans proposed employing a GATT provision that would allow the United States to withdraw all textile concessions made since the late 1940s, thus forcing all affected countries to renegotiate access to America's huge market. Nixon vetoed the proposal, arguing that it was too powerful an action and too risky to the global economy.

But the pressure on Tokyo continued to build. On July 22, the four largest American textile unions sent a message to Japan's cabinet urging them to join an international conference to settle the textile problem which they argued was destroying American jobs. On July 28, Milbur Wills warned that if the Japanese did not act, Congress would pass even more restrictive textile quotas. From July 29 to 31 in Tokyo, textiles dominated the agenda at the seventh annual "Joint Japan–U.S. Committee on Trade and Economic Affairs" among ranking cabinet officials and devoted to discussing economic issues. Stans and Ministry of International Trade and Industry minister Masayoshi Ohira represented their respective sides. But no progress was made as each side merely repeated their respective government's positions. The Americans hinted that the Senate might not ratify an agreement returning Okinawa without a textile accord. The Japanese were particularly adamant in asserting that any Okinawa for textiles swap was unacceptable. Japan's only concession was to promise to make a "fact finding" effort to determine whether textile exports were actually hurting America's industry.

Once again, both sides repeated their positions in the months leading up to the September 16 conference where the White House would present its "facts." At the three-day meeting, the MITI and Ministry of Foreign Affairs officials led by MITI's Textile Bureau Director Takahashi Shukuro squared off with a team from the departments of State, Commerce, Treasury, Labor, and Agriculture, and the U.S. Trade Representative with Commerce's Deputy Secretary Stan Nehmer serving as spokesperson. Nehmer presented an in-depth, well-documented argument that textile imports had been excessive and harmful to America's industry and employment. Without presenting counter evidence, Takahashi simply denied each of Nehmer's points. The conference ended in deadlock.

On October 2, the White House cabinet team presented Minister Yoshino Bunroku of Japan's embassy with an aide-mémoire calling for a bilateral textile accord which imposed "comprehensive ceilings" for a range of cloth and clothing products which would begin January 1, 1970 and last five years. Assistant Secretary of State Philip Trezise then flew to Tokyo for meetings from October 6 to 9 on Japanese import barriers. Once again, Tokyo rejected America's textile position and also denied that its own import barriers impeded sales of American goods in Japan. Ohira maintained that the United States should take any accusations of Japanese predatory exports or import barriers to GATT for an official finding. Japan would only negotiate a multilateral agreement.

Tokyo's official reply to the October 2 aide-mémoire was not issued until November 7. The Japanese message bluntly stated that textile imports were not hurting America's industry so no agreement was necessary. On November 10, the White House refused to consider going to GATT and insisted on a bilateral settlement as soon as possible. Worried that the textile dispute could poison the oncoming Nixon–Sato summit, Tokyo first called for a multilateral textile conference including the United States, Japan, Hong Kong, South Korea, Taiwan, Britain, and Italy. When the White House rejected that proposal, Tokyo then called for a "preliminary conference" on the textile issue to be held simultaneously with the summit in Washington. The White House agreed.

Meanwhile, starting as early as July 18, Kissinger and a secret Sato emissary, code-named "Yoshida," met periodically for the next four months to script the agreements on Okinawa and textiles that would be formally accepted at the November summit. However, two days before the summit, Yoshida called Kissinger and frantically told him Sato would have to back off from his promise to announce the specific textile figures previously agreed to at the summit; instead, the Japanese team at Geneva would agree to those same figures. Kissinger relented. However, the next night Yoshida called back to say that Sato would stick to the carefully negotiated original scenario as long as there was no reference to textiles in the joint communiqué.

Although it appeared like a major concession, Tokyo's proposal for the Geneva conference cleverly finessed the textile issue. If Nixon raised the conflict during the summit (November 17–21), Sato could simply suggest that they defer discussion until they learned the results of the Geneva Conference (November 17–22). Meanwhile, Japan's delegation at Geneva would stonewall rather than negotiate. By the time the Geneva Conference's results became known, Sato would be flying safely back to Japan.

Tokyo's skilful strategy was undercut by one unanticipated factor – Sato's promise to Nixon that, in return for a nuclear-free Okinawa, he would accept a textile agreement. On the summit's second day, according to Kissinger, "Sato explicitly promised that textiles would be resolved as the President desired. Sato declared that he took full responsibility, that it was his 'personal credo' and 'vow' to keep his word, that he committed his sincerity and all his efforts to that end."[18] But with a Japanese consensus against any textile deal, let alone a swap for Okinawa, it was also vital for Sato's reputation to keep the deal secret.

By some accounts, Sato did not promise such a deal at the summit but simply said "I will do my best" (zenchu suru), which in Japanese not only promises nothing but implies nothing will be accomplished. That scenario has been successfully refuted in *The Textile Wrangle*, an outstanding 400-page study of the dispute from beginning to end.[19] The authors argue that Sato never used the term "zenchu suru," and more likely said "If you have a problem, I will do something about it" (mondai ga areba, nantoka suru). Regardless, interviews with those American officials connected with the summit reveal that Sato clearly agreed to a swap. During the summit, Nixon happily agreed to a nuclear-free Okinawan reversion in 1972 in return for textile export restraints.

Sato completely mishandled the textile and Okinawan issues. By refusing to admit the deal, Sato

> lost also the leverage that greater openness would have given him with Japan's textile industry and bureaucracy . . . he could have argued – in Japan – that acquiescence on textiles was clearly necessary to hold up Japan's end of the broad bilateral relationship within which it was possible to get Okinawa back. By fostering the illusion he had gotten Okinawa clean, by denying and concealing the deal, he took the public urgency out of the very case for a textile settlement he continued to believe in strongly. In the short run, a more open course would have exposed Sato to strong political attack. In the longer run, people might perhaps have resigned themselves to accepting his argument that a settlement, essentially on American terms, was vital for U.S.–Japanese relations and needed to be concluded without delay.[20]

Sato thus failed profoundly as both a statesman and politician.

Sato's later failure not only to fulfill his promise but to even admit that he had made one soured the bilateral relationship. However, until Sato's betrayal became evident, Nixon remained jubilant over the summit. Nixon gleefully pronounced the summit "the most significant since the end of World War II" between the two countries.[21] Sato's rhetoric was just as inflated. Before the National Press Club he spoke of a "New Pacific Age."[22]

The Americans also must share some blame for the failure to strike a deal. Kissinger reveals that:

> To make the Sato–Nixon scenario work we were supposed to present a very tough position that would enable Sato to surface his agreement with Nixon as a compromise. However, our middle-level officials, whose knowledge of what was possible was based on the statements of their Japanese counterparts, never believed that we could achieve maximum demands. . . . Our negotiators put forward what we told them was the agreed outcome rather than the hardline position. That, of course, put Sato into the untenable position of being asked to accept the American position and evoked desperate phone calls from "Yoshida" accusing me of welshing on the promise of a tough American opening position – surely one of the very few occasions when a foreign government has complained about being given too conciliatory a proposal.[23]

Meanwhile, the American team at Geneva was bitter over the conference, denouncing their Japanese counterparts for being "typically evasive, procrastinating."[24] Nehmer stated bluntly that the "Japanese attitude in Geneva did not enhance friendly relations between the two countries. The United States is disappointed with this conference."[25]

The White House soon followed up the summit and first conference by submitting at Geneva on December 22, 1969 a highly detailed proposal that included comprehensive limits on textile imports and specific limits on twenty-eight categories based on 1968 import levels which would last five years. The Japanese rejected the proposal. The Americans then on January 2, 1970 submitted at Geneva a "compromise plan" based on the summit understanding. The second plan also included a comprehensive limit along with limits on twenty-eight categories, and a trigger mechanism in which the United States would retaliate if Japanese exports exceeded those limits. The only significant change was to make the base year 1969. The Japanese rejected this plan also. Trezise then asked for a Japanese counterproposal.

Meanwhile, Sato basked in even greater political prestige and power. The LDP gained eleven seats in the December House of Representative election, raising their total to 288 of 486. This would have been the time for Sato to cut a deal. Instead, in a New Year's day speech, he vaguely called for the dispute's resolution by "mutual compromise" and remained aloof from the negotiations in Geneva. Not surprisingly, after Tokyo's two adamant rejections of the American plans, the White House began to worry that Sato had reneged on his promise. The Japanese in turn deeply resented the continuing American efforts to impose textile restraints and increasingly believed rumors that Sato had agreed to a swap at the summit.

In February and March, four new proposals surfaced, each of which only reinforced the extreme positions. The Japanese submitted an aide-mémoire on February 2 that simply asked that they reexamine whether Japan's exports actually harmed America's textile industry. The Americans dismissed the proposal and asked for a concrete compromise based on the second plan. There followed another Japanese aide-mémoire on March 9 which reiterated objections to America's second plan without offering any specific counterproposal, although it did state for the first time that Japan would agree to specific controls where grievous damage actually occurred. Trezise rejected this Japanese message. Anger within the administration toward the Japanese deepened.

Meanwhile, the American textile industry's woes deepened in 1969 and into 1970. The Commerce Department published statistics which revealed that while domestic sales declined, imports increased by 22.7 per cent in 1969 and Japanese imports surged by 30.7 per cent.[26] House Ways and Means Chairman Mills responded to Japan's intransigence and the domestic industry's stagnation by announcing he would push through a quota bill that would exceed in severity any measures the White House was trying to negotiate. Tokyo responded with silence.

Concerned that the textile conflict could lead to a full-fledged trade war, Donald Kendall, chairman of the free trade group ECAT and president of Pepsi Cola, met with the president on March 5. Nixon had once worked as a lawyer for Pepsi Cola, and the two men were friends. The president revealed Sato's promise and gave Kendall the go-ahead to seek some concessions from Tokyo.

Meanwhile, Nixon and Kissinger worked out a compromise proposal. On March 10 the National Security Advisor took it to the Japanese embassy. The Kissinger plan had comprehensive import limits but reduced specific categories from twenty-eight to ten and dropped the trigger formula. To date, this was the first genuine concession either side had made. However, Japanese bureaucrats who opposed any deal leaked Kissinger's plan; the resulting protests on both sides of the Pacific scuttled it.

Kendall flew to Tokyo on March 11 as head of the American delegation to a U.S.–Japanese businessmen's group that periodically met to discuss issues. On March 16 he presented his own "compromise" plan to Foreign Minister Aichi and Kiichi Miyazawa who had become the new MITI chief in a January 1970 cabinet reshuffle. Kendall's plan advocated a one year freeze of Japanese textile exports at 1969 levels while an investigation of posssible damages to America's industry took place. If damages were found, the two governments would settle their dispute before a GATT panel. Japanese exports could increase after the one year limit unless the GATT panel ruled otherwise. Miyazawa and Aichi believed that Kendall's plan was Nixon's when actually the president did not even know what the ECAT chair would propose. Thus, the Japanese leaders were just about to agree to Kendall's plan when it too was leaked to the press. The resulting storm of anger from Japan's textile industry, Keidanren, Diet members, bureaucrats, and newspaper editors against any export limits caused Miyazawa and Aichi to reject the proposal. The reaction against Kendall's plan by America's textile industry and political supporters was just as vehement. Nixon repudiated Kendall's efforts.

House Ways and Means Chairman, Wilber Mills, then stepped into the fray. On April 13, Mills submitted H.R. 16920 which would impose strict limits on textile imports for five years starting in 1970 based on 1967–8 levels. Japan's exports would be cut back by 32 per cent, Hong Kong's by 40 per cent, South Korea's by 53 per cent, and Taiwan's by 62 per cent. Over one hundred other protectionist trade bills simmered in various Senate and House committees. Mills opened hearings on May 11, and a parade of textile executives and union leaders testified about the damage foreign imports were wreaking on the domestic industry. Japanese lobbyists like Michael Daniels of the American Importers Association, Nelson Stitt of the U.S.–Japan Trade Council, and Mike Masaoka of the Association on Japanese Textile Imports also testified but could not dampen the protectionist tide.

Despite these threats, Tokyo refused to budge. Instead, the Japanese dug in their heels and warned that they would demand compensation through GATT for any protectionist American laws. Miyazawa flew to Paris to meet with GATT Director General Long who asked him to accept a one-year freeze while a multilateral settlement was negotiated with GATT. Although Miyazawa had hoped for a stronger statement from Long, he now could use the director's plan to pressure Japan's industry into compliance. But the White House repudiated the Long plan.

On June 11, Sato, Aichi, Miyazawa, and Chief Cabinet Secretary Shigeru Hori met to discuss Japan's "final position" which was essentially Long's proposal. When asked, Sato denied that he had agreed to a swap. Miyazawa and Aichi then flew to Washington to meet with their counterparts from

June 22 to 24. The most serious negotiations occurred between Miyazawa and Stans, of which some took place at the commerce secretary's home. Stans countered the Japanese one-year plan with a five-year comprehensive plan with twenty-three categories. Stans implored Miyawa to split the difference with a three-year plan but the MITI chief refused. Meetings between Aichi and Secretary of State Rogers were no more successful. Kissinger journeyed once again to Japan's embassy but failed to elicit the three-year compromise. Stans then played hardball, revealing the "Sato memo" in which the prime minister had promised to cut a textile restraint deal in return for a nuclear-free Okinawa. Miyazawa refused to look at the document; he insisted that no deal had been made and the paper was a forgery – a rather serious charge! Then, to save Miyazawa's face, Undersecretary of State Alexis Johnson denied that the document was genuine even though he knew otherwise! At the final press conference, Miyazawa announced that Japan would not resume negotiations for the foreseeable future and said Japan's textile industry felt cheated by the talk of limitations.

Japanese celebrated Miyazawa's refusal to compromise. A June 26 *Asahi Shimbun* editorial captured the outpouring of Japanese nationalism: "The U.S.–Japanese textile negotiations turned out to be the first instance in which Japan rejected a U.S. demand, and could be considered the first example of 'independent foreign policy' in the postwar Japanese history of economic diplomacy. . . . The fact that Japan has managed to follow through with such an independent posture has an epoch-making significance as the cornerstone of its economic diplomacy of the 1970s."[27] In reality, Tokyo had been rejecting American proposals ever since the first American troops landed in Japan on August 22, 1945. The editorial's importance is that it reflected and reinforced the Japanese belief that a foreign policy era of newfound independence had begun – that somehow Japan was just beginning to say no when it had been adamantly doing so for a generation.

After a month's recess, hearings on the House textile quota bill resumed on June 30, 1970. As expected, it soon became a Christmas tree of protectionist measures for scores of besieged American industries. At a White House meeting on July 10, Nixon told Ways and Means Chair Mills and ranking Republican member John Byrnes that he would veto the bill unless it was limited to textile quotas and measures to strengthen the president's negotiating powers, a position he stated publicly at a July 20 news conference. Free traders hoped the bill would become so overloaded that Nixon would have to carry out his threat. The final bill that emerged in August did give the president most of what he wanted; it would have held 1971 textile imports 40 per cent below the 1969 level.

Yet, even this threat of even tougher textile quotas than those asked by the White House failed to bend Tokyo. Low level talks sputtered on with each side repeating their entrenched positions. While infuriated by Tokyo's intransigence, Nixon had lost faith in Stans's ability to cut a deal. On September 24, the president appointed his assistant, Peter Flanigan, chief negotiator. Tokyo dispatched a new ambassador, Ushiba Nobuhiko, to Washington. Both governments hoped these new faces and styles could help break the deadlock.

In late September and early October, the heat on Tokyo to compromise turned higher. GATT Chair Long urged Tokyo to accept a one-year comprehensive cap on Japanese textile exports to the United States, followed by two years of selective control. Flanigan proposed ceilings on twenty items, a trigger price mechanism, base year of July 1968–June 1969, and import growth rate proportionate with the domestic market's growth over three years ending in September 1973. A summit date was set for October 24. Tokyo finally agreed to resume serious negotiations.

At the summit, the two leaders discussed a range of bilateral and multilateral issues, with Nixon assiduously avoiding the textile dispute. When Sato finally brought it up, Nixon replied that he thought the issue had been settled at their previous summit and could not understand why the prime minister had not implemented their agreement. Sato became embarrassed and apologetic; he declared his loyalty to the president and desire to fulfill his promise. Kissinger then presented him Flanigan's plan. Sato looked it over and accepted it. Flanagan and Ushiba were designated the chief negotiators.

Unfortunately, Sato once again promised Nixon things that he lacked the will to deliver. After returning to Tokyo, Sato won a resounding victory to a unprecedented fourth term as LDP president. Yet Sato shied from capitalizing on his political base to force his party and the textile industry to accept the Flanigan plan.

The wide gap between Japan's government and industry proposals remained unbridged, and thus Tokyo had no concrete proposals when talks began on November 9. It was not until November 13 that Tokyo nailed together a compromise that largely reflected the textile industry's position. As the talks proceeded, Mills's bill worked its way through Congress. It passed the House on November 19 by a 215–172 vote, a smaller victory margin than expected. Fearing the bill would become law, Tokyo presented a "compromise" on December 1 when Ushiba proposed a 9 per cent annual growth rate cap on textile exports to the United States. Flanigan rejected the proposal. On December 10, Nixon stated that although he preferred a negotiated rather than legislated solution to the textile wrangle, he implied he would not veto the bill if it passed. The positions of Flanagan and Ushiba moved steadily closer, with differences largely over the annual growth rates for Japanese imports; Flanagan stood on a 3:5:5 per cent ratio over three years while Ushiba insisted on 3:7:7 ratio. The bill moved from the Senate Finance Committee onto the floor on December 16 whereupon it was filibustered by freetraders led by Walter Mondale of Minnesota and Jacob Javits of New York. To Japan's relief, the bill died as the session ended. With it died any need for Tokyo to concede further. Ushiba and Flanigan concluded their talks on December 30 without agreement.

All along, Japan's textile exports to the United States soared from 585,000 million square yards in 1969 to 774,000 in 1970. American textile sales stagnated, factories closed, and tens of thousands of workers lost their jobs. Yet the White House and Congress continually failed to present a united front to the Japanese.

Relieved that the pressure had deflated but fearing its eventual resurgence, MITI's Minister Miyazawa tried to convince the textile industry to accept a voluntary export cap. But the government and industry failed to agree on a figure in their talks throughout January and February. Japan lobbyist Michael Daniel resolved to break the impasse. He joined the talks in February and then returned to Washington to enlist Mills in his efforts. Mills all along had opposed the quotas his bill would have imposed and leapt at the chance to defuse the conflict. In early March, Mills and Daniels flew to Japan and urged textile industry leaders to agree to restrict exports at levels that were actually far less restrictive than Ushiba's final position in December. The plea broke the deadlock between Japan's government and industry. On March 8, after intensive talks among Japanese industry, ministry, and political leaders, Japan's textile industry announced a 5:6:6 per cent increase over three years with a base from April 1970 to March 1971 which would begin on July 1, 1971, as long as other textile exporting countries to the United States enacted similar restrictions. That same day, Tokyo declared that with the issue "settled" there was no need for further negotiations. Mills issued a statement welcoming the industry announcement.

America's textile industry erupted in protest. Nixon was embarrassed by Mills's ability to resolve an issue in two weeks that his administration had been struggling with for two years, and angry that Mills had not informed him of the negotiations and accepted a position far weaker than the White House ever considered. Nixon was in a bind. If he rejected the plan and embraced another quota bill it would be blocked by Mills's Ways and Means Committee and he would lose the Chair's support on other important issues. If Nixon acquiesced, he might well lose his "southern base" in next year's presidential election.

Three days later on March 11, Nixon harshly denounced the plan. Later that month he hinted broadly that the Okinawan reversion treaty still being negotiated might well fail to get a two-thirds Senate approval and threatened to use the "Trading with the Enemy Law" to resolve the textile fight if all else failed. On April 8, he replaced Flanigan as chief negotiator with former Treasury Secretary David Kennedy. On May 31, Kennedy and his advisors flew to the Far East to forge an agreement with the textile exporting countries on American terms. He succeeded in Taiwan but failed in South Korea, Hong Kong, and Japan.

Despite Kennedy's inability to gain agreement from all three other East Asian textile exporters, Tokyo went ahead on July 1 with its own export restraints. On July 5, Sato replaced Miyazawa with the "computerized bulldozer," Tanaka Kakuei, as MITI chief. Tanaka eventually proved to be Tokyo's most effective negotiator, both with the Americans and Japan's textile industry.

Over the next two months, the White House inflicted two "shocks" on Japan. On July 15, Nixon announced that he would visit Beijing to conduct talks with Chinese leaders and thus break two decades of American refusal to deal with China. Then on August 15, Nixon declared "a national emergency" before unveiling his New Economic Policy to reverse America's economic decline with such measures as wage and price controls, a 10 per cent tariff surcharge, and the suspension of the dollar's convertibility into gold. By declaring a national emergency, Nixon empowered himself under the 1917 Trading with the Enemy Act to impose trade restrictions unilaterally. The White House had not even hinted to Tokyo that it was considering either the China or new economic policy.

On September 8, ranking American and Japanese economic officials met at Williamsburg, Virginia to negotiate a range of outstanding economic problems including textiles. Secretary Rogers stated bluntly that "We believe that any country in chronic surplus as Japan is, has an obligation to take the necessary measures – increasing imports, eliminating export incentives, stimulating capital outflow and revaluating its exchange rate – to bring its global balance of payments into equilibrium."[28] In addition, Rogers implored the Japanese to eliminate trade and investment barriers, import more from developing countries, and restrain exports. Foreign Minister Fukuda replied with denials of a current account disequilibrium and maintained that any bilateral trade balance resulted from self-defeating American macroeconomic policies rather than Japanese neomercantilist policies. As usual, no progress was made on any of the issues raised.

The president had finally exhausted his patience on Japanese stonewalling. Nixon decided to cut the gordian knot on textile negotiations by threatening to invoke the 1917 Trading with the Enemy Act which empowered the president to regulate trade if he declared a national emergency. Nixon had declared a national emergency on August 15. On September 20, he dispatched his assistant Anthony Jurich to Tokyo with his "ultimatum" that if Japan did not settle the issue by October 15, the president would unilaterally impose restrictions based on the Trading with the Enemy Act. On September 27, the White House publicly admitted that an ultimatum had been issued. At a press conference on October 12, Nixon himself declared that he would act if the deadline passed without a settlement.

Tanaka quickly forged an elite consensus on a settlement, buying industry's compliance with promises of subsidies and protection. Late in the evening of October 15, 1971, Tanaka and Kennedy signed a "Memorandum of Understanding" which would allow Japanese man-made and wool imports of 997 million square yards from October 1, 1971 to September 30, 1972, 1.047 billion the following year, and 1.099 billion the third year, with specific limits in eighteen categories. But there were still details to work out and a final agreement was not signed until January 3, 1972.

Although it appeared as if the Americans had won, it was actually the wiley Japanese that benefited most. By stonewalling for nearly three years, the Japanese succeeded in getting the United States to abandon its "first proposal" which would have imposed limits of 508 million square yards of man-made material the first year to its final agreement of 997.7 million square yards. Meanwhile, of course, Japan's textile industry reaped enormous profits from the United States at the expense of their American rivals.

Ironically, these benefits were short-lived. Japan's exports would have eventually diminished anyway as recession and lower-priced exports from other countries squeezed its market share in the United States. Japanese man-made fiber textile exports to the United States leapt from 774 million square yards in 1970 to 1.282 billion in 1971, but then dropped to 943 million in 1972 and 650 million in 1973, and rose slightly to 690 million in 1974. But they would have suffered worse if restrictions had begun in 1969 rather than 1971.

In addition to Japan's textile industry, the only other party that clearly benefited from the agreement was Richard Nixon. Before spending limits took effect on April 7, 1972, Nixon received $363,122.50 from the textile industry and $430,000 from the clothing industry for his 1972 presidential campaign.[29] Nixon swept most of the south in the election.

The textile industry was a small and declining economic sector in each country. Yet, the conflict over Japan's textile exports consumed nearly three years of acrimonious negotiations that soured the overall relationship. Why did Washington and Tokyo allow what should have been a minor dispute to evolve into such a crisis?

Textiles were important to Nixon in a narrow political sense; southern textile interests helped elect him to the White House in exchange for a promise of protection. In a larger sense, the textile wrangle symbolized for Americans their relative economic decline, particularly compared to Japan. By standing firm on textiles, many American politicians felt vicariously that they were stemming a broader national decay. They, of course, were wrong.

It is hard not to conclude that "the textile wrangle of 1969–71 was clearly an unnecessary and wasteful exercise."[30] Both sides blundered at key points. In retrospect, a subtle behind-the-scenes White House diplomacy backed by the threat of sanctions that allowed Tokyo to forge a consensus on the inevitability of quotas close to America's first proposal would have been better than Stans's tough open approach that caused Japan's elite to mobilize in opposition. Yet Stans was not entirely to blame. Much of the "open" diplomacy of the first months of negotiations came from leaks by Japanese officials to the press and industry which in turn rallied mass opposition to any concessions. And Sato's failure even to attempt to deliver on his summit promises prolonged the negotiations and embittered relations. Nixon's understandable sense of betrayal may have sparked him to retaliate with his three "shocks." While America's stakes in the textile conflict were relatively small, the dispute was important as the opening struggle in an increasingly nationalistic American trade policy.

The turning point in America's postwar geoeconomic policies arrived on August 15, 1971 when Nixon announced his New Economic Policy. The most important effect on Japan was Nixon's determination to realign currency rates with each country's economic power. From 1949 through 1971, the yen was pegged at 360 to a dollar while Japan's economy expanded an average 10 per cent annually, or nearly four times America's rate. Japan's industries enjoyed an ever more virtuous circle of an increasingly devalued yen which made their goods more competitive abroad and reinforced the web of trade barriers at home, which increased Japan's wealth and so on.

Shortly after Nixon's announcement, the White House began negotiating with Tokyo for the yen's revaluation. Tokyo stonewalled for as long as possible, and even bought $4.4 billion in a fruitless attempt to maintain a grossly undervalued yen. At the December 1971 Smithsonian Agreement among the major economic powers, the yen was revalued 17 per cent to 308 to a dollar. Yet Japan's trade surplus continued to rise because the yen remained grossly undervalued. Japan enjoyed this exchange rate until February 1973 when the White House allowed the dollar to float against all major currencies. Japan's yen increased to an average 265 for the rest of the year but even that increase did not diminish Japan's export machine.

Meanwhile, Tokyo continued to buy dollars, increase Japanese foreign direct and portfolio investments and limit similar foreign investments in Japan to prevent the yen from rising to a level which reflected Japan's economic superpower. Fortunately for Japan, the yen rose along with a spectrum of commodity, energy, and raw material prices which helped curtail inflation in Japan and maintain Japanese competitiveness.

Despite Nixon's more nationalistic economic policies, there were no more significant trade conflicts with Tokyo after textiles. In 1973, Nixon did inadvertently fire a shot across Japan's economic bow when he threatened to boycott soybean exports to ensure low American prices after a poor harvest. Although soybean exports remained unimpeded, the threat panicked the Japanese who received over 70 per cent of their soybean imports from the United States. Tokyo responded by diversifying its soybean imports and developing foreign production with Japanese investments, particularly in Brazil. The long-term result of Nixon's ill-considered statement was even fewer American exports to Japan than might have occurred.

The postwar era's geoeconomic turning points were America's August 1971 abandonment of the gold standard and the Organization of Petroleum Exporting Countries' (OPEC) quadrupling of oil prices during November and December 1973. Nixon's action reformed the global political economy; OPEC's nearly destroyed it. The Organization of Arab Petroleum Exporting Countries (OAPEC) within OPEC led the charge to higher prices and export boycotts against some of Tel Aviv's supporters following the Arabs' defeat in the October Yom Kippur War against Israel. On October 15, 1973, OAPEC announced the boycott of oil to the United States and production cutbacks that would eventually quadruple oil prices and badly strain the western alliance. The OPEC ministers met in Teheran on December 22–23 and raised the price of an oil barrel 128 per cent from $5.12 to $11.65, on top of the 70 per cent rise in October. Altogether oil prices rose 387 per cent in two months!

Initially, no country was more damaged by the oil price increase than Japan which was dependent on foreign sources for 99 per cent of its oil needs, and 80 per cent of its total energy needs. From November 24, when OAPEC declared Japan a "hostile" state and boycotted oil exports until December 25 when OAPEC agreed to resume oil shipments, Tokyo desperately tried to fulfill the Arabs' rhetorical if not substantive demands.

Meanwhile, Kissinger just as desparately attempted to forge a united front of industrial nations against OPEC, but to no avail. On November 14 and 15, Kissinger met in Tokyo with Foreign Minister Ohira and Prime Minister Tanaka and pleaded with them to stand firm in the consortium of oil importing industrial states that he was trying to form. The Japanese leaders said they might join if Washington would guarantee Japan's oil needs. Kissinger admitted that the United States lacked the power to do so. The Japanese replied that without an oil supply guarantee they would do nothing to offend OAPEC and would continue to follow the European Community's lead in mouthing support for Palestinian self-determination and UN Resolution 242 which called for a return to the pre-June 1967 borders. To Tokyo's shock, the policy of hiding behind the European Community proved an illusion. On November 24, OAPEC declared Japan a "hostile" state and boycotted oil exports; they continued to export to the European Community.

On December 8, Foreign Minister Miki Takeo arrrived in the Middle East for an eighteen-day eight-country tour to dispense promises of aid and Palestinian support, and anti-Israeli actions. Miki's diplomatic offensive worked when on December 18 OAPEC agreed to resume oil exports and declare Japan a friendly country. Aside from the aid package and refusal to support Washington's consortium proposal, Tokyo's policy changed only in style, not substance. Kissinger was quite understanding of Tokyo's position. He writes that despite their accommodationist policy toward the Arab world, it "did not mean that the Japanese leaders personally disagreed with the substance of our Middle East policy. They never stated an explicit view to us and perhaps did not form one, because Japanese do not waste capital on matters they cannot influence."[31] Differences between Washington and Tokyo over policy toward OPEC would simmer through the rest of the Nixon White House and into the Ford and Carter administrations.

Policy Toward Japan: Geopolitical Issues

During the Nixon White House, the Ryukyu islands finally reverted to Japan. Okinawa's fate was on the agenda of Nixon's first NSC meeting on January 21, 1969, the day after his inauguration, and with the Joint Chiefs of Staff on January 27. The White House consensus was that Okinawa had to be returned but only with the stipulation that the United State retain base rights there indefinitely. Okinawa remained a key bastion in America's Pacific defenses. B-52s based in Okinawa could reach all of the Korean peninsula, much of eastern Soviet Union and China, and were currently blasting suspected enemy position across Vietnam. The Pentagon wanted to continue to keep nuclear weapons in Okinawa; most other officials thought they should be removed.

Meanwhile, in February 1969 Sato pledged before the Diet his determination to achieve Okinawa's return and to negotiate an agreement with the United States as soon as possible. Okinawa's nuclear-free reversion was to be Sato's career capstone, something he had been calling for since he assumed the prime ministership in 1964. Although he had achieved an initial commitment from President Johnson at a November 1967 summit, important details remained to be worked out, the most important of which was whether nuclear weapons would be removed. Without a nuclear-free Okinawa, Sato's career would end in ignominy rather than triumph. The mass Okinawan protests which periodically surged outside the gates of the U.S. bases whose B-52s flew missions against Indochina were as much against Sato as Washington.

On March 18, Kissinger sent Nixon a memorandum arguing that

> the political reality was that the pressures in Japan for revision were now unstoppable; agitation against our presence not only posed a physical danger to our use of the bases but also could jeopardize the political position of Sato and the governing Liberal Democratic Party, which had initiated and maintained Japan's alignment with the United States for two decades. In short, the military and political risks of seeking to maintain the status quo outweighed the political risks of having somewhat less flexibility in operating the Okinawa bases under Japanese sovereignty. Indeed our refusal to negotiate an accommodation could well lead as a practical matter to our losing the bases altogether.[32]

Nixon agreed with and acted upon Kissinger's assessment. Secretary of State Rogers visited Tokyo in July 1969 and again in August to accelerate the talks and prepare the way for Sato's summit with Nixon at the White House in November. Rogers confided on August 3 that the United States had agreed in principle to Okinawa's reversion.

Before it could forge an agreement, the White House had to finesse protests from some powerful domestic interests. The Joint Chiefs agreed on Okinawa's reversion, but continued to argue the necessity of retaining nuclear weapons at the bases. On the November 1969 summit's eve, fearing that the president might return Okinawa by executive agreement as Johnson did the Bonin islands, the Senate passed the Byrd Resolution by 63–14 which stated that no change in the Ryukyu islands' status should occur without the Senate's advice and consent.

Nixon and Sato met on November 19, 20, and 21, 1969. Seven of the joint communiqué's fifteen paragraphs dealt partly or wholly with Okinawa. Nixon agreed to Okinawa's nuclear-free reversion by 1972. The communiqué also dealt with regional security issues. Like many Americans, Nixon believed the Japanese support for the alliance, Nixon Doctrine, and regional security was soft. In return for Okinawa, Nixon wanted not just a textile agreement but an explicit Japanese statement in support of the region's web of anti-communist alliances. The communiqué stated that the "Prime minister deeply appreciated the peacekeeping efforts of the United Nations in the area and stated that the security of the Republic of Korea was essential to Japan's own security ... the maintenance of peace and security in the Taiwan area was also a most important factor for the security of Japan." Trying to promote the image of equal partnership, they claimed to have agreed on a "compromise" reversion date of May 15, half-way between Tokyo's target of April and Washington's of July 1. In a bone to Congress and the Diet, the Nixon–Sato communiqué included the statement that Okinawa's reversion would be "subject ... to the necessary legislative support." Of the communiqué's fifteen points, only one dealt with geoeconomic issues, and only two lines contained Japanese promises to reduce their trade, capital, and investment barriers.

The two governments set up a United States–Japan Consultative Committee in Tokyo to negotiate the details and a Preparatory Commission in Okinawa to handle the reversion. Negotiations over Okinawa began in June 1969 and would continue for the next three years. On May 15, 1972, Okinawa officially reverted from the United States to Japan. Many Japanese agree with Sato that Japan's sovereignty was not fully restored until that date, and thus it was only then that Japan could enjoy equal diplomatic relations with the United States.

Nixon's biggest shock to the Japanese was when he stole a march on them to China. In retrospect, the president's decision should not have been so surprising – after all he had called for it in a 1967 *Foreign Affairs* article and it flowed logically from his conception of international power. The furtive means by which he established relations with China was typical of the man, including his vindictiveness toward Prime Minister Sato. Angered over Sato's failure to fulfill his promise to resolve the textile dispute in return for Okinawa, Nixon perhaps gleefully excluded Tokyo from his plans to restore relations with China, which he announced in July 1971.

Tokyo was indeed shocked and angered over Nixon's surprise recognition of China. The reaction had more to do with his not informing them than the geopolitical rationale behind the policy shift. Sato retaliated by asserting Japan's diplomatic independence. Against American wishes, Sato dispatched top advisors to Hanoi to confer with the communist leaders. He also established diplomatic relations with Outer Mongolia which was throughly controlled by Moscow. Then, in September 1972, Sato's successor, Prime Minister Tanaka Takuei traveled to Beijing and announced

Japan's formal diplomatic recognition of the communist regime as China's legitimate government; embassies were exchanged. The United States would not do so until 1979.

Nixon's China "shock" had no practical effect on Sino-Japanese relations. Japan had enjoyed expanding economic ties with China since the early 1950s. In reviewing Japan's pre-1972 China policy, Chalmers Johnson lauds it as "one of the most skillfully executed foreign policies pursued by Japan in the postwar era – a clever, covert adaptation by Japan to the Cold War and a good example of Japan's essentially neomercantilist foreign policy."[33] From 1949 through 1972, Tokyo had pursued a brilliant "two Chinas" policy in which it balanced the conflicting demands of Washington, Taipei, and Beijing while maximizing its geoeconomic benefits from all three nations. Nixon's China "shock" was solely one of pride.

In talks between Washington and Beijing from 1971 through today, Japan has figured prominently into their calculus of the Far East power balance. During the relationship's first two years, China's leaders expressed fears that America's development of Japan into an economic superpower would eventually lead Tokyo to embark again on imperialism. Kissinger responded by arguing that the United States contained Japan within their bilateral security treaty and economic interdependence.[34] As part of their complex power balance strategy, Nixon and Kissinger encouraged Beijing's fears of Tokyo as well as Moscow in order to increase China's reliance on the United States. In 1972, Nixon actually warned Chou Enlai that he would allow Japan to acquire nuclear weapons if Beijing did not accept détente and the U.S.–Japan security treaty: "We told them that if you try to keep us from protecting the Japanese, we would let them go nuclear. And the Chinese said, 'We don't want that.'"[35]

After they restored relations, China's position shifted dramatically in regard to Japan. Kissinger recalls how Chou Enlai had initially

> described Japan as a potentially aggressive nation that might join with others to carve up China. He had accused us of deliberately reviving Japanese militarism; both privately and publicly he castigated the U.S.–Japanese Security Treaty. By February 1973, although Chou still uttered a formalistic warning about Japanese militarism, in practice he treated the Japanese as an incipient ally. China and Japan had restored diplomatic relations, encouraged by us, when Japanese Prime Minister Kakuei Tanaka visited China in September 1972. Chou Enlai now acknowledged that Japan's ties with the United States braked militarist tendencies in Japan and gave Japan an indispensable sense of security. He asked me to note that Peking had ceased its attacks on the Security Treaty; indeed,

China now urged the closest cooperation between the United States and Japan. Chairman Mao would later offer the friendly advice that to preserve Japan's dignity I should never visit Peking without also stopping in Tokyo. We had already decided that this was imperative. By the time I left office I had visited Tokyo more frequently than any other major capital.[36]

Nixon's warning to the Chinese that he might just allow Tokyo to go nuclear was not completely bluff. While concerned about Japan's growing geoeconomic power, Nixon and Kissinger apparently were fatalistic about Tokyo's possible acquisition of nuclear weapons. Both had mixed feelings about the Treaty of Nonproliferation of Nuclear Weapons which was ratified in 1969, believing "most of the major powers would eventually obtain nuclear weapons and the United States could benefit more by helping them in such efforts than by participating in an exercise in morality."[37] During the November 1969 summit, Nixon hinted to Sato that he would understand if Japan went nuclear. In March 1974, Kissinger admitted before the Joint Chiefs of Staff that: "The Japanese are mean and treacherous but they are not organically anti-American; they pursue their own interests. . . . It is essential for the U.S. to maintain a balance of power out there. If it shifts, Japan could be a big problem. . . . Japan will go nuclear at some time; we ought to let the Japanese do so without being publicly linked with it . . . it is good to keep the Chinese concerned."[38]

Nixon and Kissinger completely misunderstood Tokyo's position toward nuclear weapons. Concrete economic interests, not memories of Hiroshima and Nagasaki, made Tokyo resist any domestic or foreign pressure to increase its conventional or nuclear military capability. If Japan continued to spend only 1 per cent of GNP on defense, while the United States spent 8 or 9 per cent, then Japan could potentially enjoy seven percentage points of more GNP reinvested in strategic industries. In an increasingly interdependent world, the lighter a nation's defense burden, the greater its creation of wealth and power. Their alleged "nuclear allergy" did not inhibit Japanese from developing nuclear energy or huddling under America's nuclear umbrella. Typical was the Cabinet's reaction to the publication of the Japan Defense Agency's first White Paper in 1971. The White Paper, authored by nationalistic Director General Nakasone Yasuhiro, was actually very modest. It advocated an expanded defense to fill gaps left by Okinawa's reversion and the reduction of American forces in Japan, and expanded commitment by the Japanese people to the Self-Defence Force and its mission. In response to widespread criticism that the White Paper involved a departure from previous policy, Sato repudiated it and maintained that

Japan would not act on its suggestions. Nixon and Kissinger were brilliant practitioners of old-fashioned power balance geopolitics; however, they were novices in the wielding of geoeconomic power of which Japan was and remains the master.

GERALD FORD, 1973–77

Policymaking and Implementation

In October 1973, Gerald Ford was a loyal and clean if undistinguished Republican representative from Michigan when Nixon chose him to replace the disgraced Spiro Agnew as vice-president. Ford then became president on August 6, 1974 when Nixon resigned in the face of a probable congressional impeachment.

Ford was essentially a conservative internationalist. Like others who had served in World War II, Ford returned transformed. He later revealed that in "college I had been a real isolationist. But the war and being overseas changed my mind about the role that America should play in the world."[39] Like many who had narrowly escaped death in war, Ford felt that God had given him a second chance to work hard for the public good.[40]

Ford kept Kissinger as the administration's key foreign policymaker. With his own limited knowledge about world politics, Ford largely deferred to Kissinger's perspectives. Apparently there was no tension in Ford's role as Kissinger's mouthpiece. Ford was used to being sponsored by more powerful backers. Michigan's powerhouse Senator Arthur Vandenburg had plucked Ford from obscurity and backed him in his first political race, just as Nixon had made Ford his vice-president. Ford willingly performed his roles in the shadow of both mentors until they disappeared. Kissinger would stay with Ford until the end of his administration.

Policy Priorities

Ford's primary policies were to continue Nixon's foreign and domestic policies while tempering them with an emphasis on political honesty and openness. This, however, was a tougher balancing act than it appeared. Throughout his presidency there was a "fundamental tension . . . between the inheritance from his whole natural way of thinking – orthodox conservative Congressional Republican incrementalism – and the national vision that's Republican, Democratic, conservative, liberal, reactionary, that takes the whole scene into account."[41]

He was willing to defy public opinion when necessary. Within a month after taking office, he offended liberals by pardoning Nixon and conservatives by offering amnesty to draft evaders and war protesters. He also vetoed dozens of bills that he claimed would increase spending too high or were simply bad policy. One of Ford's aides described him as "the kind of guy who would take his shirt off his back and give it to a poor kid he saw on the street and then walk in and veto the day care program."[42]

Ford and Kissinger faced enormous international challenges. Despite Nixon's attempts to realign American power and commitments, the global power balance continued to shift toward other states, coalitions, and regions. The United States could do nothing about OPEC's quadrupling of oil prices and the resulting global stagflation. Détente had not prevented the Soviets and their Cuban auxiliaries from intervening in Ethiopia, Angola, and elsewhere.

Nowhere was the global power shift more evident than in the Far East. In April 1975, North Vietnamese troops destroyed the South Vietnamese army, entered Saigon, and unified the country under a communist dictatorship. Shortly thereafter communists took over Cambodia and Laos. During the 1970s, America's military retrenchment in the Far East coincided with a steady Soviet build up. Between 1965 and 1975, while American naval and air forces declined by 70 per cent, Soviet naval and air forces expanded by 80 per cent.[43]

While Soviet forces challenged America's throughout the Far East, Japanese corporations surpassed their American rivals throughout the region. Between 1965 and 1975, American trade with the Far East increased from $4.2 billion to $22.7 billion while Japan's soared from $4.3 billion to $31.7 billion. By 1975, Japanese direct foreign investments throughout the region exceeded America's by one-third.

Geopolitically, Ford addressed only a few issues during his two years in office. Ford and Kissinger tried to deal with Soviet nuclear power with the 1974 Vladivostok accord in which Washington and Moscow accepted limits on some weapons categories. In 1975, Ford sent marines to recapture an American ship, the "Malasquez", which had been captured by Cambodian insurgents. In submitting his 1976 budget, Ford asked for the first increase in American defense spending since 1969. Yet there were no real geopolitical innovations.

There was even less action on America's worsening geoeconomic problems. Congress empowered the president to deal with America's deteriorating economic power by initiating and passing the 1974 Trade Act. Ford, however, knew and cared little about geoeconomic conflicts. The 1974 Trade Act as a geoeconomic sword rusted in its scabbard.

Policy Toward Japan: Geoeconomic Issues

Ford's relations with Japan were largely ceremonial. He visited Japan in November 1974, and in June 1975 received Emperor Hirohito and Empress Nagako at the White House.[44] Neither Ford nor Kissinger got involved in the geoeconomic issues that arose. In 1975, Kissinger declared that relations between the United States and Japan had never been better.

Meanwhile, Japan's trade surplus with the United States continued to soar despite the yen's strengthening, from $2 billion in 1974 to $5.5 billion in 1976 and $8.1 billion in 1977. American electronics firms vainly protested Tokyo's continued neomercantilist policies in microelectronics. Part of the deal cut over returning Okinawa to Japan involved Tokyo's promise to open its microelectronic markets. In 1975, Tokyo officially "opened" Japan's electronics market by removing all tariffs and quotas. In reality, of course, the market remained carefully managed by cartels and government "administrative guidance." Throughout the 1970s, MITI and Japan's microelectronic firms worked to develop jointly first the 16K RAM, then the 64K RAM, and finally the 256K RAM semiconductor chips.

In 1976, Japan's subtle means of asserting power over the United States was revealed when the U.S. Justice Department sued the United States–Japan Trade Council for civil fraud because it had failed to register itself under the 1938 Foreign Agents Regulation Act. Although the Trade Council was completely staffed by American citizens and described itself as solely interested in improving the bilateral relationship, MITI supplied 90 per cent of its funds and it lobbied exclusively for Japanese economic interests.

Washington and Tokyo mostly cooperated during the Ford years. Ironically, in 1976, a mere four years after the bitter textile wrangle was settled, American and Japanese textile industry representatives met in Honolulu to discuss problems posed by low-priced producers from other countries. Starting in the Ford administration, American and Japanese also sat on the same side of the negotiating table during the succession of Law of the Sea conferences which culminated with the 1982 treaty. Both countries favored such principles as freedom to fish, mine, and traverse the high seas, and to sail through international straits, although they disagreed on the specifics of these broad principles. Although initially opposed, Japan followed the lead of the United States and most other countries in accepting the 200-mile exclusive economic zones (EEZs) and twelve-mile territorial sea. Both countries reluctantly bowed to the majority's assertion that deep-sea mining in the "common heritage of mankind" be regulated by a High Authority which would distribute the benefits to all other countries.

Policy Toward Japan: Geopolitical Issues

Ford's first geopolitical conflict with Japan came two months after taking office. In October 1974, retired Admiral Gene LaRocque admitted in testimony before Congress that the navy did not off-load nuclear weapons when it docked at Japanese ports. The news that the United States consistently violated Japan's nonnuclear principles sparked an explosion in Japan's media and Diet. Tokyo asked for and received a diplomatic note stating that the United States "faithfully honored its commitments to Japan," implying that it followed the prior consultation laws on troop and weapons movements in Japan required by the security treaty. Tokyo announced that it accepted Washington's explanation, and refused to answer suspicions that there was a secret bilateral agreement allowing the United States to move nuclear weapons through Japanese waters. The revelation was never discussed formally between the two governments, nor did it impede Ford's visit to Japan the following month.

Not surprisingly, given America's deteriorating geopolitical position in the Far East, the Ford White House pressed Tokyo for greater "burden sharing." Yet, Tokyo not only resisted further defense commitments, it limited even further those it had already made. In 1975, Prime Minister Miki amended the 1967 three principles of arms exports to include not only weapons but parts and fittings. In 1976, the Defense Agency issued its second White Paper, entitled the National Defense Program Outline (NDPO), in which Japan's Self Defense Force (SDF) would be increased to the point where it could defend Japan against a foreign invasion for several days while Washington rallied its forces to come to Japan's rescue. While Japanese commentators either hailed or blasted the NDPO as a step toward Japan's greater military capabilities and duties, it had no significant effect on the regional military power balance. A line in NDPO codified a practice Japan had followed for over a decade: "in maintaining the armed strength, the total amount of defense expenditure in each year shall not exceed, for the time being, an amount equivilent to 1/100th of the gross national product of the said fiscal year."[45] In other words, Japan's defense efforts would be shaped by budget principles rather than strategic threats.

While Tokyo was further limiting its defense role, Beijing was admonishing both the Japanese and Americans to do more. In 1976, Chou Enlai even called for an anti-Soviet alliance "to stretch from Japan through China, Pakistan, Iran, and Turkey to Western Europe."[46] Kissinger politely demurred.

JIMMY CARTER, 1977–81

Policymaking and Implementation

President Jimmy Carter was a liberal internationist who tried hard to realize his world view: "I was familiar with the widely accepted arguments that we had to choose between idealism and realism, or between morality and the exertion of power; but I rejected those claims. To me, the demonstration of American idealism was a practical and realistic approach to foreign affairs, and moral principles were the best foundation for the exertion of American power and influence."[47]

To staff his administration with like-minded men, Carter filled many positions with American members of the Trilateral Commission, of which he was a member. The Trilateral Commission included prominent Americans, Europeans, and Japanese who claimed to uphold ideals of multilateralism and free trade.

Carter was also careful to promote an intellectual and political balance between his Secretary of State Cyrus Vance and NSC head Zbigniew Brzezinski. The President reduced the NSC committees to two, the Policy Review Committee (PRC) with responsibilities for policies handled by one department and Special Coordinating Committee (SCC) for policies addressed by two or more bureaucracies. Overall, Carter's NSC was designed to analyze proposals from elsewhere rather than propose its own policies. Like Kennedy, Carter encouraged multiple policy views.

Despite these precautions, Carter increasingly relied on the NSC rather than the State Department. Institutionally disadvantaged like all secretaries of state, Vance's self-effacing personality further undermined his influence vis-à-vis the acerbic, ambitious, extroverted Brzezinski. While Carter and Vance communicated through memos between the White House and State Department, the president and national security advisor were right down the hall from each other and frequently played tennis. Most importantly, Carter saw himself as Zbigniew's "eager student" in world affairs.[48]

Vance and Brzezinski differed sharply over policies. The Secretary of State emphasized the increasing defusion of geopolitical and geoeconomic power around the world, and the need to deal creatively with the new array of issues and power relationships. The National Security Advisor focused on the Soviet threat and its containment. With the 1979 revolutions in Iran and Nicaragua, and Soviet invasion of Afghanistan, Brzezinski's strategy dominated. All along, despite these differences, Vance and Brzezinski, worked very closely together and seem to have avoided much of the jealousy and rivalry that frays relations between most secretaries of state and national security advisors.

The State Department became almost completely irrelevant to foreign policy after Vance resigned in protest in April 1980 after the failed raid to save the hostages in Iran. Despite his intelligence and expertise, the new Secretary of State Edward Muskie was unable to fill the void. Carter did not even bother to inform Muskie of his August decision to shift American nuclear strategy from mutually assured destruction (MAD) to a warfighting counterforce stance. Of thirty policy papers signed by Carter in late 1980, twenty-six were proposed by the NSC, three from State, and one from Defense.[49]

Carter was not merely a hands-on president, he tried micromanaging virtually every problem that came across his desk. With his engineering and naval background, Carter approached problems and policymaking rationally and systematically. Carter had "the faith of a technocrat, believing in the mechanics of objects and situations, confident he can figure out how they work."[50]

Unfortunately, the ship of state does not operate like a nuclear submarine; Carter left out the human factor. His technocratic approach ran aground on the shoals of congressional politics. Carter believed that government could make a difference; he just did not know how government worked. As Carter raced toward the White House in 1976 he ran against Washington, reviling the corruption, inefficiency, and lack of vision of all power-holders, Republican and Democrat. Unfortunately, after settling into the Oval Office, he not only believed his own rhetoric, he acted upon it. Carter equated compromise with selling out. Although he had a Democratic Congress, he ended up alienating so many powerhouses that nearly all of his proposals were mangled or shelved in committees. After one White House affront, White House Speaker Tip O'Neil angrily told Chief of Staff Hamilton Jordan, "I don't think you understand, son. The next time you do this, I'm going to ream your ass."[51] As if angering key allies were not enough, Carter overloaded the system by pushing a range of projects at once. The result was "a jumble of programs and deadlines, forced marches and sudden retreats, which blurred the thrust of his Presidency."[52]

Despite Carter's political ineptness, many praised him for his integrity and prudence in office, particularly during crises. Carter's former speechwriter, James Fallows, said this of his boss:

Carter is unusually patient, less vindictive than the political norm, blessed with a sense of perspective about the chanciness of life and the transcience of its glories and pursuits . . . when moral choices faced him, he would resolve them fairly . . . when questions of life and death, of nuclear war and human destruction were laid on his desk, he would act on them calmly, with self-knowledge, free of interior demons that might tempt him to act rashly or to prove at terrible cost that he was a man.[53]

Policy Priorities

Carter's greatest successes and failures were in foreign policy. His administration's two unequivocal triumphs were the Egyptian–Israeli Peace Treaty and the Panama Canal Treaty. Carter's efforts were essential to bringing peace between Egypt and Israel. After carefully laying the groundwork, in August 1978 he invited President Anwar Sadat and Menachim Begin to Camp David. After days of grueling negotiations, the three men announced the first of several agreements by which Israel would withdraw from the Sinai peninsula in return for full diplomatic and economic relations. That same year, Carter submitted the Panama Canal Treaty to the Senate which passed it by 68–32.

The president also improved relations with China. Chou Enlai died in January and Mao Zedong in September 1976, setting off a leadership crisis that first brought the radical Gang of Four and Hua Guofeng to power and the eclipse of the moderate faction. Only in 1978 did pragmatist leader Deng Xioaping emerge to take power and purge the radicals. The following year, in 1979, Carter felt confident enough in the hold on power of Deng's moderate faction that he agreed to open full diplomatic relations between the United States and China.

Other foreign policy initiatives had ambiguous results. The president tried to apply Trilateral Commission ideas of multilateralism to his geoeconomic policies. In particular, he encouraged Japan and West Germany to act in concert with the United States in stimulating their economies to act as "the locomotive engines of growth" for the global economy. Unfortunately, Tokyo and Bonn had their own distinct national interests and problems that made them at best reluctant and usually resistant to Carter's "locomotive" policy.

Carter fought to keep détente alive by focusing on achieving a SALT II agreement. He resisted the pressure by conservative congressmen and interest groups to counter Soviet inroads in Angola, Mozambique, and Ethiopia with American aid to anti-Soviet groups. In Vienna on June 18,

1979, President Carter and Premier Brezhnev warmly embraced after signing the SALT II treaty which imposed limits on ICBMs.

But during 1979 and 1980, the Carter White House faced a series of crises that seemed to undermine all its previous accomplishments. Key allied governments were overthrown in 1979, including Nicaragua's Somoza regime by the communist Sandinista movement and Iran's Shah by Islamic fundamentalists. Oil prices doubled during this period to around $34 a barrel, thus exacerbating the high inflation and low economic growth that had characterized the global economy since 1973.

In October 1979, Carter permitted the deposed Shah of Iran to fly to New York from Mexico for cancer treatment. On November 4, Iranians captured the American embassy in Tehran, and held hostage fifty-two American diplomats and personnel. Carter would spend much of his last years in office trying to free them through economic sanctions, negotiations, and, in April 1980, a failed military rescue attempt. Iran's leader, the Ayatollah Khomeini, finally released the hostages on January 20, 1981, 444 days after he seized them and on the day of Ronald Reagan's inauguration.

But the biggest threat to American security occurred in December 1979 when Soviet troops invaded Afghanistan to conquer that country and make it part of Moscow's empire. Many feared that the Soviet invasion was merely the first step before a invasion of Iran and attempt to take over the Persian Gulf. Carter organized some American troops into a Rapid Deployment Force and warned, in what became known as the Carter Doctrine, that any attack on the Persian Gulf would be considered an attack on the United States.

Policy Toward Japan: Geoeconomic Issues

In February 1977, a month after the inauguration, Carter tried to show the importance he attached to the bilateral relationship by dispatching Vice-President Walter Mondale to Tokyo. The following month, Prime Minister Fukuda visited Washington for a summit with Carter. There was a lot to discuss, in particular the fact that Japan's trade surplus with the United States continued to surge ever higher. The Japanese as usual adeptly turned aside any questions of the surplus with other issues like uranium processing, Carter's human rights policy, and South Korea.

Nuclear fuel processing emerged as the most important issue. At their first meeting on March 21, the talk centered on Tokyo's Tokai Mura uranium processing plant which was scheduled to begin production later that year. The United States supplied Japan with enriched uranium, and had the power under a bilateral agreement to control its uses. Carter feared the activation of

Japan's plant might contribute to nuclear proliferation, since a byproduct of the process was nuclear weapons grade plutonium. And since Carter was planning to curtail America's own plutonium production, he felt he could hardly let Japan continue its own production. Carter's anti-proliferation policy represented a sharp turn from previous administrations which had encouraged Tokyo's development of a nuclear energy industry to lessen its dependence on foreign oil. On March 30, Fukuda again led with the uranium processing issue, offering to ban reprocessing of nuclear fuels if Britain, France, West Germany, and the Soviet Union agreed to do the same. So much for Japan's alleged "nuclear allergy." No agreement was reached.

The two sides negotiated throughout the summer. The Carter administration eventually retreated on the issue, just as it would on so many other issues. On September 1, 1977, Tokyo and Washington announced an agreement by which Japan could go ahead with its nuclear processing plant. Fukuda had not only used the issue to derail discussion of trade issues, but finally won complete American support for his policy.

With the nuclear issue settled, a range of issues that had been kept on hold burst onto the policy agenda. Embattled American industries that had been petitioning the White House and Congress for relief, including steel, television, fisheries, aviation, and banking, finally got attention as Japan's trade surplus with the United States soared from $5.4 billion in 1976 to $8.1 billion in 1977. The Carter White House asked Tokyo for restraint but the Japanese refused to take any significant steps to reduce their trade surplus. In April 1977, MITI did announce that it would impose "voluntary" curbs on Japanese television exports to the United States, hardly a concession since Japanese dumping had nearly destroyed America's industry. At the London economic summit of May and Tokyo bilateral talks of November 1977, the Carter White House failed to gain Japanese promises to reduce Japan's import barriers and dumping, or even stimulate its economy. American pleas with the Japanese to practice free trade and assume international responsibilities worked no better with Carter than with any other president before or since.

Rather than press Tokyo for genuine market opening and anti-dumping measures, the Carter White House made its own unilateral concessions. In the summer, the White House agreed to remove any remaining categories on textile imports. However, a sharp surge in Japanese exports in sensitive categories that year led the White House to reimpose restrictions in 1978. Tokyo did not reciprocate by opening its own closed textile markets. Tokyo does not rein in its neomercantilist policies from foreign concessions any more than it does from foreign pleas.

On September 21, U.S. Steel filed dumping charges against Japan's Big Six steel corporations. The Carter White House promised to support America's steel industry, including leveling tariffs if dumpings were found. The threat of concrete retaliatory measures worked. Exactly one month later, the Fukuda administration announced voluntary steel export restraints, but at levels where they enjoyed large market shares; and, of course, Japan's own steel market remained closed to competitive imports.

Although pleased with Tokyo's steel agreement, the White House became disgruntled when Tokyo refused to make any concessions in other contested industries during the November talks. The White House decided that it had to make a special effort to break down Japan's diplomatic and economic walls. It dispatched USTR General Counsel Richard Rivers to Tokyo the following week with a "laundry list" of concessions it wanted from Japan and warned of retaliation should Tokyo refuse to accept them. The Ministry of Finance leaked exaggerated accounts of Rivers's list to portray Washington as making "unfair" demands upon Japan, sparking the usual outpouring of anti-Americanism from across Japan's political and economic spectrum. Unfazed, Treasury Secretary Michael Blumenthal responded by talking down the dollar to pressure Tokyo.

In mid-December, Prime Minister Fukuda dispatched the Minister for External Affairs, Ushiba Nobuhiko, to Washington with an "Eight Point Program" including tariff cuts on 124 items and expansion of quotas for citrus juice, beef, and oranges. STR Robert Strauss had the list of "concessions" analyzed by computer and found the effect on the trade imbalance to be negligible. The White House denounced the Ushiba package as completely inadequate and called for genuine market opening. The barrage of accusations and denials across the Pacific continued for the next month.

On January 11, 1978, Strauss arrived in Tokyo for talks with Ushiba over the trade deficit crisis. After two intense days of negotiation, on January 13, 1978, Strauss and Ushiba emerged to announce that Tokyo was committed to a 7 per cent growth rate for 1978, would go through with the 124 tariff cuts and quota increases it had previously promised, and, in addition, would expand import credits, send a buying mission to the United States, increase foreign aid, and increase imports of manufactured goods. In return, Washington promised to pursue noninflationary growth, improve its balance of payments, and formulate an energy policy. The Joint Statement also declared their commitment "to achieve basic equity in their trading relations by affording to major trading countries substantially equivalent competitive opportunities on a reciprocal basis." Altogether Tokyo had promised to reduce significantly its trade surplus, increase economic growth, and reduce its trade barriers.

Yet, Japan's trade surplus rose to $11.6 billion in 1978, up from $1.7 billion in 1975, despite Tokyo's promises and the yen's revaluation. The yen continued to strengthen from 253 in September 1977 to 190 by July 1979, but did little to alleviate Japan's vast global trade surplus which dipped only slightly from $14 billion in 1977 to $12.03 billion in 1978. Rather than genuinely open its own markets, Tokyo continued to respond to foreign protests against its neomercantilist policies with Orderley Marketing Agreements (OMAs) and Voluntary Export Restraints (VERs) in those industries, thus preserving its protected home markets and foreign market shares. On February 2, 1979, Japanese trade envoy Yasukawa Takeshi captured the growing contempt with which most Japanese viewed the United States, when he said: "We now even send buying missions to the United States instead of the selling missions we have always sent in the past. This reflects a 180-degree turn of Japanese trade policy and I hope Americans remember this when we talk about our trade problems."[54]

The White House failed to muster any pressure on Tokyo to live up to its own promises. In May 1979, Carter and Ohira met in Washington but failed to reach agreement on outstanding trade issues. In a speech before Congress, Ohira called for strengthening the alliance and warned against protectionism. Carter journeyed to Tokyo the following month for the Group of Seven summit which as usual focused on geopolitical rather than geoconomic issues. Throughout his last year in office, managing various geopolitical crises consumed most of the Carter White House's resources.

Policy Toward Japan: Geopolitical Issues

Carter's campaign call for withdrawing American troops from South Korea sent shock waves throughout Tokyo and the region. Although the White House later reversed its policy in late 1977, and withdrew only one division from South Korea, the uncertainty exacerbated Japan's mixed feelings over the alliance's economic benefits and psychological costs, along with doubts over how genuine America's defense commitment really was. Tokyo sent several high ranking envoys to Washington throughout 1977 to urge the Carter administration to reverse its policy, while Prime Minister Fukuda and other cabinet members raised the issue during meetings with their White House counterparts. Americans, meanwhile, increasingly deplored Japan's "free ride" on defense along with trade, investments, and technology. They noted that Tokyo opposed any further lessening of American commitments to the Far East yet refused to increase Japan's defense commitments over its own islands. Even China implored the Japanese to be more responsible. During Deng Xioaping's visit to Tokyo in October 1978, he called on Japan to increase its military power to offset Soviet regional power. In the exchange of demands across the Pacific, Carter conceded on Korea; Tokyo refused to assume any more of the defense burden.

Throughout the late 1970s, culminating with the Soviet invasion of Afghanistan, Tokyo experienced a series of tough and provocative Moscow actions. Despite Tokyo's efforts, Moscow bluntly refused to discuss the Northern Territories issue. Moscow not only used the Soviet navy to back its assertion of a 200-mile exclusive economic zone which infringed on waters claimed by Tokyo, but actually sailed its fishing boats within Japan's twelve-mile territorial sea. Meanwhile, Moscow steadily built up its Far East fleet and sailed it repeatedly through the international straits cutting through Japan. Still, Tokyo refused to increase its defense duties or capabilities.

On November 1979, the Iranian government sent a student mob to overrun the American embassy and take the personnel hostage. The Carter White House asked its allies to join sanctions against Iran. The European Community complied; Tokyo was reluctant. Japanese firms continued buying up Iranian oil which helped double prices over a few months, leaving every non-oil exporting country worse off. On December 10, 1979, Secretary of State Vance met with Foreign Minister Okita Saburo and sharply condemned Japan's actions as "insensitive" and rated them one on a scale of fourteen in terms of concern for America's hostages. Okita then blasted Vance for publicly airing American grievances, arguing that "it's one thing to express U.S. displeasure privately, but quite another to do so publicly."[55] Ronald Morse explains that: "Japan never fully appreciated the emotional nature or the 'human rights' aspect of the hostage issue in the United States. It was primarily concerned with obtaining adequate oil supplies and protecting its billion dollar petrochemical project at Bandar-Khomeini on the Persian Gulf. . . . From the beginning Japanese officials spoke of Japan being caught in a dispute between 'two friends,' presumably of equal value, and not wishing to take sides."[56]

The basis of Tokyo's policy toward the Persian Gulf was no different than its strategy anywhere else: Japan's geoeconomic interests come first. Tokyo could afford to be "insensitive" to the fate of America's hostages, the White House's delicate diplomacy toward Iran, and Japan's oil-buying splurge that doubled global oil prices. The Japanese knew that Washington would not retaliate. American criticisms would rise and fall quickly over Tokyo's policy to Iran and global oil supplies just as they had for scores of other issues in which Tokyo had rejected America's position either overtly or with empty promises. Throughout the postwar era, Tokyo could rest assured that Washington would continue to be so distracted by the range of geopolitical issues and crises bubbling across its policy agenda stove, that it would never concentrate on decisively resolving outstanding problems with Japan.

9 Japan Triumphant: The Reagan and Bush Era, 1981–93

It was an eventful twelve years, with the world and its power relations undergoing vast geopolitical and geoeconomic convulsions. The most important event, of course, was the collapse of the Soviet empire and communism. As George Kennan had predicted four decades earlier, communism and the Russian empire were doomed and would eventually crumble from their inability to develop a comfortable or meaningful economic, social, or political life for those under its sway. The western industrial democracies could accelerate that demise by achieving a virtuous cycle of economic development and political stability, by containing any Soviet psychological and political efforts to increase their influence in the west, and by negotiating constructively with Moscow on outstanding issues. This selective containment strategy would hold the Soviets at arm's length as the internal rot did its work.

From 1950 to 1969, however, the United States had abandoned Kennan's selective containment emphasis on the economic and political strengthening of the west for Paul Nitze's global containment which emphasized military alliances, nuclear and conventional forces, and brinkmanship with the Soviets anywhere around the world. A succession of confrontations and communist victories – Czechoslovakia coup (1948), Berlin blockade (1948–9), Soviet testing of an atomic bomb (1949), Chinese communist revolution (1949) – culminating with the Korean War in June 1950, seemed to discredit selective containment. But global containment was enormously expensive and led America logically into the jungled labyrinth of Vietnam.

By the late 1960s, global containment's financial, material, and psychological burdens had weakened America economically and militarily relative to its rivals. President Nixon understood this and pursued policies of selective containment which realigned American power and commitments with its genuine foreign interests. But once again, selective containment was discredited in the minds of many by Soviet aggression in Africa during the 1970s and its invasion of Afghanistan in 1979. These events coincided with a host of other geopolitical and geoeconomic blows including OPEC's quadrupling of oil prices in 1973 and further doubling in 1979 which caused global economic stagflation, communist military takeovers of South Vietnam, Cambodia, and Laos in 1975, the communist Sandinista revolution in Nicaragua in 1979, and the Islamic revolution in Iran and seizure of America's embassy that same year. In 1979, President Carter began to shift American policy back toward global containment.

Ronald Reagan won the presidency in 1980 because of his ability to convince a majority of America's voters that he would reverse the country's relative decline and restore it to greatness. Reagan's formula was quite simple: tax cuts would stimulate the economy into unprecedented levels of prosperity, generating even more revenues that would balance the budget within four years, while tripling the size of America's military and countering every Soviet or communist incursion around the world would shift the global power balance once again in Washington's favor.

Unfortunately, the policies of Reagan and his successor George Bush did not work out as planned. By piling up hundreds of billions of dollars of additional debt and diverting key financial, scientific, industrial, and human resources to the military industrial complex, Reagan's military build up weakened rather than strengthened the United States. And, most ironically, Reagan's near tripling of the defense budget may have delayed rather than hastened the Soviet collapse. Moscow's hardliners pointed to the American military threat and warned Gorbachev that it was no time for reforms.

The only true success was in a policy that Reagan initially abhorred – arms control. Reagan's INF Treaty (1987), and Bush's two START treaties (1991, 1992), eliminated or cut drastically entire classes of nuclear weapons. But arms control is an area in which everyone wins, a different type of success than the "our win, their loss" criteria by which geopolitical struggles are generally evaluated.

Although communism's failures and American containment would have eventually led to the Soviet Union's demise, Gorbachev's reforms accelerated that process. Gorbachev understood that the Soviet system was incapable of keeping up with the technological, industrial, and financial advances of the west. To make matters worse, Moscow was also committed to subsidizing communist dictatorships over the sullen peoples of East Europe, Cuba, Vietnam, and the Soviet republics, as well as other allies of dubious loyalty around the Third World. Gorbachev gambled that he could save communism in the Soviet Union through political and economic reforms and allowing the communist allies to determine their own future. But ending foreign subsidies and bringing home Soviet troops led to mass uprisings and the toppling of hated communist regimes abroad. Dismantling the Soviet Union's totalitarian regime and allowing free elections led not to communism's reform but to its demise and the independence of the "republics." Noncommunist Boris Yeltsin came to power in 1991 as president of an independent, multi-party Russia. Since then he has consolidated his power despite two coup attempts.

While America's geopolitical position soared after 1989, arguably despite rather than because of Reagan's policies, its geoeconomic decline worsened markedly between 1980 and 1992. Over twelve years, Reaganomics was largely responsible for quadrupling America's national debt, lowering economic growth and real income, sending the trade and payments deficits soaring, and converting the United States from the world's greatest creditor to greatest debtor country. When Reagan entered office in 1981, America's national debt was $976 billion; when Bush left in 1993 it was $4.2 trillion.

What priority did Japan play in American foreign policy amidst the global containment crusade against Godless Communism and the "Reagan Revolution" at home? Reaganomics severely complicated the bilateral relationship by weakening the United States and strengthening Japan. Yet, although Japan's power expanded throughout the period, it remained a secondary concern for American foreign policymakers.

During the Reagan–Bush era, Japan inherited America's role as the world's banker and by most indicators surpassed the United States in global financial, manufacturing, technological, trade, and investment power. As Japan became ever more powerful, its industries challenged America's virtually across the board. Japan's trade and investment surplus with the United States mounted steadily throughout the 1980s. Trade conflicts over specific sectors mushroomed during the 1980s and into the 1990s.

Like their predecessors, the Reagan and Bush administrations tried to counter the most egregious examples of Japanese neomercantilism. Unfortunately, they continued the American tradition of allowing its industrial, trade, and technology policies to be shaped by politics rather than long-range planning. American diplomatic efforts to win market shares in Japan for baseball bats, beef, or oranges received as much attention as semiconductors, computers, and satellites. And when the Japanese did grudgingly agree to "open" a market, the Americans usually failed to insist that the promise be kept and progress measured with an actual increase in market share. For example, after three years of efforts to open Japan's market to American baseball bats, their market share remains even today a symbolic sliver. When the White House responded to Japanese dumping, it usually did so with "voluntary export restraints". Its use of anti-dumping tariff measures was limited and sporadic.

As always, Tokyo adroitly finessed all of Washington's attempts to "level the playing field" by stonewalling negotiations until Congress or the White House threatened genuine sanctions, and then offering largely symbolic trade "concessions," all the while insisting that Japan's markets were the world's most open and American firms did not sell more in Japan because their goods were inferior and they did not try hard enough. During these twelve years, Tokyo announced ten "market opening packages," each of which it claimed had made Japan the world's most open economy. Tokyo dismissed any American or foreign accusations of unfair trade as "misunderstandings." Japan's lobbying army in Washington and the state capitals expanded throughout this time and increasingly undercut American attempts to retaliate against Japanese neomercantilism.

RONALD REAGAN, 1981–9

Policymaking and Implementation

America's forty-two presidents have risen from a variety of careers. Ronald Reagan was the first Hollywood actor to inhabit the White House. The world views of America's presidents from Truman through Carter were strongly shaped by their military experiences overseas, and often on the battlefield. Reagan spent World War II in Hollywood studios rather than at the front, playing war heroes in B movies. More than anything, Reagan's world view was shaped by the fantasized black and white morality and happy endings of his Hollywood flicks.

Reagan's domestic and foreign policies all sprang from his unswerving allegiance to a collection of simple convictions and slogans: "Government is not the solution, it's the problem;" "The Soviet Union is an evil empire;" "America is a shining city on a hill for all the world;" "We have to unleash the magic of the marketplace;" "A strong dollar equals a strong America." To achieve his goals, Reagan would "take a simple position founded on principle, give voice to it repeatedly, adhere to it stubbornly, and let others – executive branch subordinates, members of Congress, American citizens, foreigners – do the adjusting. Let them fill in the details; let them deal with the consequences. Let them worry about internal consistency. He would push the values he thought important."[1] Although these slogans and his delivery of them had a powerful mass appeal, many criticized him as "a President frozen in ideological fantasy-land."[2]

Reagan's greatest strength was his personality. Whereas most people might well dismiss anyone else of such simplistic notions and limited knowledge about the United States and the world as a crank, Reagan's sunny disposition, endless anecdotes, mastery of small talk, good looks, constant evocation and seeming personification of American myths and heroes, and ability to read speeches with conviction and animation won over a majority of the American people. Some lauded Reagan as the "Great Communicator" for his rousing speeches and small talk; others derided him as the "Great Manipulator" for his triumph of style over substance.[3]

Historians would be hard pressed to find a president who was as loose with the truth as Reagan. At press conferences and elsewhere, if he did not know the answer to a question, he often made one up, and then believed it despite all contrary evidence shown him. Among Reagan's more memorable beliefs are that "trees cause pollution" and "oil spills cure tuberculosis." He actually once told a Jewish group that he knew their suffering because he had helped liberate one of the concentration camps at the end of World War II. In reality, Reagan never left Hollywood during the war.

Not everyone was as adoring as most Americans. One distinguished political analyst noted that "Reagan's misstatements, errors of facts, and meandering mode of presentation would have led to any parliamentary leader in Europe being driven from office."[4] European leaders found it "hard to take Ronald Reagan, as a politician, altogether seriously. He was not very bright; his strong opinions were secondhand. He did not know very much about economics or world affairs. He often came to meetings very badly briefed."[5]

Although the rise of a Ronald Reagan would be inconceivable in Europe's more intellectually vigorous democracies, in American political culture, Reagan was adored rather than ridiculed by most people. Reagan was a "teflon president" against whom criticism, no matter how well-documented or argued, did not diminish his popularity. Reagan's naps at Cabinet meetings, ignorance about even the most basic issues, and ransoming of hostages never shook the faith of millions of Americans in him, and even defused congressional talk of impeachment for the Iran–Contra scandal that would have sunk most other presidents.

Reagan's teflon coating was never stronger than when 242 marines were killed in Lebanon. The American public and media continued to support him and shrugged away the botched, bloodsoaked mission as unfortunate. Just four years earlier, Carter was savaged by the press and public for the failed rescue mission of American hostages in Iran which resulted in eight dead.

Perhaps no president has been more detached from the policymaking process. Reagan reigned rather than ruled; while looking presidential he simply ratified decisions made elsewhere. As a former actor, Reagan was used to being directed and supported by a huge production ensemble. One former aide said that Reagan was not interested in policymaking: "He thinks of himself not so much as the person who decides but rather as the person who markets."[6] During meetings, Reagan was more apt to doodle or doze than try to comprehend the complex issues at stake. Generally, he would "wait for an amiable consensus to develop among advisors, who work within the boundaries of Reagan's ideology. Except for his unbudging devotion to a military buildup and opposition to tax increases, he often accepts uncritically his advisor's recommendations. . . . Reagan lacks the temperament, and often the knowledge, to choose between the competing arguments."[7] Reagan dismissed the details or even contradictions of his policies as long as they incorporated his values and priorities, and sometimes even when they did not, as when he ransomed hostages. The Tower Board investigating the Iran–Contra scandal blasted Reagan for his detached managerial style and unawareness "of the way the operation was implemented and the full consequences of U.S. participation."[8] The same criticism could apply to any of Reagan's policies.

With the void at the top, policies were shaped by fierce multi-stranded tugs of war among key advisors and cabinet heads sitting atop huge bureaucracies. During Reagan's eight years, six national security advisors and two secretaries of state served him. These men varied greatly in expertise from NSC advisor and good Reagan friend William Clark who knew almost nothing about the world to George Shultz and Al Haig who had extensive international and administrative experience. But no matter how politically adept, professional, or personally close to Reagan, these officials had to pass first through powerful chiefs of staff – Ed Meese until 1985 and Don Regan from then to the end.

Throughout Reagan's two terms, the most important aspect of the policy process was keeping it secret. As Meese put it, "We feel that it is important that the decision-making process be a matter that doesn't get a great deal of public or even internal Government attention other than from those who are directly involved, which are the members of the National Security Council, until the President makes a decision."[9]

Policy Priorities

Reagan proclaimed that "military strength, either direct or indirect, must remain an available part of America's foreign policy . . . we will not return to the days of defeatism, decline, and despair."[10] To this end, the Reagan White House embarked on a massive expansion of the defense budget; when Reagan left office it was over two and a half times its 1980 size. The United States supplied billions of weapons, supplies, and money to guerrillas in Afghanistan, Nicaragua, Angola, Cambodia, and Ethiopia, and beleaguered governments in El Salvador, Iran, and Iraq. In 1983, American troops invaded Grenada to destroy a Marxist government and Beirut with British and French troops to cover the Israeli withdrawal to southern Lebanon; they defeated the handful of enemy troops in Grenada but retreated ignominiously from Lebanon after 242 marines were killed.

Reagan's policies toward terrorists were more carrot than stick. In 1986, Reagan did order jets to bomb Libya after receiving intelligence reports that President Kadafi was behind a terrorist bombing in Berlin that killed two American soldiers. Yet the previous year, to free a TWA airliner held by terrorists, Reagan pressured Israel to free Palestinian prisoners. And then throughout 1986 and 1987, the White House ransomed American hostages in Lebanon.

Reagan's vow to free Americans held hostage in Lebanon led to his most outrageous foreign policy blunder. The Iran–Contra scandal involved a White House attempt to alleviate simultaneously three foreign policy problems: how to circumvent the law forbidding American funds to forces attempting to overthrow the Sandinista government of Nicaragua, how to free the hostages held by radical Islamic groups in Lebanon, and how to moderate the fundamentalist anti-American regime in Iran. The solution was to sell arms to Iran in return for the release of hostages, and the profits made by the arms sales would be given to the Contra forces fighting to overthrow the Sandinistas. This policy was as much a practical as legal failure. Ransoming hostages violated a basic Reagan principle and simply encouraged Islamic groups to kidnap more Americans. The arms to Iran strengthened the regime but certainly did not moderate its anti-Americanism. And the extra money to the Contras failed to translate into battlefield victories.

Also extremely controversal was Reagan's 1983 announcement of his plan to build the Strategic Defense Initiative (SDI), an anti-ICBM system that he fervently believed would protect the United States from nuclear attack and eventually render nuclear weapons obsolete. Critics maintained that SDI could cost as much as a trillion dollars and even then be quickly overwhelmed by Soviet killer satellites followed by a massive launch of their nuclear arsenal. But the president was not fazed by such arguments, assuming he was even aware of them. Thirty-five billion dollars was eventually invested in SDI between 1983 and 1992 when the program was scrapped as technically unworkable and militarily destabilizing.

The Reagan administration did score some foreign policy successes. In December 1987, the United States and Soviet Union signed the INF treaty by which both sides pledged to withdraw and destroy all intermediate range nuclear missiles from Europe. The sale of Stinger anti-aircraft missiles and other weapons to anti-Soviet forces in Afghanistan may have accelerated Moscow's decision to eventually withdraw its army in 1988. The White House's support for the Contras may have been an important factor in the Sandinista promise to hold elections in 1990 and their subsequent electoral loss to a centrist coalition of parties which then took power.

The "Reagan Revolution" that followed the 1980 election of the former California movie star and governor to the White House attempted simultaneously to cut taxes and spending, balance the budget within four years, and increase defense spending. After eight years in office, Reagan only succeeded in boosting defense spending. Meanwhile, the result of Reaganomics was economic disaster: America's national debt tripled from $975 billion in 1980 to $3 trillion in 1988, the nation became a net debtor country for the first time since the nineteenth century, the trade deficit reached $187 billion in 1987, the economy sputtered at the lowest average rate of any decade since the 1930s as American industries were ravished by high interest rates and low-priced imports at home and abroad, real income deteriorated, the tax rate remained about the same, the net national savings rate dropped from 6.9 per cent to 2.8 per cent, and federal government spending to GNP increased by one full percentage point from 24.5 per cent to 25.7 per cent.

What went wrong? The supply side theory upon which the Reagan White House based its policies was deeply flawed. According to the theory, cutting taxes would encourage more spending and investment and the resulting greater economic growth would increase tax revenues and thus balance the budget; everyone would benefit from the rising economic tide. With its 1981 Economic Recovery Tax Act (ERTA), the White House did cut income taxes 25 per cent over three years and capital gains taxes from 28 per cent to 20 per cent, and allowed businesses to speed their depreciation of assets. However, Reagan increased rather than decreased federal spending as a percentage of GNP largely by nearly tripling the defense and farm subsidy budgets over eight years. As America's national debt spiraled ever higher, the Federal Reserve Chair Paul Volker raised interest rates to encourage domestic and foreign investors to make up the revenue shortfall and cut inflation. The high interest rate policy did lower inflation rates, but at a terrible cost. The demand for dollars raised its value and thus made foreign goods cheaper and American goods more expensive in the United States and around the world. The nation's trade deficit and unemployment rate soared while its growth rate plummeted as consumers increasingly bought foreign rather than American, while businesses cut investments and consumers spending because of higher interest rates. Hundreds of billions of dollars continue to be sent abroad to service the national debt every year rather than be invested in America's economy.

Reaganomics was deeply flawed in other ways. The numbers upon which Reaganomics was based were as phony as the theory. In a fascinating interview, the Office of Management and Budget Director, David Stockman, admitted that he was forced to "cook the books" to make the deficits seem less worse than they were while the tax cuts were designed mostly to further enrich the wealthy. Reaganomic hardliners in the White House, including Reagan himself, continually thwarted Stockman's attempts to reduce the budget deficit through tax increases and spending cuts.[11] Since Congress knew the White House figures were so thoroughly discredited, every Reagan budget after 1981 appeared in Congress "dead on arrival." Although the resulting budgets negotiated between Congress and the White House were often dramatically different from the original proposals in terms of spending priorities, they never exceeded the original in total spending by more than 1 per cent. Despite his promise, Reagan never once submitted a balanced budget to Congress, and never vetoed the bill that eventually emerged.

By the end of 1985, the White House had abandoned the substance of Reaganomics, but by then it was far too late and enormous damage had been inflicted on the American economy. Fiscal conservative Jim Baker replaced radical Don Regan as Treasury Secretary, and the new chief immediately worked toward devaluing the dollar, raising taxes, and cutting spending. At the September 1985 Group of Five meeting at the Plaza Hotel in New York, the finance ministers of the United States, Japan, Germany, France, and Britain agreed to sell dollars to devalue them. Between 1985 and 1987, the dollar's value dropped from 260 to 125 yen and to lesser amounts against other currencies. Baker encouraged the Gramm–Rudman bill that which targeted deficit reductions over five years which, if not achieved, would automatically trigger across-the-board spending cuts. The 1986 Tax Reform Act (TRA) closed a range of tax loopholes and increased corporate taxes. TRA restored the overall percentage of tax revenue to GNP that ERTA had reduced.

Baker's conservative reforms helped rein in the spiraling budget and trade deficits and boost economic growth and employment. Yet, irreparable damage had already been done. Political economist I.M. Destler argues convincingly that Reaganomic's legacy is "an erosion of American strength, a result of mortgaging the economic base that underlies both domestic living standards and international power."[12]

Policy Toward Japan: Geoeconomic Issues

The Reagan administration's first strategy session to deal with Japanese neomercantilism took place a half year after taking office, in the fall of 1981. Clyde Prestowitz, who attended the meeting, revealed that it produced little discussion of strategy and no comment on objectives. While it was understood that our objective was to open the Japanese market, we did not address what was meant by open, whether it was realistic to believe we could open the market, and whether if we got what we wanted, the trade deficit would decline. Even less consideration was given to the likely Japanese response to certain initiatives. And no consideration was given to the staple issue of all negotiations: how to use a judicious mixture of carrots and sticks to achieve the objective.[13]

The biggest problem was the White House division between the dominant free trade ideologues and the minority managed-trade realists. Over time, as the trade and investment deficits with Japan soared and scores of American industries screamed for relief, the balance shifted increasingly toward the realists. Overall, the White House followed a two-track policy toward Tokyo, attempting to stem an ever greater flood of Japanese imports while negotiating for less Japanese restrictions on foreign imports and investments. Unfortunately, the political rather than strategic importance of an industry often determined whether or not the White House would support it. As a result, the White House responded to the burgeoning trade and investment deficit with a series of uncoordinated first-aid measures that stemmed some of the hemorrhaging in some industries like automobiles while allowing others like machine tools to waste away. During the early 1980s, the White House expended enormous resources trying to force Tokyo to grant access to more baseball bats, beef, and oranges while neglecting for years strategic industries like microelectronics, telecommunications, and finance.

Four months after taking office, the Reagan White House dropped its free trade ideal and cut a managed trade agreement with Tokyo over automobiles. The previous year, Japan had surpassed the United States in total automobile production and had captured 25 per cent of America's market. America's automakers were losing billions of dollars, shedding hundreds of thousands of related jobs, and seemed on the verge of collapse. After several months of negotiations, Tokyo announced on May 1 that it would restrict its automobile shipments to the United States for the next three years to 1.67 million vehicles annually. Tokyo raised its VER to 1.8 million units in 1985 and the following year to 2.3 million units. The VER benefited Japanese as well as American automakers since the limited supply meant they could raise prices at the expense of American consumers. If the White House had imposed a tariff rather than a quota, it would have not only saved America's automobile industry but diverted profits from Japan's automakers to America's treasury.

America's machine tool industry was not as lucky. On May 3, 1982, Houdaille Industries filed a petition with the U.S. Trade Representative for relief against Japan's sustained dumping assault and trade barriers which had devastated America's industry. Houdaille's request was quite modest; it simply asked the White House to revoke the tax credit for Japanese machine tools. The petition sparked a White House battle between the economic theorists and realists. The realists lost. On April 22, 1983, Reagan rejected Houdaille's petition. Houdaille shut down its machine tool division the following year.

By 1985, Japanese firms had captured 85 per cent of America's numerically controlled machine-tool market, half the total market, and surpassed the United States in total production. Only then did the Reagan administration finally accept economic realist arguments that machine tools were a strategic industry whose loss would weaken national security. The White House subsequently negotiated a VER with Tokyo which rolled back Japan's market share to 50 per cent. But this agreement was too little, too late; Japanese dumping and protection had already bankrupted most American machine tool makers.

The same year the White House rejected Houdaille's petition, it championed Harley Davidson's for relief from massive dumping by Japanese motorcycle producers. To the surprise of many, the Reagan White House accepted the petition and imposed temporary tariff hikes on Japan's producers. Harley recovered its viability within three years and actually asked the White House to rescind the tariffs a year early. Harley Davidson's turnaround is a good example of a firm capitalizing on a respite from foreign dumping to revamp itself.

Over three decades, America's television industry had been systematically destroyed by a combination of Japanese neomercantilism, U.S. business lethargy, and Washington's indifference. MITI targeted television during the early 1960s and soon Japanese firms were dumping televisions in the United States and driving American firms out of business. By the early 1980s, only Zenith still produced televisions, and clung to a tiny market sliver. The Reagan White House administered the coup de grace. In a dumping case brought by Zenith which was concluded in 1984, the U.S. Justice Department actually filed a friend of the court brief for the Japanese firms! During the 1986 Matsushita v. Zenith, the Supreme Court justices listened to one American neoclassical economist after another testify on Japan's behalf that because it was "irrational" for a firm to dump its products at a loss, dumping did not occur. The Supreme Court bought these theoretical arguments and threw out Zenith's case against Matsushita, noting the "absence of a plausible motive for the Japanese companies to engage in such a conspiracy which involved substantial profit losses and showed little likelihood of success." Dumping is rational for firms when their home market is closed to competitive imports, they are organized into a cartel, and can thus charge as much from domestic consumers as they wish. Such was the case for Japan's television manufacturers, along with most other Japanese industries.

From the early 1980s, American diplomats negotiated fruitlessly with the Ministry of Posts and Telecommunications (MPT) to open Japan's closed telecommunications market. Motorola filed complaints that its products were systematically excluded through trade barriers and buy-Japanese procurement policies by Nippon Telephone and Telegraph and other public corporations. In 1986, Tokyo finally agreed to procure some components from American telecommunications producers. By the late 1980s, Tokyo's "concession" produced an additional $300 million sales for American telecommunications firms in Japan out of a $450 billion market.

When Reagan entered the White House, America's semiconductor producers still dominated global markets despite the rapid development of Japan's industry during the 1970s; in 1981, they enjoyed a 57 per cent global share while Japan's was 33 per cent.[14] But during the 1980s, Japan's chipmakers surged ahead of their American rivals in sales and types until by 1986 Japan's global market share had doubled to 65 per cent while America's had plummeted to 27 per cent! Japan's microelectronic giants wiped out scores of small, independent American semiconductor firms, including all fourteen producers of the 1K chip, all fifteen of the 4K, all twelve of the 16K, and all but two of the 64K. The Japanese unveiled the 256K RAM before their American rivals and quickly established hegemony by selling them for $2 when they cost $3 to produce. With Japan's chipmakers in hot pursuit, American producers largely abandoned RAMs and retreated into more advanced EPROMs. By 1986, Japan's firms had conquered a dominant market share in EPROMs as well.[15] They succeeded because of classic Japanese neomercantilist policies of import protection, technology acquisition, low-interest capital, cartels, and dumping, all aided by the Reagan White House's high dollar policy and indifference.

The Reagan administration first responded uncertainly to Japan's systematic attempt to wipe out America's semiconductor industry. As it had in other Japanese dumping waves, the Reagan White House initially welcomed Japan's semiconductor assault as "market magic". And America's chipmaker industry itself hesitated to employ an anti-dumping suit against the Japanese because of the cost, time, and uncertainty of winning given the Reagan free trade rhetoric. Eventually, however, as America's semiconductor industry was driven to the brink of destruction, the administration intervened with several protectionist measures.

The first step occurred on July 22, 1982 when the Justice Department launched an anti-trust investigation of Japan's chipmakers. Tokyo responded by proposing a High Technology Working Group to finesse any possibly tough American response with Japanese promises and, if need be, symbolic "concessions." But a decisive American response never came. Clyde Prestowitz, who participated in the negotiations, argues that "if the United States had at this point simply limited the Japanese share of the U.S. market to that obtained by the U.S. companies in Japan, the superiority of the U.S. industry could probably have been maintained. Without the sales volume generally generated in the U.S. market, Japanese costs would have risen and become uncompetitive. But such a policy might have meant temporarily higher prices for consumers and was unthinkable under U.S. free trade doctrine."[16] The much ballyhooed Semiconductor Agreement of November 1982 resulted simply in the collection of statistics on the trade – Japan's dumping continued unimpeded. The two sides signed the Second Semiconductor Agreement in November 1983, but it also lacked teeth; MITI promised to "encourage" Japanese firms to use more American chips.

In 1986, America's government and semiconductor industry finally began to unite and move decisively against the Japanese. The White House filed an anti-dumping suit on 256K RAMs, while the industry filed its own on 64K RAMs and EPRONs, and another against Japan's chipmakers under Section 301 of the 1974 U.S. Trade Act unfair trade case. Meanwhile, Tokyo and Washington negotiated an overall agreement to manage the conflict. On July 30, 1986, the two sides concluded the Third Semiconductor Agreement which they officially signed on September 2. Tokyo promised to help U.S. firms sell in Japan, monitor the costs and prices of Japan's chips to the U.S. and third markets, and in a secret side letter agreed to help achieve a 20 per cent American market share in Japan within five years.

Amidst this trade war, on October 24, 1986, Japan's largest computer-maker, Fujitsu, offered to buy Fairchild Semiconductor, but dropped their attempt after Commerce Secretary Malcom Baldrige and Defense Secretary Caspar Weinberger voiced concern that the sale would imperil American national security by making the United States too dependent on Japan for strategic technology. The Japanese cried racism, pointing out that the American-based Fairchild was actually French-owned.

The Fairchild case was highly symbolic of the global tilt in geoeconomic power, strategy, and dynamism. Microelectronic and business genius Robert Noyce founded Fairchild in 1957, and with it America's most dynamic high technology center, Silicon Valley. But Fairchild, like most other American high tech firms, was a free-wheeling, entrepreneurial orphan lacking a powerful family of Japanese-style related manufacturing, research, and financial firms. It simply could not compete against Japan's microelectronic giants which were backed by industrial group behemoths. Noyce later sold out to the French firm which in turn tried to sell out to the Japanese. The fear of Japanese rather than French acquisition reflected not racism but Tokyo's economic superpower compared to Paris' economic weakness.

American sales to Japan remained stagnant despite the semiconductor accord and the yen's doubling in value by early 1987. On January 27, the White House gave Tokyo two months to prove it was in compliance with the agreement. Tokyo refused. On March 27, 1987, Reagan announced retaliatory steps against Japanese semiconductor makers by imposing 300 per cent tariffs on a range of Japanese electronic products including laptop computers and power tools. Although America's market shares continued to stagnate at home and abroad, Reagan backed off from his tough stance by publicly reducing the tariffs as a present to Prime Minister Nakasone during his visit to Washington in June 1987.

The U.S. Semiconductor Industrial Association was not just reluctant to use America's laws, institutions, and courts more vigorously because of the White House's ambivalence towards its plight. American microelectronic producers have become increasingly dependent on Japanese components for their products and operations. Japan's producers continually warn the U.S. firms that any attempt to retaliate against Japanese dumping and protection will provoke a Japanese cut-off of key shipments.

The White House policy on Japan's semiconductor dumping and protectionism, was just as ineffective as its policies toward other cases of Japanese neomercantilism. The reason, as Prestowitz reveals, was that "not realizing that the logic and structure of the Japanese market was against it, the United States kept asking for a market access defined in terms of the nature of the U.S. market, and kept feeling cheated when successive agreements yielded no results. The same situation held true with regard to dumping: U.S. demands that it be halted did not allow for the fact that Japan's industrial structure and competitive dynamics made dumping inevitable."[17]

Aside from the semiconductor pact, Prime Minister Nakasone was usually able to divert President Reagan's attention to geopolitical issues or promises of Japanese economic reforms. In April 1986, on the eve of a summit with Reagan, Nakasone nicely finessed a White House agenda packed with trade conflicts when one of his advisory committees issued the Maekawa Report which called for Japan's "internationalization" (kokusaika), including market openings, switching from export-led to domestic-led growth, and raising

Japan's quality of life. With the Maekawa Report in hand, Nakasone was able to divert the summit from geoeconomic to geopolitical issues. Once safely back in Tokyo, Nakasone said that the Maekawa Report's goals were only ideas that Japan might achieve in some future time.

The Maekawa Report's most important impact was to help popularize the buzz word "internationalization." Although the term was popular during the 1980s and into the 1990s, it meant simply reforming Japan so that its industries could compete even more fiercely in global markets. It was during this same period that Japan's "Nihonjinron" (Japan thesis) writers reached a height of publications and influence in purporting to capture the "uniqueness, purity, and superiority" of Japan's national character and culture, often by severely denigrating other cultures, nationalities, and races.[18] Some of these writers went so far as to advocate openly Tokyo policies that would accelerate America's decline and Japan's ascendance.[19] In a book coauthored with Sony President Morita Akio, LDP politician and popular novelist Ishihara Shintaro advocated that Japan play off Washington and Moscow against each other by withholding high technology from the United States or even giving it to the Soviet Union.[20] Their book's title *The Japan that Can Say No!* was ironic since from 1945 through today Tokyo has been saying "no" either bluntly or by saying "yes" and then refusing to implement free market promises to Washington.

Nakasone himself jolted the relationship on September 22, 1986 when he declared that America's economic problems stemmed from the low intelligence of its black and Hispanic population. Americans protested and Nakasone apologized for his remarks. Yet, Nakasone's beliefs echoed a national perspective. A *Japan Economic Journal* editorial candidly admitted that:

> Deep down, a majority of Japanese people agreed with their prime minister's assessment that the Japanese society is at a "higher level" in certain aspects. The Japanese belief in their own superiority seems to be more deeply ingrained than ever. . . . While the Japanese appear to have been prostrated before America, deep in their heart they have a certain enmity toward Americans. They look down on fellow Asians, but cannot abandon an obligatory feeling of affinity toward them.[21]

Policy Toward Japan: Geopolitical Issues

Japanese remained divided over fears that their security treaty with the United States might entangle them in higher military expenditures or even war, and fears that America's commitment to the defense of Japan and the Far East was weakening. Japanese anxieties that the United States was cutting back its defense commitments to East Asia started with the 1969 Nixon Doctrine, and built with America's unwillingness to stem the communist conquest of South Vietnam, Cambodia, and Laos in 1975, the revolutions in Nicaragua and Iran in 1979, and the Soviet invasion of Afghanistan that December. While those threats seemed far away, increasingly the Soviets tested the Japanese resolve to defend their country: "In 1970, Japanese jet fighters scrambled against approaching Soviet military planes 370 times; in 1976 they scrambled 528 times; in 1982 the frequency had increased to 929 times."[22]

The Reagan White House was determined to rebuild Japan's faith in America's defense commitment, something Tokyo welcomed. Unfortunately for the Japanese, the White House also asked the Japanese for a greater defense contribution. Throughout the 1980s, Washington increasingly pressured Tokyo to increase defense spending, with many Americans pointing out that Japan enjoyed an incredibly cheap if not outright free defense ride with America's nuclear and conventional forces. Japan spent an average 1 per cent of GNP on defense compared to an average 4 per cent for the NATO allies and America's 6 per cent.

Japan's ability to minimize its defense contributions reached a symbolic height during a June 1981 summit when President Reagan and Prime Minister Suzuki issued a communiqué which referred to the bilateral alliance. Japanese politicians and the media immediately denounced the reference. Foreign Minister Ito Masayoshi promptly resigned after taking responsibility for drafting the communiqué. During the same summit, Reagan asked Suzuki to develop Japan's military might to counter its growing Pacific fleet and Backfire Bomber force. Suzuki agreed to defend sea-lanes up to 1,000 miles from Tokyo Bay. After a year of negotiations, the Suzuki administration agreed to augment its F-15 Eagle Fighter force from 100 to 155 and P-3C Orion antisubmarine planes from 45 to 74.

In 1983, Edwin Reischauer, Japan expert and former ambassador to Tokyo, set off a political bombshell when he casually mentioned in an interview that American warships regularly cruise through Japan's waters and dock at its harbors while loaded with nuclear bombs. As with LaRocque's similar declaration a decade earlier, Washington assured Tokyo that it was complying with all bilateral agreements. The political protests eventually subsided.

The Suzuki and Reischauer statements aside, Reagan's presidency coincided partly with the rise of postwar Japan's most pro-defense prime minister, Nakasone Yasuhiro (1982–7). Nakasone's belief that Japan should

contribute more to the Western Alliance was sincere. Yet he found it impossible to do so. Japan's leading bureaucrats and politicians remained committed to the Yoshida Doctrine of neomercantilism and the lightest possible
defense burden. Meanwhile, Japan's Far East neighbors that were so brutally
devastated by Japanese imperialism four decades earlier protested any talk
of a greater Japanese military.

In January 1983, before leaving for a Washington summit, Nakasone secured Cabinet approval of a technology-sharing agreement with the United
States. Then during the summit, the prime minister Nakasone declared that
Japan and the United States shared a common fate (unmei kyodotai) in
which Japan would act as an "unsinkable aircraft carrier." While Nakasone's
words were music to the Reagan administration's military obsessed ears,
they caused an uproar in Tokyo where his phrases evoked images of the
wartime alliance with Nazi Germany and Japan's ultimate defeat after
blindly marching to such images. Nakasone, however, did not repudiate
his words when he returned home. Instead, his Midterm Defense Program
(fiscal year 1986–90), approved in September 1985, launched a build up
in air defense, command, control, communications, and intelligence (3CI),
and coordination among the three military branches. These budget increases
broached the psychologically important 1 per cent of GNP defense spending
level – 1.004 per cent.

Ironically, although Japan has contributed very little in money or manpower to the western alliance since the 1950s, the United States has co-
produced with Japan a range of advanced aircraft and other weapons rather
than simply exporting those products to Japan from American factories.
Coproduction has enabled the Japanese to develop cheaply a vast range
of products and technologies and enjoy wealth and jobs that it might not
otherwise have achieved. While, because of low economies of scale, it costs
Japan two to three times more than the United States to produce advanced
fighter jets, the skills, technologies, and eventual wealth acquired more than
make up the initial investment. For example, Japan used the F-15 breaking
system for its Shinkansen bullet train.

In 1987, Washington and Tokyo locked horns over Japan's plans to build
its next generation fighter-jet, the FSX, without American help. The Reagan
administration agreed in October 1987 that Tokyo could develop the FSX
from America's F-16 on its own. Affected American corporations and politicians protested that Tokyo should buy F-16s at one-third the price of developing its own advanced version. The Reagan White House reluctantly
entered bitter negotiations with Tokyo for a more equitable arrangement.
A deal was signed in November 1988 in which Tokyo agreed to concede

40 per cent of the FSX's development work to American firms, but would retain 100 per cent of the production. Congress rejected the agreement and maintained that the United States should have a significant share of production as well as development. After another half year of bargaining, the two sides finally signed an agreement on April 28, 1989 in which American firms would enjoy 40 per cent of both development and production, American technology transferred would be kept secret, and some Japanese technology would be transferred to the United States. This was perhaps the first agreement with Japan of the postwar era in which the United States seemed to gain as much as it gave away.

While eagerly accepting American technology, the Japanese have adamantly refused to part with any of their own. Japan's ability to leapfrog the United States in one high technology field after another sparked a White House determination to get access to Japanese technologies useful for military purposes. For years, the Reagan White House begged Tokyo to allow the foreign licensing of Japan's "dual use" technology. Tokyo denied these requests since most Japanese technology was now superior to America's, and it did not want American firms to enjoy the same sort of free or cheap access to technology that its own firms enjoyed from the United States. The official reason for these denials was the Japanese Constitution's Article 9.

During the mid 1980s, in addition to the FSX deal, three landmark agreements expressed the White House policy on military technology cooperation with Tokyo: the 1983 Exchange of Notes on the Transfer of Japanese Military Technologies, the 1984 Report of the Defense Science Board Task Force on Industry-to-Industry International Armaments Cooperation, and the 1988 U.S.–Japan Science and Technology Cooperation Agreement. Of the three, the 1983 agreement seemed to be the most important since it allowed for the transfer of dual use technology which could be applied to both military and civilian products, and established the Joint Military Technology Commission (JMTC) to facilitate transfers. The JMTC first met in November 1984, and by May 1985 the Pentagon had submitted a list of technologies it hoped to acquire. To Washington's disappointment, Tokyo struck various technologies off the list for various reasons. To date, Japan has transferred only three relatively minor technologies to the United States.

In 1987, Reagan announced that he would share his SDI or Star Wars anti-ICBM technology with American allies, including Japan, if they contributed their own finance, expertise, and technology to develop key areas of his scheme. Tokyo agreed to join but contributed little to SDI. Starting in November 1988, the Pentagon began granting money to Japanese firms to develop specific technologies related to SDI.

Ironically, the same year Reagan invited Japanese participation in SDI, it was revealed that a Japanese firm had licensed a vital technology to a foreign power – the Soviet Union! Toshiba Machine had sold advanced technology to the Soviet Union which would enable them to run their nuclear submarines more quietly, thus giving Moscow an advantage that would cost the United States an estimated $30–40 billion to overcome. Congress initially responded with indignation. A bill appeared that would have banned not only Toshiba Machine but the entire Toshiba group from selling in the United States, an action that might have bankrupted that Japanese corporate giant. Toshiba launched a $10 million lobbying offensive that succeeded in watering the bill down to three years of restricted sales for Toshiba Machine rather than the entire Toshiba group.

A growing chorus of senators and representatives had been protesting what they argued were the White House's technology give-aways to Tokyo while Japan enjoyed ever widening trade and investment surpluses with the United States. They warned that the result would be a "boomerang effect" in which Japanese firms would use the technology gained from SDI and FSX agreements to surge beyond their American rivals in both consumer and military products. Revelations of Toshiba Machine's violation of COCOM rules by selling advanced military technology to Moscow strengthened those who argued that the Japanese could not be trusted. The Toshiba sale was only the most notorious. Japanese firms also sold a dry dock to Moscow that when installed in Vladivostok was used for Soviet aircraft carriers.

America's trade problems peaked in 1987 when it suffered a $60 billion deficit with Japan out of a $172 billion total trade deficit. If the economists are right and there is a loss of 20,000 jobs for every billion dollars of a trade deficit, then Japan's trade surplus cost the United States 1,200,000 jobs. Yet, despite these figures, it was Japanese rather than Americans who were most bitter over the trade conflicts. One 1987 survey indicated that only 19 per cent of Americans thought relations were unfriendly while 55 per cent of Japanese thought so. Although most Americans continued to harbor positive feelings toward Japan despite the immense and growing trade surplus, there was a mirror image in which about three-quarters of citizens from each country thought blame for the problem lay on the other side of the Pacific; 73 per cent of Americans thought Japan was not doing enough to correct the trade surplus while 77 per cent of Japanese thought that Americans were blaming Japan for their own domestic problems.[23]

GEORGE BUSH, 1989–93

Policymaking and Implementation

Few men have ever assumed the presidency with better resumés. George Bush served as a Texas congressman, Republican Party Chair, ambassador to China, CIA Director, and vice-president. Strong patrons had helped him land each of those jobs. Nonetheless, once in office Bush was a doer, a hands-on operator who saw his professional duties as a series of missions accepted and accomplished.

Bush's forte was foreign policy – by his own admission he cared little for the domestic stuff. He assembled a powerful foreign policy troika: Jim Baker as Secretary of State, Brent Scowcroft as National Security Advisor, and Jim Cheney as Defense Secretary. Foreign policymaking in the Bush White House was largely a collegial affair among these men and their advisors.

But whether it was foreign or domestic policy, the Bush White House was criticized for lacking a comprehensive global view within which to analyze and act upon America's interests in a rapidly changing world – the "vision thing" as Bush derisively called it. Throughout his career, lacking a visionary anchor, Bush shifted with the political tides, from a right-wing Goldwater Republican when he first ran for office in the early 1960s, to a moderate Republican from the late 1960s through his defeat for the Republican presidential nomination in 1980, to Reaganite Republican as vice-president, and then the promoter of a "kinder gentler America" as president. Vision aside, what Bush did have was an eastern establishment patrician conception of noblesse oblige modeled on his father's big business and senate careers.

Between the 1980 and 1992 campaigns, Bush had to fight off a "wimp image" originally hurled at him by the Republican right wing. How the youngest navy combat pilot in World War II, survivor of fifty-eight missions, and winner of four medals for courage could be called a wimp is easy to understand in the context of American political culture. Mass media master Ronald Reagan was a tough act to follow. Given Reagan's decades of Hollywood and television training, anyone would be considered colorless in comparison. Which was more "presidential" in the eyes of most Americans, the real war hero Bush or celluloid hero Reagan? Add to that a concerted right wing campaign to castigate Bush's supposed "liberalism" and "wimpishness" (the two are considered synonymous by the right), and you have a negative national image.

How did these unfair accusations affect his policies? Many argue that they contributed to a deep need to prove himself in the eyes of others, either by loyally following or, rarely, boldly striking out on his own.[24] Mostly he followed. Although during the 1980 campaign George Bush had dismissed Reaganomics as "voodoo economics," he cheerfully converted after Reagan named him vice-president. Through his eight years as vice president he stood quietly by as the national debt quadrupled, economic growth slowed, and real income plunged. After winning the presidency in November 1988, Bush felt he remained beholden to the political extreme right rather than center, and thus steadfastly maintained the Reagan agenda. Tossing fiscal conservatism to the winds, he demanded repeatedly that Americans read his lips: "No new taxes!"

Policy Priorities

During Bush's 1991 "State of the Union" address, he proclaimed a "New World Order" in which "diverse nations are drawn together in common cause to achieve the universal aspirations of Mankind: peace and security, freedom and the rule of law." Revolutionary changes in international relations occurred during his watch: the Soviet empire and communism crumbled and fragile democracies emerged from the rubble, representatives of 178 countries met at Rio de Janeiro for an "Earth Summit" to debate and vote on treaties that addressed such catastrophic manmade phenomena as the greenhouse effect, destruction of the world's forests, and elimination of biodiversity, and finally America continued its socioeconomic decline relative to its major geoeconomic rivals.

Although praised as a foreign policy president, Bush's record on serving American interests abroad as this New World Order emerged was actually quite mixed. More often than not, the Bush White House tried to slow rather than shape in America's favor the revolutionary changes occurring around the world. Bush and his advisors essentially remained Cold Warriors in the New World Order they so boldly proclaimed. The problem was that "the world they all knew so well was collapsing around them, and, as it did so, the Bush team too often seemed to be a half-step behind the march of history."[25]

Bush's instinct was to help preserve rather than topple the Soviet empire and communism, and thus he supported the reactionaries rather than reformers. For the first three years of his administration, Bush coldshouldered reformer and anti-communist Boris Yeltsin, the president of the Russian Republic, and threw his support behind Soviet president Mikhail Gorbachev. During the August 1991 coup attempt against Gorbachev, Bush first seemed fatalistic about the military faction taking over and blind to Yeltsin's heroic exertions atop the tank before the Russian Parliament. After the coup was defeated and communist hardliners imprisoned, it was clear to most analysts that the political tide had shifted toward Yeltsin and the reformers. Yet Bush continued to support Gorbachev's attempts to keep the empire together. In September 1991, Bush flew to Kiev, Ukraine to stand alongside Gorbachev and urge the Ukrainian people to remain in the Soviet Union. Bush continued to support Gorbachev and disdain Yeltsin until the Soviet president was finally swept from power. Fortunately for humanity, Bush's policy of propping up the communist hardliners failed. Historians and the public overlooked Bush's bizarre policy amidst the celebration of the end of communism and the Soviet empire.

Why would Bush consistently act to delay what most Americans and other freedom-loving people around the world had dreamt of for decades? To Bush, the Soviet Union was not an evil empire but the source of political stability and peace for hundreds of nationalities who otherwise might well war against each other. There may have also been the fear that without a Cold War, the reason for being of Bush, his fellow cold warriors, and America's military industrial complex would diminish drastically. Without a visionary compass, the New World Order could be a scary and disorienting place to be.

Bush's "prudence" also got him into trouble in the Persian Gulf. The Reagan White House had tilted toward President Hussein and Iraq in its eight year war against Iran. The tilt had a sound geopolitical rationale – by propping up the weaker belligerent the war would continue to drain the finance, energy, and manpower of the two Persian Gulf states most capable of disrupting the region. The Iraq–Iran war, however, ended in 1988. Yet the Bush White House continued to supply the Hussein regime with finance, high technology, food, and political support up to the very day Iraq invaded Kuwait!

The president's diplomacy was brilliant from August 5, 1990 when he declared Iraq's invasion "will not stand" until February 19, 1991 when he ended the "one hundred hour" ground war. Over those seven months he forged a forty-two nation military alliance, received United Nations and Congressional sanction for the use of force, supervised a war which drove Iraqi forces from Kuwait with minimal allied casualties, and, through the UN, imposed a peace on Iraq which stripped it of its nuclear, chemical, and biological war fighting abilities. And yet the man Bush reviled as a "Hitler" remains firmly in power.

The Bush White House was reactionary in other foreign policy issues such as the Earth Summit, fumbling in places like Panama where ousting the

Noriega dictatorship cost the United States around $6 billion for invading and then reconstructing that country, and inadequate in promoting progressive American policies toward the North American Free Trade Agreement (NAFTA) and the GATT Uruguay Round. The White House's only unsullied successes were the START I and II nuclear weapons reduction and Conventional Forces in Europe (CFE) treaties which helped dismantle the Soviet military machine. Bush was not prudent or wise in foreign policy, he was just enormously lucky.

Despite its mixed record, at least Bush's foreign policy team was united and collegial. In contrast, like the Reagan White House, Bush's domestic policymakers were bitterly divided between ideologues and realists over what policies best served the nation's interests. And, as with Reagan, the Bush White House ideologues generally dominated.

White House Chief of Staff John Sununu, Budget Director Richard Darman, and Council of Economic Advisors Chair Michael Boskin led the neoclassical economic charge against rational American industrial, trade, and technology policies with the theoretical argument that government is the problem rather than the solution, and that tax-cuts are the cure-all for the country's socioeconomic ills. Meanwhile Commerce Secretary Robert Mosbacher and Science Advisor D. Allan Bromley desparately tried to defend and expand existing programs on the practical grounds that these investments paid off in greater American wealth and jobs, and that private industry needed assistance before it would invest in such costly technologies with uncertain long-term payoffs. After all, they argued, Tokyo successfully developed Japan's economy from rags to riches with systematic long-term industrial, trade, and technology policies. The economic realists were reinforced by bipartisan groups of congressmen led by Senator Al Gore and high tech think tanks like the National Advisory Committee on Semiconductors and Economic Policy Institute.

The economic theorists won out. Even more so than the Reagan White House, Bush's shied from any action that smacked of industrial policy. For example, the Bush White House cut funding for such Defense Advanced Research Projects Agency (DARPA) projects as HDTV, X-ray lithography, robots, and computer-aided equipment which could be used for consumer as well as military uses.

Likewise, the theorists fought those who promoted an American trade policy based on reciprocity. In 1988, Congress passed and Reagan signed the Omnibus Trade Act which granted the president ever greater powers to combat unfair trade practices. The bill's most controversial tenet was Super 301 under which the president yearly designates those countries which discriminate against American businesses and gives them eighteen months to withdraw their neomercantilist policies before the United States can retaliate with tariffs or quotas. The problem with "Super 301" is that it violates GATT's "most-favored-nation" (MFN) principle which forbids discriminating against anyone, even an unfair trader. Under GATT, a nation can either retaliate against a neomercantilist country by raising trade barriers against all countries or else must abstain from any action.

Policy Toward Japan: Geoeconomic Issues

When Bush settled into the Oval Office, American–Japanese relations remained as acrimonious as ever. The trade and investment deficits soared while Tokyo continued to stonewall talks on a range of issues. By inclination, Bush was among those who favored the old policy of giving Japan free access to American markets, technology, finance, and military protection and tolerating Japanese neomercantilism, in return for American bases in Japan. Yet rising political pressures forced him on occasion to act tough.

Somewhat apologetically, on May 25, 1989, the White House cited Japan, along with India and Brazil, as an "unfair trader" in satellites, supercomputers, and wood products under Section 301 of the 1988 Trade Act. Certainly there were dozens of other products which could be identified under Section 301. After bitter debate, the White House had settled on those three industries for fear of embarrassing Tokyo should a longer list be submitted. Negotiations were to begin by June 20. Tokyo replied by announcing it would ignore the ruling and would not negotiate under duress.

The seemingly tougher White House line was reinforced in early June 1989 when Ambassador Michael Armacost arrived in Japan and immediately established a diplomatic style and substance completely different from his predecessor, Mike Mansfield. Armacost described himself as the embassy's senior commercial officer and called on Japan to open its import and investment markets. He was also critical of the aggressive tone of Japan's mass media which routinely describes U.S.–Japan economic conflicts in warlike terms in which one side's gain is the other's loss. The ambassador did not hesitate to point out inconsistencies in Tokyo's positions such as maintaining that Japan's markets are the world's most open then claiming that a "unique" Japan did not have to restructure its economy along free market lines.

That summer, Washington and Tokyo finessed the deadlock over the three designated industries by agreeing to embark on a Structural Impediments Initiative (SII) in which both countries would identify and remove policies which inhibited free markets. American negotiators identified six goals for reforming Japan's economy: (1) prices determined by free rather than managed markets; (2) free land markets; (3) free markets for the distribution system; (4) less savings and investment and more consumption; (5) the end of exclusionary business practices; (6) and the breakup of the keiretsu oligopolies. Tokyo in turn supplied its own list of structural reforms for the United States which included calls for more savings and investments and less debt and short-term business outlooks.

In the SII negotiations, the White House attempted to enlist Japanese consumers behind their attempts to restructure Japan's markets by publicizing the lower prices and higher quality of life that would ensue. For example, during a September 1989 visit to Tokyo, U.S. Deputy Trade Representative Linn Williams stated: "We are not here just to help the U.S. The Structural Impediments Initiative is . . . also a great benefit to the Japanese people." Since 1945, Japan's consumer price index has increased twice as fast as the wholesale price index, resulting in vast windfalls for Japan's manufacturers and their distribution chains. An October 1989 study was released showing that of 122 products sold in both countries Japanese payed prices an average 41.7 per cent higher than Americans. Through import barriers and dumping, Japanese corporations have captured global markets in hundreds of products, including televisions and automobiles, yet still shamelessly gouge Japanese consumers: Japanese subcompacts cost 64 per cent more in Tokyo than New York and color televisions 100 per cent more.[26] Despite the yen's doubling after 1985, Japanese consumer prices remained exorbitant and Japan's vast trade surplus only slightly reduced. The reasons for these price discrepancies are Japanese price-fixing through cartels and other collusive practices along with government trade barriers. Tokyo countered by accelerating its already massive public relations campaign that claimed Japan's markets were the world's most open and foreigners did not sell more because their goods were inferior and they did not try hard enough.

The respective public relations campaigns by Washington and Tokyo may have had a greater effect in mobilizing their own citizens than the other side. Certainly, Washington's attempts to show the Japanese how exploited they were did not spark a consumer revolt against their oppressors, nor did most Americans fall for Tokyo's blatant propaganda that Japan was a free market paradise. A July 7–11 1989 *Businessweek/*Harris poll of 1,250 adults indicated that most Americans were very concerned about Japan's huge and intractable trade and investment supluses and neomercantilist policies.[27] Japan's huge trade surplus was deemed a very serious problem by 69 per cent of Americans and somewhat serious by a further 23 per cent, while dismissed as either not very serious or not serious at all by 4 per cent and 2 per cent, respectively. While 68 per cent of Americans judged Japanese trade barriers as the major reason for Japan's trade surplus, 38 per cent and 57 per cent also cited the inferior quality and higher prices of American goods as also important factors. Most Americans took a hard-line on how to reduce Japan's surplus with 79 per cent calling for specific import quotas for American goods in Japan, 61 per cent higher tariffs and 69 per cent quotas on Japanese imports, and 59 per cent on restricting the outflow of American technology to Japan. Furthermore, a plurality of respondents, 45 per cent, thought American-made products were superior in quality while 38 per cent thought Japanese products were better, 4 per cent thought they were equal, and only 16 per cent argued the rather sensible response that it depended on the product. Exactly two-thirds said they would be willing to pay more for an American product if it was of comparable quality to a Japanese product. Finally, 68 per cent of Americans viewed Japan's economic threat and only 22 per cent thought the Soviet military threat as the most serious foreign threat to the United States. Yet despite these worries, a vast majority of Americans continued to deeply admire Japan and the Japanese, with 73 per cent favorable and 24 per cent unfavorable toward Japan as a nation, and 80 per cent favorable and 16 per cent unfavorable toward the Japanese as people.

If one nation had ill-feelings or "bashed" the other, it was the Japanese against the Americans. A May–June 1990 *New York Times*/CBS poll revealed that 68 per cent of Japanese thought Americans were scapegoating Japan for problems rooted in the United States, while only 26 per cent thought Japanese protectionism was to blame for America's trade deficit. Only 66 per cent of Japanese had mostly friendly views of the United States while 30 per cent had unfriendly views.[28]

It was against this background of rising animosities that President Bush and Prime Minister Kaifu met for their first summit on September 2, 1989. Kaifu skilfully finessed Bush's calls for resolving bilateral trade problems by claiming Japan's markets were already the world's most open and calling for a "global partnership" to address environmental problems and Third World debt. As with so many other summits, this one ended with the usual platitudes of partnership.

U.S. Trade Representative Carla Hills was dispatched to Tokyo in October to push American views on SII and several other negotiations. During the congressional hearings for the approval of her nomination, Hills had earned the Japanese sobriquet "iron lady" for her vow to use a crow-bar if necessary to prise open Japan's closed markets. Her first visit to Japan on October 13 and 14, 1989 disappointed those who hoped she would be as tough as her rhetoric. Rather than blast Japanese neomercantilism, Hills instead adopted Tokyo's position by denouncing "managed" or "results" solutions to America's trade deficit with Japan, and even backed away from insisting upon a previous Tokyo promise to guarantee American chipmakers a 20 per cent market share. She did admit that Japanese trade barriers impeded American exports and cited a MITI decision to block baby-bottles because it included both the metric and English measurement systems. MITI claimed the two measurements would confuse Japanese mothers and hence the ban. America's trade realists criticized Hills for not arguing that Tokyo already managed its trade and investment relations with the United States, and for using baby-bottles as the example out of all the products that Japanese discriminated against.

That same month, the relationship was shaken by the translation of *The Japan That Can Say No!*, a book by Sony Chairman Morita Akio and LDP political leader Ishihara Shintaro which blasted the United States and claimed that trade conflicts were rooted in American racism rather than Japanese neomercantilism. Ishihara urged Japanese to use their high technology advantages to play off the Americans and Soviets and better extract advantages from both – as if that year's $49 billion trade surplus with the United States and American defense commitments were not enough. The book often presented contradictory information and poorly reasoned arguments. Morita, for example, claimed the standard line that Japan's markets were the world's most open while offering continual examples of how Japan's government and business collude at home and abroad.

On November 2, 1989, one of Japan's largest daily newspapers, the *Asahi Shimbun*, broke the usual cartel of silence on such practices and reported that Fujitsu had won supercomputer bids in Japan by offering bids of anywhere from three-quarters of a cent to $71! Reports followed that NEC submitted similar low bids. Fearing that the revelations would fuel Washington attempts to curb Japanese neomercantilism, Tokyo promised to investigate. The White House, however, not only did not use the opportunity to increase the heat on Tokyo for results, it did not even comment on the revelations!

A long-standing dispute between the United States and Japan was settled on January 23, 1989 when ninety-nine Japanese firms agreed to pay $32.6 million in compensation for rigged bids which discriminated against American firms. The agreement resulted from a finding in December 1988 by Japan's Fair Trade Commission that 140 Japanese construction firms had colluded to rig bids between April 1984 and September 1987 for projects at the American Yokosuka Naval Base on Tokyo Bay. The U.S. Justice Department then sued on behalf of American construction firms those Japanese firms implicated in the bid-rigging for $35 million in damages. It was a minor victory in the war Tokyo had waged against American and other foreign construction firms by denying them access to Japan and dumping bids in foreign markets.

In December 1989, Tokyo made its annual announcement about retaining the 2.3 million unit export quota on Japanese automobiles. The quota was solely a public relations ploy since it has no effect on sales of Japanese cars in the United States. Japan's share of America's automobile market has risen to nearly 30 per cent despite the quotas. Japan's automakers fill their quotas with expensive automobiles and sidestep them altogether by building automobiles with mostly Japanese components in the United States. That year transplants accounted for 22 per cent of all cars built in the United States. Honda President Kume Tadashi admitted in January 1990 that: "As a practical matter, [the quotas] will make no difference, none at all. But at this point I think it would be politically very, very difficult to back away from the quotas."[29] The statement shows how easily Washington is influenced by PR gestures rather than substance in its relationship with Tokyo.

The political and economic clout of Japan's automakers in the United States became clear on February 22, 1990 when U.S. Trade Representative Hills announced that she would fight to ensure that Japanese transplants gained entry to European Community markets. Hills stated that: "We would be remiss if we didn't stress how strongly we feel that a Japanese nameplant car made in our country is an American car. . . . If it's made here, it's an American car, and it ought not to be subjected to any kind of restriction."[30] Hills even threatened to use the 1988 Trade Act to help Japan's automakers gain greater access to European markets.

In the first half of 1990, the Bush administration initiated several "get tough" trade measures. On February 17, Federal officials opened investigations on tax underpayments by several Japanese corporations. These investigations did not begin to bear fruit for another two years when in November 1992 the Internal Revenue Service (IRS) announced that foreign firms owed $32 billion because of transfer pricing schemes. Yet it never followed up on the report by demanding repayment.

A much publicized summit in Palm Springs on March 3–4, 1990 failed to break the deadlock between the two countries. Although Bush pressed Kaifu hard for trade concessions, the prime minister merely made vague promises of facilitating Japan's "deregulation," and "internationalization." The two leaders agreed to act as partners in resolving global problems. Kaifu's promises allowed the Bush administration to avoid sanctions against Japan in supercomputers, satellites, and wood products which were threatened the previous year under Section 301 of the 1988 Trade Act.

On April 5, 1990, Tokyo and Washington signed an SII accord in which

Japan would spend more on public projects, open the distribution system to foreign businesses, stiffen anti-trust enforcement and penalties, change tax policies to open more land for commercial and residential use, provide import clearance for foreign goods within twenty-four hours, and lessen anti-competitive actions of the industrial groups. Tokyo, however, did not submit any timetables or amounts for any of its promises. The United States, in turn, promised to improve education, and savings and investment, and cut capital costs.

In announcing the deal, Prime Minister Kaifu said it would benefit Japanese consumers but would be difficult to implement and, regardless, would be the last such agreement with the United States. Japanese critics blasted the SII for American interference in Japan's internal affairs and culture. In fact, they had nothing to fear. A year of SII talks between some of the top negotiators on both sides failed to achieve anything beyond promises to enact lists of reforms. The White House message to Japanese that they could buy Japanese goods for half price in America's free markets did not spark the hoped for consumer revolt. On Capitol Hill, Senator Lloyd Bentsen's reaction to the announced deal was typical: "Put me down as a skeptic who's seen too many agreements in which the results did not match the rhetoric." Senator Max Baucus, chairman of the International Trade Subcommittee, stated that "we must judge the success or failure of [SII] . . . by its concrete contribution to expanding U.S. exports to Japan." If exports did not increase, Senator John Heinz warned, the United States should resort to "bottom-line oriented trade." Among many, economist Roger Dornbusch criticized SII for doing "little measurable good" and instead argued for a "results oriented trade policy."[31]

One week later, on April 15, with Japan's corporations firmly in mind, the White House announced that it was considering allowing the Justice Department to file anti-trust suits against the American subsidiaries of foreign firms that engaged in pricefixing, cartels, and other anti-competitive practices. Thus, for the first time, the government would retaliate against foreign firms that damaged American firms' exports or foreign investments.

Yet another contentious issue between the United States and Japan is Tokyo's practice of tying its foreign "aid" to purchases of Japanese goods and services. By one estimate, almost 70 per cent of all Japanese aid is "tied." For decades, American business executives complained that their project bids in the Third World were losing out to the "tied aid" policies of Japan and some other "donors." Yet, Washington had failed repeatedly to fight against the practice.

On May 15, 1990, the White House finally acted by announcing that henceforth it was allocating $500 million of its foreign aid budget to counter such tied aid, and identified Indonesia, Pakistan, the Philippines, and Thailand as the first recipients. Combining funds from the International Development Agency ($100 million), the Export–Import Bank ($100 million), and Loan Guarantee Authority ($300 million), the aid included packages of grants, low-interest loans, and export credits tied to purchases of American goods and services. Some in Congress criticized the Bush program as "peanuts," citing statistics that Japan's tied aid to those four countries alone was $2 billion or four times the White House's entire tied aid budget for the Third World.[32]

Negotiations on other outstanding issues continued to sputter along during 1990 and 1991, culminating with Bush's December 1991 summit with Prime Minister Miyazawa in Tokyo. During the summit, Bush unwittingly achieved memorable symbolic if not substantive results. At a state dinner, Bush vomited on Miyazawa; photos captured the prime minister tenderly holding a prostrate president. Perhaps inhibited by his illness and its embarrassing result, Bush did not press the Japanese on bilateral problems but spoke more of partnership and aid to Russia. It was left to Bush's entourage of twenty-one American corporate executives in manufacturing, finance, and energy, including the presidents of the Big Three automobile firms, to talk tough to their Japanese counterparts.

During the summit, Tokyo promised to "open" its markets to American automobiles, buy an additional $19 billion in American automobile parts, and increase local content for Japanese vehicles assembled in the United States to 70 per cent by 1994. Unlike most previous agreements, the automobile accord specified increases in "non-Japanese U.S. auto parts," thus not allowing Tokyo to include shipments from Japanese plants in the United States back home in any increased "market shares." American negotiators did not push for a genuinely "reciprocal" agreement in which Tokyo would promise to grant vehicle shares equal to the share it enjoyed in the United States. To do so would have meant America's market share in Japan rising from its current 0.5 per cent level to at least 30 per cent.

In this issue, as in so many others, Tokyo outgunned Washington not just in their immediate negotiations but in the United States. Having previously set up factories in Kentucky, Tennessee, Ohio, Indiana, and Illinois, Japan's automakers had acquired vast political clout within America's heartland to pressure Washington to accept any automobile vehicle or parts shipments to Japan regardless of nationality as contributing to the trade accord. There has been no follow through by the Bush or Clinton administrations to ensure Tokyos live up to its auto agreement. The 1992 presidential race soon consumed Bush's attentions – outstanding geoeconomic issues with Japan were placed on the backburners.

Policy Toward Japan: Geopolitical Issues

The collapse of the Soviet empire and communism diminished Washington's rationale for pressuring Tokyo for a larger Japanese defense contribution. But Washington has found other issues in which Tokyo should share a common defense burden.

On August 2, 1990, Iraq invaded Kuwait. President Bush debated with his divided advisors for three days before deciding how best to respond. British Prime Minister Thatcher was decisive in shaping Bush's decision. On August 5, after talking with her, Bush went before the press and announced that the invasion "will not stand" and asserted that the United States would do all in its power to force an Iraqi withdrawal.

The Japanese saw the situation very differently. While alarmed by the Iraqi invasion, Tokyo's initial policy was to adjust Japan's economy to the fait accompli. While Japan was still dependent on the Middle East for 70 per cent of its oil needs, it took only 5.8 per cent of its total imports from Iraq and only 5.9 per cent from Kuwait. In addition, Japan had a 142-day supply of oil, and oil itself accounted for about 70 per cent of the country's total energy needs. So even if all oil exports from those two countries were halted (which would only occur if the western powers resisted Iraq's invasion) Japan could weather the storm. Tokyo thus favored appeasement.

However, on August 5 shortly after Bush's news conference, the United States and European Community announced their embargo of all oil from Iraq and Kuwait, and urged Japan to do the same. Tokyo reluctantly complied. As the White House's attempts to forge an alliance against Iraq and build up forces in Saudi Arabia intensified, Tokyo came under increasing pressure to contribute more. On August 29, Tokyo offered to the alliance 100 medical personnel (of which only seventeen actually served), and two ship and plane loads of supplies (which did not arrive until months later). Preferring to let their western allies bear the financial and military burden, most Japanese were even opposed to these meager efforts. Prime Minister Kaifu had to plead with the Diet to make these contributions in order to avoid "international isolation" (kokusai koritsu kaihi).

The United States and European Community roundly condemned Japan's offer as grossly inadequate. The U.S. Senate unanimously resolved that Tokyo should increase its spending for American forces in Japan, extend its sea-lane defense, purchase an array of American high technology military weapons and equipment, and contribute billions of dollars to the Coalition Bush was steadily building. In late August, Tokyo upped its ante to $4 billion, of which half would go to the Coalition and half in economic aid to front-line states like Turkey, Egypt, and Pakistan. The same day this new package was announced, the House of Representatives voted 370–53 that the United States would withdraw its forces from Japan if Tokyo did not cover all of America's expenses of basing them there. Tokyo grudgingly agreed to cover 50 per cent of the costs. After the bombs began to drop, Congress again criticized Tokyo for sitting on the sidelines. In February, Tokyo announced that it would pay an additional $9 billion.

Americans and Japanese were bitter over how the other addressed the Persian Gulf War. Americans criticized Tokyo for foot-dragging and only contributing when faced with sanctions. Japanese condemned the United States for not appreciating the $9 billion it eventually supplied to the Coalition and additional $4 billion in aid to moderate Muslim states. Once again American and Japanese diplomats, politicians, and publics talked right past each other.

10 Into the Twenty-first Century: Clinton and Beyond, 1993–Future

By 1992, the world as a whole seemed a much better, safer place than just a few years earlier: the Soviet empire, Warsaw Pact, and communism had crumbled; world trade and investments expanded steadily; more countries acquired or strengthened democratic governments; Washington and Moscow signed significant nuclear and conventional arms reduction treaties; international treaties were signed to combat environmental crises like the greenhouse effect, loss of biodiversity, and ozone depletion that threaten to eventually destroy the planet.

Yet, in stark contrast, as the United States entered the 1990s, it seemed mired in an ever-worsening vicious cycle of socioeconomic decay exacerbated by political gridlock. Between 1981 and 1993, America's national debt more than quadrupled from $976 billion to $4.2 trillion; economic growth was lower than any decade since the 1930s; real wages plummeted; the trade deficit, particularly with Japan, worsened; crime, health care, racial conflict, homelessness, drug abuse, unwed mothers, education, and despair all remained much worse than in other democratic industrial countries.

And all along the politicians seemed capable only of attacking each other rather than these problems. Washington gridlock resulted from several interrelated reasons: a succession of hands-off presidents whose domestic initiatives consisted largely of calls for tax cuts and vetos (Bush alone vetoed forty-six bills) of reform measures, partisan politics, sophisticated electronic means of inciting affected special interest groups to mobilize against reforms, and a growing public apathy that the system was hopelessly stalled. Although Reagan had promised that his policies would bring "morning in America," by 1992 many Americans spelled that "mourning." A June 1992 Gallup poll revealed that 84 per cent were dissatisfied with the way things were going in the country while a CBS/*New York Times* poll indicated that 85 per cent thought the political system needed fundamental change.[1]

"Change" was the 1992 campaign theme of two of the three presidential candidates. While President Bush ran on a "Read my lips, no new taxes!" theme, his challengers, Bill Clinton and Ross Perot, campaigned against Washington's gridlock and Reaganomics' disastrous legacy. Clinton advocated such reforms as boosting economic growth by targeting strategic industries, technologies, and infrastructure, cutting government spending and debt, and boosting trade by confronting foreign neomercantilism. Perot's vision was as radical as it was simple; he called for eliminating the budget deficit within four years by spending cuts and taxes, including a 50 cent tax per gallon on gasoline. Sixty-two per cent of voters responded to the "change" theme: Clinton received 43 per cent and Perot 19 per cent of the vote, compared to only 38 per cent for Bush. Clinton recaptured this theme on the night of his November 3, 1992 electoral victory: "This election is a clarion call for our country to face the challenges of the end of the Cold War and the beginning of the next century."

POLICYMAKING AND IMPLEMENTATION

On January 5, 1993, William Jefferson Clinton became the first elected post-Cold War president. To the office, he brought a mix of strengths and weaknesses distinct from any of his predecessors. In many ways, Clinton himself symbolizes the changes he wants to transform America. As the first president born after World War II, Clinton came of age in the tumultuous, affluent, and morally ambivalent 1960s. Like former vice-president Dan Quayle and defense secretary Dick Cheney, along with his Senate nemesis Newt Gingrich, Clinton succeeded in getting a draft deferment. Unlike those Republicans who supported America's war in Vietnam but, for whatever reasons, refused to go themselves, Clinton was no hypocrite – he actively protested against the war. He just as fervently supported Johnson's Great Society legislation. A quarter century later, he still believes that policies can make things better or worse, and that government is essential to the process. But rather than an "old fashioned liberal," he now describes himself a "New Democrat" who would transform the country by slashing the national debt, converting welfare to workfare, and investing in education, infrastructure, and strategic industries and technologies.

Bill Clinton is often compared to his hero, John F. Kennedy. There are some resemblances. After Kennedy, Clinton is the youngest man ever elected to the presidency. Like Kennedy, Clinton is highly intelligent, self-confident, open-minded, and energetic. Clinton was a first-rate student, having graduated from Georgetown University, enjoyed a Rhodes scholarship at Oxford, and earned a Yale law degree. At 32 years old, he became Arkansas' youngest governor and served three terms. As an extrovert and people person, Clinton has a gift for consensus building and persuading fence sitters to take up his causes. Clinton is a genuine "Great Communicator." Unlike

Reagan, Clinton knows that communication involves not just the ability to deliver a speech, but is an endless dialectic of critical listening, thinking, and responding.

No president has demonstrated a broader, more sophisticated understanding of how a modern economy and society work than Clinton. In his statements, Clinton continually acknowledges the interrelationship of the array of socioeconomic crises facing the country, and the subsequent need for comprehensive policies to overcome those crises. A true "policy wonk," Clinton as governor and president has immersed himself in the intricacies and options of policymaking. He has attempted to create a collegial style among his policy team in which he delegates appropriate tasks while trying to monitor each policy and make the ultimate decisions. The Clinton White House is unique in that his wife Hillary and Vice-President Al Gore are his two closest policy advisors. Clinton put the First Lady in charge of developing the administration's health care policy. Gore is an expert on defense, the economy, and the environment, among other subjects, and has taken the lead in such policies as streamlining government and nurturing Russian democracy.

Yet this system and Clinton's leadership have been harshly criticized. Perhaps the most damning accusation is that Clinton tends to defer decisions on many key foreign and domestic issues.[2] As historian Gary Wills put it, Clinton "adapts so well to the present that he disregards any bearing it may have on the past or the future. . . . He is a superb tactician but a terrible strategist. He cannot connect one engagement with another."[3] Wills goes on to argue that Clinton's extroversion and need to be liked undermines effective leadership: "Clinton is an omnidirectional placater. He wants to satisfy everyone which is a surefire way of satisfying no one."

It is a good thing that Clinton is a quick study, because his foreign policy experience before winning the presidency was limited. During his first year, his foreign policy team consisted of Carter White House veteran Warren Christopher as Secretary of State, congressional military affairs expert Les Aspin as Defense Secretary, and Foreign Service officer Anthony Lake as National Security Advisor. While all three are highly intelligent and competent men, they were considered policy managers rather than bold innovators. Aspin took the blame for mistakes made in Somalia and resigned in December 1993. He was replaced in January 1994 by Defense Undersecretary William Perry.

Clinton assembled an outstanding geoeconomic policy team by eschewing economic theorists and packing his administration with first rate political economists like Laura Tyson as Economic Advisor and Robert Reich as Labor Secretary, along with such renowned congressional experts as

George Bentsen as Treasury Secretary and Leon Panetta as Office of Management Budget head, and Democratic party political operators like Ron Brown as Secretary of Commerce and Mickey Kantor as U.S. Trade Representative. Clinton created an Economic Security Council (ESC) to grapple with geoeconomic issues to balance the National Security Council emphasis on geopolitics. The ESC is chaired by Robert Rubin and includes Bentsen, Christopher, Kantor, Reich, Tyson, and Brown.

The president's ambitious policy agenda ultimately depends on congressional approval. The 1992 Congress reflected the national desire for change – no Congress since 1948 had more new members. Of the 110 freshmen representatives, 63 were Democrats and 47 Republicans. While the Democrats continued to enjoy solid majorities in both houses, Clinton could rely automatically on their votes. The majority leaders of the House and Senate, Richard Gephardt and George Mitchell, respectively, rallied the Democratic troops on most issues, although Gephardt was against NAFTA. Nonetheless, two of Clinton's most important initiatives, the debt reduction and NAFTA bills, squeaked by in Congress with the narrowest of margins.

While Clinton has created many of his own problems, they are exacerbated by historical and cultural forces far beyond his control. As cynicism deepens across the nation, presidential honeymoons with Congress, the press, and public grow correspondingly shorter. Increasing numbers of Americans simultaneously demand near instant results from the very politicians they dismiss as hopelessly corrupt and inefficient. No president has had a shorter honeymoon than Clinton. In January 1992, 74 per cent of Americans had a favorable opinion of him and 84 per cent thought he was off to a good start. Support declined precipitously over such controversies as his support for gays in the military, the aborted candidacies of Zoe Baird and Lani Guanier, a $200 haircut on the L.A airport tarmac, the announcement that revised OMB debt projections for fiscal 1994 from $237 billion to $307 billion meant that he had to scuttle his promised middle class tax cut, and continual harsh bashing by Republicans, the Christian Right, extreme right radio jockeys, and the mass media. Critical television jokes about Clinton during his first three months were five times greater than Bush's first three months four years earlier. By May, polls indicated that public support for Clinton had dropped to around 40 per cent. *Los Angeles Times* polls indicated those who consider his economic package "bold and innovative" had dropped from 50 per cent to 28 per cent from February to May while those who pegged it "tax and spend" rose from 35 per cent to 50 per cent.[4]

Clinton's popularity and the political gridlock steadily worsened. The 1994 November mid-term election resulted in a devastating defeat for the

Democratic Party. The Republicans captured both houses of Congress for the first time in forty years. Republicans Bob Dole became majority leader of the Senate and Newt Gingerich leader of the House. With their overwhelming congressional power, the Republicans have since attempted to implement another burst of Reaganomics which include massive tax cuts, increased military spending, and a balanced budget amendment. Clinton has little moral or political power to counter the Republican steamroller. Many see Clinton as a lame duck president.

POLICY PRIORITIES

Yet, despite this array of ever more formidable political obstructions, Clinton has wracked up a series of impressive geoeconomic domestic and foreign policy victories, although only by compromising with congressional opponents. However, for much of the public, these successes were overshadowed by the massive health care reform bill the White House submitted in 1994.

On February 17, 1992, the president unveiled his economic restructuring plan designed to cut the deficit and stimulate strategic industries, technologies, and infrastructure that will spur economy development. OMB Director Leon Panetta led the bill's push through the congressional labyrinth. Along the way, the White House compromised on some controversial issues; it dropped a controversial energy tax, limited a gas tax to 4.3 cents, and cut subsidies to several key economic sectors. On August 5, the House voted 218–216 for the bill; the next day, Vice-President Gore cast a tie-breaking vote in the Senate. Under Senate Minority Leader Bob Dole's leadership, the Senate Republicans voted unanimously against the bill. Politics rather than conviction shaped most Republican votes. After all, Dole himself had been instrumental in forcing through his own package of spending cuts and tax increases in 1982 and supported similar bills in 1986 and 1990. On August 10, Clinton signed the bill into law. Altogether the package is projected to decrease the projected budget deficit over the next five years by $496 billion, of which $255 billion will come from spending cuts and $241 billion from tax increases.

More than any president, Clinton understands that deepening interdependence thoroughly meshes the domestic and global economies. Economic growth at home increasingly depends on the ability of American firms to export into a heathly expanding global economy. Shortly after taking office, Clinton announced that his administration's trade policy would fall in between the "voices from two extremes" of which one "says government should build walls to protect firms from competition" and "another says government should do nothing in the face of foreign competition, no matter what the dimension and shape of that competition is, no matter what the consequences are in terms of jobs losses, trade dislocations, or crushed incomes."[5] Clinton's trade policy realism was succinctly expressed by U.S. Trade Representative Kantor: "There is no such thing as free trade – it doesn't exist. You have to have rules of the road." Referring to Japanese and other foreign complaints about the pending NAFTA accord, Kantor declared: "They're complaining because the United States is finally trying to protect the jobs of our workers and the competitiveness of our business."[6] Most Democrats and many Republicans share his "get tough" trade orientation, yet differ on specific policies. Republicans supported the NAFTA and GATT accords while Democrats favored the White House efforts to open markets bilaterally, particularly with Japan.

Yet, the administration's consensus on the means if not ends of trade policy broke down within months of the inauguration with Treasury Secretary Bentsen, National Economic Council head Rubin, Secretary of State Christopher, and Labor Secretary Reich usually advocating a softline, while U.S. Trade Representative Kantor, Commerce Secretary Brown, and Council of Economic Advisors chair Tyson generally pushed for a hardline approach. Yet none of these policymakers were ideologues, all shifted their positions according to the issue.

Clinton's trade policy has been sophisticated, systematic, and successful by White House standards. To further American exports, the Clinton White House embarked on sustained efforts in global, regional, and bilateral negotiations. But if their goals were stymied in any of those forums, the White House did not hesitate to threaten retaliation. Throughout 1993, the White House concentrated on achieving three multilateral trade agreements: the North American Free Trade Association (NAFTA), the Asia Pacific Economic Council (APEC), and General Agreement on Trade and Tariffs (GATT).

During his presidential campaign, Clinton openly supported NAFTA which builds on free trade agreements Washington signed with Mexico in 1986 and Canada in 1988. Beginning in September 1993, the White House mounted a national campaign to pressure Congress into passing NAFTA which had been signed the previous spring. Clinton argued that Congress' failure to approve NAFTA would weaken the White House's ability to negotiate successfully the pending APEC and GATT issues, and other future multilateral and bilateral conflicts. Another of Clinton's powerful arguments was that if Congress rejected the free trade accord, Mexico would turn to the Japanese. "Japanese firms would," the president colorfully maintained, "swarm over Mexico like flies on a June bug." Treasury Secretary Lloyd Bentsen echoed the president's words, arguing that if NAFTA fails "then what you see happen is that Mexico turns to Japan."[7] NAFTA was narrowly passed by the House and Senate on November 16 and 18, 1993.

Clinton wants NAFTA to be the first step toward an AFTA or "American Free Trade Agreement" that would include the entire 800 million people of the western hemisphere from Tierra del Fuego to the Arctic. In December 1994, the leaders of every government in the western hemisphere except Cuba met in Miami where they agreed to convert the entire region into one vast free trade zone by 2005.

NAFTA enhances American power in several ways. Certain NAFTA clauses strengthen the ability of American industries to compete against Japanese and other foreign rivals. Tariffs would be reduced only for those products that are made in North America largely from regional components. A television, for example, would only be considered North American if it were made in the region from locally made screens and electron guns. Automobiles would be designated local if 50 per cent or more of the component's value were local, a percentage that will rise to 62.5 per cent by 2002. This domestic content law will further spur foreign firms to set up shop somewhere in the free trade zone and buy more from local firms. The clause also inhibits foreign firms from sidestepping, say, American import barriers by transshipping goods through Mexico or Canada.

Yet NAFTA is not foolproof. Japanese firms can finesse these restrictions by either setting up their own component plants within the region or buying out North American firms. With the strong yen and lack of restrictions on foreign takeovers of American firms, Japanese corporations are rapidly gobbling up component producers. For example, the television barriers will be no problem for Asahi Glass or Nippon Electric Glass which respectively own 49 per cent of Corning Glass and 100 per cent of Owens-Illinois. Both subsidiaries make television screens.

Two days after NAFTA's passage, Clinton flew triumphantly to Seattle for the Asia Pacific Economic Conference (APEC) summit of November 19 and 20. APEC was created in 1989 as a forum in which to discuss Pacific basin issues, and includes the United States, Japan, China, South Korea, Taiwan, Canada, Australia, New Zealand, Singapore, Indonesia, Malaysia, Thailand, Brunei, and the Philippines. All of APEC's government leaders attended the 1993 summit except Malaysian Prime Minister Mohammad Mahathir, who refused to come, arguing that APEC would dilute the exclusive East Asian group that he prefers.

APEC's importance to the United States is undeniable. America's trade with the Pacific basin surpassed that with the Atlantic basin over a decade ago, and that gap continues to widen. In 1992, 40 per cent of American trade was with the fourteen other APEC members and 35 per cent with the twelve nation European Union. While the United States enjoys a slight trade balance with the European Union it suffers an $80 billion trade deficit with APEC, of which $55 billion was with Japan. In 1992, the United States exported $128 billion to and imported $202 billion from APEC, and absorbed a quarter of all APEC exports. Clinton is determined to balance that vast deficit.

The President skilfully forged an accord among the reluctant leaders in which they pledged to cut tariffs on a range of products and begin by 1996 negotiations to convert APEC into a free trade zone with uniform economic rules. In doing so, the president overcame Tokyo's objections and attempts to rally other Asian countries behind itself by acting as go-between among the western advanced industrial and poorer Asian countries. Despite Clinton's ambitions, APEC is unlikely soon to achieve its new goals given its vast diversity in culture, per capita income, and economic orientation.

Fueled by the NAFTA and APEC accords, U.S. Trade Representative Kantor successfully negotiated the remaining issues that had held up a GATT agreement since 1986. During the negotiations, the White House scored a rare though limited victory against Japan. Kantor succeeded in changing eight of the eleven proposed tenets to allow existing tough, though infrequently used, anti-dumping laws. Tokyo fiercely resisted any revisions. However, under the GATT accord, any country that loses an anti-dumping case in another country can present its case before a GATT investigative panel which can overturn the lower decision if three-quarters of the panel agree. GATT panels currently require the unanimous consent of all representatives including the country which retaliated against the foreign dumping. Although the Republicans largely favored the GATT agreement, to hurt the president they held up its passage until after the 1994 election. The Clinton administration's successful conclusion of the GATT Uruguay Round capped a string of domestic and international geoeconomic triumphs.

Meanwhile, geopolitics did not end with the Cold War. Throughout 1993 and 1994, Russia seemed to take one step forward and two backward from the three revolutions launched by Gorbachev and continued by Yeltsin: from totalitarianism to liberal democracy, from a centrally owned, planned, and managed economy to free enterprise, and from empire to nation-state. In October 1993, radical communists and nationalists in Russia's Parliament declared a revolt against Yeltsin's presidency. Yeltsin ordered the army to bombard the rebels into submission. In December 1993, Russian voters approved a democratic constitution and elected a slew of nationalists and communists to parliament that once again challenged Yeltsin's leadership. In February 1994, they granted an amnesty to all those who had participated in the August 1991 coup against Gorbachev and October 1993 coup against Yeltsin. Yeltsin could do nothing but protest the decision. All along, the Clinton White House continued to politically support Yeltsin and financially support the expansion of private enterprise in Russia by contributing $1.5 billion to a $25 billion aid program from the democratic industrial countries.

There were four other pressing geopolitical problems. In December 1992, as his last major act as president, Bush had ordered American troops into Somalia to restore order and feed millions of people who were starving to death. American support for the intervention was at first high, then dropped rapidly as Americans died in the fighting. After an ambush killed eighteen Americans in June 1993, Clinton announced that he would withdraw all American troops by March 1994. Towards Haiti, Clinton continued the Bush policy of supporting the return of democratically elected President Aristide who was overthrown and exiled by a military coup. In October 1994, Clinton broke the stalemate by ordering Haiti's invasion and Aristide's installation as president. Until February 1994, Clinton also pursued the Bush hands-off policy toward the Bosnian civil war; that month a particularly bloody shelling of a Sarajevo market caused the president to threaten military force if the Serbs did not stop the shelling and withdraw twelve miles. He supported a peace plan that would divide the region between a joint Croatian–Bosnian state and cede the rest to Serbia. To date, the fighting continues. But the most serious crisis was with North Korea which for over eighteen months rejected White House demands for it to comply with the Nonproliferation Treaty (NPT) requirements and open its nuclear facilities to inspection and desist from creating nuclear weapons. Finally, on October 18, the two sides signed an agreement in which North Korea agreed to freeze and dismantle its nuclear weapons program, allow international inspectors, resume talks with South Korea over making their peninsula nuclear-free, and rejoin the NPT, in return for a U.S. promise to give North Korea 50,000 metric tons of oil a year and build two light-breeder nuclear reactors to replace the Soviet style ones. The agreement satisfied North Korea's energy needs and the rest of the world's fears of nuclear proliferation. It will take at least a decade to implement the agreement.

There were no unambiguous victories in any of these geopolitical conflicts because none were possible. Clinton largely followed Bush's lead in trying to contain these regional conflicts without getting American troops bogged down in an unwinnable guerrilla war.

POLICY TOWARD JAPAN: GEOECONOMIC ISSUES

Presidential candidate Bill Clinton had called for a tougher policy toward unfair traders, and singled out Japan as the worst offender. In particular, he announced his intention to cut Japan's vast trade surplus in half as a percentage of gross domestic product, shift the basis of Japan's economic growth from exports to domestic consumption, and increase Japan's percentage of manufactured goods to total imports to two thirds from its current half.

The Clintons had no sooner recovered from the inaugural festivities and settled into the White House when Tokyo fired its first shot across the new administration's bow. On January 15, 1993, Foreign Ministry spokesman Hanabusa Masamichi warned that "from two-thirds to three-quarters" of the bilateral problems were America's fault and Tokyo would insist on being Washington's "equal partner" and would "assert itself a little more strongly."[8]

It took the Clinton administration more than two months after entering office before those policymakers responsible for Japan were ready to act. Clinton captured the essence of America's problems with Japan at his first news conference on March 24, 1993, arguing powerfully that

if you look at the history of American trade relationships . . . the one that never seems to change very much is the one with Japan. That is we're sometimes in a position of trade deficit, but we're often in a position of trade surplus with the European Community. We . . . once had huge trade deficits with Taiwan and South Korea, but they've changed now quite a bit; they move up and down. But the persistence of the surplus the Japanese enjoy with the United States and the rest of the world can only lead to the conclusion that the possibility of obtaining real, even access to the Japanese market is somewhat remote.[8]

In other words, all of America's major trade relationships operate largely by free market principles except that with Japan which is shaped by Tokyo's neomercantilist policies.

Clinton then admitted that inept Washington policies were partly responsible for Japan's trade surpluses. Referring to the Bush White House decision to reduce tariffs on Japanese mini-vans, Clinton blasted his predecessor for overruling "its own Customs Office and giving a $300 million a year freebie to the Japanese for no apparent reason. And we got nothing, and I emphasize, nothing in return." Tokyo responded immediately to Clinton's remarks, warning that it would appeal to GATT if the White House reclassified Japanese mini-vans as trucks which would bring higher tariffs. The White House followed up Clinton's remarks on March 31 when it released a 275-page study of forty-four countries in which the twenty-seven-page section on Japan identified it as the worst neomercantilist offender.[9]

To put pressure on Tokyo, the Clinton White House talked down the dollar's value against the yen throughout 1993's first half. On February 19 with the yen's value at 118.40, Treasury Secretary Bensten announced that he would "like to see a stronger yen," followed by similar statements by President Clinton on April 16, Commerce Secretary Brown on April 23, the Treasury Department on May 25, and U.S. Trade Representative Kantor on June 7 when the yen reached 107.27.

The effectiveness of this strategy is questionable. Theoretically, as the stronger yen cuts back Japanese exports, Tokyo is pressured to increase government spending to stimulate its stalled economy. Thus, with fewer Japanese exports and possibly greater Japanese demand for imports, American industries have an opportunity to recapture market share and profits. In reality, Japan's neomercantilist policies compensate for the stronger yen. Japan's vast surplus was merely blunted even after the yen doubled between 1985 and 1987; since then the surplus has soared. Economist William Cline estimates that for every one percentage point increase in the yen, Japan's huge global trade surplus is reduced by only $3 to $4 billion after two years, which would mean at most a $2 billion reduction in Japan's $60 billion trade surplus with the United States. For the White House to achieve its goal of halving Japan's trade surplus, the yen would have to rise to 90 to a dollar.[10] Yet, even this prediction was wildly overoptimistic. By June 1995, the yen was hovering around 98 to the dollar, yet Japan's trade surplus that year was soaring toward $65 billion.

Tokyo prepared for the mid-April summit between President Clinton and Prime Minister Miyazawa with a public relations blitz touting Japan's free markets and claiming foreigners do not sell more because they do not try hard enough and their goods are inferior. On April 12, days before his summit with Clinton, Miyazawa himself repeated the standard Japanese line that "We must never agree on managed trade. We cannot tell private industries to purchase something from this country or that country."[11] When Japanese firmly say no, they offer a compensation prize. Miyazawa added that Tokyo was considering sharing technology with the United States on magnetically levitated trains and subways and might even supply Japanese language teachers to help American businessmen.

The summit failed to achieve any agreement on curbing Japan's ever growing trade surplus. At the joint news conference ending their first summit, Miyazawa asserted that a partnership "cannot be realized with managed trade or the threat of unilateralism. . . . We can make improvements without there being any numerical targets."[12] The two leaders did agree to work on a "new framework" for relations and unveil it at a July summit.

Disappointed with the summit, the White House heated up the rhetorical war. On April 23, Commerce Secretary Brown complained that while American "exports to almost every other country . . . are up, they aren't in Japan. Where tariff reduction spurs commerce in every other market, it hasn't in Japan. Where years and years of negotiations have yielded tangible results with Canada and the E.C., for the most part, they have not in Japan." Acknowledging that the prolonged bilateral negotiations to remove Japan's tangible trade barriers left intangible ones in place, Brown concluded that results-oriented trade in which American industries are given specific market shares comparable to their shares in third markets would be one way to finesse Japanese neomercantilism.[13] On April 30, 1993, U.S. Trade Representative Kantor blasted Japan for discriminating against American firms in construction and supercomputers, while the same day Commerce Secretary Brown admitted that "only pressure is going to produce results, and only things that are measurable and monitorable are going to produce results." Japanese embassy spokesman Seiichiro Noboru immediately replied that Japan "will never accept negotiations under duress."[14]

Various Japanese officials repeatedly asserted that Tokyo would reject any American attempts to impose a result-oriented trade and appeal the issue to GATT. They also claimed that other Asian nations backed Tokyo's position for fear that the United States might also demand that they systematically reduce their own trade surpluses.

On May 19, 1993, the White House announced that henceforth American policy toward Japan would be divided among five "baskets," with one dealing with specific industry problems like automobiles, semiconductors, and so on, the second the structural differences between the two economies such as Japan's distribution system, the third on global issues like the yen's value, the fourth on foreign investment between the two countries, and the fifth on issues that span economic and military concerns like weapons sales and Japan's underwriting of American bases in Japan.[15]

The White House stated repeatedly that numerical targets were the only way to measure whether Japan's trade barriers were actually lowered. On June 5, Miyazawa once again stated that "setting numerical targets would lead to managed trade. . . . Because in a free economy no one can control exports or imports." On June 8, dismissing Japanese protests, the White House presented to Tokyo a broad proposal to open Japan's markets by setting numerical targets but would not make them legally binding and rejected the possibility of retaliating if those targets were not reached.[16] Follow up negotiations that month failed to produce any agreement on the outstanding issues.

On June 10, 1993, President Clinton named former vice-president Walter Mondale to replace Michael Armacost as the ambassador to Japan. Outgoing Armacost fired a few parting shots, denouncing Tokyo's claims of being a free trader as mere "propaganda." He hoped that Americans "are not too persuaded by some of the P.R. that's been flowing so freely recently which is designed to dismiss the problem [of Japan's immense trade and investment surpluses], or suggest that it's a product of short-term factors that will take care of themselves, or in any event the surplus will be recycled and in the long run it will go away."[17] Armacost went on to embrace President Clinton's strategy of tough results-oriented talk and action.

The show-down between the United States and Japan came in a summit between Clinton and Miyazawa amidst the G-7 summit in Tokyo between July 7 and July 10. In two nights of marathon negotiation sessions on July 8 and 9, the two sides worked out a "Framework Agreement" in which they agreed to reduce measurably Japan's trade surplus and open markets by "numerical criteria." The final deal was cut between the two leaders in a sushi restaurant. Under the Framework Agreement, Tokyo agreed to increase its imports, and identified insurance, automobiles, auto parts, telecommunications, medical technology, and intellectual property as priorities. In addition, Tokyo agreed to cut taxes and increase spending to stimulate the economy, while Washington promised to cut its budget deficit. At a joint news conference with Miyazawa, Clinton announced that "the Cold War partnership between the two countries was outdated" and called for "the rebalancing of our relationship," with economics at the forefront of changes. Miyazawa countered by arguing that "we should be patient" and "there is no need to solve it over night." Ironically, he did ask Clinton to keep up the *gaiatsu* because it was the only way to move Japan's protectionist system.

Pointing to the clause calling for measureable progress, the Clinton administration hailed the agreement as radically different from all preceding ones. Henceforth, Tokyo was committed to not just "removing" barriers but quantitatively increasing imports in volume and percentage.

Yet, as in so many previous agreements, the pact began to unravel shortly thereafter. July elections in Japan resulted in the LDP losing power for the first time. Miyazawa's LDP government was replaced by a seven party coalition headed by LDP defector Hosokawa Morihiro. Although the new government pledged its commitment to political reforms and lower prices, it reinterpreted the result-oriented "Framework Agreement" signed the previous month. Taking advantage of the agreement's ambiguous wording, Tokyo argued that it was already fully complying with any "objective criteria" to measure whether it achieved a "highly significant" trade surplus reduction over the "medium term." Tokyo rejected any "results-oriented" agreement as "managed trade." Furthermore, the Japanese continued to claim that Japan's markets were more open than America's and that it was Washington rather than Tokyo that had to liberalize its trade and industrial policies.

A new voice entered the fray in August when Ambassador Mondale arrived in Tokyo. Mondale quickly disabused Japanese hopes that he would cave in to Tokyo's economic positions like Armacost's predecessor Mike Mansfield. Instead he has inherited Armacost's title of "Mr Gaiatsu" (Mr foreign pressure). At his first news conference, Mondale warned that the United States would not hesitate to impose sanctions if Tokyo remained obstructionist on trade and investment issues.

At first Hosokawa appeared to heed these warnings. After taking office in August 1993, he created the "Advisory Group for Economic Restructuring" as part of a campaign pledge to curb bureaucratic powers, lower prices, and improve the quality of life. On November 8, 1993, Hosokawa unveiled the advisory group's report which called for eliminating 475 government economic and legal regulations which he claimed would help liberalize Japan's economy. According to Hosokawa, the principle underlying the changes was that "economic activity should be founded on the basic idea of freedom from regulations in principle, with regulated areas the exception."[18] Later that month at the APEC summit, Hosokawa presented the report as a "gift" (omiyage) to President Clinton. Even if enacted, Hosokawa's proposals would have no impact on Japan's huge trade surplus since it will do little to inhibit the "administrative guidance" (gyosei shido) with which Japan's bureaucrats carefully manage Japan's economy and decisively tip the playing field against foreign firms.

Meanwhile, Tokyo and Washington renewed their battles over specific sectors and managed to reach some agreements. One notable breakthrough was in construction. Despite Japanese promises in the late 1980s to open their construction markets, American construction firms remained largely shut out of Japan. In 1992, American firms received only $189 million of Japan's $700 billion market while Japanese firms took $1.5 billion of America's $425 billion market. These statistics grossly understated Japan's real market share because Japanese corporations have bought up dominant interests in scores of American construction companies while American attempts to buy out Japanese firms have been stymied.[19] After threatening sanctions, the White House backed away on October 26, 1993 when Tokyo made a last-minute promise to open its public sector construction market to international competition but refused to designate specific market shares or values.

The White House threatened to impose sanctions by January if Tokyo did not agree to specifics. Tokyo avoided yet another threatened American sanction by meeting the January 20, 1994 deadline for "opening" its construction industry. Two days before the sanctions' eve Tokyo presented a plan which would allow open bidding for any national construction projects worth over $7.7 million, local and prefectural projects over $25.7 million, and design and consulting projects worth over $770,000. The plan would begin April 1.

The following day, the White House announced that it would drop its threat to retaliate. U.S. Trade Representative Kantor stated that "Japan has addressed all the major U.S. concerns in the Japanese public works sector."[19] The agreement on construction theoretically "opened" a market which had already been "opened" by previous Japanese promises. Whether the latest agreement will be any more substantive than earlier deals remains to be seen.

As one set of negotiators battled over construction, another fought over rice. Since the mid-1980s, Washington and Tokyo have wrangled fruitlessly over Japan's closed rice markets with the Japanese repeatedly declaring that they would never open their country's sacred crop to foreign competition. But on November 29, 1993, the weary negotiators finally struck an accord that cracked Japan's rice market. It took another week to work out the details. Prime Minister Hosokawa symbolically announced the accord on December 7. Tokyo agreed to import 4 per cent of its 10 million ton rice market by 1995, and 8 per cent by 2001. The accord was incorporated into the GATT agreement signed in December which outlaws outright bans on agricultural imports.

News of the agreement sparked the expected opposite reactions on each side of the Pacific. Californian rice growers were jubilant, although subsequent sales have fallen far short of hopes. In Japan, protests immediately erupted from across the political spectrum with the Socialist Party threatening to quit Hosokawa's coalition government if the accord went through. Newspaper headlines blasted yet another invasion of "black ships." Hosokawa tried to patch up the political damage by announcing an economic stimulus package and postponed pushing through a political reform bill that he previously promised to enact.

As in previous agreements, Tokyo's concession was not as great as it appeared. Aside from the 1993 emergency rice imports to offset the worst harvest since 1945, there were questions of whether Japanese would actually buy foreign rice. Japan's government and rice industry have long argued that foreign rice tastes inferior to domestic rice, is soaked with cancer-causing chemicals, and would destroy Japan's traditional culture. Of course, none of these accusations is true, but nonetheless they have affected sales. When Californian rice-growers protested Tokyo's scare tactics, the government promised literally to dilute the fears it had created by blending domestic and foreign rice. California producers argued that Tokyo's real intention was to prevent Japanese consumers from conducting their own taste tests and discovering that foreign rice actually tasted better, which blind tastings persistently revealed.[20]

On January 21, the two countries signed a preliminary agreement in which both sides pledged to change their respective patent systems. But it took another seven months of hard bargaining to flesh out their initial agreements into a formal agreement. The two sides signed the patent agreement on August 16, 1994. Washington promised to grant patents for twenty years from the day they were filed rather than seventeen years from when they were rewarded, agreed to publish applications eighteen months after they were filed, and award patents on a first-to-file rather than invent basis. Tokyo agreed to accept foreign patent applications in English if a Japanese translation soon followed, and allow foreigners to correct faulty translations which were previously invalidated. Perhaps most importantly, Tokyo agreed to decide on patents within three years of their applications. Previously Japan's Patent Office had indefinitely shelved foreign applications while Japanese firms exploited their secrets.

The United States scored yet another limited victory in January. Shortly after the July 1993 summit, Tokyo had formed an advisory committee to recommend changes in the nation's copyright laws so that Japanese firms could more easily plagiarize foreign computer software and thus catch up in one of the few industries in which they trail. Tokyo had tried to enact a similar "reverse engineering" law in the mid 1980s but backed off after tough American protests. The White House protested Tokyo's latest software offensive. The protest worked. The software committee's subsequent January 1994 report did not recommend rewriting the software laws.

The White House had less success in opening Japan's semiconductor market. In 1993, for the first time since 1985, American chipmakers surpassed their Japanese rivals in global market share by 41.9 per cent to 41.4 per cent. Several important reasons were behind the turnaround. The most important was the 1986 VER which saved America's industry from complete bankruptcy by forcing Tokyo to impose floor prices worldwide and promise a 20 per cent market share in Japan for foreign producers by 1991. This allowed the breathing space in which American chipmakers could

invest in cost-cutting and new products with which to slowly climb back
in global markets. Also vital was the yen's strengthening from 265 to 108
to a dollar over those eight years. The White House thus eliminated the
two most important reasons for Japan's crushing success – dumping and an
undervalued yen. The slight 1993 shift in America's favor from their previous year's 41.5 per cent share compared to Japan's 42.3 per cent was
attributed to Japan's recession.

Yet conflicts continued despite this American comeback. In 1993, America's share of Japan's semiconductor market slipped to 19 per cent from
the previous year's 20 per cent, thus putting Tokyo in violation of the 1986
agreement which promised a 20 per cent share starting in 1991. The Clinton
administration not only wants Tokyo to restore the American market share
to 20 per cent, but to use that "results-oriented" agreement as the basis for
other industries in which foreign market share is limited by Japanese trade
and investment barriers. Tokyo is adamantly opposed to such deals and now
deeply regrets having agreed to the semiconductor agreement. The issue
remains deadlocked.

Meanwhile, negotiations stalemated over the most important issue of all
– defining the "objective criteria" called for in the Framework Agreement.
The Japanese continued to attack any attempts to achieve "results-oriented"
or "managed trade" while claiming Japan's markets were the world's most
open. A January 1994 MITI White Paper went so far as to maintain that the
low foreign trade and investment shares in Japan were actually signs of
how open Japan's markets are. Meanwhile, statistics were released showing
that Japan's 1993 trade surplus with the United States and world had surged
to $59 billion and $131 billion, respectively.

By late January 1994, Clinton White House officials were openly denouncing Tokyo's failure to abide by previous accords. Referring to Japanese
stonewalling on importing more automobiles, auto parts, telecommunications, medical equipment, and insurance policies, Undersecretary of Commerce for International Trade Jeffrey Garten complained that negotiations
had not "moved an inch" and that "we've been having a sterile, metaphysical
debate. We want results." Joan Spero, Undersecretary of State for Economic
and Agricultural Affairs, also bitterly admitted that "we had thought this
framework was different in several ways. We really saw [the Hosokawa]
government as moving toward the same kind of goals as we were. We feel
disappointment. We are back to the old formula."[21]

Then, to worsen matters, on January 21, 1994 the Hosokawa government
lost a vital vote on a package of four political reform bills in the upper house
when seventeen socialist members voted with the LDP. Hosokawa was then
faced with taking the bill back to the lower house in hopes of achieving a

two-thirds vote that would override the upper house, forming a joint-house committee to hammer out a compromise, or dissolve the lower house and call elections. Hosokawa's fragile seven-party coalition threatened to dissolve. Since 1989, two prime ministers (Takeshita and Uno) had resigned because of scandals, and two others (Kaifu and Miyazawa) resigned because they failed to achieve political reform. The defeat deeply wounded Hosokawa and rendered him unable to fulfill promises to the United States.

Amidst Japan's political deadlock and uncertainty, Treasury Secretary Bentsen arrived in Tokyo on January 22 to press Hosokawa to honor those very promises of results-oriented trade made the previous July. In meetings with Hosokawa and Finance Minister Hirohisa Fuji, he delivered a frank message from Clinton expressing his disappointment over the lack of progress in trade talks over the previous half year. He then supplemented Clinton's words with some tough talk of his own, declaring bluntly that "Japan is out of step right now. It has a continuing trade surplus. It has the lowest penetration of manufactured imports, and it has the lowest foreign investment among the major nations."[22] Fujii replied by asking Bentsen to "Trust us."

Tokyo naturally assumed that Clinton was bluffing. After all, every previous president had mouthed similar sentiments that this time the United States was committed to achieving a genuine market opening and trade deficit reduction agreement – and eventually every president had settled for "trusting" Japanese "promises." Meanwhile Japan's hold over America's political economy had strengthened yearly with increasing numbers of American firms, workers, politicians, and lobbyists dependent on their Japanese connections.

Tokyo tried some last-minute attempts to delay the final talks over numerical targets and conduct a purely ceremonial summit. Four days before the summit, a secret Hosokawa envoy, Akitane Kiuchi, met with Vice-President Gore and pleaded for more time. Gore pointed out that Tokyo had enjoyed eight months since Miyazawa had agreed to objective criteria to define exactly what that meant; time had run out. With Clinton, Kiuchi tried the same arguments that Hosokawa was politically weak and could not compromise until he was stronger. The president replied that the Prime Minister should align himself with Japanese consumers and the United States to achieve Japan's opening. The day before the summit, Foreign Minister Hata Tsutomu tried to cut a last-minute deal in separate talks with Secretary of State Christopher, Treasury Secretary Bensten, U.S. Trade Representative Kantor, National Security Advisor Lake, and even White House advisors David Gergen and Bowman Cutter. In negotiations with previous administrations, the Japanese had nearly always succeeded at their divide and rule strategy of playing the parochial interests of the departments and agencies against each other. Not this time. The Clinton White House showed a united front in speaking frankly with Hata. They also went public with their remarks.

Japan's traditional White House allies disappeared. The Pentagon was mute. Deputy Treasury Secretary Roger Altman pointed out that Japan's $131 billion trade surplus "drains growth and jobs from the rest of the world." To Tokyo's shock, even their perennial ally, the State Department, deserted them. Secretary of State Warren Christopher bluntly warned that "the United States is determined that we would redress the great imbalance in our trade and we will seek in a determined way access for American businesses in the Japanese market."[23]

Hosokawa arrived in Washington with virtually no power to delay the collision. Clinton's negotiating power was formidable. His cabinet was united behind his tough position; he would not be undercut by a department or agency succumbing to Japanese pressure. In 1993, he had scored a string of foreign economic policy success in NAFTA, APEC, and GATT, as well as his deficit reduction plan which would sharply cut Washington's red ink. The economy was expanding robustly with unemployment and inflation dropping. His popularity was rising. The Business Roundtable and Chamber of Commerce issued statements days before the summit calling on him to hang tough. And the American public was solidly behind any efforts to curtail Japanese neomercantilism.

In contrast, Hosokawa was hamstrung by Japan's political economic potentates. Hosokawa had been Japan's most popular prime minister with approval ratings at times over 70 per cent. He favored relief to Japan's exploited consumers, deregulation, and political reform. Yet he lacked the power base to push such policies through the system. Not only was the LDP opposed to his proposals, but his own seven-party coalition government was bitterly divided. To get anything through the Diet, Hosokawa had to turn to the LDP and ministry stalwarts he had vowed to fight and who were opposed to Japan's liberalization. Hosokawa had nothing to give but promises.

Despite the odds against him, Hosokawa gamely tried to divert attention away from numerical targets to Tokyo's foreign aid and $140 billion domestic stimulus package, political instability in Russia and Asian countries, the North Korean nuclear stand-off, space exploration, AIDS research, and so on. Clinton, however, just as skillfully shepherded the talks back to the central issue, dashing Hosokawa's hope that the president, like his predecessors, would make last-minute concessions to "save the relationship."

During their joint press conference after the summit, Clinton was a master of diplomatic grace and nuance. "Today we could have disguised our differences with cosmetic agreements," he stated, "but the issues between us are so important for our own nations and for the rest of the world that it is better to have reached no agreement than to have reached an empty agreement." Clinton went on to explain that "Japan's best offer did not meet the standards agreed to last July" for the opening of Japan's closed automobile, auto parts, insurance, telecommunications, and medical equipment markets. While glancing occasionally at Hosokawa, Clinton almost apologetically explained that "America's trade deficit with Japan is not very popular among the American people or the American government. It's hard to explain it, year in and year out, always getting bigger."[24] He pointed out that Tokyo had signed thirty-one "market opening" agreements with the United States over the previous twelve years and yet Japan's trade surplus continued to grow. Clinton mixed criticism of Japanese neomercantilism with praise for Hosokawa's efforts at political reform and a stimulus package. Then he invited the prime minister for a friendly breakfast the next morning.

Hosokawa admitted candidly that "in the past, Japan and the U.S. sometimes have reached ambiguous agreements which can gloss over the problems of the time, only to find them become sources of later misunderstandings between our two countries from time to time." Japanese officials later followed up Hosokawa's words by repeating their warning that they would take before GATT any unilateral American actions which curtailed Japanese exports.

Japanese cheered Hosokawa for saying "no" to the president. In fact, Japanese officials have always said no to American calls for them genuinely to open Japan's markets, while continually agreeing to the ambiguous promises to which Hosokawa alluded. The real news was that for once an American president had said no to a Japanese "yes" of empty promises.

After the news conference, Clinton stated frankly that he had "no idea of what will happen from here on in." However, he soon turned up the heat on Tokyo in several ways. First, he simply sat back and let the pressure build on the Japanese as they worried about what he might eventually do. Meanwhile, he encouraged the yen to rise further against the dollar, which in turn caused the Tokyo stock market to fall.

The White House's most concrete measure occurred on February 15 when Kantor responded to a report that Tokyo had grossly violated a 1989 agreement to open Japan's cellular phone market. Kantor set in motion the thirty-day period of additional investigation after which he could impose tariffs on Japanese firms. As Kantor pointed out, the Motorola case was a particularly blatant example of Japanese neomercantilism. For over a decade, Motorola had done everything that the experts claimed was essential to selling in Japan: invested enormous amounts in marketing and quality controls, nurtured long-term relationships, and played strictly by the rules. When these efforts failed to make any headway in Japan's carefully managed markets, Motorola turned to Washington. On March 1989, after nearly a year of negotiations, Washington finally elicited from Tokyo a promise to open its cellular phone market. As in previous agreements, Tokyo's cellular phone promise failed to open the market completely. Tokyo essentially excluded Motorola from Japan's Tokyo–Nagoya corridor by forcing it into an alliance with its competitor, IDO, which was building its own cellular phone. While IDO took Motorola's technology, Tokyo granted the American producer a limited share of the transmission base stations. As a result, Motorola was permitted to sell to only 12,000 customers out of 318,000 or 3 per cent of the Tokyo–Nagoya market. Elsewhere in Japan, where the cellular phone market is less strictly managed, Motorola was allowed to capture 49 per cent of the customers.[25]

Kantor's action was not specifically geared to Hosokawa's refusal to budge on numerical criteria; February 15, 1994 was the deadine for Tokyo's compliance with the 1989 agreement and just happened to coincide with the summit. The retaliation threat worked. On March 12, Tokyo agreed to open Japan's telecommunications industry to more Motorola products and build 159 more relay stations for their use. Clinton characterized the agreement as "a big win for everyone. Workers in the United States will gain because the agreement means more demand for cellular telephones and related equipment made in America. Japanese consumers win because they'll have access to better service and better technology at better prices. Even Japanese manufacturers may win because of the increased demand for cellular phones."[26]

Not everyone was as optimistic. Japan did not agree to numerical targets. Some wondered whether there was any reason to believe that the Japanese would honor this agreement any more than they had previous ones. Ambassador Mondale's remarks were typical of those who understood Japan. In a February 19, 1994 interview, during which he reflected on his previous half year in Tokyo, Mondale dismissed the deals he had helped cut with Tokyo as insignificant since the trade and account deficits continued to worsen. He admitted that the administration's initial hope that Hosokawa would reform the system had been disappointed: "his record over the past four or five months has not been one of an economic reformer. We don't see any difference in the position of the bureaucracy or the Government."[27]

Clinton's hard line was lauded by American businessmen, most politicians, and the public. Yet there were some prominent critics. Democratic Senator Bill Bradley dismissed it as "Japan bashing for domestic constituency, without regard to the long-term strategic interests of the country." Bradley went on to mention the need for Washington and Tokyo to cooperate on geopolitical issues involving Russia, North Korea, and China. He then claimed that the White House actions made the Japanese rather than Americans appear the world's free champions. Although it is unlikely that other governments would have trouble distinguishing whether the United States or Japan has a more open economy, Bradley's rhetoric did undercut the president. Kantor countered that while the White House respected Bradley as an ally on most issues, they could not understand the logic behind his comments. He again pointed out the reality that the "Japanese have had a sanctuary market, which they have protected for decades . . . not just to the U.S. but for other countries which has created economic and political problems in the world trading system."[28]

On March 3, Clinton signed an executive order reinstating his broad legal authority to impose trade sanctions under Super 301 of the 1988 Trade Act. Clinton's cabinet was divided over whether he should reimpose Super 301. Mondale and Tyson argued that the timing was bad given Hosokawa's fragile hold on power. The other Economic Security Council members argued for its reimposition. By reinstating Super 301, Clinton significantly boosted his negotiating power.

Super 301 requires the U.S. Trade Representative to publish an annual survey of foreign trade practices by March 31. Between then and September 30, the White House would then select and notify the most rapacious neomercantilist practitioners that they should desist or face retaliation. If the offender refused to end its predatory trade practices, the president could then either go to GATT or retaliate with higher tariffs.

The powers work. In 1989, Bush had used Super 301 to threaten retaliation against Tokyo if it did not remove barriers in telecommunications, satellites, and wood products. Tokyo reluctantly complied. However, as part of a deal cut with Tokyo, Bush then allowed Super 301 to lapse, claiming inexplicably that it inhibited rather than promoted free trade.

Clinton never got a chance to use them against Hosokawa. On April 6, Prime Minister Hosokawa resigned after he admitted to taking a million dollar loan which he never repaid. After several days of back room maneuvering and deals, Foreign Minister Tsutomu Hata became the new prime minister. Few White House officials looked forward to Hata's leadership. After all, it was Hata who once insisted that Japanese would not buy more American beef because Japanese intestines were longer and thus could not fully digest the foreign product. Somehow, Japanese intestines have no problem accommodating home-grown beef.

Although Hata clearly was not interested in opening Japan's markets, the United States lost little with Hosokawa's resignation. From the beginning, the administration's hope that Hosokawa would lead Japan into a golden age of economic and political openness was naive. In part, the policy reflected the American tendency to place bets on personalities and rhetoric rather than systems and results. Hosokawa was sincerely interested in political reforms and lower consumer prices, but not at the expense of Japan's industry or trade surpluses. And it was clear that the bureaucrats, industrialists, and politicians would never allow Hosokawa even his limited reform agenda. Yet the White House continued to cling to Hosokawa as his political support decayed and negotiations deadlocked. As Prestowitz put it,

> Hosokawa's fall demonstrates the fallacy of the view that somehow a political leader was going to emerge, be the savior, change the Japanese system, resolve the trade conflicts with the U.S. and spare us having to take difficult measures to solve the problems. The power center remains the bureaucratic mandarins and big business cartels who do not want to see the kind of changes we are advocating.[29]

Despite the clear failure of its Japan policy, the White House dared not cut Japan's gordian knot of trade, investment, and other mercantile practices by simply insisting on the trade deficit's gradual but continual reduction to balance. It was politically easier to do nothing.

All along, Japanese diplomats continued to stonewall American attempts to crack open the administration's four targeted markets – autos and auto parts, medical equipment, telecommunications, and insurance. By April 1994, the Japanese had agreed only to ease inspection rules for imported cars, review its bidding procedures for medical equipment, and adjust some insurance rules, but they adamantly refused American demands to set targets for any of the four areas.

Hata's government soon scored a significant diplomatic victory. On May 23, Tokyo agreed to allow the monitoring of Japan's markets as long as Washington gave up its right to demand that Japan expand the share for American producers. In each of the four designated industries, monitors would use seven or eight indicators to measure progress.

Shortly thereafter, to boost its image, Tokyo reannounced a symbolic victory that it had actually granted the United States in January. On May 30, Japan's Agency for Cultural Affairs announced that it would table indefinitely a proposal aired ten months earlier to revise its copyright laws so that Japanese firms could legally copy foreign computer software through a reverse engineering process called "decompilation." With Tokyo's announcement, the United States won at best a skirmish. At least those American officials charged with pressuring Tokyo on that issue could be redeployed to more central issues. But the Japanese might not need the revised law to pirate foreign software after all. Given the vague ways in which Japanese laws are written and arbitrary ways in which bureaucrats interpret them, decompilation may well be perfectly legal under existing laws. And the controversy itself diverted key American personnel, time, and energy from the central issue of numerical targets.

Meanwhile it was revealed that the Bank of Japan had spent $35 billion from January 1993 through April 1994, trying to curb the yen's rise which was inhibiting Japanese exports and growth. This very managed approach to currency markets, of course, belied Tokyo's claim that it was committed to free enterprise. Economist Fred C. Bergsten described the Bank of Japan's intervention as "the most dramatic example of managed trade in the relationship between the U.S. and Japan over the last year or so. It's very clear that the yen would have strengthened well beyond 100 in the absence of this intervention."[30] The Japanese have a clear double standard in regards to "managed trade" in which they systematically manage trade to protect or enhance their own interests while criticizing the United States and others for daring to do the same.

But the yen's fall did not just hurt Japan. Perhaps the most troubling legacy of Reaganomics' quadrupling of America's national debt between 1981 and 1993 was it made the United States dependent on foreign financiers, many of whom are Japanese. Although the White House had favored the yen's rise following the breakdown of negotiations in February, it backed away from the policy in May. As the dollar's value drops, Japanese and other foreign investors become increasingly reluctant to buy U.S. Treasury Bills. If foreign buying falls to a trickle, there would be a crisis in American currency markets and a recession. In May the Federal Reserve and other central banks worked in concert with the Bank of Japan to check the yen's rise.

In addition to these measures, the Federal Reserve raised interest rates six times during 1994. The Fed claimed the rate hikes were designed to cool an overheated economy and curb inflation. In fact, inflation was at its lowest level in years. The most important reason for the hikes was to entice Japanese investors to remain big buyers of treasury bonds. In 1993's fourth quarter, Japanese bought $6.5 billion of treasury bonds; in 1994's first quarter, the amount dropped to $3.75 billion.[31] The Fed, of course, could not admit the American economy was in Japan's pocket. Higher interest rates act like an enormous tax on America's households and businesses, slow economic growth, and lower incomes.

On June 7, the White House retreated once again when it announced it would henceforth try to score what victories it could, however limited, rather than achieve an overall breakthrough in all designated areas simultaneously. The White House pushed for limited agreements in insurance, glass, medical equipment, and telecommunications, and put on the back burner negotiations over automobiles and auto parts. As Kantor put it, "We are not going to wait to open up everything until we make deals in all sectors. But – let me be very clear – we don't intend to stop with just one or two sectors either. We see the framework negotiations as a continuing process."[32]

Late that month, on June 26, Japan's government once again fell, this time when the Socialist Party withdrew from the coaltion. Prime Minister Hata resigned just before a no-confidence vote. After three days of bargaining among all the parties, a bizarre new alliance emerged between the conservative Liberal Democratic Party (LDP) and the Socialist Party whose combined votes in the Diet made socialist Murayama Tomiichi Japan's newest prime minister. American observers rued the latest shift in Japanese politics bringing to power the two parties most opposed to opening Japan's markets.

The sectoral negotiations continued to drag on. Japanese protectionism limited American firms to less than 1 per cent of its glass market, 3 per cent of Japan's insurance market, 5 per cent of its telecommunication markets, and 20 per cent of its medical equipment market; in Europe's relatively free markets, American firms enjoyed market shares in those industries three to ten times what they were restricted to in Japan.[33]

On August 1, the White House announced it would initiate Section 301 retaliatory proceedings against Japan in those industries if Tokyo continued to stonewall negotiations. As usual, Tokyo bitterly protested. But the threat to retaliate eventually worked. On October 1, 1994, Washington and Tokyo announced trade opening agreements in insurance, medical equipment, and telecommunications. The following day, Kantor announced he would expand trade talks with Japan to include computers, wood products, paper, and financial services, all of which were supposedly opened by previous negotiations during the Reagan and Bush years.

The United States and Japan remained deadlocked over the most important bilateral competition of all – automobiles and auto parts. Two-thirds of America's trade deficit with Japan is in automobile and auto parts. In 1993, Japan's automobile makers exported 1.5 million vehicles to the United

States and sold an additional 1 million transplants for a total market share of 29 per cent of the car market and 23 per cent of the total vehicle market. In contrast, that year America's Big Three automobile makers sold only 19,335 vehicles in Japan. There has been some progress. The number of Japanese dealers selling foreign vehicles rose from fifty-five in 1988 to 530 in 1994, allowing foreign vehicles to capture about 8 per cent of the market.[34] On October 2, Clinton announced he would initiate an investigation of Japan's automobile industry under Section 301. Negotiations would begin if injury to America's automobile industry is found. Sanctions, however, could only be imposed twelve to eighteen months after negotiations begin if there is no progress.

Japan's automobile trade barriers are as powerful as they are insidious. For example, exporters of Chrysler Cherokees must comply with 238 regulations and fill out 560 pages of documents just to get the car off the ship, a bewildering bureaucratic gauntlet that jacks up prices. Then the exporter must navigate the Cherokee through an equally bewildering maze of Japan's cartelized distribution system. A Cherokee that costs $19,100 in an American showroom ends up selling for $31,372 in Japan.

Negotiations over American access to Japan's closed markets had been stalemated for 20 months before the Clinton administration finally ran out of patience. On May 17, 1995, the White House announced that if Tokyo did not open its market by June 28, the United States would impose 100 per cent tariffs worth $5.9 billion on thirteen types of Japanese luxury automobiles. The target was carefully chosen. All thirteen luxury models are produced exclusively in Japan with only tiny imputs of American parts. The tariffs would be retroactive to May 20, thus hitting shiploads of cars en route to the United States. Those American consumers able to afford such a car could just as easily buy an American or European model. The action hurts only those Americans who sell Japanese luxury cars. In 1994, of the 1.64 million vehicles Japan exported to the United States, 200,000 were the targeted 13 luxury cars. Japanese automakers have already been hurt by the rising yen. Yet, the tariff would not devastate Japanese automobile makers; luxury exports to the United State compose only 2.2 per cent of global Japanese automobile sales.

Tokyo threatened to take the United States before the WTO if the sanctions went into effect. The White House countered by threatening to go to the WTO, not just to point out Japanese discrimination in automobiles but to indict Japan's entire neomercantilist political economic system and policies. The White House would make a "nullification and impairment" case against Japan that Tokyo had nullified with nontariff barriers any advantages it gave with lower tariffs. The "nullification and impairment" case has been used twice before. In the 1970s, Washington successfully used it against Brussels' soybean subsidies. In 1982, Brussels failed in an attempt to employ it against Japan's automobile cartel, ironically because Washington refused to give support for fear it would jeopardize the alliance with Japan.

Both sides were gambling for high stakes when they threatened to take their respective complaints before the WTO. A WTO decision in Tokyo's favor would destroy Washington's bargaining power and leave Japanese neomercantilism intact. By only a few votes, Congress passed the treaty allowing the United States membership in the WTO. If the WTO ruled against the United States, pressure would mount on Congress to withdraw from the organization, an action which could destroy the WTO. A favorable WTO decision would allow Washington to retaliate against all Japanese exports until Tokyo abandoned its protectionism. The WTO's credibility would be bolstered. Yet, most observers believed that the WTO would use a narrow definition of trade barriers in deciding the case, rather than the broad range of nontariff walls identified by the White House.

Indiscreet remarks by some Japanese corporate leaders undercut Japan's position. Saito Yuzo, a Toyota executive, admitted that "if we just look at the question of cost, it is better to buy 100 per cent in the United States. But there's the problem of Japanese domestic employment. So much how to purchase depends on managerial judgement." In other words, socioeconomic goals rather than free markets shape Japan's automobile market. If a free market existed, Japanese automakers would buy exclusively from American auto-parts producers whose prices are cheaper, with comparable quality.

Tokyo also responded with a massive and ultimately successful public relations offensive before the OECD and in European and Asian capitals. The 25-nation OECD unanimously supported Tokyo. To the White House's even greater surprise and disgust, the European Union also publicly condemned and privately encouraged its actions. European Union Trade Commissioner Leon Brittan called the sanctions "illegal" and warned they could damage the world trade system. There was more than a little hypocrisy in Brittan's remarks. After all, the EU maintains its own strict quotas and domestic content laws on foreign automobiles. The real fear in Brussels was that Washington would cut a deal with Tokyo that might expand the market share of American cars in Japan at the expense of European producers. Yet, at the same time, according to Commerce Secretary Brown, "The Europeans are whispering in our ears, 'Good luck and we wish you well.' " U.S. Trade Representative Kantor remarked that Brittan "agrees with me that the Japanese market is closed, and needs opening, and our differences are mainly about tactics. . . . The Europeans are going to be a major beneficiary of our success with the Japanese. It is a little frustrating when those who benefit from what we do are publicly not supporting us." Secretary of State Christopher tried to entice Eruopean support by calling for a transatlantic economic community uniting NAFTA and the EU, but to no avail.

In the battle for world opinion, Tokyo was also successful in rallying Asian nations around the Japanese flag. To varying extents all the East and Southeast Asian nations have emulated Japanese neomercantilism and fear that if the United States successfully retaliates against Tokyo today, it might do so against them tomorrow. Tokyo deftly exploited that fear. The sole regional holdout was Singapore's senior minister and *de facto* president Lee Kuan Yew who argued that "East Asian nations should not be seen as free-riders, abusing the generosity of the industrialized world. The U.S. and Europe will no longer tolerate mercantilist practices that stress exports and restrict imports. . . . A U.S. that finds itself frustrated in Asia could look to Europe instead."

Lee pointed to the essence of geoeconomic power in an ever more interdependent world. Despite its relative decline, the United States remains the global economy's fulcrum. Other countries and regions economically depend on America's vast market more than the United States depends on them. If NAFTA and the EU united against East Asian neomercantilism, every country in the region would eventually have to dismantle its barriers and balance its trade relations. But, for now, Washington and Brussels remain distant while Japanese and regional neomercantilism are at best challenged sporadically and in specific sectors rather than systematically and forcefully.

Ironically, in December 1994 a half year before the brinkmanship over automobiles, after nearly two years of sustained efforts to open Japan's markets, the Clinton White House had quietly admitted defeat. All along Washington had forced Tokyo to sign seventeen agreements to open various markets and drop certain barriers. Yet Tokyo refused to match its words with actions. Japan's trade surplus continued to mount.

American diplomats and businessmen alike are increasingly targeting their efforts at penetrating other tough, fast growing markets in the Far East and Latin America. As Kantor put it, "We're not abandoning our efforts with Japan, because we can't afford the world's second largest economy to have sanctuary markets. But when we looked at the numbers, we saw where the action is, and it is in our own hemisphere and in Asia outside Japan."[35] Although Kantor expected American exports to Japan to rise 70 per cent to $88 billion by 2010, he predicted exports to the rest of

Asia would soar 163 per cent to $248 billion and exports to Latin America to $232 billion in the same period.

While American corporations pursue potential riches in Asia, they are already enjoying vast profits from trade and investment with Europe. A 1994 study by the Economic Strategy Institute concluded that the United States and European Union have similar economic systems that respond to market forces; overall trade between the two has largely been balanced since 1980 with shifts occurring with currency realignments. In contrast, while the United States has a largely free market system, the Far East countries carefully manage their markets and trade. The United States continually suffers immense trade deficits with the Far East. Over 75 per cent of the $1.25 billion in accumulated trade deficits since 1980 have been with Asia. American affiliates in Europe imported $32 billion from the United States while those in Asia exported $7.5 billion back to the United States. Even European investments are more beneficial than those from Asia to the United States. In 1990, European firms investing in the United States paid $7 billion in taxes while Asian firms paid only $100 million. In 1991, European firms in the United States spent $7.7 billion in research and development compared to only $1.5 billion for Asian firms in the United States.[36]

POLICY TOWARD JAPAN: GEOPOLITICAL ISSUES

Although geoeconomics overshadow the relationship, significant geopolitical differences still divide the United States and Japan. Tokyo continued to go along reluctantly with the Americans and Europeans in supporting politically and financially Russia's nascent democratic and market forces. At their summit in Tokyo in June 1993, the Group of Seven agreed on a $28 billion aid package to Russia. Yet, Tokyo has contributed even less than South Korea to the series of aid packages to Russia and refuses to give any significant aid until Moscow returns the disputed "northern territories." Given the political uncertainty in Moscow, it is extremely unlikely that Russia will comply in the foreseeable future; instead, it claims the islands are and will remain Russian.

On May 9, 1994, after over a year's negotiations, Washington and Tokyo signed yet another technology exchange agreement whereby each side's defense establishment could draw up lists of technologies it wants to obtain from the other. The agreement also allowed for joint research in relevant areas. Tokyo agreed to a Pentagon request for technology related to flat panel displays, industrial ceramics, and composite materials. It remains to be seen how much technology the Pentagon actually obtains from the agreement.

But the most important geopolitical problem was sparked in March 1993 when North Korea announced that it would no longer comply with the nuclear nonproliferation treaty requirements that it open its nuclear facilities to inspection and not build nuclear weapons. Then, in June 1993, North Korea test-fired its new Rodong missile with a range of 600 miles which could target much of Japan, including Osaka.

Washington responded by trying to coax Pyongyang into compliance by waving the stick of possible economic and military sanctions and the carrot of increased trade, diplomatic, and aid ties. On November 3, 1993, Defense Secretary Aspin announced in Tokyo a plan to build an American missile system which could be deployed in Japan to guard against regional threats. The deal involved building and selling the anti-missile system to Japan in return for Tokyo allowing American firms to license appropriate Japanese commercial patents. Aspin thus simultaneously served American geoeconomic and geopolitical interests. Throughout the stand-off with North Korea, Tokyo, along with Seoul and Beijing, cautioned Washington to avoid any tough measures toward Pyongyang that could spark its paranoid leadership into launching a war.

The crisis sputtered on until the November 1994 agreement. The diplomatic deadlock with North Korea restrained White House attempts to resolve its geoeconomic conflicts with Japan. Any American attempt to pressure North Korea into conforming to the NPT depended on cooperation from Japan, along with China, South Korea, and Russia. Economic sanctions would be meaningless unless Tokyo severed the annual $600 million to $1.8 billion of remittances from Korean-Japanese to Pyongyang, a significant percentage of North Korea's $20 billion GNP. Although Tokyo claimed that the money is remitted to the Korean people, virtually all of it ends up in Pyongyang's coffers. The loss of that hard currency could topple North Korea's economy. But Japanese fear that any crack-down on remittances could spark terrorism from among the 250,000 North Korean-Japanese or, should a war break out on the peninsula, bombs from North Korea. Tokyo is even ambiguous on whether it would allow the United States to use its bases in Japan during a second Korean War. Washington remains hobbled by the 1960 security treaty with Japan which requires the United States to come to Japan's defense but imposes no similar duty for Tokyo.[37]

Another complicating factor during the crisis was Washington's policy toward Chinese human rights practices. U.S. law requires the president to review annually China's human rights record and withdraw most-favored-nation (MFN) status if the abuses are excessive. Each administration renewed China's MFN status without controversy in the decade following the normalization of diplomatic relations with Beijing in 1979. After Chinese troops massacred pro-democracy protestors in Tiananmen Square in June 1989, pressure rose on the White House to withdraw China's MFN. The Bush administration soft-pedaled the issue, arguing that America's geo-political and geoeconomic ties with China far overshadowed how Beijing treated its dissidents.

Candidate Clinton had castigated Bush's policy as "coddling dictators." As president, however, in June 1993 Clinton announced that he too would renew China's MFN. He did warn that he would withdraw it in 1994 if Beijing did not make substantial progress on human rights. On May 29, 1994, after a rancorous year of charges and countercharges, Clinton announced that henceforth he would grant China unconditional MFN status and use quiet diplomacy to pressure Beijing on human rights. Clinton might have been able to resolve the North Korean crisis if he had made the same announcement in June 1993 in return for China's promise to exert as much pressure on Pyongyang as possible to force it back into the NPT fold. Unfortunately, Clinton remained a prisoner of his campaign rhetoric and the opportunity was lost.

Japan's own nuclear energy ambitions reemerged as an international issue in 1993. The Clinton White House joined the European Union and scores of other concerned countries in asking Tokyo to desist building breeder nuclear reactors that create rather than destroy uranium including plutonium, the material for building nuclear weapons. The White House request was quite ironic – after all, the United States had given Japan the technology to convert bomb-grade plutonium from breeder reactors. On February 20, 1994, Tokyo announced that it would postpone for twenty years its breeder reactor development program. Japan's decision may have been prompted more by unexpected developmental problems and mounting expenses than international protests. It was not until September 9, 1994, that Washington announced it would no longer aid Japan's nuclear technology.

Prime Minister Hata rekindled the controversy over Japan's nuclear energy program when he remarked in June that Japan had the capability to build nuclear bombs. The announcement provoked a chorus of horrified Far East gasps and protests. The Foreign Ministry then issued a statement insisting that "Japan does not have any expertise or experience in producing nuclear weapons. This means that Japan does not have the capability to produce them."[38]

Any "Pacific Community" sentiments Clinton had been able to stir during the November 1993 APEC summit had dissolved by the summer of 1994.

The White House's mishandling of Chinese human rights, North Korea's nuclear program, and Japanese neomercantilism, plus a May 1994 diplomatic spat over Singapore's caning of a young American vandal, prompted open criticism from virtually all Far East capitals. Asians viewed Washington as insensitive to regional conceptions of human rights and hamfisted in its diplomacy toward Pyongyang. But the biggest uproar was over trade. The White House's failure to reassure other Far East governments that it would not seek numerical targets with them pushed them into Tokyo's arms on the issue. Every government in the region, along with the European Union, condemned Clinton's numerical target scheme. Not only did they fear that they would be next if Tokyo was forced to accept numerical targets, but they also worried that Tokyo would allow more American imports at the expense of their exports to Japan. The latter fear is misplaced. Five years after Washington forced Tokyo to expand its beef import quota, Australian cattlemen sell more than American ranchers to Japan.

Despite these protests, nearly every Far East country continued to want an American military presence to deter regional powers. Yet they wanted it on their terms which included an American tolerance for neomercantilism and authoritarianism. The mixed Asian feelings toward the United States were highlighted during the latest expressions of Japanese revisionism over World War II. On May 4, 1994, the Justice Minister, Shigeto Nagano, declared publicly that Japan was not an aggressor between 1931 and 1945 and was instead trying to "liberate" Asia from western imperialism. He also called a "fabrication" the Japanese army's massacre of anywhere from 150,000 to 400,000 Chinese civilians at Nanjing in 1937. On May 6, Nagano was pressured into recanting his statements, but then was forced to resign the following day.

Nagano was simply expressing what most Japanese people believe.[39] The issue did not die with Nagano's dismissal. On May 30, a right-wing militant fired a shot at former prime minister Hosokawa for his apology over Japanese aggression in World War II. The attack followed similar assassination attempts on Nagasaki's mayor Motoshima Hiroshi in January 1990, and LDP leader Kanemaru Shin in March 1992 for their respective acknowledgements of Japanese war crimes.

The uproar forced Emperor Akihito to revise his planned two week tour of the United States in June 1994, which included a stop at Honolulu. Originally it was hinted that he might visit Pearl Harbor and apologize for Japanese aggression. But on May 17, the Imperial Household Agency stated pointedly that there would be no Pearl Harbor visit or apology. When he visited Honolulu on June 24, the Emperor did stop to lay a wreath at the National Memorial Cemetery. Akihito's sixteen-day, eleven-city tour of the

United States was largely an extended photo-op and public relations fest, marred only by a few protests by Asian-Americans demanding that he apologize for Japanese atrocities during World War II.

Despite these incidents, the widespread Japanese belief that the only wrong their country committed during World War II was to lose does not translate into the threat of renewed Japanese aggression. Japan is a well-rooted and functioning liberal democracy. The vast majority of Japanese do not want to increase the military's personnel, weapons, budget, and, most importantly, limited duties. There are no public calls for threatening Japan's neighbors with aggression.

However, these entrenched sentiments and policies could possibly change if North Korea openly brandished nuclear weapons. Pressure within Japan would build to overcome the population's alleged "nuclear allergy" and develop its own nuclear force. Even then Japan's acquisition of nuclear weapons would be unlikely given both domestic and international opposition.

AMERICA AND JAPAN INTO THE TWENTY-FIRST CENTURY

The Cold War's end has brought new challenges to the United States, and its relationship with Japan. Writing in 1989, MIT researcher Charles Ferguson argued that "the United States now faces a challenge more fundamental than any since the cold war: the simultaneous need for internal reform and for the management of a new strategic balance, namely its technological competition with Japan. If America fails it will encounter something approaching an economic crisis including severe tradeoffs between its global commitments and its domestic living standards."[40]

How will the United States respond to this challenge?

President Clinton's policy toward Japan is part of a broader set of policies designed to reverse American decline and transform the United States into the world's most prosperous and dynamic country. The policies of reducing the national debt and reordering spending priorities to target strategic industries, technologies, and infrastructure, along with his promotion of NAFTA, APEC, and GATT are all essential to the revival of America's geoeconomic and geopolitical power.

Yet, the success of these other actions will be limited as long as America's relationship with Japan remains unbalanced. And this imbalance of American liberalism and Japanese neomercantilism, and the different effects of those policies on each country's respective power, is unlikely to change.

Usually an apologist for Japan, in 1990 even Edwin Reischauer seemed to lose patience with Japanese neomercantilism, decrying Japan as "a money-bloated giant" that "had earned itself a reputation for being a thoroughly egocentric country interested only its own welfare, and yet its continued well-being or even existence depends on international cooperation and trust."[41] Most Japanese scholars admit that neomercantilism is embedded in Japan's governing triad system. Economist Nakatani Iwao stated that the

> most problematic Japanese system of all is doubtless the rigid bureaucracy. And one of the biggest problems . . . with this system is the activities of politicians aligned with private sector interest groups who take advantage of it. It is the alliance of bureaucrats, industrial and agricultural interests, and politicians that has closed Japan tight to the rest of the world. . . . The pace of change has slowed and international friction intensified by clannish bureaucrats who, with the support of industry-aligned members of the National Diet, have opposed specific reform measures even while endorsing the idea of reform.[42]

Political Scientist Inoguchi Takashi also despairs of genuine change given the governing triad's entrenched political and economic interests: "As a result of the three-way alliance, Japan became a society in which vested interests were virtually inviolable. In such a society, government policy initiatives must pass through tortuous channels before their effects can be felt, and the more ambitious the plan is, the more it will be diluted before it can be adopted. . . . Reform efforts evaporate like drops of water on a hot griddle."[43]

Over the past two generations, the causes and consequences of the geo-economic power shift between the two countries have occupied increasing amounts of each succeeding president's policy agendas. Starting with Japan's dumping of "dollar blouses" in the 1950s through the dozens of trade squabbles today over Japanese dumping and protectionism, administrations have attempted to address each separate issue as it arose rather than comprehensively understand and act against Japanese neomercantilism. During the 1980s and into the 1990s, the White House's sector by sector approach failed miserably to dent America's chronic trade deficit with Japan. Likewise starting in 1985, the attempts to "solve" the trade deficit with macroeconomic adjustments like revaluing the yen, Japan's fiscal expansion, and SII had no significant impact on Japan's vast annual surpluses.

Japan is far less protectionist today than it was previously. Yet, a former MITI Vice Minister Amaya Naohiro admitted: "almost all liberalization policies effected by Japan in the postwar period were implemented due to foreign pressure."[44] Nothing else works. Only foreign pressure can break through Japan's fortress of vested interests. The trouble with foreign pressure, as Kenneth Pyle notes, is that it "runs the risk of creating a siege mentality in Japan and thereby inflaming a narrow nationalism. . . . The external pressures for liberalization and for harmonization of Japanese institutions with international norms have created a serious dilemma for Japanese leaders, challenging central features of Japanese culture, social relations, and political structure, and arousing . . . xenophobia and ethnocentrism."[45]

Having tried everything else, America's last option in cutting through the gordian knot of Japanese neomercantilism is "results-oriented trade" in which a Japanese failure to achieve annual reductions in its trade and investment surpluses would trigger retaliatory measures. The Clinton White House, like its predecessors, has refused to exercise that option. Some fear that if the White House did systematically impose "results-oriented trade," it would spark a bilateral trade war that would eventually destroy the global economy.

Another fear is that Japan's growing geoeconomic power will inevitably translate into geopolitical power and imperial ambitions. In March 1990, Marine Corps Major-General in Japan, Henry Stackpole told a *Washington Post* correspondent that there was a Japanese threat: "The Japanese consider themselves racially superior. They feel they have a handle on the truth and their economic growth has proved that. They have achieved the Greater Asia Co-Prosperity Sphere economically, without guns." Given Japan's militaristic past, American troops would have to remain in Japan well into the twenty-first century because "no one wants a rearmed, resurgent Japan. So we are a cap in the bottle, if you will."[46]

Neither of the apocalyptic fears of global trade war or a militaristic Japan are likely. The patterns that have regulated American–Japanese relationship since 1945 will continue. Negotiations will follow the familar dance of Japanese stonewalling until threatened with sanctions and then making last-minute cosmetic "concessions." Japan's ability to soften White House and congressional policies through its lobbying and public relations power will remain formidable. Although the trade and investment surpluses will remain intractable, they may lower gradually over time. Just as the United States and Japan will manage their geoeconomic rivalry, they will remain geopolitical allies. Tokyo has even less interest in squandering its wealth on an expanded military today than it did during the Cold War. There is certainly no significant Japanese sentiment for a larger military, let alone militarism.

Pride explains much of America's policies toward Japan. In the mid nineteenth century when Britain's warships ruled the seas and its products the world's markets, America was a second-rate economic and third-rate military power. And yet it was American gunboats and diplomats which first prised open Japan. Ever since, America has been Japan's greatest partner and nemesis. American experts flocked across the Pacific in the late nineteenth century and after 1945 to tutor Japan in all aspects of modernization. The mission of modernizing Japan, which most Americans interpreted as making the Japanese "more like us," continues.

While some idealists still cling to fond hopes that Japan's Americanization will occur, others – classical economists – claim it already has. How else can Japan's dazzling economic success be explained other than by free markets? And, the liberal dogma continues, since Japan's economic growth has surpassed that of the United States then its markets must be freer. Not surprisingly, this view is identical to that of Japan's government and business associations. Hubris and myths may be the biggest obstacles in preventing Washington from realizing American interests with Japan.

In reality, almost a century and a half after Perry's warships arrived, the task of opening Japan remains incomplete. Economically, politically and culturally Japan is still only partially accessible to Americans and other foreigners. "Japanese market," of course, remains an oxymoron for American competitors which may well beat out their Japanese rivals in third markets. But the inaccessibility goes beyond the marketplace.

Over three decades ago, former prime minister Yoshida wrote that "Japan's policies *vis-à-vis* the United States must change as the nation's economic position improves with the consequent strengthening of the country's international status and self-respect. . . . But the maintenance of close bonds of friendship with the United States, based upon a deep mutuality of interests, must be one of the pillars of Japan's fundamental policy and always remain so."[47] Yoshida's foreign policy wisdom transcends national boundaries. His maxim fits the United States just as easily as Japan. And American policy toward Japan will continue to follow those guidelines.

Notes

Notes to the Introduction

1. Frederick L. Shiels, *Tokyo and Washington* (Lexington, Mass.: Lexington Books, 1980) p. 55.
2. Robert Gilpin, *The Political Economy of International Relations* (Princeton, N. J.: Princeton University Press, 1987) pp. 391–2.
3. Quoted in Akira Iriye, *Pacific Estrangement: Japanese and American Estrangement, 1897–1911* (Cambridge, Mass.: Harvard University Press, 1972) p. 9.
4. See James Fallows, *More like Us: An American Plan for American Recovery* (New York: Pantheon, 1990).
5. Roger Pineau, *The Japan Expedition, 1852–1854: The Personal Journal of Commodore Matthew Perry* (Washington, D.C.: Smithsonian Institution Press, 1968) pp. 211, 214.
6. Henry Kissinger, *Years of Upheaval* (Boston, Mass.: Little, Brown, 1982) pp. 737–8.
7. Richard Neustadt, *Alliance Politics* (New York: Columbia University Press, 1970) p. 66.
8. Akira Iriye, *Pacific Estrangement*, p. 1.

Notes to Chapter 1: Pacific Patron, 1853–94

1. Cecil Crabb, *Policy-makers and Critics: Conflicting Theories of American Foreing Policy* (New York: Praeger, 1976) p. 1.
2. William Seward, *Works*, vol. 4, p. 319.
3. James Thompson *et al.*, *Sentimental Imperialists: The American Experience in East Asia* (Honolulu: University of Hawaii Press, 1981) pp. 35–6.
4. John Witney Hall, *Japan: From Prehistory to Modern Times* (Tokyo: Charles E. Tuttle, 1971) p. 218.
5. John Foster Dulles, *Yankees and Samurai: America's Role in the Emergence of Modern Japan, 1791–1900* (New York: Harper & Row, 1965) pp. 1–6.
6. Ibid., p. 9.
7. Ibid., p. 12.
8. Ibid., p. 29.
9. Akira Iriye, *Pacific Estrangement: Japanese and American Expansion, 1897–1911* (Cambridge, Mass.: Harvard University Press, 1972) p. 8.
10. Kenneth Hagen, *This People's Navy: The Making of American Sea Power* (New York: The Free Press, 1991) p. 130.
11. Roger Pinean, *The Japan Expedition, 1852–1854: The Personal Journal of Commodore Matthew Perry* (Washington, D.C.: Smithsonian Institution Press, 1968).
12. Inazo Nitobe, *The Intercourse Between the United States and Japan* (Baltimore, Md.: Johns Hopkins University Press, 1891) p. 46.
13. Hall, *Japan*, p. 255.

14. Dulles, *Yankees and Samurai*, p. 63.
15. Thompson, *Sentimental Imperialists*, p. 67.
16. Quoted in Dulles, *Yankees and Samurai*, p. 62.
17. Quoted in ibid., p. 63.
18. Hagan, *This People's Navy*, p. 149.
19. Quoted in George H. Kerr, *Okinawa: The History of an Island People* (Rutland, Vt: Charles Tuttle, 1958) p. 4.
20. Townsend Harris, *Journal*.
21. Dulles, *Yankees and Samurai*, p. 102.
22. Both quotes from ibid., pp. 111, 117.
23. Both quotes ibid., p. 123.
24. Ibid., p. 145.
25. Nitobe, *The Intercourse Between the United States and Japan*, p. 67.
26. Henry Field, *From Egypt to Japan* (New York: 1877) p. 424.
27. Thompson, *Sentimental Imperialists*, p. 73.
28. Dulles, *Yankees and Samurai*, pp. 133–4.
29. Ibid., p. 169.
30. Ibid., p. 236.
31. Ibid., p. 251.

Notes to Chapter 2: Pacific Rival, 1894–1930

1. Among the excellent studies of this period see, Raymond Esthus, *Theodore Roosevelt and Japan* (Seattle: University of Washington, 1966); Charles E. Neu, *An Uncertain Friendship: Theodore Roosevelt and Japan, 1906–9* (1967); Akira Iriye, *Pacific Estrangement: Japanese and American Expansion, 1897–1911* (Cambridge, Mass.: Harvard University Press, 1972); Ernest May and James C. Thompson, eds, *American–East Asian Relations: A Survey* (Cambridge, Mass.: Harvard University Press, 1972); Charles E. Neu, *The Troubled Encounter: The United States and Japan* (1975).
2. Iriye, *Pacific Estrangement*, p. 35.
3. Ibid., p. 54.
4. Joshiah Strong, *New Era, or the Coming Kingdom* (New York) p. 222. For other prominent American imperial writings, see Charles Morris, *Civilization: An Historical Review of its Elements* (Chicago, 1890); Benjamin Ide Wheeler, "Greece and the Eastern Question," *Atlantic*, vol. 79 (June 1897) pp. 722–32; Alfred Thayer Mahan, *Harpers*, vol. 95 (September 1897) pp. 523–33.
5. Takahashi Kamekichi, *Nihon Kindai Hattatsushi*, vol. 1 (Tokyo: Toyokeizai shimposha, 1973) p. 23.
6. John Witney Hall, *Japan: From Prehistory to Modern Times* (Tokyo: Charles E. Tuttle, 1971) p. 300.
7. Quoted in David M. Pletcher, *The Awkward Years: American Foreign Relations under Garfield and Arthur* (Columbia: University of Missouri Press, 1962) p. 70.
8. Quoted in Iriye, *Pacific Estrangement*, p. 53.
9. Robert Beisner, *Twelve Against Empire: The Anti-Imperialists, 1989–1900* (New York: McGraw-Hill, 1968) pp. 148–50.
10. For different views, see Walter Mills, *The Martial Spirit* (Chicago: Ivan R. Dee Publishers, 1931, 1989); H. Wayne Morgan, *America's Road to Empire*

(1965); William Appleman William, *The Roots of Modern American Empire* (1969); Peter W. Stanley, *A Nation in the Making: The Philippines and the United States, 1899–1921* (1974); Richard Welch, *Response to Imperialism: The United States and the Philippine–American War* (1979); Stuart Creighton Miller, *"Benevolent Assimilation:" The American Conquest of the Philippines, 1899–1903* (1982); Lewis L. Gould, *The Spanish–American War and President McKinley* (1982).

11.   See Paul A. Varg, *The Making of a Myth: The United States and China, 1897–1912* (1968); Marilyn Blatt Young, *The Rhetoric of Empire: American China Policy, 1895–1901* (1968); Michael Hunt, *The Making of a Special Relationship: The United States and China to 1914* (1983).

12.   Frederick W. Marks, *Velvet on Iron: The Diplomacy of Theodore Roosevelt* (Linclon: University of Nebraska Press, 1979) p. 14.

13.   Arthur H. Smith, *China and America Today: A Study of Conditions and Relations* (New York: F. H. Revell, 1909) p. 54.

14.   Iriye, *Pacific Estrangement*, p. 123.

15.   Quoted in ibid., p. 198.

16.   Both quotes from ibid., 226.

17.   Alfred Dennis, *Adventures in American Diplomacy, 1896–1906* (New York: 1928) p. 242.

18.   Iriye, *Pacific Estrangement*, p. 83.

19.   Roosevelt to Spring Rice, March 19, 1904, Morison, *Roosevelt Letters*, vol. IV, p. 759.

20.   Roosevelt to Theodore Roosevelt, Jr, February 10, 1904, in ibid., vol. IV, p. 724.

21.   Esthus, *Theodore Roosevelt and Japan*, p. 101.

22.   Iriye, *Pacific Estrangement*, p. 93.

23.   Esthus, *Theodore Roosevelt and Japan*, p. 117.

24.   Quoted in Iriye, *Pacific Estrangement*, p. 98.

25.   Ibid., p. 100.

26.   Ibid., pp. 157–62.

27.   Esthus, *Theodore Roosevelt and Japan*, p. 146.

28.   Roosevelt to Hale, October 27, 1906, Morison, *Roosevelt Letters*, vol. 5, pp. 473–5.

29.   Roosevelt to George Otto Trevelyan, October 1, 1911, Morison, *Roosevelt Letters*, vol. 7, p. 1018.

30.   See Sadao Senno, "Chess Game with No Checkmate: Admiral Inoue and the Pacific War," *Naval War College Review* (January–February 1974) pp. 27–8.

31.   Homer Lea, *The Valour of Ignorance* (New York: Harper & Brothers 1942, 1909).

32.   Thomas F. Millard, *America and the Far Eastern Question* (New York: Scribners, 1909) p. 11.

33.   See any of my books on Japan.

34.   For an overview of Wilson foreign policy, see William Parsons, *Wilsonian Diplomacy: Allied–American Rivalries in War and Peace* (St Louis, Mo.: Forum Press, 1978); For an interesting psychoanalytical explanation for Wilson's policies see George and Juliette George, *Woodrow Wilson and Colonel House: A Personality Study* (1956).

35. For an excellent overview, see Roy Curry, *Woodrow Wilson and Far Eastern Policy, 1913–1921* (1957).

36. See Burton Beers, *Vain Endeavor: Robert Lansing's Attempts to End the American–Japanese Rivalry* (1962).

37. Arnold Offner, *The Origins of the Second World War: American Foreign Policy and World Politics, 1917–1941* (New York: Praeger, 1975) p. 8.

38. See Ernest May, *The World War and American Isolation, 1914–1917* (1959); Patrick Devlin, *Too Proud To Fight: Woodrow Wilson's Neutrality* (1975); John Coogan, *The End of Neutrality: The United States, Britain, and Maritime Rights, 1899–1915* (1981).

39. See Russell H. Fifield, *Woodrow Wilson and the Far East: The Diplomacy of the Shantung Question* (1952).

40. For two interesting analyses of the treaty ratification process which attribute the defeat to Wilson's psychological rigidity, see Alexander and Juliette George, *Woodrow Wilson and Colonel House*, and Edwin Weinstein, *Woodrow Wilson: A Medical and Psychological Biography* (1981).

41. Offner, *The Origins of the Second World War*, p. 42.

42. Combs, *American Foreign Policy*, p. 247.

43. For an excellent account of this period, see Akira Iriye, *After Imperialism: The Search for a New Order in the Far East, 1921–31* (Cambridge, Mass.: Harvard University Press, 1965).

44. Sadao Asada, "Japan's 'Special Interests' and the Washington Conference, 1921–22," *American Historical Review*, vol. 67 (October 1961) pp. 62–70.

45. Offner, *Origins of the Second World War*, p. 84.

46. Hall, *Japan*, p. 318.

47. Offner, *The Origins of the Second World War*, p. 72.

48. Ibid., pp. 86, 88.

Notes to Chapter 3: The Road to War, 1931–41

1. For a highly critical account of the Hoover administration policy toward the Manchuria crisis, see Justus D. Doenecke, *When the Wicked Arise: American Opinion Makers and the Manchurian Crisis, 1931–33* (Lewisburg, Pa.: Bucknell University Press, 1984). For an overview of the entire decade, see Gerald Haines, "American Myopia and the Japanese Monroe Doctrine, 1931–41," *Prologue*, vol. 13 (Spring 1981) pp. 101–14.

   For two very different views of Roosevelt's foreign policy, see the laudatory vision of Robert Dallek, *Franklin D. Roosevelt and American Foreign Policy, 1932–1945*, 2 vols (New York: Oxford University Press, 1979); and the derogatory opinion of Frederick W. Marks, *Wind Over Sand: The Diplomacy of Franklin Roosevelt* (Athens: University of Georgia Press, 1988).

2. Arnold Offner, *The Origins of the Second World War: American Foreign Policy and World Politics, 1917–1941* (New York: Praeger, 1975) p. 99.

3. Sadao Asada, "Japan's 'Special Interests' and the Washington Conference, 1921–22," *American Historical Review*, vol. 67 (October 1961) pp. 69–70.

4. Quoted in Marks, *Wind Over Sand*, p. 45.

5. Mark R. Peattie, *Ishiwara Keanji and Japan's Confrontation with the West* (Princeton: Princeton University Press, 1966) p. 80.

4

404 *Notes*

6. Quoted in Hugh de Santis, *The Diplomacy of Silence: The American Foreign Service, the Soviet Union, and the Cold War, 1933–1947* (Chicago: University of Chicago Press, 1980).

7. Marks, *Wind Over Sand*, p. 11; for a good account of Roosevelt's political perspectives, see Thomas Greer, *What Roosevelt Thought: The Social and Political Ideas of Franklin D. Roosevelt* (East Lansing: Michigan State University Press, 1958).

8. Quoted in Marks, *Wind Over Sand*, p. 260.

9. Ibid., pp. 304–5.

10. Warren Kimball, *The Most Unsordid Act: Lend Lease, 1939–1941* (Baltimore: Johns Hopkins University Press, 1969) p. 99.

11. For works on Roosevelt's advisors, see John Blum, ed., *From the Morgenthau Diaries*, 3 vols (Boston: Houghton Mifflin, 1959, 1965, 1967); John Blum, *Roosevelt and Morgenthau* (Boston: Houghton Mifflin, 1970); Stanley H. Hornbeck, *The United States and the Far East: Certain Fundamentals of Foreign Policy* (Boston: World Peace Foundation, 1942). Waldo Heinrichs, *American Ambassador: Joseph Grew and the Development of the United States Diplomatic Tradition* (Boston: Little, Brown, 1966).

12. Offner, *The Origins of the Second World War*, p. 105.

13. Franklin D. Roosevelt, *Looking Forward* (New York, NY: John Day, 1933); Franklin D. Roosevelt, *On Our Way* (New York, NY: John Day, 1934).

14. Marks, *Wind Over Sand*, p. 28.

15. Warren F. Kuehl, "Midwestern Newspapers and Isolationist Sentiment," *Diplomatic History*, vol. 3 (Summer 1979) pp. 283–306.

16. Marks, *Wind Over Sand*, p. 14.

17. See Frederick W. Marks, "Franklin Roosevelt's Diplomatic Debut: The Myth of the Hundred Days," *South Atlantic Quarterly*, vol. 84 (Spring 1985) pp. 245–6.

18. Nathaniel Peffer, *Harpers*, vol. 168 (March 1934) pp. 398–403.

19. For an excellent account of American policy toward Japan during this period, see Dorothy Borg, *The United States and the Far Eastern Crisis of 1933–38* (Cambridge, Mass.: Harvard University Press, 1964).

    For early Roosevelt views of Japan, see William L. Neumann, "Franklin D. Roosevelt and Japan, 1913–33," *Pacific Historical Review*, vol. 22 (May 1953) pp. 143–53; and Franklin D. Roosevelt, "Shall We Trust Japan?," *Asia*, vol. 23 (July 1923) pp. 475–78, 536, 528.

20. Marks, *Wind Over Sand*, p. 51; Secretary of State Cordell Hull had little effect on foreign policy, not surprising since he "made little effort to familiarize himself with foreign points of view and felt no qualms about admitting it" (Marks, ibid., p. 255). See Howard Jablon, "Cordell Hull, His 'Associates,' and Relations with Japan, 1933–36," *Mid-America*, vol. 56 (July 1974) pp. 160–74.

21. For excellent accounts of Japan's foreign policy during the 1930s, see James B. Crowley, "Japanese Army Factionalism in the Early 1930s," *Journal of Asian Studies*, vol. 21 (May 1962) pp. 309–26; James B. Crowley, "A Reconsideration of the Marco Polo Bridge Incident," *Journal of Asian Studies*, vol. 22 (May 1963) pp. 277–91; James B. Crowley, *Japan's Quest for Autonomy: National Security and Foreign Policy, 1930–1938* (Princeton: Princeton University Press, 1966).

22. Hiroyuki Agawa, *The Reluctant Admiral: Yamamoto and the Imperial Navy* (Tokyo: Kodansha International, 1979) pp. 37–8.
23. Masao Maruyama, *Thought and Behaviour in Japanese Politics* (New York: Oxford University Press, 1969).
24. Quoted in Ronald Spector, *Eagle Against the Sun: The American War with Japan* (New York, Vintage Books, 1985) p. 42.
25. Ibid., p. xvi.
26. See Ernest R. May, "U.S. Press Coverage of Japan, 1931–41," in Dorothy Borg and Okimoto Shumpei, eds, *Pearl Harbor as History: Japanese–American Relations, 1931–41* (New York: Columbia University Press, 1993) pp. 546–61.
27. Roosevelt's speech and its aftermath have been thoroughly explored. See, Dorothy Borg, "Notes on Roosevelt's 'Quarantine' Speech," *Political Science Quarterly*, vol. 72 (September 1957) pp. 405–33; John M. Haight, "Roosevelt and the Aftermath of the Quarantine Speech," *Review of Politics*, vol. 24 (April 1962) pp. 233–59; John M. Haight, "Franklin D. Roosevelt and a Naval Quarantine of Japan," *Pacific Historical Review*, vol. 40 (May 1971) pp. 203–6; Travis Beal Jacobs, "Roosevelt's Quarantine Speech," *The Historian*, vol. 24 (August 1962) pp. 483–502.
28. Quoted in Marks, *Wind Over Sand*, p. 74.
29. William Neumann, "Ambiguity and Ambivalence in Ideas of National Interest in Asia," in Alexander DeConde, ed., *Isolation and Security* (Durham: Duke University Press, 1957) pp. 133–58.
30. John W. Masland, "Commercial Influence upon American Far Eastern Policy, 1937–1941," *Pacific Historical Review*, vol. 11 (September 1942) pp. 281–99.
31. Marks, *Wind Over Sand*, p. 46.
32. Ibid.
33. Frederic R. Sanborn, *Design for War: A Study of Secret Power Politics, 1937–1941* (New York: Devin-Adair, 1951) pp. 40, 43.
34. Quoted in Robert E. Sherwood, *Roosevelt and Hopkins: An Intimate History* (New York: Harper, 1948) pp. 290–1.
35. See William L. Langer and S. Everett Gleason, *The Undeclared War, 1940–41* (New York: Harper, 1953) pp. 30–1.
36. Joseph C. Grew, *The Turbulent Era* (Boston: Houghton Mifflin, 1952) vol. 2, p. 927.
37. Henry L. Stimson and McGeorge Bundy, *On Active Service in War and Peace* (New York: Harper & Brothers, 1948) p. 173.
38. Marks, *Wind Over Sand*, pp. 112–15.
39. Both quotes from ibid., p. 95.
40. Ibid., p. 104.
41. Offner, *The Origins of the Second World War*, p. 204.
42. Ibid., p. 225; for good accounts of this diplomacy, see R. J. C. Butow, "The Hull–Nomura Conversations: A Fundamental Misconception," *American Historical Review*, vol. 65 (July 1960) pp. 822–36. R. J. C. Butow, *Tojo and the Coming of the War* (Stanford: Stanford University Press, 1961). Lester H. Brune, "Considerations of Force in Cordell Hull's Diplomacy, July 26 to November 26, 1941," *Diplomatic History*, vol. 2 (Fall 1978) pp. 389–405.
43. Dean Acheson, *Present at the Creation: My Years in the State Department* (New York: Norton, 1969) p. 24.

44. Masland, "Commercial Influence," p. 296; for other studies of the embargo, see: Irvine Anderson, "The 1941 De Facto Embargo on Oil to Japan: A Bureaucratic Reflex," *Pacific Historical Review*, vol. 44 (May 1975) pp. 201–31; Jonathan Utley, "Upstairs, Downstairs at Foggy Bottom: Oil, Exports, and Japan, 1940–41," *Prologue*, vol. 8 (Spring 1976) pp. 17–28.

45. Herbert Feis, *The Road to Pearl Harbor* (Princeton: Princeton University Press, 1975) pp. 305–11.

46. Cordell Hull, *The Memoirs of Cordell Hull*, 2 vols (New York: Macmillan, 1948), vol. 2, pp. 1069–70.

47. James MacGregor Burns, *Roosevelt: The Soldier of Freedom* (New York: Harcourt Brace, Jovanovich, 1970) p. 157.

48. For Japanese accounts that generally admit Japan's imperial ambitions and the unwillingness to accept any diplomatic solution to the crisis short of total American acquiescence, see Shigenori Togo, *The Cause of Japan*, Fumihiko Togo, trans. (New York: Simon and Schuster, 1956); Mamoru Shigemitsu, *Japan and Her Destiny: My Struggle for Peace* (New York: E. P. Dutton, 1958); Nobunaga Ike, trans. and ed., *Japan's Decision for War: Records of the 1941 Policy Conferences* (Stanford: Stanford University Press, 1967).

49. Marks, *Wind Over Sand*, p. 34.

50. Historians are sharply divided over whether Roosevelt engineered or drifted into America's entry into World War II.

 Some argue that Roosevelt did not want or seek war. See William L. Langer and S. Everett Gleason, *The Challenge to Isolation, 1937–1940* (New York: Harper, 1952); Donald F. Drummond, *The Passing of American Neutrality, 1937–1941* (Ann Arbor: University of Michigan Press, 1955); Burns, *Roosevelt: Soldier of Freedom*; Jonathan G. Utley, *Going to War with Japan, 1937–41* (Knoxville: University of Tennessee Press, 1985) pp. 177–82.

 More recent historians believe that at some point Roosevelt favored America's entry into the war, but differ over when. For a Roosevelt decision for war as early as 1940, see Sanborn, *Design for War*. For an August 1941 decision for war, see Dallek, *Franklin D. Roosevelt and American Foreign Policy*; Christopher G. Thorne, *Allies of a Kind: The United States, Britain, and the War Against Japan, 1941–1945* (New York: Oxford University Press, 1978).

 Whether or not he wanted war, Roosevelt periodically displayed a fatalism over its inevitability. Jablon, "Cordell Hull, His 'Associates,' and Relations with Japan, 1933–36."

 For other balanced accounts of the reasons for war, see Borg and Okimoto, eds, *Pearl Harbor as History*; Offner, *The Origins of the Second World War*; Jonathan G. Utley, "Diplomacy in a Democracy: The United States and Japan, 1937–41," *World Affairs*, vol. 139 (Fall 1976) pp. 130–40; Gordon Prange, *At Dawn We Slept: The Untold Story of Pearl Harbor* (New York: McGraw-Hill, 1981); Utley, *Going to War with Japan*; Gordon Prange, *Pearl Harbor: The Verdict of History* (New York: McGraw-Hill, 1986).

51. Marks, *Wind Over Sand*, pp. 278, 280.

52. Ibid., p. 263.

53. Sir George Sansom, "Liberalism in Japan," *Foreign Affairs*, vol. 19 (April 1941) pp. 551–9.

54. Offner, *The Origins of the Second World War*, p. 233.
55. Marks, *Wind Over Sand*, p. 275.
56. Morgenthau, "Morgenthau Diaries," *Collier's*, October 11, 1947, p. 74.
57. Graham T. Allison and Morton H. Halperin, "Bureaucratic Politics: A Paradigm and Some Policy Implications," in Richard H. Ullman and Raymond Tanter, eds, *Theory and Policy in International Relations* (Princeton: Princeton University Press, 1972) pp. 66–7.
58. Marks, *Wind Over Sand*, p. 71.
59. Ibid., p. 83.

Notes to Chapter 4: The Road to Peace, 1942–5

1. John Toland, *Infamy: Pearl Harbor and its Aftermath* (Garden City, NY: Doubleday, 1982), ch. 16; see also Robert Theobald, *The Final Secret of Pearl Harbor* (New York: Devin-Adair, 1954); Hamilton Fish, *FDR, The Other Side of the Coin: How We Were Tricked into World War II* (New York: Vantage Press, 1976).
2. Gordon Prange, *Pearl Harbor: The Verdict of History* (New York: McGraw-Hill, 1986); see also David Kahn, "Did FDR Invite the Pearl Harbor Attack," *New York Review of Books*, May 27, 1982, pp. 34–7; David Kahn, "The United States Views Germany and Japan in 1941," in Ernest R. May, ed., *Knowing One's Enemies: Intelligence Assessment Before the Two World Wars* (Princeton: Princeton University Press, 1984).
3. Ronald Spector, *Eagle Against The Sun: The American War with Japan* (New York: Vintage Books, 1985) pp. 93–4.
4. Ibid., p. 1.
5. Roberta Wohlstetter, *Pearl Harbor: Warning and Decision* (Stanford: Stanford University Press, 1962).
6. Ibid., pp. 387–8.
7. Quoted in Spector, *Eagle Against the Sun*, p. 96.
8. Gordon Prange, *At Dawn We Slept: The Untold Story of Pearl Harbor* (New York: McGraw-Hill, 1981) p. 736.
9. Spector, *Eagle Against The Sun*, p. 84.
10. Ibid., p. 18.
11. Alfred Hurley, *Billy Mitchell: Crusader for Air Power* (Bloomington: University of Indiana Press, 1975) p. 42.
12. Spector, *Eagle Against the Sun*, pp. 11, 12.
13. Quoted in Michael Vlahos, *The Blue Sword: The Naval War College and the American Mission, 1919–1941* (Washington, D.C., G.P.O., 1980) p. 143.
14. Spector, *Eagle Against The Sun*, p. 450.
15. Dower, *A War Without Mercy: Race and Power in the Pacific War* (New York: Pantheon Books, 1986) p. x.

    For other explorations of this theme, see Christopher Thorne, *Allies of a Kind: The United States, Great Britain, and the War Against Japan, 1941–45* (New York: Oxford University Press, 1978); Akira Iriye, *Power and Culture: The Japanese–American War, 1941–45* (Cambridge: Harvard University Press, 1981).
16. Dower, *A War Without Mercy*, p. 8.

17.	Ba Maw, *Breakthrough in Burma: Memoirs of a Revolution, 1939–1946* (New Haven: Yale University Press, 1968) p. 177.
18.	Dower, *A War Without Mercy*, p. 278.
19.	Robert Hall, ed., and John O. Gauntlett, trans., *Kokutai no Hongi: Cardinal Principles of the National Entity of Japan* (Cambridge: Harvard University Press, 1949) p. 138.
20.	Joseph Grew, *Report from Tokyo* (New York: Simon & Schuster, 1942) pp. viii, 17, 29, 30.
21.	Geoffry Gorer, "Themes in Japanese Culture," *Transactions of the New York Academy of Sciences*, 2nd ser., 5.1 November 1943, pp. 106–24; John Embree, *The Japanese* (Washington: Smithsonian Institution War Background Studies no. 7, January 23, 1943); Judith Silberpfenning, "Psychological Aspects of Current Japanese and German Paradoxa," *Psychoanalytical Review*, vol. 32, no. 1 (January 1945) pp. 73–85; Weston La Barre, "Some Observations on Character Structure in the Orient," *Psychiatry: Journal of Biology and the Pathology of Interpersonal Relations*, vol. 8, no. 3 (August 1945) pp. 319–42.
22.	Their wartime lectures and reports were later reworked into such publications as: Margaret Mead and Rhoda Metraux, eds, *The Study of Culture at a Distance* (Chicago: University of Chicago Press, 1953); Clyde Kluckhorn, *The Relation of Anthropology to Modern Life* (Boston: McGraw-Hill, 1949).
23.	Ruth Benedict, *The Chrysanthemum and the Sword* (Boston: Houghton Mifflin, 1946).
24.	Dower, *A War Without Mercy*, p. 137.
25.	Alexander Leighton, *Human Relations in a Changing World* (New York: Dutton, 1949) p. 128.
26.	John M. Blum, *V was for Victory: Politics and American Culture During World War II* (New York: Harcourt Brace Jovanovich, 1976) p. 20.
27.	Samuel Stouffer *et al.*, *Combat and its Aftermath*, pp. 34, 161, 157.
28.	Dower, *A War Without Mercy*, p. 53.
29.	Hadley Cantril, ed., *Public Opinion, 1935–46* (Princeton, NJ: Princeton University Press, 1951) p. 158.
30.	Dower, *A War Without Mercy*, p. 9.
31.	Robert Sherrod, *On to Westward*, p. 15.
32.	B. B. A. Roling and C. F. Ruter, eds, *The Tokyo Judgement: The International Military Tribunal for the Far East (I.M.T.F.E.), April 29, 1946–November 1948* (Amsterdam: APA University Press, 1977) p. 385.
33.	Edgar Jones, "One War Is Enough," *Atlantic Monthly*, February 1946, pp. 48–53.
34.	Quoted in Buell, *Master of Seapower*, p. 357.
35.	Spector, *Eagle Against The Sun*, p. 543.
36.	Quoted in ibid., p. 544.
37.	Quoted in Dower, *A War Without Mercy*, p. 115.
38.	Clay Blair, *Silent Victory: The U.S. Submarine War Against Japan* (New York: Lippincott, 1975), pp. 792, 851–2.
39.	U.S. Strategic Bombing Survey, *Final Report Covering Air-Raid Protection and Allied Subjects in Japan* (Washington: G.P.O., Report 11), p. 200.
40.	Dower, *A War Without Mercy*, p. 298.
41.	For good accounts of American diplomacy during World War II, Gaddis

Smith, *American Diplomacy During the Second World War, 1941–1945* (New York: Cooper Square, 1965); John Gaddis, *The United States and the Origins of the Cold War, 1941–47* (New York: Columbia University Press, 1972).

42. Spector, *Eagle Against The Sun*, p. 367.
43. Romanus and Sunderland, *Stillwell's Command Problems*, pp. 112, 472.
44. For an argument that the Dixie mission were "dupes" and friendship with the communists illusionary, see Tang Tsuo, *America's Failure in China* (Chicago: University of Chicago Press, 1963). For "lost opportunity" arguments see Reardon and Michael Schaller, *U.S. Crusade in China* (New York: Columbia University Press, 1979); for a balanced view, see Kenneth E. Shewmaker, *Americans and Chinese Communists, 1927–1945: A Persuading Encounter* (Ithaca: Cornell University Press, 1971).
45. Stimson, "The Decision to Drop the Bomb," p. 101.
46. Ibid., p. 102.
47. Paul Baker, ed., *The Atomic Bomb: The Great Decision* (New York: Holt, Rinehart, and Winston, 1976) p. 4.
48. Martin Sherwin, *A World Destroyed: The Atomic Bomb and the Grand Alliance* (New York: Vintage Books, 1977) p. 214.
49. Robert Ferrell, ed., *Off the Record: The Private Papers of Harry S. Truman* (New York: Norton, 1980) p. 55.
50. Samuel Morrison, "Why Japan Surrendered," *The Atlantic Monthly*, October 1960, pp. 41–7.
51. Ibid.
52. Quoted in R. J. C. Butow, *Japan's Decision to Surrender* (Stanford, Calif.: Stanford University Press, 1954) p. 100.
53. Barton Bernstein, "The Perils and Politics of Surrender: Ending the War with Japan and Avoiding the Third Atomic Bomb," *Pacific Historical Review*, February 1977, p. 5.
54. Quoted in Spector, *Eagle Against the Sun*, p. 546.
55. Quoted in Gar Alperovitz, *Atomic Diplomacy: Hiroshima and Potsdam* (New York: Simon & Schuster, 1965) p. 181.
56. Quoted in Gar Alperovitz, *Atomic Diplomacy*, p. 180.
57. Quoted in Akira Iriye, *Power and Culture: The Japanese–American War, 1941–45* (Cambridge: Harvard University Press, 1981) p. 253.
58. Morrison, "Why Japan Surrendered," p. 45.
59. William Lawrence, *Dawn Over Zero: The Story of the Atomic Bomb* (New York: Alfred A. Knopf, 1946) p. 224.
60. Barton Bernstein, "The Perils and Politics," p. 5.
61. Bernstein, "The Perils and Politics," p. 5.
62. Butow, *Japan's Decision to Surrender*, p. 208.
63. Hanson Baldwin, *Great Mistakes of the War* (New York: 1950) p. 93.
64. See, for example, ibid.
65. Morrison, "Why Japan Surrendered," p. 47.
66. Quoted in Baldwin, *Great Mistakes of the War*, p. 90.
67. Quoted in ibid., p. 91.
68. Quoted in Alperovitz, *Atomic Diplomacy*, p. 236.
69. Carroll Quigley, *Tragedy and Hope* (New York: Macmillan, 1966) p. 863.
70. Henry Stimson, "The Decision to Drop the Atomic Bomb," *Harper's Magazine*, February 1947, p. 103.

71. Ibid., p. 105.
72. Morrison, "Why Japan Surrendered," p. 47.
73. Herbert Feis, *The Atomic Bomb and the End of World War II* (Princeton: Princeton University Press) p. 194.
74. For these arguments, see P. M. S. Blackett, *Fear, War, and the Bomb* (New York: 1949); David Horowitz, "Hiroshima and the Cold War," *Liberation*, September 1965, pp. 26–7.
75. For a succinct counter to the revisionists, see Michael Amrine's review of Gar Alperovitz's *Atomic Diplomacy*, July 18, 1965, *New York Herald Tribune*, pp. 8–9.
76. Feis, *The Atomic Bomb and the End of World War II*, p. 195.
77. Gabriel Kolko, *The Politics of War: The World and United States Foreign Policy, 1945–1954* (New York: Random House, 1968) p. 538.
78. Stimson, "The Decision to Drop the Bomb," p. 102.
79. Martin Sherwin, "The Atomic Bomb and the Origins of the Cold War: U.S. Atomic Energy and Diplomacy, 1941–45," *American Historical Review*, vol. 78, no. 4 (October 1973) pp. 945–68.
80. See, for example, Kenneth Glacier, "The Decision to Use Atomic Weapons Against Hiroshima and Nagasaki," *Public Policy*, vol. 18, no. 4 (Summer 1970) pp. 465–75, 512–16; Alperovitz, *Atomic Diplomacy*, p. 238.
81. Stimson, "The Decision to Drop the Bomb," p. 98.
82. Feis, *The Atomic Bomb and the End of World War II*, p. 197.
83. See Asada Sadao, "Japanese Perceptions of the A-Bomb Decision, 1945–1980," in Joe C. Dixon, ed., *The American Military and the Far East* (Washington: G.P.O. 1980) pp. 211–19.
84. Robert Goralski, *World War II Almanac, 1931–1945* (New York: Putnam, 1981) pp. 425–9; Dower, *A War Without Mercy*, pp. 295–301.
85. Quoted in Barton Bernstein, "Roosevelt, Truman, and the Atomic Bomb, 1941–1945: A Reinterpretation," *Political Science Quarterly*, vol. 90 (Spring 1975) p. 61.
86. Spector, *Eagle Against The Sun*, p. 441.
87. Stimson, "The Decision to Drop the Bomb," p. 105.
88. Ibid.

Notes to Chapter 5: Demilitarization and Democratization, 1945–7

1. Michael Schaller, *The American Occupation of Japan* (New York: Oxford University Press, 1985) p. 52.
2. Ward and Sakamoto, "Introduction," in Ward and Sakamoto, eds, *Democratizing Japan*, p. i.
3. PWC 296b, "Japan: Economic Policies During Military Occupation," November 16, 1944, Part VII.
4. *FRUS (Foreign Relations of the United States)*, 1945, VI: 545.
5. Theodore Cohen, *Remaking Japan: The American Occupation as New Deal*, ed. by Herbert Passin (New York: 1987) p. 34.
6. Ibid., p. 17.
7. Schaller, *The American Occupation of Japan*, p. 6.
8. Michael Schaller, *Douglas MacArthur: The Far East General* (New York: Oxford University Press, 1989) p. vii.

9. Ibid., p. 74.
10. Shigeru Yoshida, *The Yoshida Memoirs* (Cambridge, Mass.: Harvard University Press, 1961) pp. 49, 287.
11. For penetrating psychological studies, see Carol M. Petillo, *Douglas MacArthur: The Philippine Years* (Bloomington, Ind.: University of Indiana Press, 1981); Richard Rovere and Arthur Schlesinger, *The MacArthur Controversy and American Foreign Policy* (New York: 1965); D. Clayton James, *The Years of MacArthur*, 3 vols (Boston: McGraw-Hill, 1970–85).
12. Schaller, *Douglas MacArthur*, p. 11.
13. Ronald Spector, *Eagle Against the Sun: The American War with Japan* (New York: Vintage Books, 1985) pp. xiv–xv.
14. Robert H. Ferrell, ed., *The Eisenhower Diaries* (New York: W. W. Norton, 1981) pp. 51, 49.
15. Schaller, *Douglas MacArthur*, pp. 72–3, 87, 119.
16. Ibid., pp. 107, 136, 119.
17. Dower, *A War Without Mercy: Race and Power in the Pacific War* (New York: Pantheon Books, 1986) p. 305.
18. Ibid., p. 300.
19. Yoshida, *The Yoshida Memoirs*, p. 63.
20. Douglas MacArthur, *Reminiscences* (New York: McGraw-Hill, 1964) pp. 283–4.
21. John Gunther, *The Riddle of MacArthur: Japan, Korea, and the Far East* (New York: Harper & Brothers, 1974) pp. 55–6.
22. MacArthur, *Reminiscences*, p. 293.
23. *Foreign Relations of the United States (FRUS)*, 1948, vol. 6, pp. 938–42.
24. Schaller, *The American Occupation of Japan*, pp. 58, 60.
25. Ibid., p. 29.
26. Yoshida, *The Yoshida Memoirs*, p. 45.
27. Whitney memo to CINC, November 8, 1946, GS file, NRAS, RG 331, Box 2055.
28. Junnosuke Masumi, *Postwar Politics in Japan, 1945–1955* (Berkeley, Calif.: Institute of East Asian Studies, University of California 1985) pp. 41–2.
29. Quoted in Richard B. Finn, *Winners in Peace: MacArthur, Yoshida, and Postwar Japan* (Berkeley, Calif.: University of California Press, 1992) p. 73.
30. Philip R. Piccigallo, *The Japanese on Trial: Allied War Crimes Operations in the East, 1945–1951* (Austin: University of Texas Press, 1987) pp. 11–12.
31. Chalmers Johnson, *Peasant Nationalism and Communist Power: The Emergence of Revolutionary China* (Stanford: Stanford University Press, 1962) pp. 207–8.
32. Dower, *A War Without Mercy*, p. 42.
33. Both quotes from ibid., p. 38.
34. Peter Williams and David Wallace, *Unit 731: The Japanese Army's Secret of Secrets* (London: Hodder and Stoughton, 1989).
35. R. John Pritchard and Sonia Magbanua Zaide, eds, *The Tokyo War Crimes Trial: The Complete Transcripts of the Proceedings of the International Military Tribunal for the Far East*, 21 vols (Garland Publishing, 1981) p. 1:390.
36. Richard Minear, *Victor's Justice: The Tokyo War Crimes Trial* (Tokyo: Charles E. Tuttle, 1971); Arnold C. Brackman, *The Other Nuremburg: The Untold Story of the Tokyo War Crimes Trials* (New York: Quill/William Morrow, 1987).

37. Hans Baerwald, *The Purge of Japanese Leaders Under the Occupation* (Berkeley, Calif.: University of California Press, 1959) pp. 92, 94.
38. Chalmers Johnson, *MITI and the Japanese Miracles* (Stanford: Stanford University Press, 1982) p. 42.
39. PJR, II:549.
40. Richard B. Finn, *Winners in Peace*, p. 126.
41. PJR, II:549.
42. Cohen, *Remaking Japan*, p. 159.
43. Ibid., p. 170.
44. Yoshida, *The Yoshida Memoirs*, p. 159.
45. Finn, *Winners in Peace*, p. 49.
46. Ibid.
47. Ibid., p. 90. FEC would not get around to approving SWNCC 228 until July 2, 1946, months after SCAP imposed its draft constitution on Japan's government.
48. Yoshida, *The Yoshida Memoirs*, p. 143.
49. Toshio Nishi, *Unconditional Democracy: Education and Politics in Occupied Japan, 1945–1952* (Stanford: Hoover Institute Press, 1982) pp. 163–4.
50. Shigeto Tsuru, *Essays on Japanese Economic Development* (Tokyo: Kinokuniya Shobo, 1958) p. 160.
51. Cohen, *Remaking Japan*, pp. 341, 345.
52. Ibid., p. 142.
53. Yoshida, *The Yoshida Memoirs*, p. 80.
54. Cohen, *Remaking Japan*, pp. 143–6.
55. MacArthur, *Reminiscences*, p. 313.
56. PRJ, II:764.
57. Dick Nanto, "The United States Role in the Postwar Economic Recovery of Japan," Ph.D. Dissertation, Harvard University (1977).
58. For an excellent account, see Ronald Dore, *Land Reform in Japan* (London: Oxford University Press, 1959) pp. 23–53.
59. Cohen, *Remaking Japan*, p. 177.
60. Andrew Gordon, *The Evolution of Labor Relations in Japan, 1953–1955* (Cambridge, Mass.: Harvard University Press, 1988) p. 331.
61. See Thomas A. Bisson, *Zaibatsu Dissolution in Japan* (Berkeley, Calif.: University of California Press, 1976) pp. 24–5.
62. Schaller, *The American Occupation of Japan*, p. 33.
63. See discussion in ibid., pp. 31–2.
64. MacArthur letter to Mr J. H. Jipson, January 24, 1948, in PRJ, II:780.
65. Schaller, *The American Occupation of Japan*, p. 31.
66. Edwin W. Pauley, *Report on Japanese Reparations to the President of the United States, November 1945 to April 1946* (DOS publication, 3174, Far Eastern Series 25, Washington, D.C.: GPO, 1946) pp. 6–7.
67. Finn, *Winners in Peace*, p. 128.
68. Cohen, *Remaking Japan*, p. 152.
69. Eleanor Hadley, *Antitrust in Japan* (Princeton: Princeton University Press, 1970) pp. 163–5.
70. Cohen, *Remaking Japan*, p. 358.
71. Johnson, *MITI and the Japanese Economic Miracle*, p. 34.
72. Yoshida, *Yoshida Memoirs*, p. 40.

73. MacArthur, *Reminiscences*, p. 302.
74. Quoted in Finn, *Winners in Peace*, p. 120.
75. Yoshida, *The Yoshida Memoirs*, p. 139.

Notes to Chapter 6: The Reverse Course, 1947–52

1. Henry Kissinger, *The White House Years* (Boston: Little, Brown, and Company, 1979) p. 135.
2. John Dower, "Reform and Reconsolidation," in Harry Wray and Hilary Conroy, eds, *Japan Examined: Perspectives on Modern Japanese History* (Honolulu: University of Hawaii, 1983) p. 347.
3. Michael Schaller, *Douglas MacArthur: The Far Eastern General* (New York: Oxford University Press, 1989) p. 154.
4. FRUS, 1949, vol. 7, pp. 743–4.
5. David Mayers, *George Kennan and the Dilemmas of U.S. Foreign Policy* (New York: Oxford University Press, 1988) pp. 320–1.
6. George Kennan quoted in David Mayers, *George Kennan*.
7. At first Kennan did not explicity distinguish between essential and peripheral American interests. Walter Lippman did and in their dialogue helped Kennan establish his containment priorities. For an excellent discussion of this conceptualization process, see Mayers, *George Kennan*, pp. 114–19.
8. Quoted in ibid., p. 179.
9. Quoted in John Gaddis, *Strategies of Containment: A Critical Appraisal of Postwar National Security Policy* (New York: Oxford University Press, 1982) p. 41.
10. Michael Schaller, *The American Occupation of Japan* (New York: Oxford University Press, 1985) p. 54.
11. FRUS 1950, vol. 6, p. 311.
12. Stewart Alsop, "We Are Losing Asia Fast," *Saturday Evening Post*, vol. 222, no. 37 (March 11, 1950) p. 29.
13. FRUS 1950, vol. I, p. 240; Gaddis, *Strategies of Containment*, p. 95.
14. Omar Bradley and Clay Blair, *A General's Life* (New York, 1983) pp. 534–5.
15. Nikita Khrushchev, *Khrushchev Remembers* (Boston: Houghton Mifflin, 1970) pp. 367–73.
16. Richard B. Finn, *Winners in Peace: MacArthur, Yoshida, and Postwar Japan* (Berkeley, Calif.: University of California Press, 1992) p. 195.
17. Ibid., p. 197.
18. FRUS, 1948, vol. 6, pp. 654–6.
19. Howard Schonberger, *Aftermath of War: Americans and the Remaking of Japan, 1945–1952* (Kent, OH: Kent State University Press, 1989) pp. 163–5.
20. Schaller, *Douglas MacArthur*, p. 151.
21. PPS, 39/1, November 23, 1948, pp. 208–11.
22. George F. Kennan, *Memoirs*, p. 393.
23. Jerome Cohen, *Japan's Economy in War and Reconstruction* (Minneapolis: University of Minnesota Press, 1949) p. 425.
24. Letter to J. H. Jipson, PRJ, II:778.

25. Schaller, *The American Occupation of Japan*, p. 116.
26. Ibid., p. 121.
27. FRUS, 1948, vol. 6, pp. 710–11.
28. FRUS, 1948, vol. 6, p. 425.
29. FRUS, 1948, vol. 6, pp. 1066–7.
30. Finn, *Winners in Peace*, pp. 220–1.
31. Kazuo Kawaii, *Japan's American Interlude* (Chicago: University of Chicago Press, 1960) p. 143; Warren Hunsberger, *Japan and the United States in World Trade* (New York: Harper & Row, 1960) p. 106; Finn, *Winners in Peace*, p. 228.
32. Theodore Cohen, *Remaking Japan: The American Occupation as New Deal* ed. by Herbert Passin (New York: 1987), p. 432.
33. Ibid., p. 223.
34. For the classic work on MITI, see Chalmers Johnson, *MITI and the Japanese Miracle* (Stanford: Stanford University Press, 1982).
35. Kennan to Lovett and Marshall, October 14, 1947, FRUS, 1947, vol. 6, pp. 536–43.
36. Quoted in Schaller, *The American Occupation of Japan*, p. 179.
37. Stewart Alsop, *Washington Post*, August 29, 1949.
38. Schaller, *The American Occupation of Japan*, p. 146.
39. PPS 51, March 29, 1949 in NSC 51, "U.S. Policy toward Southeast Asia," July 1, 1949, NSC files, MMR.
40. SWNCC 360, April 21, 1947, SWNCC Records, RG, 353.
41. NSC 41, "U.S. Policy Regarding Trade with China," February 28, 1949, NSC files, MMB, National Archives.
42. Quoted in Schaller, *The American Occupation of Japan*, p. 188. SCAP tried to encourage relations between Japan and South Korea, but to no avail. The hatred between Japanese and Koreans was still too deep to be bridged.
43. Cohen, *Remaking Japan*, p. 294.
44. Shigeru Yoshida, *The Yoshida Memoirs* (Cambridge, Mass.: Harvard University Press, 1961) p. 230.
45. Schaller, *The American Occupation of Japan*, p. 135.
46. Both quotes from Finn, *Winners in Peace*, p. 232.
47. Ibid., p. 233.
48. Quoted in ibid., p. 234.
49. Cohen, *Remaking Japan*, p. 396.
50. Finn, *Winners in Peace*, p. 235.
51. Message of February 20, 1947, PRJ, II:763.
52. Schaller, *The American Occupation of Japan*, p. 104.
53. FRUS, 1948, vol. 6, p. 691.
54. Dean Acheson, *Present at the Creation: My Years in the State Department* (New York: Norton, 1969) p. 338.
55. FRUS, 1950, vol. 6, pp. 1166–7.
56. Schaller, *The American Occupation of Japan*, p. 248.
57. Finn, *Winners in Peace*, p. 267.
58. Ibid., p. 268.
59. Quoted in William Sebald and Russell Brines, *With MacArthur in Japan: A Personal History of the Occupation* (New York: Norton, 1965) p. 278.

60. Akira Iriye, *The Cold War in Asia* (Engelwood Cliffs, NJ: Prentice Hall, 1974) p. 97.
61. Quoted in Finn, *Winners in Peace*, p. 292.
62. Baerwald, *The Purge*, p. 79.
63. Quoted in Kenneth Pyle, *The Japanese Question* (Washington, D.C.: AEI Press, 1992) p. 24.
64. Igarashi Takeshi, "Sengo Nihon 'gaiko josei' no keisei," *Kokka Gakkai Zasshi*, nos 5–8 (1984) p. 486.
65. T. J. Pempel, ed., *Uncommon Democracies: The One-Party Dominant Regimes* (Ithaca: Cornell University Press, 1990) p. 139.
66. FRUS, "Memorandum of Conversation," September 3, 1951, pp. 1326–28.
67. See Warren Cohen, "China in Japanese–American Relations," in Akira Iriye and Warren Cohen, eds, *The United States and Japan in the Postwar World* (Lexington: University of Kentucky Press, 1989) pp. 36–42.
68. Herbert Passim in Cohen, *Remaking Japan*, p. xi.
69. Ibid., p. 6.
70. Passim in ibid., p. xv.
71. Ibid., p. 13.
72. Ibid., p. 54.
73. Finn, *Partners in Peace*, p. 199.
74. Yoshida, *The Yoshida Memoirs*, p. 243.
75. Ibid., p. 195.
76. Cohen, *Remaking Japan*, p. 464.
77. Yoshida, *The Yoshida Memoirs*, p. 60.

Notes to Chapter 7: America Triumphant: The Eisenhower, Kennedy and Johnson Era, 1953–69

1. Address by John Foster Dulles, January 27, 1953, FRUS 1952–3, vol. 13, p. 360.
2. Michael Schaller, *The American Occupation of Japan* (New York: Oxford University Press, 1985) p. 296.
3. Emmet J. Hughes, *The Ordeal of Power* (New York: Dell, 1962) p. 243. See also Herbert Parmet, *Eisenhower and the American Crusades* (New York: Macmillan, 1972); Fred Greenstein, *The Hidden-Hand Presidency: Eisenhower as Leader* (New York: Basic Books, 1982).
4. Entry from July 2, 1953, in *The Eisenhower Diaries*, p. 245.
5. Matthew Ridgeway, *The Korean War* (Garden City, NY: Doubleday, 1967) p. vi.
6. Lisle A. Rose, *Roots of Tragedy: The Unites States and the Struggle for Asia, 1945–53* (Westport, Conn.: 1976) pp. 239–40.
7. Kenneth Thompson, "The Strengths and Weaknesses of Eisenhower's Leadership," in Richard A. Melanson and David Mayers, *Reevaluating Eisenhower: American Foreign Policy in the 1950s* (Chicago: University of Chicago Press, 1987) p. 25.
8. George Herring, *The Longest War: The United States and Vietnam, 1950–1975* (New York: Alfred A. Knopf, 1986) p. 57.

9. Nagai Yonosuke, *Gendai to Senryaku* (Tokyo: Bungei Shunju, 1985) p. 60.
10. Harold A. Hovey, *United States Military Assistance* (New York: Praeger Publications, 1965).
11. Quoted in Frederick Shiels, *Tokyo and Washington* (Lexington, Mass.: Lexington Books, 1980) p. 79.
12. *New York Times*, January 8, 1954.
13. FRUS, 1955–7, vol. 23, part 1, p. 202.
14. George Packard, *Protest in Tokyo* (Princeton: Princeton University Press, 1966) p. 44.
15. Dulles's memorandum for Eisenhower, "Official Visit to the United States of the Prime Minister of Japan, Mr. Nobusuke Kishi, June 12, 1957," *Declassified Documents Quarterly Catalog (DDQC)*, vol. 5 (1979), 195B.
16. Packard, *Protest in Tokyo*, p. 70.
17. Tadashi Aruga, "The Security Treaty Revision of 1960," in Warren Cohen and Akira Iriye, eds, *The United States and Japan in the Postwar World* (Lexington: University of Kentucky Press, 1989) p. 72.
18. I. M. Destler, *et al.*, *Managing An Alliance: The Politics of U.S.–Japanese Relations* (Washington, D.C.: Brookings, 1976) p. 102.
19. I. M. Destler, *et al.*, *The Textile Wrangle: Conflict in Japanese–American Relations, 1969–1971* (Ithaca, NY: Cornell University Press, 1979) p. 29.
20. *U.S. Congressional Record*, 84th Congress, 2nd sess., June 28, 1956, p. 11240.
21. Cabinet Minutes, January 18, 1957, "Minutes and Documents of the Cabinet Meetings of President Eisenhower," Reel 5 (University Publications of America, 1980).
22. Yoshida, *The Yoshida Memoirs*, pp. 123–4.
23. Akio Watanabe, "Southeast Asia in U.S.–Japanese Relations," in Cohen and Iriye, *The United States and Japan*, p. 92.
24. U.S. Department of State, FRUS, 1952–4, vol. 14, *China and Japan*, part 2 (Washington, D.C.: 1985) pp. 1300–8; John Dower, *Empire and Aftermath: Yoshida Shigeru and the Japanese Experience, 1978–1954* (New York: 1979) p. 581.
25. Discussion at the 271st Meeting of the National Security Council, "Thursday, December 22, 1955," DDRS (81) p. 497B.
26. Cohen in Akira and Cohen, *The United States and Japan*, p. 49.
27. Chalmers Johnson, *MITI and the Japanese Miracle* (Stanford: Stanford University Press, 1982) p. 247.
28. James Barber, *The Presidential Character: Predicting Performance in the White House* (Englewood Cliffs, NJ: Prentice Hall, 1992) p. 361.
29. Theodore Sorensen, *Kennedy* (New York: Bantam Books, 1965) pp. 315–16.
30. John F. Kennedy, "State of the Union Address, January 30, 1961," *John F. Kennedy, Public Papers, 1961* (Washington, D.C., 1962) p. 27.
31. Sorenson, *Kennedy*, p. 675.
32. Quoted in Seyom Brown, *The Faces of Power* (New York: 1969) p. 217.
33. Destler *et al.*, *The Textile Wrangle*, p. 31.
34. Report and Recommendations of the Task Force Ryukyus (Kayen Report), December 1961, p. 111.
35. Johnson, *MITI and Japan's Economic Miracle*, p. 251.
36. Ibid., p. 276.

37. Ito Masaya, *Ikeda Hayato, So No Sei To Shi* (Ikeda Hayato, his life and death) (Tokyo: 1966) p. 175.
38. Furukawa Jotaro, *Nit-Chu Sengo Kankei-Shi* (Postwar Sino-Japanese Relations) (Tokyo: 1981) p. 114.
39. Alfred Steinberg, *Sam Johnson's Boy* (New York: Macmillan, 1968) p. 724.
40. Barber, *The Presidential Character*, p. 73.
41. Steinberg, *Sam Johnson's Boy*, p. 724.
42. Barber, *Presidential Character*, p. 25.
43. Herring, *The Longest War*, pp. 121–3.
44. Iriye and Cohen, eds, *The United States and Japan*, p. 97.
45. U.S. Department of State, "Department of State Policy on the Future of Japan," NSC Country File, Japan, Lyndon B. Johnson Library, Austin, Texas.
46. Walter LaFeber, "Decline of Relations During the Vietnam War," in Iriye and Cohen, *The United States and Japan*, p. 101.
47. Thomas Havens, *Fire Across the Sea: The Vietnam War and Japan, 1965–1975* (Princeton: Princeton University Press) pp. 89–96.
48. Memorandum of Conversation, January 13, 1965, NSC Country File, Japan, vol. 2, LBJ Library.
49. CIA Memorandum DDRS (80), June 1966, 126A.
50. Havens, *Fire Across the Sea*, p. 138.
51. Quoted in Seymour M. Hersh, *The Price of Power: Kissinger in the Nixon White House* (New York: Summit Books, 1983) p. 381.
52. "Memorandum for the President," from Robert S. McNamara, August 30, 1967, President's Confidential File, CO 141, LBJ Library.

Notes to Chapter 8: America and Japan Neck and Neck: The Nixon, Ford, and Carter Era, 1969–81

1. Henry Kissinger, *Years of Upheaval* (Boston: Little, Brown and Company, 1982) pp. 72, 1182.
2. Oriana Fallaci, *New Republic*, December 16, 1972, p. 21.
3. Marvin and Bernard Kalb, *Kissinger* (Boston: Little, Brown and Company, 1974) p. 255.
4. Henry Kissinger, *The White House Years* (Boston: Little, Brown and Company, 1979) pp. 57, 65.
5. Ibid., p. 56.
6. Ibid., p. 69.
7. Quoted in Kissinger, *The White House Years*, p. 952.
8. Richard Nixon, "Asia after Viet Nam," *Foreign Affairs*, vol. 46 (October 1967) p. 112.
9. Kissinger, *Years of Upheaval*, pp. 735, 151.
10. Fred Bergsten, *On the Non-Equivalence of Import Quotas and "Voluntary" Export Restraints* (Brookings Institution Reprint T-009, 1975) p. 270.
11. Kissinger, *White House Years*, p. 329.
12. I. M. Destler, "Country Expertise and U.S. Foreign Policy Making," in Morton A. Kaplan and Kinhide Mushakoji, eds, *Japan, America, and the Future World* (New York: Free Press, 1976) p. 142.

13. *The United States in the Changing World Economy*, 2 vols (Washington, D.C.: GPO, December 1971).
14. C. Fred Bergsten, "The New Economics and U.S. Foreign Policy," *Foreign Affairs*, vol. 30 (January 1972) pp. 208–9.
15. I. M. Destler, *et al.*, *The Textile Wrangle: Conflict in Japanese–American Relations, 1969–1971* (Ithaca, NY: Cornell University Press, 1979) p. 7.
16. Ibid., p. 8.
17. Ibid., p. 70.
18. Kissinger, *The White House Years*, p. 336.
19. Destler, *et al.*, *The Textile Wrangle*, pp. 134–6.
20. Ibid., p. 138.
21. *New York Times*, November 23, 1969.
22. Destler, *et al.*, *The Textile Wrangle*, p. 139.
23. Kissinger, *The White House Years*, p. 337.
24. Destler, *et al.*, *The Textile Wrangle*, p. 133.
25. *Asahi Shimbun*, November 22, 1969 (evening edition).
26. Destler, *et al.*, *The Textile Wrangle*, p. 162.
27. *Asahi Shimbun*, June 26, 1970.
28. *Washington Post*, September 10, 1971.
29. Destler, *et al.*, *The Textile Wrangle*, p. 312.
30. Ibid., p. 317.
31. Kissinger, *Years of Upheaval*, p. 740.
32. Kissinger, *The White House Years*, p. 327.
33. Chalmers Johnson, "The Patterns of Japanese Relations with China, 1952–1982," *Pacific Affairs*, vol. 59 (1986) p. 405.
34. Kissinger, *The White House Years*, p. 334.
35. Quoted in Seymors M. Hersh, *The Price of Power: Kissinger in the Nixon White House* (New York: Summit Books, 1983) p. 380.
36. Kissinger, *Years of Upheaval*, p. 56.
37. Hersh, *The Price of Power*, p. 382.
38. Ibid.
39. Jerald F. terHorst, *Gerald Ford and the Future of the Presidency* (New York: The Third Press, 1974) p. 12.
40. James Barber, *The Presidential Character: Predicting Performance in the White House* (Englewood Cliffs, NJ: Prentice Hall, 1992) p. 392.
41. Barber, *Presidential Character*, p. 388.
42. *Time*, October 4, 1976, p. 23.
43. Martin Weinstein, "Trends in Japan's Foreign and Defense Policies," in William J. Barnds, ed., *Japan and the United States: Challenges and Opportunities* (New York: New York University Press, 1979) p. 167.
44. For the emperor, the highlight of his trip to the United States was his visit to Disneyland, and thereafter he sported a Mickey Mouse watch to commemorate that happy occasion.
45. Kenneth Pyle, *The Japanese Question* (Washington, D.C.: AEI Press, 1992) pp. 33–4.
46. Henry Kissinger, *Years of Upheaval*, p. 55.
47. Jimmy Carter, *Keeping Faith: Memoirs of a President* (New York: Bantam, 1982) p. 143.
48. *Washington Post*, September 16, 1977.

49. James Nation and James Oliver, *Foreign Policy Making and the American Political System* (Boston: Little, Brown and Company, 1987) p. 75.
50. William Grieder, "A Carter Album," *Washington Post*, October 24, 1976, p. A17.
51. Robert Shogan, *Promises to keep: Carter's First Hundred Days* (New York: Thomas Crowell, 1977) p. 125.
52. Ibid., p. 226.
53. James Fallows, "The Passionless Presidency: the Trouble with Jimmy Carter's Administration," *The Atlantic* (May 1976) p. 34.
54. Kyodo release, carried in FBIS/DR A & P, February 2, 1979.
55. William R. Nester, *Japan and the Third World: Patterns, Power, Prospects* (New York: St Martin's Press, 1992) pp. 215–16.
56. Ronald Morse, "Japan's Search for an Independent Foreign Policy," in Ronald Morse, ed., *The Politics of Japan's Energy Strategy* (Boulder, Colo.: Westview, 1984) p. 36.

Notes to Chapter 9: Japan Triumphant: The Reagan and Bush Era, 1981–93

1. I. M. Destler, "Reagan and the World: An 'Awesome Stubbornness,' " in Charles Jones, ed., *The Reagan Legacy: Promise and Performance* (Chatham, NJ: Chatham House, 1988) p. 259.
2. Anthony Lewis, *New York Times*, January 6, 1983, p. A26.
3. See James Tobin, "Reaganomics in Retrospect," in B. B. Kymlicka and Jean Matthews, eds, *The Reagan Revolution* (Chicago: Dorsey Press, 1988) p. 103.
4. R. W. Apple, *New York Times*, January 9, 1985.
5. Anthony King and David Sanders, "The View from Europe," in Jones, ed., *The Reagan Legacy*, p. 267.
6. James Barber, *The Presidential Character: Predicting Performance in the White House* (Englewood Cliffs, NJ: Prentice Hall, 1992) p. 262.
7. *Time*, February 6, 1984, p. 23.
8. John Tower, *Report of the President's Special Review Board* (Washington: GPO, 1988) vol. IV, p. 10.
9. Leslie Gelb, "Is Washington Big Enough for Two State Departments?" *New York Times*, February 21, 1982, p. 4.
10. *Newsweek*, April 16, 1984, p. 24.
11. William Grieder, "Stockman's Complaint," *Atlantic Monthly*, June 1982.
12. Destler, "Reagan and the World," p. 247.
13. Prestowitz, *Trading Places*, p. 273.
14. Semiconductor Industry Association, *The U.S. Crisis in Microelectronics* (San Jose, Calif.: Semiconductor Industry Association, 1987).
15. Verner, *et al.*, *The Effect of Government Targeting on World Semiconductor Competition* (Cupertino, Calif.: Semiconductor Industry Association, 1983) p. 59.
16. Prestowitz, *Trading Places*, p. 50.
17. Ibid., p. 58.
18. For an excellent analysis, see Peter Dale, *The Myth of Japanese Uniqueness*.
19. See Iida Tsuneo, *Nippon-Teki Chikaraquyosa No Sai-Hakken* (Tokyo: Nihon Keizai Shibunsha, 1979); Shimizu Ikutaro, *Nippon Yo, Kokka Tare: Kaku No*

Sentaku (Tokyo: Bungeishunjusha, 1980); Eto Jun, *1946-Nen Kempo: Sono Kosoku* (Tokyo: Bungeishujusha, 1980); Eto Jun, *Nichi-Bei Senso Was Owatte Inai* (Tokyo: Bungeishujunsha, 1987).

20. Ishihara Shintaro and Morita Akio, *The Japan That Can Say No!* (Tokyo: Kobunsha, 1989).
21. *Japan Economic Journal*, October 11, 1986.
22. Masashi Nishihara, "Japan: Regional Security," in James W. Morley, ed., *Security Interdependence in the Asia Pacific Region* (Lexington Mass.: Lexington Books, 1986) p. 72.
23. Martin Weinstein, "Trade Problems and U.S.–Japanese Security Cooperation," *The Washington Quarterly*, vol. 11 (Winter 1988) pp. 19–20.
24. Barber, *Presidential Character*, pp. 456–83.
25. Donald Snow and Eugene Brown, *Puzzle Palaces and Foggy Bottom* (New York: St Martin's Press, 1994) p. 61.
26. Waichi Sekiguchi, "U.S. Taking its Case Directly to the Japanese People," *Japan Economic Journal*, September 16, 1989; Richard Samuels, "Consuming for Production," *International Organization*, vol. 43, no. 4 (Autumn 1989) p. 625; Clyde Farnsworth, "In Japan, It's Costly to Be a Consumer," *New York Times*, November 8, 1989.
27. Mark Vamos, "What Americans Think of Japan, Inc.," *Businessweek*, August 7, 1989.
28. *New York Times*, June 6, 1990.
29. David Sanger, "Japan Seen Extending Auto Quotas," *New York Times*, January 12, 1990.
30. Clyde Farnsworth, "U.S. Backs Japan in Europe Auto Debate," *New York Times*, February 22, 1990.
31. Clyde Farnsworth, "Japanese Pledge to Lower Barriers to Trade with U.S.," *New York Times*, April 6, 1989; Charles Smith, "Tokyo Bid to Defuse Trade Tension May Backfire,"*Far Eastern Economic Review*, August 3, 1989, p. 42; Roger Dornbusch, "Misguided Efforts Won't Open Japan's Market," *Japan Economic Journal*, December 16, 1989.
32. Clyde Farnsworth, "U.S. Will Tie Aid to Exports in Bid to Curb the Practice," *New York Times*, May 16, 1990.

Notes to Chapter 10: Into the Twenty-first Century: Clinton and Beyond, 1993–Future

1. Richard Cohen, *Changing Course in Washington: Clinton and the New Congress* (New York: Macmillan, 1994) p. 18.
2. Several prominent critical accounts include: Bob Woodward, *The Agenda: Inside the Clinton White House* (New York: Simon and Schuster, 1994); John Brummet, *Highwire: From the Backroads to the Beltway: The Education of Bill Clinton* (New York: Hyperion, 1994); Elizabeth Drew, *On the Edge: The Clinton Presidency* (New York: Simon and Schuster, 1994).
3. Gary Wills, "Clinton's Troubles," *New York Review of Books*, vol. xli, no. 15, September 22, 1994, p. 7.
4. Cohen, *Changing Course in Washington*, pp. 66, 177, 179.
5. Keith Bradsher, "Middle of the Road: Clinton's Policy on Trade," *New York Times*, June 11, 1993.

6. Keith Broder, "In Twist, Protectionism is Used to Sell Trade Pact," *New York Times*, November 7, 1993.

7. Gwen Ifill, "Clinton Uses Japan to Sell Mexico Pact," *New York Times*, October 21, 1993.

8. "Transcript of Clinton's First News Conference at the White House," *New York Times*, March 24, 1993.

9. Robert Hershey, "U.S. Trade Survey Calls Japan Most Restrictive," *New York Times*, March 31, 1993.

10. Steven Greenhouse, "Yen Strategy: What the U.S. is Expecting," *New York Times*, June 25, 1993.

11. David Sanger, "Japan Leader Takes Hard Line on Trade," *New York Times*, April 13, 1993.

12. David Sanger, "Clinton and Miyazawa Hold Blunt Trade Talks," *New York Times*, April 17, 1993.

13. Andrew Pollack, "U.S. Presses Tokyo Harder," *New York Times*, April 23, 1993.

14. Keith Bradsher, "U.S. Escalates War of Words on Japan Trade," *New York Times*, April 30, 1993.

15. Keith Bradsher, "New Japan Trade Policy May Split Power Among Agencies," *New York Times*, May 19, 1993.

16. Keith Bradsher, "U.S. Says It Won't Rely on Japan Market Target," *New York Times*, June 9, 1993.

17. James Sterngold, "Tough Talk on Trade by U.S. Envoy to Japan," *New York Times*, June 11, 1993.

18. James Sterngold, "Tokyo Panel Urges Loosening of Bonds on Business," *New York Times*, November 9, 1993.

19. Keith Bradsher, "U.S. Cancels a Plan to Begin Sanctions After Japan Acts," *New York Times*, October 26, 1993.

20. Andrew Pollack, "Japan Imports Rice, but Will People Eat It?," *New York Times*, December 21, 1993.

21. James Sterngold, "Tokyo Trade Pact: Dotting the I's Proves Difficult," *New York Times*, January 16, 1994.

22. Thomas Friedman, "Bentsen Warns Japan on Stalemate in Trade Talks," *New York Times*, January 24, 1994.

23. Thomas Friedman, "U.S. Says Visit by Japanese Leader Could Turn into Confrontation," *New York Times*, February 11, 1994.

24. Gwen Ifill, "Clinton and Japan Chief Say Trade Talks Fail; U.S. Threatens Action," *New York Times*, February 12, 1994.

25. Thomas Friedman, "U.S. is Taking Action in One Japan Trade Case," *New York Times*, February 15, 1994.

26. Keith Bradsher, "Accord Will Allow U.S. Cellular Phones in Japan," *New York Times*, March 13, 1994.

27. James Sterngold, "A Hard Lesson on Trade for Mondale," *New York Times*, February 20, 1994.

28. Todd Purdum, "Bradley Rebukes Clinton on Japan," *New York Times*, February 24, 1994.

29. Thomas Friedman, "U.S. Goals on Trade Ebbing with Japan Reformer Gone," *New York Times*, April 5, 1994.

30. James Sterngold, "Japan Spares no Expense in Effort to Control Yen," *New York Times*, May 20, 1994.

31. Thomas Friedman, "Jawboning's Limits," *New York Times*, May 9, 1994.
32. Thomas Friedman, "U.S. Is Softening Stance in Talks on Japan Trade," *New York Times*, June 6, 1994.
33. Thomas Friedman, "Kantor Vows Pressure on Japan Will Continue," *New York Times*, October 3, 1994.
34. Andrew Pollack, "Japan Gives U.S. Cars a 2nd Look," *New York Times*, June 21, 1994.
35. David Sanger, "More Growth Predicted for New Markets," *New York Times*, November 4, 1994; Andrew Pollock, "U.S. Is Shifting Trade Emphasis Away from Japan," *New York Times*, November 4, 1994.
36. Thomas Friedman, "Europe, not Japan, Is Called America's Frontier for Trade," *New York Times*, June 9, 1994.
37. David Sanger, "Tokyo Reluctant to Levy Sanctions on North Koreans," *New York Times*, June 9, 1994.
38. David Sanger, "In Face-Saving Turn, Japan Denies Nuclear Know-how," *New York Times*, June 21, 1994.
39. See, Ian Buruma, *The Wages of Guilt: Memories of War in Germany and Japan* (New York: Farrar, Straus & Giroux, 1994).
40. Charles Ferguson, "America's High-Tech Decline," *Foreign Policy*, vol. 74 (Spring 1989) p. 139.
41. Edwin Reischauer, "Introduction," in Seizaburo Sato, Ken'ichi Koyama, and Shupei Kumon, eds, *Postwar Politician: The Life of Former Prime Minister Masayoshi Ohira* (Tokyo: Kodansha, 1990) p. 4.
42. Nakatani Iwao, "Sekinin Kokka, Nihon e no sentaku," *Japan Echo*, vol. 14, no. 4 (1987) pp. 7–18.
43. Inoguchi Takashi, "Zokueki shoeki ga naiju kakudai o sogai suru," *Japan Echo*, vol. 14, no. 4 (1987) pp. 56–8.
44. *Japan Economic Journal*, January 31, 1987.
45. Kenneth Pyle, *The Japan Question: Power and Purpose in a New Era* (Washington, D.C.: AEI, 1992) p. 112.
46. Fred Hiatt, *Washington Post*, March 27, 1990.
47. Shigeru Yoshida, *The Yoshida Memoirs* (Boston: Houghton Mifflin, 1962) p. 8.

Bibliography

Acheson, Dean, *Power and Diplomacy* (Cambridge, Mass.: Harvard University Press, 1958).
——, *Present at the Creation: My Years in the State Department* (New York: Norton, 1969).
Adams, Frederick C., "The Road to Pearl Harbor: A Reexamination of American Far Eastern Policy, July 1937–December 1938," *Journal of American History*, vol. 58 (June 1971) pp. 72–92.
——, *Economic Diplomacy: The Export–Import Bank and American Foreign Policy, 1934–1939* (Columbia: University of Missouri Press, 1976).
Agawa, Hiroyuki, *The Reluctant Admiral: Yamamoto and the Imperial Navy* (Tokyo: Kodansha International 1979).
Aichi, Kiichi, "Japan's Legacy and Destiny of Change," *Foreign Affairs*, vol. 48 (1969) pp. 21–38.
Akagi, Roy Hidemichi, *Japan's Foreign Relations* (Tokyo: Hokuseido Press, 1936).
Alperowtiz, Gar, *Atomic Diplomacy* (New York: Vintage Books, 1967).
Ambrose, Stephen, *Eisenhower: The President* (New York: Simon and Schuster, 1984).
——, *Rise to Globalism* (Baltimore: Penguin, 1984).
Amrine, Michael, *The Great Decision: The Secret History of the Atomic Bomb* (New York: 1959).
Anderson, Irvine H., *The Standard Vacuum and United States East Asian Policy, 1933–41* (Princeton, NJ: Princeton University Press, 1975).
——, "The 1941 De Facto Embargo on Oil to Japan: A Bureaucratic Reflex," *Pacific Historical Review*, vol. 44 (May 1975) pp. 201–31.
Arkes, Hadley, *Bureaucracy, the Marshall Plan, and the National Interest* (Princeton: Princeton University Press, 1972).
Armstrong, Anne, *Unconditional Surrender: The Impact of the Casablanca Policy Upon World War II* (New Brunswick: Rutgers University Press, 1961).
Asada, Sadao, "Japan's 'Special Interests' and the Washington Conference, 1921–22," *American Historical Review*, vol. 67 (October 1961) pp. 62–70.
Asahi, Shibum, *Pacific Rivals* (New York: John Wetherhill, 1972).
Baker, Paul, ed., *The Atomic Bomb: The Great Decision* (New York: Holt, Rinehart, and Winston, 1976).
Balentine, Joseph W., "Mukden to Pearl Harbor: The Foreign Policies of Japan," *Foreign Affairs*, vol. 27 (July 1949) pp. 651–64.
Ball, W. MacMahon, *Japan: Enemy or Ally?* (New York: 1949).
Ballou, Robert O., *Shinto, The Unconquered Enemy: Japan's Doctrine of Racial Superiority and World Conquest* (New York: Viking, 1945).
Barnds, William J., ed., *Japan and the United States: Challenges and Opportunities* (New York: New York University Press, 1979).
Barnet, Richard, *The Alliance: America–Europe–Japan. Makers of the Postwar World* (New York: Simon and Schuster, 1983).
Barnhart, Michael A., "Japanese Intelligence Before the Second World War: Best Case Analysis," in Ernest R. May, ed., *Knowing One's Enemies: Intelligence*

Assessment Before the Two World Wars (Princeton: Princeton University Press, 1984).

Bartlett, Bruce R., *Cover-Up: The Politics of Pearl Harbor, 1941–1946* (New Rochelle: Arlington House, 1978).

Bauer, Raymond A., de Sola Pool, Ithiel, and Dexter, Lewis Anthony, *American Business and Public Policy: The Politics of Foreign Trade* (New York: Atherton Press, 1964).

Behr, Edward, *Hirohito: Behind the Myth* (New York: Villard Books, 1989).

Beisner, Robert, *Twelve Against Empire: The Anti-Imperialists, 1889–1900* (New York: McGraw-Hill, 1968).

——, *From the Old Diplomacy to the New, 1865–1900* (1975).

Benedict, Ruth, *The Chrysanthemum and the Sword* (Boston: Houghton Mifflin, 1946).

Bergamini, David, *Japan's Imperial Conspiracy* (New York: Morrow, 1971).

Bernstein, Barton, ed., *Politics and Policies of the Truman Administration* (Chicago: Quadrangle Books, 1970).

——, "The Atomic Bomb and American Foreign Policy, 1941–45: A Historiographical Controversy," *Peace and Change*, vol. 2 (Spring 1944).

——, "Roosevelt, Truman, and the Atomic Bomb, 1941–1945: A Reinterpretation," *Political Science Quarterly*, vol. 90 (Spring 1975) pp. 23–69.

——, "Doomsday II: After Hiroshima Was Nagasaki Necessary?" *New York Times Magazine*, July 27, 1975.

Bisson, Thomas A., *Prospects for Democracy in Japan* (New York: 1949).

——, *Zaibatsu Dissolution in Japan* (Berkeley, Calif.: University of California Press, 1954).

Blakeslee, George H., "The Japanese Monroe Doctrine," *Foreign Affairs*, vol. 11 (July 1933) pp. 671–81.

Blum, John, ed., *From the Morgenthau Diaries*, 3 vols (Boston: Houghton-Mifflin, 1959, 1965, 1967).

——, *Roosevelt and Morgenthau* (Boston: Houghton-Mifflin, 1970).

Blum, Robert M., *Drawing the Line: The Origins of American Containment Policy in East Asia* (New York: Norton, 1982).

Bohlen, Charles, *Witness to History, 1929–1969* (New York: Norton, 1973).

Borden, William S., *The Pacific Alliance: United Foreign Economic Policy and Japanese Trade Recovery, 1947–55* (Madison: University of Wisconsin Press, 1984).

Borg, Dorothy, "Notes on Roosevelt's 'Quarantine' Speech," *Political Science Quarterly*, vol. 72 (September 1957) pp. 405–33.

——, *The United States and the Far Eastern Crisis of 1933–38* (Cambridge, Mass.: Harvard University Press, 1964).

Borg, Dorothy and Okimoto, Shumpei, eds, *Pearl Harbor as History: Japanese–American Relations, 1931–41* (New York: Columbia University Press, 1973).

Borton, Hugh, *American Presurrender Planning for Postwar Japan* (New York: 1967).

Boyle, John H., "The Drought–Walsh Mission to Japan," *Pacific Historical Review*, vol. 34 (May 1965) pp. 141–61.

Brackman, Arnold C., *The Other Nuremburg: The Untold Story of the Tokyo War Crimes Trials* (New York: Quill/William Morrow, 1987).

Brines, Russell, *MacArthur's Japan* (New York: Lippincott, 1948).

Brooks, Lester, *Behind Japan's Surrender: The Secret Struggle That Ended an Empire* (New York: 1968).

Brune, Lester H., "Considerations of Force in Cordell Hull's Diplomacy, July 26 to November 26, 1941," *Diplomatic History*, vol. 2 (Fall 1978) pp. 389–405.

Buckley, Roger, *Occupation Diplomacy: Britain, The United States and Japan, 1942–49* (Cambridge, England: 1982).

Buhite, Russell D., "Patrick J. Hurley and the Yalta Far Eastern Agreement," *Pacific Historical Review*, vol. 37 (August 1968) pp. 343–53.

——, *Soviet–American Relations, 1945–54* (Norman, Okla.: University of Oklahoma Press, 1981).

Burgess, John, "Rewriting the 'Rape of Nanking,'" *Washington Post National Weekly Edition*, February 11, 1985.

Burkman, Thomas, ed., *The Occupation of Japan: The International Context* (Norfolk, Va.: 1984).

Bush, Vannevar, *Modern Arms and Free Men* (New York: 1949).

Butow, R. J. C., *Japan's Decision to Surrender* (Stanford, Calif.: Stanford University Press, 1954).

——, "The Hull–Nomura Conversations: A Fundamental Misconception," *American Historical Review*, vol. 65 (July 1960) pp. 822–36.

——, *Tojo and the Coming of the War* (Stanford: Stanford University Press, 1961).

——, "Backdoor Diplomacy in the Pacific: The Proposal for a Konoye–Roosevelt Meeting, 1941," *Journal of American History*, vol. 59 (June 1972) pp. 48–72.

——, *The John Doe Associates: Backdoor Diplomacy for Peace* (Stanford, Calif.: Stanford University Press, 1974).

Byrnes, James F., *Speaking Frankly* (New York: Harper, 1947).

Campbell, Charles S., *The Transformation of American Foreign Relations, 1865–1900* (New York: 1976).

Cantril, Hadley, ed., *Public Opinion, 1935–46* (Princeton, NJ: Princeton University Press, 1951).

Castle, Alfred, "William R. Castle and Opposition to U.S. Involvement in an Asian War, 1939–1941," *Pacific Historical Review*, vol. 54 (August 1985) pp. 337–51.

Chase, John L., "Unconditional Surrender Reconsidered," *Political Science Quarterly*, vol. 70 (June 1955) pp. 258–79.

Clauss, Errol, "The Roosevelt Administration and Manchukuo, 1933–1941," *The Historian*, vol. 32 (August 1970) pp. 595–611.

Clemens, Diane, *Yalta* (London: Oxford University Press, 1970).

Clifford, Nicholas R., "Britain, America, and the Far East, 1937–1940: A Failure in Cooperation," *Journal of British Studies*, vol. 3 (November 1963) pp. 137–54.

Clyde, Paul H., "Historical Reflections on American Relations with the Far East," *South Atlantic Quarterly*, vol. 61 (Autumn 1961) pp. 437–49.

Coffey, Thomas M., *Imperial Tragedy* (New York: World Publishing Company, 1970).

Cohen, Jerome, *Japan's Economy in War and Reconstruction* (Minneapolis: University of Minnesota Press, 1949).

Cohen, Jerome, ed., *Pacific Partnership: United States–Japan Trade* (Lexington, Mass.: Lexington Books, 1972).

Cohen, Theodore, *Remaking Japan: The American Occupation as New Deal*, ed. by Herbert Passin (New York: Columbia University Press, 1987).

Cohen, Warren, *Dean Rusk* (Totawa, NJ: Prentice Hall, 1980).

Cohen, Warren, *New Frontiers in American–Asian Relations* (New York: Columbia University Press, 1983).

Cole, Wayne, *Roosevelt and the Isolationists, 1932–1945* (Lincoln: University of Nebraska Press, 1983).

Combs, Jerald, *American Diplomatic History: Two Centuries of Changing Interpretations* (Berkeley: University of California Press, 1983).

Compton, Arthur, *Atomic Quest* (New York: Random House, 1956).

Compton, Karl T., "If the Atomic Bomb Had Not Been Used," *The Atlantic Monthly*, vol. 78 (December 1946) pp. 54–56.

Conners, Lesley, *The Emperor's Advisor: Kinmochi Saionji* (Tokyo: Croom Helm and Nissan Institute for Japanese Studies, 1987).

Conroy, Hilary, "The Strange Diplomacy of Admiral Nomura," *Proceedings of the American Philosophical Society*, vol. 114 (June 1970) pp. 205–16.

Costello, John, *The Pacific War, 1941–45* (New York: Quill, 1981).

Coughlin, William J., "The Great Mokusatsu Mistake," *Harpers*, vol. 206 (March 1953) pp. 409–14.

Cousins, Norman, *The Pathology of Power* (New York: Norton, 1987).

Crabb, Cecil, *The Doctrines of American Foreign Policy: Their Meaning, Role, and Future* (Baton Rouge: Louisiana State University, 1982).

Craig, Gordon, and Felix, Gilbert, eds, *The Diplomats* (Princeton, NJ: Princeton University Press, 1953).

Craig, William, *The Fall of Japan* (New York: 1967).

Craigie, Robert, *Behind the Japanese Mask* (London: Hutchinson, 1946).

Craven, Frank, and Cate, James Lea, *The Army Air Forces in World War II, Volume 5: The Pacific: Matterhorn to Nagasaki, June 1944 to August 1945* (Washington, D.C.: Office of the Chief of Military History, 1944–1981).

Crow, Carl, ed., *Japan's Dream of World Empire: The Tanaka Memorial* (New York: Harper and Brothers, 1942).

Crowley, James B., "Japanese Army Factionalism in the Early 1930s," *Journal of Asian Studies*, vol. 21 (May 1962) pp. 309–26.

——, "A Reconsideration of the Marco Polo Bridge Incident," *Journal of Asian Studies*, vol. 22 (May 1963) pp. 277–91.

——, *Japan's Quest for Autonomy: National Security and Foreign Policy, 1930–1938* (Princeton, NJ: Princeton University Press, 1966).

Cumings, Bruce, *The Origins of the Korean War: Liberation and the Emergence of Different Regimes, 1945–47* (Princeton, NJ: Princeton University Press, 1981).

——, ed., *Child of Conflict: The Korean–American Relationship, 1943–53* (Seattle: University of Washington Press, 1983).

Current, R. N., "How Stimson Meant to 'Maneuver' the Japanese," *Mississippi Valley Historical Review*, vol. 40 (June 1953) pp. 67–74.

Curtis, Gerald, ed., *Japan's Foreign Policy: After the Cold War, Coping with Change* (Armonk, NY: M. E. Sharpe, 1993).

Dallek, Robert, ed., *The Roosevelt Diplomacy and World War II* (New York: Holt, Rinehart and Winston, 1970).

——, *Franklin D. Roosevelt and American Foreign Policy, 1932–1945*, 2 vols (New York: Oxford University Press, 1979).

Day, David, *The Great Betrayal* (London: Angus & Robertson, 1988).

Dennett, Tyler, "America's Far Eastern Policy," *Current History*, vol. 37 (October 1932) pp. 15–19, 125.

Department of State, *Foreign Relations of the United States*, annual volumes for 1941–51 (Washington, D.C.)

Destler, I. M., Clapp, Priscilla, Sato, Hideo, and Fukui, Haruhiro, *Managing an Alliance: The Politics of U.S.–Japanese Relations* (Washington, D.C.: Brookings Institute, 1976).

——, *The Textile Wrangle: Conflict in U.S.–Japanese Relations* (Washington, D.C.: Brookings Institute, 1979).

Dingman, Roger, "Strategic Planning and the Policy Process: American Plans for War in East Asia, 1945–50," *Naval War College Review*, vol. 32, no. 6 (November–December 1979) pp. 4–21.

——, "Farewell to Friendship: the USS *Astoria's* Visit to Japan, April 1939," *Diplomatic History*, vol. 10 (Spring 1986) pp. 121–39.

Dirkson, Herbert von, *Moscow, Tokyo, London: Twenty Years of German Foreign Policy* (Norman, Okla.: University of Oklahoma Press, 1952).

Divine, Robert, "Franklin Roosevelt and Collective Security, 1933," *Mississippi Valley Historical Review*, vol. 48 (June 1961) pp. 42–59.

——, *The Illusion of Neutrality* (Chicago: University of Chicago, 1962).

——, *The Reluctant Belligerent: American Entry into World War II* (New York: Wiley, 1965).

——, *A Second Chance: The Triumph of Internationalism in America During World War II* (New York: Athenium, 1967).

——, *Roosevelt and World War II* (Baltimore: Johns Hopkins University Press, 1969).

——, *Eisenhower and the Cold War* (New York: Oxford University Press, 1981).

Doenecke, Justus D., *When the Wicked Arise: American Opinion Makers and the Manchurian Crisis of 1931–33* (Lewisburg, Pa.: Bucknell University Press, 1984).

Donavan, Robert, *Tumultuous Years: The Presidency of Harry S. Truman* (New York: Norton, 1982).

Dorwart, Jeffrey M., *Conflict of Duty: The U.S. Navy's Intelligence Dilemma, 1919–1945* (Annapolis: Naval Institute, 1983).

Dower, John, *Empire and Aftermath: Yoshida Shigeru and the Japanese Experience, 1978–1954* (Cambridge, Mass.: Council on East Asian Studies, Harvard University, 1979).

——, "Rethinking World War II in Asia," *Reviews in American History*, vol. 12, no. 2 (June 1984) pp. 155–69.

——, *A War Without Mercy: Race and Power in the Pacific War* (New York: Pantheon Books, 1986).

Doyle, Michael, "The United States Navy – Strategy and Far Eastern Foreign Policy, 1931–1941," *Naval War College Review*, vol. 29 (Winter 1977) pp. 52–60.

Dunn, Frederick, *Peacemaking and the Settlement With Japan* (Princeton, NJ: Princeton University Press, 1973).

Elsbree, Willard H., *Japan's Role in South-East Asian Nationalist Movements* (Cambridge Mass.: Harvard University Press, 1953).

Emmerson, John K., *Arms, Yen, and Power* (New York: Dunellen Publishers, 1971).

Esthus, Raymond A., "President Roosevelt's Commitment to Britain to Intervene in a Pacific War," *Mississippi Valley Historical Review*, vol. 50 (June 1963) pp. 28–38.

Etzold, Thomas and Gaddis, John, eds, *Containment: Documents on American Policy and Strategy, 1945–50* (New York: Columbia University Press, 1978).

Evans, Medford, *The Secret War for the A-Bomb* (Chicago: University of Chicago Press, 1953).

LaFeber, Walter, *An Interpretation of American Expansion, 1860–1989* (New York: Random House, 1963).

Fagan, George V., "F.D.R. and Naval Limitation," *U.S. Naval Institute Proceedings*, vol. 81 (April 1955) pp. 411–18.

Fairbank, John K., Reischauer, Edwin, and Craig, Albert, *East Asia: Tradition and Transformation* (Boston: Houghton Mifflin, 1989).

Far Eastern Command, *Brocade Banner: The Story of Japanese Nationalism* (Civil Intelligence Section, GHQ, Far Eastern Command, September 1946).

Farley, James A., *Jim Farley's Story: The Roosevelt Years* (New York: McGraw-Hill, 1948).

Feary, Robert A., *The Occupation of Japan: Second Phase, 1948–50* (New York: Macmillan, 1950).

Feis, Herbert, "War Came at Pearl Harbor: Suspicions Considered," *Yale Review*, vol. 45 (March 1956) pp. 378–90.

——, *The Road to Pearl Harbor* (Princeton, NJ: Princeton University Press, 1975).

——, *Contest Over Japan* (New York: W. W. Norton, 1981).

Ferrell, R. H., "Pearl Harbor and the Revisionists," *The Historian*, vol. 17 (February 1955) pp. 215–33.

Fish, Hamilton, *FDR, The Other Side of the Coin: How We Were Tricked Into World War II* (New York: Vantage Press, 1976).

Fleming, D. F., *The Cold War and Its Origins*, 2 vols (London: 1961).

Frank, Isiah and Hirono, Ryokichi, eds, *How the United States and Japan See Each Other's Economy* (New York: Committee for Economic Development, 1974).

Frisch, David H., "Scientists and the Decision to Bomb Japan," in Richard S. Lewis and Jane Wilson, eds, *Alamogordo Plus Twenty-Five Years* (New York: Viking Press, 1967).

Gaddis, John, *The United States and the Origins of the Cold War, 1941–47* (New York: Columbia University Press, 1972).

——, *Strategies of Containment: A Critical Appraisal of Postwar National Security Policy* (New York: Oxford University Press, 1982).

Gallup, George, ed., *The Gallup Poll: Public Opinion, 1935–71*, vol. 1 (New York: Random House, 1972).

Gardner, Lloyd, *Architects of Illusion: Men and Ideas in American Foreign Policy* (Chicago: Quadrangle Books, 1970).

——, *Imperial America: American Foreign Policy Since 1898* (New York: Harcourt Brace Jovanovich, 1976).

Gayn, Mark, *Japan Diary* (New York: William Sloane Associates, 1948).

Gellman, Barton, *Contending with Kennan: Toward a Philosophy of American Power* (New York: Praeger Publishers, 1984).

Gibbes, Norman, "The Naval Conferences of the Interwar Years: A Study in Anglo-American Relations," *U.S. Naval War College Review*, vol. 30 (Summer 1977) pp. 50–63.

Gilpin, Robert, *American Scientists and Nuclear Policy* (Princeton, NJ: Princeton University Press, 1962).

Gimbel, John, *The Origins of the Marshall Plan* (Stanford: Stanford University Press, 1976).

Giovanni, Len, and Freed, Fred, *The Decision to Drop the Bomb* (New York: Random House, 1965).

Graebner, Norman, "Japan: Unanswered Challenge, 1931–41," in Margaret F. Morris and Sandra L. Myres, eds, *Essays on American Foreign Policy* (Austin: University of Texas Press, 1974).

——, ed., *The National Security: Its Theory and Practice, 1945–1960* (New York: Oxford University Press, 1986).

Grenville, J. A. S., ed., *The Major International Treaties, 1914–1973: A History and Guide with Texts* (London: Methuen, 1974).

Grenville, J. A. S., and Young, George, *Politics, Strategy, and American Diplomacy* (New York: Cambridge University Press, 1967).

Grew, Joseph C., "The People of Japan," in U.S. Office of Education, *Introducing the Peoples of the Far East* (Bulletin no. 7, 1945).

——, *Report from Tokyo* (New York: Simon & Schuster, 1942).

——, *Ten Years in Tokyo* (New York: Simon & Schuster, 1944).

Groves, Leslie R., *Now It Can Be Told: The Story of the Manhattan Project* (New York: Random House, 1962).

Hadley, Eleanor, *Anti-Trust in Japan* (Princeton, NJ: Princeton University Press, 1974).

Hagan, Kenneth, *American Gunboat Diplomacy and the Old Navy, 1877–1889* (1973).

——, *This People's Navy: The Making of American Sea Power* (New York: The Free Press, 1991).

Haight, John M., "Roosevelt and the Aftermath of the Quarantine Speech," *Review of Politics*, vol. 24 (April 1962) pp. 233–59.

——, "Franklin D. Roosevelt and a Naval Quarantine of Japan," *Pacific Historical Review*, vol. 40 (May 1971) pp. 203–26.

Haines, Gerald K., "American Myopia and the Japanese Monroe Doctrine, 1931–41," *Prologue*, vol. 13 (Spring 1981) pp. 101–14.

Halberstam, David, *The Best and the Brightest* (New York: Random House, 1969).

Hall, John Witney, *Japan: From Prehistory to Modern Times* (Tokyo: Charles E. Tuttle, 1968).

Harada, Kumao, *Prince Saionji and the Political Situation* (Tokyo: Iwanami Shoten, 1956).

Harriman, W. Averell, and Abel, Ellie, *Special Envoy to Churchill and Stalin, 1941–46* (New York: Random House, 1975).

Harrington, Harvey, *God, Mammon, and the Japanese* (New York: Viking Press, 1944).

Hata, Ikuhito, *The Emperor's Five Decisions* (New York: Kodansha, 1984).

Hayes, Grace, *The History of the Joint Chiefs of Staff in World War II: The War Against Japan* (Annapolis, M.E.: U.S. Naval Institute, 1982).

Hayes, Samuel P., *The Beginning of American Aid to Southeast Asia: The Griffin Mission of 1950* (Lexington, Mass.: Lexington Books, 1973).

Haynes, Richard, *The Awesome Power: Harry S. Truman as Commander in Chief* (Baton Rouge: 1973).

Heinrichs, Waldo, *American Ambassador: Joseph Grew and the Development of the United States Diplomatic Tradition* (Boston: Little, Brown, 1966).

Hellman, Donald, ed., *China and Japan: A New Balance of Power* (Lexington, Mass.: Lexington Books, 1976).

Herken, Gregg, *The Winning Weapon: The Atomic Bomb and the Cold War, 1945–50* (New York: Vintage Books, 1982).

Hess, Gary, *The United States' Emergence as a Southeast Asian Power, 1940–50* (New York: Oxford University Press, 1987).

Higham, Robin, ed., *A Guide to the Sources of United States Military History* (Hamden: Archon Books, 1981).

Hindmarsh, A. E., "The Realistic Policy of Japan," *Foreign Affairs*, vol. 13 (January 1935) pp. 262–70.

Hishida, Seiji, *Japan Among the Great Powers: A Survey of Her International Relations* (London: Longman's, 1940).

Hoopes, Townsend, *The Devil and John Foster Dulles* (Boston: Little, Brown and Company, 1973).

Hornbeck, Stanley H., *The United States and the Far East: Certain Fundamentals of Foreign Policy* (Boston: World Peace Foundation, 1942).

Horowitz, David, *The Free World Colossus: A Critique of American Foreign Policy in the Cold War* (New York: Oxford University Press, 1971).

Hughes, Emmet J., *The Living Presidency: The Resources and Dilemmas of the American Presidential Office* (New York: Coward, McCann, and Geohegan, 1972).

Hull, Cordell, *The Memoirs of Cordell Hull*, 2 vols (New York: Macmillan, 1948).

Hunsberger, Warren, *Japan and the United States in World Trade* (New York: Harper & Row, 1964).

Hunt, Michael, *Ideology and U.S. Foreign Policy* (New Haven: Yale University Press, 1987).

Hyland, William, ed., *The Reagan Foreign Policy* (New York: New American Library, 1987).

Ienaga, Saburo, *The Pacific War, 1931–45* (New York: Pantheon, 1978).

Ike, Nobunaga, trans. and ed., *Japan's Decision For War: Records of the 1941 Policy Conferences* (Stanford: Stanford University Press, 1967).

Ilchman, W. F., *Professional Diplomacy in the United States, 1779–1939* (Chicago: University of Chicago Press, 1961).

Inouye, Kyoshi, *The Emperor's Responsibilities* (Tokyo: Gendai Hyoronsha, 1975).

Iriye, Akira, "Chang Hsueh-liang and the Japanese," *Journal of Asian Studies*, vol. 20 (November 1960) pp. 33–43.

——, *After Imperialism: The Search for a New Order in the Far East, 1921–31* (Cambridge, Mass.: Harvard University Press, 1965).

——, *Across The Pacific* (Cambridge, Mass.: Harvard University Press, 1967).

——, *Pacific Estrangement: Japanese and American Expansion, 1897–1911* (Cambridge, Mass.: Harvard University Press, 1972).

——, ed., *Mutual Images: Studies in American–Japanese Relations* (Cambridge, Mass.: Harvard University Press, 1975).

——, *Power and Culture: The Japanese–American War, 1941–45* (Cambridge, Mass.: Harvard University Press, 1981).

Isaacson, Walter and Thomas, Evan, *The Wise Men: Six Friends and the World They Made* (New York: Simon and Schuster, 1986).

Jablon, Howard, "Cordell Hull, His 'Associates,' and Relations with Japan, 1933–36," *Mid-America*, vol. 56 (July 1974) pp. 160–74.

——, *Crossroad of Decision: The State Department and Foreign Policy, 1933–1937* (Lexington: University Press of Kentucky, 1983).

Jacobs, Travis Beal, "Roosevelt's Quarantine Speech," *The Historian*, vol. 24 (August 1962) pp. 483–502.

James, D. Clayton, *The Years of MacArthur*, 2 vols (New York: Houghton Mifflin, 1975).

Japan: Koseisho, *Jinko Minzokubu* [Ministry of Health and Welfare, Population, and Race Section], *Senso no Jinko ni oyobosu Eikyo* [The Influence of War on Population] and *Yamato Minzoku o Chu kaku to suru Sekai no Kento* [Investigations of Global Policy with the Yamato Race as Nucleus], originally prepared in 1942–43 and reprinted as *Minzoku Jinko Seisaku Kenkyu Shiryo* [Research Documents on Race and Population Policy], 7 vols (Bunsei Shoin, 1982).

——, *Mombusho* [Ministry of Education], ed. Dai Toa Senso to Warera [The Greater East Asia War and Ourselves, 1942].

Johnson, Chalmers, *An Instance of Treason* (Rutland, Vt.: Tuttle, 1977).

Johnson, Sheila K., *American Attitudes Toward Japan, 1941–1975* (Stanford: American Enterprise Institute and Hoover Institution, 1975).

Jonas, Manfred, *Isolationism in America, 1935–1941* (Ithaca: Cornell University Press, 1966).

Jungk, Robert, *Brighter Than a Thousand Suns* (New York: Knopf, 1958).

Kaplan, Morton A. and Mushakoji, Kinhinde, eds, *Japan, America, and the Future World Order* (New York: Free Press, 1976).

Kase, Toshihiku, *Eclipse of the Rising Sun* (London: Athlone Press, 1951).

Kato, Matsuo, *The Lost War* (New York: Knopf, 1946).

Kawai, Kazuo, "Mokusatsu: Japan's Response to the Potsdam Declaration," *Pacific Historical Review*, vol. 19 (November 1950).

——, *Japan's American Interlude* (Chicago: University of Chicago Press, 1960).

Kawakami, K. K., *Manchukuo: Child of Conflict* (New York: Macmillan, 1938).

——, "Britain's Trade War with Japan," *Foreign Affairs*, vol. 12 (April 1934) pp. 483–94.

——, *Japan in China* (London: John Murray, 1938).

——, "Far Eastern Triangle," *Foreign Affairs*, vol. 18 (July 1940), pp. 632–45.

Kennan, George F., *American Diplomacy: 1900–1950* (Chicago: University of Chicago Press, 1984).

——, *Memoirs, 1925–50* (Boston: Little, Brown, 1967).

——, *Memoirs, 1950–1963* (New York: Pantheon, 1983).

—— [X], "The Sources of Soviet Conduct," *Foreign Affairs* (July 1947).

——, "Japanese Security and American Foreign Policy, *Foreign Affairs* (October 1964).

Kerrison, Raymond, *Bishop Walsh of Maryknoll* (New York: Putnam's, 1962).

Kimball, Warren F., ed., *Churchill and Roosevelt: The Complete Correspondence*, 3 vols (Princeton: Princeton University Press, 1984).

Kissinger, Henry, *American Foreign Policy* (New York: Norton, 1977).

——, *The White House Years* (Boston: Little, Brown, 1979).

——, *Years of Upheaval* (Boston: Little, Brown, 1982).

Kitamura, Hiroshi, *Psychological Dimensions of U.S.–Japanese Relations* (Occasional Paper No. 28. Harvard Center for International Affairs, 1971).

Knebel, Fletcher, and Bailey, Charles W., *No High Ground* (New York: 1960).

Kolko, Joyce and Gabriel, *The Limits of Power: The World and United States Foreign Policy, 1945–54* (New York: 1964).

Kolko, Gabriel, *The Limits of Power: The World and United States Foreign Policy, 1945–1954* (New York: Harper and Row, 1972).

Langdon, F. C., *Japan's Foreign Policy* (Vancouver: University of British Columbia Press, 1973).

Larrabee, Eric, *Commander in Chief: Franklin D. Roosevelt, His Lieutenants, and Their War* (New York: 1987).

Larson, Deborah, *Origins of Containment: A Psychological Explanation* (Princeton, NJ: Princeton University Press, 1985).

Lasch, Christopher, "The Explosion that Froze the World," *Nation*, vol. 201, September 6, 1965.

Lauren, Paul, ed., *The China Hand's Legacy: Ethics and Diplomacy* (Boulder, Col.: Westview Press, 1987).

Leary, William M., ed., *We Shall Return: MacArthur's Commanders and the Defeat of Japan* (Lexington, Ky: 1988).

Lebra, Joyce C., ed., *Japan's Greater East Asia Co-Prosperity Sphere in World War II: Selected Readings and Documents* (New York: Oxford University Press, 1975).

Lebra, Joyce C., *Japanese Trained Armies in Southeast Asia* (Honolulu: University of Hawaii Press, 1987).

Lebra, Joyce C. and Sugiyama, Takie, *Japanese Patterns of Behavior* (Honolulu: University of Hawaii Press, 1976).

Leahy, William, *I Was There* (New York: 1950).

Leigh, Michael, *Mobilizing Consent: Public Opinion and American Foreign Policy, 1937–47* (Chapel Hill: University of North Carolina Press, 1976).

Leffler, Melvyn P., "The American Conception of National Security and the Beginnings of the Cold War, 1945–48," *American Historical Review*, vol. 89, no. 2 (April 1984) pp. 346–81.

Leuchtenburg, William F., "Franklin D. Roosevelt, 'Quarantine Address, 1937,' " in Daniel Boorstein, ed., *An American Primer*, pp. 871–81 (Chicago: University of Chicago Press, 1968).

Levine, Steven I., *The Anvil of Victory* (New York: 1987).

Lewin, Ronald, *The American Magic: Codes, Ciphers, and the Defeat of Japan* (New York: Farrar, Straus and Giroux, 1982).

Leutze, James R., *Bargaining for Supremacy* (Chapel Hill: University of North Carolina Press, 1977).

Lippman, Walter, *Public Opinion* (New York: Harcourt and Brace, 1922).

Liu, Daniel T. J., "A Review of Diplomatic Relations Between the Republic of China and the United States of America: The Sino-Japanese Conflicts, 1931–1936," *Chinese Culture*, vol. 15 (September 1974) pp. 43–75.

——, "A Study of Diplomatic Relations between China and the United States of America: The Sino-Japanese War, 1937–1941," *Chinese Culture*, vol. 15 (December 1974) pp. 11–38.

Livingston, Jon, *et al.*, *Postwar Japan: 1945 to the Present* (New York: Pantheon Books, 1974).

Louis, William R., *Imperialism at Bay* (New York: Random House, 1978).

MacArthur, Douglas, *Reminiscences* (New York: McGraw-Hill, 1964).

Maddox, Robert James, "Atomic Diplomacy: A Study in Creative Writing," *The Journal of American History*, vol. 59, March 1973, pp. 925–934.

——, *The New Left and the Origins of the Cold War* (Princeton, NJ: Princeton University Press, 1973).

Maier, Charles S., "Revisionism and the Interpretation of Cold War Origins," *Perspectives in American History*, vol. 4 (1970) pp. 313–47.

Mallory, Walter H., "The Permanent Conflict in Manchuria," *Foreign Affairs*, vol. 10 (January 1932) pp. 220–2.

Manchester, William, *American Caesar* (Boston: Little, Brown, 1978).

Manning, Paul, *Hirohito: The War Years* (New York: Dodd, Mead, 1986).

Marder, Arthur, *Old Friends, New Enemies* (New York: Oxford University Press, 1981).

Marks, Frederick W., *Velvet on Iron: The Diplomacy of Theodore Roosevelt* (Lincoln: University of Nebraska Press, 1979).

——, "The Origin of FDR's Promise to Support Britain Militarily in the Far East – A New Look," *Pacific Historical Review*, vol. 53 (November 1984) pp. 447–62.

——, "Facade and Failure: The Hull–Nomura Talks of 1941," *Presidential Studies Quarterly*, vol. 15 (Winter 1985) pp. 99–112.

——, *Wind Over Sand: The Diplomacy of Franklin Roosevelt* (Athens: University of Georgia Press, 1988).

Marx, Joseph, *Nagasaki: The Necessary Bomb?* (New York: Columbia University Press, 1971).

Masland, John W., "Missionary Influence upon American Far Eastern Policy," *Pacific Historical Review*, vol. 10 (September 1941) pp. 279–96.

——, "Commercial Influence upon American Far Eastern Policy, 1937–41", *Pacific Historical Review*, vol. 11 (September 1942) pp. 281–99.

Matray, James, *The Reluctant Crusade: American Foreign Policy in Korea, 1941–50* (Honolulu: University of Hawaii Press, 1986).

Mayers, David, *George Kennan and the Dilemmas of U.S. Foreign Policy* (New York: Oxford University Press, 1988).

Maxon, Yale C., *Control of Japanese Foreign Policy: A Study of Civil–Military Rivalry, 1930–1945* (Berkeley, Calif.: University of California Press, 1957).

McCoy, Alfred W., ed., *Southeast Asia Under Japanese Rule* (New Haven, Conn.: Yale University of Southeast Asia Studies, Monograph Series no. 22, 1980).

McDougall, Walter A., *Let the Sea Make a Noise.... A History of the North Pacific from Magellan to MacArthur* (New York: Basic Books, 1993).

McLellan, David, *Dean Acheson: The State Department Years* (New York: Dodd, Mead, and Company, 1970).

Mee, Charles L., *Meeting at Potsdam* (New York: Knopf, 1974).

——, *The Marshall Plan: The Launching of the Pax Americana* (New York: Simon and Schuster, 1984).

Melanson, Richard A., and Mayers, David, eds, *Reevaluating Eisenhower: American Foreign Policy in the Fifties* (Chicago: University of Illinois Press, 1987).

Meskill, Robert L., *Hitler and Japan: The Hollow Alliance* (New York: Atherton, 1966).

Messer, Robert, *The End of an Alliance: James F. Byrnes, Roosevelt, Truman and the Origins of the Cold War* (Chapel Hill: University of North Carolina Press, 1982).

Meyers, Ramon H. and Pettie, Mark, eds, *The Japanese Colonial Empire* (Princeton, NJ: Princeton University Press, 1984).

Minear, Richard, *Victor's Justice: The Tokyo War Crimes Trial* (Princeton, NJ: Princeton University Press, 1971).

Miscamble, Wilson, "George F. Kennan, The Policy Planning Staff and American Foreign Policy, 1947–1950" (Ph.D. dissertation, University of Notre Dame, 1980).

Montgomery, John D., *Forced to be Free: The Artificial Revolution in Germany and Japan* (Chicago: University of Chicago Press, 1957).

Montgomery, Michael, *Imperialist Japan* (London: Charles Helm, 1988).

Moore, Frederick, *With Japan's Leaders: An Intimate Record of Fourteen Years as Counsellor to the Japanese Government, Ending December 7, 1941* (New York: Scribners, 1942).

Moore, Joseph, *Japanese Workers and the Struggle for Power, 1945-1947* (Madison: University of Wisconsin Press, 1983).

Morison, Elting, *Henry L. Stimson: Turmoil and Tradition* (Boston: 1960).

Morley, James W., ed., *Forecast for Japan: Security in the 1970s* (Princeton, NJ: Princeton University Press, 1972).

——, *Deterrent Diplomacy: Japan, Germany, and the USSR* (New York: Columbia University Press, 1976).

——, *The Fatal Choice: Japan's Negotiations With the United States, 1941* (New York: Columbia University Press, 1980).

Morris, Ivan, *The Nobility of Failure: Tragic Heroes in the History of Japan* (New York: Meridian, 1976).

Morton, Louis, "The Decision to Use the Atomic Bomb," *Foreign Affairs*, vol. 35 (January 1957) pp. 334-53.

Mosley, Leonard, *Hirohito: Emperor of Japan* (Englewood Cliffs, N.J.: Prentice-Hall, 1967).

Mushakoji, Kinhide, "The Thought and Behavior of Japan's Diplomats," *Journal of Social and Political Ideas in Japan* (April 1966) pp. 19-25.

Myers, Ramon, and Peattie, Mark, *The Japanese Colonial Empire, 1895-1945* (Princeton, NJ: Princeton University Press, 1984).

Nagai, Yonosuke and Iriye, Akira, *The Origins of the Cold War in Asia* (New York: Columbia University Press, 1977).

Nathan, James, and Oliver, James, *Foreign Policy Making and the American Political System* (Boston: Little, Brown and Company, 1981).

Neils, Patricia, "Henry R. Luce and American Images of China," *Tamkang Journal of American Studies*, vol. 2 (Spring 1986) pp. 17-39.

Nelson, Anna, ed., *The State Department Policy Planning Staff Papers, 1947-1949*, 3 vols (New York: Garland Publishing Company, 1983).

Newall, William H., ed., *Japan in Asia* (Singapore: Singapore University Press, 1981).

Neu, Charles E., *The Troubled Encounter: The United States and Japan* (1975).

Neumann, William L., "Franklin D. Roosevelt and Japan, 1913-33," *Pacific Historical Review*, vol. 22 (May 1953) pp. 143-53.

——, *America Encounters Japan: From Perry to MacArthur* (Baltimore: Johns Hopkins Press, 1963).

Nitze, Paul, "The Development of NSC 68," *International Security* (Spring 1980).

Nixon, Richard, *The Memoirs of Richard Nixon* (New York: Grosset and Dunlap, 1978).

Nomura, Kichisaburo, "Japan's Demand for Naval Equality," *Foreign Affairs*, vol. 13 (October 1934) pp. 196-203.

O'Conner, Raymond, *Diplomacy for Victory: FDR and Unconditional Surrender* (New York: Macmillan, 1971).

Ogushi Toyoo, "Nippon Minzoku Sekaikan no Kakuritsu" [Establishing a Japanese Racial Worldview], *Bungei Shunju*, vol. 20, no. 1 (January 1941) pp. 24-33.

Oka, Yoshitake, *Konoe Fumimaro: A Political Biography* (Tokyo: University of Tokyo Press, 1983).

Osgood, Robert F., *The Weary and the Wary: U.S. and Japanese Security Policies in Transition* (Baltimore: Johns Hopkins University Press, 1972).

Ozaki, Robert S., *The Control of Exports and Foreign Capital in Japan* (New York: Praeger, 1972).

Pacific War Research Society, *Japan's Longest Day* (New York: Kodansha International, 1968).

Packard, Jerrold M., *Sons of Heaven* (New York: Duell, Sloan, and Pearce, 1945).

Paterson, Thomas, ed., *Cold War Critics: Alternatives to American Foreign Policy in the Truman Years* (Chicago: Quadrangle Books, 1971).

Patcher, Henry, "Revisionist Historians and the Cold War," in Irving Howe, ed., *Beyond the New Left* (New York: 1970).

Peattie, Mark R., *Ishiwara Kanji and Japan's Confrontation with the West* (Princeton, NJ: Princeton University Press, 1966).

Pelz, Stephen F., *Race to Pearl Harbor: The Failure of the Second London Conference and the Onset of World War II* (Cambridge, Mass.: Harvard University Press, 1974).

Petillo, Carol M., *Douglas MacArthur: The Philippine Years* (Bloomington, Ind.: University of Indiana Press, 1981).

Piccagallo, Philip R., *The Japanese on Trial: Allied War Crimes Operations in the East, 1945–51* (Austin: University of Texas Press, 1979).

Plesur, Milton, *America's Outward Thrust: Approaches to Foreign Affairs, 1865–1890* (1971).

Pletcher, David M., *The Awkward Years: American Foreign Relations Under Garfield and Arthur* (Columbia: University of Missouri Press, 1962).

Pogue, Forrest C., *George C. Marshall*, 3 vols (New York: Viking, 1973).

Pollard, Robert, *Economic Security and the Origins of the Cold War* (New York: Columbia University Press, 1985).

Powell, John W., "Japan's Biological Weapons, 1930–1945: A Hidden Chapter in History," *Bulletin of Concerned Asian Scholars*, vol. 12, no. 4 (October–December 1980) pp. 2–17.

——, "Japan's Germ Warfare: The U.S. Cover-Up of a War Crime," *Bulletin of Concerned Asian Scholars*, vol. 12, no. 4 (October–December, 1980).

Prange, Gordon, *At Dawn We Slept: The Untold Story of Pearl Harbor* (New York: McGraw-Hill, 1981).

Prange, Gordon, *Pearl Harbor: The Verdict of History* (New York: McGraw-Hill, 1986).

Pritchard, R. John, and Zaide, Sonia Magbanna, eds, *The Tokyo War Crimes Trial: The Complete Transcripts of the Proceedings of the International Military Tribunal for the Far East*, 21 vols (New York: Garland Publishers, 1981).

Quinlan, Robert J. "The United States Fleet: Diplomacy, Strategy and the Allocation of Ships, 1940–1941," in Harold Stein, ed., *American Civil–Military Decisions: A Book of Case Studies*, pp. 153–202 (Birmingham: University of Alabama Press, 1963).

Ramsdell, Daneil B., "Asia Askew: U.S. Best Sellers on Asia, 1931–1980," *Bulletin of Concerned Asian Scholars*, vol. 15, no. 4 (October–December 1983) pp. 2–25.

Rappaport, Armin, *Henry L. Stimson and Japan, 1931–33* (Chicago: University of Chicago Press, 1963).

Rhodes, Anthony, *Propaganda, The Art of Persuasion: World War II* (London: Chelsea Home Publishers, 1976).

Roling, B. B. A., and Ruter, C. F., eds, *The Tokyo Judgement: The International Military Tribunal for the Far East (I.M.T.F.E.), April 29, 1946–November 1948,* vol. 1 (APA University Press Amsterdam BV, 1977).

Roosevelt, Franklin D., "Shall We Trust Japan," *Asia,* vol. 23 (July 1923) pp. 475–8.

Rose, Lisle A., *Dubious Victory: The United States and the End of World War II* (Kent, Ohio: Kent State University Press, 1973).

——, *Roots of Tragedy: The United States and the Struggle For Asia* (Westport, Conn.: Greenwood Press, 1976).

Rosovsky, Henry, ed., *Discord in the Pacific: Challenges to the Japanese–American Alliance* (Washington D.C.: Columbia Books, 1972).

Rotter, Andrew J., *The Path to Vietnam: The Origins of the American Commitment to Southeast Asia* (Ithaca, N.Y.: Cornell University Press, 1987).

Royama, Masamichi, *Foreign Policy of Japan, 1914–1939* (Tokyo: Institute of Pacific Relations, 1941).

Rubin, Barry, *Secrets of State: The State Department and the Struggle Over U.S. Foreign Policy* (New York: Oxford University Press, 1987).

Samson, George, "Liberalism in Japan," *Foreign Affairs,* vol. 19 (April 1941) pp. 551–60.

——, *The Western World and Japan* (New York: Knopf, 1950).

Sato, Hideo, Clapp, Priscilla, and Fukui, Haruhiro, *Managing an Alliance: The Politics of U.S.–Japanese Relations* (Washington, D.C.: The Brookings Institute, 1976).

Schaller, Michael, *The Origins of the Cold War in Asia: The American Occupation of Japan* (New York: Oxford University Press, 1985).

——, *Douglas MacArthur: The Far Eastern General* (New York: Oxford University Press, 1989).

Schlesinger, Arthur, *The Cycles of American History* (Boston: Houghton Mifflin, 1986).

Schonberger, Howard, "The Japan Lobby in American Diplomacy, 1947–1952," *Pacific Historical Review,* vol. 46, no. 3 (August 1977) pp. 327–59.

——, "American Labor's Cold War in Occupied Japan," *Diplomatic History,* vol. 3, no. 3 (Summer 1979) pp. 249–72.

——, "General William H. Draper, the 80th Congress, and the Origins of the Reverse Course" (unpublished paper, Amherst Conference on Occupied Japan, 1980).

——, "John Foster Dulles and the China Question in the Making of the Japanese Peace Treaty," in Thomas Burkman, ed., *The Occupation of Japan: The International Context* (Norfolk, Va.: MacArthur Foundation, 1984).

Schroeder, Paul, *The Axis Alliance and Japanese–American Relations, 1941* (Ithaca: Cornell University Press, 1958).

Schulzinger, Robert, *The Wise Men of Foreign Affairs: The History of the Council on Foreign Relations* (New York: Columbia University Press, 1984).

Sebald, William, and Brines, Russell, *With MacArthur in Japan: A Personal History of the Occupation* (New York: Norton, 1965).

Sherwin, Martin J., "The Atomic Bomb as History," *Wisconsin Magazine of History,* vol. 50 (Winter 1969–70) pp. 128–34.

——, *A World Destroyed: The Atomic Bomb and the Grand Alliance* (New York: Vintage, 1975).

Sherwood, Robert E., *Roosevelt and Hopkins* (New York: Harper & Brothers, 1948).

Shigemitsu, Mamoru, *Japan and Her Destiny: My Struggle for Peace* (New York: E. P. Dutton, 1958).

Shiroyama, Saburo, *War Criminal: The Life and Death of Koki Hirota* (New York: Kodansha, 1977).

Smith, Alice Kimball, "Behind the Decision to Use the Bomb: Chicago 1944–45," *Bulletin of the Atomic Scientists*, vol. 14 (October 1958) pp. 288–312.

Smith, Gaddis, *American Diplomacy During the Second World War, 1941–1945* (New York: Cooper Square, 1965).

——, *Morality, Reason, and Power: American Diplomacy in the Carter Years* (New York: Hill and Wang, 1986).

Smith, Kingsbury, "Our Government's Plan for a Defeated Japan," *American Mercury* (January 1944) pp. 29–36.

Snow, Edgar, *The Battle for Asia* (New York: World Publishing Co., 1942).

Spector, Ronald, *Eagle Against The Sun: The American War With Japan* (New York: Vintage Books, 1985).

Sprout, Harold and Margaret, *The Rise of American Naval Power, 1776–1918* (1939).

Steel, Ronald, *Walter Lippman and the American Century* (Boston: Little, Brown and Company, 1980).

Stein, Harold, "The Rationale of Japanese Surrender," *World Politics*, vol. 15 (October 1962) pp. 138–50.

Stephan, John J., *Hawaii Under the Rising Sun: Japan's Plans for Conquest After Pearl Harbor* (Honolulu: University of Hawaii Press, 1984).

——, "The Tanaka Memorial (1927): Authentic or Spurious?" *Modern Asian Studies*, vol. 7, no. 4 (1973) pp. 733–45.

Sternsher, Bernard, "The Stimson Doctrine: FDR versus Moley and Tugwell," *Pacific Historical Review*, vol. 31 (August 1962), pp. 281–9.

Stimson, Henry L., "Henry L. Stimson Diaries" (New Haven, Conn.: Yale University Microfilm).

——, *The Far Eastern Crisis* (New York: Harper, 1936).

Stimson, Henry L. and Bundy, McGeorge, *On Active Service in War and Peace* (New York: Harper & Brothers, 1948).

Stoessinger, John, *Crusaders and Pragmatists: Movers of Modern American Foreign Policy* (New York: Norton, 1979).

Strategic Bombing Survey, *Japan's Struggle to End the War* (Washington, DC: GPO, 1946).

——, *Summary Report (Pacific War)* (Washington, DC: GPO, 1946).

Supreme Commander for Allied Powers, *The Political Reorientation of Japan, September 1945–September 1948, Report of the Government Section of SCAP* (Washington, DC: GPO, 1948).

Teller, Edward, and Leo Szilard, *The Legacy of Hiroshima* (Garden City, NY: Doubleday, 1962).

Terrill, Tom, *The Tariff, Politics and American Foreign Policy, 1874–1901* (1973).

Theoharis, "Atomic Diplomacy," *New University Thought*, vol. 5 (May–June 1967) pp. 128–34.

Thompson, James C., Peter W. Stanley, and John Curtis Perry, *Sentimental Imperialists: The American Experience in East Asia* (New York: Harper & Row, 1981).

Thorne, Christopher G., *The Limits of Foreign Policy: The West, the League, and the Far Eastern Crisis of 1931–1933* (London: Hamish Hamilton, 1972).

——, *Allies of a Kind: The United States, Great Britain, and the War against Japan, 1941–45* (New York: Oxford University Press, 1978).

——, *The Issue of War* (New York: Oxford University Press, 1985).

Tinker, Hugh, Race, *Conflict and the International Order: From Empire to United Nations* (New York: St Martin's Press, 1977).

Todorov, Tzvetan, *The Conquest of America: The Question of the Other*, translated by Richard Howard (New York: Harper & Row, 1982).

Togo, Shigenori, *The Cause of Japan*; translated by Fumihiko Togo (New York: Simon and Schuster, 1956).

Toland, John, *The Rising Sun: The Decline and Fall of the Japanese Empire, 1936–1945* (New York: Random House, 1970).

——, *Infamy: Pearl Harbor and its Aftermath* (Garden City, N.Y.: Doubleday, 1982).

Troy, Thomas, *Donovan and the C.I.A.: A History of the Establishment of the Central Intelligence Agency* (Frederick, Md: Alatheia Books, 1983).

Truman, Harry, *Memoirs*, 2 vols (New York: Doubleday, 1955–6).

Tuchman, Barbara, *Stillwell and the American Experience in China* (New York: Macmillan, 1970).

Tucker, Nancy, *Patterns in the Dust: Chinese–American Relations and the Recognition Controversy, 1949–50* (New York: 1983).

——, "American Policy toward Sino-Japanese Trade in the Postwar Years: Politics and Prosperity," *Diplomatic History*, vol. 8, no. 3 (Summer 1984) pp. 183–208.

United States Department of State, *Foreign Relations of the United States: Conferences at Washington, 1941–42, and Casablanca, 1943* (Washington, D.C.: Government Printing Office (GPO), 1968).

——, *Foreign Relations of the United States, 1931–1957* (Washington, D.C.: GPO, 1943–1986).

Utley, Jonathan G., "Diplomacy in a Democracy: The United States and Japan, 1937–41," *World Affairs*, vol. 139 (Fall 1976) pp. 130–40.

——, *Going to War with Japan, 1937–1941* (Knoxville: University of Tennessee Press, 1985).

Van der Post, Laurens, *The Prisoner and the Bomb* (New York: 1970).

Villa, Brian, "The U.S. Army, Unconditional Surrender, and the Potsdam Declaration," *Journal of American History*, vol. 63 (June 1976) pp. 66–92.

Ward, Robert E. and Frank Joseph Shulman, *The Allied Occupation of Japan, 1945–53: An Annotated Bibliography of Western-Language Materials* (Chicago: University of Chicago Press, 1974).

Weinstein, Franklin B., ed., *United States–Japan Relations and the Security of East Asia* (Boulder, Col.: Westview Press, 1978).

Weinstein, Martin, *Japan's Postwar Defense Policy, 1947–1968* (New York: Columbia University Press, 1971).

Weston, Rubin Francis, *Racism in U.S. Imperialism: The Influence of Racial Assumptions on American Foreign Policy, 1893–1946* (Columbia: University of South Carolina Press, 1972).

White, Theodore, *In Search of History* (New York: Harper & Row, 1978).

Wildes, Harry Emerson, *Typhoon in Tokyo: The Occupation and its Aftermath* (New York: Columbia University Press, 1954).

Wilkins, Mira, *The Emergence of the Multinational Enterprise: American Business Abroad from the Colonial Era to 1914* (Cambridge University Press, 1970).

Williams, Peter and Wallace, David, *Unit 731: The Japanese Army's Secret of Secrets* (London: Hodder and Stoughton, 1988).

Willoughby, Charles A. and Chamberlain, John, *MacArthur, 1941–51* (New York: 1955).

Wilcox, Robert, *The Secret War* (New York: Morrow, 1987).

Williams, William, *The Roots of the Modern American Empire* (1969).

Wilmot, H. P., *Empires in the Balance: Japanese and Allied Pacific Strategies to April 4, 1942* (Naval Institute Press, 1982).

Winnacker, Rudolph A., "The Debate about Hiroshima," *Military Affairs*, vol. 11 (Spring 1947) pp. 25–30.

Winkler, Allan M., *The Politics of Propaganda: The Office of War Information, 1942–1945* (New Haven, Conn.: Yale University Press, 1978).

Witney, Courtney, *MacArthur: His Rendevous with History* (New York: 1965).

Wohlstetter, Roberta, *Pearl Harbor: Warning and Decision* (Standford, Calif.: Stanford University Press, 1982).

Wolf, Robert, ed., *Americans as Proconsuls: The United States Military Government in Germany and Japan* (Carbondale, Ill.: 1984).

Wray, Harry, and Hilary Conroy, *Japan Examined: Perspectives on Modern Japanese History* (Honolulu: University of Hawaii Press, 1983).

Yoshida, Shigeru, *The Yoshida Memoirs* (Cambridge, Mass.: Harvard University Press, 1961).

Yoshihashi, Takehiko, *Conspiracy at Mukden: The Rise of the Japanese Military* (New Haven, Conn.: Yale University Press, 1963).

Young, A. Morgan, *Imperial Japan* (New York: Morrow, 1938).

Ziegler, Janet, *World War II: Books in English, 1945–1965* (Stanford, Calif.: Hoover Institution Press, 1971).

Index

The Contributors

June Ahn is a graduate student and Dean's Fellow in Urban Education in the Rossier School of Education at the University of Southern California. He studies the structural, social, and socio-psychological dynamics of education organizations and technology.

Bruce D. Baker is an Associate Professor in the Department of Educational Theory, Policy, and Administration in the Graduate School of Education at Rutgers University in New Brunswick, NJ. His recent research focuses on state aid allocation policies and practices, with particular attention to the equity and adequacy of aid for special student populations.

David P. Baker is a Professor of Education and Sociology in the College of Education at Pennsylvania State University.

Eva L. Baker is a Distinguished Professor of Education at UCLA, Graduate School of Education & Information Studies. She directs the Center for Research on Evaluation, Standards, and Student Testing (CRESST). Dr. Baker was recently the president of the American Educational Research Association and is currently a member of the National Academy of Education.

Nina Bascia is a Professor and Chair of the Department of Theory & Policy Studies at the Ontario Institute for Studies in Education of the University of Toronto (OISE/UT).

Clive R. Belfield is an Assistant Professor in the Department of Economics at Queens College, City University of New York. Dr. Belfield writes on the economics of education, with an emphasis on the economics of pre-schooling.

Mark Berends is a Professor of Sociology and Director of the Center for Research on Educational Opportunity at the University of Notre Dame.

Tara Béteille is a doctoral candidate in the Economics of Education program at Stanford University and a Stanford Graduate Fellow.

Geoffrey D. Borman is a Professor of Education at the University of Wisconsin-Madison, a Senior Researcher with the Consortium for Policy Research in Education, and the lead analyst for the Center for Data-Driven Reform in Education at Johns Hopkins University.

Kathryn M. Borman is a Professor of Anthropology and lead researcher at the Alliance for Applied Research in Anthropology and Education, Department of Anthropology the University of South Florida.

Dominic J. Brewer is the Clifford H. and Betty C. A Professor in Urban Leadership and a Professor of Education in Economics and Policy at the University of South California. He is a labor economist specializing in economics of education and education policy.

Mary Alice Callahan is currently a doctoral student University of California, Berkeley, studying education policy. She was a teacher for 24 years and continue work with the California Federation of Teachers be a state vice president and as a member of the Am Federation of Teachers program and policy council.

Eric M. Camburn is an Assistant Professor at the University of Wisconsin and a Senior Researcher at the Consortium Policy Research in Education. His research focuses on public schools and their improvement, including programmatic efforts to improve instruction and learning organizational factors that promote such improvement

Steve Cantrell is a Senior Program Officer for & Melinda Gates Foundation. Previously he the Regional Educational Laboratory–Midwest Chief Research Scientist for Los Angeles Unified District.

Martin Carnoy is the Vida Jacks Professor of Education Stanford University. His research focuses on the value of education, on the underlying political of educational policy, and on the financing and allocation aspects of educational production.

Tino A. Castañeda is a doctoral student in Educational Leadership and Policy Studies at the University of Washington, Seattle. He is currently working as a researcher on a national study of educational leadership.

Lora Cohen-Vogel earned her Ph.D. from Vanderbilt University and is currently an Assistant Professor at Florida State University. Her teaching and research focus on educational policy and politics, with particular attention to issues in teacher preparation, recruitment, and retention.

Richard Correnti is an Assistant Professor and a Research Scientist at the Learning Research Development Center at the University of Pittsburgh. His research interests focus on instruction received by students, including how to measure instructional delivery on a large scale, variability in students' accumulated instruction, and how instruction influences student learning.

Bridget A. Cotner is a graduate student in the Measurement, Research, and Evaluation Program in the College of Education, the University of South Florida.

Linda Darling-Hammond is the Charles E. Ducommun Professor of Education at Stanford University where her research, teaching, and policy work focus on issues of teaching quality, school reform, and educational equity. She is former president of the American Educational Research Association and a member of the National Academy of Education.

Amanda Datnow is Professor and Director of Education Studies at the University of California, San Diego. She was formerly a faculty member at the University of Southern California and at the Ontario Institute for Studies in Education. Her research focuses on the politics and policies of school reform, particularly with regard to the professional lives of educators, and issues of equity.

Laura M. Desimone is an Associate Professor at the University of Pennsylvania Graduate School of Education. She studies education policy effects on teaching and learning in the core academic subjects, with a focus on comprehensive school reform, standards-based reform, and teachers' professional development.

Maressa L. Dixon is a graduate student in Applied Anthropology at the University of South Florida.

George Farkas is a Professor in the Department of Education at the University of California, Irvine. His research interests include labor markets, schooling and human resources, demography, statistical research methods, evaluation research, and economic sociology.

Michael J. Feuer is the executive director of the Division of Behavioral and Social Sciences and Education in the National Research Council (NRC) of the National Academies, where he is responsible for a broad portfolio of studies and other activities aimed at improved economic, social, and educational policymaking.

Robert E. Floden is a University Distinguished Professor of Teacher Education, Measurement and Quantitative Methods, Educational Psychology, and Educational Policy at Michigan State University. He is Associate Dean for Research, director of the Institute for Research on Teaching and Learning and co-director of Teachers for a New Era (TNE).

Barbara Foorman is the Francis Eppes Professor of Education and Director of the Florida Center for Reading Research at Florida State University.

Timothy G. Ford is a doctoral candidate and Erickson Research Fellow in the Curriculum, Teaching, and Educational Policy program at Michigan State University. His primary research interests center on the sociology of education, in particular the relationship between policy and the social organization of schooling and parenting and adolescent development.

Rachel Fulcher-Dawson is a graduate student in educational policy at Michigan State University.

Bruce Fuller is Professor of Education and Public Policy at the University of California, Berkeley. He served as a legislative aide and education advisor to one California governor, then as research sociologist at the World Bank. Fuller previously taught comparative policy and cultural studies at Harvard University.

Adam Gamoran is a Professor of Sociology and Educational Policy Studies and the director of Wisconsin Center for Education Research at University of Wisconsin, Madison. His research interests include school organization, stratification and inequality in education, and resource allocation in school systems.

Patricia Gándara is Professor of Education in the Graduate School of Education and Information Studies at UCLA, and co-director of The Civil Rights Project/Proyecto Derechos Civiles at UCLA. Her research focuses on educational equity and access for low income and ethnic minority students, language policy, and the education of Mexican origin youth.

Mona Ghali is a graduate student at the Ontario Institute for Studies in Education, the University of Toronto.

Louis M. Gomez is the Aon Professor of Learning Sciences and co-director of the National Science Foundation-sponsored Center for Learning Technologies in Urban Schools (LeTUS) at Northwestern University.

The Editors

Gary Sykes is a Professor of Teacher Education and Education Policy at Michigan State University. He specializes in educational policy relating to teaching and teacher education. His research interests center on policy issues associated with the improvement of teaching and teacher education, on the development of leadership preparation programs, and on educational choice as an emerging policy issue.

Barbara Schneider is a John A. Hannah University Distinguished Professor in the College of Education and Department of Sociology at Michigan State University. She holds research appointments at the University of Chicago and NORC, where she is Principal Investigator of the Data Research and Development Center (DRDC). She has published 12 books and over 100 articles and reports on family, social context of schooling, and sociology of knowledge. Professor Schneider is currently conducting a collaborative study with the Michigan Department of Education on using administrative data to make state education policy decisions. She was selected by the American Sociological Association as the editor of *Sociology of Education*.

David N. Plank is Executive Director of Policy Analysis for California Education (PACE), an independent policy research center based at the University of California-Berkeley, Stanford University, and the University of Southern California. He was previously a professor at Michigan State University, where he founded and directed the Education Policy Center. He received his Ph.D. from the University of Chicago in 1983. In addition to his work on education policy in the U.S., he has served as a consultant in the areas of educational policy and finance to international organizations including the World Bank, the UNDP, the OECD, USAID, and the Ford Foundation, and also to governments in Africa and Latin America.

M. Cecilia Gómez is a doctoral student in the School of Education at the University of California, Davis. Her research interests include the schooling of English-Spanish bilingual students, language policy, second/third and heritage language acquisition, teacher education, and Spanish in the U.S.

Preston C. Green, III is an Associate Professor of Education and Law in the College of Education and Dickerson School of Law at Pennsylvania State University. His research focuses on the legal issues surrounding school choice and educational access.

Bridget K. Hamre is the Research Coordinator in the National Center for Research on Early Childhood Education at the University of Virginia. Her primary research interests lie in integrating psychological and educational theory and methodology.

Jane Hannaway is currently Principal Research Associate and Director of the Education Policy Center at the Urban Institute. She is also the overall Principal Investigator of the National Center for Analysis of Longitudinal Data in Education Research (CALDER) project.

Eric A. Hanushek is the Paul and Jean Hanna Senior Fellow at the Hoover Institution of Stanford University. He is an expert on educational policy, specializing in the economics and finance of schools.

James C. Hearn is a Professor of Higher Education in the Institute of Higher Education at the University of Georgia. His research focuses on postsecondary education policy and organization.

Thomas Hehir is Professor and Director of the School Leadership Program in the Harvard Graduate School of Education. An advocate for children with disabilities in the education system, he has written on special education, special education in the reform movement, due process, and least restrictive environment issues.

Joan L. Herman is Director of the National Center for Research on Evaluation, Standards, and Student Testing (CRESST) at UCLA. Her research has explored the effects of accountability and assessment on schools and teachers and the design of assessment systems to support school planning and instructional improvement.

Carolyn D. Herrington is a Professor of Educational Policy and Director of the Learning Systems Institute Center on Educational Policy at Florida State University. Prior to that, she served as Dean of the College of Education at the University of Missouri. Her work focuses on the policy and politics of educational reform with an emphasis on the state as the agent of analysis.

Frederick M. Hess is Resident Scholar and Director of Education Policy Studies at the American Enterprise Institute for Public Policy Research. He is a faculty associate at the Harvard University Program on Education Policy and Governance and serves on the Review Board for the Broad Prize in Urban Education.

Meredith I. Honig is an Assistant Professor of Educational Leadership and Policy Studies at the University of Washington, Seattle. Dr. Honig's research and teaching focus on policy design, policy implementation, and organizational change in cities.

Rebecca Jacobsen is an Assistant Professor of Teacher Education at Michigan State University. Her background is in politics and education where she has focused on public opinion and its impact on education policy.

Christy Marie Johnson has an MBA and Master's in Education from Stanford University, where her focus was on human capital, strategy, and organization. Prior to graduate school she taught mathematics, economics, and European history at a public high school and consulted with several nonprofits. In 2005, she was Junior Achievement's national teacher of the year.

Nathan D. Jones is a doctoral candidate at Michigan State University pursuing a joint degree in Education Policy and Special Education. His research interests focus on teacher quality and the sociology of education, particularly related to the role of colleagues in influencing the practices and beliefs of early career teachers.

David Kaplan is a Professor of Quantitative Methods in the Department of Educational Psychology at the University of Wisconsin, Madison and holds an affiliate faculty appointment in the interdisciplinary Prevention Sciences Program.

Venessa Keesler is a graduate student in the Measurement and Quantitative Methods program at Michigan State University. Her research interests include policy analysis using state administrative data and rural education.

Spyros Konstantopoulos is an Assistant Professor of Educational Research Measurement and Evaluation at the Lynch School of Education at Boston College. His research interests include the extension and application of statistical methods to issues in education, social science, and policy studies.

Julia E. Koppich is a San Francisco-based education consultant and President of J. Koppich & Associates. She has taught at the Graduate School of Education at the University of California at Berkeley and at the School of Education at Stanford University. Her areas of specialization include education policy analysis and public sector labor relations.

T. Austin Lacy is a doctoral student at the Institute of Higher Education at the University of Georgia. His most recent research focuses on state science and technology policies affecting universities.

Douglas Lee Lauen is an Assistant Professor of Public Policy at the University of North Carolina at Chapel Hill who specializes in educational policy, research methods, and urban school reform.

Chong-Jae Lee is a Professor of Educational Policy and Administration in the Department of Education at Seoul National University. He served as President of the Korean Education Development Institute (KEDI) from 2002-2005 and as the President of the Korean Society for the Study of Educational Administration (KSEA).

Heesook Lee is a Visiting Postdoctoral Scholar in the College of Education at Florida State University. She holds a Ph.D. from Seoul National University in Korea and has conducted research at the Korean Educational Development Institute for several years. Her current work in education focuses on the returns to higher education using meta-analysis

Jing Lei is an Assistant Professor of Instructional Design, Development and Evaluation in the School of Education at Syracuse University.

Henry M. Levin is the William H. Kilpatrick Professor of Economics and Education at Teachers College, Columbia University.

Jane Clark Lindle is the Eugene T. Moore Distinguished Professor of Educational Leadership at Clemson University and researches the micropolitical influences of accountability policy on the practices of school leaders and teachers. Recently her work has appeared in *Educational Policy, International Journal of Educational Management,* and the *Journal of School Leadership.* Lindle is a past editor of *Educational Administration Quarterly.*

Susanna Loeb is an Associate Professor of Education at Stanford University. She specializes in the economics of education, and the relationship between schools and federal, state, and local policies. Her work focuses particularly on school finance and teacher labor markets.

Catherine A. Lugg is an Associate Professor of Education in the Department of Theory, Policy, and Administration, Graduate School of Education, at Rutgers, the State University of New Jersey. Her research interests include educational politics and history, and the influence social movements and political ideology have on educational politics and policy.

Adam Maier is a doctoral candidate in the educational policy program at Michigan State University. His research

interests include teacher preparation policy, teacher labor markets, and the connections between the two.

Betty Malen is a Professor in the Department of Education Policy Studies at the University of Maryland, College Park. Her research examines the political determinants and the substantive effects of prominent education reforms (e.g., choice, decentralization, professionalization of teaching, school reconstitution) and analyzes the micropolitics of schools.

Martha McCarthy is the Chancellor's Professor and Chair of the Education Leadership and Policy Studies department at Indiana University, Bloomington. Her primary research interests pertain to church/state relations involving schools, free expression rights, equity concerns, privatization of education, and curriculum censorship.

Kathryn A. McDermott is an Associate Professor of Education and Public Policy and Administration at the University of Massachusetts Amherst. Her current research is on the formation and implementation of state-level education policy.

Sarah-Kathryn McDonald is Executive Director of the Data Research and Development Center and a Senior Research Scientist for the National Opinion Research Center at the University of Chicago.

Lorraine M. McDonnell is a professor of political science at the University of California, Santa Barbara, and the 2008-09 president of the American Educational Research Association. Within a general focus on the politics of education policy, her past research has examined school-level responses to federal and state policies, the role of teacher unions, the politics of student testing, and the potential of deliberative democracy to foster public participation in schools.

C. Kent McGuire is the dean of the College of Education at Temple University, Director of the Center for Research in Human Development and Education, and a Professor in the Educational Administration Program, Department of Educational Leadership and Policy Studies.

Michael K. McLendon is an Associate Professor of Public Policy and Higher Education and Director of the Program in Higher Education Leadership and Policy at Peabody College, Vanderbilt University. McLendon's research focuses on state politics, governance, and finance of higher education.

Julie F. Mead is an Associate Professor of Educational Leadership and Policy Analysis at the University of Wisconsin, Madison. She researches legal aspects of special education and parental school choice initiatives.

Leigh Mesler is a graduate student in Human Development and Social Policy at Northwestern University. Her research interests include studying policy implementation and the effects of policy on teachers and students in urban schools.

Roslyn Arlin Mickelson is Professor of Sociology and Public Policy at the University of North Carolina at Charlotte. Mickelson's research focuses upon the political economy of schooling and school reform, particularly the relationships among race, ethnicity, gender, class, and educational processes and outcomes.

Robert J. Miller is a Research Scientist at the University of Michigan. His main fields of interest are educational policy, organizational theory, and the analysis of school effectiveness.

Michael Mintrom is an Associate Professor of Political Studies at the University of Auckland. Over the past decade he has published extensively on the politics of educational reform.

Dana L. Mitra is Assistant Professor in the department of Education Policy Studies at Pennsylvania State University. Her research interests include student voice, youth-adult partnerships, and high school reform.

Karen Mundy is an Associate Professor of Adult Education and Community Development at the Ontario Institute for Studies in Education (OISE) of the University of Toronto.

Jeannie Oakes is Director of Education and Scholarship at the Ford Foundation. Until Fall 2008, she was Presidential Professor in Educational Equity at UCLA's Graduate School of Education and Information Studies, where she directed UCLA's Institute for Democracy, Education, and Access and the University of California's All Campus Consortium on Research for Diversity.

Jennifer O'Day is a Managing Research Scientist and policy analyst in the Education Program of the American Institutes for Research. She has carried out research and written extensively in the areas of systemic standards-based reform, educational equity, and capacity building strategies.

Rodney T. Ogawa is a professor of education at the University of California, Santa Cruz. His research examines the impact of school organization and educational reform on teachers.

V. Darleen Opfer is a Senior Lecturer in Educational Research Methods and School Improvement at Cambridge University. Her research focuses on aspects of educational politics and the policy process.

Martin Orland is the Director of Evaluation and Policy Research at WestEd. Orland directs a nationwide staff of methodologists, research scientists, content experts, and

evaluators whose goal is to help address critical needs in the fields of education and human development.

Hyun-Jeong Park is an assistant professor in the Department of Education at Seoul National University, Korea. Her primary interests are in international comparisons of competencies and empirical analysis of the student-level and school-level effects on student achievements.

Vicki Park is a doctoral candidate at the University of Southern California's Rossier School of Education and a research associate with the Center on Educational Governance. Her research interests center on educational policy and administration with an emphasis on K-12 urban school reform, and Asian American students' schooling experiences.

P. David Pearson is Professor and Dean of the Graduate School of Education at the University of California, Berkeley. His research interests include practice and policy in literacy instruction and assessment.

Robert C. Pianta is Dean of the Curry School of Education, Novartis Professor of Education, and Director of the Center for Advanced Study of Teaching and Learning at the University of Virginia.

Therese D. Pigott is an Associate Professor of Research Methodology in the School of Education at Loyola University Chicago. Her interests are meta-analysis methodology and the application of missing data to research synthesis.

Margaret L. Plecki is Associate Professor of Educational Leadership and Policy Studies at the University of Washington, Seattle. Her teaching and research interests focus on school finance policy, the economics of education, teaching quality, educational leadership, and state and local education policy.

Jennifer King Rice is an Associate Professor in the Department of Education Policy Studies at the University of Maryland. Her research draws on the discipline of economics to explore education policy questions concerning the efficiency, equity, and adequacy of U.S. public education.

Andrea K. Rorrer is an Assistant Professor in the Department of Educational Leadership and Policy Studies and the Director of the Education Policy Center at the University of Utah.

Lisa Rosen is a Research Associate (Assistant Professor) at the Center for Urban School Improvement at the University of Chicago. Her research and writing bring the tools of anthropology to bear on questions surrounding educational policy formation and implementation, school improvement, and institutional development, particularly in urban settings. She will be joining the faculty of Michigan State University in the Fall of 2009.

James E. Rosenbaum is a Professor of Sociology, Education, and Social Policy at Northwestern University. His books include *Crossing the Class and Color Lines*, and *Beyond College for All*, which was awarded the Waller Prize in Sociology.

Brian P. Rowan is the Burke A. Hinsdale Collegiate Professor and a Research Professor at the Institute of Social Research at the University of Michigan. His research interests center on the organization of American education, paying special attention to the nature of teachers' work, how it is managed in school settings, and how teaching affects student learning.

William H. Schmidt is a University Distinguished Professor and currently co-director of the Education Policy Center, co-director of the U.S.-China Center for Research on Educational Excellence and co-director of the Promoting Rigorous Outcomes in Mathematics and Science Education (PROM/SE) project at Michigan State University.

Alan H. Schoenfeld is the Elizabeth and Edward Conner Professor of Education at the University of California at Berkeley. Schoenfeld's research deals with thinking, teaching, and learning, with an emphasis on mathematics.

Lawrence J. Schweinhart is an early childhood program researcher, author, and speaker. He has conducted research at the High/Scope Educational Research Foundation in Ypsilanti, Michigan, since 1975 and has served as its president since 2003.

Linda Skrla is Professor of Educational Administration and Associate Dean for Research, P-16 Initiatives, and International Programs at Texas A&M University. Her research interests focus on school leadership and social justice, feminism, and qualitative research methodology.

Marshall S. Smith is the director of the Education program at the William and Flora Hewlett Foundation. He has taught at Harvard, the University of Wisconsin at Madison, and Stanford, where he was also the Dean of the School of Education, and he has served in senior education policy positions in both the Carter and Clinton administrations.

Matthew L. Smith currently works at the International Development Research Centre in Ottawa, Canada. He holds degrees from the University of California at San Diego, Edinburgh University, and the London School of Economics and Political Science, where he recently received his PhD.

James P. Spillane is the Spencer T. and Ann W. Olin Professor in Learning and Organizational Change in the School of Education and Social Policy at Northwestern University.

Jennifer L. Stephan is a doctoral student in Human Development and Social Policy at Northwestern University. Her research interests include educational policy and factors promoting success in higher education.

David O. Stovall is an Associate Professor of Educational Policy Studies at the University of Illinois at Chicago. He studies the influence of race in urban education, community development, and housing.

Christopher B. Swanson is the director of the EPE Research Center, a division of Editorial Projects in Education, which publishes *Education Week*. His research on high school graduation rates aims to provide educational leaders and the public with independent, actionable information on this critical issue.

Carlos Alberto Torres is professor of social sciences and comparative education at the University of California Los Angeles. He is the Founding Director of the Paulo Freire Institutes in Sao Paulo, Brazil, Buenos Aires, Argentina, and UCLA. He has been a visiting professor in universities in North America, Latin America, Europe, Asia, and Africa, lectured across the globe and recently completed a 10-year term as Director of the Latin America Center at UCLA.

Karolyn Tyson is an Associate Professor in the Department of Sociology at the University of North Carolina at Chapel Hill.

Richard Van Heertum is currently teaching in the education and history departments at CUNY/College of Staten Island. He recently completed his Ph.D. in education and cultural studies at the University of California Los Angeles, where his dissertation focused on cynicism and democracy.

Sandra Vergari is an Associate Professor in the Department of Educational Administration and Policy Studies at the University at Albany, State University of New York. Her research focuses on K-12 education reform politics and policy.

Maris A. Vinovskis is the Bentley Professor of History, Research Professor at ISR, and Professor of Public Policy at the Gerald R. Ford School of Public Policy at the University of Michigan.

Ruth Chung Wei is a post-doctoral scholar at the Stanford University School of Education, conducting research on teacher education and teacher quality issues, performance assessment, and classroom assessment.

David L. Weimer is a Professor of Public Affairs and Political Science in the Robert M. La Follette School of Public Affairs at the University of Wisconsin, Madison.

His research focuses broadly on policy craft, institutional design, and health policy.

Martin West is an Assistant Professor of Education, Political Science, and Public Policy at Brown University. His research examines the politics of education reform efforts and their effectiveness in improving student achievement.

Frankie Keels Williams is associate professor and co-ordinator for the Higher Education Doctoral Program in Educational Leadership at Clemson University.

John F. Witte is a Professor of Public Affairs and Political Science in the Robert M. La Follette School of Public Affairs at the University of Wisconsin, Madison.

Yong Zhao is a University Distinguished Professor of Educational Psychology and Educational Technology at Michigan State University. He directs the Center for Teaching and Technology and the U.S.-China Center for Research on Educational Excellence. He is also executive director of the Confucius Institute at MSU.

The Reviewers

Jacob Adams
Motoko Akiba
Ann Allen
Kathryn Anderson-Levitt
David P. Baker
W. Steven Barnett
Susan J. Bodilly
Barbara T. Bowman
Mark Bray
Marie Brennan
Jere Brophy
Claudia Buchmann
Katrina E. Bulkley
William J. Carbonaro
Martin Carnoy
Dorinda Carter
James G. Cibulka
David T. Conley
Jerusha Conner
Mark Constas
Nesta Devine
John B. Diamond
Jaap Dronkers
Nell K. Duke
Garrett A. Duncan
Margaret Eisenhart
David N. Figlio
William A. Firestone
Lamont A. Flowers
Ericka Frankenberg
Douglas Fuchs
Margaret E. Goertz
Brian Gong
Jay P. Greene
Eric Grodsky
James Guthrie

Floyd M. Hammack
Douglas N. Harris
Thomas Hatch
Jeffrey Henig
Stephen P. Heyneman
Guanglei Hong
Susan Moore Johnson
Phillip Jones
Sean Kelly
Joyce King
James Ladwig
Douglas Lee Lauen
Kerstin LeFloch
Benjamin Levin
Henry M. Levin
Christopher A. Lubienski
Betty Malen
Paul Manna
Helen Marks
Martha McCarthy
Kathryn A. McDermott
Patrick McEwan
Patrick McGuinn
Michael K. McLendon
Hugh Mehan
Karen Miksch
Michael Mintrom
David H. Monk
Chandra Muller
Yas Nakib
Aaron M. Pallas
Joseph Petrosko
Donald Peurach
Joy Kreeft Peyton
Lawrence O. Picus

Sean F. Reardon
Nicolas Retana
Lauren Morando Rhim
Susan L. Robertson
Steven M. Ross
Andrew J. Rotherham
Richard Rothstein
Richard Ruiz
John L. Rury
Judyth Sachs
Laura Salganik
Evan Schofer
Roberta Y. Schorr
Michael W. Sedlak
Yossi Shavit
Dorothy Shipps
Robert E. Slavin
Marshall S. Smith
Mary Lee Smith
Jeffrey Smith
Brian Stecher
Gail L. Sunderman
Jonathan A. Supovitz
Larry E. Suter
Paul Teske
Sandra Tonnsen
John Tyler
Julie K. Underwood
Jeffrey C. Valentine
Tyll van Geel
Arthur E. Wise
Adam E. Wyse
Tara J. Yosso
Peter A. Youngs
Kenneth M. Zeichner
Ron Zimmer